Welcome to MODERN CURRICULUM PRESS Phonics

Celebrating More Than 50 Years of Success!

Creating successful readers has been the goal of Modern Curriculum Press Phonics for over fifty years. Since its early beginnings, this tried and true program has helped over 55 million children learn how to read. Today, MCP Phonics is ready to give our next generation of learners the solid foundation they need to become lifelong readers. Teachers can rely on MCP Phonics as a proven program based on current research and best practices for teaching phonics in today's classroom.

The tools that help children learn to read . . .

- **Student books** for kindergarten–third grade.
- A comprehensive **Teacher's Resource Guide** for each level.
- **Phonics Picture Cards** for kindergarten and first/second grade.
- **Phonics Word Cards** for first–third grade.
- A **Phonics and Reading Library** for each level featuring books from MCP Ready Readers and Early Chapter Books programs.
- A complete set of **assessment** tools including pretests and posttests and a direct connection to MCP's new assessment tool, Phonemic Awareness and Phonics Assessment (PAPA).

Teachers want to know . . .

D1444984

MODERN CURRICULUM PRESS

Phonics
LEVEL K

LEVEL K

How does MCP Phonics deliver systematic and explicit phonics instruction?

Level K of MCP Phonics presents the letters and sounds of the alphabet in a systematic sequence of instruction that fosters strong phonemic awareness, phonics, and early literacy skills.

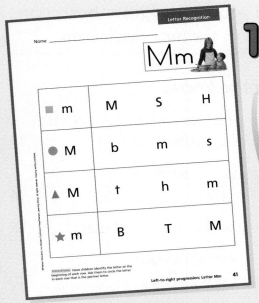

1 Start each lesson with **letter recognition** activities to strengthen alphabetic awareness.

2 Reinforce letter recognition with **handwriting** activities to develop understanding that print conveys meaning.

3 Develop students' ability to hear, focus on, and recognize phonemes in spoken words with **phonemic awareness** activities.

4 Help students make connections between spoken sounds and their corresponding printed symbols with **sound to symbol** activities.

A bath is not for me!

A horse is for me.

8 Apply newly learned phonemic awareness and phonics concepts to reading with fun and decodable **Take-Home Books**.

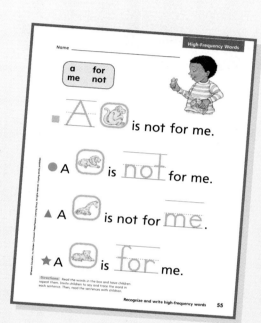

7 Improve reading fluency with practice in key **high-frequency** words.

6 Measure students' understanding of skills and concepts with **review** pages.

5 Reinforce sound to symbol correspondences and strengthen emerging reading and writing skills with fun **Picture Dictionary** pages.

LEVEL A

MCP Phonics Level A focuses on explicit and systematic instruction in consonants, short and long vowels, and high-frequency words.

1 Begin instruction with **phonemic awareness** activities to teach children the sound a vowel makes.

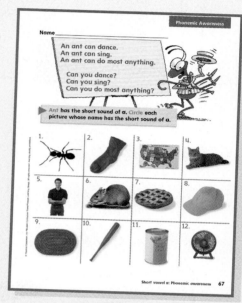

LEVEL A

2 Move into activities that teach **sound to symbol** relationships so children see the letter or letters that represent the sound.

3 Provide essential practice in combining phonemes and phonograms into words with **blending** lessons.

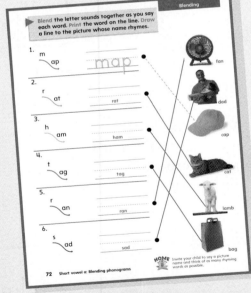

LEVEL A

4 Continue with **spelling** activities that target specific skills and encourage children to make the connection between hearing and reading words.

LEVEL B

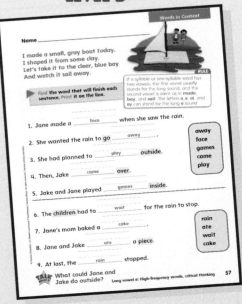

5 Practice high-frequency words (highlighted in the Teacher's Resource Guide) and newly learned decoding skills to read sentences in **words in context** activities.

MCP Phonics LEVELS B and C

focus on long and short vowels, vowel pairs, diphthongs, and digraphs, as well as compound words, prefixes, and suffixes. High-frequency word instruction continues in Level B.

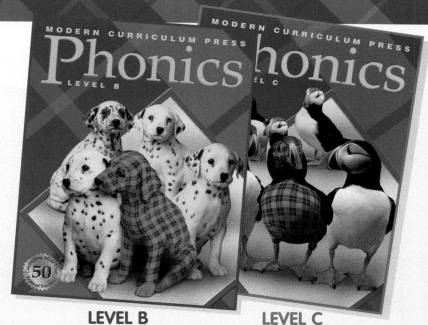

LEVEL B   **LEVEL C**

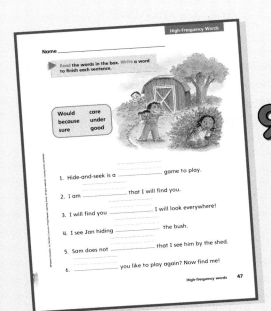

LEVEL B

9 Continue instruction in selected **high-frequency words** to provide children with the tools they need to be successful readers.

8 Provide opportunities for individual reading success with highly decodable **Take-Home Books**.

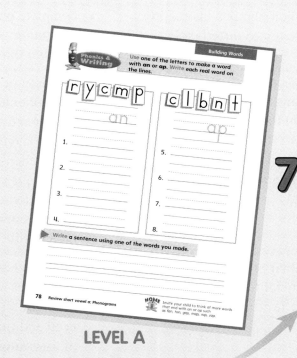

LEVEL A

7 Apply newly learned phonics skills to make new words with fun **Word Building** activities.

LEVEL C

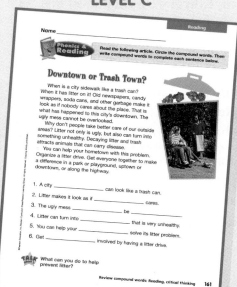

6 Encourage fluency and build comprehension while providing skills practice with engaging **Phonics & Reading** passages.

What is the research base that supports MCP Phonics?

The new **MCP Phonics** program is based on current research that stresses the importance of phonics and effective teaching methods for phonics.

The National Reading Panel and Put Reading First say. . .	The new MCP Phonics provides. . .
• Phonemic awareness instruction is most effective when children are taught to manipulate phonemes by using the letters of the alphabet.	• sound to letter instruction, beginning with letter recognition in kindergarten that moves in a logical sequence from hearing the sounds letters make to associating the sounds with the letters in words.
• Children with phonological and phonemic awareness skills are likely to have an easier time learning to read and spell.	• series of lessons on individual skills that first focus on phonemic awareness, then give a broader emphasis on phonological awareness.
• Systematic and explicit phonics instruction improves kindergarten and first-grade children's word recognition, spelling, and reading comprehension.	• systematic and explicit instruction and practice in phonemic and phonological awareness, sound to symbol relationships, blending, syllabication, and other phonics and word study skills.
• Systematic and explicit phonics instruction is most effective when introduced early.	• complete phonics instruction in **student books** beginning with kindergarten and continuing through third grade.
• Phonics instruction is not an entire reading program for beginning readers. Children also need to work on their knowledge of the alphabet, listen to stories and informational texts read aloud, read texts both out loud and silently, and write letters, words, and stories.	• a variety of activities that help children transition from phonics to reading, including read-aloud fiction and nonfiction **unit openers** that encourage oral language, **reading passages** with comprehension questions, decodable **Take-Home Books** for group and independent reading, instruction on different **types of writing**, and a **Phonics and Reading Library** for each level that includes little books and chapter books.
• Systematic and explicit phonics instruction is particularly beneficial for children who are having difficulty learning to read.	• a comprehensive **Teacher's Resource Guide** for each level with lesson plans and activities for different types of learners and for children who need additional support, as well as a complete set of **assessment tools** for each unit.
• Repeated and monitored oral reading improves reading fluency and overall reading achievement.	• many opportunities for children to read aloud with teacher guidance using highly decodable text targeting phonics skills.

Listed here are some of the resources used to develop the new edition of MCP "Plaid" Phonics.

Research Resources

Adams, Marilyn Jager. *Beginning to Read.* 1990. Cambridge, MA: Massachusetts Institute of Technology.

Allington, Richard L., editor. *Teaching Struggling Readers.* 1998. Newark, DE: International Reading Association.

Ambruster, Bonnie and Jean Osborn. *Put Reading First: The Research Building Blocks for Teaching Children to Read.* 2001. Developed by the Center for the Improvement of Early Reading Achievement (CIERA) from the findings of the National Reading Panel. Washington D.C. Partnership for Reading. National Institute for Literacy. www.nifl.gov

Baumann, J.F., J.V. Hoffman, A.M. Duffy-Hester, and J.M. Ro. "The First R Yesterday and Today: U.S. Elementary Reading Instruction Practices Reported by Teachers and Administrators." *Reading Research Quarterly 35: 343–353, 2000.*

Beck, Isabel and Connie Juel. "The Role of Decoding in Learning to Read" in *What Research Has To Say About Reading Instruction.* Samuels, S. Jay and Alan E. Farstrup, editors. 1992. Newark, DE: International Reading Association.

Ericson, Lita, and Moira Fraser Juliebö. *The Phonological Awareness Handbook for Kindergarten and Primary Teachers.* 1998. Newark, DE: International Reading Association.

Hiebert, E.H. *Text Matters in Learning to Read.* November 1, 1998. CIERA Report #1-001. Ann Arbor, MI: Center for the Improvement of Early Reading Achievement, University of Michigan.

Juel, Connie, and Cecilia Minden-Cupp. *Learning to Read Words: Linguistic Units and Strategies.* September 30, 1998. CIERA Report #1-008. Ann Arbor, MI: Center for the Improvement of Early Reading Achievement, University of Michigan.

Morrow, L.M. *Literacy Development in the Early Years: Helping Children Read and Write,* 4th ed., 2001. Needham Heights, MA: Allyn & Bacon.

Preventing Reading Difficulties in Young Children, National Research Council. 1998. Washington, D.C.: National Academy Press.

Report of the National Reading Panel: Teaching Children to Read. An Evidence-Based Assessment of the Scientific Research Literature on Reading and Its Implications for Reading Instruction. Reports of the Subgroups. December 2000. National Reading Excellence Initiative, an activity of the National Institute for Literacy. www.nationalreadingpanel.org

Samuels, S. Jay, Nancy Schermer, and David Reinking. "Reading Fluency: Techniques for Making Decoding Automatic" in *What Research Has To Say About Reading Instruction.* Samuels, S. Jay and Alan E. Farstrup, editors. 1992. Newark, DE: International Reading Association.

Strickland, Dorothy S., and Lesley Mandel Morrow, editors. *Beginning Reading and Writing.* 2000. New York, NY: Teachers College Press.

Strickland, Dorothy S. *Teaching Phonics Today: A Primer for Educators.* 1998. Newark, DE: International Reading Association.

Yopp, H. "Developing Phonemic Awareness in Young Children," *The Reading Teacher* 45: 696–703, 1992.

What phonics skills do I need to teach?

MCP Phonics Scope and Sequence

	Kindergarten (Level K)	Grade 1 (Level A)	Grade 2 (Level B)	Grade 3 (Level C)
Phonemic Awareness				
Identify and isolate initial and final consonant sounds of spoken words	◆	◆	◆	◆
Identify and isolate initial vowel sounds of spoken words	◆	◆	◆	◆
Identify and isolate medial consonant and vowel sounds of spoken words	◆	◆	◆	◆
Segment phonemes in words	◆	◆	◆	◆
Blend phonemes into words	◆	◆	◆	◆
Phonological Awareness				
Recognize and produce rhyming words	◆	◆	◆	◆
Blend onset-rimes into words	◆	◆		
Understand that spoken words are composed of sounds which are represented by alphabetic letters	◆	◆	◆	◆
Print Knowledge and Concepts of Print				
Develop concept of letter, word	◆	◆		
Develop concept of sentence, paragraph	◆	◆		◆
Track print left to right, top to bottom on page, front to back of book	◆	◆		
Match spoken to printed words	◆	◆		
Develop awareness that print conveys meaning	◆	◆		
Alphabetic Awareness				
Know the order of the alphabet	◆	◆		
Know capital and lowercase letter names and distinguish between the two	◆	◆		
Know letter/sound relationships	◆	◆		
Write letters of the alphabet, both capitals and lowercase	◆	◆		
Emerging Reading/Writing Skills				
Print own name	◆	◆		
Write using pictures, some letters	◆	◆		
Oral language development	◆	◆		
Visual discrimination	◆	◆		
Phonics Decoding Strategies				
Use phonics and structural analysis to decode words	◆	◆	◆	◆
Use semantic, syntactic, and graphophonic clues to identify words and their meanings	◆	◆	◆	◆
Phonics and Decoding Skills				
Sound to symbol correspondence	◆		◆	◆
Blend sounds to make words	◆	◆		
Blend onset-rime to make words	◆	◆		
Initial consonants	◆	◆	◆	◆
Medial consonants		◆	◆	◆
Final consonants	◆	◆	◆	◆
Hard and soft c and g		◆	◆	◆
Consonant blends		◆	◆	◆
Consonant digraphs		◆	◆	◆
Short vowels	◆	◆	◆	◆
Long vowels		◆	◆	◆
Y as a vowel		◆	◆	◆
r-controlled vowels		◆	◆	◆
Vowel pairs		◆	◆	◆
Vowel digraphs		◆	◆	◆
Vowel diphthongs		◆	◆	◆
Words ending in le			◆	◆
Phonograms (word families)	◆	◆	◆	◆
Common word patterns (CVC, CVCe, etc.)		◆	◆	◆
Fluency				
Repeated readings	◆	◆	◆	◆

MCP Phonics provides instruction in

- ★ Alphabetic awareness
- ★ Phonological awareness, phonemic awareness, phonics
- ★ Decoding strategies and skills
- ★ High-frequency words
- ★ Spelling
- ★ Vocabulary
- ★ Comprehension
- ★ Writing
- ★ Study Skills
- ★ Fluency

	Kindergarten (Level K)	Grade 1 (Level A)	Grade 2 (Level B)	Grade 3 (Level C)
Word Analysis				
Plural endings			◆	◆
Base words		◆	◆	◆
Inflectional endings		◆	◆	◆
Suffixes			◆	◆
Prefixes			◆	◆
Contractions		◆	◆	◆
Compound words			◆	◆
Syllabication and common syllable patterns for word identifications			◆	◆
Spelling				
Building words (phonograms)		◆	◆	
Vowels: short, long, r-controlled, digraphs, diphthongs, unusual vowel spellings		◆	◆	◆
Consonants: single, double, blends, digraphs, silent, unusual consonant spellings		◆	◆	◆
Endings on nouns and verbs		◆	◆	◆
Syllable constructions		◆	◆	◆
Affixes		◆	◆	◆
Apostrophes in contractions		◆	◆	◆
Vocabulary				
Picture clues	◆	◆	◆	
High-frequency words	◆	◆	◆	
Synonyms			◆	◆
Antonyms			◆	◆
Homonyms			◆	◆
Multiple-meaning words (homographs)				◆
Comprehension				
Reading words in context	◆	◆	◆	◆
Critical thinking	◆	◆	◆	◆
Speaking and listening skills	◆	◆	◆	◆
Writing				
A sentence		◆		
Description: an event, a place, a picture		◆	◆	◆
Diary entry				◆
Directions			◆	
e-mail message				◆
Friendly letter		◆	◆	
Informative paragraph				◆
Interview				◆
Journal entry				◆
Letter to the editor				◆
Lists		◆		
Log entry			◆	
Main idea and details				◆
Narrative paragraph				◆
News story			◆	◆
Postcard		◆		◆
Poem				◆
Report (preparation for)				◆
Story				◆
Study Skills				
Dictionary alphabetical order				◆
Dictionary guide words				◆
Locating words in the dictionary				◆

How does MCP Phonics make planning a lesson easy?

Identifies the skill-driven learning goals for the lesson, providing direction and structure, as well as a measure for meeting state standards

Features research-based, built-in activities in each lesson that target, teach, and build phonemic and phonological awareness skills

Provides an array of multisensory teaching options and activities to address different learning styles

Offers unparalleled on-the-spot support for English language learners with a specially designed instructional model that provides tips, suggestions, and activities

Provides additional suggestions for practicing skills with the student book, and **applying** them to immediate reading opportunities

---

Lesson 31 Pages 69–70

Short Vowel a

Skill Focus

Children will

★ recognize the short sound of *a*.
★ understand that *a* stands for /a/.
★ write uppercase and lowercase *Aa*.
★ apply what they have learned by reading and writing.

▶ Teach

Phonemic Awareness: Phoneme Categorization Say the word *map*, elongating the medial short *a* sound: *maaaap*. Then say the word naturally. Encourage children to repeat the word. Review that the sound they hear in the middle of *map* is short *a*. Next, say groups of three words. Ask children to clap each time they hear a word that has the sound of short *a*.

- hat   pan   pin
- map   mop   mat

Sound to Symbol Write the words *bat, can,* and *pan* on the board. Read each word slowly, blending the individual phonemes before saying the words naturally: *bbbaaattt, cccaaannn, pppaaannn*. Discuss how the words are the same. (*The letter a stands for the short a sound.*)

Distribute copies of Blackline Master 13 and have children select the *a* letter card. As you read the following words, have children listen for short *a* and identify the position in which they hear the sound by placing their *a* card in the correct box on the blackline master. Use the following words: *rag, hat, apple, cap, ax.*

	a	

Handwriting Write *Aa* on the chalkboard and use the models on page 70 to review how to form the letters. Have children follow along with their fingers on their desktops.

▶ Practice and Apply

Sound to Symbol As children complete page 69, encourage them to say the correct picture name softly to themselves by blending the phonemes.

Writing Note short *a* words in children's writing and check for correct spelling.

Reading Use *Haddie's Caps,* MCP Phonics and Reading Library, Level A, to provide additional practice in reading words with the short *a* sound.

69

Sound to Symbol

Name _____

➤ Say the name of each picture. Circle its name.

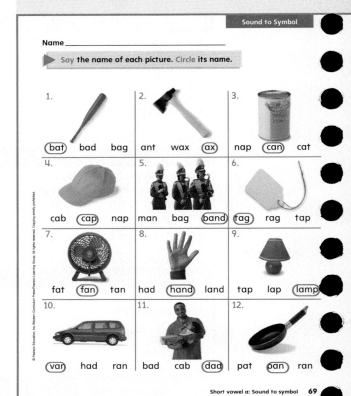

1. (bat) bad bag
2. ant wax (ax)
3. nap (can) cat
4. cab (cap) nap
5. man bag (band)
6. (tag) rag tap
7. fat (fan) tan
8. had (hand) land
9. tap lap (lamp)
10. (van) had ran
11. bad cab (dad)
12. pat (pan) ran

Short vowel a: Sound to symbol **69**

FOCUS ON ALL LEARNERS

ESL/ELL ENGLISH LANGUAGE LEARNERS

Use everyday objects whose names contain the sound of short *a* to identify children's comprehension of and ability to identify the sound of short *a*.

- Display an object. Ask a volunteer to name it and the vowel sound. Provide assistance naming objects if necessary.
- When all objects have been named, choose one and write its name plus two other words on the chalkboard. Have a volunteer underline the correct word and tell why the word was chosen.

AUDITORY/KINESTHETIC LEARNERS GROUPS

Write these word pairs on the board: *fat, bag; pat, cat; wag, sap; fan, man;* and *tap, lap.* Read them aloud. When you say a rhyming pair, the children pantomime the action.

VISUAL LEARNERS GROUPS

Materials: chart paper, drawing paper, crayons or markers

Draw a hat, a fan, and a cap at the top of a chart. Label the pictures. Touch a word and ask if children can make a rhyming word by changing the beginning letter. As children suggest words, write them in a list.

MCP Phonics Teacher's Resource Guides provide research-based methods for teaching skills and strategies along with a wide variety of activities that address diverse learning styles and connections to other areas of the curriculum.

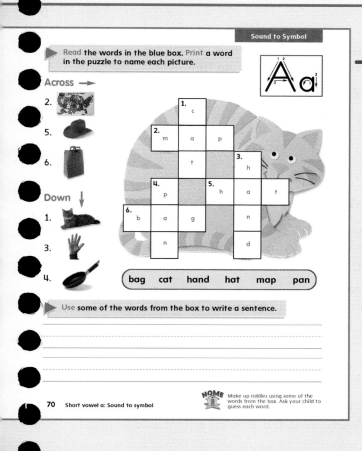

Sound to Symbol

Read the words in the blue box. Print a word in the puzzle to name each picture.

Across →

2.
5.
6.

Down ↓

1.
3.
4.

bag cat hand hat map pan

Use some of the words from the box to write a sentence.

70   Short vowel a: Sound to symbol

HOME Make up riddles using some of the words from the box. Ask your child to guess each word.

CURRICULUM CONNECTIONS

Provides opportunities to tap other areas of the curriculum through a wide variety of activities

SPELLING

Materials: index cards.

Have children copy one of the list words *bag, can, cat, fan, ham,* and *map* onto one side of each index card. Then have them draw a picture of the word on the back of the card. Have them show one picture at a time to a partner, who should say and spell the word.

WRITING

Have children write two sentences that tell about a cat that has a cap. Ask them to include some other short *a* words in their sentences.

PORTFOLIO

TECHNOLOGY   **AstroWord** Short vowel *a*

Connects teachers and students to phonics instruction on CD-ROM

KINESTHETIC LEARNERS PARTNERS

Materials: Phonics Picture Cards: apple (45), bag (47), cap (48), cat (49), ham (50), hand (51), hat (52), pig (59), sun (67), box (70), boat (108), broom (123)

Shuffle the Picture Cards. Have partners work together to remove any cards with names lacking the short *a* sound.

CHALLENGE

Materials: paper ruled into 1-inch squares

Children can work in pairs to make word chains. Have one child write the letters for a short *a* word in the squares on the paper. Then have the partner write another word, using a letter from the first word as its first or last letter. Have them continue, taking turns.

EXTRA SUPPORT/INTERVENTION

Materials: Letter Cards: Aa, Bb, Cc, Hh, Ff, Mm, Pp, Tt

Write *cat* on the board and have children make the word with letter cards. Have them change the first letter to make new words and read each word. See Daily Phonics Practice, page 312.

Integrating Phonics and Reading

Guided Reading
Draw children's attention to the cover of the book and ask them what they think the book will be about. You may wish to use the activity in the English Language Learners section below.
First Reading Ask children to identify each hat and what Haddie does as she wears it.
Second Reading Ask children to identify the short *a* words in the story. You may want to add these words to the classroom Word Wall.
Comprehension
After reading, ask children the following questions:
• How does each of Haddie's caps fit the action she is doing? *Inference/Comparisons*
• Which of Haddie's caps is your favorite? Why? *Reflective Analysis/Personal Response*
ESL/ELL English Language Learners
After children have looked through the book, ask them what is on Haddie's head in each picture.(*A hat*) Explain that *cap* means almost the same thing as *hat*.

Presents a guided or shared reading mini-lesson that enables students to apply newly learned skills to decodable text and build fluency

How does MCP Phonics fit into my classroom reading instruction?

The new **MCP Phonics** offers more meaningful skills practice and activities to address the needs of all learners.

Flexible Choices

One of the most outstanding features of MCP Phonics, and one that makes MCP Phonics a very easy program to use, is its flexibility. MCP Phonics can be quickly incorporated into class reading time…

★ to support phonics instruction in any basal reading or guided reading program.

★ independently as a stand-alone phonics program.

Using MCP Phonics . . .

to support core reading programs

- Teach lessons from MCP Phonics as the phonics component of your reading program.

- Assign practice pages to reinforce phonics concepts presented in your program.

- Use Words in Context pages, Phonics and Reading, and Take-Home Books for practice in applying newly learned skills to decodable texts.

- Enhance instruction for all learning types by using suggested activities presented in Focus on All Learners in the Teacher's Resource Guide.

- Assess knowledge of skills and concepts with built-in assessment tools, review lessons, and unit checkups.

as a stand-alone Phonics Program

- Use the Assessment Tools in MCP Phonics to determine students' needs and then match instruction to specific lessons.

- Teach lessons in the order in which they are presented or select skill blocks of lessons according to teacher preference to provide basic phonics instruction.

- Assign lessons as independent practice or for homework.

- Enhance instruction with Daily Phonics Practice Activities in the Teacher's Resource Guide.

- Use Words in Context pages, Phonics and Reading, and Take-Home Books for practice in applying newly learned skills to decodable texts.

Technology

Teachers who want to move beyond the workbook and reinforce specific phonics skills may choose to use a technology program called AstroWord*, featuring in-depth phonics instruction on CD-ROM. This tool is especially helpful in tailoring lessons for children who need help and those who have different learning styles.

*AstroWord Copyright ©1998 Pearson Education, Inc.

How does MCP Phonics help my students apply their skills to reading, writing, and language arts?

From Phonics to Reading and Writing

By taking full advantage of the features offered in **MCP Phonics**, teachers can move children from phonics instruction into authentic reading and a variety of language arts activities to build fluency.

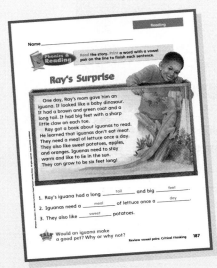

LEVEL B (Grade 2)

Apply newly learned phonics skills to reading stories and nonfiction passages in **Phonics and Reading** activities, Levels A, B, C.

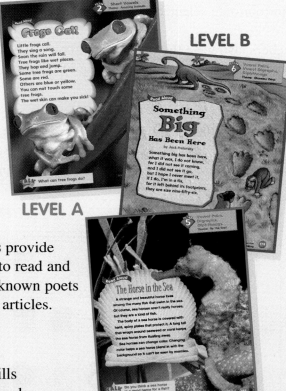

LEVEL B

LEVEL A

LEVEL C

In all levels **Unit Openers** provide opportunities for children to read and talk about poems by well-known poets or high-interest nonfiction articles.

LEVEL A (Grade 1)

Reinforce targeted skills and high-frequency words with beautifully illustrated, decodable **Take-Home Books** at all levels.

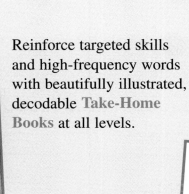

Provide more opportunities for children to build words and extend practice to writing activities with special **Phonics and Writing** pages, Levels A, B, C.

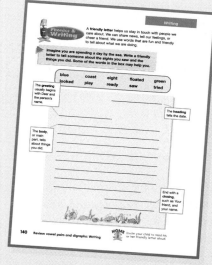

LEVEL C (Grade 3)

The new MCP Phonics and Reading Libraries for Grades K-3

The **Phonics and Reading Library** for grades K–3 features collections of titles from MCP's *Ready Readers* and *Early Chapter Books* programs. All the titles are featured at point-of-use in the MCP Phonics Teacher's Resource Guide and provide essential application of skills to reading. Titles can be used in a variety of ways to support balanced literacy: as part of a classroom independent reading library or reading center, or to foster early literacy skills with guided and shared reading activities that develop confidence, fluency, and comprehension.

These books may be used . . .

★ with the lessons in the Teacher's Resource Guide.

★ as part of a classroom independent reading library or reading center.

★ to reinforce selected phonics skills.

Teachers also have the option to purchase multiple copies of each book to guide reading with a group of children.

Guiding Students' Reading

In addition to thematic unit introductions, Take-Home Books, and engaging reading passages, MCP Phonics offers more choices for reading with a unique feature called **Integrating Phonics and Reading** that uses books from MCP Phonics and Reading Libraries.

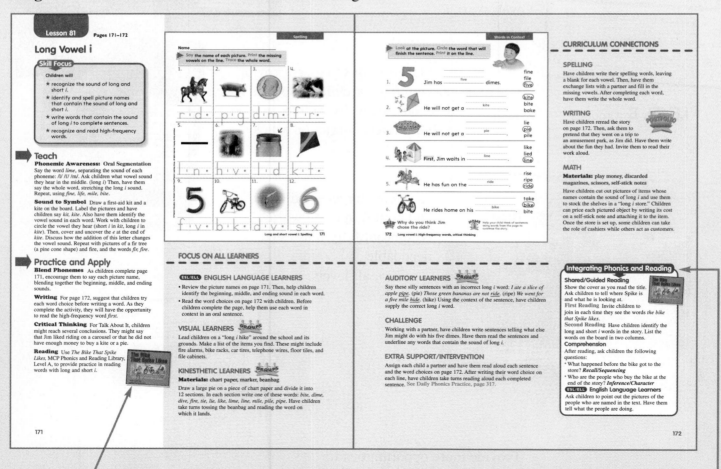

At the end of each lesson in the Teacher's Resource Guide, a book from the **MCP Phonics and Reading Library** is recommended for practice in applying the phonological awareness, phonics, or word study skill taught in the lesson.

Integrating Phonics and Reading enhances instruction and builds fluency with a small-group reading activity that reinforces the specific skills presented in the lesson. This mini-lesson describes how to use each little book or chapter book with children in multiple readings. An activity is also suggested for English language learners.

How does MCP Phonics incorporate high-frequency word instruction?

As children begin to read, they will often encounter words they cannot decode using phonics skills they know. These words are commonly called "high-frequency words." Many state guidelines now require that as early as kindergarten, children memorize and read selected high-frequency words.

MCP Phonics . . .

★ teaches the most common high-frequency words beginning at Level K.

★ builds a comprehensive and cumulative list by the end of Level B.

★ teaches and provides practice for words individually and in context.

★ reinforces high-frequency words in reading passages.

★ assesses selected high-frequency words in Pretests, Posttests, and Unit Checkups.

★ helps to build fluency through repeated readings of high-frequency words.

Level K	Level A			Level B		
a	about	I	saw	about	girl	saw
are	after	in	says	after	go	scare
at	are	into	sees	again	good	see
can	as	is	she	along	grow	she
do	because	it	some	always	has	should
for	blue	just	takes	any	have	some
go	by	knows	that	anywhere	her	something
have	called	like	the	around	here	song
here	come	little	their	because	his	sure
I	could	live	them	before	holding	that
is	do	long	then	began	house	their
it	does	look	there	behind	inside	then
like	down	love	they	believe	into	there
look	each	made	time	beyond	laugh	these
me	finds	make	to	bought	likes	they
my	first	many	too	boy	listen	things
not	for	more	trees	build	little	this
on	friend	most	two	buy	look	today
see	from	my	under	care	loved	together
the	get	no	up	children	might	too
to	glad	not	use	choose	my	two
we	go	now	very	climb	near	under
with	goes	of	want	come	new	usually
you	going	off	was	could	nice	very
	got	on	water	decided	often	wants
	grow	one	were	different	once	was
	have	only	when	does	one	watch
	he	other	where	down	only	water
	help	our	which	edge	other	we
	her	out	why	enough	our	were
	here	over	with	even	outside	what
	his	people	you	ever	over	when
	home	runs	your	every	own	where
	how	said		everything	people	with
				favorite	piece	would
				finally	pours	you
				find	probably	your
				first	said	
				friends		

How will MCP Phonics help my English Language Learners?

ESL/ELL **English language learners** need additional support and alternative teaching methods to help them succeed.

Each lesson in the MCP Phonics Teacher's Resource Guides provides flexible strategies for adapting the pages for native-English speakers and English language learners in the same classroom. These strategies incorporate recommendations from SDAIE (Specially Designed Academic Instruction in English) and CALLA (Cognitive Academic Language Learning Approach), which include:

1. Analyze material from the student's point of view.
2. Provide background experience and personalize the lesson.
3. Identify and teach essential vocabulary.
4. Present lesson orally.
5. Use a variety of visuals.
6. Simplify grammatical structures and paraphrase.
7. Reinforce language learning while teaching content.
8. Teach study skills text aids.
9. Use manipulative materials and hands-on activities.
10. Monitor student's progress.

Four Stages of Language Acquisition

Language learners move through a series of predictable stages as they acquire a new language. Although the terminology and number of stages vary among language professionals, most recognize four stages. Individual language acquisition will vary as language learners develop. The strategies provided for MCP "Plaid" Phonics take into account the following stages.

1 Pre-Production Stage

Children at this stage of language acquisition have an extremely limited command of English, although they understand more English than they can produce. They often use gestures, yes or no answers, nods or shakes of their heads to communicate. At this stage, instruction may be most effective in native-language or formal English classes.

2 Early Production Stage

Children at this stage comprehend more spoken English, but they still are unable to respond fluently. Communication is beginning, but responses are likely to be of the short-answer variety and may be awkward in grammar and structure.

3 Speech Emergence Stage

Children at this stage can follow along for most classroom and daily routines, but they are limited by vocabulary and inconsistent grammatical structures. There's an emphasis on acquiring verbal fluency.

4 Intermediate Fluency Stage

Children at this stage are well on their way to achieving dual-language fluency. They can comprehend more, can respond more fluently using the conventions of English, and can make themselves understood in a variety of settings, social and academic.

Strategies for the English-Speaking Classroom

Try these language acquisition strategies with your English language learners.

Gestures

★ Limit unconscious, random hand movements. For example, a hand gesture or symbol such as the "V" (peace sign) can be confusing to some children, and, in some cultures, may have different linguistic or cultural connotations.

★ Do use gestures to act out what you are trying to communicate.

Repetition and Consistency

★ Children at the pre-production and early production stages thrive on repetition to familiarize themselves with classroom rhythms.

★ When comprehension fails, class routines and activity formats give ELLs contextual clues on how to proceed.

Visuals

★ Use pictures, objects, and realia, or real-world clues, to convey meaning; to name an object; to indicate color, size, and shape.

★ Pantomime or bring videos to illustrate conceptualized vocabulary such as verbs and adjectives.

High-frequency Vocabulary

★ ELLs acquire everyday words before specialized or content vocabulary. Bring in familiar household objects and use items in the classroom to model lesson content.

★ Take advantage of other high-frequency vocabulary, such as sight words and proper names, to illustrate target sounds.

★ Look for good sources of daily vocabulary that use target sounds in your classroom and school community and from the children.

Encouraging Input

★ Support all response and oral input.

★ Model native pronunciation naturally and indirectly by repeating the target word(s) in context after the speaker has finished.

★ If additional pronunciation practice is needed, set aside small group time to reinforce this area.

Adapting Conceptual Activities

★ Activities such as word searches, crossword puzzles, mazes, and so on, contain words printed in vertical or diagonal patterns that may confuse the letter-order patterns children are learning.

★ Incorporate conceptual activities after children master the concepts to reinforce word recognition, comprehension, or pronunciation.

Peer Practice

★ Have ELLs work in pairs with more English-proficient children to afford one-on-one learning.

★ Have ELLs cooperate on worksheet activities and read stories aloud in small groups.

★ Monitor pair work for participation.

How do I assess my students' needs in phonics?

Today's teachers know that ongoing assessment is the key to identifying students' strengths, teaching to their needs, and measuring their progress in acquiring phonics skills. **MCP Phonics** provides several ways to assess students' reading skills that can be used as a guide to meaningful, effective instruction.

Formal Assessment Tools

★ **Pretests** identify each student's strengths and needs, allowing teachers to structure lesson plans.

★ **Posttests** evaluate a student's overall mastery of skills and identify specific areas that require reteaching.

★ The **Performance Assessment Profile** identifies the specific skills on the pre- and posttests and provides suggestions for reteaching activities in the Teacher's Resource Guide.

Informal Assessment Tools

★ **Review pages** can be found at different points within a series of lessons to help check mastery of skills.

★ **Take-Home Books** provide reading practice targeted to specific skills.

★ A two-page **Unit Checkup** at the end of each unit can be used as a quick assessment.

★ Suggestions for **Student Portfolios** are provided with the lessons in the Teacher's Resource Guide.

★ A **Student Progress Checklist** is provided with each unit to keep track of each student's mastery of skills.

Phonemic Awareness and Phonics Assessment (PAPA)

This normed, standardized tool enables teachers to

★ Analyze each student's phonemic awareness and phonics skills.

★ Administer assessment in only 30 minutes to individuals, groups, or the entire class.

★ Raise standardized test scores by driving effective instruction.

Once skills have been assessed, the PAPA Teacher's Resource Guide provides a correlation of results to MCP Phonics lessons.

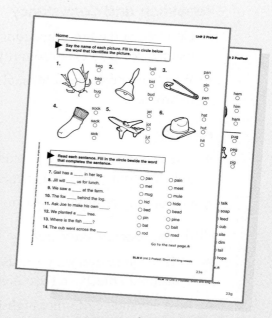

A **pretest** and a **posttest** are provided at the beginning of each unit.

How can I adapt MCP Phonics for summer school?

To easily adapt MCP Phonics for summer school students who need help with reading...

★ assess student needs using unit reviews in the MCP Phonics student books, pretests in the Teacher's Resource Guides, and the PAPA program.

★ target instruction to specific skills using the student book table of contents to select one or two two-page lessons for each day.

★ plan for 20 minutes of a 90-minute block for reading and language arts to do a quick review and additional instruction in phonics.

Following is a chart that outlines suggested basic skills to cover in MCP Phonics, Levels A through C (Grades 1–3), during each week of a six-week summer school program.

WEEK	LEVEL A (GRADE 1)	LEVEL B (GRADE 2)	LEVEL C (GRADE 3)
1	**Unit 1**	**Unit 2**	**Unit 2**
Day 1	Initial Consonants	Short Vowel a	Short Vowel a
Day 2	Initial Consonants	Short Vowel a	Short Vowel i
Day 3	Initial Consonants	Short Vowel i	Short Vowel o
Day 4	Medial Consonants	Short Vowel i	Short Vowel u
Day 5	Final Consonants	Short Vowel o	Short Vowel e
2	**Unit 1**	**Unit 2**	**Unit 2**
Day 1	Short Vowel a	Short Vowel o	Long Vowel a
Day 2	Short Vowel a	Short Vowel u	Long Vowel i
Day 3	Short Vowel a	Short Vowel u	Long Vowel o
Day 4	Short Vowel i	Short Vowel e	Long Vowel u
Day 5	Short Vowel i	Short Vowel e	Long Vowel e
3	**Unit 2**	**Unit 3**	**Unit 3**
Day 1	Short Vowel i	Long Vowel a	Consonant Blends
Day 2	Short Vowel o	Long Vowel a	Consonant Blends
Day 3	Short Vowel o	Long Vowel i	Consonant Digraphs
Day 4	Short Vowel o	Long Vowel i	Consonant Digraphs
Day 5	Short Vowel u	Long Vowel o	R-Controlled Vowels
4	**Unit 2**	**Unit 3**	**Units 4 and 5**
Day 1	Short Vowel u	Long Vowel o	R-Controlled Vowels
Day 2	Short Vowel u	Long Vowel u	Vowel Digraphs
Day 3	Short Vowel e	Long Vowel u	Vowel Digraphs
Day 4	Short Vowel e	Long Vowel e	Vowel Diphthongs
Day 5	Short Vowel e	Long Vowel e	Vowel Diphthongs
5	**Unit 3**	**Unit 4**	**Units 4 and 6**
Day 1	Long Vowel a	Consonant Blends	Plurals
Day 2	Long Vowel a	Consonant Blends	Endings
Day 3	Long Vowel i	Consonant Digraphs	Endings
Day 4	Long Vowel i	Consonant Digraphs	Suffixes
Day 5	Long Vowel o	R-controlled Vowels	Suffixes
6	**Unit 3**	**Units 4 and 6**	**Unit 5**
Day 1	Long Vowel o	R-controlled Vowels	Prefixes
Day 2	Long Vowel u	Vowel Digraphs	Prefixes
Day 3	Long Vowel u	Vowel Digraphs	Base Words/Syllables
Day 4	Long Vowel e	Diphthongs	Syllables
Day 5	Long Vowel e	Diphthongs	Syllables

How can MCP Phonics help struggling readers in an after-school program?

MCP Phonics can be used in a variety of ways to provide instruction and additional practice. This flexibility makes it a perfect tool for teachers who want to give students additional support in reading skills.

Reinforce phonics in 15 minutes after school

★ Assess students to determine in which skills they need additional instruction. Use the pretests and posttests in the Teacher's Resource Guide, review lessons and Unit Checkups in the student books, and PAPA (Phonemic Awareness and Phonics Assessment).

★ Select lessons to target specific reading skills by using the detailed table of contents in the student book.

★ Adapt MCP Phonics to any basal reading program to give students additional practice. Again, use the table of contents as a guide for selecting specific lessons that correlate to the day's lessons.

★ Use MCP Phonics as a stand-alone program for students who need additional phonics instruction. Present skills in the order shown in the table of contents, or rearrange them. The two-page lesson format will provide as much or as little instruction as time allows.

Select skills to correlate to basal reading lessons taught during class time.

Use MCP Phonics as a stand-alone phonics program. Use lessons in order, or present lessons in an order that best fits with classroom reading instruction.

Pull out lessons to target skills for extra instruction. For example, these lessons will help a student who needs practice with short vowel *a* sound to symbol and blending.

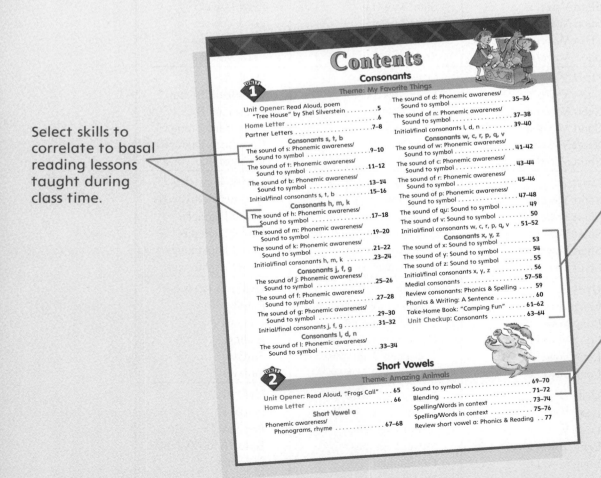

Contents

Consonants

UNIT 1 — Theme: My Favorite Things

MODERN CURRICULUM PRESS

Phonics
LEVEL C

ELWELL • MURRAY • KUCIA

TEACHER ADVISORY BOARD

Dr. Elsie Dabbs Heller
Kennett, MO

Emily Hendricks
Lafayette, IN

Debie Jarvie
Montville Township, NJ

Ellen Johnston
Dallas, TX

Meg Kouretsos
Chicago, IL

Cindy O'Linn
Hollywood, FL

Sr. Mary Jean Raymond, O.S.U.
Cleveland, OH

Frank Russomanno
Newark, NJ

Patricia Sears
Virginia Beach, VA

Ann E. Straw
Los Altos, CA

Fran Threewit
Kenwood, CA

Sonjia M. Wilson
Portland, OR

MODERN CURRICULUM PRESS
Pearson Learning Group

The following people have contributed to the development of this product:
Art and Design: Stephen Clarke, Dorothea Fox, Sherri Hieber-Day, Denise Ingrassia, Judy Mahoney, Karen Mancinelli, Elbaliz Méndez, Dan Thomas, Daniel Trush
Editorial: Leslie Feierstone-Barna, Teri-Crawford Jones, Cindy Kane
Manufacturing: Lori Servidio, Cristina Tamen
Marketing: Alison Bruno
Production: Irene Belinsky, Lissy Díaz, Joanne Saito, Suellen Leavy, Susan Levine
Publishing Operations: Thomas Daning, Vince Esterly, Magali Iglesias, Kate Matracia

PHOTOGRAPHS: All photos © Pearson Learning unless otherwise noted.
Cover: *t.* Kennan Ward/Corbis. *b.* Frans Lanting/Minden Pictures. Page 3: *frgd.* Mark L. Stephenson/Corbis; *mdgd.* Kevin Fleming/Corbis; *bkgd.* Getty Images, Inc. 24: Ariel Skelley/Corbis Stock Market. 35: Paul Rocheleau. 36: Lawrence Migdale/Photo Researchers, Inc. 49: *t.* Gary W. Carter/Corbis; *b.* Dan Guravich. 50: *t.* W. Perry Conway; *m.* Jim Zuckerman/Corbis; *b.* W. Perry Conway/Corbis. 74: PhotoDisc, Inc./Getty Images, Inc. 78: Stuart Westmorland/Corbis. 87: *b.* Sue Gregory/Wristies, Inc. 88: *t.* Schomburg Center for Research in Black Culture; *b.* Anne W. Meggitt. 91: Steve Vidler/SuperStock, Inc. 92: *l.* Spencer Grant/PhotoEdit; *r.* FPG International. 123: *t.* Ron Garrison/The Zoological Society of San Diego; *b.* Wolfgang Kaehler. 124: *t.* Stephanie Maze/Corbis; *b.* Richard T. Nowitz. 127: *frgd.* Stone; *bkgd.* Jeffrey L. Rotman/Corbis. 146: Randi Faris/Corbis. 147: *t.* Tom Stack & Associates; *b.* WaterHouse, Inc. 148: *t.* Fred Bavendam/Minden Pictures; *b.* Stuart Westmorland/Corbis. 151: Barrett & MacKay Photography. 161: Parker-Boon Productions for Silver Burdett Ginn. 164: E.R. Degginger/Color-Pic, Inc. 193: John N. Domoney.

REBUS PHOTOS: All photos © Pearson Learning unless otherwise noted.
Babies: SuperStock, Inc. *Barn*: Jeff Gnass/Corbis Stock Market. *Batter*: SuperStock, Inc. *Bird*: ZEFA Germany/Corbis. *Boat*: SuperStock, Inc. *Bride*: Naideau/Corbis Stock Market. *Bridge*: Susan Van Etten/PhotoEdit. *Bug*: Imagery. *Bunny*: Stephen Krasemann/Stone. *Camel*: Four by Five/SuperStock, Inc. *Chicks*: David A. Wagner/Corbis Stock Market. *City*: SuperStock, Inc. *Clown*: Alan Epstein/FPG International. *Crow*: Tom Ulrich/Stone. *Cry*: Norbert Shafer/Corbis Stock Market. *Deer*: SuperStock, Inc. *Doe*: Maresa Pryor/Animals Animals. *Duck*: S. Nielsen/Imagery. *Elephant*: James Balog/Stone. *Fin*: Jack Grove/PhotoEdit. *Fire*: Mats Lindgren/Stone. *Fish*: Zig Leszczynski/Animals Animals. *Fly*: Rod Planck/Stone. *Fox*: Darrell Gulin/Stone. *Goal*: Ann Summa Photography. *Grasshopper*: SuperStock, Inc. *Hen*: D. MacDonald/PhotoEdit. *Hill*: SuperStock, Inc. *House*: Tom McCarthy/PhotoEdit. *Jays*: Natural Selection Stock Photography, Inc. *Ladies*: SuperStock, Inc. *Mole*: Robert Maier/Animals Animals. *Monkey*: Zig Leszczynski. *Monkeys*: John Bracegirdle/Masterfile. *Nurse*: George W. Disario/Corbis Stock Market. *Pansies*: Gary Randall/FPG International. *Parrot*: Ron Kimball Photography. *Pig*: Don Mason/Corbis Stock Market. *Ponies*: Robert Maier/Animals Animals. *Puppies*: Tim Davis/Stone. *Row*: Ariel Skelley/Corbis Stock Market. *Sail*: Robert Pearcy/Earth Scenes. *Scarecrow*: SuperStock, Inc. *Sky*: John Lemker/Earth Scenes. *Snail*: F.E. Unverhau. *Snake*: SuperStock, Inc. *Spider*: SuperStock, Inc. *Squirrel*: E.R. Degginger/Animals Animals. *Swing*: Dorey A. Cardinale/Parker-Boon Productions for Silver Burdett Ginn. *Tent*: Richard Price/FPG International. *Tiger*: Zig Leszczynski/Animals Animals. *Train*: Walter C. Lankenau/Evergreen Graphics. *Trunk*: Art Wolfe/Stone. *Tub*: David Young-Wolff/PhotoEdit. *Turkey*: Ralph A. Reinhold/Animals Animals. *Turkeys*: Natural Selection Stock Photography, Inc. *Volcano*: Robert Reiff/FPG International. *Web*: J.C. Stevenson/Animals Animals. *Wheat*: Kevin Morris/Stone. *Yard*: Dorey A. Cardinale/Parker-Boon Productions for Silver Burdett Ginn. *Zebra*: Patti Murray/Animals Animals.

ILLUSTRATIONS: Page 140: Elizabeth Allen. 110: Meryl Anderson. 45: Bob Berry. 154: Gary Bialke. 105, 145: Lisa Blackshear. 3, 137, 139: Denny Bond. 196: Greta Buchart. 102, 172, 192: Annette Cable. 81: Penny Carter. 47: Cat Graphics. 166: Michael Chesworth. 129: Chi Chung. 108, 195: Daniel Clifford. 185: Raúl Colón. 40: Nancy Doniger. 93: Julie Durrell. 115, 135, 178: Doris Ettlinger. 1, 2, 114: Peter Fasolino. 23: Siri Weber Feeney. 4, 111, 169, 170, 197: Dennis Hockerman. 205, 206: Laura Jacobsen. 4, 14, 122, 131, 163, 181, 182: Meredith Johnson. 80: John Kanzler. 200: Wallace Keller. 113: Anne Kennedy. 29, 171: Terry Kovalcik. 2, 72: Holly Kowitt. 66: Darcia Labrosse. 153: Jeff Le Van. 136, 160: Anthony Lewis. 53: Lori Lohstoeter. 8, 56, 107: Diana Magnuson. 73: Shelley Matheis. 94, 168: Anni Matsick. 32, 62: Erin Mauterer. 157: Patrick Merrell. 1, 15: Andy Myer. 95: Mary Newell. 6, 128, 130: Pearson Learning. 30: Donna Perrone. 77: Mike Reid. 26: Janet Skiles. 12: Michael Sloan. 53k, 83, 85: Teri Sloat. 158: Jessica Wolk Stanley. 76: Tom Stanley. 41: Winson Trang. 191: Amy Wummer. 55, 189: Amy Young. 116: Jerry Zimmerman. Rebus art: Stephen Clarke, P.T. Pie Illustrations, Pearson Learning.

ACKNOWLEDGMENTS: "Changing" from *The Llama Who Had No Pajama: 100 Favorite Poems*, copyright © 1981 by Mary Ann Hoberman, reprinted by permission of Harcourt, Inc. Reprinted by permission of Gina Maccoby Literary Agency in the British Commonwealth. Copyright © 1959, renewed 1987, 1998 by Mary Ann Hoberman. "The Spangled Pandemonium" from *Beyond the Paw Paw Trees* by Palmer Brown. Copyright © 1954 by Palmer Brown. Used by permission of HarperCollins Publishers. Edite Kroll Literary Agency for the British Commonwealth. Excerpt from the poem "Reply to Someone Who Asked…" in *A Week in the Life of Best Friends* by Beatrice Schenk de Regniers. Copyright © 1986 by Beatrice Schenk de Regniers. Used by permission of Marian Reiner.

ZB Font Method Copyright © 1996 Zaner-Bloser

NOTE: Every effort has been made to locate the copyright owner of material reprinted in this book. Omissions brought to our attention will be corrected in subsequent printings.

Printed in the United States of America

8 9 10 11 VOO3 11 10

ISBN 0-7652-2627-8 (Teacher Resource Guide)
ISBN 0-7652-2622-7 (Full Color Edition - Pupil)
ISBN 0-7652-2623-5 (Black and White Edition - Pupil)

1-800-321-3106
www.pearsonlearning.com

Contents

UNIT 1

Consonants, Hard and Soft c and g

Theme: Celebrations

Short and Long Vowels

Theme: Friends and Family

Compounds, Blends, and Digraphs, Y as a Consonant and a Vowel, r-Controlled Vowels

Theme: What an Imagination!

Contractions, Plurals, Suffixes
Theme: A Working World

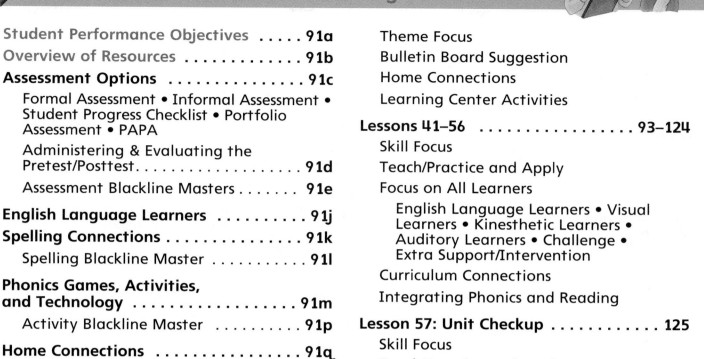

Vowel Pairs, Digraphs, Diphthongs
Theme: By the Sea

Prefixes, Base Words, Suffixes, Syllables
Theme: Taking Care of Our Earth

Synonyms, Antonyms, Homonyms, Dictionary Skills
Theme: Express Yourself!

UNIT 1

Consonants, Hard and Soft c and g
THEME: CELEBRATIONS

CONTENTS

In Unit 1, children will review consonant sounds and hard and soft *c* and *g* within the context of the theme "Celebrations." As children begin to understand and learn to apply the concept that consonant sounds can be used to help read words, they will be able to

► Recognize and use initial consonants to read and write words

► Recognize and use medial consonants to read and write words

► Recognize and use final consonants to read and write words

► Distinguish the hard and soft sounds of *c*

► Distinguish the hard and soft sounds of *g*

Overview of Resources

LESSON	MCP PHONICS AND READING LIBRARY, LEVEL C PROGRAM	TITLE	DAILY PHONICS PRACTICE
Unit Opener			
1: Initial consonants	RR, Stg Five, Bk 3	*Carrots Don't Talk*	212
2: Medial consonants	RR, Stg Three, Bk 4	*Dinner by Five*	212
3: Final consonants	RR, Stg Five, Bk 28	*Mother's Helpers*	212
4: Hard and soft *c* and *g*	RR, Stg Four, Bk 7	*Miss Muffett and the Spider*	213
5: Hard and soft *c* and *g*	RR, Stg Three, Bk 24	*The Cat That Broke the Rules*	213
6: Review consonant sounds; hard and soft *c* and *g*	FC, Set 1	*The Day the Sky Turned Green*	212–213
7: Review consonants; hard and soft *c* and *g*; Take-Home Book: "Come Celebrate"			212–213
8: Unit Checkup			212–213

RR–Ready Readers   Stg–Stage   Bk–Book

Assessment Options

In Unit 1, assess children's ability to read and write words with initial, medial, and final consonants, including hard and soft *c* and *g*. Use the Unit Pretest and Posttest for formal assessment. For ongoing informal assessment, you may wish to use children's work on the Review pages, Take-Home Books, and Unit Checkups. Encourage children to evaluate their own work and to participate in setting goals.

ESL/ELL Consonant sounds, especially final consonant sounds, may be problematic for English language learners. Note pronunciation difficulties as they occur, but assess performance based upon children's ability to distinguish specific sounds when pronounced by a native speaker. For additional support for English language learners, see page 5j.

FORMAL ASSESSMENT

Use the Unit 1 Pretest, on pages 5e–5f, to help assess a child's knowledge at the beginning of a unit and to plan instruction.

ESL/ELL Before administering the Pretest, gather together items or pictures of items that match the visuals on pages 5e–5f. Select an item and have volunteers name it. Ask other children to write the word on the board and identify the initial, medial, or final consonant. Some children may have difficulty understanding the directions. Read them aloud and model how to complete the test pages.

Use the Unit 1 Posttest, on pages 5g–5h, to help assess mastery of unit objectives and to plan for reteaching, if necessary.

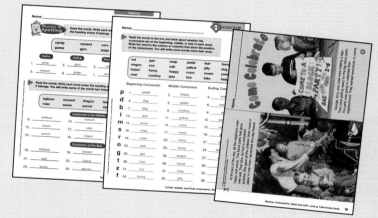

INFORMAL ASSESSMENT

Use the Review pages, Unit Checkup, and Take-Home Books in the student book to provide an effective means of evaluating children's performance.

Unit 1 Skills	Review pages	Checkups	Take-Home Books
Initial consonants	17–18	21–22	19–20
Medial consonants	17–18	21–22	19–20
Final consonants	17–18	21–22	19–20
Hard and Soft *c*	17–18	21–22	19–20
Hard and Soft *g*	17–18	21–22	19–20

STUDENT PROGRESS CHECKLIST

Use the checklist on page 5i to record children's progress. You may wish to cut the sections apart to place each child's checklist in his or her portfolio.

PORTFOLIO ASSESSMENT

This logo appears throughout the teaching plans. It signals opportunities for collecting children's work for individual portfolios. You may also want to include the Pretest and Posttest, the Review pages, the Unit Checkup, Phonics & Reading, and Phonics & Writing pages.

PHONEMIC AWARENESS AND PHONICS ASSESSMENT

Use PAPA to obtain an itemized analysis of children's decoding skills.

PAPA Skills	MCP Phonics Lessons in Unit 1
Beginning sounds	Lessons 1, 6
Ending sounds	Lessons 3, 6
Letter sounds	Lessons 4–6

Pretest and Posttest

DIRECTIONS

To help you assess children's progress in learning Unit 1 skills, tests are available on pages 5e–5h.

Administer the Pretest before children begin the unit. The results of the Pretest will help you identify each child's strengths and needs in advance, allowing you to structure lesson plans to meet individual needs. Administer the Posttest to assess children's overall mastery of skills taught in the unit and to identify specific areas that will require reteaching.

ESL/ELL Support English language learners by implementing any of the following suggestions before or during test taking, as appropriate.

- Practice test-taking skills with children. Skills such as filling in test circles may be new to some children. Ask a peer-mentor, teacher aide, or faculty coworker to work one-on-one with children to relieve test anxiety.
- Simplify tasks for the test-taker. Break down tasks into steps or relieve children of certain steps so that they can focus on one or two tasks at a time.
- Administer the test orally. Name the picture clues and read the word choices aloud so that children can hear the vowel sounds.

PERFORMANCE ASSESSMENT PROFILE

The following chart will help you identify specific skills as they appear on the tests and will enable you to identify and record specific information about an individual's or the class's performance on the tests.

Depending on the results of each test, refer to the Reteaching column for lesson-plan pages where you can find activities that will be useful for meeting individual needs or for daily phonics practice.

Answer Keys

Unit 1 Pretest, page 5e (BLM 1)

1. b	5. l	9. x	13. cube
2. v	6. g	10. t	14. certain
3. p	7. r	11. b	15. gift
4. g	8. d	12. v	16. cage

Unit 1 Pretest, page 5f (BLM 2)

17. hard c	21. soft c	25. hard g
18. hard c	22. hard g	26. hard g
19. soft c	23. soft g	
20. hard c	24. soft g	

Unit 1 Posttest, page 5g (BLM 3)

1. c	5. t	9. t	13. celery
2. s	6. b	10. l	14. act
3. r	7. p	11. p	15. sugar
4. b	8. l	12. g	16. giant

Unit 1 Posttest, page 5h (BLM 4)

17. hard c	21. hard c	25. hard g
18. hard c	22. hard g	26. hard g
19. soft c	23. soft g	
20. soft c	24. soft g	

Performance Assessment Profile

Skill	Pretest Questions	Posttest Questions	Reteaching	
			Focus on All Learners	Daily Phonics Practice
Initial consonants	1, 4, 8, 11	1, 4, 8, 11	7–8, 17–20	212
Medial consonants	6, 9, 12	6, 9, 12	9–10, 17–20	212
Final consonants	2, 3, 5, 7, 10	2, 3, 5, 7, 10	11–12, 17–20	212
Soft c	14, 19, 21	13, 19, 20	13–18	213
Hard c	13, 17, 18, 20	14, 17, 18, 21	13–18	213
Soft g	16, 23, 24	16, 23, 24	13–18	213
Hard g	15, 22, 25, 26	15, 22, 25, 26	13–18	213

Name _____

> ▶ **Fill in the circle below the consonant that completes each picture's name.**

1. 
a ○
b ○
h ○
__ike

2. 
v ○
h ○
r ○
fi__e

3. 
g ○
p ○
f ○
jee___

4. 
p ○
g ○
c ○
__oat

5. 
d ○
m ○
l ○
pretze__

6. 
y ○
m ○
g ○
wa__on

7. 
r ○
k ○
f ○
dee___

8. 
t ○
g ○
d ○
__og

9. 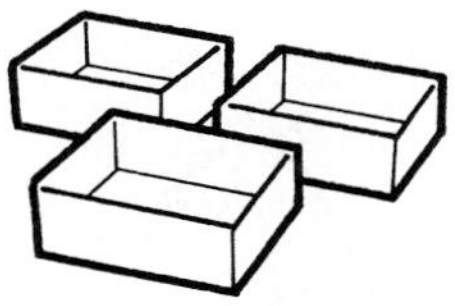
x ○
k ○
s ○
bo__es

10. 
l ○
t ○
r ○
ca__

11. 
d ○
b ○
t ○
___oat

12. 
f ○
v ○
n ○
se__en

> ▶ **Fill in the circle beside the word that has the same c or g sound as the word at the left.**

13. bacon   ○ ice   ○ cube   ○ celery

14. fence   ○ curtain   ○ certain   ○ come

15. good   ○ page   ○ gift   ○ magic

16. engine   ○ again   ○ getting   ○ cage

Go to the next page. →

BLM 1 Unit 1 Pretest: Initial, medial, and final consonants; hard and soft c and g

Name _____

> Say each word. Fill in the circle under the picture that has the same **c** sound.

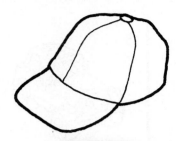

	hard c	**soft c**
17. doctor	○	○
18. corn	○	○
19. recess	○	○
20. vacuum	○	○
21. prince	○	○

> Say each word. Fill in the circle under the picture that has the same **g** sound.

	hard g	**soft g**
22. got	○	○
23. page	○	○
24. age	○	○
25. garden	○	○
26. tag	○	○

Possible score on Unit 1 Pretest is 26. Number correct _____

BLM 2 Unit 1 Pretest: Hard and soft c and g

Name _____

> **Fill in the circle below the consonant that completes each picture's name.**

1. 
___up
- ○ j
- ○ l
- ○ c

2. 
hor___e
- ○ h
- ○ s
- ○ p

3. 
doo___
- ○ r
- ○ b
- ○ f

4. 
___alloon
- ○ g
- ○ m
- ○ b

5. 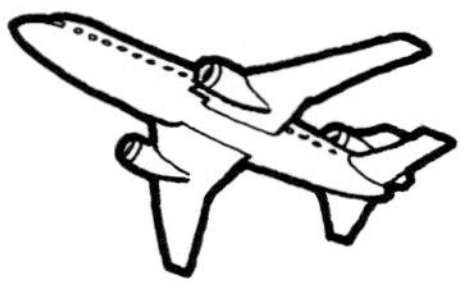
je___
- ○ t
- ○ y
- ○ r

6. 
ca___in
- ○ l
- ○ g
- ○ b

7. 
ro___e
- ○ g
- ○ p
- ○ f

8. 
___amp
- ○ l
- ○ g
- ○ c

9. 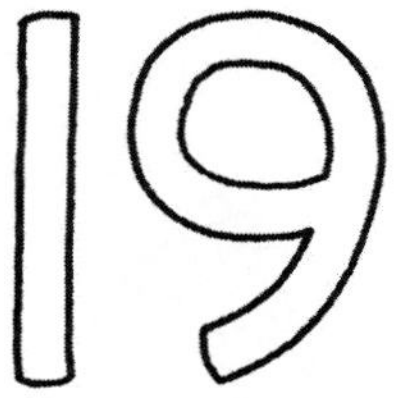
nine___een
- ○ d
- ○ t
- ○ l

10. 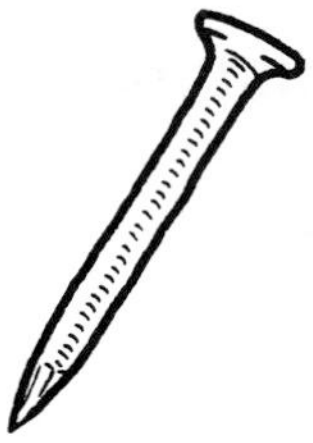
nai___
- ○ y
- ○ f
- ○ l

11. 
___encil
- ○ b
- ○ p
- ○ n

12. 
dra___on
- ○ d
- ○ g
- ○ c

> **Fill in the circle beside the word that has the same c or g sound as the word at the left.**

13. cereal   ○ coat   ○ corn   ○ celery

14. cow   ○ act   ○ pencil   ○ price

15. flag   ○ sugar   ○ page   ○ gym

16. large   ○ gold   ○ giant   ○ pig

Go to the next page. →

BLM 3 Unit 1 Posttest: Initial, medial, and final consonants; hard and soft *c* and *g*

Name_____

> Say each word. Fill in the circle under the picture that has the same **c** sound.

	hard c	**soft c**
17. carrot	○	○
18. come	○	○
19. cell	○	○
20. mice	○	○
21. cute	○	○

> Say each word. Fill in the circle under the picture that has the same **g** sound.

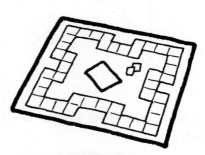   

	hard g	**soft g**
22. gone	○	○
23. pigeon	○	○
24. orange	○	○
25. igloo	○	○
26. eagle	○	○

Possible score on Unit 1 Posttest is 26. Number correct _____

BLM 4 Unit 1 Posttest: Hard and soft *c* and *g*

Student Progress Checklist

Make as many copies as needed to use for a class list. For individual portfolio use, cut apart each child's section. As indicated by the code, color in boxes next to skills satisfactorily assessed and insert an *X* by those requiring reteaching. Marked boxes can later be colored in to indicate mastery.

Student Progress Checklist

Code: ■ Satisfactory   ☒ Needs Reteaching

Student: _____ _____ Pretest Score: _____ Posttest Score: _____	**Skills** ☐ Initial Consonants ☐ Medial Consonants ☐ Final Consonants ☐ Hard and Soft *c* ☐ Hard and Soft *g*	**Comments / Learning Goals**
Student: _____ _____ Pretest Score: _____ Posttest Score: _____	**Skills** ☐ Initial Consonants ☐ Medial Consonants ☐ Final Consonants ☐ Hard and Soft *c* ☐ Hard and Soft *g*	**Comments / Learning Goals**
Student: _____ _____ Pretest Score: _____ Posttest Score: _____	**Skills** ☐ Initial Consonants ☐ Medial Consonants ☐ Final Consonants ☐ Hard and Soft *c* ☐ Hard and Soft *g*	**Comments / Learning Goals**
Student: _____ _____ Pretest Score: _____ Posttest Score: _____	**Skills** ☐ Initial Consonants ☐ Medial Consonants ☐ Final Consonants ☐ Hard and Soft *c* ☐ Hard and Soft *g*	**Comments / Learning Goals**

BLM 5 Unit 1 Checklist

Throughout Unit 1 there are opportunities to assess English language learners' ability to read and write words with initial, medial, and final consonant sounds, including soft and hard *c* and *g*. Recognizing and pronouncing consonant sounds can be especially problematic for English language learners. Many children's home languages lack final consonant sounds or lack the final consonant sounds found in English. English language learners will need many opportunities to listen to and practice saying English consonant sounds before they can reasonably be expected to reproduce them without error. Take note of pronunciation difficulties as they occur, and assess children's progress based on their ability to distinguish consonant sounds when pronounced by a native speaker.

Lesson 1, pages 7–8 Some English language learners may be learning the Roman alphabet for the first time, so discriminate form from size between uppercase and lowercase letters.

Lesson 2, pages 9–10 Words in Hmong, Vietnamese, Cantonese, Korean, and Khmer are monosyllabic. Prolonging the medial consonant sound may lead children to say each word as two. Double middle consonants are uncommon in many languages; have children practice saying and writing words such as *hammer, kitten,* and *balloon.*

Lesson 3, pages 11–12 In Spanish, the consonants *p, g,* and *f* are not used in the final position. Children can practice their pronunciation by listening to and repeating the following words: *soap, map, cup; bug, bag, log;* and *leaf, beef, elf.*

Lesson 4, pages 13–14 Children who speak Korean, Khmer, Hmong, and Vietnamese may confuse the hard *g* with initial hard *c* or *k*. Children whose home languages are Tagalog, Korean, Hmong, Khmer, or Vietnamese may have difficulty differentiating /j/ or soft *g* and the sound of *sh* or *ch*. Children who speak Russian or Spanish may also confuse soft *g* (/j/) and *ch*.

Lesson 5, pages 15-16 Children who speak Korean, Khmer, Hmong, and Vietnamese may confuse a hard *c* with an initial hard *g*. Confirm pronunciation through word pairs such as *cold, gold*. English language learners whose home languages are Tagalog, Cantonese, Korean, Khmer, or Vietnamese may not make the *s* sound of soft *c* in an initial position and instead say /z/. Verify that children pronounce correctly the initial sounds of *city, celery,* and *zoo.*

Spelling Connections

INTRODUCTION

The Unit Word List is a list of selected spelling words drawn from this unit. The words are grouped by initial, medial, and final consonants and hard and soft *c* and *g*. To incorporate spelling into your phonics program, use the activity in the Curriculum Connections section of each teaching plan.

ESL/ELL It is recommended that English language learners reach the intermediate fluency level of English proficiency before focusing on spelling.

For English language learners, introduce 6–8 words at a time. Help children understand the words' meaning by using visuals or realia.

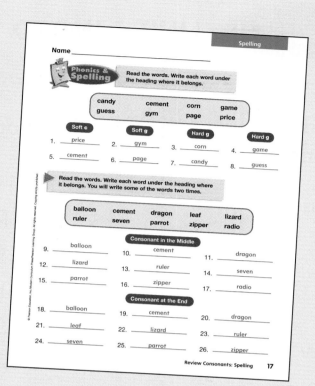

1. Administer pretests of the words, some of which have not yet been formally introduced. Dictation sentences are provided.

2. Provide practice.

3. Reassess. Dictation sentences are provided.

A final review that covers the consonants, including soft *c* and *g* is provided on page 18.

DIRECTIONS

Make a copy of Blackline Master 6 for each child. After administering the pretest for consonant sounds and hard and soft *c* and *g*, give children a copy of the appropriate word list.

Children can work with a partner to practice spelling the words orally and identifying the consonant in each word. You may want to challenge children to make new words by substituting consonants. Children can write words of their own on *My Own Word List* (see Blackline Master 6).

Have children store their list words in an envelope in their books or notebooks. Alternatively, you may want to suggest that students keep a separate spelling notebook, listing words with similar patterns. Another idea is to build Word Walls with children and display them in the classroom. Each section of the wall can focus on words with a single phonics element. The walls will become a good resource for children to use when they are writing.

Unit Word List

Initial, Medial, Final Consonants
balloon
lizard
ruler
seven
window
zipper

Hard and Soft *c, g*
candy
price
corn
game
gym

Name _____

UNIT 1 WORD LIST

Initial, Medial, Final Consonants

balloon

lizard

ruler

seven

window

zipper

Hard and Soft c, g

candy

price

corn

game

gym

page

My Own Word List

My Own Word List

BLM 6 Unit 1 Spelling Words

51

Phonics Games, Activities, and Technology

The following collection of ideas offers a variety of opportunities to reinforce phonics skills while actively engaging children. The games, activities, and technology suggestions can easily be adapted to meet the needs of your group of learners. They vary in approach so as to consider children's different learning styles.

CELEBRATION CONCENTRATION

Have children brainstorm a list of favorite celebrations as you write them on the chalkboard. Invite children to take a vote to choose eight names from the list. Provide each child with eight index cards, as well as a blue and a red marker or crayon. Invite children to copy the name of one celebration on each card, using red to write every consonant in each word and blue for all vowels. After discussing the consonant sounds found in the initial, medial, and final positions of the words, invite children to use the cards to play concentration with a partner. Two players put their cards face down between them and take turns turning over two cards at a time. If the two cards match, the player gets to keep them and gets another turn. If the cards do not match, the player turns them face down again. Players take turns until all cards are matched.

CELEBRATE C

On a large sheet of construction paper, invite children to draw a large, open *C* such as the one at right. Have them divide it into three sections as shown, labeling the sections *Hard, Soft,* and *Hard and Soft.* Invite children to write words with hard and/or soft *c* in the appropriate spaces. Children may want to decorate their pages by drawing pictures of some of their words. A similar activity can be done to focus on the sounds of *g*.

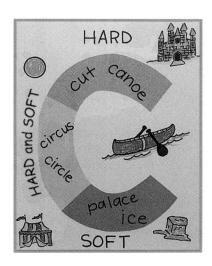

TONGUE-TWISTER TIME

Begin each day with a tongue twister featuring words with the same initial consonant sound. As you say the twister of the day, have children repeat it, saying the words faster each time. Then, write the tongue twister on chart paper and invite a volunteer to use a marker to highlight the initial consonant that is repeated. Here is one to get you started: *Busy Betty buys bagels, biscuits, berries, and bunches of bananas by the bushel.*

SEPARATING SOUNDS

Tell children that information can often be organized into categories and shown in a Venn diagram. Draw a large Venn diagram on butcher paper. Label one circle *Hard Sounds,* the other circle *Soft Sounds,* and the area where they intersect *Both Sounds.* Provide a list of the following words: *goat, canvas, garage, circus, George, cactus, doctor, process, cement, gorge, bicycle, recess, corn, circle, gum, orange, carriage, engine,* and *golden.* Challenge children to write the words in the correct section of the diagram. They can also add words of their own. You may wish to display the diagram on a Word Wall.

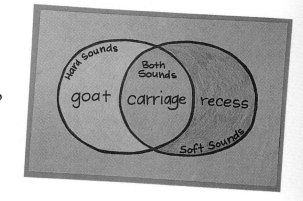

"HI, MY NAME IS . . ." RAP

Have children work independently to choose a consonant to feature in the initial position in words to complete the rap as shown at the right. As each child recites his or her rap, the others can clap to the beat.

Hi, my name is _____.
My partner's name is _____.
We work in _____.
And we sell _____.

Hi, my name is Hannah.
My partner's name is Hal.
We work in Houston.
And we sell hamsters.

MYSTERY LETTER

Have students help you write the consonants on separate sheets of paper. Tape one letter to each child's back without letting the child see it. Then, have children work in pairs. One child acts out the meanings of words that begin with the letter on his or her partner's back. Clues are given until the letter is guessed. The same is done for the other partner. Change the letters on children's backs and repeat the activity two more times to focus on medial and final consonants.

HOT POTATO

In advance, cut up 1-inch squares of tagboard. Choose a consonant to write on each square and put the squares in a colored sock. Close the top with a rubberband. Invite children to sit in a circle to play "hot potato." Play music as children pass the "potato" around. When the music stops, the child with the sock opens it, pulls out a letter, and says two words, one with the letter in the initial position and one with the letter in the final position. To make the game more challenging, play a round requiring children to say words with letters in the medial position.

PICTURE SORTS

Invite children to cut several pictures from magazines. Encourage them to work with a partner or in a small group to sort the pictures in various ways. As children first say the name of each picture, have them concentrate on analyzing the sounds in the picture name. Then, have them sort and resort the pictures according to initial, medial, and final consonant sounds. You might want to suggest that they list the words in each group before resorting, so they can later explain their groupings.

COMMON CONSONANT GRAPH

Use butcher paper to make a bar graph, listing all consonants in order in a vertical column on the left side of the graph and numerals in a horizontal row along the top of the graph. Tell children they will use the graph to discover the number of consonants in their first names. Invite children to predict which three consonants they think will be the most common and write their predictions on the chalkboard. Then, have each child place a square next to each consonant in his or her first name. When the graph is complete, discuss the results to see how accurate their predictions were.

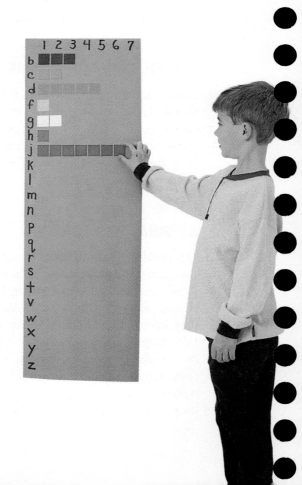

GIFT BOX TOSS

Cover a box with wrapping paper. Have children tape consonant letters to each side. Use the box for a small-group activity. Each child takes a turn tossing the box and choosing one consonant from the side facing up. Challenge the child to say and spell a word with the consonant in the initial, medial, or final position.

IMAGINE A CIRCUS!

To review words with hard and soft *c* and *g*, write the following words on slips of paper and put them in a hat: *huge, price, orange, came, gum, gather, circle, clown, candy, flag, game, giraffe, arrange, large, canvas,* and *got.* Invite children to imagine they are at a circus. Begin by having a volunteer take a slip of paper from the hat and use the word in a question related to the circus. For example, if the word *price* is chosen, the question might be asked *What is the price for a ticket?* The volunteer who correctly identifies the *c* or *g* in the word as hard or soft is the next one to choose a word.

CELEBRATE CONSONANTS

Make copies of the "Celebrate Consonants" game board on Blackline Master 7. Children can use the game board to create games that focus on the use of words with consonants. A spinner or number cube can be used to determine the number of spaces to move, or two players can move every other balloon from Start to Finish. Game markers, such as buttons, can be used to move along the board. Here are some suggestions for use.

- Write a consonant on each balloon. As players land on a balloon, they say a word with the consonant in the initial, medial, or final position.
- Write words on the balloons. Players read the word landed on and say another word that begins with the same consonant. The game can also focus on words that have the same medial or final consonant.
- Write words with a missing letter in the initial, medial, or final position for players to identify.
- Write words with *c* and *g* for players to read and identify as a soft or hard sound.
- On each balloon, write a set of scrambled letters that spell a word with *c* or *g* for players to identify.

The following software products reinforce children's understanding of short vowels.

DK I Love Spelling!
Recommended for ages 7–11, this program provides hours of intergalactic learning fun. As children travel from planet to planet, they build spelling skills through interactive games and puzzles. They see 5,000 key words and 50 different spelling-pattern word groups.

** DK Publishing, Inc.
   95 Madison Avenue
   New York, NY 10016
   www.DK.com

KidWorks™ Deluxe
Children ages 4–9 are provided with a variety of tools in this multimedia creativity kit to expand their reading, writing, and creativity skills. After writing and illustrating their own stories, children can choose to have the story read back to them or record their own story.

** Sunburst Technology
   1900 South Batavia Ave.
   Geneva, IL 60134
   (800) 321-7511
   www.sunburst.com

Name _____

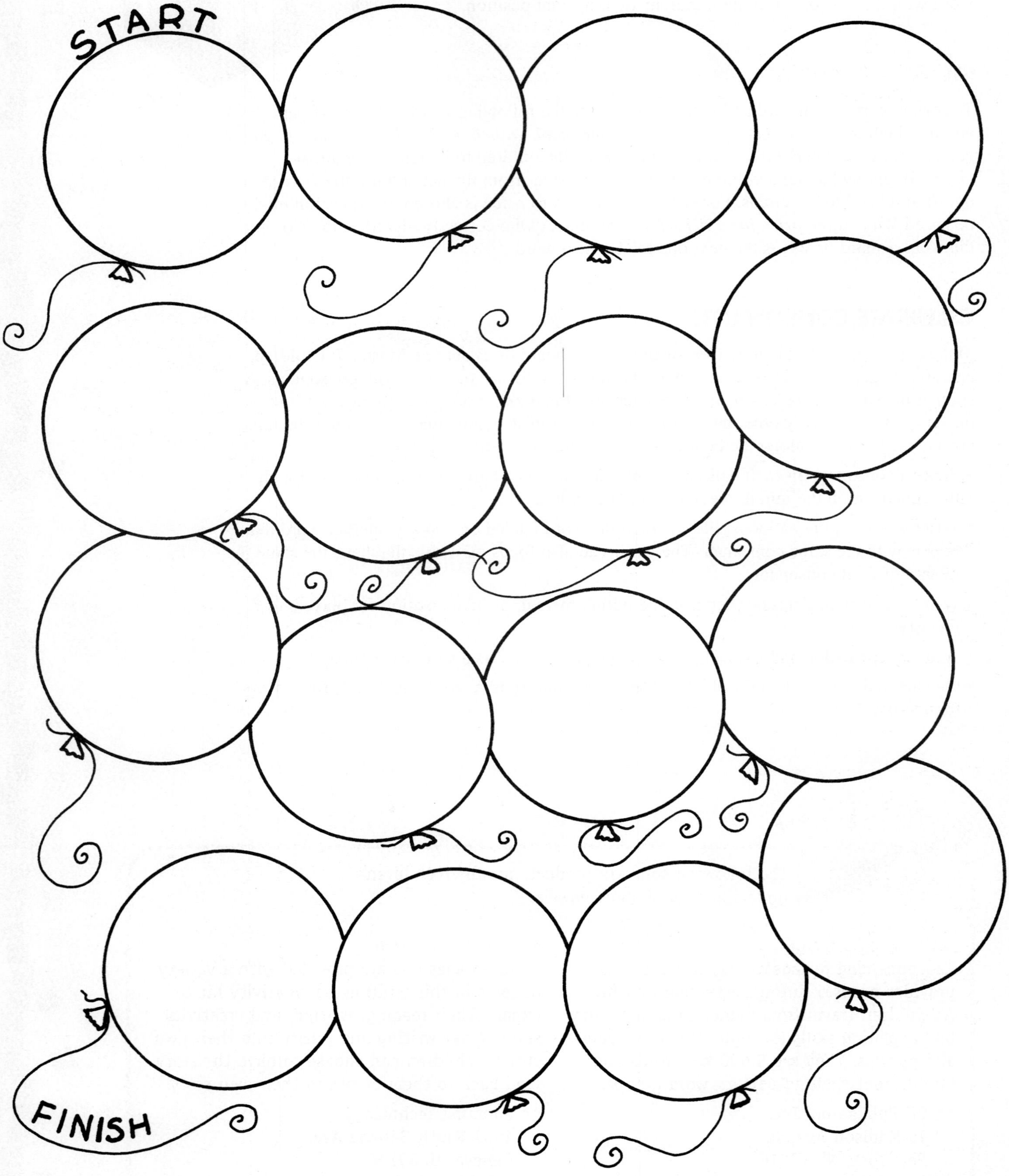

START

FINISH

Home Connections

The Home Connections features of this program are intended to involve families in their children's learning and application of phonics skills. Three effective opportunities to make connections between home and school include the following.

- **HOME LETTER**
- **HOME NOTES**
- **TAKE-HOME BOOKS**

HOME LETTER

A letter is available to be sent home at the beginning of Unit 1. This letter informs family members that children will be learning to read and write words with initial, medial, and final consonants as well as words with hard and soft *c* and *g* within the context of the unit theme, "Celebrations." The suggested home activity focuses on making a mobile to celebrate a child's favorite day. This activity promotes interaction between child and family members while supporting children's learning of reading and writing words with consonant sounds. The letter, available in both English and Spanish, also suggests theme-related books family members can read together.

HOME NOTES

Whenever the Home logo appears within the student book, a phonics activity is suggested to be done at home. The activities are simple to do, requiring little or no preparation or special materials, and are meant to reinforce the targeted phonics skill.

TAKE-HOME BOOKS

Within the student book are Take-Home Books that can be cut out and assembled. The story language in each book reinforces the targeted phonics skills. The books can then be taken home and shared with family members. In Unit 1, one Take-Home Book is available, focusing on consonants, hard and soft *c* and *g*, and the theme "Celebrations."

Home Notes in Spanish are also available for both teachers and parents to download and use from our website, www.PlaidPhonics.com.

Initial, Medial, and Final Consonants; Hard and Soft c and g

Skill Focus

Assess Prior Knowledge

To assess children's prior knowledge of consonants, use the pretest on pages 5e–5f.

Unit Focus

Build Background

- Write the theme "Celebrations" on the board. Say the word and help children find it on page 5. Invite children to talk about celebrations in which they have taken part.

- Draw children's attention to the picture on the page. Explain that Chinese New Year is a time when people have fun and wish their families and friends good luck.

- Read the text aloud as children follow along. Point out that Chinese New Year is celebrated in many cities around the world, not just in China. The festivities usually include a colorful parade with people wearing dragon and lion costumes. The dragon symbolizes good luck and wealth, and the lion symbolizes beauty and power. Invite children to identify other aspects of Chinese New Year celebrations mentioned in the selection.

Introduce Consonants

- Display an alphabet chart and remind children that letters are vowels or consonants. Then, have children identify the consonants. As they name each letter, have them say the sound it makes.

- Point to the word *Celebrations* on the board. Have children identify the consonants in the word. Tell children they will learn more about consonants as they work on the lessons in this unit.

Critical Thinking Ask children to imagine themselves doing the actions described in the selection. Then, have volunteers respond to the Talk About It question.

Read Aloud

CHINESE NEW YEAR

Colorful dancing lions and dragons weave down the street. There is music and dancing. People wave and cheer. It's Chinese New Year!

People celebrate Chinese New Year for 15 days. It is a time to wish their friends and family good luck.

Part of celebrating Chinese New Year is eating a special meal. People wear the color red to bring happiness. They also decorate their homes with special flowers to bring good luck.

Maybe the best part of Chinese New Year is lucky money. Money is placed into little red packets. A good luck message is written on the front. Then the packets are given to children.

TALK about It What part of Chinese New Year would you like the best? Why?

Unit 1 • Introduction
Critical Thinking 5

THEME FOCUS

CELEBRATIONS

Ask children to think about the theme of this unit, "Celebrations." Have them name some events people celebrate, such as birthdays, weddings, anniversaries, and holidays. Encourage children to talk about holidays that originated in our own country, such as Thanksgiving, as well as celebrations that come to us from other countries, such as Cinco de Mayo.

CHARADES

Ask volunteers to pantomime the activities people enjoy during a particular celebration such as a Memorial Day parade, a birthday party, or an Independence Day picnic. Challenge others to identify the celebration and write its name on the board. Then, have children identify the consonants in the name.

LET'S CELEBRATE!

Invite the class to create their own special celebration. Have children choose a name and a date for their celebration and plan activities for people to do. Ask children to put their plan in writing and circle the consonants in the words they use.

HOME LETTER

Dear Family,

In this unit about "Celebrations," your child will learn about consonants that appear at the beginning, middle, and end of words. Your child will also learn about the hard and soft sounds for the letters **c** and **g** in words such as coat, circus, giraffe, and gate. As your child becomes familiar with identifying consonants, you might try these activities together.

▶ Make a mobile to celebrate your child's favorite day. With your child, draw pictures or cut pictures from magazines. Punch a hole in the pictures and tie them to a coat hanger. Ask your child to name each picture and identify any consonants at the beginning, middle, or end of the name.

▶ Your child might enjoy reading these books with you. Look for them in your local library.

Children Just Like Me: Celebrations!
by Anabel Kindersley

Light the Candle! Bang the Drum! by Ann Morris

Sincerely,

Estimada familia:

En esta unidad, que trata sobre "Celebrations" ("Celebraciones"), su hijo/a estudiará las consonantes que aparecen al principio, mitad y final de las palabras. También aprenderá los sonidos fuertes y débiles de las letras **c** y **g** en palabras como coat (abrigo), circus (circo), giraffe (jirafa) y gate (puerta). A medida que su hijo/a se vaya familiarizando con la identificación de consonantes, pueden hacer las siguientes actividades juntos.

▶ Construyan una escultura con partes movibles para celebrar el día favorito de su hijo/a. Juntos, dibujen o recorten ilustraciones de revistas. Perforen un hueco en la ilustración y uníanla a un perchero. Pidan a su hijo/a que nombre cada ilustración e identifique las consonantes al principio, mitad o final del nombre.

▶ Ustedes y su hijo/a disfrutarán leyendo estos libros juntos. Búsquenlos en su biblioteca local.

Children Just Like Me: Celebrations!
de Anabel Kindersley

Light the Candle! Bang the Drum!
de Ann Morris

Sinceramente,

6
Unit 1 • Introduction

HOME CONNECTIONS

- The Home Letter on page 6 is intended to acquaint family members with the phonics skills children will be studying in this unit. Children can tear out page 6 of their book and take it home.
- You may want to suggest that children complete the activities on the page with a family member. Encourage children to look in the library for the books suggested and read them with family members.

LEARNING CENTER ACTIVITIES

WRITING CENTER

Work with children to make a calendar for the school year that highlights occasions they can celebrate, such as birthdays, holidays, and school vacations. Trips, assemblies, or other special events can be added as they are planned. Provide materials for children to use to write and decorate greeting cards for favorite celebrations. Display the cards for everyone to read.

SCIENCE CENTER

Celebrate the seasons that take place during the school year, beginning with autumn. Have children prepare seasonal displays with artwork, poems, and items that represent the season and its holidays. Include a calendar in each display, marking the beginning and end of the season.

MATH CENTER

Have children locate sports scores in several newspapers and make a list of them. Children can celebrate the winning teams' victories by doing the following for each game score listed: subtract the losing team's score from the winning team's score to find out by how many points the game was won.

BULLETIN BOARD

Ask children to cut out pictures of people celebrating various occasions. Display the pictures on a bulletin board under the title "Celebrations All Year." Have volunteers take turns describing one of the pictures for others to guess. Then, tell children to write a caption for each picture, identifying the consonants in the words they use.

6

Initial Consonants

Skill Focus

Children will

★ identify initial consonants from auditory and visual clues.

★ identify words with particular initial consonants in context.

ESL/ELL Some English language learners may be learning the Roman alphabet for the first time, so discriminate form from size between uppercase and lowercase letters.

Teach

Phonemic Awareness: Phoneme Identity
Say words that begin with the same initial consonant sound, such as *hammer, hello, hamburger.* Have children take turns repeating the words you have said and adding another word with the same beginning sound to continue the series. Repeat the exercise with words that have other initial consonants.

Sound to Symbol Write *boat, ball,* and *bird* on the board. Read the words aloud, stressing the initial consonant sound, and ask what sound children hear at the beginning of each word. (/b/) Change each small *b* to a capital *B* and have a child read the words aloud again. Point out that the small and the capital (lower and uppercase) letters stand for the same sound.

Practice and Apply

Sound to Symbol Be sure children can identify each of the pictures on page 7. Encourage them to say each picture name to themselves before deciding on the consonant that stands for the beginning sound.

For page 8, review the consonant sounds of *q* and *y.* Write the words *queen* and *yes* on the board and read them aloud, stressing their initial consonant sounds. Have volunteers come to the board and circle the initial consonant of each word. Point out that the letter *q* is usually followed by the letter *u.*

Reading Use *Carrots Don't Talk!,* MCP Phonics and Reading Consonant and Vowel Skills Library, Level C, to provide additional practice in reading words with initial consonants.

Name _____

▶ Say the name of each picture. Write the capital and small letter for the beginning sound of each picture.

1. cup — C c	2. gold — G g	3. pie — P p	4. bird — B b
5. volcano — V v	6. house — H h	7. deer — D d	8. jar — J j
9. fish — F f	10. ladder — L l	11. zebra — Z z	12. tooth — T t
13. window — W w	14. map — M m	15. ruler — R r	16. sandwich — S s

Initial consonants: Sound to symbol   **7**

FOCUS ON ALL LEARNERS

ESL/ELL ENGLISH LANGUAGE LEARNERS

Help English language learners associate initial consonants with their sounds. Write a consonant on the board, say its name, and model its sound. Find an object in the room whose name begins with the target sound. Write the word on the board, say it, and have children repeat. Ask a child to circle the initial consonant and find another object or picture whose name begins with the same sound.

VISUAL LEARNERS

Play "I Spy" by having children take turns providing clues to describe an object. The clue should include a word with the same beginning sound in the object's name, for example: "I spy something whose name begins with the same sound as *dog.* It has a knob and can be opened and closed." (*door*)

KINESTHETIC LEARNERS PARTNERS

Materials: bingo game cards, game markers

Give children bingo cards with consonants written in the spaces. As words are called, children cover letters representing initial sounds. Play until someone calls out "bingo!"

> Circle each word that begins with **q, s, v, w, y,** or **z.**

1. The (Quinns) (were) excited about their (summer) (vacation.)
2. They (were) going to (Washington,) D.C., for (seven) days.
3. (Susan) (wanted) to (visit) the home of the President.
4. (Zack) couldn't (wait) to (see) their cousins (Vincent) and (Sally)
5. Mom (said) they (would) all see the (Washington) Monument.
6. Dad (was) (sure) they (would) like to (sail) on the river.
7. The whole family (wanted) to (visit) the (zoo.)
8. (Zack) (said) the (zebra) (was) his (very) favorite animal.
9. His (sister) (wanted) to see a (wolf) (with) (yellow) eyes.
10. (Soon) it (was) time for the (Quinns) to go.

> Choose two of the sentences above. Write the numbers of the sentences in the left-hand corners of the boxes. Then draw a picture to go with each sentence.

8 Initial consonants: Words in context

HOME Say aloud: *Quinns, summer, visit, wolf, yellow, zoo.* Invite your child to name another word with the same beginning sound as each of these words.

CURRICULUM CONNECTIONS

SPELLING

Use these words and sentences as a pretest for writing words with initial, medial, and final consonants.

1. **balloon**   Fill the **balloon** with air.
2. **seven**   One week is **seven** days.
3. **ruler**   This **ruler** is 12 inches long.
4. **lizard**   A **lizard** has a long tail.
5. **window**   I opened the **window.**
6. **zipper**   My coat has a **zipper.**

WRITING

Have children write tongue twisters using words that start with the same consonant, such as *Ten tiny turtles took taxis to Texas.*

TECHNOLOGY   **AstroWord** Consonant Sounds and Letters

AUDITORY LEARNERS   PARTNERS

Materials: index cards

Make two sets of word cards. One set includes the words *sailboat, ladder, deer, jar, zebra, teeth.* The other set includes *lamp, dollar, jam, zipper, time, sandwich.* One child reads a word from set one. The partner reads the word from set two with the same beginning sound.

CHALLENGE

Material: timer

Ask children to write as many words as they can with the same initial consonant sound within a given period of time. Explain that they should begin writing when you start the timer and stop when the timer sounds. At the end of each round, have children make a class list of the words they have written. Depending on the words listed, you may want to discuss initial consonants that stand for different sounds. (c, g)

EXTRA SUPPORT/INTERVENTION

Materials: butcher paper or chart paper

Involve children in beginning or continuing a Word Wall that involves the writing and grouping of words that begin with the same consonant and the same consonant sound. See Daily Phonics Practice, page 212.

Integrating Phonics and Reading

Guided Reading
Have children look at the cover and read the title. Discuss what the book may be about.
First Reading Help children identify whom the boy is talking to and what he is doing on each page.
Second Reading Have children identify the words on each page that begin with a consonant. Ask them to name each consonant.

Comprehension
After reading, ask children these questions:
- What does the girl think about the boy's story about the talking carrot, dog, and tree? How do you know? *Inference/Character*
- How do you think the girl feels on the last page? What do you think she will do or say? *Reflective Analysis/Personal Response*

ESL/ELL English Language Learners
Have children use the pictures and their own words to tell the story. Prompt with questions such as: *Who is talking in this picture?*

Medial Consonants

Skill Focus

Children will

★ identify medial consonants from auditory and visual clues.

★ identify and write words with medial consonants to complete sentences.

ESL/ELL Words in Hmong, Vietnamese, Cantonese, Korean, and Khmer are monosyllabic. Prolonging the medial consonant sound may lead children to say each word as two. Double middle consonants are uncommon in many languages; have children practice saying and writing words such as *hammer*, *kitten*, and *balloon*.

Teach

Phonemic Awareness: Phoneme Isolation
Say a word with a medial consonant, such as *ladder*, stressing the medial consonant sound. Call on a child to repeat the word and identify the medial consonant sound. Repeat the exercise, using these words: *ruler, summer, seven, yellow, dragon, button, diner, spider, lizard*.

Sound to Symbol Ask children to help you complete words that have medial consonants. Write *pa_er* on the board and say the word *paper*. Have a volunteer name the missing letter and write it in the blank. Continue with the words *money, button, forest, frozen, palace,* and *body*. Finally, focus on the word *button*, pointing out that in some words the medial consonant sound is represented by double consonants. Give additional examples, such as *ladder, balloon, letter, rabbit, hammer, zipper*.

Practice and Apply

Sound to Symbol Have children name the first item on page 9 (*balloon*). Have them say the word again, stressing the middle consonant sound. (*balllloon*) Ask a volunteer to identify the consonant that stands for this sound. (*l*) For the activity, suggest that children say each word to themselves, stressing the middle sound and listening for it.

Writing For the exercise on page 10, suggest that children read each sentence with their word choice in place to make sure it makes sense in context.

Critical Thinking On page 10, discuss the Talk About It question. Have children review what the family did and saw while they were at the zoo.

Reading Use *Dinner by Five*, MCP Phonics and Reading Consonant and Vowel Skills Library, Level C, to provide additional practice in reading words with medial consonants.

Name _____

▶ Say the name of each picture. Write the consonant that stands for the sound you hear in the middle of each word.

1. balloon — l	2. ladder — d	3. letter — t	4. wagon — g
5. slippers — p	6. hammer — m	7. zipper — p	8. mitten — t
9. camel — m	10. parrot — r	11. dragon — g	12. seven — v
13. spider — d	14. tiger — g	15. button — t	16. radio — d

Medial consonants: Sound to symbol   **9**

FOCUS ON ALL LEARNERS

- -

ESL/ELL ENGLISH LANGUAGE LEARNERS

Verify whether children can identify medial consonants before introducing words. Then, teach single and double medial consonants, using words English language learners know.

• Write *wagon, camel,* and *seven* on the board. Pronounce each word slowly, tracking it with your finger, and stopping on the medial consonant as you stress the medial sound. Have children repeat the words. Ask volunteers to name and circle the medial consonant.

• Write *balloon, ladder, hammer,* and *zipper* on the board, pronouncing each word as you write it. Invite volunteers to name and circle the middle consonants in each word. Explain that some words have two of the same consonants that stand for one sound.

KINESTHETIC/VISUAL LEARNERS PARTNERS

Material: index cards

Have partners make word cards for *miner, diner, color, tulip, tiger, dragon, letter, kitten, supper, clippers, spider, glider*. Have them arrange the cards face down and play a game of "Concentration," matching words with the same medial consonant sound.

▶ Look at the picture. Read the sentence. Circle the word that will finish the sentence. Write it on the line.

1. Mom took my _____baby_____ sister and me to the zoo.
   (baby)   bunny

2. The zoo is in the center of our _____city_____.
   cousin   (city)

3. First we saw a _____tiger_____ at the zoo.
   (tiger)   tulip

4. Then we came to the pond where the _____beaver_____ lives.
   honey   (beaver)

5. Next we saw a big cat called a _____leopard_____.
   It was covered with spots!
   (leopard)   lemon

6. After that we saw a _____lizard_____ beside a cactus.
   (lizard)   peanut

7. I got to ride on a _____camel_____.
   parrot   (camel)

8. As we left, my sister _____waved_____ good-bye to the animals.
   (waved)   wagon

TALK About It Do you think the family had fun at the zoo? Why?

HOME Help your child to use three of the answer words in a sentence.

10   Medial consonants: Words in context, critical thinking

CURRICULUM CONNECTIONS

SPELLING

Write the words *balloon, lizard, letter, parrot, zipper,* and *seven* in one column on the board. Form another column with the words *supper, hazy, pillow, hurry, clever,* and *battle.* Have one group of volunteers circle the middle or double consonant in each word. Then, have others draw lines to connect the words having the same middle consonant sounds and spellings.

WRITING

Have children write riddles for words with a medial consonant. For example: *I am a number below ten. My middle consonant is v. What am I?* (seven)

MATH

Ask children to make a list of items whose names have a medial consonant. Then, have them group the items according to medial consonant. Finally, have children list the consonants in order of increasing frequency.

TECHNOLOGY   **AstroWord** Consonant Sounds and Letters

VISUAL/AUDITORY LEARNERS   GROUPS

Make a four-column chart on the board, using each of the following words as column headers: *letter, balloon, funny,* and *wiggle.* Say the words *tiger, mitten, wagon, city, button, yellow, tiny, canoe, salad, molar, banner,* and *struggle.* As you say each word, call on a volunteer to write it in the column headed by the word with the same medial consonant sound.

CHALLENGE

Assign each child a consonant. Then, challenge children to list as many words as they can that have the middle sound made by the consonant they have been assigned. Set a time limit for children to make their lists.

EXTRA SUPPORT/INTERVENTION

Ask children to raise their hands when they hear a pair of words with matching middle consonant sounds. Use word pairs such as the following: *arrow/narrow; rider/tiger; wagon/dragon; hammer/swimmer; fixes/foxes; robot/motor.* See Daily Phonics Practice, page 212.

Integrating Phonics and Reading

Guided Reading

Have children look at the cover of *Dinner by Five* and discuss what the characters are doing. What do children think the title of the book means?

First Reading Point out the clock and other picture clues that help tell the story.

Second Reading Help children identify words in the story that have medial consonants, such as *dinner, pizza,* and *salad.*

Comprehension

After reading, ask children these questions:

• How did Kim, Mike, and Dad each help with dinner? *Recall/Making Comparisons*

• Why do you think Kim and Mike decided to make dinner? *Inference/Plot*

ESL/ELL English Language Learners
Discuss with children what pizza and salad are and how they are made.

Final Consonants

Skill Focus

Children will

★ identify final consonants from auditory and visual clues.

★ identify and write words with final consonants to complete sentences.

ESL/ELL In Spanish, the consonants *p, g,* and *f* are not used in the final position. Children can practice their pronunciation by listening to and repeating the following words: *soap, map, cup; bug, bag, log;* and *leaf, beef, elf.*

Teach

Phonemic Awareness: Phoneme Isolation
Seat children in a circle. Say a word such as *coat.* Ask a child to repeat the word, isolate the ending sound /t/, and say a word that begins with the sound, such as *top.* The next child isolates the ending sound /p/ and says a word that begins with that sound, such as *pen.* Continue until each child has had a chance to offer a word.

Sound to Symbol Remind children that they can hear consonant sounds at the beginning, in the middle, and at the end of words. On the board, write the words *mop, tap,* and *step.* Have a child isolate the final sound (/p/) and circle the letter that stands for this sound in the words on the board.

Repeat the activity, using words with other final consonants, such as *pan, spin, den (n); bus, gas, toss (s);* and *cat, spot, sit (t).*

Practice and Apply

Sound to Symbol Have children name the first item pictured on page 11. (*coat*) Say the word again, stressing the final consonant sound. Ask a child to name the letter that stands for that sound. (*t*) Suggest that children say each word to themselves, stressing the final sound and listening for it.

Writing For the sentences on page 12, be sure children understand that they are to fill in only one circle for each sentence. Remind them to write their answer choice on the line.

Critical Thinking After reading the sentences on page 12, discuss with children the Talk About It question. Ask them to compare their school day with Ben's school day.

Reading Use *Mother's Helpers,* MCP Phonics and Reading Consonant and Vowel Skills Library, Level C, to provide additional practice in reading words with final consonants.

Name _____

> Look at the letter in each row. Then, say the name of each picture. Color the pictures whose names **end** with the sound of the letter.

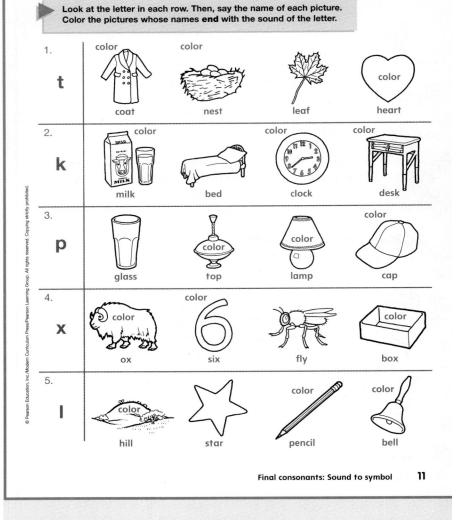

Final consonants: Sound to symbol   **11**

FOCUS ON ALL LEARNERS

ESL/ELL ENGLISH LANGUAGE LEARNERS
English language learners may need help with words ending in *p* or *g,* such as *soap, map, cup; bug, bag, log.*

- Write *p* and *g* on the board and list the words under their final consonant.
- Point to a word, say it, and model the final sound. Have children repeat after you.
- Ask a volunteer to go to the board, circle the letter that stands for the final sound, and name the letter.
- For page 11, you may want to orally preview the picture names with children, stressing the ending sound.
- For page 12, orally preview the first sentence, then read the three word choices. Have children orally try each word in the sentence and select the word that matches the picture clue.

AUDITORY LEARNERS GROUPS
Say words, omitting the final consonant sound. Ask volunteers to add the final sound. Use words such as *elephan*(t); *mailbo*(x); *cookboo*(k); *seve*(n); *astronau*(t); *sailboa*(t); *bedroo*(m); *garde*(n); *lizar*(d); *balloo*(n).

Look at the picture. Fill in the circle beside the word that will finish the sentence. Write the word on the line.

1. Ben rides the ___bus___ to school.
   - ○ bug
   - ○ bud
   - ● bus

2. He is wearing his red ___cap___.
   - ○ cat
   - ● cap
   - ○ car

3. Ben carries his lunch in a ___bag___.
   - ○ bat
   - ○ bad
   - ● bag

4. Today he has a ___ham___ sandwich.
   - ● ham
   - ○ hat
   - ○ had

5. Ben writes with his new ___pen___.
   - ○ pet
   - ● pen
   - ○ peg

6. He labels a ___map___ with it.
   - ● map
   - ○ man
   - ○ mat

7. After school, Ben plays with his ___cat___.
   - ○ car
   - ● cat
   - ○ cap

8. At eight o'clock he goes to ___bed___.
   - ○ beg
   - ○ bet
   - ● bed

TALK About It How is your school day like Ben's?

HOME Ask your child to think of words ending with the letters *t*, *k*, *p*, *x*, and *l*.

12 Final consonants: Words in context, critical thinking

CURRICULUM CONNECTIONS

SPELLING

Use the following words and sentences as a posttest for writing words with initial, medial, and final consonants.

1. **balloon** Tie a string on the **balloon**.
2. **ruler** Use a **ruler** to measure.
3. **seven** What is **seven** times three?
4. **window** Close the **window**.
5. **lizard** The **lizard** is a reptile.
6. **zipper** My suitcase has a **zipper**.

WRITING

Ask children to write a journal entry about a typical day at school. Have them identify final consonants in words they used.

PORTFOLIO

SOCIAL STUDIES

Ask partners to list words associated with a holiday that end in consonants. For example, Thanksgiving: *pilgrim, pumpkin*. Call on volunteers to identify the end consonants.

TECHNOLOGY **AstroWord** Consonant Sounds and Letters

KINESTHETIC/VISUAL LEARNERS INDIVIDUAL

Materials: index cards, envelopes

On cards, write words with final consonants. Place each card inside an envelope so that when the card is removed, the beginning letters of the word appear first. Invite a volunteer to slide the word card out of the envelope so that the letters gradually appear and guess the final consonant before looking.

CHALLENGE

Challenge children to write as many words as they can that begin and end with the same consonant and consonant sound, such as *kick, dad, mom, deed, river*.

EXTRA SUPPORT/INTERVENTION

Materials: letter cards

Make letter cards for children to use to build words that end with the same consonant. Begin by having them build the word *cap*. Then, have them change the first two letters to make new words such as *top, rip*, or *pup*. See Daily Phonics Practice, page 212.

Integrating Phonics and Reading

Guided Reading

Have children look at the cover of *Mother's Helpers* and read the title. Invite them to talk about ways to help a family member.

First Reading Have children describe the things Rick and Lora do at the museum.

Second Reading Have children identify story words with final consonants.

Comprehension

After reading, ask children these questions:
- How did Rick's feelings about the museum change? *Inference/Character*
- Would you like to do what Lora and Rick did? Why or why not? *Reflective Analysis/ Personal Response*

ESL/ELL **English Language Learners**

Draw a question mark on the board. Explain that it is used at the end of a sentence to show a question. Say *Will you work here?* Ask where Lora and Rick's mother is going to work.

Hard and Soft c and g

Skill Focus

Children will

★ distinguish between the hard and soft c and g sounds.

★ sort words with hard or soft c or g.

ESL/ELL Children who speak Korean, Khmer, Hmong, and Vietnamese may confuse the hard g with initial hard c or k. Children whose home languages are Tagalog, Korean, Hmong, Khmer, or Vietnamese may have difficulty differentiating /j/ or soft g and the sound of sh or ch. Children who speak Russian or Spanish may also confuse soft h (/j/) and ch.

▶ Teach

Phonemic Awareness: Phoneme Categorization

Explain that you will say sets of three words. Children are to identify which word has a different beginning consonant sound from the other two. Use these words:

- **corn   celery   coat**
- **cereal   center   cow**
- **giant   gull   germ**
- **got   goat   ginger**

Sound to Symbol Point out that some consonants can have two sounds. Write *corn* and *celery* on the board. Read the words aloud as you underline the *c* in each. Ask in which word *c* stands for the sound of *s* as in *say*. (*celery*) In which word does *c* have the sound of *k* as in *kite?* (*corn*) Explain that *c* usually has the soft sound of *s* when it is followed by *e, i,* or *y*. The letter *c* has the hard sound of *k* when it is followed by *a, o,* or *u.*

Do the same exercise with the words *goat* and *ginger.* Have children identify the word in which *g* stands for the hard sound of *g* (*goat*) and for the sound of *j* as in *jam* (*ginger*). Explain that when *g* is followed by *e, i,* or *y,* the *g* is usually soft and has the sound of *j*. Otherwise, *g* has a hard sound.

Practice and Apply

Sound to Symbol Review the rule at the top of page 13. Suggest that children compare the *c* sound in each word with the *c* sound in *cap* or in *cereal.*

Review the rule on page 14. Suggest that children label the hard *g* column "as in *got*" and the soft *g* column "as in *giant.*"

Reading Use *Miss Muffett and the Spider,* MCP Phonics and Reading Consonant and Vowel Skills Library, Level C, to provide additional practice in reading words with hard and soft c.

13

Name_____

Say each word in the box below. Write the words that contain a hard **c** sound under the picture of the cap. Write the words that contain a soft **c** sound under the picture of the cereal.

RULE When the letter **c** is followed by the vowels **a**, **o**, or **u**, it has a hard sound. Hard **c** has a **k** sound. When **c** is followed by **e**, **i**, or **y**, it usually has a soft sound. Soft **c** has an **s** sound.

cat	cot	cut
lace	city	fancy

actor	cattle	cinema	cub	doctor	pencil
candy	celery	coat	cymbal	grocery	price
carriage	cellar	corn	decide	palace	recess
		cow	decorate		

actor	grocery
doctor	decide
coat	cymbal
decorate	cellar
candy	price
cub	palace
cattle	recess
cow	cinema
carriage	celery
corn	pencil

Hard and soft c: Sound to symbol   **13**

FOCUS ON ALL LEARNERS

ESL/ELL ENGLISH LANGUAGE LEARNERS

Display items (or pictures of items) whose names are words with hard or soft *c* sounds, such as *pencil, cup, celery, candy.* Label the items with their names. Hold up each item and say its name, modeling correct pronunciation. Ask English language learners to repeat the word, then sort the items according to whether the *c* in its name is hard or soft. Repeat the exercise for words with hard or soft *g*, such as *game, sugar, orange,* and *page.* For pages 13 and 14, read aloud the rules, then apply the rules by modeling the first two items on each page.

KINESTHETIC/AUDITORY LEARNERS PARTNERS

Have partners play tic-tac-toe with *c* and *g* instead of *x* and *o.* One child in each pair will be *c* and the other will be *g.* Players take turns saying a word with their letter, telling whether the letter sound is soft or hard, and writing *c* or *g* in the tic-tac-toe grid.

AUDITORY LEARNERS GROUPS

Have children form a "hard sound" group and a "soft sound" group. Read aloud words from pages 13 and 14 as members of the appropriate group raise their hands when they hear hard or soft *c* and *g* sounds.

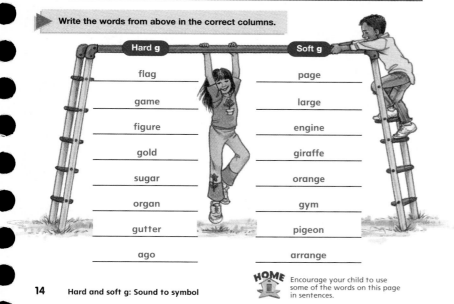

Say the words in each box. Draw a line to connect the words that have the same **g** sound.

RULE

When the letter **g** is followed by the vowels **a**, **o**, or **u**, it has a hard sound. When **g** is followed by **e**, **i**, or **y**, it usually has a soft sound. Soft **g** has the sound you hear at the beginning of **jam**.

gain   **g**ot   **g**um
a**g**e   **g**iant   **g**ypsy

1.
page — game
flag — engine

2.
figure — large
gold — giraffe

3.
orange — gym
sugar — organ

4.
gutter — ago
pigeon — arrange

Write the words from above in the correct columns.

Hard g	Soft g
flag	page
game	large
figure	engine
gold	giraffe
sugar	orange
organ	gym
gutter	pigeon
ago	arrange

HOME Encourage your child to use some of the words on this page in sentences.

14   Hard and soft g: Sound to symbol

CURRICULUM CONNECTIONS

SPELLING

Use the following words and sentences as a pretest for writing words with hard or soft *c* and *g*.

1. **candy**   This **candy** is chocolate.
2. **price**   What is the **price** of gold?
3. **corn**   Jen bought two cans of **corn**.
4. **game**   I know a new **game**.
5. **gym**   We ran laps around the **gym**.
6. **page**   Read the first **page**.

WRITING

Provide children with story starters, such as the following: the giant and the gold; the pigeon in a wig; the cow at the cinema; the giraffe in a gym suit. Have volunteers read their stories to the class.

PORTFOLIO

SOCIAL STUDIES

Have children list "city" and "country" words with hard and soft *c* and *g*. City words might be *offices, traffic,* and *gym*. Country words might be *cattle, wagon,* and *fences*.

TECHNOLOGY   **AstroWord** Consonant Sounds and Letters

Integrating Phonics and Reading

Guided Reading
Have children look at the cover of *Miss Muffett and the Spider* and read the title. Discuss why Miss Muffett looks upset.

First Reading Have children describe who Miss Muffett asks for help in getting rid of the spider.

Second Reading Ask children to identify story words with hard and soft *c* sounds.

Comprehension
After reading, ask children these questions:
• Why did Miss Muffett want to get rid of the spider? *Cause and Effect/Inference*
• Why did Miss Muffett have a bigger problem at the end of the story? *Personal Response/Inference*

ESL/ELL English Language Learners
On each page, have children identify the words that contain the letter *c*. Help them pronounce each word and then determine whether the *c* sound is hard or soft.

VISUAL LEARNERS   GROUPS

Have children write the words below on the board, replace the first letter of each with *c* or *g*, and read the new words. Use the words *name* (*game/came*), *boat* (*goat/coat*), *hood* (*good*), *hem* (*gem*), *term* (*germ*), *went* (*cent*), *pity* (*city*), *rub* (*cub*). Ask children to tell whether the *c* or *g* sound is hard or soft.

CHALLENGE

Suggest that children work with partners to create tongue twisters using words with hard or soft *c* and *g*. As an example, write the following on the board: *Cyrus the cyclist cycled in circles at the circus.*

EXTRA SUPPORT/INTERVENTION

Materials: self-stick notes

Choose words from pages 13 and 14 to write on self-stick notes. Have children read and sort the words by the hard and soft sounds of *c* and *g*. Once sorted, have children look back at their completed pages 13 and 14 to see in which groups the words were written. **See Daily Phonics Practice, page 213.**

Hard and Soft c and g

Skill Focus

Children will

★ distinguish between hard and soft *c* and *g*.

★ identify words with the hard and soft *c* and *g* sounds.

ESL/ELL Children who speak Korean, Khmer, Hmong, and Vietnamese may confuse a hard *c* with an initial hard *g*. Confirm pronunciation through word pairs such as *cold, gold*. English language learners whose home languages are Tagalog, Cantonese, Korean, Khmer, or Vietnamese may not make the *s* sound of soft *c* in an initial position and instead say /z/. Verify that children pronounce correctly the initial sounds of *city, celery,* and *zoo*.

Teach

Phonemic Awareness: Phoneme Categorization Explain that you will say sets of three words. Children are to identify which word has a different middle consonant sound from the other two. Use these words:

- engine   pigeon   sugar
- organ   pages   figure
- become   recess   decide
- circus   local   fancy

Sound to Symbol Review the rules for the hard and soft sounds of *c* and *g*. Then, write the words *city, coin, ceiling, cork, rice,* and *cactus* on the board. Call on volunteers to circle the *c* in each word and identify it as having a hard or a soft sound. Repeat the activity for the hard and soft *g* sound, using the words *age, gem, guess, doghouse, gym, gate,* and *general*.

Practice and Apply

Sound to Symbol As children complete the top of page 15, remind them to circle only words with the soft *c* or *g* sound. For the bottom, suggest first looking for words that have a *c* or *g*.

Critical Thinking For the Talk About It question, have children review the sentences and discuss the things they would have enjoyed doing.

Writing For page 16, remind children that each word in the box will be used only once. To find the answer, have children write the boxed letters in order, starting from the top.

Reading Use *The Cat That Broke the Rules,* MPC Phonics and Reading Consonant and Vowel Skills Library, Level C, to provide additional practice in reading words with hard and soft *c* and *g*.

15

Name _____

▶ Circle each word that has the soft **c** sound or the soft **g** sound.

> **RULE**
> When the letter **c** or **g** is followed by **e, i,** or **y,** the **c** or **g** usually has a soft sound.
> ra**c**e   pa**g**e

(ice)   can   (lace)   came   (fancy)   (gym)
gate   (giant)   (rice)   (large)   (huge)   wig
(rage)   (center)   (celery)   because   coyote   (general)
hug   (city)   (judge)   (page)   (face)   cookies
game   (engine)   (dance)   leg   (ceiling) (police)
(fence)   garden   (stage)   guess   (magic)   (place)
tag   (nice)   (bridge)   (giraffe) (gem)   cover

▶ Circle each word that has the hard sound of **c** or **g**.

1. Everyone had a (good) time at (Carol's) birthday party.
2. The (guests) (came) dressed in fancy (costumes).
3. Lance was a (detective) who solved (crimes).
4. Janice wore a (colorful) (gown) and an orange (wig).
5. A magician did (tricks) and (juggled) (cans).
6. The children played (games) and had (sack) races.
7. (Carol's) mother (gave) them (cake) and ice (cream).
8. (Carol) (gasped) as she opened her (cards) and presents.
9. (Curtis) (gave) her a (goldfish) in a bowl.
10. (Gary) the (cat) looked at it (closely).
11. He thought he (could) (catch) the fish for dinner.
12. The children laughed when (Gary) was (carried) outside.

 TALK about it Do you think everyone had a good time at the party? Why or why not?

Hard and soft c and g: Words in context, critical thinking   **15**

FOCUS ON ALL LEARNERS

ESL/ELL ENGLISH LANGUAGE LEARNERS

- Review the rule at the top of page 15. Then, choose two words from the first and second row of words in the first activity to model the pronunciation of the hard and soft *c* and *g*.

- With books closed, print on the board several words from page 15. Say the words one at a time, and ask English language learners to identify which sound of *c* or *g* each one contains.

- For page 16, make sure that children understand what to do. You may wish to model the first item.

KINESTHETIC/AUDITORY LEARNERS GROUPS

Materials: index cards

Arrange the class in groups. Have each group write words with hard and soft *c* and *g* on index cards, four words for each sound (16 cards in all). Then, have groups exchange cards and see how quickly they can read and sort the cards by the sounds of *c* and *g*.

AUDITORY LEARNERS PARTNERS

Have partners take turns providing clues about a word, including whether the word has soft or hard *c* or *g*. Here is an example: *My word has a soft c sound and is the name of frozen water.* (ice)

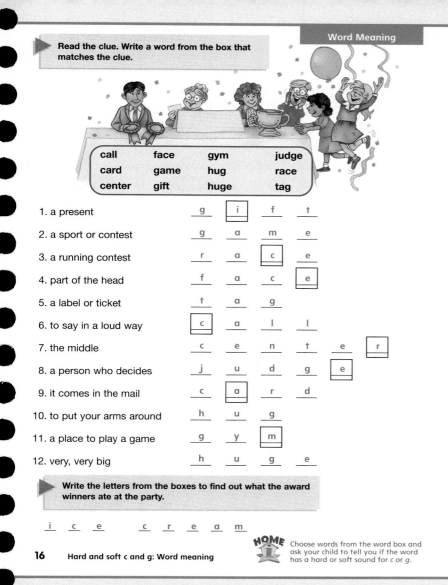

> **Word Meaning**
>
> Read the clue. Write a word from the box that matches the clue.

call	face	gym	judge
card	game	hug	race
center	gift	huge	tag

1. a present   g   **i**   f   t
2. a sport or contest   g   a   m   e
3. a running contest   r   a   **c**   e
4. part of the head   f   a   c   **e**
5. a label or ticket   t   a   g
6. to say in a loud way   **c**   a   l   l
7. the middle   c   e   n   t   e   **r**
8. a person who decides   j   u   d   g   **e**
9. it comes in the mail   c   **a**   r   d
10. to put your arms around   h   u   g
11. a place to play a game   g   y   **m**
12. very, very big   h   u   g   e

> Write the letters from the boxes to find out what the award winners ate at the party.

 i c e   c r e a m

16   Hard and soft c and g: Word meaning

Choose words from the word box and ask your child to tell you if the word has a hard or soft sound for c or g.

CURRICULUM CONNECTIONS

SPELLING

Use the following words and sentences as a posttest for writing words with hard and soft c and g.

1. **candy**   Dell bought some **candy**.
2. **price**   The **price** is two dollars.
3. **corn**   We ate **corn** on the cob.
4. **game**   The board **game** is on the shelf.
5. **gym**   Here is the **gym**.
6. **page**   Pat turned the **page**.

WRITING

Ask children to write about an event that happened at the party described on page 15. Have them underline words with c or g.

MATH

Have children list items included in the party described on page 15, such as *cake, ice cream, cards, bingo, magician, costumes,* and *goldfish.* Have them assign a cost to each item and list them from the most to the least expensive.

 **AstroWord** Consonant Sounds and Letters

VISUAL LEARNERS   GROUPS

Divide children into four teams. Have each team search the classroom for the names of items and words in print that have hard or soft c or g, such as *ceiling, lace, goldfish, giraffe.* Children can list their words on a Word Wall under appropriate headings.

CHALLENGE

Challenge children to work in pairs to write sentences that contain as many words as possible with hard and soft c and g sounds. Invite partners to read their sentences for the class. Here is an example: *Carla danced a jig across the bridge.*

EXTRA SUPPORT/INTERVENTION

Read words and sentences with children as necessary as they do the activities on pages 15 and 16. Help them determine whether the sound they hear in the words they read is the hard or soft sound of c or of g. See Daily Phonics Practice, page 213.

Integrating Phonics and Reading

Guided Reading

Have children look at the cover of the book and read the title. Ask them what rules a cat might break. **First Reading** Have children identify what Leo the cat does at the library.

Second Reading Help children identify story words that have the hard and soft g sound.

Comprehension

After reading, ask children these questions:
- Why did Leo want to go to the library? *Recall/Cause and Effect*
- How would you feel about a cat at your library? *Inference/Personal Response*

ESL/ELL English Language Learners

On each page, have children identify the words that contain the letter c or g. Help them pronounce each word and then determine whether the letter has a hard or soft sound.

Phonics and Spelling / Phonics and Writing

Review Consonants

Skill Focus

Children will

★ spell and write words with initial, medial, and final consonants, including hard and soft *c* and *g*.

★ write a journal entry using words with initial, medial, and final consonants, including words with hard and soft *c* and *g*.

Teach

Phonics and Spelling Write the following on the board: *_adder, ru_er, penci_*. As you say each word, have a volunteer supply the missing consonant. (*ladder, ruler, pencil*) Have the child identify the position of the letter *l* in the words. (ladder: *beginning*, ruler: *middle*, pencil: *end*)

Review the rules for hard and soft *c* and *g*. Then, write the following on the board: *_olor, _elery, _own, _ym*. Say each word (*color, celery, gown, gym*) and ask a volunteer to supply the missing letter and identify the sound as either hard or soft *c* or *g*. (color: *hard* c, celery: *soft* c, gown: *hard* g, gym: *soft* g)

Practice and Apply

Phonics and Spelling For the first activity on page 17, suggest that children read aloud each word in the list to hear the *c* or *g* sound before they sort the words. For the second activity, point out that there are 10 words in the list and 18 word blanks, so most of the words will be used twice.

Phonics and Writing Before children write their journal entries, have them brainstorm about celebrations they have been to, while you list their ideas on the board. Then, review the information in the callout boxes. Remind children to include in their entries some of the words in the box at the top.

Reading Use *The Day the Sky Turned Green*, MCP Phonics and Reading Library, Level C, to provide additional practice in reading words with hard and soft *c* and *g*.

The Day the Sky Turned Green

Name _____

Phonics & Spelling Read the words. Write each word under the heading where it belongs.

candy	cement	corn	game
guess	gym	page	price

Soft c
1. price
5. cement

Soft g
2. gym
6. page

Hard c
3. corn
7. candy

Hard g
4. game
8. guess

Read the words. Write each word under the heading where it belongs. You will write some of the words two times.

balloon	cement	dragon	leaf	lizard
ruler	seven	parrot	zipper	radio

Consonant in the Middle
9. balloon
10. cement
11. dragon
12. lizard
13. ruler
14. seven
15. parrot
16. zipper
17. radio

Consonant at the End
18. balloon
19. cement
20. dragon
21. leaf
22. lizard
23. ruler
24. seven
25. parrot
26. zipper

Review Consonants: Spelling   **17**

FOCUS ON ALL LEARNERS

ESL/ELL ENGLISH LANGUAGE LEARNERS

• For page 17, model the first item in each activity, thinking aloud. For example: *I want a word with the soft c sound. I look in the box.* Candy *starts with a hard c sound.* Cement *starts with a soft c sound. I will write* cement.

• For page 18, show English language learners examples of journal entries and explain that any kind of writing can go in a journal. They should feel free to express their ideas in whatever way they wish. Review the words in the box and provide children with labeled pictures to help them understand those that are unfamiliar.

KINESTHETIC LEARNERS GROUPS

Materials: index cards

Have each group make a set of alphabet letter cards. One member begins by forming a spelling word with the cards and then challenges other members to make new words by replacing one or more consonants. Then, repeat the process, using another spelling word.

Phonics & Writing

A journal is a special book where you can keep any kind of writing—words, lists, drawings, poems, stories, even doodles. A **journal entry** is something you write in a journal.

▶ Write a journal entry about a celebration you have been to. Some of the words in the box may help you.

| balloon | games | party | birthday | cake | gym |
| slice | holiday | candles | magic | family | fun |

Your entry can be **notes, lists,** or **whole sentences.**

Start your entry with the date.

Make doodles or drawings if you want to.

18 Hard and soft c and g: Writing

Ask your child to read the journal entry he or she wrote.

CURRICULUM CONNECTIONS

SPELLING

Use the following words and dictation sentences to review the spelling words from Unit 1.

1. **balloon**   I blew up a red **balloon**.
2. **ruler**   I used a **ruler** to measure it.
3. **seven**   A flock of **seven** birds flew by.
4. **window**   I will wash the **window**.
5. **zipper**   The **zipper** on my coat is stuck.
6. **lizard**   Sam named his **lizard** "Dino."
7. **candy**   The **candy** was too sweet.
8. **price**   What is the **price** of that hat?
9. **gym**   We play in the **gym** every day.
10. **corn**   My uncle grows **corn** on a farm.
11. **game**   We played a **game** of baseball.
12. **page**   I read the last **page** of the book.

MUSIC

Play recordings of parade music or marches. Ask children to describe what they picture and how the music makes them feel.

TECHNOLOGY   **AstroWord** Consonant Sounds and Letters

VISUAL LEARNERS GROUPS

Materials: paper strips

Write the words from page 17 on strips of paper and place them in a box. Seat children in a circle. One child selects a strip and reads the word aloud. The word is passed to the next child, who names and spells another word that begins with the same consonant. The next child selects a new strip.

CHALLENGE

Challenge children to write their journal entries on a separate sheet of paper as short stories, including as many words with hard and soft *c* and *g* as they can. Invite volunteers to read their stories aloud.

EXTRA SUPPORT/INTERVENTION

Materials: two index cards per child

Have each child write the letter *s* on one card and the letter *h* on the other. Tell children that you will say a word with *c* or *g*. If the *c* or *g* sound is hard, children should raise their *h* card. If the sound is soft, they should raise their *s* card. Use the words *cement, candy, price, corn, ice, place, because, guess, game, page, good.* See Daily Phonics Practice, pages 212–213.

Integrating Phonics and Reading

The Day the Sky Turned Green

Guided Reading
Have children read the title and look at the cover. Discuss the illustration, and have children share their ideas about what the book will be about.

First Reading Invite children to use the illustrations and words to describe what happens to Roberto and how Champ helps him.

Second Reading Have children identify the initial and final consonants of story words.

Comprehension
After reading, ask children these questions:
• Who is telling the story? *Recall/Details*
• How would you describe Champ? *Reflective Analysis/Personal Response*

ESL/ELL English Language Learners
Use gestures, sounds, and pantomime to illustrate the meanings of selected story words, such as *growl, whine, explode,* and how a tornado moves.

Take-Home Book

Review Consonants; Hard and Soft c and g

Skill Focus

Children will

★ read words with initial, medial, and final consonants, including hard and soft *c* and *g*, in the context of a story.

★ reread for fluency.

Teach

Build Background

- Remind children that the theme of this unit is "Celebrations." Ask them to name some of the celebrations they have read and talked about in this unit.

- Write the word *celebrate* on the board and read it aloud. Have children name some events they celebrate with friends, family, or classmates. Write children's ideas around the word *celebrate* to form a web. Tell children they are going to read a book about a celebration known as a block party.

Phonemic Awareness: Phoneme Isolation
Have children identify the letter at the beginning of the word *celebrate*. (*c*) Ask a child to say the word again and tell whether the *c* is soft or hard. (*soft*) Invite children to offer examples of other words that have hard and soft *c* and *g* sounds.

Practice and Apply

Read the Book Help children tear out and fold the pages to make their Take-Home Books. Ask them to look through their books, then talk about the pictures. Read the story together. Discuss what they learned about celebrations.

Sound to Symbol Label three columns on the board: *beginning, middle, end.* Read aloud or have volunteers read the book. Have children identify words that have initial, medial, or final consonants. Ask volunteers to write the words on the board in the correct column, read them aloud, and circle the appropriate consonants.

Have children read the book again to find words with soft and hard *c* and *g*. Children can sort the words by their *c* and *g* sounds.

Reread for Fluency Have children reread the book to increase their fluency and comprehension. Children can take their books home to read with family members.

19

Name _____

George, Amy, and José were making a sign. They were getting ready for the big block party. The party was going to celebrate their neighborhood. They wanted everybody to come.

1

COME TO A BLOCK PARTY! FOOD FUN PETS 2–6 SAT.

FOLD

At the end of the day, all the neighbors were happy and proud. The block party had gone very well. Then Mrs. Ito had a wonderful surprise. She gave all the children birds made of paper to help them remember this day forever.

4

Review Consonants; Hard and soft c and g: Take-home book   **19**

FOCUS ON ALL LEARNERS

ESL/ELL ENGLISH LANGUAGE LEARNERS

Give English language learners a list of words to find in the story and sort according to these categories: Hard *c*: *come, decorate, music, came, colorful, contests, corn, cats.* Soft *c*: *celebrate, rice.* Hard *g*: *going, juggled, games, good, great, gone, gave.* You may wish to model selecting one word in each category. Encourage children to match words with items in the illustrations when applicable.

VISUAL LEARNERS

Materials: construction paper, markers

Have children make book covers for favorite stories. Remind them to include the title of the story. Then, have children display their covers and have classmates identify initial, medial, and final consonants in the titles.

KINESTHETIC/VISUAL LEARNERS

Have children take turns reading aloud from the story. After reading a sentence, the reader chooses one word from the sentence and writes it on the board. A volunteer identifies a consonant at the beginning, middle, or end of the word. Then, that child continues with the next sentence from the story.

The children all helped to decorate the street. They hung streamers and balloons that waved in the breeze. Music filled the air. It was almost time for the party.

Everyone came. Mr. Addo told stories. Mrs. Stone juggled colorful balls. There were games and contests, too.

The adults brought the food. There were hotdogs and hamburgers and corn, beans, and rice. Everything tasted so good!

The pet parade was a great hit. There were dogs and cats and a lizard or two. There was a parrot that could talk. There was a soft rabbit. The children paraded through the street with their pets. Everyone waved as they went by.

20 Review Consonants; Hard and soft c and g: Take-home book

CURRICULUM CONNECTIONS

LANGUAGE ARTS

Suggest that children write a list of questions they would like to ask the author of the Take-Home Book. Then, have them underline consonants in the initial, medial, and final positions of some of the words they used.

ART

Materials: chart paper, crayons or markers

Have children choose a favorite book and draw a series of pictures to depict the story sequence. Ask them to write a brief caption under each picture, including words with soft and hard *c* and *g* sounds.

MATH

Materials: chart paper, markers

As a class or in small groups, encourage children to create a picture graph to tabulate the number of books they have read so far this year. As the year goes on, they can add symbols next to their names to show the increase in the total number of books read.

TECHNOLOGY **AstroWord** Consonant Sounds and Letters

AUDITORY LEARNERS

Slowly read aloud sentences from the story. Periodically pause on a word and have children identify the beginning, middle, or final consonant. If the consonant is *c* or *g,* have children tell whether it has a hard or a soft sound.

CHALLENGE

Challenge children to use encyclopedias and other resource materials to make a list of national celebrations. Then, have them choose their favorite celebration and write a paragraph explaining why they like it.

EXTRA SUPPORT/INTERVENTION

Invite children to retell the Take-Home Book story in their own words. On the board, write key words they use. Then, have them identify the consonants in the initial, medial, and final positions in the words. See **Daily Phonics Practice, pages 212–213.**

Unit Checkup

Review Consonants; Hard and Soft c and g

Skill Focus

Children will

★ review consonants in initial, medial, and final positions in words.

★ distinguish the hard and soft sounds of c and g in words.

Teach

Phonemic Awareness: Phoneme Isolation
On the board, write *Beginning, Middle,* and *Final.* Say a word, such as *wagon,* and ask children to identify the consonants that stand for the sounds they hear at the beginning, middle, and end of the word. (*w, g, n*) Write the consonants under the corresponding headings on the board. Use the words *rabbit, pedal, seven, comic, magic, melon, zipper, parrot, cement.*

Sound to Symbol Review the rules for the hard and soft *c* and *g* sounds. Then, write the words *ice, can, lace, came, nice,* and *cover* on the board. Ask volunteers to circle the *c* in each word and identify it as having a hard or soft sound.

Repeat the activity for the hard and soft *g* sound, using the words *rage, hug, large, leg, gem, tag,* and *huge.*

Practice and Apply

Assess Skills For page 21, be sure children understand that the consonants they are looking for in the words are listed along the left-hand side of the page in dark letters. Ask a volunteer to read them aloud.

For the activity at the top of page 22, make sure that children understand that they are to fill in only one circle per item. Suggest that children try both words in the sentence to determine which one makes the most sense. For the activity at the bottom of page 22, have children say the words quietly to themselves in order to hear whether the sounds are hard or soft.

Name _____

Read the words in the box and think about whether the consonants are at the beginning, middle, or end of each word. Write the word in the column or columns that show the position of the consonants. You will write some words more than once.

vat	gas	soap	pedal	leaf	hurry
wagon	zoo	cab	yellow	jiffy	dog
hated	funny	happy	room	music	comic
near	cowboy	jazz	tow	bike	hazy

	Beginning Consonant		Middle Consonant		Ending Consonant
p	1. pedal	2. happy		3. soap	
d	4. dog	5. pedal		6. hated	
b	7. bike	8. cowboy		9. cab	
l	10. leaf	11. yellow		12. pedal	
m	13. music	14. comic		15. room	
s	16. soap	17. music		18. gas	
r	19. room	20. hurry		21. near	
n	22. near	23. funny		24. wagon	
g	25. gas	26. wagon		27. dog	
t	28. tow	29. hated		30. vat	
z	31. zoo	32. hazy		33. jazz	
f	34. funny	35. jiffy		36. leaf	

Initial, medial, and final consonants: Assessment   **21**

FOCUS ON ALL LEARNERS

ESL/ELL ENGLISH LANGUAGE LEARNERS

• For page 21, select a word from the box and write it on the board. Point to and say the word. Have English language learners repeat. Call on volunteers to circle the consonants at the beginning, middle, and end of the word. Ask children to say the sounds that the consonants stand for.

• For page 22, model the first item. Then, explain how to list your word choice in the correct column at the bottom of the page.

KINESTHETIC LEARNERS GROUPS

Materials: index cards, timer

Have children copy words with *c* and *g* from page 22 on index cards. Then, have them take turns reading and sorting the words as you time them.

VISUAL LEARNERS GROUPS

Send teams on a word hunt in search of words with a specific consonant, such as words with the hard *g* sound or words with double consonants in the middle. Suggest that teams chart their results.

UNIT 1 CHECKUP

▶ **Fill in the circle beside the word that belongs in each sentence.**

1. Alice ___ a package for her birthday.   ● got   ○ gym
2. She was ___ that it was from Carl.   ○ curtain   ● certain
3. The package was ___!   ● huge   ○ hug
4. Alice tried to ___ what was in it.   ○ gem   ● guess
5. She ___ opened the enormous box.   ○ cement   ● carefully
6. A ___ orange kite was inside.   ● giant   ○ garden
7. "I ___ believe it," Alice exclaimed.   ○ cent   ● can't
8. "I'll ___ Carl right away to thank him."   ● call   ○ cell

▶ **Write all of the word choices listed above in the correct columns.**

9. **Hard c**
curtain
carefully
can't
call

10. **Soft c**
certain
cement
cent
cell

11. **Hard g**
got
hug
guess
garden

12. **Soft g**
gym
huge
gem
giant

22   Hard and soft c, g: Assessment

STUDENT PROGRESS ASSESSMENT

To help you evaluate the progress children have made with consonants, review the observational notes you made as children were working through the activities in the unit.

PORTFOLIO ASSESSMENT

Review the materials children have collected in their portfolios. Have interviews with children to discuss their written work and the progress they have made since the beginning of the unit. Use their work to help you evaluate how well they apply the phonics skills they have learned.

DAILY PHONICS PRACTICE

For children who need additional practice with consonants, quick reviews can be found on pages 212–213 in Daily Phonics Practice.

PHONICS POSTTEST

To assess children's mastery of consonants, use the posttest on pages 5g–5h.

AUDITORY LEARNERS   PARTNERS

One child reads aloud a word from pages 21–22. His or her partner writes the word and circles initial, medial, and final consonants whose sounds are heard. If the word has a *c* or *g,* he or she also determines whether the *c* or *g* is soft or hard. Partners take turns reading words and identifying consonants.

CHALLENGE

Suggest that children work together to write a sentence using words that include all the consonants. For example: *The quick brown fox jumps over the lazy dog.*

EXTRA SUPPORT/INTERVENTION

Materials: bingo game boards, game markers

Provide blank bingo game boards and have children choose words from pages 21 and 22 to write in the spaces. To play, call out clues such as the following: *Cover a word that has the consonant* p *in the middle position.* Play until someone calls out "bingo!" and then repeat. See Daily Phonics Practice, pages 212–213.

Teacher Notes

UNIT 2

Short and Long Vowels

THEME: FRIENDS AND FAMILY

CONTENTS

UNIT 2 RESOURCES

TEACHING PLANS

Student Performance Objectives

In Unit 2, children will review short and long vowel sound associations for *a, e, i, o,* and *u* within the context of the theme "Friends and Family." As children begin to understand and learn to apply the concept that consonant and vowel sounds can be blended together to form words, they will be able to

▶ Identify the short *a, e, i, o,* and *u* vowel sounds in words and picture names

▶ Discriminate among short vowel sounds in words

▶ Recognize and pronounce the long vowel sounds of *a, e, i, o,* and *u*

▶ Distinguish between short and long vowels

▶ Identify spellings for long vowel sounds

Overview of Resources

| LESSON | MCP PHONICS AND READING LIBRARY, LEVEL C | | DAILY PHONICS PRACTICE |
	PROGRAM	TITLE	
Unit Opener			
9: Short *a*	RR, Stg Five, Bk 11	*A Giant-Sized Day*	213
10: Short *i*; Review short *a, i*	RR, Stg Five, Bk 12	*The Princess and the Wise Woman*	213
11: Short *u*; Review short *a, i, u*	RR, Stg Five, Bk 15	*Cubby's Gum*	213
12: Short *o*; Review short *a, i, u, o*	RR, Stg Five, Bk 13	*Toast for Mom*	213
13: Short *e*; Review short *a, i, u, o*	RR, Stg Five, Bk 14	*Something Everybody Needs*	213
14: Review short vowels	RR, Stg Five, Bk 16	*Julie's Mornings*	213
15: Long *a*	RR, Stg Four, Bk 9	*Who Has a Tail?*	214
16: Long *i*; Review long *a, i*	RR, Stg Four, Bk 13	*The Princess Who Couldn't Cry*	214
17: Long *u*; Review long *a, i, u*	RR, Stg Three, Bk 37	*My Sister June*	214
18: Long *o*; Review long *a, i, u, o*	RR, Stg Five, Bk 13	*Toast for Mom*	214
19: Long *e*; Review long *a, i, u, o, e*	RR, Stg Four, Bk 17	*Red and I Visit the Vet*	214
20: Review long and short vowels	RR, Stg Five, Bk 17	*This Room Is a Mess!*	213–214
21: Review short and long vowels; Take-Home Book: "Animal Homes"			213–214
22: Unit Checkup			213–214

RR–Ready Readers   Stg–Stage   Bk–Book

Assessment Options

In Unit 2, assess children's ability to read and write words with short and long vowel sounds. Use the Unit Pretest and Posttest for formal assessment. For ongoing informal assessment, you may wish to use children's work on the Review pages, Take-Home Books, and Unit Checkups. Encourage children to evaluate their own work and to participate in setting goals for their own learning.

ESL/ELL Short and long vowel sounds may be especially problematic for English language learners. Note pronunciation difficulties as they occur, but assess performance based upon children's ability to distinguish specific sounds when pronounced by a native speaker. For additional support for English language learners, see page 23j.

FORMAL ASSESSMENT

Use the Unit 2 Pretest, on pages 23e–23f, to help assess a child's knowledge at the beginning of a unit and to plan instruction.

ESL/ELL Before administering the Pretest, gather together items (or pictures of them) that match the visuals on page 23e. Select an item and have volunteers name it. Ask other children to write the word on the board and read it aloud, emphasizing the vowel sound. Some children may have difficulty understanding the test directions. Read them aloud and model how to complete the test pages.

Use the Unit 2 Posttest, on pages 23g–23h, to help assess mastery of unit objectives and to plan for reteaching, if necessary.

INFORMAL ASSESSMENT

Use the Review pages, Unit Checkup, and Take-Home Books in the student book to provide an effective means of evaluating children's performance.

Unit 2 Skills	Review pages	Checkups	Take-Home Books
Short *a, i, u, o, e*	35–36, 47–48	51–52	49–50
Long *a, i, u, o, e*	47–48	51–52	49–50

STUDENT PROGRESS CHECKLIST

Use the checklist on page 23i to record children's progress. You may want to cut the sections apart to place each child's checklist in his or her portfolio.

PORTFOLIO ASSESSMENT

This logo appears throughout the teaching plans. It signals opportunities for collecting children's work for individual portfolios. You may also want to include the Pretest and Posttest, the Review pages, the Unit Checkup, Phonics & Reading, and Phonics & Writing pages.

PHONEMIC AWARENESS AND PHONICS ASSESSMENT

Use PAPA to obtain an itemized analysis of children's decoding skills.

PAPA Skills	MCP Phonics Lessons in Unit 2
Short Vowels	Lessons 9–14, 20
Long Vowels	Lessons 15–20

Pretest and Posttest

DIRECTIONS

To help you assess children's progress in learning Unit 2 skills, tests are available on pages 23e–23h.

Administer the Pretest before children begin the unit. The results of the Pretest will help you identify each child's strengths and needs in advance, allowing you to structure lesson plans to meet individual needs. Administer the Posttest to assess children's overall mastery of skills taught in the unit and to identify specific areas that will require reteaching.

ESL/ELL Support English language learners by implementing any of the following suggestions before or during test taking, as appropriate.

- Model procedures for marking test answers. Complete several items together or in small groups to make sure children understand test-taking procedures.

- Conduct the test one-on-one with children who are unable to read independently in English or who need special pacing. Provide frequent support for their efforts.

- For items 7–30, tell children that correct answers may have short or long vowel sounds. They should choose the word that makes the most sense in the context of the sentence.

PERFORMANCE ASSESSMENT PROFILE

The following chart will help you identify specific skills as they appear on the tests and will enable you to identify and record specific information about an individual's or the class's performance on the tests.

Depending on the results of each test, refer to the Reteaching column for lesson-plan pages where you can find activities that will be useful for meeting individual needs or for daily phonics practice.

Answer Keys

Unit 2 Pretest, page 23e (BLM 8)

1. bug	6. hat	11. bed
2. bell	7. pain	12. pine
3. pin	8. meet	13. bait
4. sock	9. mule	14. road
5. jet	10. hid	

Unit 2 Pretest, page 23f (BLM 9)

15. nap	21. stove	27. bike
16. whale	22. lead	28. bus
17. met	23. drive	29. bat
18. huge	24. big	30. Pete
19. hot	25. lake	
20. dug	26. joke	

Unit 2 Posttest, page 23g (BLM 10)

1. top	6. pig	11. sit
2. pen	7. take	12. dime
3. ham	8. soap	13. tail
4. rug	9. feed	14. hope
5. net	10. cute	

Unit 2 Posttest, page 23h (BLM 11)

15. time	21. late	27. seen
16. robe	22. ten	28. hat
17. sun	23. lock	29. bun
18. sail	24. green	30. five
19. pick	25. map	
20. juice	26. pet	

Performance Assessment Profile

Skill	Pretest Questions	Posttest Questions	Reteaching	
			Focus on All Learners	**Daily Phonics Practice**
Short *a*	6, 15, 29	3, 25, 28	25–26, 35–36, 47–50	213
Short *i*	3, 10, 24	6, 11, 19	27–28, 35–36, 47–50	213
Short *u*	1, 20, 28	4, 17, 29	29–30, 35–36, 47–50	213
Short *o*	4, 19	1, 23	31–32, 35–36, 47–50	213
Short *e*	2, 5, 11, 17	2, 5, 22, 26	33–36, 47–50	213
Long *a*	7, 13, 16, 25	7, 13, 18, 21	37–38, 47–50	214
Long *i*	12, 23, 27	12, 15, 30	39–40, 47–50	214
Long *u*	9, 18	10, 20	41–42, 47–50	214
Long *o*	14, 21, 26	8, 14, 16	43–44, 47–50	214
Long *e*	8, 22, 30	9, 24, 27	45–50	214

Name _____

> Say the name of each picture. Fill in the circle below the word that identifies the picture.

1. 
beg ○
bag ○
bug ○

2. 
bell ○
bid ○
bud ○

3. 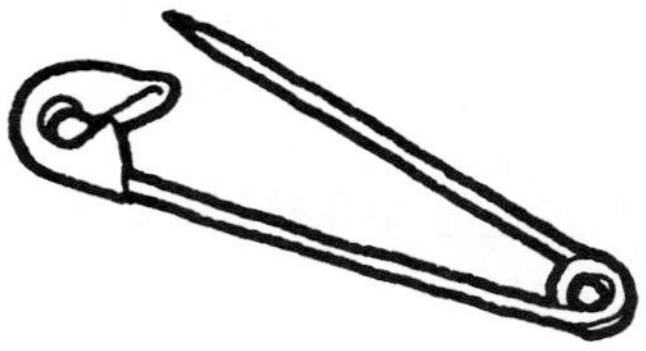
pan ○
pin ○
pen ○

4. 
sock ○
sack ○
sick ○

5. 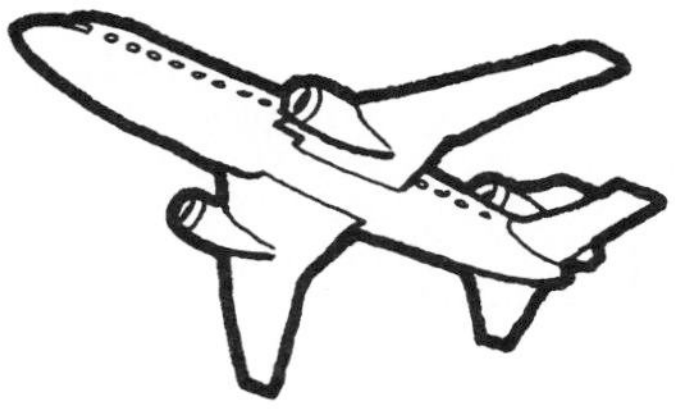
jet ○
jot ○
jut ○

6. 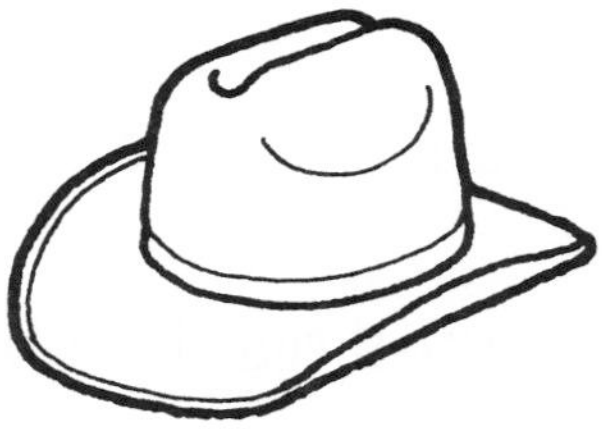
hat ○
hut ○
hit ○

> Read each sentence. Fill in the circle beside the word that completes the sentence.

7. Gail has a _____ in her leg. ○ pan   ○ pain

8. Jill will _____ us for lunch. ○ met   ○ meet

9. We saw a _____ at the farm. ○ mug   ○ mule

10. The fox _____ behind the log. ○ hid   ○ hide

11. Ask Joe to make his own _____. ○ bed   ○ bead

12. We planted a _____ tree. ○ pin   ○ pine

13. Where is the fish _____? ○ bat   ○ bait

14. The cub went across the _____. ○ rod   ○ road

Go to the next page.→

BLM 8 Unit 2 Pretest: Short and long vowels

Name _____

> **Read each sentence. Fill in the circle next to the word that completes the sentence.**

15. Jake took a ____ after school.   ○ nap   ○ name

16. The ____ came up on the beach.   ○ what   ○ whale

17. Jean ____ us at the end of the road.   ○ meet   ○ met

18. We have quite a ____ load of logs.   ○ huge   ○ hug

19. It was a very ____ summer.   ○ heat   ○ hot

20. The badger ____ a deep hole.   ○ dug   ○ dune

21. Tom burned his thumb on the hot ____.   ○ stove   ○ stop

22. The band will ____ the parade.   ○ led   ○ lead

23. Mom will ____ me to dance class.   ○ drive   ○ drip

24. My new coat is too ____ for me.   ○ bite   ○ big

25. We went swimming in the ____.   ○ lake   ○ lack

26. Luke told a funny ____.   ○ joke   ○ jot

27. Sue got a new green ____.   ○ bike   ○ bid

28. Bill rides the ____ to school.   ○ bug   ○ bus

29. Steve brought his ____ to the game.   ○ bat   ○ bait

30. My dog ____ can do many tricks.   ○ pet   ○ Pete

Possible score on Unit 2 Pretest is 30. Number correct _____

BLM 9 Unit 2 Pretest: Short and long vowels

23f

Name _____

> Say the name of each picture. Fill in the circle below the word that identifies the picture.

1.	tap ◯ top ◯ tip ◯	2.	pen ◯ pan ◯ pin ◯	3.	hem ◯ him ◯ ham ◯
4.	rig ◯ rug ◯ rag ◯	5.	net ◯ not ◯ nut ◯	6.	pug ◯ peg ◯ pig ◯

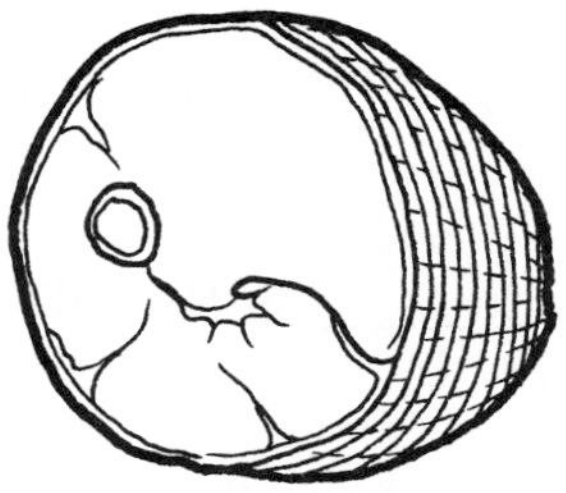

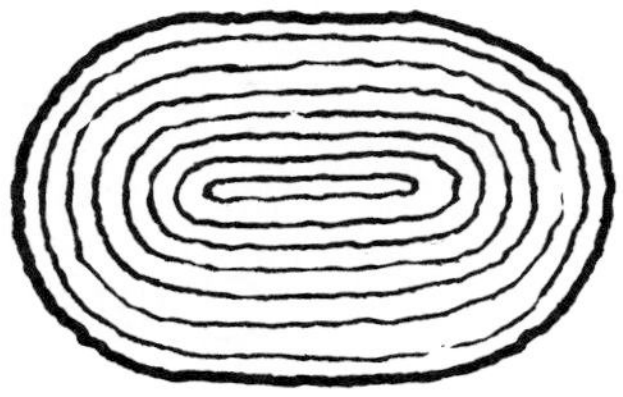

> Read each sentence. Fill in the circle beside the word that completes the sentence.

7. Mrs. Jones likes to _____ a walk after dinner.   ◯ take   ◯ talk

8. Sue washed her hands with _____.   ◯ sop   ◯ soap

9. John will _____ his cat.   ◯ fed   ◯ feed

10. The puppy is _____.   ◯ cute   ◯ cub

11. Mom and Dad ____ next to each other.   ◯ sit   ◯ site

12. A _____ is ten cents.   ◯ dime   ◯ dim

13. The dog wagged its _____.   ◯ tall   ◯ tail

14. I _____ I will get a new bike.   ◯ hop   ◯ hope

Go to the next page.→

BLM 10 Unit 2 Posttest: Short and long vowels

Name _____

> ▶ Read each sentence. Fill in the circle next to the word that completes the sentence.

15. It is _____ for a test! ○ Tim ○ time

16. I wear a _____ to stay warm before bed. ○ robe ○ rob

17. The _____ is shining. ○ sun ○ suit

18. The boat has a _____. ○ salt ○ sail

19. Pam will _____ a number. ○ pick ○ pike

20. I'll drink grape _____. ○ just ○ juice

21. The bus was _____. ○ lad ○ late

22. Sue will count to _____. ○ ten ○ team

23. I have the key to open the _____. ○ lock ○ let

24. Ann put on her _____ coat. ○ green ○ grass

25. Use a _____ to find your way. ○ main ○ map

26. Jane likes to _____ her puppy. ○ peat ○ pet

27. Have you _____ my new toy? ○ seen ○ set

28. A ____ will keep my ears warm. ○ hail ○ hat

29. Tom ate the last _____. ○ bun ○ ban

30. The _____ fish swim around the bowl. ○ five ○ fan

Possible score on Unit 2 Posttest is 30. Number correct _____

BLM 11 Unit 2 Posttest: Short and long vowels

Student Progress Checklist

Make as many copies as needed to use for a class list. For individual portfolio use, cut apart each child's section. As indicated by the code, color in boxes next to skills satisfactorily assessed and insert an *X* by those requiring reteaching. Marked boxes can later be colored in to indicate mastery.

Student Progress Checklist

Code: ■ Satisfactory   ☒ Needs Reteaching

Student: _____ _____ Pretest Score: _____ Posttest Score: _____	**Skills**	**Comments / Learning Goals**
	☐ Short *a* ☐ Long *a* ☐ Short *i* ☐ Long *i* ☐ Short *u* ☐ Long *u* ☐ Short *o* ☐ Long *o* ☐ Short *e* ☐ Long *e*	
Student: _____ _____ Pretest Score: _____ Posttest Score: _____	**Skills** ☐ Short *a* ☐ Long *a* ☐ Short *i* ☐ Long *i* ☐ Short *u* ☐ Long *u* ☐ Short *o* ☐ Long *o* ☐ Short *e* ☐ Long *e*	**Comments / Learning Goals**
Student: _____ _____ Pretest Score: _____ Posttest Score: _____	**Skills** ☐ Short *a* ☐ Long *a* ☐ Short *i* ☐ Long *i* ☐ Short *u* ☐ Long *u* ☐ Short *o* ☐ Long *o* ☐ Short *e* ☐ Long *e*	**Comments / Learning Goals**
Student: _____ _____ Pretest Score: _____ Posttest Score: _____	**Skills** ☐ Short *a* ☐ Long *a* ☐ Short *i* ☐ Long *i* ☐ Short *u* ☐ Long *u* ☐ Short *o* ☐ Long *o* ☐ Short *e* ☐ Long *e*	**Comments / Learning Goals**

BLM 12 Unit 2 Checklist

Throughout Unit 2 there are opportunities to assess English language learners' ability to read and write words with short and long vowel sounds. Recognizing and pronouncing vowel sounds can be especially problematic for English language learners. Children's home languages vary from having five pure vowel sounds in Spanish to 35 syllabic vowels in Cantonese. English language learners will need many opportunities to listen to and practice saying English vowel sounds before they can reasonably be expected to reproduce them without error. Take note of pronunciation difficulties as they occur, and assess children's progress based on their ability to distinguish vowel sounds when pronounced by a native speaker.

Lesson 9, pages 25–26 Korean and Russian speakers may pronounce /ya/ after certain consonants, making the *ca* of *camp* sound like the *kya* series in *brickyard*.

Lesson 10, pages 27–28 Children whose home language is not English may pronounce short *i* like the *ee* in *see* or the *ea* in *meat*. Practice *mitt, meat; lips, leaps; six, seeks;* and so on.

Lesson 11, pages 29–30 Children who speak Spanish, Tagalog, or some Asian languages may pronounce short *u* like the *o* in *hot*.

Lesson 12, pages 31–32 Native speakers of Spanish, Tagalog, and some Asian languages may pronounce in the same way the sounds of short *o*, short *a*, and short *u*. Practice *hot, hat, hut; lock, lack, luck.*

Lesson 13, pages 33–34 Since no vowel sound similar to short *e* exists in Korean, offer additional practice and support with *pen, net, leg, bed, red, belt, tent,* and other words from the lesson.

Lesson 15, pages 37–38 Children who speak languages other than English may confuse long *a* with short *e*; practice *let, late; red, rake; tell, tale.* Native speakers of Spanish may write *e* instead of long *a* in words.

Lesson 16, pages 39–40 Children who speak Asian languages or Spanish may clip the long *i* and pronounce it like short *a*, for example, pronouncing *glide* as *glad.* Practice with *mine, man; bike, back; flight, flat.*

Lesson 17, pages 41–42 Children who speak Cantonese or Vietnamese may pronounce a "round" *u*. Spanish speakers may have trouble with the /yu/ sound of long *u* as in *music* or *cube* (saying *moosic* or *coob*).

Lesson 18, pages 43–44 Speakers of Asian languages may confuse long *o* with the sound of *aw* as in *awful*; practice *low, law; so, saw;* and so on.

Lesson 19, pages 45–46 Children who speak languages other than English may assimilate long *e* and short *i*; practice *feet, fit; Pete, pit; beat, bit.*

Spelling Connections

INTRODUCTION

The Unit Word List is a list of selected spelling words drawn from this unit. The words are grouped by short and long vowel sounds. To incorporate spelling into your phonics program, use the activity in the Curriculum Connections section of each teaching plan.

ESL/ELL It is recommended that English language learners reach the intermediate fluency level of English proficiency before focusing on spelling.

For English language learners, introduce 6–8 words at a time. Help children understand the words' meanings by using visuals or realia.

The spelling lessons utilize the following approach for each vowel sound.

1. Administer pretests of the words, some of which have not yet been introduced. Dictation sentences are provided.

2. Provide practice.

3. Reassess. Dictation sentences are provided.

A midunit review that focuses on words with short-vowel sounds is provided in Lesson 14.

An end-of-the-unit review that covers long-vowel words is provided on page 48.

DIRECTIONS

Make a copy of Blackline Master 13 for each child. After administering a pretest for a group of vowel sounds, give children a copy of the appropriate word list.

Children can work with a partner to practice spelling the words orally and identifying the vowel sound in each word. You may want to challenge children to make new words by substituting the vowel sounds. Children can write words of their own on *My Own Word List* (see Blackline Master 13).

Have children store their list words in an envelope in their books or notebooks. Alternatively, you may want to suggest that children keep a spelling notebook, listing words with similar patterns. Another idea is to build Word Walls with children and display them in the classroom. Each section of the wall can focus on words with a single phonics element. These walls will become a good resource for children to use when they are writing.

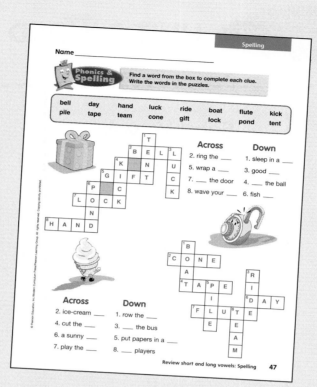

Unit Word List

Short Vowels *a, i*
hand
glass
back
kick
gift
dish

Short Vowels *u, o, e*
bus
luck
lock
pond
tent
bell

Long Vowels *a, i*
sail
tape
day
pile
time
ride

Long Vowels *u, o, e*
flute
cube
boat
cone
meat
seal

Name _____

 **Phonics & Spelling**

UNIT 2 WORD LIST

Short Vowels
a, i

hand

glass

back

kick

gift

dish

Short Vowels
u, o, e

bus

luck

lock

pond

tent

bell

Long Vowels
a, i

sail

tape

day

pile

time

ride

Long Vowels
u, o, e

flute

cube

boat

cone

meat

seal

My Own Word List

My Own Word List

BLM 13 Unit 2 Spelling Words

Phonics Games, Activities, and Technology

The following collection of ideas offers a variety of opportunities to reinforce phonics skills while actively engaging children. The games, activities, and technology suggestions can easily be adapted to meet the needs of your group of learners. They vary in approach so as to consider children's different learning styles.

RHYME TIME

In advance, write words with short and long vowels on slips of paper, such as *bag, cake, seek, hen, brick, fin, bone, top, gum, flute*. Place the words in a container. Have children sit in a circle. Ask the first player to pick a slip of paper from the container and read the word. Have the container passed to the right and have that child say a word that rhymes with the first player's word. Continue around the circle, allowing each child to say another word that rhymes. When no more rhyming words can be identified, have the player who is holding the container pick another word. Continue until all words have been picked from the container.

HINK PINKS

Hink pinks are rhyming word pairs that help children attend to the spelling-pattern rhyme relationship in words and give children a purpose for manipulating and pairing words that rhyme. Work with children to create hink pinks to write and illustrate or to describe in riddles for their classmates to guess. Here are some examples of hink pinks that feature both short and long vowel sounds: *drab crab, fake snake, wet pet, beast feast, quick chick, bright light, crop flop, cold gold, crunch lunch, rude dude*.

PLAY CHARADES

Write the following long and short vowel action words on slips of paper: *fan, ride, hear, greet, rest, leap, skip, find, lock, yell, jump, smile, clap, write, paint, read, climb, jog, wink, smell, sniff, hum, strut, sing*. Or choose words your class needs to focus on. Put the slips of paper in a hat. Begin by inviting one child to choose a slip of paper and silently read the word. The child identifies the vowel sound and acts out the word for the others to guess. The one who guesses correctly chooses the next word.

I EAT MY PEAS WITH HONEY

Write the poem at the right on the chalkboard. Invite children to come to the board and circle the words that rhyme (*honey/funny; life/knife*); have the long *e* sound (*eat, peas, keeps*); have the short *i* sound (*with, it*); and have the short *u* sound (*funny, but*). Then, ask children to identify the vowel sounds in any remaining words. Invite some volunteers to substitute the word *peas* in the poem with the name of another food with a short or long vowel sound. Then, they can reread the poem for the group, inserting the new food name, for example, *beans, grapes, cheese bites, fish sticks*.

> I eat my peas with honey.
> I've done it all my life.
> The peas taste kind of funny,
> But it keeps them on the knife.

VOWEL HOUSE

Provide children with two pieces of construction paper—one white and one another color. Tell children they will be making a vowel house. Using the colored construction paper, encourage children to draw a house or apartment building that has four large windows and a door. Help them cut the windows and door in the middle or on three sides so that they flap open and shut as shown. Next, children can paste the house onto the white piece of paper, making sure they do not paste the windows or doors shut. Have some children focus on short vowel words and others on words with long vowels to "live" in the house. First, have them label the house Short Vowel House or Long Vowel House. Then, inside each window and door, tell children to write one or more words that have the appropriate vowel sounds in them.

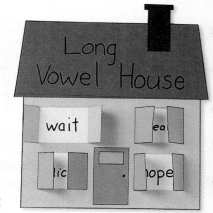

WORD SCAVENGER HUNT

Around the room, scatter cards with words featuring short vowel sounds. Children can form five teams and hunt for words having a specific vowel sound. When the hunt has ended, ask each team to display and read the words they found. These words can then be added to an existing word wall. Feature words with long vowel sounds for a future hunt.

PHONOGRAM TIC-TAC-TOE

Have partners draw a nine-square tic-tac-toe grid on paper and write a short vowel phonogram in each square, for example: *at, en, ip, ost, ump, and, ent, id, ot*. To play, partners take turns choosing a phonogram to name and spelling a word that ends with the phonogram. If correct, an *X* or *O* can be written over the phonogram.

MAKE A WORD

Provide children with sets of letter cards. Begin by having them build words with short vowel sounds, such as *ran, set, bit, cot,* and *cub*. Then, have children manipulate letter cards to substitute letters that stand for each short vowel sound with letters that spell the long vowel sound, creating words such as *rain, seat, bite, coat,* and *cube*.

PLANTING WORDS

In advance, work with a small group of children to construct a cardboard tree with five branches or draw one on a large sheet of butcher paper. Label each branch with a vowel. Cut leaf shapes from paper, attach a circle of tape to the back, and on them write words with vowel sounds you wish children to review. Invite children to take a leaf, read the word, identify the vowel sound, and attach the leaf to the appropriate branch. Continue until all leaves are placed on the tree. Then, have children sort the words on each branch into groups of short and long vowel sounds. The leaves can be removed and reattached for future play.

SENTENCE BUILDING

Write the following phrases on cards: *ride on a bus, see a whale, eat a peach, climb up stairs, go to the beach, sail a boat, comb hair, train a seal, wave a flag, wrap a gift, ride a bike, chase a cat, watch a bull*. Invite children to take turns choosing a phrase to read and use in a sentence. Challenge children to use two phrases in nonsense sentences, if they like. Then, encourage children to write phrases of their own.

WORDS AROUND THE HOUSE

Have children use milk cartons that have been washed and dried to create small houses with removeable roofs. Invite children to brainstorm things in their homes as you list the items on the board. When the list is complete, ask children to come to the board and circle words with short and long vowels. Provide children with paper strips and encourage them to copy the words onto the strips. They can store their words in their "houses" and play matching word games they create with a partner.

MAKE FLIP BOOKS

Distribute copies of Blackline Master 14 to make flip books with children. First, brainstorm different short and long vowel phonograms and list them on the chalkboard. Then, have children cut out the rectangles, and help them assemble the -ive flip book, by fastening it on the two dots with yarn or staples. Then, have children choose a phonogram to write on the large blank rectangles. On each set of smaller rectangles, children can write initial consonants, blends, or digraphs that, when combined with their phonogram, make words. When children have each completed their three original flip books, have them share the books with partners or in small groups.

CATEGORY APARTMENT BUILDING

Have children draw the outline of a three-story apartment building on a sheet of paper, as shown, with space for a roof at the top and three rows of windows. Have children label an area at the far left of each floor *long*, *short*, and *both*. Invite each child to select a category and write its name on the roof of their apartment drawing. Then, have children think of words that relate to their category and write them in the remaining windows of the apartment. Tell children to decide if each word has a long vowel sound, a short vowel sound, or a combination of the two and then write it on the appropriate floor. Suggested categories might include plant, mammals, birds, colors, cities, states, foods.

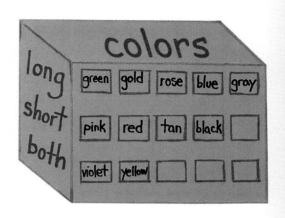

The following software products reinforce children's awareness of vowels, consonants, and other phonemic elements.

Reader Rabbit® 3
This product, the last in the *Reader Rabbit* series, is designed to teach six- to eight-year-olds writing skills such as who, what, where, when, and how through a series of games centered around Reader Rabbit's job as a newspaper reporter.

** Riverdeep The Learning Company
    500 Redwood Blvd.
    Novato, CA 94947
    (800) 825-4420
    www.learningcompanyschool.com

Leapfrog Leappad® Pro
Children ages 6 and up will have their reading abilities pushed to the next level by this more "sophisticated" version of the Leappad. The program features a wide selection of interactive books that improve reading comprehension, increase vocabulary, and teach word definitions and pronunciations.

**Leapfrog
    6401 Hollis Street, Suite 150
    Emeryville, CA
    www.leapfrog.com

Make Flip Books

: d	:	i v e		
: f	: h	: l	:dr	
• •	• •			
• •	• •	• •	• •	
• •	• •			
• •	• •	• •	• •	

BLM 14 Unit 2 Activity

Home Connections

The Home Connections features of this program are intended to involve families in their children's learning and application of phonics skills. Three effective opportunities to make connections between home and school include the following.

- **HOME LETTER**
- **HOME NOTES**
- **TAKE-HOME BOOKS**

HOME LETTER

A letter is available to be sent home at the beginning of Unit 2. This letter informs family members that children will be learning to read and write words with short and long vowel sounds within the context of the unit theme, "Friends and Family." The suggested home activity focuses on making a collage of activities that a child shares with family or friends. This activity promotes interaction between child and family members while supporting children's learning study of short and long vowel sounds. The letter, available in both English and Spanish, also suggests theme-related books family members can enjoy reading together.

HOME NOTES

Whenever the Home logo appears within the student book, a phonics activity is suggested to be done at home. The activities are simple to do, requiring little or no preparation or special materials, and are meant to reinforce the targeted phonics skill.

TAKE-HOME BOOKS

Within the student book are Take-Home Books that can be cut out and assembled. The story language in each book reinforces the targeted phonics skill. The books can then be taken home and shared with family members. In Unit 2, one Take-Home Book is available, focusing on each of the short and long vowels *a, e, i, o,* and *u* as well as the unit theme, "Friends and Family."

Home Notes in Spanish are also available for both teachers and parents to download and use from our website, www.PlaidPhonics.com.

Short and Long Vowels

Skill Focus

Assess Prior Knowledge

To assess children's prior knowledge of short and long vowels, use the pretest on pages 23e–23f.

Unit Focus

Build Background

- Write the theme "Friends and Family" on the board, read it aloud, and help children locate it on page 23.

- Direct children to the illustration on the page and discuss what is happening in the picture. Have children describe what the two children are doing.

- Read the poem "A Friend" aloud as children follow along. Ask children how the children in the picture are showing they are friends. Suggest that they are sharing an activity and they are having fun. Encourage children to exchange ideas about the kinds of things friends do when they visit each other's homes.

Introduce Vowels

- Write *a, e, i, o,* and *u* on the board. Have children identify the letters and point out that they are called vowels. Ask what the other letters of the alphabet are called. (*consonants*)

- Remind children that vowels can have two sounds: short and long. Then, reread the poem "A Friend." Afterward, say the words *me, she, he, case,* and *may* slowly, stressing the long vowel sounds: *meee, sheee, heee, caaase,* and *maaay.* Explain that children will learn more about vowel sounds as they do the lessons in this unit.

Critical Thinking Ask children to think about the things they do with their friends. Then, ask volunteers to respond to the Talk About It question.

Read Aloud

A Friend
by Beatrice Schenk de Regniers

Whoever we are,
Whatever we be,
We're friends 'cause I'm me
We're friends 'cause she's she.
(Or because he is he—
Whatever, whatever the case may be.)
A friend
is a friend
is a friend!

UNIT 2 Short and Long Vowels
Theme: Friends and Family

TALK About It What special things do you do with your friends?

Unit 2 • Introduction
Critical Thinking **23**

THEME FOCUS

HOME SWEET HOME

Ask children to discuss how the illustration on page 23 relates to the theme "Friends and Family." Prompt children with questions such as *What do you think makes a friend a friend? How can friends be like family?*

AROUND THE NEIGHBORHOOD

Have children think of words that name things in or around their neighborhood. List the words children offer only if their vowel sounds are short or long, such as *streets* (long *e*), *homes* (long *o*), and *grass* (short *a*). Display them around the room. Then, invite each child to choose a word and say another word with the same vowel sound.

HIGH-RISE WORD WALL

Draw two high-rise buildings on mural paper and divide each building into five floors. Label the floors *a, e, i, o,* and *u.* Invite children to write words with long vowel sounds in one building and words with short vowel sounds in the other.

Dear Family,

In this unit about "Friends and Family," your child will learn about the vowels **a, e, i, o,** and **u** and the sounds they make. As your child becomes familiar with vowel sounds, you might try these activities together.

► Make a collage of activities that your child shares with family or friends. With your child, identify the activities whose names have short vowel sounds. Help him or her to draw pictures or cut pictures from magazines and glue them on paper. Then repeat the activity to illustrate long vowel sounds.

► With your child, read the poem on page 23 and identify the words with long and short vowel sounds.

► Your child might enjoy reading these books with you. Look for them in your local library.

26 Fairmount Avenue
by Tomie De Paola

Horrible Harry Moves Up to Third Grade
by Suzy Kline

Sincerely,

_____

Estimada familia:

En esta unidad, que trata sobre "Friends and Family" ("Amigos y familia"), su hijo/a estudiará las vocales **a, e, i, o** y **u** y sus sonidos. A medida que su hijo/a se vaya familiarizando con los sonidos de las vocales, pueden hacer las siguientes actividades juntos.

► Construyan un collage de las actividades que su hijo/a comparte con la familia y amigos. Juntos, identifiquen las actividades en cuyos nombres hay vocales con sonidos breves. Ayuden a su hijo/a hacer dibujos o recortar ilustraciones de revistas y pegarlas sobre papel. Después, repitan la actividad para ilustrar las vocales con sonidos largos.

► Lean con su hijo/a el poema en la página 23 e identifiquen las palabras con sonidos breves y con sonidos largos.

► Ustedes y su hijo/a disfrutarán leyendo estos libros juntos. Búsquenlos en su biblioteca local.

26 Fairmount Avenue de Tomie De Paola
Horrible Harry Moves Up to Third Grade de Suzy Kline

Sinceramente,

_____

(24)
Unit 2 • Introduction

* The Home Letter on page 24 is intended to acquaint family members with the phonics skills children will be studying in this unit. Children can tear out page 24 and take it home.

* You may want to suggest that children complete the activities on the page with a family member. Encourage children to look in the library for the books suggested and read them with family members.

LEARNING CENTER ACTIVITIES

WRITING CENTER

Encourage children to write a "shapely" description of a dream house. Explain that as they write, they should make their sentences form the shape of a house. If possible, display some examples of "shapely" writing for the class to use as models.

SOCIAL STUDIES CENTER

Provide reference materials children can use to learn about families around the world. Encourage children to draw or collect pictures to display in a center. Have them label each picture with the country in which the family lives.

MATH CENTER

Have children build miniature houses, using cardboard, craft sticks, glue, and other art materials. When children finish building, have them measure and record the length, width, and height of their houses.

SCIENCE CENTER

Invite children to brainstorm words that name homes for animal families, focusing on words with short and long vowel sounds, such as *den, nest, hive, cave, hole, tree,* and *lodge.* Have each child choose a home to describe in a riddle for classmates to guess.

BULLETIN BOARD

Have children cut out or draw pictures of friends and families for a "Friends and Family" bulletin board. Children can brainstorm different activity words for each category, such as: Friends: play, share, laugh, talk; Family: eat, sleep, clean, play. Have children label their pictures.

Short Vowel a

Skill Focus

Children will

★ identify picture names that have the sound of short *a*.

★ read and write words in context that have the sound of short *a*.

ESL/ELL Korean and Russian speakers may pronounce /ya/ after certain consonants, making *ca* of *camp* sound like the *kya* series in *brickyard*.

Teach

Phonemic Awareness: Phoneme Categorization Say the word *bag*, elongating the short *a* sound: (*baaag*) Have children repeat the vowel sound they hear. Identify the sound as the short *a*. Then, say groups of three words. Tell children to identify the word in each group that has the short *a* sound.

- hit   hat   hot
- bag   bug   beg
- pen   pan   pin

Sound to Symbol Write the word *bat* on the board and say it, elongating the medial sound. (*baaat*) Tell children that the sound of *a* in *bat* is the short *a* sound. Point out that the vowel *a* is between two consonants. Then, ask children to come to the board, erase the beginning consonant, and write a different consonant to make new words with the short sound of *a*. (*cat, fat, hat, mat, pat, rat, sat*)

Practice and Apply

Phonemic Awareness As children complete the top of page 25, have them say each picture name, listening for short *a*.

Sound to Symbol Before children solve the puzzle, have them read all the words in the box to themselves, listening for short *a*.

For page 26, ask children to read each word with the letter *a* and listen for the sound. Remind them to write only the words that have the short *a* sound.

Critical Thinking Review what the people in the sentences did at the beach. Then, have children discuss the Talk About It question, sharing their experiences with beach activities.

Reading Use *A Giant-Sized Day*, MCP Phonics and Reading Consonant and Vowel Skills Library, Level C, to provide additional practice in reading words with short *a*.

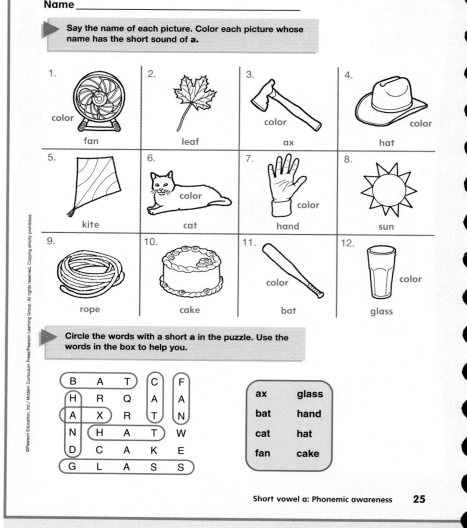

Name _____

▶ Say the name of each picture. Color each picture whose name has the short sound of **a**.

1. fan (color)	2. leaf	3. ax (color)	4. hat (color)
5. kite	6. cat (color)	7. hand (color)	8. sun
9. rope	10. cake	11. bat (color)	12. glass (color)

▶ Circle the words with a short **a** in the puzzle. Use the words in the box to help you.

```
B  A  T     C  F
H  R  Q  A  A  N
A  X  R  T  N
N  H  A  T  W
D  C  A  K  E
G  L  A  S  S
```

ax	glass
bat	hand
cat	hat
fan	cake

Short vowel a: Phonemic awareness   **25**

FOCUS ON ALL LEARNERS

ESL/ELL ENGLISH LANGUAGE LEARNERS

Bring a baseball cap into class. Show it to children and say the word *cap*, elongating the short *a*. Have children repeat. Use the word *cap* to model short *a*. If children are unsure about the vowel sound of a word pictured on page 25, they can compare its sound with that in *cap*. Likewise, children can compare the vowel sounds of the words on page 26 with the sound of *a* in *cap*.

KINESTHETIC/AUDITORY LEARNERS **GROUPS**

Play a version of Simon Says by having children pantomime an action only when the command includes a word with the short *a* sound. Include commands such as *dig in the sand, bat a ball, shake hands,* and *take a nap*.

VISUAL LEARNERS PARTNERS

Have each child write five short *a* words. Then, have partners trade papers, read each word aloud, and use each in a sentence.

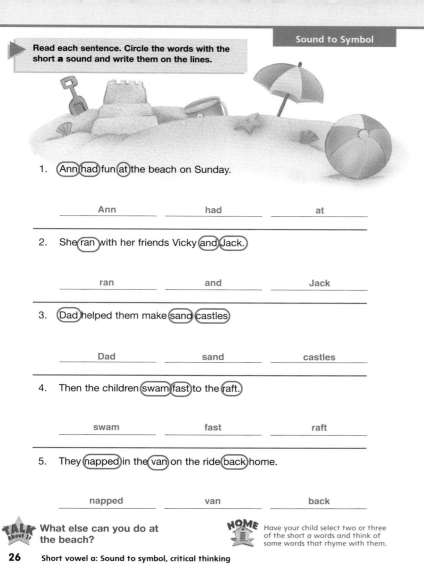

Read each sentence. Circle the words with the short **a** sound and write them on the lines.

Sound to Symbol

1. (Ann) (had) fun (at) the beach on Sunday.

   Ann _____ had _____ at

2. She (ran) with her friends Vicky (and) (Jack.)

   ran _____ and _____ Jack

3. (Dad) helped them make (sand) (castles)

   Dad _____ sand _____ castles

4. Then the children (swam) (fast) to the (raft.)

   swam _____ fast _____ raft

5. They (napped) in the (van) on the ride (back) home.

   napped _____ van _____ back

TALK What else can you do at the beach?

HOME Have your child select two or three of the short *a* words and think of some words that rhyme with them.

26 Short vowel a: Sound to symbol, critical thinking

CURRICULUM CONNECTIONS

SPELLING

Use the following words and sentences as a pretest for writing words with short *a* and *i*.

1. **hand**   I held my sister's **hand**.
2. **glass**   Pat drank a **glass** of milk.
3. **back**   Stan ran **back** to camp.
4. **kick**   Hal will **kick** the ball to Sam.
5. **gift**   I liked the **gift**.
6. **dish**   The **dish** is on the table.

WRITING

Have children reread page 26. Ask them to continue the story by writing about another place the characters visit on another day. Have children underline the short *a* words they used.

PORTFOLIO

SCIENCE

Have children investigate animals that live in the sand, such as hermit crabs. Suggest that groups present their findings in a bulletin board with labels and captions.

TECHNOLOGY   **AstroWord** Short Vowels: *a, i*

AUDITORY LEARNERS **GROUPS**

Have children sit in a circle. Ask one child to say a word with short *a*. The child next to him or her repeats the word and says another short *a* word. The next child repeats the first two words and offers another, and so on. Continue as long as possible and then begin again with another child and another word.

CHALLENGE

Ask children to make their own word search puzzles, using words with the short *a* sound. Suggest that they select a theme for their puzzles, such as "at the beach."

EXTRA SUPPORT/INTERVENTION

Materials: index cards

Make word cards with words that have the phonograms *-ab, -ack, -ad, -am, -ag, -at*. Ask children to sort the words into word families. Have them talk about how the words in each family are alike and different. Ask: *How are all the word families alike?* See Daily Phonics Practice, page 213.

Integrating Phonics and Reading

Guided Reading

Have children look at the cover illustration and read the title. Ask them to discuss what they think the story will be about.

A Giant-Sized Day

First Reading Ask children where the giant is and what he is doing in each picture.

Second Reading Have children identify the short *a* words in the story. You may want to add them to the classroom Word Wall.

Comprehension

After reading, ask children these questions:

- What makes Clad decide to go to the beach? *Recall/Cause and Effect*
- Why does Clad take a little nap at the end of the story? *Recall/Inference*

ESL/ELL **English Language Learners**

Have children retell the story in their own words. Help them identify story words with short *a*.

26

Short Vowel i

Skill Focus

Children will

★ identify and write words with short *i*.

★ match rhyming short *i* words.

★ sort words according to vowel sounds.

ESL/ELL Children whose home language is not English may pronounce short *i* like the *ee* in *see* or the *ea* in *meat*. Practice *mitt, meat; lips, leaps; six, seeks;* and so on.

Teach

Phonemic Awareness: Phoneme Substitution Have children change the short *a* sound in the following words to the short *i* sound and say the new word. Use the words *pan, sap, sack, lamp, mast, tan, bag,* and *hat*.

Sound to Symbol Write the words *pig, if, fish,* and *zip* on the board. Have volunteers use colored chalk to highlight the vowel *i* in each word. Then, have them read the words aloud. Ask children to name the short vowel sound they hear. (*short i*) Ask children to name other words that have short *i* and add them to the list on the board.

Practice and Apply

Sound to Symbol As children do the exercise at the top of page 27, remind them to say the words to themselves in order to hear their letter sounds. Help children understand that the words all have the short *i* sound.

As children complete the bottom of page 27, remind them that rhyming words often share some of the same letters, called phonograms. Point out the following examples on the page and ask children what letters are the same in each word pair: *kick-sick, pig-big, dip-tip*.

Review the rule at the top of page 28. To help children distinguish between the short *a* and short *i* sounds, remind them to compare the sound of each word in the box with the vowel sounds in *cat* and *fish*.

Reading Use *The Princess and the Wise Woman,* MCP Phonics and Reading Consonant and Vowel Skills Library, Level C, to provide additional practice in reading words with short *i*.

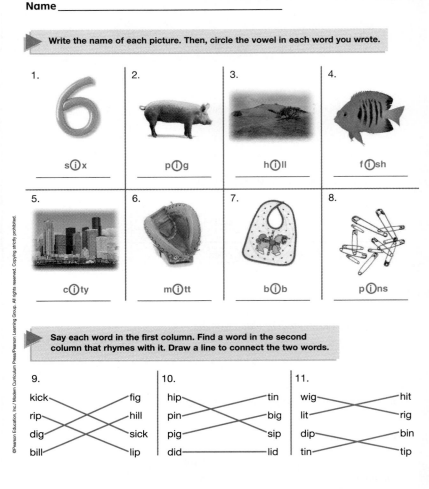

Name _____

Write the name of each picture. Then, circle the vowel in each word you wrote.

1.	2.	3.	4.
s(i)x	p(i)g	h(i)ll	f(i)sh

5.	6.	7.	8.
c(i)ty	m(i)tt	b(i)b	p(i)ns

Say each word in the first column. Find a word in the second column that rhymes with it. Draw a line to connect the two words.

9.
kick — fig
rip — hill
dig — sick
bill — lip

10.
hip — tin
pin — big
pig — sip
did — lid

11.
wig — hit
lit — rig
dip — bin
tin — tip

Short vowel i: Sound to symbol, rhyme   **27**

FOCUS ON ALL LEARNERS

- -

ESL/ELL ENGLISH LANGUAGE LEARNERS

• Read the directions for page 27 aloud. Ask children to paraphrase the task for you. Have them complete the page individually, then review answers together aloud.

• Use the bottom of page 27 to have English language learners practice rhyming words and short *i* phonograms.

• On page 28, review the short vowel rule at the top.

• Invite volunteers to say the names of the two pictures aloud. Have volunteers write answers on the chalkboard.

VISUAL LEARNERS

Have children brainstorm phrases using rhyming short *i* words. Examples include *mill on a hill* or *pig does a jig*. List children's ideas on the board. Ask children to choose a phrase and draw a picture.

KINESTHETIC/VISUAL LEARNERS

On the board, write a short *i* word such as *dish*. Ask a child to use one of the letters in another short *i* word, written vertically. Have children continue adding short *i* words, writing them horizontally or vertically to create a crossword puzzle.

Say the words in the box below. Write the words with a short **a** sound under the picture of the cat. Write the words with a short **i** sound under the picture of the fish.

RULE
If a word or syllable has only one vowel and it comes at the beginning of the word or between two consonants, the vowel usually has a short sound.
ant   f**i**n

lamp	late	Jim	gift	if	back
bike	cake	cat	ham	died	zip
hit	map	rain	an	sip	tick
ask	dime	fish	milk	ran	at
pin	dish	wax	will	rap	flat

Short a

lamp	an
ask	ran
map	rap
cat	back
wax	at
ham	flat

Short i

hit	milk
pin	will
dish	if
Jim	sip
fish	zip
gift	tick

28   Review short vowels a, i

 HOME Ask your child to think of some names for the cat and the fish using short *a* and short *i* words.

CURRICULUM CONNECTIONS

SPELLING

Use the following words and dictation sentences as a posttest for words with the short vowels *i* and *a*.

1. **hand**   Hold out your **hand**.
2. **glass**   Pour milk in the **glass**.
3. **back**   Stan ran **back** to camp.
4. **kick**   **Kick** the ball to me.
5. **gift**   Jim opened his **gift**.
6. **dish**   Put the **dish** in the sink.

WRITING

Challenge children to write rhyming couplets, featuring words with short *i*. Encourage them to brainstorm lists of rhyming words before they begin to write.

SCIENCE

Invite children to make a chart with five headings: *Sight, Touch, Taste, Hearing,* and *Smell.* Have children write words with short *i* or short *a* that name things they see, touch, taste, hear, and smell.

TECHNOLOGY   AstroWord Short Vowels: *a, i*

Integrating Phonics and Reading

Guided Reading

Have children leaf through the book and point out the princess and the wise woman. Ask them to predict how the woman will help the princess.

First Reading Ask what the princess wants to do and how the wise woman helps her.

Second Reading Have children identify words with the short *i* sound.

Comprehension

After reading, ask children these questions:

- What does the wise woman tell the princess to do on each day? *Recall/Sequence*
- Why does the wise woman think the princess is ready for her trip? *Inference/ Cause and Effect*

ESL/ELL **English Language Learners**

Help children identify the exact words said by characters in the story. Explain that they can tell which words are spoken because the words are enclosed in quotation marks.

AUDITORY/KINESTHETIC LEARNERS **PARTNERS**

Have partners write commands for "Short *i* Simon Says." The commands should include a short *i* word, such as *put your hands on your hips, touch your chin,* or *pucker your lips.* Collect the commands children have written and play a class game. You should also include commands that do not have a short *i* word. Children are "out" if they act on commands without a short *i* word.

CHALLENGE

Ask children to look at the short *i* words they sorted at the bottom of page 28. Challenge them to begin a rhyming dictionary or a class Word Wall by writing rhyming words for some of these words.

EXTRA SUPPORT/INTERVENTION

Materials: index cards

Have children help make word cards for *blink, slip, rip, spin, slid, lift, jig, spill, twist.* Display the cards and invite children to take turns choosing a word to act out for others to guess. See Daily Phonics Practice, page 213.

Short Vowel u

Skill Focus

Children will

★ identify picture names that have the short sound of *u*.

★ change short *u* words to words with short *i* and words with short *a*.

ESL/ELL Children who speak Spanish, Tagalog, or some Asian languages may pronounce short *u* like the *o* in *hot*.

Teach

Phonemic Awareness: Phoneme Categorization Say the word *rug*, stressing the short *u* sound. (*ruuug*) Tell children that the vowel sound they hear in *rug* is short *u*. Then, say groups of three words. Ask children to identify the word in each group with the short *u* sound.

- **big**   **bug**   **bag**
- **tack**   **tick**   **tuck**
- **hum**   **ham**   **him**

Sound to Symbol Write the words *bug, nut,* and *cup* on the board. Read each word slowly with children. Then, ask them to identify the letter that stands for the short vowel sound. (*u*)

Help children see how the short vowel rule on page 28 applies to the words, pointing out that each word has one syllable and one vowel between two consonants. Then, have children suggest other short *u* words that fit the same pattern.

Sound to Symbol: Phoneme Substitution Write the word *bug* on the board and have children read the word aloud. Call on a volunteer to change the vowel to *i* and write the new word. Ask children to read the word. (*big*) Then, have another child erase the vowel and write short *a*. Have children read the new word. (*bag*)

Practice and Apply

Sound to Symbol As children complete the top of page 29, have them say each word aloud in order to hear the letter sounds.

Writing As children complete the bottom of page 29, suggest they try each word in the sentence before choosing the one that makes the most sense.

Spelling For page 30, point out that children form each new word by changing the vowel to the one shown in the heading at the top.

Reading Use *Cubby's Gum*, MCP Phonics and Reading Consonant and Vowel Skills Library, Level C, to provide additional practice in reading words with short *u*.

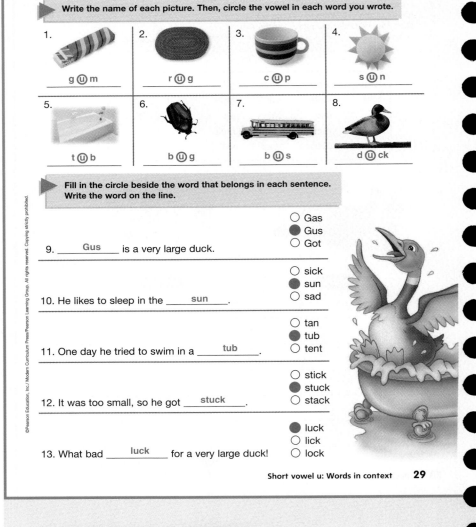

Words in Context

Name _____

Write the name of each picture. Then, circle the vowel in each word you wrote.

1. g u m
2. r u g
3. c u p
4. s u n
5. t u b
6. b u g
7. b u s
8. d u ck

Fill in the circle beside the word that belongs in each sentence. Write the word on the line.

9. ___Gus___ is a very large duck.
   - ○ Gas
   - ● Gus
   - ○ Got

10. He likes to sleep in the ___sun___.
    - ○ sick
    - ● sun
    - ○ sad

11. One day he tried to swim in a ___tub___.
    - ○ tan
    - ● tub
    - ○ tent

12. It was too small, so he got ___stuck___.
    - ○ stick
    - ● stuck
    - ○ stack

13. What bad ___luck___ for a very large duck!
    - ● luck
    - ○ lick
    - ○ lock

Short vowel u: Words in context   **29**

FOCUS ON ALL LEARNERS

ESL/ELL ENGLISH LANGUAGE LEARNERS

- Read aloud the directions for the first activity on page 29. Ask a volunteer to model item 1. Have children complete items 2–8 individually before reviewing answers.

- Verify children's ability to write short *u* words in context using the second activity on page 29. Read the directions aloud and model the tasks. Read the sentence in item 1 without saying the answer. Have children fill in the circle before the correct word. Then, have children write the word. Continue the two-step process as children complete items 10–13. Review answers.

- For page 30, read the directions and model the first item.

AUDITORY LEARNERS   GROUPS

Draw a large tic-tac-toe grid on the board. Form two teams: "Bugs" and "Cats." The Bug team members write short *u* words, and the Cat team members write short *a* words. Teams alternate writing words on the grid to play tic-tac-toe. Play again with the teams "Ducks" and "Fish."

Cubby's Gum

Say each word. Change the short **u** to short **a**. Write the new word in the first column. Then, change the short **a** to short **i**. Write the new word in the second column.

	Short a word	Short i word
1. fun	fan	fin
2. us	as	is
3. bug	bag	big
4. hum	ham	him
5. hut	hat	hit
6. but	bat	bit
7. luck	lack	lick
8. tuck	tack	tick
9. bun	ban	bin
10. lump	lamp	limp
11. bud	bad	bid
12. rug	rag	rig
13. must	mast	mist
14. stuck	stack	stick
15. truck	track	trick
16. pun	pan	pin

HOME Pick a few groups of words and help your child think of rhymes for each word such as *fun/bun, fan/pan, fin/pin*.

30 Review short vowels a, i, u: Spelling

CURRICULUM CONNECTIONS

SPELLING

Use the following words and sentences as a pretest for writing words with short vowels *u, o, e*.

1. **bus**   We ride a **bus** to school.
2. **luck**   Wish me **luck** on my test!
3. **lock**   Please **lock** the door.
4. **tent**   The **tent** is by the lake.
5. **bell**   The school **bell** rang.
6. **pond**   Fish live in the **pond**.

WRITING

Invite children to write an adventure in which Gus the duck experiences some good luck. Have them include as many short *u* words as they can in their story.

SCIENCE/FINE ARTS

Have small groups make lists of animal names with the short *u* sound, such as *slug, duck, pup, bug, cub,* and *puffin.* Ask each group to create drawings showing each animal in its natural home.

TECHNOLOGY   **AstroWord** Short Vowels: *e, u*

KINESTHETIC LEARNERS **GROUPS**

Materials: construction paper, tape, beanbag

Have children write the phonograms *-um, -ug, -up, -un, -ub, -uff,* and *-unk* on squares of construction paper and tape them to the floor. Then, have children take turns tossing a beanbag onto the squares and saying a word with the phonogram on which the beanbag has landed.

CHALLENGE

Materials: paper, stapler, scissors

Challenge children to make flipbooks of words with short *a, i,* or *u* phonograms that change into other words with short *a, i,* or *u* phonograms. Invite children to share their flipbooks with their classmates.

EXTRA SUPPORT/INTERVENTION

Materials: letter cards

Have children use letter cards that you provide to build words with short *u*. Start by having them build the word *bug.* Change the *g* to *d* to make *bud,* the *d* to *n* to make *bun, n* to *s* to make *bus,* and so on. See Daily Phonics Practice, page 213.

Integrating Phonics and Reading

Guided Reading

Have children look at the title and the cover. Ask them to predict what will happen in the story they are about to read.

First Reading Have children identify the gum in each picture and talk about the trouble it is causing.

Second Reading Have children identify words with short *a, i,* and *u* sounds.

Comprehension

After reading, ask children these questions:

• What does Cubby do with his gum that causes problems in the story? *Recall/Cause and Effect*

• Why does everyone laugh at Cubby at the end of the story? *Inference/Plot*

ESL/ELL English Language Learners

Draw an exclamation point on the board and explain it is used to express strong feeling. Read the sentence *Someone got bubble gum in my flute!* with expression.

Short Vowel o

Skill Focus

Children will

★ identify and write short *o* words in the context of a paragraph.

★ write words with short *a, i, o,* or *u* to complete sentences.

ESL/ELL Native speakers of Spanish, Tagalog, and some Asian languages may pronounce in the same way the sounds of short *o*, short *a*, and short *u*. Practice *hot, hat, hut; lock, lack, luck.*

► Teach

Phonemic Awareness: Phoneme

Categorization Say the word *not*, elongating the short *o* sound. (*noooot*) Then, say the word naturally. Identify the vowel sound as short *o*. Then, have children identify the short *o* word in each of these groups.

- **goat　got　go**
- **mop　moon　mole**
- **loose　lock　loaf**

Sound to Symbol: Phoneme Substitution

Write the following words on the board: *cot, top, pop.* Have children read the words. Call on volunteers to come to the board, erase the vowel, and make a new word by writing *a, i,* or *u*. Encourage children to read the words aloud.

► Practice and Apply

Sound to Symbol As children complete the top of page 31, encourage them to say each picture name in order to hear the letter sounds.

Writing For the bottom of page 31, suggest children read the paragraph aloud to themselves, listening for the short *o* sound.

On the top of page 32, suggest that children try all the vowels with the consonants in the word before writing their new words.

For the sentences on page 32, suggest that children try their word choice in the sentence first before deciding which word makes the most sense.

Critical Thinking After reading the story, discuss with children whether Max makes a good pet. Encourage them to support their answers.

Reading Use *Toast for Mom*, MCP Phonics and Reading Consonant and Vowel Skills Library, Level C, to provide additional practice in reading words with short *o*.

Name _____

▶ Write the name of each picture. Then, circle the vowel in each word you wrote.

1.	2.	3.	4.
b ⊙ x	t ⊙ p	l ⊙ ck	d ⊙ ll

5.	6.	7.	8.
f ⊙ x	s ⊙ ck	p ⊙ p	m ⊙ p

▶ Read the paragraph. Underline the words with the short **o** sound. Then write the words on the lines.

A Summer Picnic

The <u>Todd</u> family went <u>on</u> a picnic one summer day. Although the sun was shining brightly, it was <u>not</u> too <u>hot</u>. They ate a big lunch with hamburgers, juice, and salad. After lunch, <u>Dot</u> and Tim helped <u>Mom</u> search for unusual <u>rocks</u>. They stored these in a big <u>box</u>. Dad and <u>Bobby</u> went to the <u>pond</u> with their <u>dog</u> to watch the ducks. They saw a toad <u>hop</u> in the grass. It was a great day!

9. ___Todd___	10. ___on___	11. ___not___
12. ___hot___	13. ___Dot___	14. ___Mom___
15. ___rocks___	16. ___box___	17. ___Bobby___
18. ___pond___	19. ___dog___	20. ___hop___

Short vowel o: Sound to symbol　**31**

FOCUS ON ALL LEARNERS

ESL/ELL ENGLISH LANGUAGE LEARNERS

- Review the rule for short vowel sounds. Use several c-v-c pattern words as examples: *pop, hot, fox, cat, sip,* and *run*. Ask children to supply additional words.

- Read the directions for the activities on page 31 aloud. Ask children to work with a partner to identify the pictures and read the paragraph. Review answers as a group.

- For page 32, read the directions for the first activity aloud. Then, model the first item. Review answers as a group.

- For the second activity, read the words in the box together. Then, model the first item. Have children work with a partner to complete items 10–20.

VISUAL LEARNERS GROUPS

On the board, make a four-column chart, labeled *-ob, -ot, -ock,* and *-op*. Ask children to think of words for each column. Then, have children take turns providing clues about their words for the others to guess. When a word is guessed, add it to the chart.

Make two new words by changing the vowel in each word to a, i, u, or o.

1. cat   _cut_   _cot_
2. bad   _bid_   _bud_
3. tip   _tap_   _top_
4. lock   _lick_   _luck_
5. on   _an_   _in_
6. big   _bag_   _bug_
7. ham   _him_   _hum_
8. fun   _fan_   _fin_

Find the word in the box that will finish each sentence. Write the word on the line.

9. I love my tabby _cat_, Max.
10. He sleeps _on_ the rug in my room.
11. Sometimes Max plays with a paper _bag_.
12. He likes to _run_ in and out of it.
13. I gave _him_ some string to play with, too.
14. It was _fun_ to see Max try to catch it.
15. Once Max was very _bad_.
16. He jumped on _top_ of the counter.
17. He made some milk _tip_ over.
18. I was going to _mop_ the floor.
19. Then Max started to _lick_ up the milk.
20. He cleaned the mess _in_ a hurry!

bad	bag	cat
fun	him	in
lick	mop	on
run	tip	top

 Do you think Max is a good pet? Why or why not?

HOME Ask your child to write a story using some of the words from the box.

32 Review short vowels a, i, u, o: Words in context

CURRICULUM CONNECTIONS

SPELLING

Materials: index cards, markers

Make letter cards for *k, l, c, o* and arrange them in a pocket chart. Ask a volunteer to arrange the letters to spell a short *o* word. (*lock*) Continue with the word *pond* and other short *o* words. Review words with short *u* as well.

WRITING

Have each child recall a summertime event and create a word web of short *a, i, u,* and *o* words that tell about it. Then, have them write about the event.

SOCIAL STUDIES

Draw a large house shape on butcher paper with lines dividing it into puzzle pieces, one per child. Cut apart the pieces, marking the front of each. Children can decorate their pieces with short *a, i, o,* or *u* words and pictures to tell about their homes. When ready, have children reassemble the puzzle.

TECHNOLOGY   **AstroWord** Short Vowels: *i, o*

AUDITORY LEARNERS   GROUPS

Form teams to represent short *a*, short *i*, and short *u*. As you say short *o* words, a member from each team replaces the short *o* sound with the team's vowel sound and says the new word. If no word is possible, the team says "pass." Say the words *not, lock, jog, on, top, rob, hot, sock, rock, cot, bog,* and *flop.*

CHALLENGE

Challenge children to make up a crossword puzzle using words with short *o.*

EXTRA SUPPORT/INTERVENTION

Materials: letter cards

Write the word *hot* on the board and have children make the word with letter cards. Then, have them change the first letter to make and read new words. Repeat with the words *hop* and *sock.* **See Daily Phonics Practice, page 213.**

Integrating Phonics and Reading

Guided Reading

Toast for Mom

As children look at the cover of the book, ask them what they think the book will be about. Invite children to talk about making and eating toast.

First Reading Have children tell what happened each time Rose made toast.

Second Reading Have children identify story words with short *a, i, u,* and *o* sounds.

Comprehension

After reading, ask children these questions:

- Why didn't Rose pay more attention to the toast? *Inference/Cause and Effect*
- Did the story turn out the way you expected? Explain. *Personal Response/Reflective Analysis*

ESL/ELL English Language Learners

Ask children to use the illustrations to tell in their own words what happened in the beginning, middle, and end of the story.

Short Vowel e

Skill Focus

Children will

★ identify the short e sound from auditory and visual clues.

★ identify and discriminate among the sounds of short *a, i, o, u,* and *e* in words.

ESL/ELL Since no vowel sound similar to short *e* exists in Korean, offer additional practice and support with *pen, net, leg, bed, red, belt, tent,* and other words from the lesson.

Teach

Phonemic Awareness: Phoneme Isolation
Say the word *bed,* stretching the sound of each phoneme as in *bbbeeeddd.* Have children repeat the word. Ask them what vowel sound they hear in the middle of the word. (*short e*) Then, say the following words and have children identify the short vowel sound in each: *pan, him, duck, not.* Have children repeat each word and substitute the short *e* sound, as in *bed,* and say the new word. (*pen, hem, deck, net*)

Sound to Symbol Repeat the words *pen, hem, deck,* and *net.* Ask children to identify the vowel sound they hear. (*short e*) Have volunteers write the words on the board and circle each vowel *e* as you repeat each word, elongating the medial sound. (*peeen, heeem, deeeck, neeet*) Call on a child to explain how the short vowel rule applies to the words. (*A word or syllable with one vowel at the beginning or between two consonants is usually short.*)

Practice and Apply

Sound to Symbol As children complete the first activity on page 33, encourage them to say each picture name to themselves, listening for the short *e* sound. For the second activity, suggest that children compare the sounds of each of the words in the box with the sounds of the picture name before determining which words rhyme.

Writing For page 34, suggest that children say each word, listening for the short vowel sound, before writing the word in the correct list. Remind children to write a word of their own at the end of each list.

Reading Use *Something Everyone Needs,* MCP Phonics and Reading Consonant and Vowel Skills Library, Level C, to provide additional practice in reading words with short *e.*

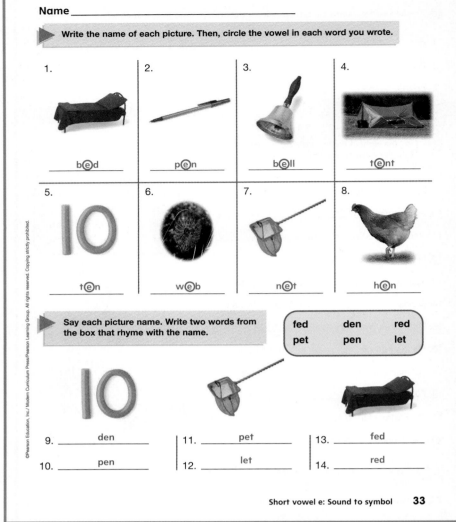

Name _____

Say each picture name. Write two words from the box that rhyme with the name.

fed	den	red
pet	pen	let

9. _____ den _____   11. _____ pet _____   13. _____ fed _____

10. _____ pen _____   12. _____ let _____   14. _____ red _____

Short vowel e: Sound to symbol   **33**

FOCUS ON ALL LEARNERS

ESL/ELL ENGLISH LANGUAGE LEARNERS

• Teach c-v-c pattern words containing short *e* before completing the activities on page 33. Begin by pointing out that short *e* often occurs between two consonant sounds; examples to write and pronounce include *wet* and *best.*

• On the board, write *red, men, set.* Have English language learners read the words aloud with you. Ask children to say a rhyming word for each that begins with *b* (*bed, Ben, bet*).

• Read aloud the directions for the activities on page 33. Ask English language learners to work with a partner to complete items 1–14. Write answers on the chalkboard; correct them as a group.

• Read the directions and model the activity on page 34.

AUDITORY/KINESTHETIC LEARNERS

Materials: small bell

One child in each group holds the bell while another says a word. If the word has the short *e* sound, the bell is rung. The bell is passed to the next child, and another group member offers a word.

Read the words in the box. Write the words with the same short vowel sound in the correct list. Then, write your own word with the same vowel sound on the last line.

top	fit	bus	cab	cup
jet	pen	pig	rock	wig
tub	box	tag	step	map
bed	him	nut	pot	sad

short a

cab
tag
map
sad
___

short e

step
jet
pen
bed
___

short i

wig
fit
pig
him
___

short o

rock
top
box
pot
___

short u

bus
cup
tub
nut
___

34 Review short vowels a, e, i, o, u

 Ask your child to list the words in the box in alphabetical order.

CURRICULUM CONNECTIONS

SPELLING

Use these words and sentences as a posttest for writing words with short vowels *u, o,* and *e.*

1. **luck**   Rick has good **luck** fishing.
2. **bus**   The **bus** arrived on time.
3. **lock**   The key fits the **lock**.
4. **pond**   We swam in the **pond**.
5. **bell**   The **bell** rang every hour.
6. **tent**   Our **tent** is near the lake.

WRITING

Have children use the pictures on page 33 for story ideas. For example, *A night spent in a tent. A bell that keeps ringing. Ten special friends on an adventure. A spider mends a hole in its web.*

FINE ARTS

Provide magazines, construction paper, scissors, markers, and glue for children to use to create a collage of "home" words. Suggest they cut out as many words with short vowels as possible for the theme "Friends and Family."

TECHNOLOGY   **AstroWord** Short Vowels: *e, u*

Integrating Phonics and Reading

Guided Reading

After children have looked over the cover and read the title, ask what they think everyone needs. You may also wish to use the activity for English language learners, below.

First Reading Ask children to explain why and how Nell made her seeder.

Second Reading Have children identify words in the story with short *a, i, u, o,* and *e.*

Comprehension

After reading, ask children these questions:

• What happened at the beginning, middle, and end of the story? ***Recall/Sequence***

• Why do you think Nell liked to make things people really needed? ***Inference/Character***

ESL/ELL **English Language Learners**

Have children tell in their own words how Nell made her seeder. Remind them to use sequence words: *first, then, next,* and *finally.*

AUDITORY LEARNERS   PARTNERS

Have partners work separately to write three or four riddles for the other to guess. The answers should have the short *e* sound. For example: *It is a bird's home.* (nest) *It is something you write with.* (pen or pencil) *You can find it on a beach.* (shell) *This comes after nine.* (ten)

CHALLENGE

Materials: poster board, game spinner or die, game markers

Challenge children to work together to create board games featuring words with short vowel sounds. Children should decide how the game will look and what the rules will be. Then, they can teach others to play.

EXTRA SUPPORT/INTERVENTION

Materials: tag board, scissors, stapler, markers

Have children make flipbooks of short *e* word families. Each book should feature a different phonogram and initial letters for word building. Phonograms might include *-eck, -ed, -ell, -ent, -est, -et.* See Daily Phonics Practice, page 213.

Phonics and Reading / Phonics and Writing

Review Short Vowels

Skill Focus

Children will

★ read and write words with the short vowels *a, e, i, o,* and *u* in context.

★ write a descriptive paragraph using words with short vowel sounds.

▶ Teach

Phonemic Awareness: Phoneme Isolation
Say each of the following words and have children identify the short vowel sound they hear in each one: *pack, hill, jump, job, best.* After each vowel sound is identified, ask volunteers to offer other words with the same vowel sound.

Sound to Symbol Write these words on the board, leaving out the vowels: *glad, test, kick, box, club.* Say each word and call on children to write the vowel in place. Then, have volunteers come to the board and write rhyming words (with the same phonograms) under each word. (*bad, dad, sad; best, nest, pest; lick, pick, sick; fox, lox, ox; cub, rub, tub*)

▶ Practice and Apply

Phonics and Reading For the exercise on page 35, suggest that children look in the selection for words to complete the sentences.

Critical Thinking After reading the selection, discuss the Talk About It question with children. Have children talk about the ways in which living in a tree house might be different from living in a house on the ground.

Phonics and Writing Before children begin writing their descriptive paragraphs on page 36, review the information in the callout boxes. Remind children to include some of the words in the box at the top in their writing.

Reading Use *Julie's Mornings,* MCP Phonics and Reading Consonant and Vowel Skills Library, Level C, to provide additional practice in reading words with short vowels.

Name_____

 **Phonics & Reading**   Read the story. Use words with short vowels to finish the sentences.

Living in the Trees

Squirrels, birds, and monkeys can all make their homes in trees. Did you know that some people build homes in trees, too? Of course, people do not build nests as birds do! They build tree houses.

Some people live in their tree houses all the time. Others build tree houses to have a place just to relax. Many parents build tree houses so their children can have a fun place to play. There are even tree houses that can be rented for a very different kind of vacation!

Whether a tree house is just for fun or a place to live, it must be built with care. It is important to pick only the strongest branches of a tree to hold up the tree house. The branches must not move around too much in the wind, or the house will move too!

1. People do not build ____nests____ as birds do.

2. Some people ____live____ in their tree houses all the time.

3. Other people build tree houses to have a place ____just____ to relax.

4. Many parents build tree houses so their children ____can____ have a fun place to play.

5. The branches that hold up the tree house must ____not____ move around in the wind.

 TALK About It What do you think it would be like to live in a tree house?

Review short vowels: Reading, critical thinking   **35**

FOCUS ON ALL LEARNERS

ESL/ELL **ENGLISH LANGUAGE LEARNERS**
Read the selection aloud and have English language learners underline these words in the text: *nests, not, just, can, fun, rented, must, pick, wind.* After reading, write the underlined words on the board. Say each word and have children repeat. Then, have children identify the vowel sounds of the words and sort them by vowel sound.

KINESTHETIC LEARNERS **GROUPS**
Materials: large index cards

Write words from Lessons 9–13, with the letters scrambled, each on a separate card. Have children form teams. Display one scrambled word and have a child from each team unscramble the word and write it on the board. The first person to write the word correctly earns a point for the team.

AUDITORY LEARNERS **GROUPS**
Say pairs of words that have the same initial and final sounds but different short vowels, such as *cap/cup, set/sit, top/tap, hit/hut, leg/log.* Ask children to identify the two short vowels.

Phonics & Writing

A **descriptive paragraph** uses words to create a picture for the reader. The words tell how something feels, looks, sounds, smells, and tastes. One sentence gives the topic. The other sentences give details about the topic.

> Write a descriptive paragraph about a trip you would like to take with friends or family. Some of the words in the box may help you.

trip	sun	picnic	pond
city	swam	tent	fun
bus	napped	hot	fish

Begin with a **topic sentence** that tells what you are describing.

Give **details** about the topic in the other sentences.

Use some **describing words** to make a clear picture of your topic.

36 Review short vowels: Writing

HOME Ask your child to read the descriptive paragraph to you and point out the words with short vowel sounds.

CURRICULUM CONNECTIONS

SPELLING

Use the following words and sentences as a mid-unit review of spelling words with short vowels.

1. **hand**   I held my brother's **hand**.
2. **glass**   The **glass** broke.
3. **back**   Sue patted me on the **back**.
4. **kick**   Tell Bill to **kick** the ball.
5. **gift**   Uncle Joe sent me a **gift**.
6. **dish**   Please pass the salad **dish**.
7. **bus**   We rode the **bus** to the zoo.
8. **luck**   Good **luck** on the test.
9. **lock**   I will **lock** the door.
10. **tent**   Let's pitch the **tent** here.
11. **bell**   I heard the **bell** ring.
12. **pond**   Ducks swam on the **pond**.

WRITING

Have children write about what it would be like to live in a tree house. Ask volunteers to share their work with the class.

 **TECHNOLOGY** **AstroWord** Short Vowels: *a, i; i, o; e, u*

Integrating Phonics and Reading

Guided Reading

Have children discuss things they do and see in the morning. Then, have them leaf through the book. Ask: *What do you think the story will be about?*

First Reading Have children describe what happens on each day in the story.

Second Reading Have children identify story words with short vowel sounds.

Comprehension

After reading, ask children these questions:
- Why does Julie paint her room twice? *Recall/Plot*
- Did the story end the way you thought it would? Explain. *Reflective Analysis/ Personal Response*

ESL/ELL English Language Learners

Point out to children that the story tells what Julie did every day. Help children locate the names of days in the story and tell what happened.

VISUAL LEARNERS *PARTNERS*

Have several children come to the board at one time. Name a specific short vowel sound and have each child write a word with that sound. Ask children to use their words in sentences. Classmates can check the spellings and tell whether the sentences make sense.

CHALLENGE

Challenge children to start with one of the words from the box on page 36 and make as many new short vowel words as they can by changing one letter at a time. For example: *sun–fun–bun–but–bat–fat–fit–sit–set.*

EXTRA SUPPORT/INTERVENTION

Before children attempt to write words in context on page 35, read each sentence aloud with them, leaving out the short vowel answers. Then, have children look through the selection to help them find words to complete the sentences. Help children define words that are unfamiliar. See Daily Phonics Practice, page 213.

Long a

Skill Focus

Children will

★ identify the long *a* sound.

★ recognize that the long *a* sound is represented by different spellings.

★ read and write words in context that have the long *a* sound.

ESL/ELL Children who speak languages other than English may confuse long *a* with short *e*; practice *let, late; red, rake; tell, tale.* Native speakers of Spanish may write *e* instead of long *a* in words.

Teach

Phonemic Awareness: Phoneme Categorization Say the word *make*, stressing the *a* sound. (*maaake*) Ask children what vowel sound they hear. (*a*) Tell them that this sound of *a* is called long *a*. Then, say four groups of words. Have children identify the word in each group that has the long *a* sound.

- **lake**   **like**   **lack**
- **clam**   **claim**   **climb**
- **mad**   **made**   **mud**
- **ran**   **run**   **rain**

Sound to Symbol Write the words *make, hay,* and *rain* on the board and read them aloud. Ask what vowel sound children hear. (*long* a) Have them name the vowels in each word. Explain that when a word with one syllable has two vowels, the first vowel usually has the long sound and the second one is usually silent. Remind children that *y* sometimes acts as a vowel as well as a consonant. Have volunteers identify the silent vowel in each word.

Practice and Apply

Sound to Symbol For page 37, tell children to say the name of the picture to themselves, listening to the letter sounds. Then, have them find the word that names the picture. For page 38, suggest that children read each word in the sentence carefully, listening for the long *a* sound.

Critical Thinking Review what happened at the baseball game and what Dave did. Then, have children discuss the Talk About It question.

Reading Use *Who Has a Tail?*, MCP Phonics and Reading Consonant and Vowel Skills Library, Level C, to provide additional practice in reading words with long *a*.

Name _____

Circle the word that names each picture.

RULE
If a one-syllable word has two vowels, the first vowel usually stands for the long sound, and the second vowel is silent. If the first vowel is **a**, the word has the long **a** sound.

cake   train   hay

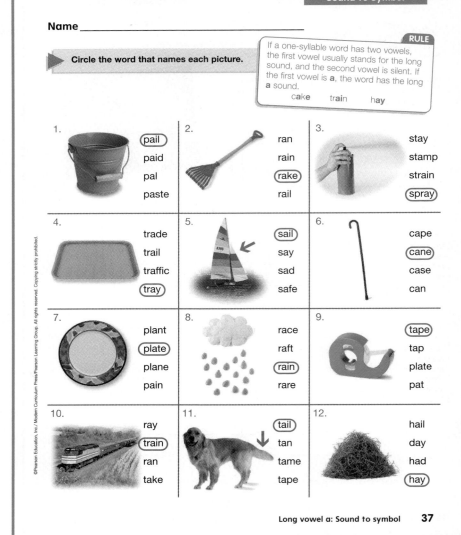

1. (pail) / paid / pal / paste

2. ran / rain / (rake) / rail

3. stay / stamp / strain / (spray)

4. trade / trail / traffic / (tray)

5. (sail) / say / sad / safe

6. cape / (cane) / case / can

7. plant / (plate) / plane / pain

8. race / raft / (rain) / rare

9. (tape) / tap / plate / pat

10. ray / (train) / ran / take

11. (tail) / tan / tame / tape

12. hail / day / had / (hay)

Long vowel a: Sound to symbol   **37**

FOCUS ON ALL LEARNERS

ESL/ELL ENGLISH LANGUAGE LEARNERS

Teach children guidelines for spelling words with long *a* by reviewing the rule on page 37.

- Ask a volunteer to read or explain the rule.
- Make a three-column list on the board; label columns *e, i,* and *y*. Have children supply words with long *a* where *e* is the second (silent) vowel; repeat for *i* and *y*.
- Read aloud the directions for the worksheet on page 37. Have children complete items 1–6 in pairs. Have them complete items 7–12 individually. Review answers aloud.
- For page 38, read the directions aloud. Then, model the first item by reading the sentence aloud and identifying the words with the long *a* sound. Have children complete the page individually or with a partner.

VISUAL LEARNERS

Materials: words cards for long and short *a*, bag or box

Place the word cards in a bag or box. Have children take turns choosing a card, reading the word, and identifying the word as having either a long *a* sound or a short *a* sound. Suggest that children sort the cards into short *a* and long *a* piles.

Read each sentence. Underline the words with the long *a* sound. Then, write them on the lines below the sentence.

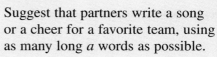

1. Kate could hardly wait until the first of May.

   Kate _____   wait _____   May _____

2. She and Gail would see their first baseball game.

   Gail _____   baseball _____   game _____

3. The Braves would play the Jays.

   Braves _____   play _____   Jays _____

4. When the day finally came, it looked like rain.

   day _____   came _____   rain _____

5. Just in case, the girls decided to take their gray caps.

   case _____   take _____   gray _____

6. They arrived late and paid at the gate.

   late _____   paid _____   gate _____

7. They raced to claim their places.

   raced _____   claim _____   places _____

8. A batter named Dave got on first base.

   named _____   Dave _____   base _____

9. He waved when he made it to home plate.

   waved _____   made _____   plate _____

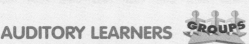 **Why do you think Dave waved?**

 Ask your child to use other long *a* words, or words from the page, to continue the story.

38   Long vowel a: Words in context, critical thinking

CURRICULUM CONNECTIONS

SPELLING

Use these words and sentences as a pretest for writing words with long vowels *a* and *i*.

1. **sail**   We pulled the **sail** tight.
2. **tape**   I needed **tape** to wrap a gift.
3. **day**   On what **day** will you come?
4. **pile**   Make a **pile** of papers.
5. **time**   It is **time** to go home.
6. **ride**   May I **ride** your bike?

WRITING

Suggest that partners write a song or a cheer for a favorite team, using as many long *a* words as possible.

MATH

Ask children to name games they like. Record responses along the bottom of a bar graph on the board. Use bars to show the number of votes for each game. Have children use the data to select the most popular and least popular games.

 **AstroWord** Long Vowels: *a, i*

AUDITORY LEARNERS GROUPS

On the board, make a three-column chart. Label the columns *ai, ay, a_e.* Have children take turns saying a word with long *a* and writing the word in the column with the correct spelling for the vowel sound.

CHALLENGE

Have children write sentences that ask classmates to do something. Each sentence should contain two long *a* words. For example: *Say* your *name. Play* a *game.*

EXTRA SUPPORT/INTERVENTION

Materials: cutouts of baseballs

Have children write long *a* words on the baseballs. Ask them to attach the baseballs to a bulletin board. Invite pairs of children to work together, taking turns pointing to words and reading them aloud. See Daily Phonics Practice, page 214.

Integrating Phonics and Reading

Guided Reading

Have children look at the cover and title and tell what they think the book will be about. Invite them to describe the peacock's tail on the cover.

First Reading Ask children to name the animal tails and the objects they are compared to.

Second Reading Have children identify the long and short *a* words in the story.

Comprehension

After reading, ask children these questions:

• How are the tails like the objects they are compared to? *Inference/Visualization*

• Did you know any of the animals before you turned the page? Name the animals. *Reflective Analysis/Personal Response*

ESL/ELL English Language Learners

Have children point to each tail in the pictures. Encourage them to pantomime how the tail resembles the object it is compared to.

Long i

Skill Focus

Children will

★ identify the long *i* sound.

★ recognize that the long *i* sound is represented by different spellings.

★ write words that have the long *i* sound to complete sentences.

ESL/ELL Children who speak Asian languages or Spanish may clip the long *i* and pronounce it like short *a*, for example, pronouncing *glide* as *glad*. Practice with *mine/man; bike/back; flight/flat.*

Teach

Phonemic Awareness: Phoneme Isolation
Say the word *like,* stressing the long *i* sound. (*liiike*) Then, say the word naturally. Ask children what vowel sound they hear. (*i*) Explain that the vowel sound is long *i*. Invite children to name other words with long *i*.

Sound to Symbol Write *rice* and *pie* on the board and read the words aloud. Ask: *What vowel sound does each word have?* (*long* i) Explain that the long *i* sound can be spelled in different ways. Words like *rice* and *dime* (*i,* consonant, *e*) have the long *i* sound. Words with *ie* such as *pie* and *tie* also have long *i*. Point out that, like words with the long *a* vowel sound, words with the long *i* sound may have two vowels that make the vowel sound.

Practice and Apply

Sound to Symbol Review the rule at the top of page 39. Ask children to read the example words and identify the vowel that is silent. As children complete the page, encourage them to say each picture name, listening for the vowel sound. Point out that some of the picture names have short *i* and some have long *i*. Discuss how each pair of words is the same and different.

Writing For page 40, suggest that children try their word choice in the sentence to see whether it makes sense before writing it on the line.

Reading Use *The Princess Who Couldn't Cry,* MCP Phonics and Reading Consonant and Vowel Skills Library, Level C, to provide additional practice in reading words with long *a* and long *i*.

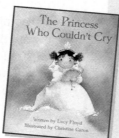

Name _____

> Circle the word that names each picture.

RULE
If a one-syllable word has two vowels, the first vowel usually stands for the long sound, and the second vowel is silent. If the first vowel is **i**, the word has the long *i* sound.

> bike   dime   pie

1. kit / (kite)
2. (ride) / rid
3. pine / (pin)
4. (rip) / ripe
5. bit / (bite)
6. fir / (fire)
7. (Tim) / time
8. (pile) / pit
9. (dime) / dim
10. (sit) / site
11. fine / (fin)
12. (slide) / slid

Long and short vowel i: Sound to symbol   **39**

FOCUS ON ALL LEARNERS

ESL/ELL ENGLISH LANGUAGE LEARNERS

• Write *pin, fin, rid, hid, dim, bit* on the board and say the words. Help English language learners identify the vowel sound of the words as short *i*. Then, add an *e* to each word. Read the words and explain that addition of *e* changes the short *i* to long *i*. Model with the words *pin* and *pine*.

• State the rule for long vowel sounds on page 39. Help children identify the long and silent vowels in the example words.

• Read the directions for page 40 aloud. Model the first sentence by reading it aloud and telling children how you would select a word from the box. Have children read the completed sentence.

• For the activity at the bottom of the page, do the first item with children by reading each word and asking if they hear a long vowel sound. If they do, ask what vowel sound they hear.

VISUAL/KINESTHETIC LEARNERS   GROUPS

Materials: index cards, colored chalk

Draw a kite on the board. Have each child write one long *a* word, one short *i* word, and two long *i* words each on cards. Place the cards in a pile. Have children take turns choosing a card. If the word has the long *i* sound, the child writes the word on the kite.

▶ **Find the word in the box that will finish each sentence. Write the word on the line.**

1. Kay got a new ___kite___ to fly.

2. It came in the ___mail___ from Mike.

3. A big smile was on Kay's ___face___.

4. The kite had a long ___tail___.

5. It had blue and red ___stripes___.

6. It also had ___five___ yellow stars.

7. Kay had to ___tie___ a string to it.

8. She flew it on a very windy ___day___.

9. The wind stopped, and the kite ___came___ down.

10. Then it began to ___rain___, and Kay ran home.

11. She carefully put the kite ___away___.

12. Kay ___smiled___ at the thought of flying it again.

> away
> came
> day
> face
> five
> kite
> mail
> rain
> smiled
> stripes
> tail
> tie

▶ **Circle each word that has a long vowel sound.**

13. (whale) (pie) (pail) big pig (fine)
14. jam (blame) (nine) (bike) (dime) gas
15. hit (save) fist (pipe) trip man
16. sand (mice) (plate) fish cat trash
17. (ate) (name) dish (five) (game) snap
18. ran hand map (rain) (pain) (line)

40   Long vowels a, i: Words in context

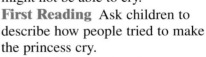

HOME With your child, take turns saying as many words as you can that have the long a sound.

CURRICULUM CONNECTIONS

SPELLING

Use the following words and sentences as a posttest for writing words with long *a* and *i*.

1. **sail**   The boat has a colorful **sail**.

2. **tape**   Put **tape** on the package.

3. **day**   The **day** is windy.

4. **pile**   Rake the leaves into a **pile**.

5. **time**   What **time** is it?

6. **ride**   Let's take a **ride**.

WRITING

Help children use long vowel words to write a *diamante* poem.

lines 1, 7: name the opposites
lines 2, 6: two adjectives for each word
lines 3, 5: three *-ing* words naming actions
line 4: two nouns for each word

Example:
NIGHT
Dark, silent
Ending, sleeping, dreaming,
Sunset, dusk, sunrise, sunshine
Waking, rising, smiling
Bright, alive
DAY

 **AstroWord** Long Vowels: *a, i*

Integrating Phonics and Reading

Guided Reading

As children look at the cover, ask them what they think the book will be about. Talk about why someone might not be able to cry.

First Reading Ask children to describe how people tried to make the princess cry.

Second Reading Have children identify the long and short *i* words in the story.

The Princess Who Couldn't Cry

Written by Lucy Floyd
Illustrated by Christine Caron

Comprehension

After reading, ask children these questions:

• Why do you think it is important for the princess to be able to cry? *Inference/Character*

• Was it wrong of the queen to play a trick on the princess? Explain. *Reflective Analysis/Personal Response*

ESL/ELL **English Language Learners**

Write *try* and *tried* on the board and say the words. Have children find another story word in which the *y* has been changed to *i* before adding *-ed*. (*cry/cried*)

KINESTHETIC/AUDITORY LEARNERS   GROUPS

Give the following commands, one at a time, for children to act out. Ask a volunteer to write on the board the word in the command that has the long *i* sound. Say: **Hide** your hands. Clap four **times**. **Wipe** your desk. **Pile** three books. **Bite** an apple. Step and **slide**. Hold up **five** fingers. **Smile!**

CHALLENGE

Ask children to think of short *i* and long *i* pairs such as *slid* and *slide*, *kit* and *kite*, *fin* and *fine*. Challenge them to use both words in a single sentence. Here is an example: *I slid down the slippery slide.*

EXTRA SUPPORT/INTERVENTION

Materials: construction paper, yarn, paper bow-tie shapes

Have children cut small kite shapes from construction paper and attach lengths of yarn to them for tails. Then, have children write long *i* words on the bow-tie shapes and tape them to the tails of their kites. See *Daily Phonics Practice, page 214.*

Long U

Skill Focus

Children will

★ identify the long *u* sound.

★ recognize that the long *u* sound is represented by different spellings.

★ distinguish among long *a*, long *i*, and long *u* sounds in words.

ESL/ELL Children who speak Cantonese or Vietnamese may pronounce a "round" *u*. Spanish speakers may have trouble with the /yoo/ sound of long *u* as in *music* or *cube* (saying *moosic* or *coob*).

Teach

Phonemic Awareness: Phoneme Categorization Say the word *tube*, stressing the long *u* sound. (*tuuube*) Identify the vowel sound as long *u*. Then, say four groups of three words. Ask children to identify the word in each group that has the long *u* sound.

- tray   true   trunk
- hog   hug   huge
- cute   cat   cut
- glow   glue   glee

Sound to Symbol Write *suit, glue,* and *use* on the board and read the words aloud. Ask what vowel sound children hear. (*long* u) Have children name the vowels in each word. Remind them that when a word with one syllable has two vowels, the first one usually stands for the long sound and the second one is usually silent. Ask a child to identify the silent vowel in each word.

Tell children that long *u* has two sounds: /yoo/ as in *cute* and /oo/ as in *suit* and *tune*. Point out that both follow the long vowel rule.

Practice and Apply

Sound to Symbol/Writing For page 41, ask children to try each word in the sentence before deciding which one makes the most sense.

For the word sort on page 42, children can compare the vowel sounds in the words with the vowel sounds in *cane, bike,* and *tube*.

Critical Thinking Ask children what Luke does to prepare for the concert and how he feels before the concert begins. Then, discuss the Talk About It question.

Reading Use *My Sister June,* MCP Phonics and Reading Consonant and Vowel Skills Library, Level C, to provide additional practice in reading words with long and short *u*.

41

Name _____

Look at the picture. Circle the word that names the picture. Then, complete the sentence by writing the word on the line.

RULE
If a one-syllable word has two vowels, the first vowel usually stands for the long sound, and the second vowel is silent. If the first vowel is **u**, the word has the long **u** sound. Long **u** can have the sound of **oo**, as in **blue**, or **yoo**, as in **cute**.
tube   glue   fruit

1. luck / (Luke)   _____Luke_____ will play a song at his concert.

2. sun / (Sue)   He will play the song with _____Sue_____.

3. (flute) / flunk   They will play the _____flute_____.

4. sit / (suit)   Luke will wear his new _____suit_____.

5. (cut) / cute   He will also get his hair _____cut_____ for the concert.

6. (hug) / huge   After the concert, his dad will give him a big _____hug_____.

7. fun / (fruit)   Then Luke will have _____fruit_____ juice and cookies.

TALK About It How do you think Luke will feel after the concert?

Long and short vowel u: Words in context, critical thinking   **41**

FOCUS ON ALL LEARNERS

ESL/ELL ENGLISH LANGUAGE LEARNERS

The following exercise can help English language learners identify and spell words with the long *u* sound.

- Say groups of three words and have children name the two that rhyme. For example: *blue, Sue, run; flute, tub, suit; cut, use, fuse; rule, luck, mule.*

- Display familiar items whose names have the long *u* sound, such as *glue, ruler, tube,* and *cube.* Have children identify the items and write their names on the board.

- Write *glue, flute, suit,* and *cube* on the board. Review the rule on page 41. Ask children to identify the silent vowel that makes the *u* long.

- For page 42, review the long *a, i,* and *u* sounds before children begin. Model identifying and writing one word in each category.

VISUAL/AUDITORY LEARNERS

Write on the board the song title "The Tune of the Happy Flute." Ask children to identify words with the long *u* sound. Invite partners to brainstorm and write other song titles, using words with long *u*. You may wish to repeat the activity, having children use words with long *a* and *i*.

Say each word in the box and listen for the long vowel sound. Then, write the word in the correct column.

cane	tune	dime	stay	ride	mule	fine
bike	lake	pail	use	tape	lie	came
tube	pie	suit	tuba	like	cube	rain

Long a **Long i** **Long u**

1. cane
2. lake
3. pail
4. stay
5. tape
6. came
7. rain

8. bike
9. pie
10. dime
11. ride
12. like
13. lie
14. fine

15. tube
16. tune
17. suit
18. use
19. tuba
20. mule
21. cube

Say each word. Write two words that rhyme with it.

lake   **like**   **suit**

22. _____ 24. _____ 26. _____
23. _____ 25. _____ 27. _____

 HOME Ask your child to add more rhyming words to the lists above.

42   Review long vowels a, i, u

CURRICULUM CONNECTIONS

SPELLING

Use these words and sentences as a pretest for writing words with long vowels *u, o, e.*

1. **flute**   Julian plays the **flute**.
2. **cube**   Lucy ate a sugar **cube**.
3. **boat**   Can you row in a **boat**?
4. **cone**   Scoop the yogurt into a **cone**.
5. **meat**   This recipe uses **meat**.
6. **seal**   Watch the **seal** perform.

WRITING

Have children make a poster announcing the music concert described in the sentences on page 41. Suggest that they name performers, tunes, and musical instruments.

PORTFOLIO

MUSIC

Write these headings on the board: *Instruments with Strings, Instruments You Blow, Instruments You Strike.* Ask children to name instruments for each category. Circle words with long *a, i,* or *u.*

TECHNOLOGY   **AstroWord** Long Vowels: *e, u*

AUDITORY/KINESTHETIC LEARNERS **GROUPS**

Play Simon Says by giving commands for children to carry out only if a word with the long *u* sound is heard (otherwise, they should stand still). Include commands such as: *Play a flute. Sing a tune. Trace a cube. Ride a mule. Pick fruit. Pour juice. Play a tuba. Make a huge circle.*

CHALLENGE

Challenge children by having them think of new song lyrics to go with a familiar tune. Encourage them to use long *u* words.

EXTRA SUPPORT/INTERVENTION

Offer support by reading aloud the word choices from page 41 to help children hear the difference in the vowel sounds. For page 42, read each word individually and limit the choice of columns to two. See Daily Phonics Practice, page 214.

Integrating Phonics and Reading

Guided Reading
Have children look at the cover and the title. Talk about things brothers and sisters do together. Then, ask what children think the book will be about.

My Sister June

First Reading Have children identify things Jessica Beth did that June got blamed for.
Second Reading Ask children to identify the long and short *u* words in the story.
Comprehension
After reading, ask children these questions:
- Why wasn't June blamed for what Jessica Beth did to her room? *Inference/Cause and Effect*
- Would you like to have June as a sister? *Reflective Analysis/Personal Response*

ESL/ELL **English Language Learners**
Have children use picture clues to tell what happened to June because of something Jessica Beth had done.

Long o

Skill Focus

Children will

★ identify the long o sound.

★ recognize that the long o sound is represented by different spellings.

★ distinguish among the sounds of long *a, i, o,* and *u* in words.

ESL/ELL Speakers of Asian languages may confuse long o with the sound of *aw* as in *awful;* practice *low/law, so/saw,* and so on.

▶ Teach

Phonemic Awareness: Phoneme Identity
Say the words *bone, goat,* and *toe,* elongating the vowel sound. Have children repeat, also stressing the vowel sounds: *booone, goooat, toooe.* Ask children to name the vowel sound. Identify it as long o. Repeat the words and ask volunteers to name words that rhyme.

Sound to Symbol Write the words *tone, boat,* and *doe* on the board and have children read them aloud. Call on volunteers to underline the letters that stand for the long o sound in each word. Then, help children apply the rule for long vowel sounds by naming the silent vowel in each word.

Write the word *row* on the board and ask children to identify the letters that stand for the long o sound. (*-ow*) Explain that although *w* is a consonant, it becomes silent in some words when paired with the vowel *o.* Help children list other words with the same *-ow* spelling and sound. (*bow, know, bowl, show, low, mow, sow*)

Rhyming Words Review long vowels *a, i, u, o* by writing the following words on the board: *coat, lake, cube, pie.* Have children read the words and identify the long vowel sounds. Then, invite children to name a word that rhymes with each word on the board, such as *goat, bake, tube, tie.*

▶ Practice and Apply

Sound to Symbol For page 43, suggest that children name the picture and look for the letters that stand for those sounds.

Writing As children complete page 44, encourage them to say each word in the box softly to themselves until they find the word that rhymes. You may wish to point out that each word in a box is used only once.

Reading Use *Toast for Mom,* MCP Phonics and Reading Consonant and Vowel Skills Library, Level C, to provide additional practice in reading words with long and short *o.*

Sound to Symbol

Name _____

RULE
If a one-syllable word has two vowels, the first vowel usually stands for the long sound, and the second vowel is silent. If the first vowel is **o**, the word has the long **o** sound.

bone   goat   toe

▶ Circle the name of each picture.

1. ripe / rap / (rope) / rode
2. (row) / ray / rod / rule
3. (soap) / soak / sap / sip
4. (bow) / bone / bun / box
5. hive / hop / hay / (hose)
6. (robe) / rope / rob / rod
7. bone / bat / (boat) / bite
8. tone / (toe) / toad / tie
9. cane / (cone) / can / came
10. (doe) / den / dock / duck
11. corn / cook / (coat) / cube
12. got / (goal) / game / gas

Long vowel o: Sound to symbol   **43**

FOCUS ON ALL LEARNERS

ESL/ELL **ENGLISH LANGUAGE LEARNERS**
Assess English language learners' familiarity with the sound of long o by reviewing the rule on page 43 and using words in context.

- Write these sentences on the board:

  I'll **row** the **boat** and toss the **rope.**

  I **hope** the **toad** got out of the **road.**

- Help volunteers read the sentences aloud and identify words with the long o sound.

- Pantomime, or have children pantomime actions from the sentences.

KINESTHETIC LEARNERS **PARTNERS**

Materials: index cards

Have partners write these long o words on cards: *toad, road, cone, stone, doe, toe, row, low, goat, boat, rope,* and *hope.* Then, have them place the cards face down to form a grid. To play, have children take turns turning over two cards at a time to find a rhyming pair. If the words rhyme, the player keeps the cards and tries again. If not, the cards are returned to their face down position and the next player takes a turn.

Say each word. Find the word in the box that rhymes with it. Then, write the rhyming word on the line.

1.

| cone | coat | row |
| rode | hope | pole |

load ___rode___
boat ___coat___
hoe ___row___
bone ___cone___
soap ___hope___
hole ___pole___

2.

| pail | late | made |
| lake | way | save |

wait ___late___
day ___way___
sale ___pail___
cake ___lake___
paid ___made___
wave ___save___

3.

| like | hive | ride |
| mine | bite | pie |

dive ___hive___
lie ___pie___
line ___mine___
bike ___like___
tied ___ride___
kite ___bite___

4.

| tune | tube | mule |
| rude | cute | use |

June ___tune___
rule ___mule___
mute ___cute___
cube ___tube___
fuse ___use___
dude ___rude___

44 Review long vowels a, i, u, o

 HOME Help your child use rhyming words from the page to make up sentences such as *I like the bike.*

CURRICULUM CONNECTIONS

SPELLING

Make a four-column chart on the board and label the columns *bone, goat, toe, row.* Say words with long *o* and invite children to work together to write words in the column with the same spelling pattern. Use *boat, cone, doe, slow, hoe, croak, chose, throw.* Then, have children add words of their own.

WRITING

Engage children in making "backward crosswords." First, ask them to create a crossword puzzle using long *o* words. Then, have them swap puzzles and write the clues.

 PORTFOLIO

SOCIAL STUDIES

Invite children to create a map of the neighborhood around the school. Explain that their maps should show buildings, stores, benches, and any other landmarks. Have children use as many long *o, a, i,* or *u* words as possible.

 **TECHNOLOGY** **AstroWord** Long Vowels: *i, o*

VISUAL/AUDITORY LEARNERS GROUPS

Have children write the following words on the board: *coat, bowl, toe, soap, doe, road, rope, cone,* and *bone.* Members of the group take turns providing clues about a word for the others to guess, such as *What do you wear when it is cold?* (coat)

CHALLENGE

Challenge children to choose a word from page 44, add a letter to form a second word, add another to form a third word. Letters can be rearranged, but each new word must contain all the letters of the previous word. (Examples include the words *hoe, hope, phone; tune, tunes,* and *sunset.*)

EXTRA SUPPORT/INTERVENTION

Write these words on the board: *rob, do, hop, cot, rod, got,* and *slop.* Ask children to add the letter *e* or *a* to form new words. Have children say each new word aloud. (*robe, doe, hope, coat, goat, slope*) See Daily Phonics Practice, page 214.

Integrating Phonics and Reading

Guided Reading

If you used this book in Lesson 12, review the story with children. If not, have them look at the cover and tell what the book will be about.

First Reading Have children tell why the toast was cold each time it was made.

Second Reading Ask children to identify the long and short *o* words in the story.

Comprehension

After reading, ask children these questions:
- Why was Rose too busy to watch the toast? *Recall/Making Comparisons*
- What would you tell Rose to help her do all the things she wanted to do? *Reflective Analysis/Personal Response*

ESL/ELL English Language Learners

Have children use picture and word clues to retell the story. Ask simple questions about each page, such as, *Who is this? What is she doing?*

Long e

Skill Focus

Children will

★ identify the long e sound.

★ recognize that the long e sound is represented by different spellings.

★ read and write long e words in context.

★ distinguish among the sounds of long *a, i, u, o,* and *e* in words.

ESL/ELL Children who speak languages other than English may assimilate long *e* and short *i*; practice *feet, fit; Pete, pit; beat, bit.*

Teach

Phonemic Awareness: Phoneme Identity
Say the words *seal, feet, stream, clean, cheap, beast, heat, seed, queen, sweep,* and *street.* Have children repeat each word and say its vowel sound. Identify the vowel sound as long *e.* Ask children to name other words with the long *e* sound.

Sound to Symbol Write these incomplete words on the board: n_t, n_ _t. Have a volunteer write *e* in the first word, read it aloud, and identify the vowel sound. (*net, short* e) Have another child write *ea* in the second word, read it aloud, and identify the vowel sound. (*neat, long* e) Ask a child to apply the long vowel rule to the word *neat.* (*In a one syllable word with two vowels, the first vowel usually stands for the long sound and the second vowel is silent.*)

Words in Context Next, write the following sentences on the board. Ask children to complete the sentences with the words *net* and *neat.* Discuss how they know which word belonged in each sentence.

• **Use a ____ to catch the fish.** *(net)*
• **Your room is very ____.** *(neat)*

Practice and Apply

Sound to Symbol As children complete pages 45 and 46, encourage them to listen for the vowel sound in each word or picture name before deciding on a choice. Suggest they apply the long vowel rule to each of the words they choose.

Critical Thinking Have children identify the animals Pete sees at the zoo and the one that is his favorite. Then, discuss children's responses to the Talk About It question.

Reading Use *Red and I Visit the Vet,* MCP Phonics and Reading Consonant and Vowel Skills Library, Level C, to provide additional practice in reading words with long and short *e.*

Red and I Visit the Vet

Name _____

Look at the picture. Circle the word that names the picture. Then, complete the sentence by writing the word on the line.

RULE
If a one-syllable word has two vowels, the first vowel usually stands for the long sound, and the second vowel is silent. If the first vowel is **e**, the word has a long **e** sound.
Pete   leaf   jeep

1. Pet / **Pete**
   ____Pete____ likes to visit the zoo.

2. **seals** / sells
   He thinks the ___seals___ are funny.

3. set / **seat**
   Pete finds a ___seat___ to watch them play.

4. tent / **teeth**
   He likes the lion with its big ___teeth___.

5. **meat** / met
   The lion likes to eat ___meat___.

6. **eagle** / enter
   Pete's favorite animal is the ___eagle___.

7. trend / **tree**
   It sits high up in a ___tree___.

8. fell / **feet**
   Pete's ___feet___ hurt at the end of the day.

TALK About It What is your favorite animal at the zoo? Why?

Long vowel e: Words in context, critical thinking   **45**

FOCUS ON ALL LEARNERS

ESL/ELL ENGLISH LANGUAGE LEARNERS
Materials: index cards

• Print words with short vowels, such as *set,* on index cards, one word per card.

• Have children select a card, read the word aloud, and identify the short vowel sound they hear. Break up tasks if necessary.

• Ask children to replace the short vowel with long *e* and say the new word. (*seat*) Allow time for English language learners to change the short vowel word to a long one. Allow children to write the words to help them visualize the change.

• Other word options include *bet, bad, red, fed, lid, sun, sell.*

KINESTHETIC LEARNERS GROUPS

Have children give one another commands to act out, using words with long *e.* For example: *Shake your* **feet**. *Touch your* **teeth**. *Sit in your* **seat**. *Make a* **peep**. *Puff out your* **cheeks**. Have children identify the long *e* word in sentences they use.

Say the name of each picture. Color the animals whose names contain the long vowel sound shown at the beginning of each row.

1. **Long a** — jay, color snail, cat, color whale

2. **Long i** — color tiger, color mice, kitten, pig

3. **Long u** — skunk, color mule, duck, puppy

4. **Long o** — fox, color goat, color doe, ox

5. **Long e** — color seal, hen, color bee, eagle color

HOME
Invite your child to use each of the words with a long vowel sound in a sentence.

46 Review long vowels a, e, i, o, u

CURRICULUM CONNECTIONS

SPELLING

Use these words and sentences as a posttest for writing words with long vowels *u, o, e.*

1. **seal** The **seal** swam after a fish.
2. **meat** Put **meat** in the salad.
3. **flute** A **flute** is an instrument.
4. **boat** I hope my **boat** will float.
5. **cone** A tepee has a **cone** shape.
6. **cube** A **cube** has six equal sides.

WRITING

Challenge children to write a limerick featuring words with long *e.* Example:

There once was a lazy **sheep**
Who did **sleep** in the **seat** of a **jeep.**
He woke up at **three**
To the buzz of a **bee**
And **leaned** on the horn, which went **BEEP!**

TECHNOLOGY **AstroWord** Long Vowels: *e, u*

VISUAL/AUDITORY LEARNERS GROUPS

Materials: paper, crayons or markers

Write silly captions on the board, such as: *a seal that can **teach, sheep** in a **jeep,** a **bee** with big **feet,** a **queen** with no **teeth.*** Ask children to add others, using words with long *e.* Then, have them choose a caption to illustrate, trade drawings, and match the picture they get to its caption.

CHALLENGE

The long *e* sound is found in onomatopoetic words, such as *eek, meow, peep, creak,* and *beep.* Ask children to think of similar words with long *e* or make up sound-effect words to write and illustrate. You may wish to include words with other long vowel sounds.

EXTRA SUPPORT/INTERVENTION

Materials: tag board, paper fasteners, scissors

Provide materials for children to use to make word wheels featuring words with the phonograms *-eep, -eal, -eak, -eat, -eed,* or *-eet.* Children can trade wheels with a partner to read. See Daily Phonics Practice, page 214.

Integrating Phonics and Reading

Guided Reading

Red and I Visit the Vet

Have children look over the cover and read the title. Invite them to offer ideas about why someone might take a pet to a vet.

First Reading Have children tell what Dr. Chen did during Red's checkup.

Second Reading Ask children to identify the long and short *e* words in the story.

Comprehension

After reading, ask children these questions:

- What did you learn about how a vet gives a dog a checkup from this story? *Recall/Main Idea and Details*
- Why do you think Dr. Chen asked Red questions? *Reflective Analysis/Prior Knowledge*

ESL/ELL English Language Learners

Remind children that Red's owner answers the questions Dr. Chen asks. Have children find questions the vet asked and the answers the girl gave.

Phonics and Spelling / Phonics and Writing

Review Short and Long Vowels

Skill Focus

Children will

★ write words with short and long vowel sounds.

★ write a numbered list using words with short and long vowel sounds.

Teach

Phonics and Spelling Review the rule that if a word has only one vowel that comes at the beginning or is between two consonants, the vowel usually has the short sound, as in *hop*. If a word with one syllable has two vowels, the first vowel usually stands for the long sound and the second vowel is silent, as in *hope*.

Write the words *hand, gift, bus, lock,* and *tent* on the board. Ask a child to read them aloud and say whether they have long or short vowel sounds. (*short*) Then, say the following words and have volunteers write them under the words with the same vowel sounds: *pond, glass, dish, bell, luck.* Invite children to add words to each column.

Repeat the activity for long vowels, using the words *sail* (tape), *pile* (time), *flute* (cube), *boat* (cone), *meal* (seat).

Practice and Apply

Phonics and Spelling Make sure children understand how to do a crossword puzzle. When children have completed the puzzles, ask them what they notice about the vowel sounds in the answers. (*The words in the top puzzle have short vowels. Those in the bottom puzzle have long vowels.*)

Phonics and Writing Before children write their lists, have them brainstorm ideas. List their ideas on the board. Remind them that their lists should begin with a topic, and each item should be numbered and begin on a new line.

Reading Use *This Room Is a Mess,* MCP Phonics and Reading Consonant and Vowel Skills Library, Level C, to provide additional practice in reading words with short and long vowels.

This Room Is a Mess!

Written by Anne Patterson
Illustrated by Pamela R. Levy

Spelling

Name _____

Phonics & Spelling Find a word from the box to complete each clue. Write the words in the puzzles.

| bell | day | hand | luck | ride | boat | flute | kick |
| pile | tape | team | cone | gift | lock | pond | tent |

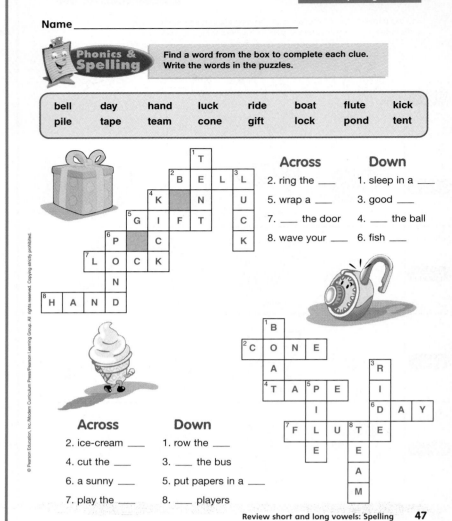

Across
2. ring the ___
5. wrap a ___
7. ___ the door
8. wave your ___

Down
1. sleep in a ___
3. good ___
4. ___ the ball
6. fish ___

Across
2. ice-cream ___
4. cut the ___
6. a sunny ___
7. play the ___

Down
1. row the ___
3. ___ the bus
5. put papers in a ___
8. ___ players

Review short and long vowels: Spelling   **47**

FOCUS ON ALL LEARNERS

ESL/ELL ENGLISH LANGUAGE LEARNERS

Materials: letter cards a, i, u, o, e; colored chalk

• On the board, draw a chart, two rows high and five columns wide. Label the rows *Long Vowels* and *Short Vowels.* Label each column with one of the five vowels.

• Ask a child to choose a card, say a word that has the long sound of that letter, and write the word in the chart on the board. Repeat the activity for short vowels. You may wish to model selecting and reading a card for a short and a long vowel before you begin.

• Review the completed chart with children by reading the words aloud. Make any corrections, explaining why the word was not correct.

KINESTHETIC/AUDITORY LEARNERS

Have children form a starting line across one side of the classroom. Say a word for each child in turn. The child should identify the vowel sound and spell the word. If correct, the child takes one short or one long step forward, depending on the vowel sound in the word. Play until everyone reaches the other side.

Phonics & Writing

Making **lists** can help you learn. They can help you organize your thoughts and remember important facts and ideas. Items on a list are often numbered.

▶ Make a list of some things you like to do at home. Some of the words in the box may help you.

read	help	cook	play	ball	cat
dog	home	like	best	things	book

Begin by writing the **topic** of your list.

_____

Begin each item on a new line.

Number the items on your list.

_____
_____
_____
_____
_____
_____
_____
_____
_____

48   Review short and long vowels: Writing

HOME Ask your child to read the list and identify the words with long and short vowels.

CURRICULUM CONNECTIONS

SPELLING

Use these words and sentences to review spelling words with long vowels.

1. **sail** The ship will **sail** at dawn.
2. **tape** This **tape** is very sticky.
3. **day** What a beautiful **day**!
4. **pile** That's a big **pile** of leaves.
5. **flute** Will you play your **flute**?
6. **cube** A **cube** has six sides.
7. **ride** Can you **ride** a bike?
8. **cone** Joan has an ice-cream **cone**.
9. **seal** A **seal** is a good swimmer.
10. **meal** Breakfast is an important **meal**.
11. **time** What **time** is school out?
12. **boat** The toy **boat** sank.

MATH

Invite pairs of children to write lists of math words: short vowel sounds and long vowel sounds. Compile a class list. Words might include: *sum, add, cent; base, cone, feet.*

TECHNOLOGY   **AstroWord** Short Vowels: *a, i; i, o; e, u.* Long Vowels: *a, i; e, u; i, o*

Integrating Phonics and Reading

Guided Reading
Have children look at the cover and the title. Ask what some of the items are in the illustration.
First Reading Have children describe how Magda cleaned up her room.
Second Reading Have children find short and long vowel sounds in story words.

Comprehension
After reading, ask children these questions:
• Why did Amado want Magda to clean up her room before Mom got home? *Cause and Effect/Inference*
• Do you think Magda and Amado get along? Explain. *Reflective Analysis/Personal Response*

ESL/ELL **English Language Learners**
Remind children that when Magda first tries to clean up her room, she puts her things into groups. Invite children to identify the groups using picture and word clues.

VISUAL/KINESTHETIC LEARNERS   **GROUPS**

Have children take turns pantomiming puzzle clues for either puzzle on page 47. The child who answers the clue correctly pantomimes the next clue. Continue until the puzzle is complete.

CHALLENGE

Challenge children to work together to make their own crossword puzzles using words with either long or short vowel sounds. Make photocopies of the puzzles and distribute them for others to complete.

EXTRA SUPPORT/INTERVENTION

Materials: index cards

Use index cards to make letter cards. Engage children in a vowel substitution activity. For example, have children form the word *bag*. Then, have them change the vowel to form *big*. Continue by building words *beg, bug, bog*. Do the same for long vowel words, such as *male, mile, mule, mole*. See Daily Phonics Practice, pages 213–214.

Take-Home Book

Review Short and Long Vowels

Skill Focus

Children will

★ read short and long vowel words in the context of a story.

★ reread for fluency.

Teach

Build Background

- Remind children that the theme of this unit is "Friends and Family." Ask them to share information they have learned about the different kinds of homes families live in and the kinds of things friends and families do together.

- Write these animal names on the board: *beaver, spider, chipmunk*. Ask children to share what they know about the homes of these animals. Point out that they will be reading a book about animal homes.

Phonemic Awareness: Phoneme Isolation
Say the animal names you have written, elongating the vowel sounds. (*beeeaver, spiiider, chiiipmuuunk*) Call on children to identify the vowel sound(s) they hear. (*long* e, *long* i, *short* i, *short* u)

Practice and Apply

Read the Book Help children tear out and fold the pages to make their Take-Home Books. Have children look through the book and talk about the pictures. Then, read the story together. Afterward, discuss what children have learned about animal homes.

Sound to Symbol On the board, draw a chart of two rows and five columns. Label the rows *Long Vowels* and *Short Vowels*. Label each column with one of the five vowels. Have children reread the story to find words with short and long vowel sounds. When each spot in the chart is filled, review the words with the class.

Reread for Fluency Have children reread the book to increase their fluency and comprehension. Tell children to take their books home to read with family members.

Name _____

Animal Homes

Animals live in many different kinds of homes. Some animals build their homes, while others live in trees or under the ground. Some animals that build their own homes are beavers and spiders. Beavers build their homes from sticks and mud. Many spiders spin webs and live in or near the webs.

1

FOLD

Some animals have two homes that are very far apart. Monarch butterflies and Arctic terns are two kinds of animals that travel a long way to a warmer winter home.

Every year, some monarchs make a trip of 3,000 miles to their winter homes in Mexico. The Arctic terns travel even farther. Each winter they fly from their homes near the North Pole to warmer homes near the South Pole. Their trip is over 10,000 miles long each way!

4

Review short and long vowels: Take-home book   **49**

FOCUS ON ALL LEARNERS

- -

ESL/ELL ENGLISH LANGUAGE LEARNERS

Use these suggestions to support English language learners as they read the Take-Home Book.

- Help children identify the animals in each picture and describe what they are doing.

- Work with children to make a story web or a main idea chart to help them organize their ideas.

- Read the story together.

- Have children identify the vowel sounds in familiar story words.

VISUAL/KINESTHETIC LEARNERS

Materials: large sheets of drawing paper, game markers, dice

Arrange children in groups. Have each group draw a large frog on one side of a sheet of paper and a large snake on the other. Ask children to write short vowel words on the frog and long vowel words on the snake. To use the drawings in a game, have players toss a die to see how many words they are to read aloud and cover with game markers. Have them play until all words are covered.

Other animals make their homes in trees. Some owls look for holes high up in trees. Then they build their nests in the holes. Raccoons often make their homes in hollow logs or stumps. Squirrels often use old tree trunks for their dens.

Some animals make their homes underground. Chipmunks live in long tunnels that they dig in the ground. They hollow out the middle of the tunnel for a nest. Prairie dogs also dig tunnels underground. The tunnels connect to each other to form large "towns" with many entrances. Thousands of prairie dogs can live in one prairie dog town.

50 Review short and long vowels: Take-home book

CURRICULUM CONNECTIONS

MATH

Point out that the story gives facts about animal homes that are expressed using numbers:

"Thousands of prairie dogs can live in one prairie dog town. Every year, monarchs make a trip of 3,000 miles to their winter homes in Mexico."

Provide reference sources about animals and their homes. Ask children to find other facts about animals that are conveyed in terms of numbers.

SCIENCE

Ask children to explain how a story about animal homes related to the theme "Family and Friends." Begin a discussion about animals that live in zoos or wildlife parks. Have children talk about what these captive animals need to make their human-made homes as comfortable and safe as their natural habitats.

WRITING

Invite children to imagine they are one of the animals in the story. Have them write a paragraph about the ways in which their home is well suited to their needs.

 **AstroWord** Short Vowels: *a, i; i, o; e, u.* Long Vowels: *a, i; i, o; e, u*

AUDITORY/VISUAL LEARNERS

Have partners take turns reading pages of the story aloud. After reading a page, the reader identifies words that have short or long vowel sounds. The listener identifies the vowel sound in each word.

CHALLENGE

Materials: reference books about animals

Invite children to write their own book about an animal home. Suggest that they choose an animal with a name that has a short or long vowel sound.

EXTRA SUPPORT/INTERVENTION

Materials: Take-Home Books

Ask children to use a highlighter to mark words in their Take-Home Books that they are uncertain about. Then, work with children to review the pronunciation and meaning of the words they highlighted. See Daily Phonics Practice, pages 213–214.

Unit Checkup

Review Short and Long Vowels

Skill Focus

Children will

★ identify short and long vowel sounds in words.

★ read and write words with short and long vowel sounds.

★ distinguish among the sounds of short and long *a, i, u, o,* and *e* in words.

Teach

Phonemic Awareness: Phoneme Isolation
Remind children that each of the vowels *a, i, o, u,* and *e* each has a short and a long sound. Then, say the following word pairs and call on volunteers to identify the vowel sounds they hear: *cap/cape; seat/set; pine/pin; hop/hope; tub/tube.* Invite children to offer similar word pairs that illustrate the short and long sound of each vowel.

Sound to Symbol Write the five vowels on the board. Ask a child to choose a vowel and say and write a word with the short sound of that vowel. Then, ask another child to say and write a word with the long sound of the vowel. Urge children to write more than one word to represent different spellings for the long vowel sound. Do the same activity for each of the other vowels. If necessary, remind children of the rules for short and long vowel sounds.

Practice and Apply

Assess Skills For the first activity on page 51, have children say each picture name to themselves and listen for the vowel sound. Children may wish to review the short and long vowel rules as they work on the activity. For the second exercise, you may wish to complete the first item with children. When they finish the activity, review children's responses as a class.

For page 52, make sure children understand that only one circle should be filled in for each item. Have them say each word in order to hear the vowel sounds.

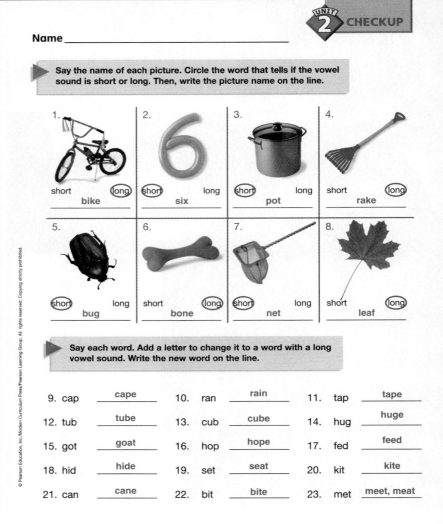

Name _____

Say the name of each picture. Circle the word that tells if the vowel sound is short or long. Then, write the picture name on the line.

1. short (long)   bike
2. (short) long   six
3. (short) long   pot
4. short (long)   rake
5. (short) long   bug
6. short (long)   bone
7. (short) long   net
8. short (long)   leaf

Say each word. Add a letter to change it to a word with a long vowel sound. Write the new word on the line.

9. cap   cape
10. ran   rain
11. tap   tape
12. tub   tube
13. cub   cube
14. hug   huge
15. got   goat
16. hop   hope
17. fed   feed
18. hid   hide
19. set   seat
20. kit   kite
21. can   cane
22. bit   bite
23. met   meet, meat

Short and long vowels: Assessment   **51**

FOCUS ON ALL LEARNERS

ESL/ELL ENGLISH LANGUAGE LEARNERS

Review long and short vowel sounds by using words in context and rhyming words.

• On the board, write the sentence *Billy bakes sweet hot pies and donuts to send over the deep blue sea to his Uncle Jack.*

• Read the sentence aloud. Make sure children understand the meaning of the sentence. Then, have English language learners underline the words with long vowel sounds and circle the words with short vowel sounds.

• If a child has difficulty with a specific vowel sound, reinforce and review the applicable lesson(s).

• Have English language learners who are ready for a challenge name words that rhyme with these words: *Billy, bakes, sweet, hot, send, deep, blue, sea,* and *Jack.*

KINESTHETIC LEARNERS

Send partners on a scavenger hunt for words that have a particular vowel sound. After a given period of time, have each pair of children share their words and add them to an existing Word Wall.

> Say the first word in each row. Fill in the circle beside the word with the same vowel sound.

1.	**can**	○ mail	● gas	○ name	○ tape
2.	**rust**	○ suit	○ mule	● hum	○ use
3.	**deep**	● peak	○ went	○ sled	○ elf
4.	**milk**	○ pipe	○ hike	○ file	● hill
5.	**cute**	○ nuts	● fuse	○ shut	○ dull
6.	**clock**	○ cone	○ goat	● dot	○ soak
7.	**desk**	○ peel	● neck	○ leap	○ tree
8.	**last**	○ cake	○ rain	● bank	○ same
9.	**fire**	○ hid	○ ship	○ fill	● kite
10.	**job**	● plot	○ note	○ soap	○ rode
11.	**mug**	○ glue	○ cube	○ flute	● luck
12.	**flake**	○ black	● race	○ ask	○ fan
13.	**will**	● mist	○ shine	○ white	○ dime
14.	**send**	○ seen	○ meat	● bet	○ jeep
15.	**joke**	○ box	○ spot	○ rock	● coat

52   Short and long vowels: Assessment

ASSESS UNDERSTANDING OF UNIT SKILLS

STUDENT PROGRESS ASSESSMENT

Refer to the observational notes you made as children worked on the activities in this unit. Your notes will help you assess the progress children made with short and long vowels.

PORTFOLIO ASSESSMENT

To evaluate children's written work, review the contents of their portfolios. Schedule interviews with children in order to discuss what they have learned about short and long vowels and to identify the areas that still need work.

DAILY PHONICS PRACTICE

You may wish to use the quick reviews on pages 213–214 in Daily Phonics Practice with children who need additional practice with short and long vowels.

PHONICS POSTTEST

Use the posttest on pages 23g–23h to assess children's mastery of short and long vowels.

AUDITORY LEARNERS GROUPS

Play a game of "Vowel Volleyball." One team, the Longs, begin by saying a word with a long vowel sound. The other team, the Shorts, say a word with the short sound for the same vowel within five seconds or the Longs score a point and serve again.

CHALLENGE

Challenge children to write a mystery story, using the words from the first activity on page 51. For example, something could happen to a *bike*. The number *six*, a *net*, and a *rake* could be clues readers can use to solve the mystery.

EXTRA SUPPORT/INTERVENTION

Materials: index cards

Write words with short and long vowel sounds, each on a separate card. Ask children to sort the words according to short and long vowel sounds. Then, have them sort the words again according to the spelling of each vowel sound. See Daily Phonics Practice, pages 213–214.

Teacher Notes

UNIT 3

Compounds, Blends, and Digraphs, Y as a Consonant and Vowel, r-Controlled Vowels

THEME: WHAT AN IMAGINATION!

CONTENTS

Student Performance Objectives

In Unit 3, children will be introduced to compound words, syllables, consonant blends and digraphs, *y* as a consonant and a vowel, and *r*-controlled vowels within the context of the theme "What an Imagination!" As children begin to understand and learn to apply the concepts involved in longer words, they will be able to

▶ Identify the two words in compound words

▶ Identify the number of syllables in words

▶ Identify *r, l,* and *s* blends and the sounds they make in words

▶ Identify *y* as a vowel and a consonant

▶ Identify and read words with consonant digraphs

▶ Identify syllables with blends and digraphs

▶ Read words that contain an *r*-controlled vowel

Overview of Resources

LESSON	MCP PHONICS AND READING LIBRARY, LEVEL C PROGRAM	TITLE	DAILY PHONICS PRACTICE
23: Compound words	RR, Stg Five, Bk 30	*The Junkpile Robot*	214
24: Syllables	RR, Stg Five, Bk 28	*Mother's Helpers*	215
25: *r* Blends	RR, Stg Four, Bk 13	*The Princess Who Couldn't Cry*	215
26: *l* Blends	RR, Stg Four, Bk 3	*Looking for Angus*	215
27: *s* Blends	RR, Stg Five, Bk 29	*A Pot of Stone Soup*	215
28: Final blends	VFC, Set 2	*A Helping Hand*	215
29: *Y* as a vowel	RR, Stg Four, Bk 10	*The Night Sky*	215–216
30: *Y* as a vowel and a consonant	RR, Stg Four, Bk 11	*The Fourth of July*	215–216
31: Consonant digraphs	RR, Stg Five, Bk 9	*Suki and the Case of the Lost Bunnies*	216
32: Consonant digraphs	NC, Set 1	*One Step at a Time*	216
33: Syllables	NC, Set 4	*The Living Desert*	215
34: Review consonant blends & digraphs	RR, Stg Four, Bk 26	*Squirrels*	215–216
35: *R*-controlled vowels	RR, Stg Five, Bk 19	*Friends Forever*	216–217
36: *R*-controlled vowels	RR, Stg Five, Bk 20	*Fern and Burt*	216–217
37: Syllables with *r*-controlled vowels	RR, Stg Five, Bk 21	*The Monster Under the Bed*	215–217
38: Review *r*-controlled vowels	RR, Stg Five, Bk 22	*Carla Gets a Pet*	216–217
39: Take-Home Book: "They Had an Idea!"			215–217
40: Unit Checkup			214–217

RR—Reader Readers   Stg—Stage   Bk—Book   NC—Next Chapters   VFC—Very First Chapters

Assessment Options

In Unit 3, assess children's ability to read and write compound words and multisyllabic words; words with *r, l,* and *s* blends, *y* as a vowel and a consonant, consonant digraphs, and *r*-controlled vowels. Use the Unit Pretest and Posttest for formal assessment. For ongoing informal assessment, you may wish to use children's work on the Review pages, Take-Home Books, and Unit Checkups. Encourage children to evaluate their own work and to participate in setting goals for their own learning.

ESL/ELL The skills covered in this unit may be especially problematic for English language learners. Note pronunciation difficulties as they occur, but assess performance based upon children's ability to distinguish specific sounds when pronounced by a native speaker. For additional support for English language learners, see page 53j.

FORMAL ASSESSMENT

Use the Unit 3 Pretest, on pages 53e–53f, to help assess a child's knowledge at the beginning of a unit and to plan instruction.

ESL/ELL Before administering the Pretest, gather together items or pictures of items that are named by the less familiar words on page 53e. Select an item and have volunteers name it. Ask other children to write the word on the board and identify the target phonics element (consonant blend, consonant digraph, *r*-controlled vowel, and so on). Read directions aloud and model how to complete the test pages.

Use the Unit 3 Posttest, on pages 53g–53h, to help assess mastery of unit objectives and to plan for reteaching, if necessary.

INFORMAL ASSESSMENT

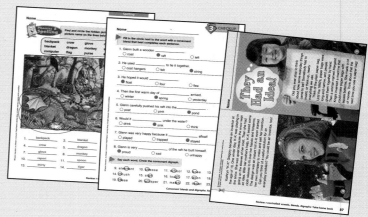

Use the Review pages, Unit Checkup, and Take-Home Books in the student book to provide an effective means of evaluating children's performance.

Unit 3 Skills	Review pages	Checkups	Take-Home Books
Compound words		89–90	87–88
Syllables		89–90	87–88
Consonant blends	66, 77–78	89–90	87–88
Sounds of *y*	70, 85–86	89–90	87–88
Consonant digraphs	77–78	89–90	87–88
r-Controlled vowels	85–86	89–90	87–88

STUDENT PROGRESS CHECKLIST

Use the checklist on page 53i to record children's progress. You may wish to cut the sections apart to place each child's checklist in his or her portfolio.

PORTFOLIO ASSESSMENT

This logo appears throughout the teaching plans. It signals opportunities for collecting student work for individual portfolios. You may also want to include the Pretest and Posttest, the Review pages, the Unit Checkup, Phonics & Reading, and Phonics & Writing pages.

PHONEMIC AWARENESS AND PHONICS ASSESSMENT

Use PAPA to obtain an itemized analysis of children's decoding skills.

PAPA Skills	MCP Phonics Lessons in Unit 3
Deleting sounds	Lessons 23, 33, 37
Consonant blends	Lessons 25–28, 34
Consonant digraphs	Lessons 31–32, 34
Long vowels	Lessons 29, 30
r-Controlled vowels	Lessons 36–38

Pretest and Posttest

DIRECTIONS

To help you assess children's progress in learning Unit 3 skills, tests are available on pages 53e–53h.

Administer the Pretest before children begin the unit. The results of the Pretest will help you identify each child's strengths and needs in advance, allowing you to structure lesson plans to meet individual needs. Administer the Posttest to assess children's overall mastery of skills taught in the unit and to identify specific areas that will require reteaching.

ESL/ELL Support English language learners by implementing any of the following suggestions before or during test taking, as appropriate.

• Model procedures for marking test answers. Complete several items together or in small groups to make sure children understand test-taking procedures.

• Conduct the test one-on-one with children who are unable to read independently in English or who need special pacing. Provide frequent support for their efforts.

• Administer the test orally. Try reading aloud the word choices so that children can hear the sounds of consonant blends, the letter *y*, consonant digraphs, syllables, and *r*-controlled vowels in words.

PERFORMANCE ASSESSMENT PROFILE

The following chart will help you identify specific skills as they appear on the tests and will enable you to identify and record specific information about an individual's or the class's performance on the tests.

Depending on the results of each test, refer to the Reteaching column for lesson-plan pages where you can find activities that will be useful for meeting individual needs or for daily phonics practice.

Answer Keys

Unit 3 Pretest, page 53e (BLM 15)

1. flashlight	8. computer
2. snowflake	9. caterpillar
3. grasshopper	10. elephant
4. watermelon	11. envelope
5. butterfly	12. laughing
6. playground	13. clarinet
7. fancy	14. celebration

Unit 3 Pretest, page 53f (BLM 16)

15. carton	21. urgent	27. blend
16. birthday	22. digraph	28. digraph
17. pretty	23. blend	29. digraph
18. snorkel	24. blend	30. blend
19. herd	25. digraph	31. blend
20. yawn	26. digraph	

Unit 3 Posttest, page 53g (BLM 17)

1. overcoat	8. children
2. pancake	9. entertainment
3. sailboat	10. potato
4. outdoors	11. telephone
5. treetop	12. salamander
6. moonlight	13. crocodile
7. another	14. discuss

Unit 3 Posttest, page 53h (BLM 18)

15. cord	21. nurse	27. blend
16. why	22. blend	28. blend
17. over	23. digraph	29. digraph
18. yes	24. digraph	30. blend
19. bird	25. blend	31. digraph
20. garden	26. digraph	

Performance Assessment Profile

Skill	Pretest Questions	Posttest Questions	Reteaching	
			Focus on All Learners	Daily Phonics Practice
Compound words	1, 2, 3, 4, 5, 6	1, 2, 3, 4, 5, 6	55–56	214
Syllables	7, 8, 9, 10, 11, 12, 13, 14	7, 8, 9, 10, 11, 12, 13, 14	57–58, 75–76, 83–84	215
Consonant blends	23, 24, 27, 30, 31	22, 25, 27, 28, 30	59–66, 77–78, 87–88	215
Sounds of *y*	17, 20	16, 18	67–70, 87–88, 71–74,	215–216
Consonant digraphs	22, 25, 26, 28, 29	23, 24, 26, 29, 31	77–78, 87–88	216
r-Controlled vowels	15, 16, 18, 19, 21	15, 17, 19, 20, 21	79–82, 85–88	216–217

Name _____

> **Fill in the circle beside the compound word in each row.**

1. ○ cover   ○ laughing   ○ flashlight   ○ invisible

2. ○ wrinkle   ○ snowflake   ○ discover   ○ computer

3. ○ deliver   ○ weather   ○ merchant   ○ grasshopper

4. ○ person   ○ watermelon   ○ united   ○ release

5. ○ butterfly   ○ impossible   ○ helpful   ○ beginning

6. ○ friendly   ○ bicycle   ○ important   ○ playground

> **In each box, fill in the circle beside the word that has the number of syllables shown at the top.**

7. **2**	8. **3**	9. **4**	10. **3**
○ terrific	○ alike	○ little	○ people
○ fancy	○ computer	○ sidestroke	○ plush
○ leaf	○ stranger	○ caterpillar	○ elephant
11. **3**	12. **2**	13. **3**	14. **4**
○ iceberg	○ recycle	○ careful	○ telephone
○ household	○ laughing	○ helicopter	○ concert
○ envelope	○ sly	○ clarinet	○ celebration

Go to the next page. →

BLM 15 Unit 3 Pretest: Compound words and syllables

Name_____

> Read the first word in each row. Fill in the circle beside the word that
> has the same sound as the underlined letter or letters in the first word.

15. p<u>ar</u>t	○ carton	○ fern	○ bird	○ hurt
16. d<u>ir</u>ty	○ barking	○ dined	○ birthday	○ short
17. pon<u>y</u>	○ toys	○ pretty	○ holiday	○ shy
18. s<u>or</u>t	○ surfer	○ loafer	○ hurdle	○ snorkel
19. al<u>er</u>t	○ herd	○ chorus	○ park	○ short
20. <u>y</u>ellow	○ purify	○ chimney	○ yawn	○ happily
21. h<u>ur</u>t	○ snore	○ fear	○ forest	○ urgent

> Read the word in each box. Fill in the circle by **digraph** if the word
> contains a digraph or by **blend** if the word contains a blend.

22.	share	○ digraph ○ blend	27.	sleeve	○ digraph ○ blend
23.	crane	○ digraph ○ blend	28.	laugh	○ digraph ○ blend
24.	plant	○ digraph ○ blend	29.	birthday	○ digraph ○ blend
25.	watch	○ digraph ○ blend	30.	scrape	○ digraph ○ blend
26.	phone	○ digraph ○ blend	31.	flavor	○ digraph ○ blend

Possible score on Unit 3 Pretest is 31. Number correct _____

BLM 16 Unit 3 Pretest: Consonant blends, sounds of *y*, consonant digraphs, *r*-controlled vowels

Name _____

> Fill in the circle beside the compound word in each row.

1. ○ telling   ○ music   ○ overcoat   ○ author

2. ○ different   ○ pancake   ○ teacher   ○ compare

3. ○ sailboat   ○ machine   ○ agree   ○ morning

4. ○ lion   ○ lumber   ○ outdoors   ○ ended

5. ○ setting   ○ treetop   ○ mountain   ○ parent

6. ○ needle   ○ classes   ○ animal   ○ moonlight

> In each box, fill in the circle beside the word that has the number of syllables shown at the top.

7. **3**	8. **2**	9. **4**	10. **3**
○ vowel	○ children	○ nickel	○ lemon
○ another	○ strong	○ eagle	○ explain
○ camel	○ peach	○ entertainment	○ potato
11. **3**	12. **4**	13. **3**	14. **2**
○ telephone	○ salamander	○ crocodile	○ mouth
○ swimmer	○ introduce	○ rocket	○ discuss
○ become	○ spearmint	○ happen	○ electric

Go to the next page. →

BLM 17 Unit 3 Posttest: Compound words, syllables

Name_____

> ▶ Read the first word in each row. Fill in the circle beside the word that has the same sound as the underlined letter or letters in the first word.

15. h<u>or</u>n   ○ father   ○ cord   ○ purse   ○ large

16. fl<u>y</u>   ○ beauty   ○ why   ○ boy   ○ baby

17. bak<u>er</u>   ○ over   ○ care   ○ dark   ○ morning

18. <u>y</u>arn   ○ city   ○ apply   ○ yes   ○ every

19. f<u>ir</u>st   ○ bird   ○ for   ○ start   ○ year

20. h<u>ar</u>d   ○ hurry   ○ work   ○ sir   ○ garden

21. h<u>ur</u>t   ○ heart   ○ nurse   ○ park   ○ more

> ▶ Read the word in each box. Fill in the circle by **digraph** if the word contains a digraph or by **blend** if the word contains a blend.

22.	stove	○ digraph ○ blend	27.	proof	○ digraph ○ blend
23.	teeth	○ digraph ○ blend	28.	crisp	○ digraph ○ blend
24.	show	○ digraph ○ blend	29.	chew	○ digraph ○ blend
25.	blame	○ digraph ○ blend	30.	grip	○ digraph ○ blend
26.	know	○ digraph ○ blend	31.	wrap	○ digraph ○ blend

Possible score on Unit 3 Posttest is 31. Number correct _____

BLM 18 Unit 3 Posttest: Consonant blends, sounds of *y*, consonant digraphs, *r*-controlled vowels

Student Progress Checklist

Make as many copies as needed to use for a class list. For individual portfolio use, cut apart each child's section. As indicated by the code, color in boxes next to skills satisfactorily assessed and insert an *X* by those requiring reteaching. Marked boxes can later be colored in to indicate mastery.

Student Progress Checklist

Code: ■ Satisfactory   ☒ Needs Reteaching

Student: _____	Skills	Comments / Learning Goals
_____	☐ Compound Words	
Pretest Score: _____	☐ Syllables	
Posttest Score: _____	☐ Consonant Blends	
	☐ Sounds of *y*	
	☐ Consonant Digraphs	
	☐ *r*-controlled Vowels	

Student: _____	Skills	Comments / Learning Goals
_____	☐ Compound Words	
Pretest Score: _____	☐ Syllables	
Posttest Score: _____	☐ Consonant Blends	
	☐ Sounds of *y*	
	☐ Consonant Digraphs	
	☐ *r*-controlled Vowels	

Student: _____	Skills	Comments / Learning Goals
_____	☐ Compound Words	
Pretest Score: _____	☐ Syllables	
Posttest Score: _____	☐ Consonant Blends	
	☐ Sounds of *y*	
	☐ Consonant Digraphs	
	☐ *r*-controlled Vowels	

BLM 19 Unit 3 Checklist

Throughout Unit 3 there are opportunities to assess English language learners' ability to read and write compound words, multisyllabic words, words with consonant blends, words with the letter *y*, words with consonant digraphs, and words with *r*-controlled vowels. Recognizing and pronouncing words with these phonic elements may be especially problematic for English language learners. Take note of pronunciation difficulties as they occur, and assess progress based on their ability to distinguish letter sounds when pronounced by a native speaker.

Lesson 23, pages 55–56 If your English language learners speak Hmong, Vietnamese, or Cantonese which are monosyllabic languages, they may need additional practice with the concept of compound words. Spanish speakers may also require practice with compound words, since few words in their native language are formed in this manner.

Lesson 25, pages 59–60 Native speakers of Vietnamese, Hmong, Korean, Khmer, and Cantonese may confuse *r* blends and *l* blends. Have children practice pronouncing *grow, glow; braid, blade; fright, flight;* and so on.

Lesson 26, pages 61–62 Spanish speakers may pronounce a short *e* before *sl* words, since Spanish lacks initial *s* blends. Check to see that children do not separate the two consonants with a *schwa* sound (where *blow* might sound like *below*).

Lesson 27, pages 63–64 Khmer, Hmong, Cantonese, Korean, and Vietnamese do not contain initial *s* blends. Spanish speakers will likely pronounce a short *e* before all *s* blends. Russian speakers might pronounce a voiced *z* sound in some blends.

Lesson 28, pages 65–66 Native speakers of Cantonese, Khmer, or Korean will be familiar with *ng*, but not with other final blends. Speakers of Tagalog or Spanish may "clip" the blends, pronouncing only the first consonant of each.

Lesson 29, pages 67–68 Children who speak Spanish will have little difficulty with the long *e* sound of *y*. For other English language learners, treat the different sounds as two different sounds for one letter: *bunny, sorry, sunny; shy, fry, why.*

Lesson 31, pages 71–72 Native speakers of Vietnamese, Khmer, Korean, or Hmong may confuse *ch* with *sh* or initial *j*. Offer additional oral and listening practice, having the children clearly pronounce *chair, share; chip, ship; chilly, jelly; cheap, jeep;* and so forth.

Lesson 32, pages 73–74 Most English language learners will be familiar with voiced and unvoiced sounds and silent letters. Practice *kn* and *gn* orally with native speakers of Chinese, Vietnamese, and Spanish: *knot, knee, knife, know, gnaw.*

Lesson 33, pages 75–76 Since Vietnamese, Hmong, and Cantonese are monosyllabic, native speakers of these languages may require additional support and oral practice with words containing more than one syllable.

Lesson 35, pages 79–80 There is no sound in Spanish similar to the English sound for the letter combinations *ir, er,* and *ur*. In Spanish, each combination stands for a distinct sound. Spanish-speaking children may initially pronounce *bird* like *beard* or *letter* like *let air.*

Lesson 36, pages 81–82 In Spanish, each of the *r*-controlled letter combinations stands for a distinct sound. Practice with *part, hard; first, third; under, her; purse, burn; cord, torn.*

Lesson 37, pages 83–84 Many Asian languages, such as Hmong, are monosyllabic and native speakers may pronounce two-syllable words in English as separate words.

Spelling Connections

INTRODUCTION

The Unit Word List is a list of selected spelling words drawn from this unit. The words are grouped by these categories: vowels in compounds and syllables; blends; final blends and sounds of *y*; consonant digraphs and syllables with blends and digraphs; and *r*-controlled vowels. To incorporate spelling into your phonics program, use the activity in the Curriculum Connections section of each teaching plan.

ESL/ELL It is recommended that English language learners reach the intermediate fluency level of English proficiency before focusing on spelling. For English language learners, introduce 6–8 words at a time. Use visuals or realia to help children understand the words' meanings.

The spelling lessons utilize the following approach for each type of word or phonics element.

1. Administer a pretest of the words, some of which may not have yet been introduced. Dictation sentences are provided.

2. Provide practice.

3. Reassess. Dictation sentences are provided.

A midunit review of spelling words can be found on page 78 of the teacher's edition. An option for creating an end-of-the-unit review of Unit 3 spelling words can be found on page 86 of the teacher's edition.

DIRECTIONS

Make a copy of Blackline Master 20 for each child. After administering the pretest for word study and phonics elements, give each child a copy of the appropriate word list.

Children can work with a partner to practice spelling the words orally and identifying the phonics elements in each word. You may want to challenge children to make new words by substituting blends and digraphs or by creating new compound words. Children can write words of their own on *My Own Word List* (see Blackline Master 20).

Have children store their list words in an envelope in their books or notebooks. Alternatively, you may want to suggest that children keep a spelling notebook, listing words with similar patterns. Another idea is to build Word Walls with children and display them in the classroom. Each section of the wall can focus on words with a single phonics element. The walls will become a good resource for children to use when they are engaged in writing.

Unit Word List

Vowels in Compounds and Syllables
sunshine
overcoat
backpack
pencil
monkey
dragon

Blends with *r, l, s*
broom   flag
crow   swing
glove   spoon

Final Blends; *y* as a Vowel or Consonant
king   why
shelf   years
carry   yellow

Consonant Digraphs; Syllables with Blends and Digraphs
echo
know
blanket
telephone
wheel
teacher

r-Controlled Vowels
tiger   favorite
park   thirty
hurry   garden

Name _____

 **Phonics & Spelling**

Unit 3 WORD LIST

Vowels in Compounds and Syllables

sunshine

overcoat

backpack

pencil

monkey

dragon

Blends r, l, s

broom

crow

glove

flag

swing

spoon

Final Blends; y as a Vowel and as a Consonant

king

shelf

carry

why

year

yellow

Consonant Digraphs; Syllables with Blends and Digraphs

echo

know

blanket

telephone

wheel

teacher

r-Controlled Vowels

tiger

park

hurry

favorite

thirty

garden

My Own Word List

Phonics Games, Activities, and Technology

The following collection of ideas offers a variety of opportunities to reinforce phonics skills while actively engaging children. The games, activities, and technology suggestions can easily be adapted to meet the needs of your group of learners. They vary in approach so as to consider children's different learning styles.

COMPOUND-WORD RACE

Write the following words on cards: *any, thing, some, day, time, snow, man, up, down, foot, in, out, ball, side, stairs, town, one, every,* and *mail.* Make a copy of the game board "Word Race" on Blackline Master 21. Have children play with a partner or in a small group. Players begin by placing the word cards face down in a pile in the New Cards box. Players take turns choosing a card from the top of the stack and using it to form a compound word. If successful, the player places the word card in the Used Card box and moves a game marker along the track the same number of spaces as syllables in the word. Continue playing until everyone reaches Finish.

MOVING ALONG WITH SYLLABLES

In advance, prepare a list of familiar one-, two-, three-, and four-syllable words. You might use imaginative or funny words to go with the unit theme. Have children form a line across one side of the room. Read a word for each child to repeat and tell the number of syllables. If correct, the child moves forward the same number of steps as syllables, imitating the movements of an imaginary creature. If incorrect, the next child attempts to tell the number of syllables. Play until everyone reaches the other side of the room.

ESL/ELL This activity can be adapted for English language learners by using only familiar words, mostly of one or two syllables.

DEFINING COMPOUNDS

Lighthouse: a house that weighs so little I can pick it up

Pineapple: an apple that grows on a pine tree

Turtleneck: the part of the turtle that holds the head up

Invite children to review compound words they know. You might list several fun compounds on the board as they dictate. Then, invite children to choose as many compound words as they wish and invent definitions based on the words that form the compound. For example, *supermarket* could mean "a store where superheroes shop." Suggest that children add an illustration to each of the definitions they write. Set aside time for some fun sharing.

NAMES WITH Y

How many children in your class have names that end with the vowel *y*? Ask those children whose names end with *y* to write their names on the chalkboard. Just for the day, have all children add *y* to their names and write them on the board as well. For the remainder of the day, have children call each other and you by names that end with *y*.

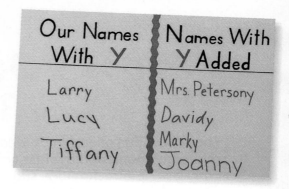

Our Names With Y	Names With Y Added
Larry	Mrs. Petersony
Lucy	Davidy
Tiffany	Marky
	Joanny

MAKE A WORD

Write the following blends on separate cards: *bl, cl, gl, br, dr, cr, tr, sl, st,* and *sn*. Write these phonograms on another set of cards: *um, ain, ock, ush, ob, eam, ack, ap,* and *ip*. Put the cards in envelopes labeled *Blend* and *Phonogram*. Invite children to work in pairs to make words by mixing and matching the cards. Children can list the words they make on paper to determine how many words they can make.

ESL/ELL Pair English language learners with more English-proficient peers to do this and the following word-building exercises.

Y SEARCH

Invite each child to fold a piece of paper to form three columns. At the top of each column, have children write one of the following heads: *y*: long *i* sound; *y*: long *e* sound; consonant *y*. Then, invite children to look through favorite books to find words with *y* and write each word they find in the appropriate column on the chart. Suggest that children compile their words to make a class Word Wall.

R-CONTROLLED CIRCLE GAME

Write the *r*-controlled vowels *ar, er, ir, or,* and *ur* on separate cards and place them in a box. Seat children in a circle and give the box to one child, who begins by choosing a card from the box, saying a word with the vowel sound, and calling on a volunteer to use the word in a sentence. The vowel card is then returned to the box and is passed on to the next child.

ACTION WORD RACE

Write action words that contain consonant blends, digraphs, or *y* as a vowel on cards. Make a copy of the Word Race game board on Blackline Master 21 so partners or small groups can play a game. Have the word cards placed face down in the New Cards box. Players take turns removing a card from the top of the stack, reading the word, and performing the action. The player then moves a game marker one space for each syllable in the word and places the word card in the Used Card box. Play until everyone reaches Finish. Words for the cards might include *blow, breathe, creep, clap, drive, fly, frown, grab, sway, skip, slither, smile, spin, stomp, trot, cry, spy, carry, write, push, laugh, cough, whine,* and *kneel*.

ESL/ELL This activity can be adapted for English language learners by using simple picture-word cards that children have made beforehand. Words such as *smile, frown, cry, kneel,* and *push* might be effectively conveyed by simple drawings.

SYLLABLE RACE

Invite children to use the game board "Word Race" on Blackline Master 21 to play another game. Write on cards words with one to four syllables that reflect the humorous/ imaginative theme of the unit. To play, children place the word cards face down on the New Card box. One child picks a card, reads the word aloud, and names the number of syllables it has. If the group agrees, the player moves a marker one space for each syllable. Play continues until everyone has reached Finish.

R-CONTROLLED SQUARES

Invite children to make consumable game cards such as the one shown. As you say words aloud, have children listen for the vowel sounds. If the word has an *r*-controlled vowel, encourage children to write it in the appropriate column. If there is no *r*-controlled vowel, children write nothing. Continue reading words until children have filled a column. Check their answers by having them read their words aloud.

er	or	ur	ar	ir
feather	horse	purse	large	thirsty
	more	hurry	yarn	
	cord		garden	
	storm			

REVISIT A FAMILIAR RHYME

Write the following rhyme on the board and recite it with children.

> Way down south, where bananas grow,
> A grasshopper stepped on an elephant's toe.
> The elephant cried with tears in his eyes,
> "Why don't you pick on someone your own size?"

Invite children to read and circle words with each of the following phonetic elements: blends with *r*, *s*, *l* (*grow, stepped, grasshopper, cried*); consonant digraphs (*elephant, where, south, why, with, pick*); compound words (*grasshopper, someone*); three-syllable words (*bananas, grasshopper, elephant*); words with *y* (*way, eyes, why, you, your*). As they circle a word, have them point out the element, and isolate its sound or in the case of the compound words, name the words from which they are made. Just for fun, invite children to substitute the compound word in the rhyme with another compound word and reread the rhyme.

TECHNOLOGY

The following software products reinforce children's understanding of advanced phonics skills

Kid Phonics™ 2
As they work through seven activities and interactive games, children start with sounding out words and progress to building sentences. Concepts taught include prefixes, suffixes, silent letters, homonyms, and more.

** Sunburst Technology
1900 South Batavia Ave.
Geneva, IL 60134
(800) 321-7511
www.sunburst.com

Turbo "Twist"™ Spelling
This program, intended for ages six and up, covers a wide range of phonics including consonant blends and digraphs, short and long vowels, double vowels, *-ed*, *-s*, and *-ing* endings, *j* sound, silent *e*, *oo*, compound words, suffixes, and *ai*, *sh*, and *ch* sounds.

** Leapfrog
6401 Hollis St., Suite 150
Emeryville, CA 94608
(800) 883-7430
www.leapfrog.com

Name _____

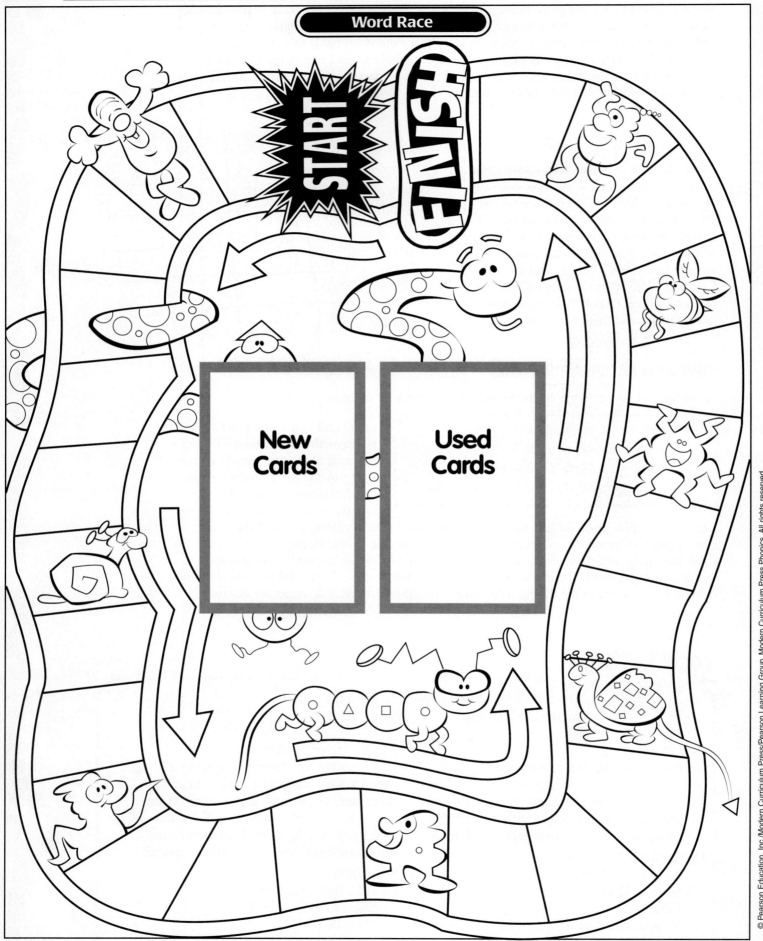

Word Race

New Cards

Used Cards

BLM 21 Unit 3 Activity

Home Connections

The Home Connections features of this program are intended to involve families in their children's learning and application of phonics skills. Three effective opportunities to make connections between home and school include the following.

- **HOME LETTER**
- **HOME NOTES**
- **TAKE-HOME BOOKS**

HOME LETTER

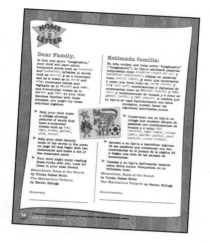

A letter is available to be sent home at the beginning of Unit 3. This letter informs family members that children will be learning to read and write compound words, multisyllable words, consonant blends, *y* as a consonant and vowel, consonant digraphs, and *r*-controlled vowels within the context of the unit theme, "What an Imagination!" The suggested home activity focuses on reading the poem, "The Spangled Pandemonium" and finding words with consonant blends. This activity promotes interaction between child and family members while supporting children's learning of reading and writing words with consonant blends. The letter, available in both English and Spanish, also suggests theme-related books family members can look for in a local library and enjoy reading together.

HOME NOTES

Whenever the Home logo appears within the student book, a phonics activity is suggested to be done at home. The activities are simple to do, requiring little or no preparation or special materials, and are meant to reinforce the targeted phonics skill.

Home Notes in Spanish are also available for both teachers and parents to download and use from our website, www.PlaidPhonics.com.

TAKE-HOME BOOKS

Within the student book, are Take-Home Books that can be cut out and assembled. The story language in each book reinforces the targeted phonics skills. The books can then be taken home and shared with family members. In Unit 3, one Take-Home Book is available, focusing on compound words, multisyllable words, consonant blends, *y* as a consonant and vowel, consonant digraphs, and *r*-controlled vowels as well as the theme "What an Imagination!"

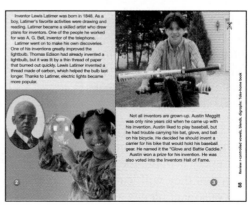

Compounds, Syllables, Blends and Digraphs, Y as a Consonant and Vowel, R-Controlled Vowels

Skill Focus

Assess Prior Knowledge

To assess children's prior knowledge of compound words, syllables, consonant blends and digraphs, *y* as a consonant and a vowel, and *r*-controlled vowels, use the pretest on pages 53e–53f.

Unit Focus

Build Background

- On the board, write the theme title, "What an Imagination!" Read the title aloud and have children find it on page 53. Talk about the meaning of the word *imagination*. Ask children to name imaginary people, places, and things.

- Read the poem aloud as children follow along silently. Afterward, ask children what they liked best about the poem. Have them relate the illustration to the action described in the poem.

Introduce Consonant Blends and Syllables

- Read the poem again and ask children to identify words that start with two or three consonants, such as *spangled, slithered, glibly, crawled, climbed, scrambled,* and *stay.* Help children pronounce the words, stressing the initial sounds. Point out that the sounds of the letters that begin the words blend together.

- Reread the first verse of the poem slowly and have children clap with you for every syllable they hear in each word. Tell children that they will learn more about syllables and consonant blends as they work on the exercises in this unit.

Critical Thinking Discuss the animals children typically see at a zoo. Then, ask for responses to the Talk About It question. Talk about why the Spangled Pandemonium is an imaginary creature.

Read Aloud

The Spangled Pandemonium
by Palmer Brown

The Spangled Pandemonium
Is missing from the zoo.
He bent the bars the barest bit,
And slithered glibly through.

He crawled across the moated wall,
He climbed the mango tree,
And when his keeper scrambled up,
He nipped him in the knee.

To all of you a warning
Not to wander after dark,
Or if you must, make very sure
You stay out of the park.

For the Spangled Pandemonium
Is missing from the zoo,
And since he nipped his keeper,
He would just as soon nip you.

TALK About It Would you see a Spangled Pandemonium at the zoo? Why or why not?

Unit 3 • Introduction
Critical Thinking **53**

THEME FOCUS

WHAT AN IMAGINATION!

Draw children's attention to the actions of the Spangled Pandemonium as described in the poem. Ask if this imaginary creature reminds children of any real animals. Have them use a dictionary to find out the meanings of *spangled* and *pandemonium.* Discuss how the illustrations suit the theme "What an Imagination!"

WRITE ON!

Invite children to write an additional verse for the poem, telling where the Spangled Pandemonium was spotted next. Encourage children to read their verses aloud.

LITTLE WORDS

Write the word *imagination* on the board. Ask children to use their knowledge of words to see how many smaller words they can spell by using the letters in *imagination,* such as *in, nation, nag, ton, gnat, mat.* Create a Word Wall of *imagination* words.

Dear Family,

In this unit about "Imagination," your child will learn about compound words such as sunshine and basketball; syllables in words such as pen/cil; **y** as a consonant and as a vowel as in carry and why; consonant blends and digraphs as in blanket and echo; and r-controlled vowels as in garden and bird. As your child becomes familiar with these concepts, you might try these activities together.

► Help your child make a collage showing pictures of words that have r-controlled vowels such as star, tiger, turkey, garden, park, soccer.

► Help your child identify some of the words in the poem on page 53 that begin with two consonants and make a list of the consonant pairs.

► Your child might enjoy reading these books with you. Look for them in your local library.

Meanwhile, Back at the Ranch by Trinka Hakes Noble

The Mysterious Tadpole by Steven Kellogg

Sincerely,

_____

Estimada familia:

En esta unidad, que trata sobre "Imagination" ("Imaginación"), su hijo/a estudiará palabras compuestas como sunshine (rayos del sol) y basketball (baloncesto); sílabas en palabras como pen/cil (lápiz); **y** como una consonante y como una vocal como en carry (llevar) y why (por qué); combinaciones y digramas de consonantes como en blanket (manta) y echo (eco); y combinaciones de vocales y **r** como en garden (jardín) y bird (pájaro). A medida que su hijo/a se vaya familiarizando con estos conceptos, pueden hacer las siguientes actividades juntos.

► Construyan con su hijo/a un collage que muestre dibujos de palabras con combinaciones de vocales y **r** como star (estrella), tiger (tigre), turkey (pavo), garden (jardín), park (parque), soccer (fútbol).

► Ayuden a su hijo/a a identificar algunas de las palabras que comienzan con dos consonantes en el poema de la página 53 y hagan una lista de las parejas de consonantes.

► Ustedes y su hijo/a disfrutarán leyendo estos libros juntos. Búsquenlos en su biblioteca local.

Meanwhile, Back at the Ranch de Trinka Hakes Noble

The Mysterious Tadpole de Steven Kellogg

Sinceramente,

_____

54 Unit 3 • Introduction

BULLETIN BOARD

Children can use a variety of art materials to create imaginary creatures inspired by the subject of "The Spangled Pandemonium." Display children's work on a bulletin board and invite them to create captions telling about their creatures.

HOME CONNECTIONS

- The Home Letter on page 54 will acquaint family members with the phonics skills children will be studying in this unit. Children can tear out page 54 and take it home.

- You may want to suggest that children complete the activities on the page with a family member. Encourage children to look in the library for the books suggested and read them with family members.

LEARNING CENTER ACTIVITIES

WRITING CENTER

Have children write a paragraph describing an imaginary land where an imaginary animal or object can be found. (See the Theme Connections Bulletin Board idea.) Call on volunteers to share their descriptions with the class.

SCIENCE CENTER

Suggest that children learn about inventions of the past and present. Provide reference materials children can use to find out how an inventor of their choosing used his or her imagination to create something new. Ask children to record the name of the inventor, the name and date of the invention, and details explaining how and why the invention came about.

MATH CENTER

Challenge children to use words or ideas from the poem on page 53 to write word problems for classmates to solve. For example, "If the mango tree is 18 feet tall and the Spangled Pandemonium climbed 4 inches in 3 seconds, how long did it take the creature to reach the top of the tree?" *(162 seconds or 2 minutes and 42 seconds)*

Compound Words

Skill Focus

Children will

★ match compound words with their meanings.

★ identify the two words within a compound word.

★ identify short and long vowel sounds in compound words.

ESL/ELL If your English language learners speak Hmong, Vietnamese, or Cantonese, which are monosyllabic languages, they may need additional practice with the concept of compound words. Spanish speakers may also require additional practice, since few words in their native language are formed in this manner.

Teach

Introduce Compound Words Say the pairs of words below. Ask children to put each pair of words together to form a new word.

- day *and* time
- fire *and* place
- bath *and* tub
- sail *and* boat
- tree *and* top
- back *and* pack
- post *and* card
- water *and* fall

Write the word *daytime* on the board. Explain that *daytime* is a compound word. A compound word is two or more words joined together to make a new word. Have a volunteer identify the two words in *daytime* (*day* and *time*).

Write the following on the board: *fire____, sail____, sun____, ____cake, ____tub, ____hive*. Challenge children to add another word to each word to form a compound word. Examples may include *fireplace, sailboat, sunshine, cupcake, bathtub, beehive*.

Practice and Apply

Sound to Symbol Have children read the rule for compound words at the top of page 55 and apply it to the words *home* and *work*. Then, have them do the exercise. Suggest that children draw a line between the two words within each compound word. Also review short and long vowel sounds.

Writing For page 56, suggest that children cross out words as they use them, since each word is used only once. Remind them that the clue for each compound word contains the smaller words used in the compound.

Reading Use *The Junkpile Robot*, MCP Phonics and Reading Word Study Skills Library 2, Level C, to provide practice in identifying and using compound words.

Name _____

Say each compound word. On the lines, write the two words that make up the compound word. Then, circle the words with short vowel sounds. Underline the words with long vowel sounds.

RULE
A **compound word** is made up of two or more words joined together to make a new word. **Homework** is **work** you do at **home**.

1. teapot — tea — pot
2. sunshine — sun — shine
3. seagull — sea — gull
4. beehive — bee — hive
5. beanbag — bean — bag
6. pancake — pan — cake
7. wayside — way — side
8. airway — air — way
9. necktie — neck — tie
10. milkweed — milk — weed
11. peanuts — pea — nuts
12. treetop — tree — top
13. waterfall — water — fall
14. overcoat — over — coat

Compound words **55**

FOCUS ON ALL LEARNERS

ESL/ELL ENGLISH LANGUAGE LEARNERS

Give English language learners practice with compound words by having them identify objects whose names are compound words.

- Use familiar objects to introduce words such as *chalkboard, notebook, doorknob, flagpole, shoelace, bookshelf,* and so on.

- Write the words on the board as items are named. Say the words for children to repeat.

- Break each word into its component words, saying, for example: *What do you call the **lace** in your **shoe**?*

- As children respond, check to see that they pronounce the two component words together, without pausing between them.

KINESTHETIC LEARNERS

Materials: index cards

Have partners refer to pages 55 and 56 to write words on index cards that can be paired to form compound words. Suggest they mix the cards, then lay them face down. Each partner turns over two cards at a time to try to make a compound word. If a word is made, the partner keeps the cards.

▶ Read each clue. Match each compound word from the box to its clue. Write the word on the line.

backpack	backyard	bathtub	countertop	dustpan
outside	overhead	paintbrush	raincoat	rattlesnake
seashell	snowflake	shoelace	treetop	waterfall

1. a brush for painting _____paintbrush_____

2. the top of a tree _____treetop_____

3. opposite of inside _____outside_____

4. a coat worn in rain _____raincoat_____

5. a pan to scoop dust _____dustpan_____

6. a shell near the sea _____seashell_____

7. a flake of snow _____snowflake_____

8. a tub for a bath _____bathtub_____

9. a snake with a rattle _____rattlesnake_____

10. the top of the counter _____countertop_____

11. a pack on your back _____backpack_____

12. the back of the yard _____backyard_____

13. over your head _____overhead_____

14. water that falls _____waterfall_____

15. a lace for a shoe _____shoelace_____

 Make up clues your child can answer with compound words, such as *a boat that sails. (sailboat)*

56 Compound words

CURRICULUM CONNECTIONS

SPELLING

Use these words and sentences as a pretest for writing compound words and two-syllable words.

1. **sunshine** We sat in the **sunshine.**
2. **overcoat** There is Tim's **overcoat.**
3. **backpack** This is a new **backpack.**
4. **pencil** Liz put the **pencil** down.
5. **monkey** The **monkey** climbed the tree.
6. **dragon** The **dragon** flew high in the sky.

WRITING

Have partners create new compound words by joining two words that do not usually go together. Children can write the definitions and create illustrations to make a class dictionary entitled *A Compound Imagination.*

SCIENCE

Ask children to list compound words that name plants or animals, such as *sunflower* and *grasshopper.* Have children choose a word to illustrate for a bulletin-board display.

TECHNOLOGY **AstroWord** Compound Words

Integrating Phonics and Reading

Guided Reading

Have children look at the cover and read the title. Then, have them preview the illustrations. Ask what they think the book will be about.

The Junkpile Robot

First Reading Encourage children to describe the main character and tell why it is called J. R.

Second Reading Have children identify compound words in the story.

Comprehension

After reading, ask children these questions:

• Why was everyone running after J. R.? *Recall/Cause and Effect*

• Did the story turn out the way you expected? Explain. *Reflective Analysis/Personal Response*

ESL/ELL English Language Learners

Have children locate and say compound words they find in the story. Ask them to identify each of the shorter words that form the compound word.

AUDITORY LEARNERS GROUPS

Say a word that can be used to form a compound word, such as *sun.* Call on a child to supply the other word and say the new compound word; for example, *set, sunset.* Then, ask the same child to name a word and call on a classmate to use it to form a compound word. Continue the exercise until all children have had a chance to participate.

CHALLENGE

Challenge children to design a Word Wall by writing compound words in categories, such as words related to food, school subjects, sports, clothing, homes, and weather.

EXTRA SUPPORT/INTERVENTION

It might be helpful for you to read the words on pages 55 and 56 aloud with children before they do the exercises. See Daily Phonics Practice, page 214.

Syllables

Skill Focus

Children will

★ identify the number of vowel sounds in words.

★ recognize that the number of vowel sounds and the number of syllables in a word are the same.

Teach

Introduce Syllables On the board, write the words *milk, pencil, nail,* and *treetop.* Ask children to identify the number of vowels they see in each word. *(1, 2, 2, 3)* Have volunteers identify the vowels.

Say each word and ask children to identify the number of vowel sounds they hear in each word. *(1, 2, 1, 2)* Call on volunteers to identify the vowel sounds. *(short* i; *short* e *and short* i; *long* a; *long* e *and short* o) Explain that the number of vowels and the number of vowel sounds in a word can be different. For example, *nail* has two vowels and one vowel sound.

Tell children that words are made of one or more parts or syllables. Explain that one vowel sound is heard in each syllable. Then, ask volunteers to identify the number of syllables in the words on the board. *(1, 2, 1, 2)*

Practice and Apply

Phonological Awareness Before children begin the activity on page 57, have them read the hint at the top of the page. Suggest they say each picture name softly to themselves and listen for the vowel sounds. Remind them to write the number of syllables in the box.

Sound to Symbol Make sure children understand how to do the exercise on page 58. Invite a volunteer to restate the directions. Remind children that it is the number of vowel *sounds* and not the number of vowels that determines the number of syllables in a word.

Reading Use *Mother's Helpers,* MCP Phonics and Reading Word Study Skills Library 2, Level C, to provide additional practice in identifying syllables.

Name _____

Say the name of each picture. Write the number of syllables you hear in the box.

HINT

Words are made of syllables. You hear one vowel sound in each syllable.

1. nest `1`	2. dragon `2`	3. robot `2`	4. seven `2`
5. pencil `2`	6. hose `1`	7. money `2`	8. clock `1`
9. turkey `2`	10. monkey `2`	11. sled `1`	12. blanket `2`
13. letter `2`	14. fish `1`	15. candy `2`	16. giant `2`

Syllables: Phonological awareness   **57**

FOCUS ON ALL LEARNERS

ESL/ELL **ENGLISH LANGUAGE LEARNERS**

Give English language learners practice with two-syllable words by reviewing compound words from the previous lesson.

• Write *sail, boat,* and *sailboat* on the board. Have a child read the words aloud.

• Have children identify the vowel sounds in *sail* and *boat.* Explain that each vowel sound stands for a syllable. Ask how many vowel sounds/syllables are in *sail* and *boat.* (1 in each word) Repeat for *sailboat.* (2)

• Then, have children identify familiar two-syllable classroom or household objects, such as *pencil* and *window.*

AUDITORY LEARNERS   GROUPS

Have children take turns saying their first names. Ask the rest of the class to identify the number of syllables they hear in each name. Do the same with their surnames.

KINESTHETIC LEARNERS   GROUPS

As you read the following words aloud, have children clap their hands or tap their desks each time they hear a syllable: *beads, cabin, rabbit, music, pie, picnic, robot, peppermint, umbrella,* and *Saturday.*

Look at each word. Write the number of vowels you **see** in the first column. Say the word. Write the number of vowels you **hear** in the second column. Then, write the number of syllables in the third column.

	Vowels You See	Vowels You Hear	Number of Syllables
1. basket	2	2	2
2. jeep	2	1	1
3. milk	1	1	1
4. rabbit	2	2	2
5. basement	3	2	2
6. music	2	2	2
7. beans	2	1	1
8. hillside	3	2	2
9. mailbox	3	2	2
10. peanuts	3	2	2
11. picnic	2	2	2
12. ate	2	1	1
13. pancake	3	2	2
14. sailboat	4	2	2
15. tune	2	1	1
16. rode	2	1	1
17. treetop	3	2	2
18. cabin	2	2	2

 Ask your child to tell you a story using six words on this page.

CURRICULUM CONNECTIONS

SPELLING

Use these words and sentences as a spelling posttest for writing multisyllabic and compound words.
1. **pencil**   Do you have my **pencil?**
2. **monkey**   The **monkey** watched us.
3. **dragon**   What color is a **dragon?**
4. **sunshine**   Mike likes the **sunshine.**
5. **overcoat**   I put my **overcoat** on a hook.
6. **backpack**   My **backpack** is red.

WRITING

Ask children to write word riddles using clues that tell how many syllables the word has, what vowel sounds it has, and what the word means. For example: *I have two syllables with long* a *and short* o. *You drop letters into me. What am I?* (mailbox)

TECHNOLOGY   **AstroWord** Multisyllabic Words

VISUAL LEARNERS

Materials: paper bags, index cards

Have partners write five one-syllable words and five two-syllable words on cards and label paper bags with the numerals 1 and 2. Have children shuffle the cards and turn them over. In turn, have children choose a card, read the word, and place the card in the bag that matches the number of syllables it has. Suggest that partners trade word cards with other classmates and repeat the activity.

CHALLENGE

Challenge children to identify the number of vowels, vowel sounds, and syllables in the names of each of the 50 United States.

EXTRA SUPPORT/INTERVENTION

Suggest to children that they say each word they encounter on pages 57 and 58 and tap on desks for each syllable they hear. Supervise them as they work and make sure that they can correctly distinguish among vowels, vowel sounds, and syllables. See Daily Phonics Practice, page 215.

Integrating Phonics and Reading

Guided Reading

Have children look at the cover and read the title. Talk about ways in which children can help their parents. Then, have children predict how the children in the story help their mother.

First Reading Pause at different points in the book to ask children how Lora and Rick are helping their mother.

Second Reading Have children identify the number of syllables in selected story words.

Comprehension

After reading, ask children these questions:
• Why do you think Lora and Rick's mother took them to the museum? ***Recall/Cause and Effect***
• Do you think Lora and Rick will return to the museum? Why or why not? ***Making Predictions/Inference***

ESL/ELL English Language Learners
Have children use word and picture clues to describe what Lora and Rick did in the museum.

R Blends

Skill Focus

Children will

★ define a consonant blend.

★ identify the sounds made by the initial blends *br, cr, dr, fr, gr,* and *tr.*

★ read and write words with initial *r* blends.

ESL/ELL Native speakers of Vietnamese, Hmong, Korean, Khmer, and Cantonese may confuse *r* blends and *l* blends. Have children practice pronouncing *grow, glow; braid, blade; fright, flight;* and so on.

Teach

Phonemic Awareness: Phoneme Categorization Explain that you will say groups of three words. Children are to identify which word has a different beginning sound from the other two. Use these groups of words:

- **train   tack   talk**
- **dish   drain   dear**
- **form   farm   from**

Sound to Symbol Write *train* on the board. Say the word, stressing the *tr* blend: *tttrrrain.* Tell children that the *tr* sound is called a consonant blend. A consonant blend is two or more consonants that come together in a word. The sounds blend together, but each sound is still heard. *R* blends are consonant blends in which the second consonant is *r.*

On the board, write the words *cane, dive, boom, fee, gate,* and *tip.* Have children rewrite the words, adding an *r* after the first consonant. Ask volunteers to read each new word and identify each initial *r* blend. (*crane, drive, broom, free, grate, trip*)

Practice and Apply

Sound to Symbol Review the rule at the top of page 59. Say each picture name with children before they begin the activity at the top of the page. Suggest that children say each picture name in order to hear the *r* blend.

Writing For the activity at the bottom of page 59, have children read each sentence with their word choice to make sure it makes sense. For page 60, suggest that children check to make sure that their word choice matches the picture and the clue.

Reading Use *The Princess Who Couldn't Cry,* MCP Phonics and Reading Library, Super Skills Collection, Level C, to provide additional practice in identifying *r* blends.

59

Name _____

> **RULE**
> A **consonant blend** is two or more consonants that come together in a word. Their sounds blend together, but each sound is heard. Listen for the **r** blends in the following words.
> **gr**ass   **cr**y

Write the name of each picture. Circle the **r** blend that stands for the beginning sound.

1. (br)o o m
2. (fr)u i t
3. (cr)o w
4. (pr)e t z e l
5. (dr)u m
6. (tr)a i n

Find the word or words in the box that will complete each sentence. Write the words on the lines.

brother	crowds	dream	friends	from
practice	prize	proud	trumpet	try

7. My _____brother_____ Tim and I play in the school band.

8. We both play the _____trumpet_____.

9. We will _____practice_____ hard for the big parade.

10. There will be a _____prize_____ for the best band.

11. We _____dream_____ of winning it.

12. _____Crowds_____ of people will watch _____from_____ the sidewalks.

13. All our _____friends_____ will cheer for us.

14. We will _____try_____ hard to make them _____proud_____ of us.

Consonant blends with r: Sound to symbol   **59**

FOCUS ON ALL LEARNERS

ESL/ELL ENGLISH LANGUAGE LEARNERS

Assess English language learners' ability to hear *r* blends.

- On the board, write the six *r* blends in a row. Review the sound of each, using familiar words from the lesson. Point out that *r* is always the second letter.

- For additional listening discrimination practice, say a series of words and have children clap only when they hear an *r* blend. Words may include *pour, prank, grow, block, friend, grab, brick, crow.*

- Write words with initial *r* blends under the correct headings on the board. Invite children to add words of their own.

KINESTHETIC LEARNERS GROUPS

Have children play "categories." One child announces an *r*-blend category, such as *br.* Children then snap their fingers or clap their hands to a beat as they take turns saying a word that begins with the blend. (*brown, broom, bright,* and so on) Repeat the game with a new *r*-blend category.

Read each clue. Find a word in the box that matches the clue. Write the word on the line. Circle the **r** blend that stands for the beginning sound.

frame	crow	broom	bridge	grapes
train	truck	drum	grasshopper	bride

1. You can cross over me.

I am a ___(br)idge___.

2. I ride on the road.

I am a ___(tr)uck___.

3. I hold a picture.

I am a ___(fr)ame___.

4. I am a big black bird.

I am a ___(cr)ow___.

5. We are fruits on the vine.

We are ___(gr)apes___.

6. You sweep the floor with me.

I am a ___(br)oom___.

7. I ride on tracks.

I am a ___(tr)ain___.

8. It is my wedding day.

I am a ___(br)ide___.

9. I am a green bug.

I am a ___(gr)asshopper___.

10. You play me with sticks.

I am a ___(dr)um___.

60 Consonant blends with r: Words in context

HOME Ask your child to name other words that begin with the *r* blends *br, cr, dr, fr, gr,* and *tr.*

CURRICULUM CONNECTIONS

SPELLING

Use these words and sentences as a pretest for writing words with *r, l,* and *s* blends.

1. **broom**   Put the **broom** in the closet.
2. **crow**   A **crow** sat on a fence post.
3. **glove**   Where is my **glove?**
4. **flag**   Raise the **flag** on the pole.
5. **swing**   The baby likes the new **swing.**
6. **spoon**   Use a **spoon** to stir the soup.

WRITING

Reread the sentences on page 59. Have children write a story about what happens during or after the big parade. Suggest that they use some *r*-blend words in their stories.

FINE ARTS

PORTFOLIO

Have children draw scenes that feature things whose names begin with *r* blends. For example, a scene might show a crow spying on a grasshopper. Suggest that children identify the *r* blends in their pictures.

TECHNOLOGY   **AstroWord** Consonant Blends & Digraphs

Integrating Phonics and Reading

Guided Reading
Have children look at the cover illustration and read the title. Then, have children leaf through the book and predict what the story is about.
First Reading Ask children to identify and describe each of the characters in the story.
Second Reading Help children identify words in the story that begin with *r* blends.

The Princess Who Couldn't Cry

Comprehension
After reading, ask children these questions:
• Why did the queen ask the farmer for help?
  Recall/Drawing Conclusions
• How might you have helped the Princess cry?
  Creative/Personal Response

ESL/ELL English Language Learners
Have children use the words and pictures to name different ways people tried to make the Princess cry, such as: *tell sad, sad tales* and *play sad, sad tunes.*

AUDITORY LEARNERS GROUPS

Invite the group to tell a round-robin story about a trip they take by train or driving a truck. Encourage them to use *r*-blend words whenever possible as they tell their story.

CHALLENGE

Ask children to begin a class Word Wall by listing words that start with the *r* blends *br, cr, dr, fr, gr,* and *tr.* Encourage children to add words with other *r* blends to the wall.

EXTRA SUPPORT/INTERVENTION

Materials: index cards

Write *r*-blend words from the lesson on index cards. Have children read the words and sort them into groups according to initial blends. Suggest that children add words of their own to the groups. See Daily Phonics Practice, page 215.

L Blends

Skill Focus

Children will

★ use visual and auditory clues to identify *l* blends and the sounds they stand for.

★ read and write words with initial *l* blends.

ESL/ELL Spanish speakers may pronounce a short *e* before *sl* words, since Spanish lacks initial *l* blends. Check to see that children do not separate the two consonants with the schwa sound (where *blow* sounds like *below*).

Teach

Phonemic Awareness: Phoneme Isolation
Say the words *lock* and *clock,* emphasizing the initial consonant sounds. Ask children to identify these consonant sounds. Help them hear how the letters *cl* blend so that, although the consonants are sounded together, each individual consonant sound can be heard. Repeat with other word pairs, such as: *love/glove; lag/flag; late/plate.*

Sound to Symbol Write *plate, glove,* and *flag* on the board. Read the words aloud, elongating the sounds of the initial blends. Then, ask a child to circle the blend in each word. Identify *pl, gl,* and *fl* as *l* blends. Tell children that the letters *c, b,* and *s* also join with *l* to form blends. Write *cl, bl, fl, gl, pl,* and *sl* on the board and have children name words that start with these blends, such as *clam, blue, flap, glad, play, slam.*

Practice and Apply

Sound to Symbol For page 61, tell children that each picture name begins with an *l* blend. Have them say each picture name so that they can hear the sound of the blend.

Writing For the activity at the top of page 62, have children compare the *l* blends at the beginning of the numbered words with the words listed in the clock. For the activity at the bottom of the page, suggest that children read each sentence with their word choice to make sure the word makes sense in context.

Reading Use *Looking for Angus,* MCP Phonics and Reading Library, Super Skills Collection, Level C, to provide additional practice in identifying *l* blends.

Name _____

> Write the name of each picture. Circle the **l** blend that stands for the beginning sound in its name.

RULE
Remember that in a **consonant blend** the sounds of the consonants blend together, but you can still hear each sound. Listen for the **l** blends in the following words.
black   **pl**ant

1. (fl) ag	2. (pl) ate	3. (cl) ock
4. (bl) ocks	5. (gl) ass	6. (sl) ed
7. (pl) ants	8. (fl) y	9. (gl) obe
10. (sl) ippers	11. (bl) anket	12. (cl) own
13. (fl) ashlight	14. (gl) ove	15. (pl) ug

Consonant blends with l: Sound to symbol   **61**

FOCUS ON ALL LEARNERS

ESL/ELL ENGLISH LANGUAGE LEARNERS

Assess English language learners' oral proficiency with *l* blends by doing the following exercises.

• Adapt the Phonemic Awareness and Sound to Symbol activities for small groups of English language learners.

• Use short words beginning with *l* to give children practice reading and saying various *l* blends. Include word pairs such as *late/plate; lock/block; loud/cloud; lip/slip; lag/flag;* and *lad/glad.*

• Use realia and visual aids to help children understand different meanings for words such as *fly, plant, block, play,* and *close.*

KINESTHETIC LEARNERS GROUPS

Materials: butcher paper, beanbag

Divide a large sheet of paper into six sections labeled *fl, gl, sl, pl, cl,* and *bl.* Have each child toss a beanbag onto the paper and say a word that begins with the blend in the square on which the beanbag lands.

For each word, find two words in the clock with the same **l** blend. Write them on the lines.

1. clock _____clean_____ _____clip_____

2. black _____blue_____ _____block_____

3. flat _____flag_____ _____fly_____

4. glad _____glow_____ _____glue_____

5. plant _____play_____ _____please_____

6. sled _____sleep_____ _____slide_____

Clock words:
block	glow
flag	blue
sleep	play
clean	please
slide	glue
fly	clip

Read each sentence carefully. Find the word in the glass that will complete the sentence. Write the word on the line.

7. The wind was _____blowing_____ as Flora left school.

8. The sky was covered with stormy _____clouds_____ .

9. It was too cold to _____play_____ outside.

10. Flora _____slipped_____ her hands into her pockets.

11. She had left her _____gloves_____ at home.

12. Flora's house was six _____blocks_____ away.

13. She was _____glad_____ when she finally arrived.

14. Her mom gave her a _____glass_____ of warm milk.

15. Flora sat _____close_____ to the fireplace to get warm.

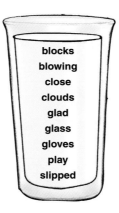

Glass words:
blocks
blowing
close
clouds
glad
glass
gloves
play
slipped

62 Consonant blends with l: Words in context

HOME Ask your child to add one new word to each group of words at the top of the page.

CURRICULUM CONNECTIONS

SPELLING

Write *l*-blend words on slips of paper and give one to each child. Have children go to the board and write their word with the letters scrambled. Invite volunteers to unscramble the words and circle the *l* blend.

WRITING

Ask children to write poems using *l*-blend words that rhyme. Here is an example:
   The shining sun began to glow,
   As gentle winds began to blow.
Invite children to share their poems.

MATH

Have children use words that begin with an *l* blend to write math problems. For example:
   Flora has twelve dollars. She plans to buy slippers for $4.50 and a clock for $6.95. How much money will she have left after her purchase?
Children can trade problems with partners to read and solve. (*55 cents*)

TECHNOLOGY **AstroWord** Consonant Blends & Digraphs

AUDITORY LEARNERS *GROUPS*

Invite children to work together to create tongue twisters, using words with *l* blends. Start them off with one or two of the following examples: *Plump plovers pluck plumage. Flipping flounders flap and float. Sleds slide on slippery sleet.* Challenge children to say one another's tongue twisters quickly three times.

CHALLENGE

Materials: tagboard, scissors, paper fasteners, markers

Suggest that children make *l*-blend word wheels to share with classmates. There can be one word wheel for each of the blends: *bl, cl, fl, gl, pl,* and *sl.*

EXTRA SUPPORT/INTERVENTION

Materials: index cards

Write the words from the box at the bottom of page 62 on individual cards so that children can focus on one word at a time as they search for a match to complete each sentence. See Daily Phonics Practice, page 215.

Integrating Phonics and Reading

Guided Reading
Have children look at the cover illustration and read the title. Then, ask them to predict who or what Angus is and what will happen.
First Reading Ask children to describe how and where the children looked for Angus.
Second Reading Help children identify words in the story that begin with *l* blends.

Comprehension
After reading, ask children these questions:
• Why does the little girl say Angus doesn't eat, sleep, swim, or hear? *Recall/Cause and Effect*
• Did the ending of the story surprise you? Why or why not? *Reflective Analysis/Personal Response*

ESL/ELL English Language Learners
Explain how speech balloons are used to show the words each character says. Assign three children the roles of the characters in the story and help them read the story aloud.

S Blends

Skill Focus

Children will

★ use visual and auditory clues to identify *s* blends and the sounds they stand for.

★ read and write words with initial *s* blends.

ESL/ELL Khmer, Hmong, Cantonese, Korean, and Vietnamese do not contain initial *s* blends. Spanish speakers will likely pronounce a short *e* before all *s* blends. Russian speakers might pronounce a voiced *z* sound in some blends.

Teach

Phonemic Awareness: Phoneme Isolation
Say the words *sweet* and *star,* stressing the initial consonants. Have children identify the consonant sounds. Ask: *What beginning consonant do both words have? (s)* Identify *sw* and *st* as *s* blends. Point out that in *s* blends, the letter *s* comes before the other letter or letters in the blend.

Sound to Symbol Write these words on the board: *tar, kid, wing, led, pot,* and *nail.* Call on volunteers to add an *s* to the beginning of each word. Have children read each new word and identify its initial *s* blend. *(star, skid, swing, sled, spot, snail)*

Point out that *s* blends can also have three letters. Write the words *spring, stream,* and *screen* on the board. Say the words and have children identify the consonants they hear at the beginning of each. *(spr, str, scr)*

Practice and Apply

Sound to Symbol For page 63, have children review the rule at the top of the page. Suggest they say each picture name in order to hear the initial consonant sounds.

Writing For the first activity on page 64, have children read each sentence with both word choices before deciding which makes more sense. For the activity at the bottom of the page, suggest that children read each word aloud, listening for the *s* blend.

Reading Use *A Pot of Stone Soup,* MCP Phonics and Reading Library, Super Skills Collection, Level C, to provide additional practice in identifying *s* blends.

Name _____

▶ Write the name of each picture. Circle the **s** blend that stands for the beginning sound.

> **RULE**
> Remember that in a **consonant blend** the sounds of the consonants blend together, but you can still hear each sound. Listen for the **s** blends in the following words.
> **str**aw   **sp**ell   **sn**ip

1. (str)awberry
2. (sn) ail
3. (sk)ate
4. (sw)eater
5. (st)ool
6. (sl)ed
7. (st)amp
8. (sn) ake
9. (sp)ider
10. (sq)uirrel
11. (st)ar
12. (sp)oon
13. (sw)ing
14. (sk)y
15. (sc)arecrow

Consonant blends with s: Sound to symbol   **63**

FOCUS ON ALL LEARNERS

ESL/ELL ENGLISH LANGUAGE LEARNERS

Assess English language learners' ability to read, write, and say words with *s* blends.

- On the board, write words that can be preceded by the letter *s.* Words may include *nail, tar, lip, cat, pill, lap, tone, wing, mile, kin,* and *pot.*
- Have children read a word aloud, write an *s* in front of the word, and say the new word. Model pronunciation of the *s* blends and review the target sounds chorally.
- To give children extra practice, bring in to class items whose names have *s* blends, such as *sweater, skirt, spoon,* and *stamp.*

KINESTHETIC LEARNERS GROUPS

Ask children to generate commands that include words with *s* blends. Children can take turns giving a command for the others to act out, such as *Look at the **sky**. **Squash** a bug. **Smell** a flower. Make a **strange** face.*

AUDITORY LEARNERS GROUPS

Say an *s*-blend word, such as *spray.* Call on a child to name the letters in the blend. Then, have the same child say another word with an *s* blend and continue around the room.

▶ **Read each sentence. Circle the word that will complete the sentence. Write the word on the line.**

1. Our first camping trip was (special / slender). _____special_____
2. We (stamp, spent) five days in the mountains. _____spent_____
3. Our trip was in early (string, spring). _____spring_____
4. The weather was (still / spill) quite chilly. _____still_____
5. We wore (scatters, sweaters) under our coats. _____sweaters_____
6. We also wore two pairs of (stockings / snails). _____stockings_____
7. I tripped on a (stump / sport) while hiking. _____stump_____
8. My ankle became very (swollen / squirrel). _____swollen_____
9. We all (swept, screamed) when we saw a snake. _____screamed_____
10. The snake just (splashed, slithered) away. _____slithered_____

▶ **Read each word. Circle the s blend that is used in the word. Write the word on the line.**

11. skid _____skid_____   12. stamp _____stamp_____
13. smile _____smile_____   14. spray _____spray_____
15. scale _____scale_____   16. stream _____stream_____
17. sniff _____sniff_____   18. spell _____spell_____
19. sweep _____sweep_____   20. scrub _____scrub_____
21. smell _____smell_____   22. snow _____snow_____

64 Consonant blends with s: Words in context

 HOME Help your child use s-blend words from the page to make up silly sentences, such as *The slender squirrel smiled.*

CURRICULUM CONNECTIONS

SPELLING

Use the following words and sentences as a posttest for writing words with *r, l,* and *s* blends.

1. **broom**   Bill put the **broom** down.
2. **spoon**   I got a **spoon** from the drawer.
3. **crow**   A **crow** is a large black bird.
4. **glove**   I found my **glove.**
5. **flag**   I carried a **flag** in the parade.
6. **swing**   Kim pushed the **swing.**

WRITING

Have children write a postcard to a friend about a camping trip, using *s*-blend words. Suggest they draw a scene on one side of an index card and write a note on the other.

SCIENCE

Invite children to read about animals whose names begin with *s* blends, such as *scorpion, sloth, scallop, skunk, snake, stork,* and *swan.* Then, have children decide how they want to share their information with the class.

TECHNOLOGY **AstroWord** Consonant Blends & Digraphs

VISUAL LEARNERS **PARTNERS**

Materials: drawing paper

Have partners create realistic or fanciful cartoon-like drawings of subjects whose names have *s* blends, such as a *sluggish sloth, a snail on skates, squirrels sledding, a swollen snowman, a spider on a stump.* Ask children to write captions that identify the *s* blends their drawings illustrate.

CHALLENGE

Have children work with partners to create crossword puzzles with initial *s* blends. Make photocopies of the puzzles and challenge classmates to solve them.

EXTRA SUPPORT/INTERVENTION

Write words that begin with the letter *s,* but not an *s* blend. Guide children as they add a letter to form a new word that begins with an *s* blend. Words may include: *sell (spell, swell); sing (swing, sting, string); say (sway, stay, stray, spray); seam (scream, stream).* See Daily Phonics Practice, page 215.

Integrating Phonics and Reading

Guided Reading

Have children look at the cover and read the title. Then, invite children to discuss what they think the story will be about.

First Reading Have children tell how Ned tricked the woman into feeding him.

Second Reading Help children identify words in the story that begin with *s* blends.

Comprehension

After reading, ask children these questions:

• Why do you think the woman gave Ned what he needed for his soup? *Inference/Cause and Effect*

• What kind of soup did Ned really make? *Recall/Inference*

ESL/ELL **English Language Learners**

After children have looked through the book, have them use picture and word clues to name the different ingredients Ned used in his soup.

Final Consonant Blends

Skill Focus

Children will

★ identify final consonant blends and the sounds they stand for.

★ read and write words with final consonant blends.

ESL/ELL Native speakers of Cantonese, Khmer, or Korean will be familiar with *ng*, but not with the other final blends. Speakers of Tagalog or Spanish may "clip" the blends, pronouncing only the first consonant of each.

Teach

Phonemic Awareness: Phoneme Isolation
Review the initial *r, s,* and *l* blends that children have learned. Tell them that consonant blends can come at the end of words as well as the beginning. Say the following words and have children listen carefully to the ending sounds: *fast, milk, sink, wing.* Ask a child to identify the final consonant blends. *(st, lk, nk, ng)*

Sound to Symbol Write these words on the board: *tent, lamp, gift,* and *desk.* Say each word, stressing the final consonant blend. Then, have volunteers identify the consonant blend that stands for the final sound in each word. *(nt, mp, ft, sk)* Ask children to name other words they know that end with the blends *nt, mp, ft,* and *sk.*

Practice and Apply

Sound to Symbol Review the rule at the top of page 65 for final consonant blends. Suggest that children say each word in order to hear the final consonant blend.

Writing For the activity at the top of page 66, have children read the poem aloud. For the activity at the bottom of the page, suggest that children use the poem at the top of the page as a model and look for words in the box that rhyme.

Reading Use *A Helping Hand,* MCP Phonics and Reading Library, Super Skills Collection, Level C, to provide additional practice in identifying final consonant blends.

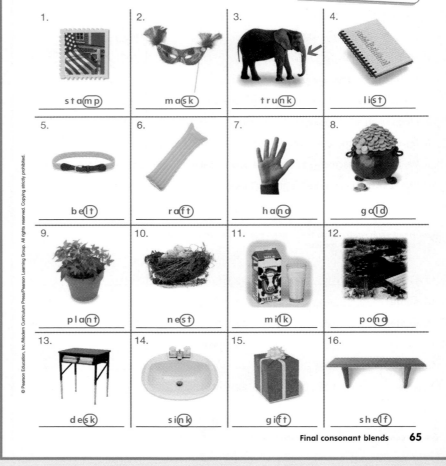

Sound to Symbol

RULE
Sometimes consonant blends are at the ends of words. Listen for the consonant blends in the following words.
be**nd**   pa**st**

Name _____

Write the name of each picture. Circle the consonant blend that stands for the ending sound.

1. sta**mp**
2. ma**sk**
3. tru**nk**
4. li**st**
5. be**lt**
6. ra**ft**
7. ha**nd**
8. go**ld**
9. pla**nt**
10. ne**st**
11. mi**lk**
12. po**nd**
13. de**sk**
14. si**nk**
15. gi**ft**
16. she**lf**

Final consonant blends   65

FOCUS ON ALL LEARNERS

- -

ESL/ELL ENGLISH LANGUAGE LEARNERS

Materials: bingo markers, consonant blend cards *mp, sk, nk, lk, lf, st, lt, ft, nt, nd, ld*

Adapt the activity on page 65 to develop English language learners' comprehension of final blends.

- Play a game of bingo by calling out the name of a picture clue on page 65 and having children cover it with a marker. Have children repeat the word and say the final blend.

- Vary and reinforce with final blend cards. Display cards one at a time; have children cover the picture clues with markers.

- Pair English language learners with a more English-proficient partner to do the activity as originally intended.

KINESTHETIC LEARNERS

Materials: index cards

Write several words on index cards, including words that have final consonant blends and words that do not. Have partners decide how to sort the cards and explain their reasoning to you.

> Read the poem. Underline the words with the **fl** consonant blend. Then write the words on the lines. Use each word only once.

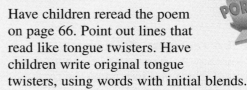

THE FLY AND THE FLEA

A fly and a flea flew up in a flue.
Said the fly to the flea, "What shall we do?"
"Let's fly," said the flea.
"Let's flee," said the fly.
So they fluttered and flew up the flue.

1. _____fly_____
2. _____flea_____
3. _____flew_____
4. _____flue_____
5. _____flee_____
6. _____fluttered_____

> Write your own nonsense poem. Choose words from the box or your own words with beginning or ending consonant blends. Write the words on the lines.

chimp	chomp	jump	stamp	stomp	cling
skunk	snail	snake	stew	sled	spoon
grabbed	grapes	grew	gruff	sped	spider
spin	spoke	twiggy	twirled	twisted	sloth

7. A _____ and a _____ _____ in a _____.

8. Said the _____ to the _____, "What shall we do?"

9. "Let's _____," said the _____ to the _____.

10. "Let's _____," said the _____ to the _____.

11. So they _____ and _____ up the _____.

66 Review consonant blends

 HOME Ask your child to read his or her poem to you, stressing the words with consonant blends.

AUDITORY LEARNERS GROUPS

As you say the following words, have volunteers replace the final sound in each word with a blend and say the new word. Use: *fat (fast), ran (rang, raft, ramp), shell (shelf), mill (milk, mist, mink), den (desk, dent), lit (lift, list, limp, link), set (send, self).*

CHALLENGE

Challenge children to find more final blends *(sp, ct, pt)* and list as many words as they can that end in each. Caution them that combinations with *r (rk, rt)* are not blends. In addition, point out that when one consonant is silent *(would, walk),* it is not a blend. Suggest that children use a dictionary.

EXTRA SUPPORT/INTERVENTION

Before children begin page 65, say each picture name with them. Make sure they hear the final consonant blend in each word. See Daily Phonics Practice, page 215.

CURRICULUM CONNECTIONS

SPELLING

Use these words and sentences as a pretest for writing words with final blends and words with *y* as a consonant.
1. **king**   The **king** sat on a throne.
2. **shelf**   The cat naps on a high **shelf.**
3. **carry**   I will **carry** the books.
4. **why**   **Why** are you going now?
5. **year**   Will you be nine next **year?**
6. **yellow**   Look for a **yellow** bird.

WRITING

Have children reread the poem on page 66. Point out lines that read like tongue twisters. Have children write original tongue twisters, using words with initial blends.

PORTFOLIO

SOCIAL STUDIES

Point out that the word *stamp* begins and ends with a blend. Ask children to design stamps featuring words that begin and end with a blend. Have children share their work.

TECHNOLOGY **AstroWord** Consonant Blends & Digraphs

Integrating Phonics and Reading

Guided Reading

Have children look at the cover and read the title. Then, discuss how a dog might help someone in a wheelchair.
First Reading Have children describe the different kinds of helping dogs.
Second Reading Help children identify story words that end with consonant blends, such as *find, lost, strong, different, lift.*

Comprehension

After reading, ask children these questions:
• Why are dogs such good helpers? *Recall/ Inference*
• What new things did you learn about dogs? *Reflective Analysis/Personal Reaction*

ESL/ELL English Language Learners
Use the question at the beginning of each chapter to help children build background on what the chapter will be about. Ask the question, then help children read the answer, using the picture clues to gather information.

A Helping Hand

Y as a Vowel

Skill Focus

Children will

★ distinguish between the two vowel sounds of *y*.

★ read and write words with *y* as a vowel.

ESL/ELL Children who speak Spanish will have little difficulty with the long *e* sound of *y*. For other English language learners, treat the different sounds as two different sounds for one letter: *bunny, sorry, sunny; shy, fry, why.*

▶ Teach

Phonemic Awareness: Phoneme Categorization Say the word *pony*, elongating the final long *e* sound. Have children name the final vowel sound they hear. (long *e*) Repeat with the word *try*, elongating the final long *i* sound. Next, say groups of three words. Ask children to identify the two words in each group that have the same final vowel sound.

• **fly**	**bunny**	**dry**
• **copy**	**sky**	**shy**
• **funny**	**try**	**pony**
• **muddy**	**why**	**penny**

Sound to Symbol On the board, write *fly, dry,* and *sky.* Have children say the words and name the vowel sound they hear. (long *i*) Ask which letter stands for this sound. (*y*) Explain that *y* can be a consonant or a vowel, depending on where it is in a word. When it is the only vowel at the end of a syllable or a one-syllable word, *y* has the long *i* sound. Repeat the activity with *copy, funny,* and *pony* to show that *y* can also have the long *e* sound. Explain that when *y* is the only vowel at the end of a word with more than one syllable, it usually has the long *e* sound.

▶ Practice and Apply

Sound to Symbol Read aloud the rules on pages 67 and 68. For the first activity on both pages, have children say the words to themselves so that they can hear the vowel sounds.

Writing For the second activity on page 67, have children make sure they write a complete sentence in answer to each question. For the second activity on page 68, suggest that children cross out each word choice as it is used.

Reading Use *The Night Sky,* MCP Phonics and Reading Library, Super Skills Collection, Level C, to provide additional practice in identifying *y* as a vowel.

Name _____

> Add **y** to each blend to make a word. Write the word on the line.

RULE
When **y** is the only vowel at the end of a syllable or a word of one syllable, **y** has the long **i** sound.
trying   shy

1. fr _____ fry
2. cr _____ cry
3. tr _____ try
4. dr _____ dry
5. sk _____ sky
6. sl _____ sly
7. fl _____ fly
8. spr _____ spry

> Read each question. Use one or more of the words you just made to answer it. Write your answer on the lines. Use a complete sentence.

9. Where do you look to see clouds?

   You look in the sky to see clouds.

   _____

10. Why do we use umbrellas when it rains?

    We use umbrellas to keep us dry.

    _____

11. What can an airplane do in the sky?

    An airplane can fly in the sky.

    _____

12. What sometimes happens if you fall and hurt yourself?

    Sometimes, I cry if I fall and hurt myself.

    _____

Y as a vowel: long i, Sound to symbol   **67**

FOCUS ON ALL LEARNERS

- -

ESL/ELL **ENGLISH LANGUAGE LEARNERS**

Use familiar words to help English language learners recognize, and distinguish between the two vowel sounds for *y*.

• On the board, write words that children will likely recognize, such as *my, try, why, any,* and *funny.* Include names of classmates as appropriate, such as *Tommy* or *Christy.*

• Ask volunteers to say the words and identify their vowel sounds of *y.* Have children sort the words by vowel sound.

• Remind children that they have also learned words in which *y* is silent. Use *day, play,* and *may* as examples.

KINESTHETIC LEARNERS

Materials: chart paper, markers

Have children look at books in your classroom and list words in the titles that end in *y.* Tell children to create a Word Wall with the words, grouping them according to their *y*-vowel sound.

VISUAL LEARNERS GROUPS

Ask children to fold a sheet of paper in half and write the word *try* on one half and *funny* on the other. Call out words that end with *y.* Have children write each word under the word with the same sound for *y.*

Say each word in the box and listen for the **y** sound. Write the words in the correct column.

RULE

When **y** is the only vowel at the end of a word with more than one syllable, it usually has the long **e** sound.
pretty   quickly

bunny	cry
every	grocery
trying	muddy
shy	sky
swiftly	why

Y = Long i

sky

why

cry

shy

trying

Y = Long e

every

grocery

muddy

swiftly

bunny

Find a word in the box below to complete each sentence. Write the word on the line.

1. My _____family_____ likes to do things together.

2. Sometimes we go to the _____library_____.

3. There are so _____many_____ books to choose from.

4. Dad likes _____history_____ books about ancient Egypt.

5. I like books with lots of _____funny_____ jokes.

6. Mom likes books about _____pretty_____ gardens.

7. Once we checked out more than _____twenty_____ books.

8. It was difficult to _____carry_____ them!

carry
family
funny
history
library
many
pretty
twenty

68   Y as a vowel: Long i and e, Words in context

 HOME Ask your child to use some words that end in *y* to describe an activity that your family likes to do together.

AUDITORY LEARNERS **GROUPS**

Ask questions using words with *y* as a vowel, such as **Why** are people **shy**? **Why** does a **bunny** hop? How does a bird **fly**? What **story** do you like? Ask children to identify the words in each sentence that use *y* as a vowel. Then, invite children to ask similar questions of their own.

CHALLENGE

Challenge children to collect *y*-as-a-vowel words in which the *y* is in the medial position. Encourage them to find examples for both sounds of *y*, such as *ladybug, everyone; myself, cycle*. Add their words to the class Word Wall.

EXTRA SUPPORT/INTERVENTION

Materials: word cards with vowel-*y* words

Have children sort the word cards into two piles: one for *y* that sounds like long *e*, and one for *y* that sounds like long *i*. Then, help children read each set of words aloud. See Daily Phonics Practice, pages 215–216.

CURRICULUM CONNECTIONS

SPELLING

Write the words *carry* and *why* on the board. Ask children to write on the board lesson words for each of the following clues: "I'm looking for a word that ends like *carry* and names a small animal that hops." (*bunny*) "I'm looking for a word that ends like *why* and means bashful." (*shy*) Invite children to give clues of their own.

WRITING

Ask children to write instructions for finding a book in the library. Suggest that they may either write their instructions as an informational paragraph or as a numbered list of steps. Urge them to include words with *y* as a vowel. Invite children to share their writing with classmates.

SOCIAL STUDIES

Have children look through the index of cities in a road atlas for city names in which *y* is used as a vowel. Suggest they list the city names and identify the vowel sound of *y* heard in each.

 **TECHNOLOGY**   **AstroWord** Long Vowels: *e, u*; Long Vowels: *i, o*

Integrating Phonics and Reading

Guided Reading

Have children look at the cover and read the title. Then, encourage them to talk about why the people in the illustration are looking at the sky.

 The Night Sky

First Reading Have children describe in their own words how the seven sisters ended up as stars.

Second Reading Help children identify words in the story that have *y* as a vowel.

Comprehension

After reading, ask children these questions:

• Why is the star that the boy turned into far from the sisters? *Inference/Characters*

• Why do you think people told this story? *Reflective Analysis/Genre*

ESL/ELL **English Language Learners**

Explain that *The Night Sky* is a story told by Native Americans, the first people to live in this country. Have children use illustration and text clues to identify the setting and other details of the story.

Y as a Vowel and a Consonant

Skill Focus

Children will

★ distinguish between the different vowel sounds of *y* in words.

★ identify *y* as a consonant in words.

★ read and write words with *y* as a vowel and as a consonant.

▶ Teach

Phonemic Awareness: Phoneme Identity
Ask volunteers to say words that end with the same vowel sound as *try. (fly, sky, why, cry)* Repeat the activity for words that end with the same vowel sound as *every. (baby, pony, party, funny)* Then, point out that *y* can also be used as a consonant. Ask volunteers to name words that begin with the same consonant sound heard in *yarn. (yard, yam, yolk, yellow, year)*

Sound to Symbol Write the words *yam, yet,* and *yell* on the board. Read each word slowly, elongating the initial *y* sound: *yyyam, yyyet, yyyell.* Have children repeat the sound they hear at the beginning of each word. Explain that when *y* comes at the beginning of a word, it is a consonant.

To review what children have learned about *y* as a vowel, write the words *fly* and *empty* on the board. Ask children to identify the vowel sound they hear at the end of each word. *(long* i, *long* e) Have volunteers explain the rules for *y* as a vowel.

▶ Practice and Apply

Sound to Symbol For the activity at the top of page 69, remind children to listen carefully to the sound of *y* in each word. For the activity at the bottom of page 69, suggest that children isolate the *y* sound in the first word and listen for that sound in the other words.

Reading/Writing For the activity on page 70, suggest that children say each underlined word softly to themselves before deciding which column it goes in.

Reading Use *The Fourth of July,* MCP Phonics and Reading Library, Super Skills Collection, Level C, to provide additional practice in identifying *y* as a vowel and as a consonant.

Name _____

▶ Say the name of each picture. Find the name in the box. Write it on the line. Circle the names that have **y** as a consonant.

> **RULE**
> When **y** comes at the beginning of a word, it is a consonant.
> **y**olk

yo-yo	bunny	yarn	cry	fly	yes
penny	pony	pretty	yard	sky	try

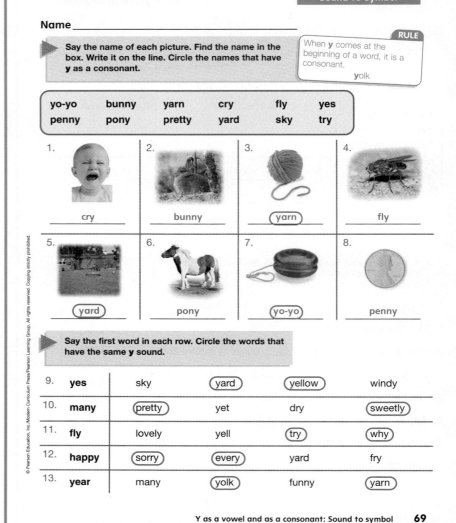

1. cry	2. bunny	3. (yarn)	4. fly
5. (yard)	6. pony	7. (yo-yo)	8. penny

▶ Say the first word in each row. Circle the words that have the same **y** sound.

9.	**yes**	sky	(yard)	(yellow)	windy
10.	**many**	(pretty)	yet	dry	(sweetly)
11.	**fly**	lovely	yell	(try)	(why)
12.	**happy**	(sorry)	(every)	yard	fry
13.	**year**	many	(yolk)	funny	(yarn)

Y as a vowel and as a consonant: Sound to symbol   **69**

FOCUS ON ALL LEARNERS

ESL/ELL ENGLISH LANGUAGE LEARNERS

Use familiar words to help English language learners recognize and distinguish between the sounds of *y* as a vowel and consonant.

• On the board, list these (or similar) familiar words in random order: *fly, sky, dry; baby, funny, story; you, yellow, yes.*

• Ask volunteers to point to a word, read it aloud, circle the *y*, and say whether the *y* is used as a vowel or a consonant.

• Help children sort the words according to vowel sound.

AUDITORY/KINESTHETIC LEARNERS GROUPS

Materials: 2 or 3 bells

Have the class form teams. Provide each team with a bell to be passed from player to player. Read aloud lesson words with *y*. The first player to ring the bell and correctly identify *y* as either a consonant or a vowel scores a point for his or her team.

VISUAL LEARNERS PARTNERS

Have partners devise their own codes for words, using symbols or numbers to represent letters. Then, have them use their codes to write words with *y*. Challenge pairs to trade codes and words. Time them to see which pair decodes the words the fastest.

Read the story. Underline each word that has a **y**.
Then, write the words in the correct columns.

Goody's Ice Cream

One afternoon <u>my</u> brother and I saw a plane go over our <u>yard</u>.
"Isn't it a <u>beauty</u>, Craig?" I <u>yelled</u> over the noise.
"Where is it now?" I heard Craig <u>cry</u> out.
"Over there, in the <u>sky</u> above the <u>yellow</u> house," I said. "Do <u>you</u> see it <u>yet</u>?"
"I would like to <u>fly</u> a plane like that one," said Craig.
"Let's <u>try</u> to save so we can have our own plane when we grow up. Here's <u>twenty</u> cents to start," I said.
Just then, from down the street came the jingling of a bell and the sound of a whistle. We both knew that it was <u>Goody</u>, the person who sold ice cream. The ice-cream bars were big and thick and <u>creamy</u>. Craig looked at me. "<u>Why</u> not?" I said. "It is <u>very</u> hot and <u>dry</u>."
We stood eating our ice cream. Craig said, "We'd better start soon to save for the airplane, or we'll be <u>fifty</u> <u>years</u> old before we get it."
"<u>Yes</u>," I said. "We'd better start <u>early</u> tomorrow."

Y = a consonant	Y = long e	Y = long i
yard	beauty	my
yelled	twenty	cry
yellow	Goody	sky
you	creamy	fly
yet	very	try
years	fifty	Why
Yes	early	dry

70 Review y as a vowel and as a consonant

HOME Make up a story with your child using some of the words in the columns.

CURRICULUM CONNECTIONS

SPELLING

Use the following words and sentences as a posttest for writing words with final blends, *y* as a vowel, and *y* as a consonant.

1. **king**   The **king** announced a holiday.
2. **why**   **Why** don't we take the bus?
3. **carry**   Josh will **carry** the box.
4. **shelf**   Put the cans on the **shelf.**
5. **year**   In what **year** were you born?
6. **yellow**   Sherry lives in the **yellow** house.

WRITING

Have children continue the story on page 70 by telling what happens once the characters have enough money for their plane. Ask children to circle words with *y* as a consonant or a vowel.

PORTFOLIO

TECHNOLOGY

AstroWord Long Vowels: *e, u;*
Long Vowels: *i, o*

AUDITORY LEARNERS **GROUPS**

Materials: tape recorder, tape

Record the story on page 70. Have children listen to the story and list all the words they hear that have the letter *y*. Ask children to sort the words according to whether the *y* is a consonant or a vowel.

CHALLENGE

Invite children to compose sentences using as many words from pages 69 and 70 in each sentence as they can. For example: *My yellow pony can fly like the wind.* Then, have children circle the words with *y* as a vowel and underline the words with *y* as a consonant.

EXTRA SUPPORT/INTERVENTION

Materials: two index cards per child

Write the word *vowel* on one card and the word *consonant* on the other. Provide each child with a pair of cards. As you recite words from the lesson, have children hold up the word card that shows how *y* is used in the words. See Daily Phonics Practice, pages 215–216.

Integrating Phonics and Reading

Guided Reading

Have children read the title and look at the cover. Invite them to talk about things they have seen and done in celebration of the Fourth of July.

First Reading Have children identify the Fourth-of-July activities described in the story.

Second Reading Help children identify story words that have *y* as a vowel or a consonant.

Comprehension

After reading, ask children these questions:
• What do people do to celebrate the Fourth of July? *Recall/Summarize*
• Do you think the story is a good description of the Fourth of July? Why or why not? *Reflective Analysis/Personal Response*

ESL/ELL **English Language Learners**

Have children locate the word *big* on page 3 of the story. Explain that the word *big* can mean large or it can mean very important. Then, have them read the sentence aloud and identify how *big* is used.

Consonant Digraphs

Skill Focus

Children will

★ identify a consonant digraph as two consonants together that represent one sound.

★ read and write words with consonant digraphs.

ESL/ELL Native speakers of Vietnamese, Khmer, Korean, or Hmong may confuse *ch* with *sh* or initial *j*. Offer additional oral and listening practice, having the children clearly pronounce *chair, share; chip, ship; chilly, jelly; cheap, jeep.*

Teach

Phonemic Awareness: Phoneme Isolation
Explain that you will say the pairs of words below. Ask children to tell what sound they hear at the beginning of the words in each pair.

- **chair/chin**   • **sheep/shake**
- **these/those**   • **wheel/when**

Say these word pairs and ask children what sound they hear at the end of the words in each pair:

- **peach/teach**   • **teeth/wreath**
- **fish/dish**   • **rough/tough**

Sound to Symbol Write the words *wheel, chair, dish, teach, write, ticket,* and *echo* on the board and read them aloud. Ask volunteers to circle two consonants either at the beginning, middle, or end of each word. *(wh, ch, sh, ch, wr, ck, ch)* Explain that each of the letter pairs *wh, ch, sh, wr,* and *ck* is a consonant digraph, a pair of consonants that together represent one sound. Ask volunteers to identify the sound of each consonant digraph.

Practice and Apply

Sound to Symbol Read aloud the rule for a consonant digraph at the top of page 71. For the activities on the page, suggest that children read each word aloud and listen carefully to hear the sound represented by the consonant digraph.

Writing For the first activity on page 72, suggest that children read each sentence with their word choice for sense. For the second activity, tell children that words appear across or down.

Reading Use *Suki and the Case of the Lost Bunnies,* MCP Phonics and Reading Library, Super Skills Collection, Level C, to provide additional practice with consonant digraphs.

Name _____

RULE
A **consonant digraph** consists of two consonants that together represent one sound.
knit   bo**th**   **sch**ool

▶ Write the name of each picture. Then circle the digraph.

1.	2.	3.	4.
cherry	wheel**ch**air	si**gn**	du**ck**

5.	6.	7.	8.
di**sh**	ta**ck**	**kn**ot	**wr**ap

▶ Say each word. Then circle the consonant digraph.

9. s**ch**eme	10. **wh**eel	11. kit**ch**en	12. **wr**ite
13. bir**th**day	14. **th**rew	15. ni**ck**el	16. pea**ch**es
17. nor**th**	18. fini**sh**	19. mo**th**er	20. rou**gh**
21. benea**th**	22. **ch**oke	23. **kn**it	24. e**ch**o
25. **kn**ow	26. **ch**ord	27. **th**i**ck**	28. far**th**er
29. tele**ph**one	30. **sh**ake	31. **wr**ist	32. **ch**ocolate
33. bo**th**er	34. ti**ck**et	35. **wh**eat	36. **ch**orus
37. tou**gh**	38. si**gn**	39. s**ch**ool	40. **gn**aw

Consonant digraphs: Sound to symbol   **71**

FOCUS ON ALL LEARNERS

ESL/ELL ENGLISH LANGUAGE LEARNERS

Confirm English language learners' ability to produce the target sounds correctly; model and practice pronunciation by using familiar objects or picture clues from the Student Edition.

- Introduce one or two digraphs at a time to focus children's efforts on producing individual target sounds correctly.

- Print digraphs on the board. Display appropriate objects or picture clues. Model the sounds, and then say the words.

- Urge frustrated learners to direct their efforts toward correct production of the sounds, listening carefully to your models.

VISUAL LEARNERS GROUPS

Write the following rows of words on the board:

- **rain   more   tart   pin   hop   hip   tap**
- **coal   mud   lap   sit   pat   bean   bird**

Ask volunteers to choose a word from the first row and replace the initial consonant with a digraph to make a new word. Then, have children choose a word from the second row and replace the final consonant with a digraph to make a new word.

▶ Read each riddle and circle the word to complete the riddle.
Write the word on the line, then circle the consonant digraph.

1. What happens when a bowl of fruit is embarrassed?
   The _____(ch)erries_____ turn red!   (cherries) teeth   bananas

2. Why are fish so smart?
   They travel in a _____s(ch)ool_____.   group   (school) scheme

3. What's the best thing to put into a pie?
   Your _____tee(th)_____!   (teeth)   knife   fork

4. What bird lowers its head the fastest?
   A _____du(ck)_____!   swan   sheep   (duck)

5. What did the barber say after the near accident?
   "That was a close _____(sh)ave_____!"   (shave)   shower one

6. What always talks back to you?
   An _____e(ch)o_____!   actor   chorus (echo)

7. How do you know owls are curious?
   They're always asking _____(wh)o_____.   (who)   whine   how

8. Why is the sun bright?
   It _____(sh)ines_____!   bright   (shines) shows

▶ Find and circle the words in the puzzle. Use the words in the box to help you.

chorus	nickel
elephant	scheme
gnaw	shower
knife	teeth
laugh	whine

```
E  L  E  P  H  A  N  T
T  A  Z  V  W  L  M  E
N  U  S  C  H  E  M  E
I  G  L  L  I  F  Y  T
C  H  B  G  N  A  W  H
K  N  I  F  E  G  X  L
E  Q  C  H  O  R  U  S
L  S  H  O  W  E  R  Z
```

72 Consonant digraphs: Words in context

HOME Ask your child to identify the consonant digraphs in the words in the word box.

CURRICULUM CONNECTIONS

SPELLING

Use the following words and sentences as a pretest for consonant digraphs and blends.

1. **echo**   Listen for the **echo.**
2. **know**   Do you **know** the answer?
3. **blanket**   Dad folded the **blanket.**
4. **telephone** The **telephone** rang twice.
5. **wheel**   The **wheel** rolled away.
6. **teacher**   My neighbor is a **teacher.**

WRITING

Have children write riddles, using words with consonant digraphs. Encourage children to share their riddles.

HEALTH

Have children list foods whose names have consonant digraphs, such as *fish, chicken, spinach, squash, cherries,* and *peaches.* Help children list the words in food groups: Dairy, Meat–Protein, Fruit–Vegetable, Grains.

TECHNOLOGY   **AstroWord** Consonant Blends & Digraphs

AUDITORY LEARNERS GROUPS

Materials: a wrapped box

Seat children in a circle. Have one child hold a wrapped box and finish the following sentence with a word that has a consonant digraph: *In the wrapped box is a _____.* The box is passed to the next child who repeats the sentence and adds another word with a consonant digraph. Continue the game, passing the box around the circle.

CHALLENGE

Challenge children to write tongue twisters featuring words with consonant digraphs. Use the following as an example: *Shy Sheila sells seashells by the seashore.*

EXTRA SUPPORT/INTERVENTION

As children do the activities on pages 71 and 72, read the words and sentences aloud with them to help them hear the sounds of the consonant digraphs. See Daily Phonics Practice, page 216.

Integrating Phonics and Reading

Guided Reading

Have children look at the cover illustration and read the title. Then, ask what clues help children predict what the story will be about.

First Reading Have children describe the things Suki found before she found what Sam wanted.

Second Reading Help children identify story words that contain consonant digraphs, such as *things, when, chair, kitchen, bathroom.*

Comprehension

After reading, ask children these questions:
• Why couldn't Sam explain what he wanted? *Inference/Character*
• How would you describe Suki? Was she good at finding lost things? *Reflective Analysis/Personal Response*

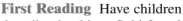
ESL/ELL English Language Learners

Help children identify each object Suki found by pointing to an object in a picture and asking *What is this?* Have children answer by finding and pointing to the word that names the object.

Consonant Digraphs

Skill Focus

Children will

★ identify consonant digraphs at the beginning, in the middle, and at the end of words.

★ read and write words with consonant digraphs.

ESL/ELL Most English language learners will be familiar with voiced and unvoiced sounds and silent letters. Practice *kn* and *gn* orally with native speakers of Chinese, Vietnamese, and Spanish: *knot, knee, knife, know, gnaw.*

Teach

Phonemic Awareness: **Phoneme Isolation**
Explain that you will say groups of three words. Ask children to identify the consonant digraph that they hear at the beginning, middle, or end of the words in each group. Use these words:

- **chair**   **peach**   **matches**
- **shake**   **dishes**   **brush**
- **think**   **with**   **father**

Sound to Symbol   Remind children that a consonant digraph is two or more consonants that together represent one sound. Then, write the words *cheese, teacher,* and *reach* on the board. Say each word aloud, stressing the *ch* sound. Ask children what consonant digraph appears in each word. *(ch)* Call on volunteers to underline the *ch* in each word. Remind children that a consonant digraph can be at the beginning, in the middle, or at the end of a word. Then, have children say words with consonant digraphs and identify whether the digraph is at the beginning, in the middle, or at the end of the word.

Practice and Apply

Writing   For the activity at the top of page 73, suggest that children read each sentence with their word choice in place to make sure the word makes sense.

Sound to Symbol   For the activities at the bottom of page 73 and on page 74, suggest that children look for a pair of consonants that together represent one sound.

Reading   Use *One Step at a Time,* MCP Phonics and Reading Library, Super Skills Collection, Level C, to provide additional practice in identifying consonant digraphs.

Name _____

▶ Choose a word from the box to complete each sentence. Write the word on the line.

1. I love my new elementary _____school_____.

2. My classroom _____teacher_____ is very nice.

3. Her name is Ms. _____White_____.

4. She _____knows_____ how to make learning fun.

5. I like doing _____math_____ problems.

6. In October I was sick with a bad _____cough_____.

7. My _____mother_____ made me stay in bed.

8. My teacher _____wrote_____ me a letter.

9. Everyone in my class _____signed_____ it.

10. Someone drew a picture of an _____elephant_____ on it.

11. The picture made me _____laugh_____.

12. I _____thought_____ it was very funny.

cough
elephant
knows
laugh
math
mother
school
signed
teacher
thought
White
wrote

▶ Say each word. Write its consonant digraph on the line.

13. rough	gh	14. kitchen	ch	15. Ralph	ph
16. choice	ch	17. wrong	wr	18. tough	gh
19. know	kn	20. chemical	ch	21. sign	gn
22. gnaw	gn	23. knife	kn	24. patch	ch
25. phone	ph	26. wrist	wr	27. Kathy	th

Consonant digraphs: Words in context   **73**

FOCUS ON ALL LEARNERS

ESL/ELL ENGLISH LANGUAGE LEARNERS

Continue practicing pronunciation of digraphs while teaching spelling and recognition of lesson vocabulary.

- Assess English language learners' ability to hear the differences among target and similar sounds with a "Same or Different" activity. Use word pairs such as *this, dish; three, thread; ten, them; beach, catch,* and so on.

- Write words on the board with the target digraphs in different positions, such as *threw, mother,* and *south.* Have children identify the consonant digraph. Then, say the words together.

KINESTHETIC LEARNERS

Have children work in pairs to create word-search puzzles that contain words with consonant digraphs. Pairs of children can try to solve each other's puzzles.

VISUAL LEARNERS

Materials: colored chalk

Write the following words on the board, omitting the consonant digraphs: *(wr)ong, (kn)ot, in(ch), fi(sh)ing, o(th)er, si(gn), (wh)ere, rou(gh), qui(ck)ly, gra(ph).* Ask volunteers to use colored chalk to write a digraph to complete each word.

Say each word and circle its consonant digraph. Write the word in the column that tells whether the consonant digraph is at the beginning, middle, or end of the word.

bea**ch**	ano**th**er	bir**th**day	starfi**sh**	cat**ch**
chin	**ch**oose	**ch**orus	cou**gh**	di**sh**es
elep**h**ant	**kn**ow	lau**gh**ed	mat**ch**es	mo**th**er
nor**th**	pa**th**	pea**ch**es	ra**th**er	tou**gh**
shell	si**gn**	**th**rew	toge**th**er	**wh**eel
whine	**wh**ite	wi**sh**	wi**th**	**wr**ite

Beginning	**Middle**	**End**
threw	together	beach
write	another	north
shell	matches	cough
know	birthday	path
chin	peaches	with
white	mother	catch
wheel	dishes	starfish
whine	laughed	tough
chorus	rather	wish
choose	elephant	sign

74 Consonant digraphs: Sound to symbol

 HOME Have your child make up questions that include two or more words from the box, such as *Is a starfish on the beach?*

CURRICULUM CONNECTIONS

SPELLING

Write the spelling words *know, wheel,* and *teacher* on the board. Have children say each word and identify the consonant digraph. Then, have volunteers write *chin, knife, knew, whine, peach,* and *white* under the spelling words with the same digraphs. Talk about the positions of the digraphs in the matched words.

WRITING

Ask children to write about humorous things that have happened in the classroom. Have them check their writing for words with consonant digraphs.

SOCIAL STUDIES

Have children work in groups to create a map of an imaginary place. Suggest they use words with consonant digraphs to label streets, landmarks, and shops. For example: *Washington School, The Cheese Shop, Peachtree Street, cabbage patch, Children's Library, White Sand Beach,* and so on.

TECHNOLOGY **AstroWord** Consonant Blends & Digraphs

AUDITORY LEARNERS **GROUPS**

Have children repeat each of the following sentences after you and identify the words that have the same consonant digraph sound. Use these sentences: *The washed dishes are on the shelf. The chicken checked to see which nest was best. She sells seashells by the seashore. Chucky chomps on peaches, cheese, and cherries. White whales whistle while they swim.*

CHALLENGE

Challenge children to write groups of words that contain the same consonant digraph but in a different position in each word; for example, *third, birthday, bath.*

EXTRA SUPPORT/INTERVENTION

Materials: index cards

Choose words from pages 73 and 74 to write on index cards. Have children read and sort the words according to consonant digraphs and then according to the position of the digraphs within the words. See Daily Phonics Practice, page 216.

Integrating Phonics and Reading

Guided Reading

Have children look at the cover and read the title. Discuss how people once traveled west by wagon.

First Reading Encourage children to choose an exciting event to retell in their own words.

Second Reading Help children identify story words that end with consonant digraphs, such as *whined, brother, buckets, shirt, wrinkled.*

Comprehension

After reading, ask children these questions:

• What are some of the reasons the trip west was so hard? *Recall/Cause and Effect*

• Imagine you are Sarah or Jack. What would you say about the trip to a new home? *Reflective Analysis/Personal Reaction*

ESL/ELL **English Language Learners**

Help children summarize by turning each chapter title into a question, such as *What happened at the fork in the road?* Prompt by asking *What happened first?*

Syllables

Skill Focus

Children will

★ recognize that the number of vowel sounds and the number of syllables in a word are the same.

★ identify the number of syllables in words.

★ write multisyllabic words to complete sentences.

ESL/ELL Since Vietnamese, Hmong, and Cantonese are monosyllabic, native speakers of these languages may require additional support and oral practice with words containing more than one syllable.

Teach

Introduce Syllables Write *pail, pencil,* and *umbrella* on the board. Have children identify the number of vowels in each word. *(2, 2, 3)* Ask volunteers to circle the vowels. Then, say each word and have children identify the number of vowel sounds in each word. *(1, 2, 3)* Ask children to compare the number of vowels and the number of vowel sounds in each word. For example, *pail* has two vowels but only one vowel sound.

Remind children that words can be divided into one or more syllables. One vowel sound is heard in each syllable. Ask children how many syllables each of the words on the board has. *(1, 2, 3)*

Practice and Apply

Sound to Symbol Before children do the activity on page 75, read aloud the rule at the top of the page. To make sure children understand the directions, model how to do the first item.

Writing For the activity at the top of page 76, make sure children understand that they are to complete each sentence with a two-syllable word from the choices to the right of each sentence. For the activity at the bottom of page 76, ask a volunteer to read the poem aloud. Then, have children identify the number of syllables in all the words in the poem.

Reading Use *The Living Desert,* MCP Phonics and Reading Word Study Skills Library 2, Level C, to provide additional practice in identifying syllables.

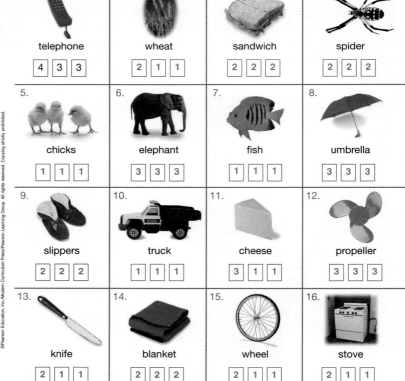

Name _____

Say the name of each picture. In the first box under the name, write the number of vowels you see in the word. In the second box, write the number of vowel sounds you hear. In the third box, write the number of syllables. The first one is done for you.

RULE
Words can be divided into one or more syllables. You hear one vowel sound in each syllable.

1. telephone **4 3 3**	2. wheat **2 1 1**	3. sandwich **2 2 2**	4. spider **2 2 2**
5. chicks **1 1 1**	6. elephant **3 3 3**	7. fish **1 1 1**	8. umbrella **3 3 3**
9. slippers **2 2 2**	10. truck **1 1 1**	11. cheese **3 1 1**	12. propeller **3 3 3**
13. knife **2 1 1**	14. blanket **2 2 2**	15. wheel **2 1 1**	16. stove **2 1 1**

Syllables: Sound to Symbol   **75**

FOCUS ON ALL LEARNERS

- -

ESL/ELL ENGLISH LANGUAGE LEARNERS

Assess English language learners' awareness of syllables in words by reviewing words that name familiar objects.

● Explain orally the relationship between vowel sounds and syllables. Give examples of words from the lesson.

● Provide familiar two-syllable words by having children name two-syllable clothing items they are wearing, such as *sweater, sweatshirt,* and *jacket.* Have them clap for each vowel sound.

● Read the poem on page 76 aloud. Have English language learners say each line after you. Then, help them identify the number of syllables in the words in each line.

KINESTHETIC LEARNERS

As you say a word aloud, have children jump in place each time they hear a vowel sound. Then, have them identify the number of syllables in the word.

VISUAL/AUDITORY LEARNERS

Materials: dictionaries

Have children take turns choosing a word from the dictionary, saying the word aloud, and asking a partner to name the number of vowel sounds heard in the word.

► **Circle the two-syllable word that makes sense in the sentence. Write the word on the line.**

1. Friday was ____Mother's____ birthday.
2. I baked a ____cherry____ cake.
3. The cake had ____thirty____ candles.
4. Mom loved her ____presents____.
5. I ____painted____ her a picture.
6. Dad gave her a blue ____sweater____.
7. Grandmother ____knitted____ her a red scarf.

(Mother's)	my	problem
chicken	fudge	(cherry)
(thirty)	six	forest
(presents)	gifts	little
(painted)	drew	player
kitchen	dress	(sweater)
never	bought	(knitted)

► **Read the poem. Then, complete each sentence by writing the correct word from the poem on the line.**

Jack Be Nimble

Jack be nimble,
Jack be quick.
Jack jump over
The candlestick.

8. A one-syllable word that means *fast* is ____quick____.
9. The two-syllable word in the title of the poem is ____nimble____.
10. The three-syllable word in the poem is ____candlestick____.
11. A two-syllable word that means *above* or *across* is ____over____.

76 Syllables: Words in context

 Ask your child to read sentences 1–7 and identify all of the two-syllable words.

CURRICULUM CONNECTIONS

SPELLING

Use these words and sentences as a posttest for writing words with consonant digraphs and syllables with blends and digraphs.

1. **echo**   The **echo** was loud and clear.
2. **blanket**   The **blanket** on my bed is green.
3. **know**   I **know** the answer.
4. **telephone** Here is the **telephone.**
5. **wheel**   A **wheel** is round.
6. **teacher**   Mr. Sanchez is a piano **teacher.**

WRITING

Suggest that children write a birthday poem for a family member. Provide materials so children can make cards and write their poems inside.

FINE ART

Have children make mobiles of theme-related items with multisyllabic names. Children can draw or cut out pictures of the items, paste them on tagboard, and hang them from coat hangers.

TECHNOLOGY **AstroWord** Multisyllabic Words

Integrating Phonics and Reading

Guided Reading
Direct children to look at the cover and read the title. Then, invite them to tell what they know about the desert and the animals that live there.

First Reading Ask children to describe some of the plants and animals that live in a desert.
Second Reading Have children identify the number of syllables in selected story words.
Comprehension
After reading, ask children these questions:
• Name some ways living things survive in a desert. *Recall/Main Ideas and Details*
• What new facts did you learn about the desert? *Reflective Analysis/Personal Response*
ESL/ELL **English Language Learners**
Review the names of different animals in the text by showing children a picture and asking: *What animal is this?* or *Is this a (name of animal)?* Have children respond in a complete sentence, such as *That is a (name of animal).*

AUDITORY/VISUAL LEARNERS GROUPS

Materials: small slips of paper, paper bag

Give each group a bag and slips of paper. Have children write the numbers *1, 2,* and *3* on the slips and put them in the bag. Have children take turns drawing a number, saying a word with that number of syllables, and returning the number to the bag.

CHALLENGE

Have children code nursery rhymes by writing the number of syllables in each line. For example, the first line of "Humpty Dumpty," which is *Humpty Dumpty sat on a wall,* would be *2, 2, 1, 1, 1, 1.*

EXTRA SUPPORT/INTERVENTION

Work with children to complete the lesson pages successfully. Encourage them to "think aloud" by saying words softly to themselves and tapping out the syllables of each word. See Daily Phonics Practice, page 215.

Phonics and Reading / Phonics and Writing

Review Consonant Blends and Digraphs

Skill Focus

Children will

★ select words with consonant blends and consonant digraphs to complete sentences.

★ write a paragraph for a research report using words with consonant blends and digraphs.

Teach

Phonics and Reading Review the difference between a consonant blend and a consonant digraph. Point out that in a consonant blend, the two consonant sounds blend together, but each consonant is heard, as the letters *sp* in *spell*. In a consonant digraph, the two consonants together represent one sound, as the letters *kn* in *knit*.

Say these words, one at a time: *laugh, friend, snake, shop, blink, write.* Have children write each word and tell whether it has a consonant blend or a consonant digraph. (laugh-*digraph*, friend-*blend*, snake-*blend*, school-*digraph*, blink-*blend*, write-*digraph*)

Practice and Apply

Phonics and Reading Make sure children understand that they should complete the sentences on page 77 with story words that have consonant blends or digraphs.

Critical Thinking For the Talk About It question at the bottom of page 77, suggest that children reread the opening paragraph of the story. Discuss what kind of person Tony is.

Phonics and Writing Before children begin writing, use the callouts on page 78 to review the structure of a research report. Remind children to try to include some of the words from the box in their paragraph.

Reading Use *Squirrels,* MCP Phonics and Reading Library, Super Skills Collection, Level C, to provide additional practice in reading words with consonant blends and digraphs.

Name _____

 **Phonics & Reading**   Read the story. Then, use words with consonant blends or digraphs to finish the sentences.

What an Imagination!

My friend Tony likes to make people laugh. He invents funny stories and jokes to tell. Everyone knows that he has quite an imagination!

One day at recess, Tony said, "You won't believe what happened yesterday when I was walking home from school. Suddenly, I saw a bird with brightly colored feathers. It looked at me and said, 'Hi, Tony! Hi, Tony!' When I blinked, it was gone."

We all laughed and said, "What an imagination you have!"

When we were back in class, Mrs. Kelly asked, "Did anyone see the newspaper story about the parrot that escaped from a pet store yesterday? Luckily, someone recognized the bird and told the owner where to find it. The parrot had the same name as you, Tony."

"See, it wasn't my imagination!" Tony told us. "I just got one fact wrong. The bird wasn't talking to me. It was talking to itself!"

1. Tony likes to make people _____laugh_____.

2. He invents funny _____stories_____ and jokes to tell.

3. Everyone _____knows_____ that Tony has quite an imagination.

4. Tony saw a bird on his way home from _____school_____.

5. The bird had brightly colored _____feathers_____.

6. When Tony _____blinked_____, the bird was gone.

7. The class told Tony, "_____What_____ an imagination you have!"

8. Tony said he just got one fact _____wrong_____.

TALK About It Why didn't Tony's friends believe his story right away?

Review consonant blends and digraphs: Reading, critical thinking   **77**

FOCUS ON ALL LEARNERS

ESL/ELL ENGLISH LANGUAGE LEARNERS

Use the story on page 77 to review consonant blends and digraphs with English language learners.

• Photocopy the story, one copy per child.

• Tell children to scan the story and highlight words they recognize that contain consonant blends or digraphs. Have those who need additional support work together, using digraph and blend cards you prepared. Children in this group should locate target words only.

• Ask children to print target story words on the board. Invite volunteers to underline the letters that stand for each blend or digraph. Model pronunciation of the sound or sounds, rather than the full word. Have children repeat the words chorally.

KINESTHETIC LEARNERS   INDIVIDUAL

Materials: newspapers, magazines, scissors, glue

Have children search through printed materials and cut out words that have consonant blends or digraphs. Children can glue the words onto paper to create collages or combine them with other words to form sentences.

Phonics & Writing

A **research report** gives facts and details about a topic. When you write a research report, you find and collect information about a topic that interests you. The information may come from people, books, magazines, newspapers, or the Internet.

▶ Write one paragraph for a research report about tigers. The paragraph might be about where tigers live, how they get their food, or something else that interests you about tigers. Some of the words in the box may help you.

white	know	stripes	claws	gnaw
tropics	hunt	travel	protect	must

Give your report a **title**.

Include the **main idea** in your first sentence.

Include **details** about the main idea in the other sentences.

78 Review consonant blends and digraphs: Writing

HOME Ask your child to read the report he or she wrote and identify the words with consonant blends and digraphs.

CURRICULUM CONNECTIONS

SPELLING

Use these words and sentences for a midunit cumulative spelling review.

1. **overcoat** — Dad wore his **overcoat.**
2. **backpack** — Carry a **backpack** on the hike.
3. **pencil** — The point on my **pencil** broke.
4. **monkey** — The **monkey** climbed the tree.
5. **dragon** — Does a **dragon** breathe fire?
6. **broom** — Greg used a **broom** to sweep.
7. **blanket** — The **blanket** kept me warm.
8. **glove** — I can't find my **glove.**
9. **flag** — The **flag** waves in the wind.
10. **crow** — A big **crow** landed on the roof.
11. **swing** — We took turns on the **swing.**
12. **spoon** — I need a **spoon** to eat my soup.
13. **sweater** — Have you seen my **sweater?**
14. **king** — The **king** made a new law.
15. **shelf** — Don put his books on the **shelf.**
16. **carry** — Can you **carry** my bag for me?
17. **why** — **Why** is the sky blue?
18. **year** — The **year** starts in January.
19. **echo** — We heard an **echo** in the valley.
20. **know** — I **know** where to find acorns.
21. **telephone** — He'll answer the **telephone.**
22. **wheel** — Who invented the **wheel?**
23. **teacher** — Our **teacher** gave us new books.

AUDITORY LEARNERS 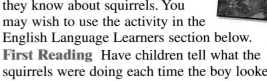 GROUPS

Materials: consonant blend and digraph cards, paper clip

Place the consonant blend and digraph cards face up on the floor or on a table. Have children take turns tossing a paper clip onto the cards, saying a word that has the digraph or blend on which the clip lands, and then using the word in a sentence.

CHALLENGE

Materials: highlighter marking pen

Challenge children to invent and write an imaginary story. Suggest that children use ideas both from stories they have heard or read and from real-life events or experiences. When children have finished writing, they should use a marker to highlight story words that have consonant blends or digraphs.

EXTRA SUPPORT/INTERVENTION

Materials: highlighter marking pen

Read the story on page 77 with children and have them use a marker to highlight words with consonant blends and digraphs. Suggest they refer to the highlighted words to help them complete the sentences on the page. See Daily Phonics Practice, pages 215–216.

Integrating Phonics and Reading

Guided Reading

Have children look at the cover and read the title. Ask them to tell what they know about squirrels. You may wish to use the activity in the English Language Learners section below.

First Reading Have children tell what the squirrels were doing each time the boy looked.

Second Reading Help children identify story words that have consonant blends and digraphs.

Comprehension

After reading, ask children these questions:

- Did the boy have an active imagination? Why or why not? *Inference/Character*

- Do you think the boy in the story liked squirrels? Why or why not? *Reflective Analysis/Drawing Conclusions*

ESL/ELL **English Language Learners**

Point out to English language learners that the last word in every second and fourth line rhymes. Read aloud an example. Then, ask children to read other rhyming lines.

R-Controlled Vowels

Skill Focus

Children will

★ identify the sounds of *ar, er, ir, or,* and *ur* in words.

★ read and write words that contain *r*-controlled vowels.

ESL/ELL There is no sound in Spanish similar to the English sound for the letter combinations *ir, er,* and *ur*. In Spanish, each combination stands for a distinct sound. Spanish-speaking children may initially pronounce *bird* like *beard* or *letter* like *let air*.

Teach

Phonemic Awareness: Phoneme Identity
Say the word *torn,* elongating the *r*-controlled vowel sound: *tooorrrn.* Have children repeat the vowel sound. Next, say groups of three words. Ask children to identify the words in each group that have the same vowel sound.

• corn	horn	toad
• first	fist	thirst
• last	park	bark
• hurt	spurt	punch
• tent	term	germ

Sound to Symbol Explain that when a vowel is followed by the letter *r,* it has a sound that is different from its usual long or short sound. Write the words *bark, term, first, corn,* and *spurt* on the board. Ask volunteers to say each word and identify the vowel that is paired with *r* in each one. Point out that *er, ir,* and *ur* have the same sound.

Practice and Apply

Sound to Symbol Read aloud the rule at the top of page 79. For the first exercise, tell children that the vowel sound they hear in each word is represented by a vowel followed by the letter *r.*

Writing For the activity at the bottom of page 79, suggest that children read the sentences aloud in order to hear the *r*-controlled vowel sound. For the crossword puzzle on page 80, tell children that each clue describes a word in the box and that each word is used in the puzzle only once.

Reading Use *Friends Forever,* MCP Phonics and Reading Library, Super Skills Collection, Level C, to provide additional practice in identifying *r*-controlled vowels.

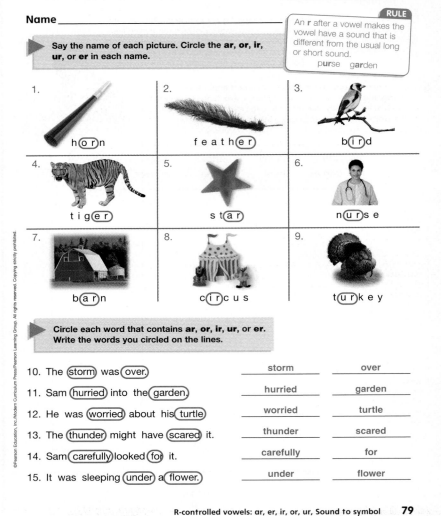

Sound to Symbol

Name _____

> Say the name of each picture. Circle the **ar, or, ir, ur,** or **er** in each name.

RULE
An **r** after a vowel makes the vowel have a sound that is different from the usual long or short sound.
pu**r**se ga**r**den

1. h**o**rn
2. feath**er**
3. b**ir**d
4. tig**er**
5. st**ar**
6. n**ur**se
7. b**ar**n
8. c**ir**cus
9. t**ur**key

> Circle each word that contains **ar, or, ir, ur,** or **er.** Write the words you circled on the lines.

10. The storm was over.   storm   over
11. Sam hurried into the garden.   hurried   garden
12. He was worried about his turtle.   worried   turtle
13. The thunder might have scared it.   thunder   scared
14. Sam carefully looked for it.   carefully   for
15. It was sleeping under a flower.   under   flower

R-controlled vowels: ar, er, ir, or, ur, Sound to symbol   **79**

FOCUS ON ALL LEARNERS

ESL/ELL ENGLISH LANGUAGE LEARNERS

Practice words with *r*-controlled vowels by having English language learners complete activities in writing.

• Ask children to complete the first activity on page 79 with an English-proficient partner. Explain that they should print each picture name and circle its vowel + *r* combination.

• In small groups, review the activity orally. Verify correct spelling and clear pronunciation of the target words.

• Encourage English language learners to complete the activity at the bottom of page 79 individually. Suggest that they circle each vowel + *r* combination in the words they write.

KINESTHETIC LEARNERS GROUPS

Materials: egg carton, markers, paper clips

Write the five vowel + *r* combinations at random in the hollows of the egg carton. Have children take turns tossing a paper clip into the carton and saying a word with the vowel + *r* combination on which their paper clip lands.

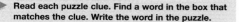

► Read each puzzle clue. Find a word in the box that matches the clue. Write the word in the puzzle.

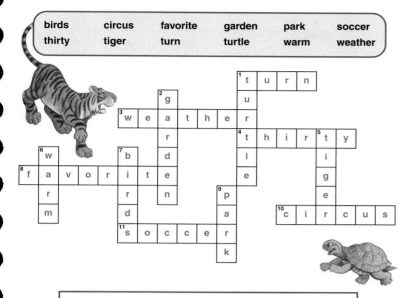

birds   circus   favorite   garden   park   soccer
thirty   tiger   turn   turtle   warm   weather

Across
1. move right or left
3. cloudy, windy, or sunny
4. 30
8. most well liked
10. where clowns are found
11. game to kick the ball into the goal

Down
1. an animal with a hard shell
2. plants and flowers
5. a striped wild animal
6. not cool, not hot
7. blue jays and robins
9. a place to play

80 R-controlled vowels: ar, er, ir, or, ur

CURRICULUM CONNECTIONS

SPELLING
Use these words and sentences to give children practice writing words with *r*-controlled vowels.

1. **tiger**   A **tiger** is a large cat.
2. **park**   Let's go to the **park.**
3. **hurry**   **Hurry,** or we will be late.
4. **favorite**   Winter is my **favorite** season.
5. **thirty**   I counted **thirty** monkeys.
6. **garden**   Hank worked in the **garden.**

WRITING
Invite children to write stories about a wild storm during which unbelievable events occur. Have them underline words with *r*-controlled vowels.

PORTFOLIO

SOCIAL STUDIES
Help children find out how the words *Thursday* (named for *Thor,* the Norse god of thunder) and *Saturday* (named for *Saturn,* the Roman god of farming and agriculture) got their names.

TECHNOLOGY **AstroWord** *r*-Controlled Vowels

VISUAL LEARNERS GROUPS
Give each group of children a list of words with *r*-controlled vowels, such as: *purple, circle, bird, park, turtle, car, warm, farm, garden, corn, morning, nurse,* and *barn.* Have the first player read the list and give a clue for a word. The child who guesses the word gets the list, chooses a different word, and gives a new clue. Play continues until all the words are used. Example clues include *Name a color made from blue and red.* (purple) *Name a shape that is round.* (circle)

CHALLENGE
Challenge children to select words from pages 79 and 80 and write as many words that rhyme with them as they can. Then, have children use the words to write rhyming couplets.

EXTRA SUPPORT/INTERVENTION
Write the words from the word box on page 80 on the board in random order. Have children circle *er, ir, or, ar,* and *ur* in the words, and then read the words aloud. See Daily Phonics Practice, pages 216–217.

Integrating Phonics and Reading

Guided Reading
As children read the title and look at the cover, ask them what they think makes a good friend. Tell the class that in this book they will read about a very special kind of friendship.

First Reading Ask children to describe how Mouse and Lion became best friends.
Second Reading Help children identify words in the story that have *r*-controlled vowels.

Comprehension
After reading, ask children these questions:
• Why do you think Lion let Mouse go? *Inference/Drawing Conclusions*
• Were there any surprises in the story? If so, what were they? *Reflective Analysis/Details*

ESL/ELL English Language Learners
Say aloud story words with *r*-controlled vowels, modeling pronunciation. Have children repeat the words after you.

R-Controlled Vowels

Skill Focus

Children will

★ identify the sounds of *ar, er, ir, or,* and *ur* in words.

★ read and write words that contain *r*-controlled vowels.

ESL/ELL In Spanish, each of the *r*-controlled letter combinations stands for a distinct sound. Practice with *part, hard; first, third; under, her; purse, burn; cord, torn.*

Teach

Phonemic Awareness: Phoneme Isolation
Have children listen as you slowly say each of the following sentences. Ask children to repeat the words in each sentence that have the same *r*-controlled vowel sound and then isolate the sound.

• **Do dogs *bark* in the *park* when it is *dark*? (ar)**

• **Can a *turtle* jump a *purple hurdle*? (ur)**

• **Can a *horse* eat *corn* with a *fork*? (or)**

Sound to Symbol Write *am, spot, bid, cod, bun, cat, pat, hut,* and *skit* on the board. Have children say each word and identify the short vowel sound. Ask volunteers to create new words by inserting an *r* after the vowel in each word and writing the new word on the board. *(arm, sport, bird, cord, burn, cart, part, hurt, skirt)* Have children say each pair of old and new words and compare how the vowel sounds change when *r* is added.

Practice and Apply

Sound to Symbol For the first activity on page 81, read the directions aloud and do the first item with children to make sure they understand what to do.

Writing For the second activity on page 81, have children reread each sentence with the word choice in place to make sure the sentence makes sense. For page 82, suggest that children look for the *r*-controlled vowel combination in each word to make sure they write it in the correct column.

Reading Use *Fern and Burt*, MCP Phonics and Reading Library, Super Skills Collection, Level C, to provide additional practice in identifying *r*-controlled vowels.

FERN AND BURT

Name _____

▶ Circle the **ar, or, ir, ur,** or **er** in each numbered word. Then, find the word in the box with the same beginning letter and vowel sound. Write it on the line.

bark	bore	Burt	cord	dart	first	circus
hurdle	leader	herd	purse	shore	startle	thirty

1. f(ir)   ___first___
2. b(ur)n   ___Burt___
3. lett(er)   ___leader___
4. c(or)n   ___cord___
5. h(ur)t   ___hurdle___
6. c(ir)cle   ___circus___
7. d(ar)k   ___dart___
8. st(ar)   ___startle___
9. b(or)n   ___bore___
10. sh(or)t   ___shore___
11. th(ir)d   ___thirty___
12. h(er)   ___herd___
13. b(ar)n   ___bark___
14. p(ur)ple   ___purse___

▶ Find a word on the ribbon to complete each sentence. Write the word on the line.

15. My ___mother___ has a green thumb.

16. She loves to work in her ___garden___.

17. Our backyard is beautiful during the ___summer___.

18. It is ___bursting___ with colorful flowers!

19. There are ___orange___, yellow, and pink flowers.

20. Mom once won ___third___ place at a flower show.

21. Her eyes ___sparkled___ as she received her prize.

bursting
garden
mother
orange
sparkled
summer
third

R-controlled vowels: ar, er, ir, or, ur, Sound to symbol   **81**

FOCUS ON ALL LEARNERS

ESL/ELL ENGLISH LANGUAGE LEARNERS

Use this activity with English language learners to assess their command of *r*-controlled vowels.

• Bring in ten items or pictures, two for each vowel sound.

• Prepare five index cards: *ar, or, ir, er, ur.*

• Each child names an item and pairs it with the correct card.

• Review words and vowel + *r* combinations. If children have reached the intermediate level of proficiency, confirm spelling of target words by having them spell aloud.

KINESTHETIC LEARNERS GROUPS

Materials: paper plates, markers, beanbags

Write the five vowel + *r* combinations on separate plates. Make one or more sets. Scatter the plates on the floor. Invite children to toss a beanbag and say a word with the vowel + *r* combination shown on the plate where the beanbag lands.

VISUAL LEARNERS PARTNERS

Suggest that pairs of children make word puzzles for one another to solve. Each puzzle should include a clue and a row of squares for each letter in the word; for example, *the hottest season* (summer).

Sound to Symbol

Read the sentences. Underline each word that contains **ar, or, ir, ur,** or **er.** Then write the words you underlined in the correct boxes below.

1. Rita made a special <u>birthday</u> <u>card</u> <u>for</u> a friend.
2. <u>First</u>, she <u>decorated</u> it with blue and red <u>stars</u>.
3. Then, she wrote a <u>clever</u> little <u>verse</u>.
4. In the <u>morning</u>, Rita <u>hurried</u> to the mailbox.
5. <u>Darla</u> received many <u>surprises</u> on Friday.
6. Mom and Dad gave <u>her</u> a <u>purse</u>, a <u>furry</u> kitten, and a red <u>sweater</u>.
7. She got a yellow <u>bird</u> from Aunt <u>Shirley</u>.
8. <u>Darla</u> really likes the <u>large</u> and <u>colorful</u> greeting from Rita.

ir
birthday
First
bird
Shirley

er
clever
verse
her
sweater

or
for
decorated
morning
colorful

ar
card
stars
Darla
large

ur
hurried
surprises
purse
furry

82   R-controlled vowels: ar, er, ir, or, ur, Sound to symbol

 Ask your child to think of one more word to add to each gift box.

CURRICULUM CONNECTIONS

SPELLING

Have children draw five columns on a sheet of paper and label them *ar, er, ir, or,* and *ur.* As you call out words with *r*-controlled vowels, children write each word in the appropriate column.

WRITING

Have children write riddles about words with *r*-controlled vowels to share with a partner. Children may wish to make open-the-flap books, so that the answers are revealed in an interesting way.

MATH

Have children use the following guidelines to prepare a list of twelve *r*-controlled words.

1/3 of the words have *ar* (4 words)
1/12 of the words have *er* (1 word)
1/6 of the words have *ir* (2 words)
1/4 of the words have *or* (3 words)
1/6 of the words have *ur* (2 words)

TECHNOLOGY  **AstroWord** *r*-Controlled Vowels

---

AUDITORY LEARNERS **GROUPS**

Materials: bingo game board, game markers

Have children choose words from pages 81 and 82 to write in the spaces on their bingo game cards. To play, call out words from these pages and have children cover the words they have written. The child who has bingo wins the round.

CHALLENGE

Provide children with *r*-controlled word frames and have them add letters to write complete words. Examples: __*arm* (charm, harm, alarm); __*orn* (horn, corn, born); __*urt* (curt, hurt, spurt); __*ern* (stern, fern, tern); __*irt* (dirt, flirt, skirt).

EXTRA SUPPORT/INTERVENTION

Materials: index cards

Write several words from pages 81 and 82 on separate cards for children to read and sort according to vowel + *r* combinations. See Daily Phonics Practice, pages 216–217.

Integrating Phonics and Reading

Guided Reading

Have children look at the cover, read the title, and leaf through the book. Then, invite them to predict what the story will be about.
First Reading Have children describe the conflict between Fern and Burt and how it was resolved.
Second Reading Help children identify words in the story that contain *r*-controlled vowels.

Comprehension

After reading, ask children these questions:
• Why did Fern and Burt go looking for things to wear? *Recall/Drawing Conclusions*
• What do you think was the moral of the story? *Inference/Drawing Conclusions*

ESL/ELL **English Language Learners**

Point out that the words the characters say in the story are enclosed in quotation marks, and point out several examples. Then, ask volunteers to act out the story using each character's exact words.

Syllables

Skill Focus

Children will

★ identify the number of syllables in one-, two-, and three-syllable words.

★ recognize that the number of vowel sounds and the number of syllables in a word are the same.

★ read and write multisyllabic words, including some that contain *r*-controlled vowels.

ESL/ELL Many Asian languages, such as Hmong, are monosyllabic, and native speakers may pronounce two-syllable words in English as separate words.

Teach

Introduce Syllables Write the word *part* on the board and say it aloud. Ask a volunteer to circle the letters that make the vowel sound. *(ar)* Then, ask children how many syllables are in the word. *(one)* Remind children that each syllable in a word has one vowel sound. When a vowel is paired with the letter *r*, the two letters have one vowel sound.

Write the words *letter, garden, circus, turkey,* and *shortly* on the board. Ask children how many syllables are in each word. *(two)* Then, ask volunteers to identify whether they hear an *r*-controlled vowel sound in the first or second syllable. Continue in a similar way with the words *yesterday, dangerous,* and *factory.*

Practice and Apply

Sound to Symbol Ask a volunteer to read aloud the rule at the top of page 83. Read the directions aloud and do the first item with children to make sure they understand how to do the activity.

For page 84, tell children that each word in the box will be used once. Suggest that children check off or cross out words as they use them.

Reading Use *The Monster Under the Bed,* MCP Phonics and Reading Library, Super Skills Collection, Level C, to provide additional practice in identifying the number of syllables in words.

Name _____

> Say the name of each picture. In the box, write the number of syllables you hear in the picture name. Then, color the pictures whose names have two syllables.

RULE
The letters **ar, or, ir ur,** and **er** each have one vowel sound. A word has as many syllables as it has vowel sounds.

1. fork | 1
2. turkey color | 2
3. finger color | 2
4. computer | 3
5. toaster color | 2
6. letter color | 2
7. star | 1
8. garden color | 2
9. corn | 1
10. turtle color | 2
11. wheelbarrow | 3
12. circus color | 2

R-controlled vowels: Syllables, Sound to symbol　**83**

FOCUS ON ALL LEARNERS

ESL/ELL ENGLISH LANGUAGE LEARNERS

Assess English language learners' awareness of syllables in words by reviewing words from the lesson.

- With children, read aloud the words in the box on page 84. Encourage children to tap out each syllable.
- Draw a three-column chart on the board. Label the columns *1, 2,* and *3,* representing the number of syllables in a word.
- Have children write the words from page 84 in the appropriate columns.

KINESTHETIC LEARNERS GROUPS

Say words for children to write on the board. Then, have them draw lines between syllables and identify the letter(s) that represent the vowel sound in each one. Use the words *river, surface, market, afternoon, corner, dirty,* and *letter.*

VISUAL LEARNERS GROUPS

Write these word groups on the board: *tiger, turkey, moose; grasshopper, hornet, butterfly; sweater, skirt, shirt; storm, thunder, lightning; green, blue, purple.* Have children identify the number of syllables in each word, words with *r*-controlled vowels, and what the words in each group have in common.

► Write the word that matches the meaning. Then say the word. Write the number of syllables in the box.

1. wind, rain, and lightning ___thunderstorm___ [3]
2. the day a person is born ___birthday___ [2]
3. the day before today ___yesterday___ [3]
4. red and blue mixed ___purple___ [2]
5. a floor covering ___carpet___ [2]
6. the day after Friday ___Saturday___ [3]
7. the opposite of *tall* ___short___ [1]
8. the number after 12 ___thirteen___ [2]
9. musical instrument with strings ___guitar___ [2]
10. to surprise and frighten ___startle___ [2]
11. a person who grows crops ___farmer___ [2]
12. an animal with a bushy tail ___squirrel___ [2]
13. corn that is popped ___popcorn___ [2]
14. a plant with feathery leaves ___fern___ [1]
15. a thing liked the best ___favorite___ [3]
16. a place where things are made ___factory___ [3]
17. very shiny ___sparkling___ [2]
18. a meal eaten at night ___supper___ [2]
19. the opposite of *boy* ___girl___ [1]
20. ships dock here ___port___ [1]
21. a celebration ___party___ [2]

Word Box
birthday
carpet
factory
farmer
favorite
fern
girl
guitar
party
popcorn
port
purple
Saturday
short
sparkling
squirrel
startle
supper
thirteen
thunderstorm
yesterday

84 R-controlled vowels: Syllables, Word meaning

HOME Ask your child to identify the *r*-controlled vowel in each word in the box.

CURRICULUM CONNECTIONS

SPELLING

Draw five columns on the board and label them *ar, er, ir, or, ur.* Have volunteers write each word you say in the column indicating the spelling of the vowel sound. Say the words *tiger, park, hurry, favorite, thirty,* and *garden.* Ask children to suggest their own words to add to the chart.

WRITING

Extend the unit theme "What an Imagination!" by having children write a tall tale suggested by words from pages 83 and 84. Ask them to circle any *r*-controlled words they use.

MATH

Assign a numeral to each letter of the alphabet: *a=1; b=2, c=3,* and so on. Have children use the code to write a message for a classmate to decode. Each message should include at least one word with an *r*-controlled vowel sound. Here is an example: *1-18-5 25-15-21 9-14 20-8-9-18-4 7-18-1-4-5? (Are you in third grade?)*

TECHNOLOGY **AstroWord** *r*-Controlled Vowels

AUDITORY LEARNERS   GROUPS

Materials: spinner marked *1, 2, 3, vowel + r*

Have children form two teams. To play, teams take turns spinning the spinner and saying a word with one, two, or three syllables or a word with an *r*-controlled vowel. One point is given for each correct response. Two points are taken away for each incorrect response.

CHALLENGE

Write the following categories on the board and challenge children to think of one-, two-, and three-syllable words to fit each category: animals, sports, colors, weather, foods, computer terms.

EXTRA SUPPORT/INTERVENTION

Before children begin each section of the lesson, read the words aloud slowly so children can hear each syllable pronounced distinctly. See Daily Phonics Practice, pages 215–217.

Integrating Phonics and Reading

Guided Reading

Have children read the title and describe the cover. Then, ask them to speculate about what happens in the story. You may wish to use the activity in the English Language Learners section below.

First Reading Have children summarize the story that Mama Monster was reading.

Second Reading Have children identify the number of syllables in selected story words.

Comprehension

After reading, ask children these questions:
* What did Morris the Monster do when he heard a strange noise? *Recall/Details*
* What do you think makes this story unusual? Why? *Reflective Analysis/Setting, Characters*

ESL/ELL **English Language Learners**

Have children use the pictures to retell the story in their own words. You may wish to prompt with questions such as: *What is Morris doing now? How does Morris feel in this picture?*

Phonics and Spelling / Phonics and Writing

Review R-Controlled Vowels

Skill Focus

Children will

★ spell and write words that contain *r*-controlled vowels.

★ write a narrative paragraph using words that contain *r*-controlled vowels.

▶ Teach

Phonics and Spelling Review with children the fact that an *r* after a vowel makes the vowel have a sound that is different from the usual long or short vowel sound. Then, draw a five-column chart with these headings: *ar, er, ir, or, ur.*

Ask volunteers to say the sound of each *r*-controlled vowel. Then, have children sort words by placing them in the correct column of the chart. Write words on the board, such as *storm, star, turn, firm, fern, hurry, morning, verse, first, bird, purse, large, color,* and *clever.*

▶ Practice and Apply

Phonics and Spelling Make sure that children are able to read the words in the box on page 85 before they begin the activity. When children have finished writing the words in alphabetical order, you may wish to have them identify words that have *r*-controlled vowels.

Phonics and Writing Before children begin writing, invite them to brainstorm ideas about the funny things that have happened to them. Review the guidelines given in the boxes to help children develop the structure of their story clearly and express their ideas in an interesting way.

Reading Use *Carla Gets a Pet,* MCP Phonics and Reading Library, Super Skills Collection, Level C, to provide additional practice in reading words with *r*-controlled vowels.

Name _____

Phonics & Spelling Find and circle the hidden pictures. Then write each picture name on the lines below in alphabetical order.

backpack	crow	glove	report	thirty
blanket	dragon	monkey	spoon	tiger
computer	flag	purse	swing	wheel

1. backpack
2. blanket
3. computer
4. crow
5. dragon
6. flag
7. glove
8. monkey
9. purse
10. report
11. spoon
12. swing
13. thirty
14. tiger
15. wheel

Review r-controlled vowels: Spelling   **85**

FOCUS ON ALL LEARNERS

ESL/ELL ENGLISH LANGUAGE LEARNERS

Materials: letter cards *ar, er, ir, or, ur;* colored chalk

Confirm recognition of and discrimination between *r*-controlled vowel sounds by having English language learners help you complete a chart with words they know.

- On the board, draw a chart with five columns. Label the columns with the five *r*-controlled vowels.

- Shuffle the letter cards. Ask a volunteer to draw a card and write a word that contains the *r*-controlled vowel in the appropriate column. Have the child read the word aloud.

- Ask children to analyze the completed chart after all have participated. Review words aloud and correct any errors.

KINESTHETIC/AUDITORY LEARNERS

Have partners make a tic-tac-toe grid on paper and write an *r*-controlled vowel in each of the nine spaces. To play, have children take turns saying and spelling a word with the *r*-controlled vowel before writing an *X* or *O* in the space.

Phonics & Writing

A **narrative paragraph** tells a story about something that really happened. The events, characters, and setting are real. Often the writer is the main character. Using descriptive words helps bring the story alive.

Write a narrative paragraph about one of the funniest things that ever happened to you. Some of the words in the box may help you.

laughter	favorite	purple	turn	later	yesterday
party	garden	short	dark	first	for

Start your paragraph with a **topic sentence** that tells who, when, and where.

Use words like **first, then,** and **later** to make the order of the story clear.

Use words that tell how things **looked, sounded, smelled, tasted,** and **felt.**

HOME Ask your child to read his or her story to you and identify the words with r-controlled vowels.

CURRICULUM CONNECTIONS

SPELLING

Use the following words and sentences to review Unit 3 spelling words with *r*-controlled vowels. Note: A cumulative test for spelling words with consonant blends, digraphs, *y* as a vowel and consonant, and compound words can be found on page 78.

1. **tiger**   A **tiger** has stripes.
2. **park**   Let's play in the **park.**
3. **hurry**   Please **hurry** or we'll be late.
4. **favorite**   What is your **favorite** food?
5. **thirty**   I have **thirty** seashells.
6. **garden**   Roses grew in the **garden.**

MATH

Have children find words with *r*-controlled vowels and sort them by spelling (*ar, er, ir, or, ur*). Then, have children arrange the words in each group from the one with the fewest letters to the one with the most letters. For example, the list might start with *or, for, born* and end with *organization.*

TECHNOLOGY   **AstroWord** *r*-Controlled Vowels

AUDITORY LEARNERS   GROUPS

Have children number a sheet of paper from 1 through 10, skipping every other line. Dictate words containing *r*-controlled vowels for them to write, pausing after each word for children to check spelling and to circle the *r*-controlled vowel. Use the words *chart, fern, first, work, burst, shark, serve, shirt, world,* and *hurry.*

CHALLENGE

Challenge children to create a list of rhyming words with *r*-controlled vowels, such as *bark, dark, lark, mark, park,* and *shark,* and then use the words to write a rhyming couplet.

EXTRA SUPPORT/INTERVENTION

Materials: index cards

For children who need support, use index cards to make a set of letter cards and guide them as they build words with *r*-controlled vowels. See *Daily Phonics Practice,* pages 216–217.

Integrating Phonics and Reading

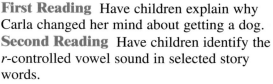

Guided Reading

Have children look at the cover and read the title. Then, involve children in a discussion of the different kinds of pets people have and how they take care of them.

First Reading Have children explain why Carla changed her mind about getting a dog.

Second Reading Have children identify the *r*-controlled vowel sound in selected story words.

Comprehension

After reading, ask children these questions:

- How did Carla show her mother she could take care of a pet? *Recall/Character*
- How do you think Carla felt when King ran away? *Reflective Analysis/Personal Response*

ESL/ELL **English Language Learners**

Point out that story events take place in a certain order. Then, invite children to retell what happened in the beginning, middle, and end of the story, using picture clues to help them.

Take-Home Book

Review Blends, Digraphs, R-Controlled Vowels

Skill Focus

Children will

★ read words with consonant blends, consonant digraphs, and *r*-controlled vowels in the context of a story.

★ reread for fluency.

Teach
Build Background

• Remind children that the theme of this unit is "What an Imagination!" Then, invite children to share anecdotes or ideas relating to the theme.

• Ask children if they ever think about who invented things they use every day. Have them look around the room and name items that had to be invented, such as the chalkboard, electric lights, and so on. Explain that children will be reading a book about people who had the imagination to invent some very useful things.

Sound to Symbol Help children review consonant digraphs, consonant blends, *y* as a consonant and a vowel, and *r*-controlled vowels. Write *glass, wheel, horn, yarn,* and *fly* on the board. Call on volunteers to identify the word with the consonant blend *(glass)*, the consonant digraph *(wheel)*, the *r*-controlled vowel *(horn, yarn)*, *y* as a consonant *(yarn)*, and *y* as a vowel *(fly)*.

Practice and Apply

Read the Book Help children tear out and fold the pages to make their Take-Home Books. Encourage children to look through the book and talk about the pictures. Then, read the story together.

Sound to Symbol Write these headings on the board: *Blends, Digraphs, r-Controlled Vowels.*

Have children look through the book and identify words with consonant blends *(long, square, snow, sleeve, traffic, play)*, consonant digraphs *(then, that, design, sign, should)*, and *r*-controlled vowels *(paper, inventor, narrow, first, started, third)*. Ask children to write each word under its heading and identify the appropriate phonics element in each.

Reread for Fluency Have children reread the book to increase their fluency and comprehension. Encourage children to take their books home to read and share with family members.

Review r-controlled vowels, blends, digraphs: Take-home book   **87**

FOCUS ON ALL LEARNERS

ESL/ELL ENGLISH LANGUAGE LEARNERS

After helping children make their Take-Home Books, do the following activities with English language learners.

• Read the story together.

• Ask children to point to and name the invention in each photograph and describe what it is used for.

• You may wish to help children make a main-idea chart to help organize their ideas.

• Have children identify the consonant blends, consonant digraphs, and *r*-controlled vowels in familiar story words.

KINESTHETIC LEARNERS PARTNERS

Have partners take turns reading aloud pages of the Take-Home Book. As one child reads, the partner should follow the text and clap every time a word with an *r*-controlled vowel is read. Have children repeat the activity focusing first on consonant blends and then on consonant digraphs.

VISUAL LEARNERS *INDIVIDUAL*

Ask children to write their own captions for the pictures in the Take-Home Book. Have them underline any consonant blends, consonant digraphs, or *r*-controlled vowels in words they use.

(2)

Inventor Lewis Latimer was born in 1848. As a boy, Latimer's favorite activities were drawing and reading. Latimer became a skilled artist who drew plans for inventors. One of the people he worked for was A. G. Bell, inventor of the telephone.

Latimer went on to make his own discoveries. One of his inventions greatly improved the lightbulb. Thomas Edison had already invented a lightbulb, but it was lit by a thin thread of paper that burned out quickly. Lewis Latimer invented a thread made of carbon, which helped the bulb last longer. Thanks to Latimer, electric lights became more popular.

(3)

Not all inventors are grown-up. Austin Meggitt was only nine years old when he came up with his invention. Austin liked to play baseball, but he had trouble carrying his bat, glove, and ball on his bicycle. He decided he should invent a carrier for his bike that would hold his baseball gear. He named it the "Glove and Battie Caddie." Austin won a prize for his invention. He was also voted into the Inventors Hall of Fame.

88 Review r-controlled vowels, blends, digraphs: Take-home book

CURRICULUM CONNECTIONS

LANGUAGE ARTS

Suggest that children write a poem about one of the inventions described in the Take-Home Book. Explain that the poem can be serious or funny. Invite children to share their work with the class. Collect the poems together in a class book and display it in the Reading Center for all to enjoy.

SOCIAL STUDIES

Have children brainstorm a list of items they use every day. Then, have each child choose one or more items from the list and do some research to find out how it was invented and who invented it. Suggest that children use reference books, as well as Internet sources. Invite children to share what they discovered with the class.

SCIENCE

Invite children to work together to write a description for a new invention. Suggest that they build models, using paper, cardboard, boxes, twist ties, string, and other available materials. Display children's inventions during a class "Invention Convention."

TECHNOLOGY **AstroWord** Consonant Blends & Digraphs; r-Controlled Vowels

AUDITORY LEARNERS GROUPS

Have partners take turns reading the pages of the story aloud. After reading each page, the reader identifies words that have consonant blends, consonant digraphs, or r-controlled vowels. The listener identifies the specific letters that make up the phonics element in each word.

CHALLENGE

Challenge children to come up with an invention of their own. Suggest that it can be something serious or something silly. Then, have them describe their inventions in a paragraph or two and include an illustration.

EXTRA SUPPORT/INTERVENTION

Materials: index cards

Make letter cards out of index cards. Use the letter cards to build words from the story that contain r-controlled vowels. As each word is formed, have children substitute letters to form other words with the same vowel + r combination. Repeat the activity with words that contain consonant blends and consonant digraphs. See Daily Phonics Practice, pages 215–217.

Unit Checkup

Review Compounds, Blends, Y as a Vowel and Consonant, Consonant Digraphs, R-Controlled Vowels

Skill Focus

Children will

★ use words with consonant blends in context.

★ identify consonant digraphs in words.

★ read and sort words with *y* as a vowel and consonant.

★ identify *r*-controlled vowels in words.

★ identify compound words in the context of a story.

▶ Teach

Phonemic Awareness: Phoneme Isolation
Have volunteers say words that end with the same vowel sound as *fly*. (*try, spy, why*) Repeat the activity for words that end like *pony*. (*baby, every, very*) Then, remind children that *y* can also be used as a consonant.

Have children identify the consonant digraph that they hear as you say these word groups.

- **chain**   **bench**   **matches** *(ch)*
- **shadow**   **wishes**   **rush** *(sh)*
- **thing**   **north**   **birthday** *(th)*

Ask children to identify the *r*-controlled vowel sound heard as you say these word groups.

- **lord**   **pork**   **morning** *(or)*
- **first**   **squirrel**   **bird** *(ir)*
- **smart**   **spark**   **arm** *(ar)*

Sound to Symbol Write the following word pairs on the board: *skin, desk; stamp, fast; spin, wasp; starve, feast.* Ask volunteers to identify the initial and final blends common to both. (*sk, st, sp, st*)

▶ Practice and Apply

Assess Skills For the first activity on page 89, have children read each sentence with their word choice to make sure it makes sense. For the second activity, suggest that children look for a pair of consonants in each word that stand for one sound.

For page 90, review the directions for each activity to make sure children understand what to do.

89

Name _____

▶ Fill in the circle next to the word with a consonant blend that best completes each sentence.

1. Glenn built a wooden _____.
   ○ coat   ● raft   ○ left

2. He used _____ to tie it together.
   ○ coat hangers   ○ felt   ● string

3. He hoped it would _____.
   ● float   ○ four   ○ flee

4. Then the first warm day of _____ arrived.
   ○ winter   ● spring   ○ yesterday

5. Glenn carefully pushed his raft into the _____.
   ○ post   ○ pink   ● pond

6. Would it _____ under the water?
   ○ drink   ● sink   ○ think

7. Glenn was very happy because it _____ afloat!
   ○ played   ○ trapped   ● stayed

8. Glenn is very _____ of the raft he built himself.
   ● proud   ○ sad   ○ unhappy

▶ Say each word. Circle the consonant digraph.

9. ele(ph)ant   10. (ch)eese   11. s(ch)ool   12. (kn)ee   13. e(ch)o

14. (th)ree   15. si(gn)   16. tou(gh)   17. (wr)en   18. (ch)eck

19. (th)ese   20. (wh)isper   21. mat(ch)   22. ti(ck)et   23. bir(th)day

Consonant blends and digraphs: Assessment   **89**

FOCUS ON ALL LEARNERS

ESL/ELL ENGLISH LANGUAGE LEARNERS

Incorporate kinesthetic learning into your Unit Checkup.

- Prepare questions using a variety of assessment strategies, such as incomplete sentences, same-or-different, and so on. Print on separate cards and place one each in an envelope.

- Place the envelopes in different places around the classroom.

- Ask English language learners to number sheets of paper to correspond to your games. Have children go to an envelope, open it, and print the answer to the word game on their paper.

KINESTHETIC LEARNERS GROUPS

Materials: index cards, boxes

Have children label boxes *digraphs, blends,* r-*controlled vowels, compound words,* y *as a vowel,* y *as a consonant.* Then, have children write words from the lesson on cards and ask classmates to sort them by placing them in the correct boxes.

VISUAL LEARNERS PARTNERS

Have partners play "I Spy" with the words on pages 89 and 90. One player chooses a word and gives a clue; for example, *I spy a compound word that starts with a blend.* The partner then looks for that word on the pages and identifies it. (*treetops*)

> Look at the words in the box. Write each word in the correct column.

beauty	every	fry	spry	year	yesterday

Y = a consonant	**Y = long e**	**Y = long i**
1. year	2. beauty	3. spry
4. yesterday	5. every	6. fry

> Say the first word in each row. Circle the word with the same r sound.

7.	**farm**	(parking)	worst	third	burn
8.	**corn**	purse	cough	fire	(forty)
9.	**tiger**	(clerk)	alarm	snore	park
10.	**squirrel**	wrote	morning	(birthday)	like

> Read the paragraph. Circle the compound words. Write the words on the lines.

Last (weekend,) my family and I went to the zoo. The day was bright with (sunshine,) so we didn't need our (overcoats.) My sister wanted to see the monkeys. The (zookeeper) told us to look for them in the (treetops.) All we could see were (peanut) shells falling from the trees. When we looked up, there were the monkeys!

11. weekend	12. sunshine	13. overcoats
14. zookeeper	15. treetops	16. peanut

90 R-controlled vowels, compounds, y as a vowel: Assessment

ASSESS UNDERSTANDING OF UNIT SKILLS

STUDENT PROGRESS ASSESSMENT

Review the observational notes you made as children worked through the activities in this unit. Your notes will help you evaluate the progress children have made with the phonics skills in this unit.

PORTFOLIO ASSESSMENT

Review the materials children have collected in their portfolios. You may wish to have interviews with children to discuss their written work and the progress they have made since the beginning of the unit. As you review children's written work, evaluate how well they apply the phonics skills they have learned. Have them set future goals.

DAILY PHONICS PRACTICE

For children who need additional practice with the unit skills, quick reviews are provided on pages 214–217 in Daily Phonics Practice.

PHONICS POSTTEST

To assess children's mastery of the unit skills, use the posttest on pages 53g–53h.

AUDITORY LEARNERS GROUPS

Create a small baseball diamond in a part of the classroom, labeling home plate and the bases. Children take turns "at bat." Give a blend, digraph, or vowel + *r* for the child to match with a word (first base); spell the word (second base); use the word in a sentence (third base). A correct response from the next player sends the child to home plate.

CHALLENGE

Challenge children to list words that feature three of the unit phonics elements, for example, a compound word that has a blend and a digraph, like *flashlight*. Have children share their lists with the class.

EXTRA SUPPORT/INTERVENTION

Help children review the unit by completing the pages with them orally, letting them read the items and answer choices aloud to you. See Daily Phonics Practice, pages 214–217.

Teacher Notes

UNIT 4

Contractions, Plurals, Suffixes

THEME: A WORKING WORLD

CONTENTS

Student Performance Objectives

In Unit 4, children will review and extend their understandings of contractions, plurals, inflected endings, comparatives, and suffixes within the theme "A Working World." As children practice using structural analysis to decode words, they will be able to

▶ Identify contractions and the words from which they are formed

▶ Identify when to add -s and -es to make plural forms

▶ Add inflectional endings -s, -ed, -ing to base words

▶ Add suffixes -ful, -less, -y, -ly, -ness, -er, -est, -able, -ible, -ion, -ment, and -en to base words

▶ Identify words that require spelling changes when adding a suffix

▶ Identify the base words of words with suffixes

▶ Identify syllables in words with suffixes

Overview of Resources

LESSON	MCP PHONICS AND READING LIBRARY, LEVEL C PROGRAM	TITLE	DAILY PHONICS PRACTICE
41: Contractions	RR, Stg Five, Bk 29	*A Pot of Stone Soup*	217
42: Contractions	RR, Stg Five, Bk 5	*Three Wishes*	217
43: Plurals -s, -es (ss, x, ch, sh)	RR, Stg Five, Bk 4	*Winter's Song*	218
44: Plurals of words ending in y	RR, Stg Five, Bk 9	*Suki and the Case of the Lost Bunnies*	218
45: Plurals -es for words ending f and fe	NC, Set 4	*Gray Wolf*	218
46: Ending and Suffixes	NC, Set 4	*How Mother Nature Got Her Job*	218–219
47: Doubling final consonants	RR, Stg Five, Bk 6	*Moon Stories*	218–219
48: Suffixes and endings: words ending in e	RR, Stg Five, Bk 7	*Bedtime at Aunt Carmen's*	218–219
49: Suffixes and endings: words ending in e	RR, Stg Five, Bk 8	*The Fox and the Crow*	218–219
50: Review suffixes and endings	RR, Stg Five, Bk 2	*All About Bats*	218–219
51: Suffixes -ful, -ly, -less, -ness, -er, -est	RR, Stg Five, Bk 10	*Sarah's Lovely Songs*	219
52: Suffixes -ion, -ment, -en, -able, -ible	NC, Set 4	*At Home on the Earth*	219
53: Review suffixes; syllables in words with suffixes and endings	NC, Set 3	*Josh and T.J.*	218–219
54: Review suffixes; words with suffixes and endings	NC, Set 3	*The Plant That Almost Ate the World*	218–219
55: Review contractions, plurals, suffixes, and endings	FC, Set 2	*Let's Build a Playground*	217–219
56: Take-Home Book: "Working in a Zoo"			217–219
57: Unit Checkup			217–219

RR—Reader Readers   Stg—Stage   Bk—Book   FC—First Chapters   NC—Next Chapters

Assessment Options

In Unit 4, assess children's ability to read and write contractions and words with plural forms, inflectional endings, and comparative forms. Use the Unit Pretest and Posttest for formal assessment. For ongoing informal assessment, you may wish to use children's work on the Review pages, Take-Home Books, and Unit Checkups. Encourage children to evaluate their own work and to participate in setting goals for their own learning.

ESL/ELL The skills in this unit may be problematic for English language learners. Note pronunciation difficulties as they occur, but assess performance based upon children's ability to distinguish specific sounds when pronounced by a native speaker. For additional support for English language learners, see page 91j.

FORMAL ASSESSMENT

Use the Unit 4 Pretest, on pages 91e–91f, to help assess a child's knowledge at the beginning of a unit and to plan instruction.

ESL/ELL Before administering the Pretest, review the concepts orally with children, using charts or the chalkboard to summarize and practice rules for forming plurals, contractions, or adding endings to base words. Read directions aloud and model how to complete the test pages.

Use the Unit 4 Posttest, on pages 91g–91h, to help assess mastery of unit objectives and to plan for reteaching, if necessary.

INFORMAL ASSESSMENT

Use the Review pages, Unit Checkup, and Take-Home Books in the student book to provide an effective means of evaluating children's performance.

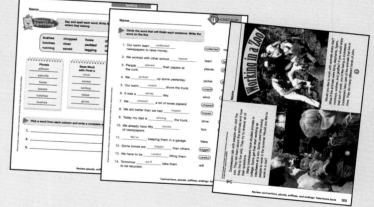

Unit 4 Skills	Review pages	Checkups	Take-Home Books
Contractions	121–122	125–126	123–124
Plurals -s, -es	111–112, 121–122	125–126	123–124
Inflectional endings -s, -ed, -ing; Comparatives -er, -est	111–112, 121–122	125–126	123–124
Doubling final consonants	111–112, 121–122	125–126	123–124
Words ending in e	111–112, 121–122	125–126	123–124
Suffixes -ful, -ly, -less, -ness, -er, -est, -y	121–122	125–126	123–124
Suffixes -en, -able, -ible, -ion	121–122	125–126	123–124
Syllables/Suffixes	121–122	125–126	123–124

STUDENT PROGRESS CHECKLIST

Use the checklist on page 91i to record children's progress. You may want to cut the sections apart to place each child's checklist in his or her portfolio.

PORTFOLIO ASSESSMENT

This logo appears throughout the teaching plans. It signals opportunities for collecting student work for individual portfolios. You may also want to include the Pretest and Posttest, the Review pages, the Unit Checkup, Phonics & Reading, and Phonics & Writing pages.

PHONEMIC AWARENESS AND PHONICS ASSESSMENT

Use PAPA to obtain an itemized analysis of children's decoding skills.

PAPA Skills	MCP Phonics Lessons in Unit 4
Deleting sounds	Lessons 53, 54

Pretest and Posttest

DIRECTIONS

To help you assess children's progress in learning Unit 4 skills, tests are available on pages 91e–91h.

Administer the Pretest before children begin the unit. The results of the Pretest will help you identify each child's strengths and needs in advance, allowing you to structure lesson plans to meet individual needs. Administer the Posttest to assess children's overall mastery of skills taught in the unit and to identify specific areas that will require reteaching.

ESL/ELL Support English language learners by implementing any of the following suggestions before or during test taking, as appropriate.

• Model procedures for marking test answers. Complete several items together or in small groups.

• Conduct the test one-on-one with children who are unable to read independently in English or who need special pacing. Provide frequent support for their efforts.

• Use word lists, charts, and word wheels to provide pretest familiarity with the answer choices.

• Most English language learners have little experience forming contractions using an apostrophe, as this form does not exist in many languages other than English. Provide frequent opportunities to develop a base knowledge of this concept.

PERFORMANCE ASSESSMENT PROFILE

The following chart will help you identify specific skills as they appear on the tests and will enable you to identify and record specific information about an individual's or the class's performance on the tests.

Depending on the results of each test, refer to the Reteaching column for lesson-plan pages where you can find activities that will be useful for meeting individual needs or for daily phonics practice.

Answer Keys

Unit 4 Pretest, page 91e (BLM 22)

1. they've	7. we've	12. brushes
2. can't	8. I'm	13. ducks
3. here's	9. knives	14. elves
4. they'll	10. cherries	15. watches
5. it's	11. lilies	16. stories
6. we're		

Unit 4 Pretest, page 91f (BLM 23)

17. moving	26. home-less
18. cooler	27. fruit-ful
19. harmful	28. soft-en
20. breakable	29. stick-y
21. careless	30. teach-er
22. tasted	31. sad-ness
23. kindness	32. thank-less
24. softly	33. grace-ful
25. shortest	34. fast-est

Unit 4 Posttest, page 91g (BLM 24)

1. don't	7. they're	12. clouds
2. I'm	8. we've	13. shelves
3. they'll	9. puppies	14. bunches
4. you've	10. lives	15. ferries
5. he's	11. dishes	16. boxes
6. that's		

Unit 4 Posttest, page 91h (BLM 25)

17. quickly	26. taste-less
18. tallest	27. sink-a-ble
19. colorful	28. fol-low-ing
20. running	29. kind-ly
21. usable	30. dream-er
22. helpless	31. hard-en
23. worked	32. sick-ness
24. darkness	33. spoon-ful
25. noisier	34. small-est

Performance Assessment Profile

Skill	Pretest Questions	Posttest Questions	Reteaching Focus on All Learners	Daily Phonics Practice
Contractions	1–8	1–8	93–96, 121–124	217
Plurals -s	13	12	97–98, 121–124	218
Plurals -es (ss, x, ch, sh)	12, 15	11, 14, 16	97–98, 121–124	218
Plurals -s, -es (y)	10, 11, 16	9, 15	99–100, 121–124	218
Plurals for f, fe	9, 14	10, 13	101–102, 121–124	218
Suffixes with no spelling changes	18–21, 23–25	17–19, 22–24	103–104, 111–116, 121–124	218–219
Suffixes with spelling changes	17, 22	20–21, 25	105–112, 121–124	218–219
Syllables in words with suffixes	26–34	26–34	117–124	218–219

Name _____

> **Fill in the circle beside the contraction for each set of words.**

1.	they have	○ theyve	2.	can not	○ can't
		○ they've			○ ca'nt
3.	here is	○ here's	4.	they will	○ the'll
		○ her's			○ they'll
5.	it is	○ its	6.	we are	○ w'are
		○ it's			○ we're
7.	we have	○ we've	8.	I am	○ I'm
		○ weve			○ Im

> **Fill in the circle beside the correct plural form of the word.**

9.	knife	○ knifes	10.	cherry	○ cherries
		○ knives			○ cherrys
11.	lily	○ lilies	12.	brush	○ brushs
		○ lilys			○ brushes
13.	duck	○ duckes	14.	elf	○ elfs
		○ ducks			○ elves
15.	watch	○ watchies	16.	story	○ stories
		○ watches			○ storys

Go to the next page.→

BLM 22 Unit 4 Pretest: Contractions, plurals

Name _____

> Read each sentence. Fill in the circle beside the word choice that best completes the sentence.

17. The windshield wipers are _____ too slowly. ○ move ○ moving

18. It is _____ in the shade than in the sun. ○ cooler ○ coolest

19. A ladybug will eat _____ insects that hurt plants. ○ harmful ○ harmless

20. Do not drop the glass. It's _____. ○ breaking ○ breakable

21. Sara made some _____ mistakes. ○ careless ○ caring

22. Those pancakes _____ delicious. ○ tasteful ○ tasted

23. It is good to treat all animals with _____. ○ kinder ○ kindness

24. Mary hummed the song _____ to herself. ○ soft ○ softly

25. That puppy has the _____ legs I have ever seen. ○ shortest ○ shorter

> Fill in the circle beside the word in each box that is correctly broken into syllables.

26.	27.	28.
○ home-less ○ homel-ess	○ fru-itful ○ fruit-ful	○ sof-ten ○ soft-en
29.	30.	31.
○ stic-ky ○ stick-y	○ tea-cher ○ teach-er	○ sad-ness ○ sa-dness
32.	33.	34.
○ than-kless ○ thank-less	○ grace-ful ○ gra-ceful	○ fast-est ○ fas-test

Possible score on Unit 4 Pretest is 34. Number correct _____

BLM 23 Unit 4 Pretest: Suffixes

91f

Name _____

> ► **Fill in the circle beside the contraction for each set of words.**

1.	do not	○ don't ○ dont	2.	I am	○ I'am ○ I'm
3.	they will	○ the'yll ○ they'll	4.	you have	○ you've ○ youve
5.	he is	○ he's ○ hes	6.	that is	○ that's ○ tha'ts
7.	they are	○ they're ○ theye	8.	we have	○ we've ○ w'eve

> ► **Fill in the circle beside the correct plural form of the word.**

9.	puppy	○ puppys ○ puppies	10.	life	○ lives ○ lifes
11.	dish	○ dishies ○ dishes	12.	cloud	○ cloudes ○ clouds
13.	shelf	○ shelfs ○ shelves	14.	bunch	○ bunches ○ bunchs
15.	ferry	○ ferrys ○ ferries	16.	box	○ boxes ○ boxs

Go to the next page. →

Name _____

> Read each sentence. Fill in the circle beside the word choice that best completes the sentence.

17. Dan's sled goes very _____.   ○ quicker   ○ quickly

18. Molly is the _____ girl in the class.   ○ tallness   ○ tallest

19. Adam's drawing is _____.   ○ colorful   ○ coloring

20. Mom is _____ to catch the bus.   ○ runing   ○ running

21. This old pen is still _____.   ○ usable   ○ useable

22. A baby chick is _____.   ○ helper   ○ helpless

23. Nancy _____ hard to finish the test.   ○ worked   ○ workable

24. The owl's eyes glowed in the _____.   ○ darkly   ○ darkness

25. The city is _____ than the country.   ○ noisier   ○ noise

> Fill in the circle beside the word in each box that is correctly broken into syllables.

26.	○ taste-less ○ tast-eless	27.	○ sink-a-ble ○ sink-ab-le	28.	○ fol-lo-wing ○ fol-low-ing
29.	○ kind-ly ○ ki-ndly	30.	○ drea-mer ○ dream-er	31.	○ harde-n ○ hard-en
32.	○ sick-ness ○ sic-kness	33.	○ spoonf-ul ○ spoon-ful	34.	○ small-est ○ sma-llest

Possible score on Unit 4 Posttest is 34. Number correct _____

BLM 25 Unit 4 Posttest: Suffixes

Student Progress Checklist

Make as many copies as needed to use for a class list. For individual portfolio use, cut apart each child's section. As indicated by the code, color in boxes next to skills satisfactorily assessed and insert an *X* by those requiring reteaching. Marked boxes can later be colored in to indicate mastery.

Student Progress Checklist

Code: ■ Satisfactory   ☒ Needs Reteaching

Student: _____ _____ Pretest Score: _____ Posttest Score: _____	**Skills** ☐ Contractions ☐ Plurals *-s, -es (ss, x, ch, sh)* ☐ Plurals *-s, -es (y)* ☐ Inflectional Endings *-s, -ed, -ing* ☐ Comparatives *-er, -est* ☐ Doubling Final Consonant ☐ Words Ending in *e* ☐ Suffixes *-ful, -y, -ly, -less, -ness* ☐ Suffixes *-ion, -ment, -en, -able, -ible* ☐ Syllables with Suffixes	**Comments / Learning Goals**
Student: _____ _____ Pretest Score: _____ Posttest Score: _____	**Skills** ☐ Contractions ☐ Plurals *-s, -es (ss, x, ch, sh)* ☐ Plurals *-s, -es (y)* ☐ Inflectional Endings *-s, -ed, -ing* ☐ Comparatives *-er, -est* ☐ Doubling Final Consonant ☐ Words Ending in *e* ☐ Suffixes *-ful, -y, -ly, -less, -ness* ☐ Suffixes *-ion, -ment, -en, -able, -ible* ☐ Syllables with Suffixes	**Comments / Learning Goals**

BLM 26 Unit 4 Checklist

ESL/ELL English Language Learners

Throughout Unit 4 there are opportunities to assess English language learners' ability to read and write contractions and words with plural forms, inflectional endings, comparatives, and suffixes. Recognizing and pronouncing words with these phonic elements may be especially problematic for English language learners. Take note of pronunciation difficulties as they occur, and assess progress based on children's ability to distinguish specific sounds when pronounced by a native speaker.

Lesson 41, pages 93–94 Native speakers of Spanish may be familiar with contractions (*al, del*), but not with the apostrophe used to show the letters that are left out. Provide plenty of visual examples, converting uncontracted forms to contracted forms.

Lesson 42, pages 95–96 English language learners may not be fully aware of the baseline beneath the letters of a contracted word and may, therefore, confuse the apostrophe with a comma. Reinforce written punctuation through practice.

Lesson 43, pages 97–98 The ability to distinguish between sibilant sounds such as those of *x, z, ss, sh,* or *ch* is dependent on the phonetics of the speaker's first language. English language learners may have difficulty perceiving meaningful differences between certain pairs of these sounds.

Lesson 44, pages 99–100 English language learners may have no experience in forming plurals of words ending in *y* and making spelling changes accordingly. Point out that the sound of *y* and *ie* is the same.

Lesson 46, pages 103–104 Many languages other than English do not use inflectional endings to mark verb tenses. Children may need help understanding that these endings tell when the action of the verb takes place.

Lesson 47, pages 105–106 English language learners may not hear the difference between the sound of a final *-n* and that of a final *-ng* and say *runin* instead of *running*. Demonstrate the position of the open mouth as you model each sound; practice with *plan, planning; turn, turning;* and *clean, cleaning*.

Lesson 48, pages 107–108 Children who speak languages in which syllables normally end in vowels may find it difficult not to pronounce the "silent *e*" because they want to add a neutral vowel following the final consonant. Have children practice writing and saying *hide, ride, frame, take,* and so on.

Lesson 49, pages 109–110 Unlike English, some languages distinguish consonants that are aspirated, or pronounced with a puff of air, from those that are not. Children may experience some confusion with the inflectional ending *-ed* in various contexts. Provide oral practice as needed.

Lesson 50, pages 111–112 Note that *er* in Spanish stands for a different sound from *er* in English, and children may say *late air* for *later*, and so on. If necessary, provide oral practice with words such as *taller, harder, faster,* and *longer*.

Lesson 51, pages 113–114 Children whose home language is Cantonese, Hmong, Vietnamese, Korean, or Khmer come from monosyllabic-language backgrounds. Overstressing the suffixes for clarity may mislead English language learners into thinking two-syllable words are two separate words.

Lesson 54, pages 119–120 Native speakers of Spanish will have little difficulty making the sound of *y*, since *y* in Spanish also functions as a vowel and a consonant. Other English language learners should consider the different sounds as they do long and short vowel differences—as two sounds for the same letter.

Spelling Connections

INTRODUCTION

The Unit Word List is a list of selected spelling words drawn from this unit. The words are grouped by these categories; contractions, plurals and inflectional endings, and suffixes. To incorporate spelling into your phonics program, use the activity in the Curriculum Connections section of each teaching plan.

ESL/ELL It is recommended that English language learners reach the intermediate fluency level of English proficiency before focusing on spelling. For English language learners, introduce 6–8 words at a time. Help children understand the words' meanings by using visuals or realia.

The spelling lessons utilize the following approach for each category of words.

1. Administer a pretest of the words, some of which have not yet been introduced. Dictation sentences are provided.

2. Provide practice.

3. Reassess. Dictation sentences are provided.

A midunit review focusing on contractions, plurals, and words with inflectional endings appears in Lesson 50 on page 112 of the teacher's edition. An end-of-unit test focusing on words with suffixes appears in Lesson 55 on page 122 with the option of giving a cumulative test by including the words on page 112.

DIRECTIONS

Make a copy of Blackline Master 27 for each child. After administering the pretest for each category of words, give each child a copy of the appropriate word list.

Children can work with a partner to practice spelling the words orally and identifying the phonics elements in each word. You may want to challenge children to add inflectional endings and suffixes to words other than those on the spelling list. Children can write words of their own on *My Own Word List* (see Blackline Master 27).

Have children store their list words in an envelope in their books or notebooks. You may want to suggest that children keep a spelling notebook, listing words with similar patterns. Another idea is to build Word Walls with children and display them in the classroom. Each section of the wall can focus on words with a single phonics element. The walls will become a good resource for children to use when they are engaged in writing.

Unit Word List

Contractions
there's
couldn't
you'll
they've
I'd
let's

Plurals and Inflectional Endings
pillows
foxes
babies
knives
dressed
opening

Suffixes
illness
likable
brighten
slowly
restful
useless

Name _____

Phonics & Spelling Say and spell each word. Write the words on the note pad where they belong.

bushes	chopped	foxes	gives	losses
lunches	nicer	padded	pencils	pillows
running	saved	tagging	takes	writing

Plurals
pillows
pencils
foxes
losses
lunches
bushes

Base Word with Final e
nicer
saved
writing
takes
gives

Final Consonant Doubled Before Adding Ending
running
tagging
chopped
padded

Pick a word from each column and write a complete sentence that uses the word.

1. _____
2. _____
3. _____

Review plurals, suffixes, and endings: Spelling **121**

Name _____

 **UNIT 4 WORD LIST**

Contractions

there's
couldn't
you'll
they've
I'd
let's

Plurals and Inflectional Endings

pillows
foxes
babies
knives
dressed
opening

Suffixes

illness
likable
brighten
slowly
restful
useless

My Own Word List

BLM 27 Unit 4 Spelling Words

911

Phonics Games, Activities, and Technology

The following collection of ideas offers a variety of opportunities to reinforce phonics skills while actively engaging children. The games, activities, and technology suggestions can easily be adapted to meet the needs of your group of learners. They vary in approach so as to consider children's different learning styles.

GROUP CONTRACTION CONCENTRATION

Write each of the following contractions and word pairs on separate sheets of paper: *there is, there's; it is, it's; they have, they've; you would, you'd; do not, don't; I would, I'd;* and *we are, we're.* Give the papers to 14 volunteers who stand across the front of the room with the blank side of the paper facing the rest of the group. Children play concentration by asking two children at a time to turn around their words. If a match of a word pair and contraction is made, the two children stand off to the side. Play until all matches have been made.

JOBS WITH -ING

Ask children to name careers and brainstorm verbs that describe what people do in these jobs, such as *drive, sing, act, serve, teach, sell, help, make, bake, repair, clean, rescue, build, design, write, paint, print,* and *protect.* After you have created a list of 18 words, provide copies of Blackline Master 28, "A Working World." Have children work in pairs to copy each word in one of the circles on the game board. To play a game, partners take turns choosing a word on the board and spelling aloud the *-ing* form, dropping final *e* as necessary. As words are chosen and correctly spelled, ask children to cover them with game markers, buttons, or circles cut from paper.

SPIN AND SPELL

Make a large game spinner by attaching an arrow to the center of a paper plate. Draw lines to make six sections on the plate, and write one of these suffixes in each section: *-er, -est, -ful, -ness, -less, -ly.* Write several base words from the lessons in Unit 4 across the chalkboard. Children take turns spinning the arrow and choosing a word on the board to which the suffix can be added. The new word is written on the board under the base word. Pay attention to necessary spelling changes as words are written.

ONE WOLF, TWO

Invite children to work in pairs to fold a sheet of paper into 16 squares. Write the following words on the board: *wolf, leaf, calf, knife, elf, loaf, scarf, shelf.* Invite partners to write the words in eight of the squares and write the plural forms of the words in the remaining eight squares. Children can draw objects of the words if they wish. Then, have them cut apart the squares and use them to play a matching game. To play, have them mix up the cards and place them face down in a pile. Each player can take two cards. They take turns asking one another for a card to make a match. If no match can be made, the player can take a card from the pile. Play until singular and plural forms of all the words have been paired.

-S OR -ES?

Make available a set of base word cards to which *-s* or *-es* must be added to form the plural. You might include words such as *box, dress, class, dog, card, patch, dish, six, brush, door, watch, puppet, clock, glass, letter, gift,* and *egg.* Partners can use the cards to sort the words into two groups, those words requiring *-s* and those requiring *-es.* Children can write the plural forms on paper in two groups to verify.

WORD PUZZLES

Write on strips of paper or index cards words that have suffixes and no spelling changes. Then, cut each card, splitting the base word from the suffix with an irregular edge. Put the cards in a decorative envelope and invite children to piece the words together like puzzles.

NEW SHOES?

Write the poem at the right on the chalkboard or on chart paper. After reading the poem aloud with children, invite them to find the words that end with *-y.* Encourage them to figure out which of those words are base words with a suffix added. Invite children to underline each word and spell the base word. You might also have children find the two contractions in the poem and spell the two words that make each contraction.

> My shoes are new and squeaky shoes,
> They're very shiny, creaky shoes.
> I wish I had my leaky shoes
> That mother threw away.
> I liked my old brown leaky shoes
> Much better than these creaky shoes,
> These shiny, creaky, squeaky shoes
> I've got to wear today.

CAREER TRAITS

Write the following words on the chalkboard: *cheery, lucky, healthy, thoughtful, hopeful, adaptable, lively, careful, helpful, playful, kindly, likable, artful, graceful, tricky, friendly, sensible, bravest, speedy.* Ask children which of these traits describe them. Ask for a few examples of careers that they think might require some of the same traits. Then, provide pairs of children with a copy of Blackline Master 28, "A Working World." Have partners copy the words from the board to write in the circles on the game board. To play a game, partners take turns choosing a word, spelling the base word, and naming a career that requires such a trait. Children can color in the circles as words are used.

PENNY HOCKEY

Provide each child with a 2-×-12-inch strip of heavy tagboard or posterboard. First, have children write the suffixes *-ful, -ly, -less,* and *-able* across the strip, leaving two inches at each end. Then, have them fold each end to make the strip stand as shown. To play penny hockey, give each pair a penny and have partners stand up their suffix strips facing one another to form "goals" on either end of a desk. Then, using one finger, a player must flick the penny to the other side of the desk, trying to hit the suffix strip. If the penny misses, the other player takes a turn. If the penny hits the strip, the child names a word with the suffix that has been hit by the penny. Players get one point for getting the penny in the goal and a second point if they can name a word that has the suffix. Have children keep score with tally marks. Repeat the game with the suffixes *-en, -ible, -ion, -ment,* and *-y.*

SPELLING SYLLABLES

Invite children to choose a partner. Say the following words one at a time, emphasizing the syllable breaks: *healthy, tricky, useless, darken, sadly, neatness, cleaning, illness, brighten, teacher, oldest, shipment, lovable, smoothest, slowly, bumpy, coldest, foxes, restful.* As each word is said, invite one child in a pair to spell the first syllable of the word and the partner to spell the second syllable. Once children are comfortable with the procedure, two pairs of children can do the activity together, asking one another to spell syllables in words.

IT'S IN THE BAG

Write the following words on slips of paper: *dresses, daisies, spoonful, quickness, colorless, gladly, youngest, longer, windy, napping, smiled, frighten, likable, sensible, movement, invention.* Put the words in a paper bag. Invite children to sit in a circle. Play music as children pass the bag around. When the music stops, the child with the bag must remove a slip, read the word, and spell the base word. Play continues until all words have been read.

WHERE DO YOU WORK?

Write the following words associated with careers on the board: *office, school, company, factory, truck, bakery, greenhouse, farm, zoo, museum, ranch, hotel, train, fire station, hospital, library, store, restaurant.* Ask children to describe the kind of work that goes on in each of these locations. Then, provide partners with a copy of Blackline Master 28, "A Working World." After partners copy each word from the board in a circle on the sheet, have them take turns tossing a button onto the game board and spelling the plural form of the word on which the button landed.

CONTRACTION BUILDERS

Provide children with sets of letter cards and an apostrophe card. As you say two words, such as *you have, is not, he is, I am, will not, can not, would not, she will, we have,* see how quickly children can use the letter cards to form the corresponding contraction. Children can follow a similar procedure with a partner by taking turns telling each other a word pair from which to build a contraction.

TECHNOLOGY

The following software products reinforce children's understanding of a variety of phonics skills.

Word Munchers® Deluxe
Word recognition, rhyming, and phonics are the skills practiced as children (ages 8–12) zoom through mazes with a "munching" character. The mazes contain words and objects to be munched according to rules displayed on the screen.

** Riverdeep The Learning Company
   500 Redwood Blvd.
   Novato, CA 94947
   (800) 825-4420
   www.learningcompanyschool.com

Phonics, Reading and Writing Excelerator
This four-disc set is packed with more than 30 individual lessons and over 200 activities. Each program is designed to help first-time readers with basic skill sets, while reinforcing key concepts like uppercase and lowercase letters, phonics, word formation, sentence structure, and creative composition.

** Topics Entertainment
   1600 SW 43rd St.
   Renton, WA 98055
   (425) 656-3621
   www.topics-ent.com

Name _____

BLM 28 Unit 4 Activity

91p

Home Connections

The Home Connections features of this program are intended to involve families in their children's learning and application of phonics skills. Three effective opportunities to make connections between home and school include the following.

- **HOME LETTER**
- **HOME NOTES**
- **TAKE-HOME BOOKS**

HOME LETTER

A letter is available to be sent home at the beginning of Unit 4. This letter informs family members that children will be learning to read and write contractions, plurals, and words with suffixes and endings within the context of the unit theme, "A Working World." The suggested home activity focuses on pictures in magazines that show different kinds of work people do. This activity promotes interaction between child and family members while supporting children's learning of reading and writing contractions and words with endings. The letter, available in both English and Spanish, also suggests theme-related books family members can find in the library and enjoy reading together.

HOME NOTES

Whenever the Home logo appears within the student book, a phonics activity is suggested to be done at home. The activities are simple to do, requiring little or no preparation or special materials, and are meant to reinforce the targeted phonics skill.

TAKE-HOME BOOKS

Within the student book are Take-Home Books that can be cut out and assembled. The story language in each book reinforces the targeted phonics skills. The books can be taken home and shared with family members. In Unit 4, one Take-Home Book is available, focusing on contractions, plurals, and suffixes as well as the unit theme, "A Working World."

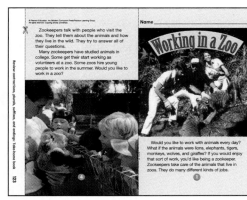

Home Notes in Spanish are also available for both teachers and parents to download and use from our website, www.PlaidPhonics.com.

Pages 91–92

Contractions, Plurals, and Suffixes

Skill Focus

Assess Prior Knowledge

To assess children's prior knowledge of contractions, plurals, and suffixes, use the pretest on pages 91e–91f.

Unit Focus

Build Background

- Write the theme title "A Working World" on the board, read it aloud, and help children find it on page 91. Engage children in a discussion about different kinds of work and the people who do it. Invite children to talk about workers they know.

- Ask children if they can identify the animal skeleton in the picture on page 91. Tell them that it is the skeleton of a dinosaur called Tyrannosaurus rex or T. Rex. The bones were found in South Dakota by a scientist named Susan Hendrickson.

- Read the text aloud. Point out that fossils help scientists determine what life was like millions of years ago.

Introduce Plurals and Suffixes

- Write the words *fossils* and *scientists* on the board. Explain that the words, called plurals, mean "more than one." Ask children to find other plurals in the selection.

- Write *called* and *trying*. Underline *-ed* in *called*, and *-ing* in *trying*. Have children find other story words with the endings *-ed* and *-ing*.

- Write the word *you're* on the board. Explain that *you're* is a contraction, or two words written as one. An apostrophe is used to show that a letter is missing from the second word. Invite children to identify the two words that make up *you're*. (*you are*) Have them find another contraction. (*you've*)

Critical Thinking Discuss the kinds of things a dinosaur hunter does. Then, ask volunteers to respond to the Talk About It question.

Read Aloud

The Dinosaur Hunters

Imagine that you've just discovered the complete skeleton of a brand-new dinosaur. You'd be famous!

Scientists who study ancient life are called paleontologists (pay-lee-on-TAH-luh-gists). They study fossils — traces of living things that are sometimes found in rocks. Much of their time is spent working in labs or museums. When these scientists do go on a dinosaur "dig," they might spend hours carefully chipping one piece of bone from a rock. Finding a complete skeleton is remarkable.

Still, you might get lucky. That happened to fossil collector Susan Hendrickson. She discovered the finest skeleton of a giant T. Rex ever found. It was nicknamed "Sue" in her honor.

TALK About It Do you think you would like to become a dinosaur hunter? Why or why not?

Unit 4 • Introduction
Critical Thinking 91

THEME FOCUS

A WORKING WORLD!

Reread the unit theme. Then, write these categories on the board: *Medicine, Sports, Food, Science, Communication,* and *Transportation.* Invite children to name careers for each of the categories. Then, have children suggest other categories and offer the names of careers for each of them.

CONTRACTION GUESSING GAME

Have partners provide clues describing a job and ask classmates to guess what the job is. Write the following sentence frames on the board for children to use as they give their clues.

You'll see me _____.   I'm a person who _____.
Example: You'll see me in a field. I'm a person who plows.

ROLE-PLAYING WORK

Have partners or small groups act out different work situations. Suggest roles such as police officer/driver, teacher/students, coach/players, clerk/shopper, waiter/customer.

HOME LETTER

Dear Family,

In this unit about "A Working World," your child will learn about contractions, plurals, and suffixes. As your child becomes familiar with these skills and concepts, you might try these activities together.

▶ With your child, draw pictures or cut pictures from magazines to illustrate different kinds of careers. Glue them on sheets of paper, one career per sheet. Then help your child label each page. Staple the sheets together or tie them together with yarn.

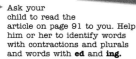

▶ Ask your child to read the article on page 91 to you. Help him or her to identify words with contractions and plurals and words with **ed** and **ing.**

▶ Your child might enjoy reading these books with you. Look for them in your local library.

Library Lil by Suzanne Williams

Breakout at the Bug Lab by Ruth Horowitz

Sincerely,

_____

Estimada familia:

En esta unidad, que trata sobre "A Working World" ("Un mundo trabajador"), su hijo/a estudiará contracciones, plurales y sufijos. A medida que su hijo/a se vaya familiarizando con estas destrezas y conceptos, pueden hacer las siguientes actividades juntos.

▶ Con su hijo/a, hagan dibujos o recorten fotos que ilustren diferentes tipos de profesiones. Péguenlos sobre hojas de papel. Después, ayuden a su hijo/a a escribir un título para cada ilustración. Engrapen juntas las hojas o átenlas con un cordón de estambre.

▶ Pidan a su hijo/a que les lea el artículo en la página 91. Ayúdenlo/a a identificar palabras con contracciones, palabras en plural y palabras que terminan en **ed** y **ing.**

▶ Ustedes y su hijo/a disfrutarán leyendo estos libros juntos. Búsquenlos en su biblioteca local.

Library Lil de Suzanne Williams

Breakout at the Bug Lab de Ruth Horowitz

Sinceramente,

_____

92
Unit 4 • Introduction

- The Home Letter on page 92 will acquaint family members with the phonics skills children will be studying in this unit. Children can tear out page 92 and take it home.

- You may want to suggest that children complete the activities on the page with a family member. Urge children to look in the library for the books suggested and read them with family members.

LEARNING CENTER ACTIVITIES

WRITING CENTER

Have children write character sketches of people they know in the "working world." Suggest that they interview the people to discover what a typical workday is like. Then, have them use their notes to write an "on-the-job" description of the person. Suggest that children include a drawing or photograph of the person at work. Use children's character sketches to make a display entitled "Our Working World."

SCIENCE CENTER

Have children think about science careers and write down the name of the career they think would be most interesting, such as astronaut, inventor, medical researcher, tornado chaser, zoo director, and veterinarian. Compile a class list to determine if there is a favorite career.

MATH CENTER

Have children imagine they are chefs and they must prepare a lunch for a group of 25 children. What should they serve? Invite children to work in small groups to create a menu, figure out the quantity of food they will need for each item, and determine the cost. Suggest that children refer to newspaper ads to check the prices of food items.

BULLETIN BOARD

Create a bulletin board display with a picture of Earth in the center and the title "A Working World." Show "spokes" of yarn from the center to other circles. Have children write the names of careers ending with *-er* in each circle and draw pictures to illustrate their ideas.

Contractions

Skill Focus

Children will

★ identify contractions and the two words from which they are made.

★ write contractions to complete sentences.

ESL/ELL Native speakers of Spanish may be familiar with contractions (al, del), but not with the apostrophe used to show the letters that are left out. Provide plenty of visual examples, converting uncontracted forms to contracted forms.

Teach

Introduce Contractions List the following word pairs on the board: *did not, you have, we will, that is.* Explain that each of these pairs of words can be written as a contraction. Tell children that a contraction is a short way of writing two words. It is formed by putting two words together and leaving out one or more letters. An apostrophe is used to show where the letters were left out. Next to each word pair write its contraction: *didn't, you've, we'll, that's.* Then, ask children to tell how the contractions compare to the words. *(Some letters are left out. There is an apostrophe in the contraction.)*

Have children name the letters that were left out when each contraction was written *(o, ha, wi, i).* Point to the apostrophe in one of the contractions and call on a volunteer to explain its purpose. *(to show where one or more letters have been left out)* You may wish to give an example of an exception such as the word *won't,* in which the *ill* in *will* is changed to *o.*

Practice and Apply

Writing Have children read the rule on page 93 and explain how it applies to the words *I'm* and *we'll.* Make sure children understand the directions on pages 93 and 94. Invite volunteers to state the directions in their own words.

For the activity at the bottom of page 94, suggest that children read each sentence with their choice of contraction in place to be sure that the sentence makes sense.

Reading Use *A Pot of Stone Soup,* MCP Phonics and Reading Word Study Skills Library 1, Level C, to provide additional practice in identifying contractions.

Name _____

> Read each contraction. Write the two words that make each contraction. Then write the letter or letters that were left out.

DEFINITION

A **contraction** is a short way of writing two words. It is formed by putting two words together and leaving out one or more letters. Use an apostrophe (') to show where something is left out.
I am = I'm   we will = we'll

Contraction	Two Words	Letters Left Out
1. isn't	is not	o
2. there's	there is	i
3. haven't	have not	o
4. wouldn't	would not	o
5. you've	you have	ha
6. it's	it is	i
7. let's	let us	u
8. don't	do not	o
9. they've	they have	ha
10. couldn't	could not	o
11. he's	he is	i

Contractions: 't, 's, 've   **93**

FOCUS ON ALL LEARNERS

ESL/ELL ENGLISH LANGUAGE LEARNERS

Assess whether English language learners recognize and understand both uncontracted and contracted forms of words.

- Model for children the uncontracted form of selected word pairs by using each word in a sentence set in an everyday context, such as "Tomorrow *we will* have recess in the park"; or "This is *not* a nice day." Write the sentences on the board. Use gestures, props, and facial expressions to convey meanings.

- Model the same sentences spoken with the contracted forms. Write the sentences on the board. Say the sentences with and without contractions to contrast. Have children repeat.

VISUAL LEARNERS

Have partners write nine contractions on a tic-tac-toe grid and *X*s and *O*s on self-stick notes. Players take turns naming the two words that form one of the contractions on the grid and placing an *X* or an *O* on the matching contraction.

Contractions

Find a contraction in the word box to match each pair of words. Write the contraction on the line.

1.
isn't	
I'm	
I've	
we're	

_I'm_ — I am
isn't — is not
_we're_ — we are
_I've_ — I have

2.
it's	
wouldn't	
weren't	
didn't	

weren't — were not
wouldn't — would not
_it's_ — it is
didn't — did not

3.
let's	
wasn't	
we'll	
you'll	
you're	

you'll — you will
you're — you are
let's — let us
wasn't — was not
_we'll_ — we will

4.
shouldn't	
aren't	
that's	
they'll	
won't	

that's — that is
they'll — they will
won't — will not
aren't — are not
shouldn't — should not

Complete each sentence using a contraction from the box below.

| we'll | It's | aren't | won't | I've |

5. _____It's_____ going to be a fine day for a hike.

6. _____I've_____ been looking forward to it.

7. First _____we'll_____ walk through the forest.

8. I hope the trails _____aren't_____ muddy.

9. We _____won't_____ get home until evening.

 HOME Ask your child which words make up the contractions in the word boxes.

CURRICULUM CONNECTIONS

SPELLING

Use these words and sentences as a pretest for writing contractions.

1. **there's**   **There's** a bee on my shoulder.
2. **couldn't**   Ron **couldn't** wait to eat lunch.
3. **you'll**   **You'll** have fun at the zoo.
4. **they've**   **They've** just gotten off the boat.
5. **I'd**   **I'd** like to tell you a story.
6. **let's**   **Let's** go for a walk.

WRITING

Suggest that children write their own stories about something they enjoy doing outdoors. Encourage children to use contractions in their writing.

SOCIAL STUDIES

Talk about tips about what to take along and what to do for people who are going on a hike in the forest. Have children list their ideas. Tips might include: *wear hiking boots or sturdy shoes, take a jacket, carry water and food, take along a trail map or compass,* and *don't hike alone.*

KINESTHETIC LEARNERS   GROUPS

Write six contractions and corresponding word pairs each on a sheet of paper. Have twelve volunteers stand, each holding the blank side of a paper toward the group. Children then take turns playing a game of "Concentration," asking two volunteers at a time to turn around their papers to see whether they match.

CHALLENGE

Have children write a list of questions that contain contractions. Tell children to exchange papers with classmates and write answers that contain contractions.

EXTRA SUPPORT/INTERVENTION

Help children successfully begin page 93 by working with them to complete some of the items. For the first activity on page 94, suggest that children first draw lines to connect matching pairs. See Daily Phonics Practice, page 217.

Integrating Phonics and Reading

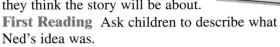

Guided Reading

Ask a volunteer to read the title and invite children to discuss the cover. Then, ask children what they think the story will be about.

First Reading Ask children to describe what Ned's idea was.

Second Reading Have children identify selected contractions in the story.

Comprehension

After reading, ask children these questions:
- Why did the woman think Ned's soup tasted just like her own? *Recall/Drawing Conclusions*
- How would you describe Ned's personality? *Reflective Analysis/Character*

ESL/ELL English Language Learners

Point out that in this story each of the character's exact words are enclosed in quotation marks. Point out several examples. Then, have children take the parts of the characters and read the story aloud.

Contractions

Skill Focus

Children will

★ identify contractions in context and write the two words from which they are made.

★ identify and write the contractions that can be made from two words.

★ write a short story using contractions.

ESL/ELL English language learners may not be fully aware of the baseline beneath the letters of a contracted word and may, therefore, confuse the apostrophe with a comma. Reinforce written punctuation through practice.

Teach

Phonological Awareness: Oddity Task
Say each group of three words below and ask children to raise their hands when they hear a contraction. As each contraction is identified, call on volunteers to identify the two words that make it.

- **fast**   **didn't**   **table**
- **she**   **laugh**   **you've**
- **they've**   **could**   **cannot**

Sound to Symbol On the board write *I will, was not, I am, we have, that is.* Ask children to write the contraction that stands for each pair of words. Then, have them circle the letter(s) in each uncontracted form that were replaced by an apostrophe. Finally, have volunteers write other contractions on the board, followed by the words from which they are made.

Practice and Apply

Reading Suggest that children first read the story on page 95 and then go back to circle contractions. To build background, point out that the word *paleontologist* was used in the article on page 91.

Critical Thinking Discuss with children the kinds of things scientists do and how they go about their work. Then, have them respond to the Talk About It question at the bottom of page 95.

Writing When children finish writing their stories, ask volunteers to name the contractions they used and the words they stand for.

Reading Use *Three Wishes,* MCP Phonics and Reading Word Study Skills Library 1, Level C, to provide additional practice in identifying contractions.

Name _____

▶ Read the story and circle each contraction. On the lines at the bottom of the page, write the two words that make up each contraction you circled.

A Puzzling Situation

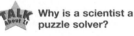

"(There's) *T. rex!*" said Sam excitedly as he and Alice ran up the stairs in the museum.

"How do scientists put these bones together?" asked Alice.
"(It's) like a puzzle," said a man behind them. "(I'm) Dr. West, museum paleontologist. (I'd) be happy to help you."

"(Let's) see *Triceratops!*" exclaimed Alice as they walked to the next skeleton.

"(Here's) an interesting dinosaur," said Sam. "How did you know where each bone would fit?"

"(That's) a good question," said Dr. West. "It (isn't) easy, but (we're) able to use computers to help us with the bones (we've) found. Then (we're) ready to solve the puzzle!"

"(Wouldn't) that be fun to try!" said Alice.

"(You're) both welcome to watch us someday," said Dr. West. "(You'd) really enjoy it."

"I think (I'll) be a paleontologist. Then (I'd) be a puzzle solver!" said Sam.

"(We'll) both be puzzle solvers," said Alice quickly. "(I'd) like to be a paleontologist, too!"

1.	there is	2.	it is	3.	I am
4.	I would	5.	let us	6.	here is
7.	that is	8.	is not	9.	we are
10.	we have	11.	we are	12.	would not
13.	you are	14.	you would	15.	I will
16.	I would	17.	We will	18.	I would

 Why is a scientist a puzzle solver?

Contractions: 't, 's, 've, 'm, 're, 'll, 'd, critical thinking   **95**

FOCUS ON ALL LEARNERS

- -

ESL/ELL ENGLISH LANGUAGE LEARNERS

Assess English language learners' ability to form and use contractions by reviewing at random contracted forms.

- On the board, write word pairs that make up contractions, using an equal sign to show that the contracted form means the same thing as the uncontracted form. Have volunteers complete the contractions for you. Model where to place and to write the apostrophe.

- Read aloud the directions on pages 95 and 96 and model how to do each activity. If necessary, complete the activities with children, having them repeat the answers chorally.

AUDITORY LEARNERS   GROUPS

Write several word pairs on the board, such as *do not, he is, you are, will not, they have, are not,* and *it will.* Say each word pair, ask a child to point to the words, say a contraction for the word pair, and use the contraction in a sentence.

VISUAL LEARNERS GROUPS

Write contraction equations on the board for children to complete, such as *I + will =, he + is =, they + are =, we + have =, did + not =.* Ask children to write their own equations.

Write the contraction that can be made from the two words.

1. I am	I'm	2. are not	aren't
3. can not	can't	4. should not	shouldn't
5. could not	couldn't	6. did not	didn't
7. he is	he's	8. we will	we'll
9. does not	doesn't	10. let us	let's
11. here is	here's	12. you will	you'll
13. I have	I've	14. will not	won't
15. you are	you're	16. they have	they've
17. she is	she's	18. we have	we've
19. I will	I'll	20. it is	it's

Write a story using five of the contractions that you wrote above.

_____

_____

_____

_____

_____

_____

_____

96 Review contractions

HOME Ask your child to read the story he or she wrote, and name the words that make up each contraction.

CURRICULUM CONNECTIONS

SPELLING

Use these words and sentences as a posttest for writing contractions.

1. **there's**   **There's** an airplane in the sky.
2. **couldn't**   Eva **couldn't** find her pencil.
3. **you'll**   I think **you'll** enjoy the book.
4. **they've**   **They've** just returned home.
5. **I'd**   Dad asked what **I'd** like to do.
6. **let's**   **Let's** play a guessing game.

WRITING

Suggest that children think about what they would like to know about paleontology and write a letter posing questions to Dr. West. When children have finished, have them circle the contractions.

SCIENCE

Ask children to name dinosaur facts that they think are true. List them on the board. Then, have children use resources to verify whether the facts are true. Review children's results as a class.

KINESTHETIC LEARNERS GROUPS

Have children form teams and line up at the board. Say two words that can make a contraction. The first person in each team writes the words, the second person writes the contraction, and the third person writes the missing letters. The first team to finish earns a point. Continue with other words.

CHALLENGE

Challenge children to write riddles in which they use contractions. For example: _It has teeth, but it can't chew. (comb)_ Invite children to share their riddles with the class.

EXTRA SUPPORT/INTERVENTION

Materials: index cards

Use index cards to make letter and apostrophe cards. Invite children to use the cards to build two words you say and then replace one or more letters with the apostrophe to form a contraction. See Daily Phonics Practice, page 217.

Integrating Phonics and Reading

Guided Reading

Ask a volunteer to read the title aloud. Then, invite children to talk about what they would wish for if they could wish for anything they wanted.

First Reading Have children describe the three wishes in the order in which they were made.

Second Reading Have children identify the contractions in the story.

Comprehension

After reading, ask children these questions:

• Why did the man get angry at his wife? _Recall/Cause and Effect_

• Did the story turn out the way you expected? Explain. _Reflective Analysis/Personal Response_

ESL/ELL English Language Learners

Read a page of the book as children listen for contractions. If they hear one, have them raise a hand. Call on a volunteer to find, point to, and read the contraction in the text.

Plurals -s, -es

Skill Focus

Children will

★ read and identify words with the plural suffixes -s and -es.

★ distinguish between the use of -s and -es to form plurals.

ESL/ELL The ability to distinguish between sibilant sounds such as those of *x, z, ss, sh,* or *ch* is highly dependent on the phonetics of the speaker's first language. English language learners may have difficulty perceiving meaningful differences between certain pairs of these sounds. Practice word pairs within noted areas of difficulty.

Teach

Introduce Plurals with -s and -es Say the words *book* and *books* and ask children which word means one and which means more than one. On the board, write *trees, pencils,* and *crayons.* Ask volunteers to identify the letter that was added to the end of each word to make it mean "more than one." *(-s)* Explain that the plural of most words is formed by adding *-s.*

Then, write *boxes, bushes, glasses,* and *branches* on the board. Have children identify the letters that were added to each word to make it plural. *(-es)* Point out that when a word ends in *x, sh, ss,* or *ch,* the letters *-es* are added to make the plural.

Practice and Apply

Sound to Symbol Read aloud the rule on page 97 and explain how it applies to the words *pear* and *box.* For the activity on page 97, suggest that children say the picture name before they decide which word to circle.

Writing Read aloud the rule on page 98 and explain how it applies to the example words. For the first activity on the page, suggest that children look at the ending of each word before they write its plural form. Read aloud the definition in the middle of the page. Point out that the plural endings on words are suffixes. The word without the plural ending is called a base word.

Reading Use *Winter's Song,* MCP Phonics and Reading Word Study Skills Library 1, Level C, to provide additional practice in identifying words with plural endings.

97

Name _____

▶ Circle the word that names each picture. Then color the pictures that show more than one.

> **RULE**
> When **s** or **es** is added to a word it forms the plural. Plural means "more than one." See how the ending **s** or **es** makes these words mean more than one.
> one pear   two pear**s**
> one box   many box**es**

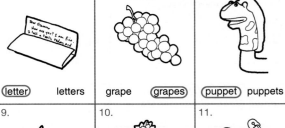

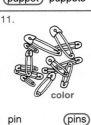

1. color	2. color	3.	4. color
box **(boxes)**	brick **(bricks)**	**(coat)** coats	dish **(dishes)**
5.	6. color	7.	8. color
(letter) letters	grape **(grapes)**	**(puppet)** puppets	egg **(eggs)**
9. color	10.	11. color	12.
star **(stars)**	**(gift)** gifts	pin **(pins)**	**(watch)** watches

Plural endings: -s, -es, Sound to symbol   **97**

FOCUS ON ALL LEARNERS

ESL/ELL **ENGLISH LANGUAGE LEARNERS**

Assess whether English language learners understand that *-s* or *-es* is used to show that a word refers to more than one.

• Introduce singular and plural by holding a single pencil, saying "pencil," then holding up several pencils and saying "pencils," stressing the final *-s* and pointing to all the pencils.

• In many languages nouns do not change form to indicate number. Help English language learners to understand the motivation for writing words with *-s* or *-es* by giving examples.

KINESTHETIC LEARNERS

Materials: index cards

Make word cards for lesson words such as *bunch, glass, dress, patch, dish, lunch, letter, egg,* and *box* and two cards each for *s* and *es.* Have two teams take turns choosing a word card and forming its plural with an *s* or *es* card.

VISUAL LEARNERS   INDIVIDUAL

Invite children to write paragraphs about a walk in the woods, using plural forms of such words as *branch, fox, bush, tree, bird,* and *squirrel.* Have children exchange papers and read each other's paragraph to see how their walks compare.

Write the plural form of the word in parentheses.

> **RULE**
> If a word ends in **ss, x, ch,** or **sh,** add the ending **es** to make it mean more than one.
>
> | | |
> |---|---|
> | one porch | two porch**es** |
> | one class | many class**es** |
> | one fox | three fox**es** |
> | one brush | some brush**es** |

1. five (cross) _____crosses_____
2. some (glass) _____glasses_____
3. those (box) _____boxes_____
4. cake (mix) _____mixes_____
5. seven (dress) _____dresses_____
6. few (church) _____churches_____
7. three (ax) _____axes_____
8. many (dish) _____dishes_____

Underline the word in each sentence that means more than one. Then write its base word on the line.

> **RULE**
> The word to which a suffix or ending is added is called the **base word.**

9. Kim is busy packing <u>boxes</u>. _____box_____
10. She is using <u>bunches</u> of paper. _____bunch_____
11. She carefully wraps the good <u>dishes</u>. _____dish_____
12. She puts paper around the <u>glasses</u>. _____glass_____
13. Then she packs her <u>dresses</u>. _____dress_____
14. Her favorite is the one with <u>patches</u> on it. _____patch_____
15. She does not pack her <u>paintbrushes</u>. _____paintbrush_____
16. She ties them together in <u>batches</u>. _____batch_____
17. She needs them for her art <u>classes</u>. _____class_____
18. She studies during her <u>lunches</u>. _____lunch_____

 HOME Ask your child to think of more words with plural forms ending in -es.

98 Plurals: Words ending in ss, x, ch, and sh, Words in context

---

CURRICULUM CONNECTIONS

SPELLING

Use these words and sentences as a pretest for writing plurals and words with inflected endings.

1. **pillows**   The **pillows** feel soft.
2. **foxes**   Some **foxes** have red fur.
3. **babies**   The **babies** are finally asleep.
4. **knives**   These **knives** are not sharp.
5. **dressed**   Sarah **dressed** her doll.
6. **opening**   Dad is **opening** the window.

WRITING

Have children create imaginary shopping lists for a trip to the supermarket. Explain that their lists should include both singular and plural words. When they have finished their lists, ask children to underline the plural words they used. Then, have them circle the -s or -es ending in each plural.

 TECHNOLOGY   **AstroWord** Base Words and Endings

AUDITORY LEARNERS **GROUPS**

Materials: small box wrapped in white paper

Label a covered box by writing *s* on three sides and *es* on the other three sides. Have children sit in a circle and take turns tossing the box (as though rolling a die). The child uses the *s* or *es* ending on the side of the box facing up to spell a plural word.

CHALLENGE

Invite children to make up rhymes using plurals that end in *-s* or *-es.* Explain that the poems can be silly or serious. Here is an example: *I saw four goats. They were rowing four boats. The man held two boxes. Inside were two foxes.*

EXTRA SUPPORT/INTERVENTION

Materials: pictures of singular and plural objects

Provide children with pictures of plural and singular objects. Ask them to sort the pictures into two groups: those that show one item and those that show more than one item. Help them name each plural object and label the picture. Then, have children sort the plurals according to *-s* or *-es* endings. See Daily Phonics Practice, page 218.

Integrating Phonics and Reading

Guided Reading

Ask children to read the title and look at the cover. Have them talk about what a winter's song might be. You may also wish to use the English Language Learners activity below.

First Reading Have children describe examples of winter's song as illustrated in the story.

Second Reading Ask children to identify plural nouns used in the story.

Comprehension

After reading, ask children these questions:
- What different sounds make up a winter's song? *Recall/Comparisons*
- Do you think the children in the story like winter? Why or why not? *Inference/Details*

ESL/ELL **English Language Learners**

Tell children that some words in the story express exactly how things sound. Point out examples, such as *rumble, crash,* and *swoosh.* Then, ask children to find other similar words in the story.

Plurals of Words Ending in y

Skill Focus

Children will

★ identify when to add *-s* and when to add *-es* to form the plural of nouns ending in *y*.

★ read and write the plural forms of words ending in *y* in context.

ESL/ELL English language learners may have no experience in forming plurals of words ending in *y* and making spelling changes accordingly. Point out that the sound of *y* and *ie* is the same.

Teach

Introduce Plurals of Words Ending in y

Use letter cards to build the words *gift, day, watch,* and *box*. Ask children to use additional letter cards to change the words to their plural forms. *(gifts, days, watches, boxes)*

Write the words *toy* and *berry* on the board. Give volunteers the opportunity to spell the plural form of the words orally. Then, write *toys* and *berries* on the board. Lead children to see that some words must be changed before adding *-es* to form the plural. Then, ask what was changed in the word *berry* to make it plural. *(The y was changed to i and -es was added.)*

Explain that if a word ends in a consonant and *y*, the *y* is changed to *i* and *-es* is added to make it plural. If a word ends in a vowel and *y*, the word stays the same and an *-s* is added to make it plural.

Practice and Apply

Writing Read aloud the rule at the top of page 99 and explain how it applies to the example words. For the first activity on page 99 and for the activity on page 100, suggest that children look at the ending of each base word before they decide how to write its plural form. Encourage children to refer to the rule if they are uncertain.

For the second activity on page 99, remind children that when they write the base word for a word whose spelling has changed, they need to change the spelling back to what it was before the plural suffix was added.

Reading Use *Suki and the Case of the Lost Bunnies,* MCP Phonics and Reading Word Study Skills Library 1, Level C, to provide additional practice in identifying the plural forms of words that end in *y*.

Name _____

> Write the plural form of the word in parentheses.

> **RULE**
> If a word ends in a consonant and **y,** change the **y** to **i** and add **es.** If a word ends in a vowel and **y,** just add **s.**
> one baby   two bab**ies**
> one jay   many jay**s**

1. three (cherry)   cherries
2. some (lily)   lilies
3. eight (fairy)   fairies
4. those (fly)   flies
5. two (party)   parties
6. nine (tray)   trays
7. few (boy)   boys
8. many (chimney)   chimneys
9. four (day)   days
10. all (turkey)   turkeys

> Underline the word with a suffix in each sentence that means more than one. Then write its base word on the line.

11. Lucy and Mom went downtown to buy groceries.   grocery
12. They always had fun on shopping days.   day
13. Lucy saw some puppies in a pet store window.   puppy
14. Two ladies worked in the store.   lady
15. One woman said Lucy could pet the puppies.   puppy
16. "They're as soft as bunnies," Lucy said.   bunny
17. Just then two boys came into the store.   boy
18. Their families came in, too.   family
19. They had traveled from one of the nearby cities to buy a puppy.   city

Plurals: -s, -es with words ending in y, Words in context   **99**

FOCUS ON ALL LEARNERS

ESL/ELL ENGLISH LANGUAGE LEARNERS

Teach the plural endings of words that end in *y* by using the activity at the top of page 99.

- Write *boy, day, tray, chimney,* and *turkey* on one side of the board, and *cherry, lily, fairy, fly,* and *party* on the other. Present the rule to children by using these words as specific examples. Ask volunteers to give the plural of each word. As volunteers pronounce each plural, write it beside the singular form.

- Carefully pronounce and reiterate each plural form. Point out the vowel + *y* or consonant + *y* ending for each word.

- Have children work in pairs to read and write the plurals in items 1–10 on page 99. Have volunteers say the words aloud.

KINESTHETIC LEARNERS

Materials: index cards

Use index cards to make letter cards. Have children work in groups of three. One child gathers letters that spell a word ending in *y* and mixes the cards. Another child unscrambles the letters to make the word. The third child adds and manipulates letters to change the word to its plural form.

Look at each picture. Then read the word below the line. Change the word to mean more than one. Write the new word on the line.

Animals

puppies
(puppy)

monkeys
(monkey)

turkeys
(turkey)

jays
(jay)

bunnies
(bunny)

ponies
(pony)

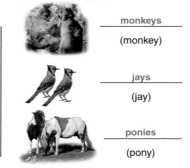

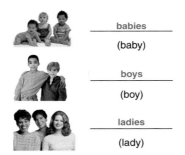

Flowers

daisies
(daisy)

lilies
(lily)

pansies
(pansy)

People

babies
(baby)

boys
(boy)

ladies
(lady)

100 Plurals: -s, -es with words ending in y

SPELLING

Have children unscramble words you write on the board. Begin with the letters *i a b b s e* for the word *babies*. Continue with the words *ladies, flies, pansies, ponies, stories,* and *cities.*

WRITING

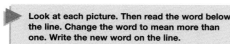

Ask children to write a counting book that could be used to teach preschoolers the numbers one through ten. Suggest that the book feature an animal whose name ends in *-y* on each page. Possibilities include *monkey, pony, turkey, puppy, kitty, bunny, donkey, fly, canary,* and *blue jay.* Share the number books with a preschool class.

SCIENCE

Have children use field guides to find out facts about wild turkeys, blue jays, canaries, or other birds they see around the school or their homes. Ask children to share their findings with the class.

TECHNOLOGY   **AstroWord** Base Words and Endings

VISUAL LEARNERS   PARTNERS

Have partners use the plurals of words ending in *y* to complete sentences. Provide sentence frames such as the ones below.

1. The _____ are sleeping.
2. What are the _____ doing?
3. Catch those _____!
4. The large _____ are from the farm.

CHALLENGE

Ask children to write silly sentences using pairs of plural words that rhyme. Here are some examples: *There were **flies** buzzing around the **pies**. Blue jays are musical **birds** whose songs never have any **words**.*

EXTRA SUPPORT/INTERVENTION

Help children complete both sections of page 99. Have them read each item aloud and say the answer before writing it. See Daily Phonics Practice, page 218.

Integrating Phonics and Reading

Guided Reading

Call on volunteers to read the title and describe what is happening in the cover illustration. Then, invite them to predict what the story will be about.

First Reading Have children describe all the different bunnies Suki found.

Second Reading Have children identify plural forms of story words ending in *y*.

Comprehension

After reading, ask children these questions:

• How does Suki Wong describe herself? *Recall/Character*

• What did Sam mean when he said his bunnies hop up and down? *Inference/Details*

ESL/ELL English Language Learners

Point out that Suki Wong found many bunnies, but none of them were the ones that Sam lost. Invite children to leaf through the book and use word and picture clues to describe the bunnies Suki found.

Plural -es for Words Ending in f and fe

Children will

★ read and write the plural forms of words ending in *f* or *fe*.

★ write the plural forms of words ending in *f* or *fe* to complete sentences.

★ match words ending in *f* and *fe* and their plurals with definitions.

Teach

Introduce Plurals of Words Ending in f and fe Write these words on index cards: *leaf, wolf, calf, elf, knife, wife, life, leaves, wolves, calves, elves, knives, wives, lives.* Distribute the cards. Ask each child to read the word and tell whether it names one or more than one. Then, have children display their cards and walk around the room to match singular words with plural forms.

Write the words *leaf* and *life* on the board. Point out that *leaf* ends in *f* and *life* ends in *fe*. Explain that if a word ends in *f* or *fe*, the *f* or *fe* is changed to *v* and *-es* is added to make the word plural. Ask children to write the plural forms of *leaf* and *life* on the board. Walk them through the steps if needed.

Write the words *wolf, scarf, wife,* and *knife* on the board. Ask volunteers to write the plural form of each word.

Practice and Apply

Writing Read aloud the rule at the top of page 101 and explain how it applies to the example words. For the first activity on page 101, point out that children will be writing the plural form of each word in parentheses. Suggest that they pay particular attention to how each word ends before deciding how to write its plural form. For the activity at the bottom of the page, suggest that children read each sentence with their word choice in place to make sure the sentence makes sense.

Read the hint at the top of page 102 with children. You may wish to review how to complete a crossword puzzle.

Reading Use *Gray Wolf,* MCP Phonics and Reading Word Study Skills Library 1, Level C, to provide additional practice in identifying the plural forms of words that end in *f* or *fe*.

101

Name _____

> Write the plural form of the word in parentheses on the line.

RULE
If a word ends in **f** or **fe**, change the **f** or **fe** to **v** before adding the ending **es**.
one thief   several thie**ves**
one life   nine li**ves**

1. these (leaf) _____leaves_____   2. six (calf) _____calves_____
3. those (wolf) _____wolves_____   4. few (knife) _____knives_____
5. four (shelf) _____shelves_____   6. several (elf) _____elves_____
7. two (half) _____halves_____   8. few (wife) _____wives_____
9. ten (thief) _____thieves_____   10. many (life) _____lives_____

> Write a word from the box below to complete each sentence. Then write its base word on the line.

calves	knives	leaves
lives	loaves	scarves
shelves	wives	wolves

11. Long ago, pioneers led hard _____lives_____.   life

12. The men built _____shelves_____ to store things on.   shelf

13. They built barns for the cows and their _____calves_____.   calf

14. They had to protect the animals from _____wolves_____.   wolf

15. Pioneer _____wives_____ worked as hard as their husbands.   wife

16. Each week they baked _____loaves_____ of bread.   loaf

17. They used _____knives_____ to cut the bread into thick slices.   knife

18. They made medicine from _____leaves_____ and roots.   leaf

19. At night, the women knitted warm _____scarves_____.   scarf

Plurals: -es with words ending in f and fe, Words in context   **101**

FOCUS ON ALL LEARNERS

ESL/ELL ENGLISH LANGUAGE LEARNERS

This activity gives English language learners extra practice reading and writing the plural forms of words ending in *f* or *fe*.

• On the board, write *half, shelf, life,* and *wife,* along with their plural forms. Help children identify the similarities between these words and their plural forms. (*Two of the words end in* f *and two end in* fe. *All plural forms end in* ves.)

• Underline the final letters in each word (*f, fe, ves*). Say the final sounds of each word clearly, pointing to the underlined letters as you do so. Have children repeat after you.

KINESTHETIC LEARNERS

Have groups line up in teams in front of the board. Draw on the board a large box for each team. Have team members, in turn, fill their boxes by writing the plural form of the words you say. Use these words: *leaf, calf, half, knife, loaf, shelf, wife, elf, life.*

VISUAL LEARNERS PARTNERS

Materials: index cards

Partners make word cards by writing singular and plural forms of words ending in *f* and *fe* each on an index card. They can use the cards to play "Concentration," matching both forms of a word.

Read each clue. Find the word in the box that matches the clue. Then, write the word in the crossword puzzle.

HINT
Singular means one. Plural means more than one.

Crossword grid answers:
1. ELF
4. THIEVES
7. SCARVES
9. WIFES
12. FOXES
13. TURKEYS

elf	thieves	scarves	foxes	loaves
wife	scarf	turkeys	lives	wolf
shelves	axes	elves	car	

Across

1. singular form of elves
4. plural form of thief
7. plural form of scarf
9. singular form of wives
12. plural form of fox
13. plural form of turkey

Down

2. plural form of life
3. plural form of shelf
5. plural form of elf
6. plural form of loaf
8. singular form of scarves
9. singular form of wolves
10. plural form of ax
11. singular form of cars

102 Plurals: -es with words ending in f and fe

 HOME Ask your child to give the singular and plural forms for names of objects around the home.

CURRICULUM CONNECTIONS

SPELLING

Invite children to choose plural forms of words from pages 101 and 102. Suggest they scramble the letters and write the scrambled words on the board. They can call on classmates to unscramble and rewrite the words.

WRITING

PORTFOLIO

Suggest that children write a list of questions they would ask an elf. Encourage them to use plural forms of words ending in *f* and *fe* in their writing. Some examples might include: *How are the lives of elves different from our lives? Why might elves hide among leaves?* Have children interview each other about life as an elf.

SOCIAL STUDIES

Have children find out some facts about wolves and people. Ask: *What kind of characters are most of the wolves in fairy tales? How has our attitude toward wolves changed over time?*

TECHNOLOGY **AstroWord** Base Words and Endings

AUDITORY LEARNERS **GROUPS**

Have children form two teams. Say a word ending in *-ves* and ask a member of the first team to spell the base word and write it on the board. If the word is spelled correctly, continue with a new word for team two. If the word is incorrect, a member from team two can try to spell the word.

CHALLENGE

Challenge children to create word-search puzzles using singular and plural forms of words ending in *f* and *fe*. Make photocopies and distribute the puzzles for classmates to solve.

EXTRA SUPPORT/INTERVENTION

Before children begin page 102, review with them how to complete a crossword puzzle and the meaning of *singular* and *plural*. See Daily Phonics Practice, page 218.

Integrating Phonics and Reading

Guided Reading
Ask a volunteer to read the title. Then, have children turn to the table of contents and read the chapter titles. Ask children to predict what the story will be about.

First Reading Ask children to tell the story in their own words.
Second Reading Ask children to identify plural forms of story words ending in *f* and *fe*.
Comprehension
After reading, ask children these questions:
• Name some things Cally did to let Gray Wolf know she would not harm her. *Recall/Inference*
• Do you think the story was realistic? Explain. *Reflective Analysis/Personal Response*
ESL/ELL English Language Learners
Look at the glossary with children. Explain that a glossary is a list of story words and their definitions. Ask children to find an unfamiliar word in the glossary and read its definition.

Endings and Suffixes

Skill Focus

Children will

★ form new words by adding the endings -s, -ed, and -ing to base words.

★ form new words by adding the suffixes -er and -est to base words.

ESL/ELL Many languages other than English do not use inflectional endings to mark verb tenses. Children who speak such languages may need help understanding that these endings tell when the action of the verbs takes place.

Teach

Introduce Endings Write the word *work* on the board. Add -*s* to make it *works*. Then, erase the -*s* and add -*ed* to make it *worked*. Erase the -*ed* and add -*ing* to make it *working*. Then, write *plays, played,* and *playing* on the board. Ask volunteers to circle the endings -*s*, -*ed*, and -*ing*.

Write *taller* and *tallest* on the board and use the words in sentences to show how the ending -*er* is used to compare two things and -*est* is used to compare more than two things. Explain that -*er* and -*est* are word parts called suffixes. A suffix is added to a base word to make a new word.

Write *teach* and *teacher* on the board to show that -*er* can be added to a word to change its meaning to "a person who."

Practice and Apply

Writing For page 103, point out to children that they are adding endings to base words in the first activity and isolating the base words in the second activity.

Read aloud the definition at the top of page 104. For the first activity, suggest that children determine how many things are being compared in each sentence before deciding which suffix to add.

Read aloud the rule in the middle of page 104. Point out that adding the suffix -*er* to the words in this activity changes their meanings so that they name people who are doing something.

Reading Use *How Mother Nature Got Her Job,* MCP Phonics and Reading Word Study Skills Library 1, Level C, to provide additional practice in identifying words with suffixes.

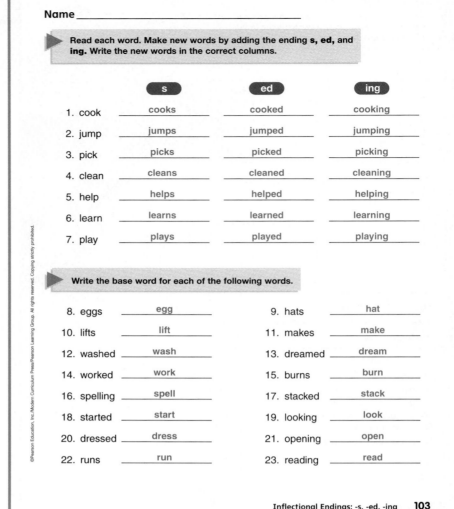

Name _____

▶ Read each word. Make new words by adding the ending **s, ed,** and **ing.** Write the new words in the correct columns.

	s	ed	ing
1. cook	cooks	cooked	cooking
2. jump	jumps	jumped	jumping
3. pick	picks	picked	picking
4. clean	cleans	cleaned	cleaning
5. help	helps	helped	helping
6. learn	learns	learned	learning
7. play	plays	played	playing

▶ Write the base word for each of the following words.

8. eggs	egg	9. hats	hat
10. lifts	lift	11. makes	make
12. washed	wash	13. dreamed	dream
14. worked	work	15. burns	burn
16. spelling	spell	17. stacked	stack
18. started	start	19. looking	look
20. dressed	dress	21. opening	open
22. runs	run	23. reading	read

Inflectional Endings: -s, -ed, -ing   **103**

FOCUS ON ALL LEARNERS

ESL/ELL ENGLISH LANGUAGE LEARNERS

The activities on page 103 provide English language learners with practice identifying and manipulating inflectional endings.

• Introduce the meaning of -*ed* (to show action that has already taken place) by giving clue words such as *yesterday* or *last week*. Some children may find expressing sequence of action confusing.

• Read aloud the directions for both activities on page 103; have children complete items 1–7 in small groups; review aloud together. Then, complete items 8–23 on the board.

AUDITORY LEARNERS GROUPS

Have groups list words that mean "a person who. . .", such as *teacher, singer, worker, farmer,* and *painter.* Then, have children share their ideas about the work these people do. Encourage the use of words with suffixes -*er* and -*est*.

VISUAL LEARNERS PARTNERS

Have children write equations that show the addition of the endings -*s*, -*ed*, -*ing*, -*er*, or -*est* to base words: *think + s = _____*. Ask them to write subtraction equations as well: *tallest – est = _____*. Suggest that partners trade equations to solve.

DEFINITION

Read each sentence. Add **er** or **est** to each word below the line. Write the new word on the line.

A **suffix** is a word part that is added to the end of a base word to make a new word.
The suffix **er** may be used to compare two things. The suffix **est** may be used to compare more than two things.

1. Lisa is _____taller_____ than her sister Nancy.
   (tall)

2. Nancy is _____older_____ than Lisa.
   (old)

3. Their little sister Joy is

   the _____youngest_____ of the three.
   (young)

4. Joy is also the _____shortest_____.
   (short)

5. "Lisa may be tall," says Joy, "but I'm

   _____smarter_____ than she is!"
   (smart)

RULE

Add the suffix **er** to each word. Write the new word on the line.

The suffix **er** sometimes means a *person who.* A teacher is a person who teaches.

6. teach _____teacher_____

8. sing _____singer_____

10. work _____worker_____

12. farm _____farmer_____

7. perform _____performer_____

9. play _____player_____

11. report _____reporter_____

13. print _____printer_____

104 Suffixes: -er, -est, Words in Context

 HOME Ask your child to make sentences that use the words on the lines above.

CURRICULUM CONNECTIONS

SPELLING

On the board, draw five columns headed *-s, -ed, -ing, -er,* and *-est.* Say words with the endings for volunteers to write in the appropriate columns. Begin with the spelling words *dressed, opening, pillows, foxes, knives,* and *babies.*

WRITING

Suggest that children write sentences that compare the heights and ages of people they know by using the base words *tall, short, young,* and *old* and the suffixes *-er* and *-est.* Children may wish to draw pictures to illustrate their sentences.

PORTFOLIO

MATH

Invite children to measure objects in the classroom and record the names of the objects and their lengths (to the nearest inch or centimeter) on chart paper. Then, have them use words with *-er* and *-est* to compare the size and shape of the objects they have measured.

TECHNOLOGY **AstroWord** Suffixes

KINESTHETIC LEARNERS **PARTNERS**

Materials: small objects of different sizes and shapes, a bag

Place a dozen items in a bag. Invite partners to take turns pulling out an item and comparing it to the preceding one, using the comparative form *-er.* (smaller, brighter, straighter, newer) Then, have them choose items that can be described with the comparative form *-est.*

CHALLENGE

Just for fun, suggest that children add *-er* to action words to invent new words that mean "one who." Have them write each word along with a definition, such as: *zoom + er; zoomer, one who travels at high rates of speed: lift + er; lifter, one who lifts heavy objects on the job.*

EXTRA SUPPORT/INTERVENTION

Help children identify the base words at the bottom of page 103 by having them read the words and cover the endings before writing their responses. See Daily Phonics Practice, pages 218–219.

Integrating Phonics and Reading

Guided Reading

Ask volunteers to read the title and describe the cover. Then, involve children in a discussion of what is meant by the term "Mother Nature."

First Reading Have children describe what happened when Demeter became Mother Nature.

Second Reading Ask children to identify story words with inflectional endings and suffixes.

Comprehension

After reading, ask children these questions:

- Why was Demeter Dunn chosen to be Mother Nature? *Recall/Character*
- If you were given the chance to be Mother Nature, what would you do? *Creative/Personal Response*

ESL/ELL English Language Learners

Review chapters 8 and 9. Discuss how Demeter's attitude about being Mother Nature changed. Read aloud dialog in which this change occurs.

Doubling Final Consonants

Skill Focus

Children will

★ identify base words that require doubling a final consonant before adding an ending or a suffix.

★ form new words by adding an ending or a suffix.

★ identify the base words of words with an ending or a suffix.

ESL/ELL English language learners may not hear the difference between the sound of a final *-n* and that of a final *-ng* and say *runin* instead of *running*. Demonstrate the position of the open mouth as you model each sound; practice with *plan, planning*; *turn, turning*; and *clean, cleaning*.

Teach

Introduce Doubling Final Consonants

Ask a volunteer to write the word *slow* on the board. Call on children to add *-er, -est, -ed,* and *-ing* and write the new words. Ask whether they needed to change the base word when they added the suffixes. *(no)*

Write the words *bigger* and *biggest* on the board. Have children tell what they notice about the base word when the suffixes were added. *(The final consonant is doubled.)* Explain that when a word with a short vowel ends in a single consonant, the consonant is usually doubled before adding an ending or a suffix that begins with a vowel.

Practice and Apply

Writing Read aloud the rule at the top of page 105 and explain how it applies to the example words. For the first activity on the page, remind children to double the final consonant of each circled word before adding an ending or a suffix.

For the activity at the top of page 106, suggest that children read each sentence with their new word in place to make sure it makes sense. Remind children that they may have to double the final consonant before adding *-ed, -ing, -er,* or *-est* to a word. For the activity at the bottom of the page, suggest that children divide each word between the double consonants to find the base word.

Reading Use *Moon Stories,* MCP Phonics and Reading Word Study Skills Library 1, Level C, to provide additional practice in identifying words with suffixes.

105

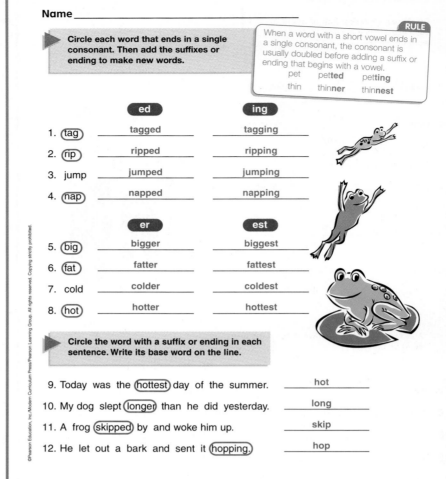

Name _____

> Circle each word that ends in a single consonant. Then add the suffixes or ending to make new words.

RULE
When a word with a short vowel ends in a single consonant, the consonant is usually doubled before adding a suffix or ending that begins with a vowel.
pet   pet**ted**   pet**ting**
thin   thin**ner**   thin**nest**

	ed	**ing**
1. (tag)	tagged	tagging
2. (rip)	ripped	ripping
3. jump	jumped	jumping
4. (nap)	napped	napping

	er	**est**
5. (big)	bigger	biggest
6. (fat)	fatter	fattest
7. cold	colder	coldest
8. (hot)	hotter	hottest

> Circle the word with a suffix or ending in each sentence. Write its base word on the line.

9. Today was the (hottest) day of the summer. _____hot_____

10. My dog slept (longer) than he did yesterday. _____long_____

11. A frog (skipped) by and woke him up. _____skip_____

12. He let out a bark and sent it (hopping.) _____hop_____

Suffixes and endings: Doubling the final consonant   **105**

FOCUS ON ALL LEARNERS

ESL/ELL ENGLISH LANGUAGE LEARNERS

Have children practice adding *-ed, -ing, -er,* and *-est* to base words requiring doubling of final consonants.

• Read aloud the rule on page 105. On chart paper, write the base words in items 1 through 8. Apply the rule for doubling final consonants by having children hold up one finger if a base word ends in a single consonant and two fingers if the word ends in two consonants.

• Read each base word aloud. Have volunteers say and then spell the new words before writing them.

KINESTHETIC LEARNERS

Materials: index cards

Have partners write on the cards base words to which suffixes or endings can be added. Then, have children work together sorting the cards into two groups: words that require spelling changes when a suffix or ending is added and words that do not.

AUDITORY LEARNERS   *INDIVIDUAL*

Review the folk tale of the race between the tortoise and the hare. Have children retell the story, using words such as *faster, fastest, runner, running, slower, stopped,* and *started*.

▶ Complete each sentence by adding the correct suffix or ending to the word in parentheses. Write the word on the line.

1. Ed was tired of _____sitting_____ on the bench. (sit)
2. He _____begged_____ the coach to let him play. (beg)
3. "I'm _____putting_____ you in the game," said the coach. (put)
4. On his first try, Ed just _____tipped_____ the ball. (tip)
5. Then he _____batted_____ the ball past the pitcher. (bat)
6. He began _____running_____ and reached home plate. (run)
7. "Ed's our _____hottest_____ player!" said the coach. (hot)
8. Ed was proud to be a _____winner_____. (win)

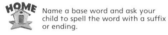

	RUNS	HITS	ERRORS	1	2	3	4	5	6	7	8	9
Home	8	10	4	1	0	1	1	2	1	2		
Visitor	6	8	3	1	2	0	1	0	1			

▶ Write the base word for each of the following words.

9. shopper _____shop_____
11. tagged _____tag_____
13. fanned _____fan_____
15. dripping _____drip_____
17. chopper _____chop_____
19. cutting _____cut_____
21. quitting _____quit_____

10. swimmer _____swim_____
12. stopper _____stop_____
14. petted _____pet_____
16. rubbed _____rub_____
18. biggest _____big_____
20. bigger _____big_____
22. hopping _____hop_____

106 Suffixes and endings: Doubling the final consonant

 Name a base word and ask your child to spell the word with a suffix or ending.

SPELLING

Have children write word equations to show suffixes or endings being added to base words that require spelling changes. Here is an example: *skip + p + ed = skipped.*

WRITING

Have children write a poem about summer, using words with suffixes. Below is an example:

Summer
Hottest, sunniest
swimming, playing ball
trying to keep cool
Vacation

SOCIAL STUDIES

Ask children to name jobs related to sports, including those whose names have the *-er* suffix, such as *player, announcer, coach, referee, umpire, sportswriter, broadcaster, photographer,* and *cheerleader.* Talk about the responsibilities that come with each job.

 **AstroWord** Suffixes

AUDITORY LEARNERS

Have children form two teams. As you say words with suffixes or endings, members of each team take turns calling out "double" if the final consonant in the word is doubled when a suffix or ending is added, or "no change" if no spelling change is made. A team scores a point for each correct call.

CHALLENGE

Challenge children to prepare an activity like the one at the top of page 106 for classmates to complete. The sentences should form a coherent story, and the answer words should be provided in a word bank in random order.

EXTRA SUPPORT/INTERVENTION

Write the following on the board: *fan_ed, beg_ed, beg_ing, tip_ed, tip_ing, hot_er, hot_est, big_er, big_est.* Then, have children use colored chalk to write the doubled consonant and read the word. See Daily Phonics Practice, pages 218–219.

Integrating Phonics and Reading

Guided Reading
Have children read the title, look at the cover, and leaf through the book. Then, invite them to predict what the story will be about.
First Reading Have children describe what Father Sky did to help the moon.
Second Reading Ask children to identify story words with suffixes or endings.
Comprehension
After reading, ask children these questions:
• What does the moon do after Father Sky removes the pin? *Recall/Sequence*
• Do you think this story explains effectively why the moon moves across the sky? Why or why not? *Reflective Analysis/Plot*
ESL/ELL English Language Learners
Invite children to use picture and word clues to retell the story or parts of the story in their own words.

Suffixes and Endings: Words Ending in e

Skill Focus

Children will

★ identify base words that require dropping the final e before adding a suffix or ending.

★ form new words by adding suffixes or endings to base words ending in e.

ESL/ELL Children who speak languages in which syllables normally end in vowels may find it difficult not to pronounce the "silent e" because they want to add a neutral vowel following the final consonant. Have children practice writing and saying *hide, ride, frame, take,* and so on.

Teach

Introduce Dropping the Final e On the board, write *driver, smiled, writing,* and *finest.* Ask volunteers to circle the endings or suffixes and identify the base words. (*drive, smile, write, fine*) Ask how many vowels are in each of the base words. (*two*) Which vowel in each word is silent? (*the final* e) Ask what happens to this silent e when suffixes or endings are added. (*It is dropped.*) Tell children that when a word ends in a silent e, you drop the e before adding an ending or a suffix that begins with a vowel, such as *-er, -ing,* and *-est.*

Write the words *trace, place,* and *lace* on the board. Ask volunteers to erase the final e and add the suffix *-ing.* Repeat with the suffix *-ed.*

Practice and Apply

Writing Read aloud the rule at the top of page 107 and explain how it applies to the words *take* and *large.* You may wish to do the first item in the activity aloud with children to make sure they understand what to do.

Before children begin the activity on page 108, review the rule at the top of the page. Point out that in the activity children will be doing, all the base words end in silent e and all of the suffixes begin with a vowel.

Reading Use *Bedtime at Aunt Carmen's,* MCP Phonics and Reading Word Study Skills Library 1, Level C, to provide additional practice in identifying words with suffixes.

Name _____

Read each sentence. Add a suffix or ending to each word. Then circle the word that completes the sentence.

> **RULE**
> When a word ends in silent **e**, drop the **e** before adding a suffix or ending that begins with a vowel.
> take tak**ing**
> large larg**est**

1. May-ling _____ her music every afternoon.

   practice + es = ⬭(practices) _____ close + es = _____ closes

2. Fluffy is the _____ cat I've ever seen!

   ripe + est = _____ ripest _____ cute + est = ⬭(cutest)

3. Chef Edna _____ cucumbers for a salad.

   trace + es = _____ traces _____ slice + es = _____ ⬭(slices)

4. Dale makes up stories because she wants to be a _____ .

   write + er = ⬭(writer) dive + er = _____ diver

5. Mike has a job _____ leaves for his neighbor.

   hide + ing = _____ hiding _____ rake + ing = _____ ⬭(raking)

6. Carlos _____ an insect for his science fair project.

   examine + ed = ⬭(examined) invite + ed = _____ invited

Suffixes and endings: Words ending in e, Words in context   **107**

FOCUS ON ALL LEARNERS

ESL/ELL ENGLISH LANGUAGE LEARNERS

Model for English language learners how to identify base words with a final e and how to apply the rule on page 107.

• Explain the rule on page 107; ask children why the e is called silent. (*It is not pronounced orally.*)

• Read aloud the answer choices for items 1–6 and have children underline the base words. Then, have children complete one item at a time.

KINESTHETIC LEARNERS GROUPS

On the board, make a chart with five columns headed with the suffixes *-es, -ed, -ing, -er,* and *-est.* Have children take turns thinking of a base word, adding the suffixes to the base word, and writing the new words in the appropriate columns.

VISUAL LEARNERS PARTNERS

Write the words *bake, smile, tame, cute, wave,* and *fine* and the endings or suffixes *-es, -ed, -ing, -er,* and *-est* on the board. Ask children to choose three words, mentally add suffixes to them, and write sentences, leaving a blank for each of the new words. Have partners exchange papers and complete each other's sentences.

Make new words by adding the suffixes or endings shown below. Write the new words in the correct columns.

RULE
When a word ends in silent e, drop the e before adding es, ed, ing, or est.
hope hop**ing**
large larg**est**

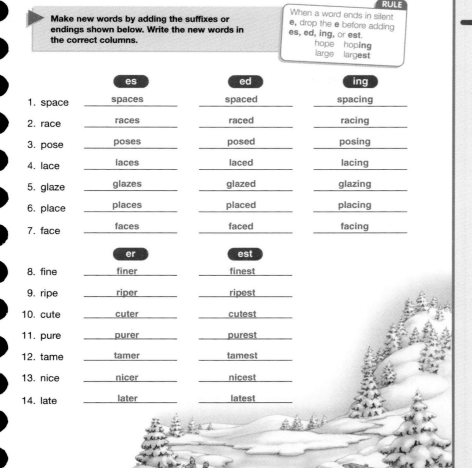

	es	**ed**	**ing**
1. space	spaces	spaced	spacing
2. race	races	raced	racing
3. pose	poses	posed	posing
4. lace	laces	laced	lacing
5. glaze	glazes	glazed	glazing
6. place	places	placed	placing
7. face	faces	faced	facing

	er	**est**
8. fine	finer	finest
9. ripe	riper	ripest
10. cute	cuter	cutest
11. pure	purer	purest
12. tame	tamer	tamest
13. nice	nicer	nicest
14. late	later	latest

108 Suffixes and endings: Words ending in e

HOME Say a base word. Then say a suffix or ending and ask your child to spell the new word.

CURRICULUM CONNECTIONS

SPELLING

On the board, write the spelling word *dressed* and the words *bakes, cracking, ripest, slices, licks,* and *raking.* Have children sort out the words that had a silent *e* dropped before the suffix was added and spell the base words that end in silent *e.*

WRITING

Have children write riddles about jobs, using words with suffixes whose base words end in silent *e,* such as the following example: *You do a lot of slicing in this job.* (cook)

MATH/SOCIAL STUDIES

Ask children to name people who keep their school running, such as teachers, principal, secretaries, lunchroom workers, custodians, and bus drivers. Help children find out how many employees are in each category. Choose a method to record the numbers, such as a tally chart, table, or graph.

TECHNOLOGY **AstroWord** Suffixes

AUDITORY LEARNERS **GROUPS**

Give verbal clues about words from pages 107 and 108 for children to guess, for example: *I'm thinking of a word with the suffix -es. It begins with a blend and means "cuts into pieces."* (slices) Have children continue by selecting words and giving their own clues.

CHALLENGE

Suggest that children write a story, using some of the words that have suffixes on page 108. Challenge children to use as many of the words as they can. Encourage them to have fun by writing a silly or a make-believe story.

EXTRA SUPPORT/INTERVENTION

Materials: index cards

Use index cards to make letter cards. Guide children as they build words that end in silent *e.* Then, have them manipulate the letter cards to remove the *e* and add the letters *-es, -ed, -ing, -er,* or *-est* to form new words. See Daily Phonics Practice, pages 218–219.

Integrating Phonics and Reading

Guided Reading
Call on volunteers to read the title and talk about what the cover illustration shows. Then, invite children to predict what the story will be about.

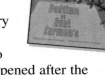

First Reading Ask children to describe each of things that happened after the children went to bed.
Second Reading Ask children to identify words with suffixes used in the story.
Comprehension
After reading, ask children these questions:
• Why did Edgar get out of bed to sleep on the couch? *Recall/Drawing Conclusions*
• Were you satisfied with the way the story ended? Why or why not? *Reflective Analysis/Personal Response*
ESL/ELL **English Language Learners**
Make sure children understand that the words *I* and *me* refer to the narrator of the story. Invite children to read the text as if they were the main character telling a story about themselves.

Suffixes and Endings: Words Ending in e

Skill Focus

Children will

★ identify base words that require dropping a final e before adding a suffix or an ending.

★ form new words by adding suffixes or endings to base words ending in e.

★ write words with suffixes or endings to complete sentences.

ESL/ELL Unlike English, some languages distinguish consonants that are aspirated, or pronounced with a puff of air, from those that are not. English language learners from those language backgrounds may experience some confusion with the inflectional ending -ed in various contexts. Provide oral practice as needed.

▶ Teach

Introduce Suffixes and Endings: Words Ending in e Have children name words that end in silent e and write the words on the board. Ask what happens to the final e when -es, -ed, -ing, -er, or -est is added. (*The final e is dropped.*) Ask volunteers to demonstrate by adding a suffix to each of the words on the board.

Write the words *rattled, larger, hoping, takes,* and *wisest* on the board. Have volunteers circle the suffixes and write the base words. Ask children what had to be added to the base words when the suffix was dropped. (*The final e had to be added.*)

▶ Practice and Apply

Writing Point out that on page 109 children will be writing base words for words that have suffixes. Remind them that when a base word ends in a silent e, the e has to be replaced when the suffix is dropped.

For page 110, suggest that children try each base word with more than one possible suffix before deciding on the one that makes the most sense in the context of the sentence.

Critical Thinking For the Talk About It question, tell children that there is no wrong answer. Encourage them to use their imaginations.

Reading Use *The Fox and the Crow,* MCP Phonics and Reading Word Study Skills Library 1, Level C, to provide additional practice in identifying words with suffixes.

109

Name _____

▶ Write the base word for each word below.

1. taking ____take____　　2. hiding ____hide____

3. shining ____shine____　　4. chased ____chase____

5. bravest ____brave____　　6. used ____use____

7. places ____place____　　8. baker ____bake____

9. traced ____trace____　　10. hoping ____hope____

11. safer ____safe____　　12. largest ____large____

▶ Read each sentence. Circle the word that has a suffix or ending and write its base word on the line.

13. Carl was (shaking) his bank. ____shake____

14. "I need a (larger) baseball mitt," he said. ____large____

15. "I want the (latest) model." ____late____

16. Nothing (rattled) when he shook the bank. ____rattle____

17. He had spent almost all of his money on ice (skates) ____skate____

18. "I only (practiced) on them once," he said. ____practice____

19. "Mom told me the lake seldom (freezes)" ____freeze____

20. Carl thought baseball was the (finest) game. ____fine____

21. He could have (used) the mitt all summer. ____use____

22. "I should have been (wiser)" he said. ____wise____

Suffixes and endings: Words ending in e, Words in context　**109**

FOCUS ON ALL LEARNERS

ESL/ELL **ENGLISH LANGUAGE LEARNERS**

- Have volunteers take turns naming words ending with -es, -ed, -ing, -er, and -est from the story at the bottom of page 109. Have the group repeat each word chorally.

- Read the story aloud. Then, ask volunteers to each read a sentence. Have children clap whenever they hear a word that ends with -es, -ed, -ing, -er, or -est.

- Write the words on the board and underline the suffixes.

KINESTHETIC LEARNERS

On the board, draw five trees with equal numbers of branches. Write a suffix on the trunk of each tree: -es, -ed, -ing, -er, and -est. Have a child stand in front of each tree. When you say "Go!" have children write a different word with their suffix on each branch. The first player to fill in his or her branches wins.

VISUAL LEARNERS

Write words such as *nicer, hoped, tracing, bravest,* and *chases* on the board. Seat four children in a circle. The first child reads a word and writes it on paper. The next child writes the base word. The third adds a new suffix to the base word. The fourth chooses a new word and begins again.

▶ **Read each sentence. Complete the sentence by adding the correct suffix or ending to the word in parentheses. Write the new word on the line.**

1. Dan has a little brother _____named_____ Tim. (name)

2. Dan usually _____likes_____ to baby-sit for Tim. (like)

3. One day Dan's parents _____arranged_____ to go to a wedding. (arrange)

4. Dan had planned to go ice _____skating_____ that day. (skate)

5. His parents _____hoped_____ he'd baby-sit for Tim. (hope)

6. Dan hated _____changing_____ his plans. (change)

7. Then Mother had an idea that _____saved_____ the day. (save)

8. "How about _____taking_____ Tim with you?" she asked. (take)

9. Dan _____agreed_____ that it was a good idea. (agree)

10. "Taking Tim is _____nicer_____ than not going," said Dan. (nice)

11. Tim was happy to be _____invited_____ along. (invite)

12. "You'll be the _____cutest_____ kid on skates!" said Dan. (cute)

13. They had the _____finest_____ weather for skating. (fine)

14. The boys _____glided_____ swiftly over the ice. (glide)

TALK About It What do you think happened next?

HOME Help your child think of sentences using words from the page to continue the story.

110 Suffixes and endings: Words ending in e, critical thinking

---

CURRICULUM CONNECTIONS

SPELLING

Use these words and sentences as a posttest for writing plurals and words with inflected endings.

1. **pillows**   Mom bought new **pillows.**
2. **foxes**   **Foxes** have long bushy tails.
3. **babies**   Two **babies** are crying.
4. **knives**   Please wash the **knives.**
5. **dressed**   He **dressed** as a clown.
6. **opening**   Who is **opening** the door?

WRITING

Have children continue the story on page 110, telling what happens to Dan and Tim when they are skating. Suggest that partners check each other's spelling of silent *e* words with endings.

FINE ARTS

Display art prints or posters that depict winter scenes. Invite children to write captions for each picture. Then, have children read their captions. The class guesses which scene is being described.

TECHNOLOGY  **AstroWord** Suffixes

Integrating Phonics and Reading

Guided Reading
Have volunteers read the title and share their thoughts about the cover illustration. Then, invite children to predict what the story will be about.

First Reading Ask children to describe how Fox tricked Crow into dropping the cheese.
Second Reading Ask children to identify words with suffixes used in the story.

Comprehension
After reading, ask children these questions:
• What made Crow drop the cheese? *Recall/Inference*
• What is the moral of the story? *Reflective Analysis/Genre*

ESL/ELL English Language Learners
Have children identify the two main characters in the story. *(Fox and Crow)* Then, ask them to suggest words that could be used to describe each of the characters.

AUDITORY LEARNERS **PARTNERS**

Display the following words and sentences: *bake, chase, ripe, fine, freeze; Your pear is ____ than mine. The cat is ____ the mouse. Dad ____ a pie this morning. The lake ____ in winter. She is the ____ skater of all.* Have children work with partners to read aloud and complete the sentences by choosing a base word and adding a suffix.

CHALLENGE

Challenge pairs of children to create a crossword puzzle, using base words that end in silent *e*. Explain that their clues should be words that have had suffixes added; for example: *1. base word for used*. Suggest that children share their puzzles with classmates to solve.

EXTRA SUPPORT/INTERVENTION

Do the activities on page 109 with children. For items 1–12, have them underline the suffix in each word before writing the base word. Remind them that all the base words they write will end with silent *e*. See Daily Phonics Practice, pages 218–219.

Phonics and Reading / Phonics and Writing

Review Suffixes and Endings

Skill Focus

Children will

★ write words with endings and suffixes to complete sentences about a story.

★ write a diary entry using words with endings and suffixes.

ESL/ELL Note that *er* in Spanish stands for a different sound from *er* in English, and children may say *late air* for *later,* and so on. Listen for native-language interference; if necessary, provide oral practice with words such as *taller, harder, faster,* and *longer.*

Teach

Phonics and Reading Remind children that a suffix is a word part that is added to a base word. If a base word with a short vowel ends in a single consonant, the consonant is usually doubled before the suffix or ending is added. If the base word ends in a silent *e,* and the suffix or ending begins with a vowel, the *e* is dropped before the suffix or ending is added.

Write these words on the board: *stopping, uses, dancer, branches, gladdest, helped,* and *newer.* Call on children to read each word, identify the ending or suffix, and write the base word.

Then, write these words on the board: *work, tall, shop, win, bake, smile.* Ask volunteers to add an ending or a suffix to each word. If the base word needs to be changed before the ending is added, have children explain what is changing and why.

Practice and Apply

Phonics and Reading After children have read the selection on page 111, encourage them to identify words in the story that have endings or suffixes. Suggest that children look in the story for words to complete the sentences.

Critical Thinking For the Talk About It question at the bottom of page 111, have children talk about whether they themselves would like Aunt Carmen's job as a museum tour guide.

Phonics and Writing Before children begin writing their diary entries on page 112, review the information in the callout boxes.

Reading Use *All About Bats,* MCP Phonics and Reading Word Study Skills Library 1, Level C, to provide additional practice in reading words with suffixes.

111

Name _____

 **Phonics & Reading**   Read the paragraphs. Then write the correct word on the line to complete each sentence.

The Dino Guide

My name is Rosa Gonzales. When I grow up I want to be just like my aunt Carmen! Aunt Carmen works in a natural history museum as a tour guide. That means she helps people understand the things they are looking at. My aunt's job is in the best part of the museum. She gives tours of the dinosaur exhibits. We call her the "Dino Guide."

Aunt Carmen says that the largest dinosaurs were more than 130 feet tall. They could have looked in the windows of a six-story building. My aunt is often invited to talk about dinosaurs at schools. She's been promising to bring a dinosaur egg to my class! She says the egg was found in a nest on the ground. It is only about 7 inches across. That is much smaller than I would expect a dinosaur's egg to be. Who could have thought that a dinosaur could begin its life inside an egg that size?

1. Aunt Carmen _____works_____ in a natural history museum.

2. She helps people understand the things they are _____looking_____ at.

3. She gives _____tours_____ of the dinosaur exhibits.

4. The _____largest_____ dinosaurs were more than 130 feet tall.

5. They could have _____looked_____ in the windows of a six-story building.

6. She's been _____promising_____ to bring a dinosaur egg to my class.

7. The egg is only about 7 _____inches_____ across.

8. It is much _____smaller_____ than I would expect.

TALK About It Do you think Aunt Carmen likes her job? Why or why not?

Review suffixes and endings: Reading, critical thinking   **111**

FOCUS ON ALL LEARNERS

ESL/ELL ENGLISH LANGUAGE LEARNERS

Use the story on page 111 to review endings and suffixes.

● Photocopy the story, one copy per child. You may wish to enlarge the print.

● Tell English language learners to scan the story and highlight words they recognize that have endings or suffixes. Have children who need additional support work together.

● Have children print target story words on the board. Invite volunteers to circle each suffix and write the base word.

KINESTHETIC LEARNERS   INDIVIDUAL

Materials: children's magazines, highlighters

Provide paragraphs copied or cut from magazines. Have children read one or two paragraphs and highlight and list words that have the suffixes *-s, -es, -ed, -ing, -er,* and *-est.*

VISUAL LEARNERS   GROUPS

Have each child write the suffixes *-s, -ed, -ing, -er,* and *-est* on a sheet of paper along with a word that ends in each suffix. Then, have children pass their papers on to another group member to read each word and add five more. Continue until children have added words to each person's page.

Phonics & Writing

When you write in a diary, you are writing for yourself. You can make an entry in a diary when you want to remember things or express yourself. Writing a **diary entry** can also help you sort out your feelings or think about things that happened.

Imagine you are a travel writer. In your diary, describe some things you saw on your last trip. Some of the words in the box may help you.

traveling	writer	faster	days
monkeys	wolves	learned	cooking
worked	starting	bigger	coldest

Write the day or date at the beginning of your entry.

Write about the things you saw and how you felt about them.

Remember you are writing for yourself.

HOME Ask your child to read the diary page to you and identify the words with suffixes and endings.

112   Review suffixes and endings: Writing

CURRICULUM CONNECTIONS

SPELLING

Use these words and sentences for a cumulative midunit spelling review.

1. **there's**   **There's** a horse in the room!
2. **couldn't**   Anna **couldn't** go with us.
3. **you'll**   I think **you'll** like this movie.
4. **they've**   **They've** already seen it.
5. **I'd**   Dad thought **I'd** be late.
6. **let's**   **Let's** make up a song.
7. **pillows**   We sat on **pillows.**
8. **foxes**   The four baby **foxes** played.
9. **babies**   The twin **babies** were alike.
10. **knives**   Where are the steak **knives?**
11. **dressed**   Ben was **dressed** as a frog.
12. **opening**   Mona is **opening** the trunk.

MATH AND SOCIAL STUDIES

After children have finished writing their diary entries, have them locate their destinations on a map of the United States or on a world map. Help them figure out how far they'd have to travel to reach each place they visited.

AUDITORY LEARNERS GROUPS

Materials: copies of bingo game boards, game markers

Have children write the suffixes *-s, -es, -ed, -ing, -er,* and *-est* in the spaces on the game boards. As you say words with suffixes, children cover the suffix heard in the word. Play until someone has bingo and then begin a new game.

CHALLENGE

Materials: poster board, game markers, spinners or dice

Challenge children to work together to create a game board featuring a path with words with suffixes written in each space. Allow children to write the rules for playing and supply game markers and spinners or dice.

EXTRA SUPPORT/INTERVENTION

Provide clues for a word with a suffix and have children guess the word. Here is an example: *This word is made from the base word* large *and the suffix* -est. *(largest)* Then, ask children to write the word on the board. See Daily Phonics Practice, pages 218–219.

Integrating Phonics and Reading

Guided Reading

Have children look at the cover and read the title. Ask them to discuss what they know about bats. Invite children who have seen bats to share their experiences.

First Reading Ask children to describe where bats live and how they survive.

Second Reading Have children identify selected story words that have suffixes or endings.

Comprehension

After reading, ask children these questions:

• In what ways do bats help people? ***Recall/Details***

• Did your ideas about bats change after reading the story? Explain. ***Reflective Analysis/ Personal Response***

ESL/ELL English Language Learners

Invite children to leaf though the book and use word clues to describe what the bats are doing in each picture. If necessary, point out the key words in the upper left-hand corner of the pages.

112

Suffixes

Skill Focus

Children will

★ read and write words with the suffixes *-ful, -ly, -less, -ness,* and *-y.*

★ add the suffixes *-ful, -ly, -less, -ness,* and *-y* to base words to complete sentences.

ESL/ELL Children whose home language is Cantonese, Hmong, Vietnamese, Korean, or Khmer come from monosyllabic language backgrounds. Overstressing the suffixes for clarity may mislead English language learners into thinking two-syllable words are two separate words.

Teach

Introduce Suffixes *-ful, -ly, -less, -ness,* and *-y* Write the words *slowly, hopeful, sickness, helpless,* and *bumpy* on the board. Ask volunteers to underline the base words. Then, ask children what the part of the word that is not underlined is called. *(a suffix)* Have volunteers identify each of the suffixes. *(-ly, -ful, -ness, -less,* and *-y)* Circle each suffix as it is identified.

Remind children that adding a suffix to a base word changes the word's meaning or how it is used. Then, discuss the meaning of each word on the board. *(in a slow way, full of hope, being sick, without help, having bumps)*

Practice and Apply

Writing Read aloud the rule at the top of page 113. For the activity on that page, point out that children may want to try several suffixes before choosing the one that helps form the best word for the sentence. For the second activity on page 114, suggest that identifying the suffix in each word will help children find the base word.

Critical Thinking For the Talk About It question discuss what the doctor told Jan to do. Invite children to share what they do to get better when they are sick.

Reading Use *Sara's Lovely Songs,* MCP Phonics and Reading Word Study Skills Library 1, Level C, to provide additional practice in identifying words with suffixes.

Name _____

> **Read each sentence. Add the suffix ful, less, y, ly, or ness to the word below the line. Write the new word on the line.**

> **RULE**
> When a **suffix** is added at the end of a base word, it changes the base word's meaning or the way it is used.
>
> Hope**ful** means **full of hope.**
> Slow**ly** means **in a slow way.**
> Help**less** means **without help.**
> Sick**ness** means **being sick.**
> Bump**y** means **having bumps.**

1. Jan was sick, and food seemed _____**tasteless**_____ to her.
   (taste)

2. She was _____**thirsty**_____, but it was hard to swallow.
   (thirst)

3. "Your face is pale and looks _____**colorless**_____," said Mother.
   (color)

4. "I hope the doctor can see you _____**quickly**_____."
   (quick)

5. Jan's _____**illness**_____ turned out not to be serious.
   (ill)

6. "Medicine will help you," the doctor said _____**kindly**_____.
   (kind)

7. "You must be _____**careful**_____ to get plenty of rest."
   (care)

8. "I don't like being sick," Jan said _____**sadly**_____.
   (sad)

9. Mother gave her a _____**spoonful**_____ of medicine.
   (spoon)

10. Jan felt _____**sleepy**_____ and took a nap.
    (sleep)

 TALK About it What can Jan do to get better?

Suffixes: -y, -ly, -ness, -ful, -less, critical thinking   **113**

FOCUS ON ALL LEARNERS

ESL/ELL ENGLISH LANGUAGE LEARNERS

Assess whether English language learners understand what a suffix is and how it changes a word's meaning.

• Ask English language learners what a suffix is. If children are unsure, review the rule at the top of page 113.

• On the board, write *-ly, -ful, -less, -ness,* and *-y;* add them to words to form suffix equations such as *quick + ly = quickly.*

• Write words such as these on the board: *thankful, restless, sickness, needy, sweetly.* Have children brainstorm the meaning of each word, based on its suffix. *(full of thanks, without rest, being sick, having need, in a sweet way)* Use the words in context sentences if children have difficulty.

KINESTHETIC LEARNERS GROUPS

Materials: poster board, paper fastener

Make a spinner, divided into five sections. Attach an arrow and write a suffix *(-ly, -ful, -less, -ness,* and *-y)* in each section of the spinner. Have children form teams and then have team members take turns spinning the spinner and using the suffix the spinner lands on to write a word on the board.

► **Read each word. Make new words by adding the suffixes. Write the new words in the correct columns.**

	y	**less**	**ful**
1. tear	teary	tearless	tearful
2. need	needy	needless	needful
3. fruit	fruity	fruitless	fruitful
4. cheer	cheery	cheerless	cheerful
5. trust	trusty	trustless	trustful

	ly	**ness**
6. sick	sickly	sickness
7. neat	neatly	neatness
8. loud	loudly	loudness
9. quick	quickly	quickness
10. bright	brightly	brightness

► **Write the base word for each of the words below.**

11. kindness	kind		12. gladly	glad
13. tricky	trick		14. harmless	harm
15. spoonful	spoon		16. rainy	rain
17. useful	use		18. sadness	sad
19. homeless	home		20. kindly	kind

114 Suffixes: -y, -ly, -ness, -ful, -less

 Choose a base word and a suffix and ask your child to say the new word.

See Daily Phonics Practice, page 219.

CURRICULUM CONNECTIONS

SPELLING

Use these words and sentences as a pretest for writing words with suffixes.

1. **illness** Amy's **illness** did not last long.
2. **likable** What a **likable** puppy!
3. **brighten** Flowers will **brighten** the room.
4. **slowly** He walked home **slowly.**
5. **restful** Classical music can be **restful.**
6. **useless** This broken wrench is **useless.**

WRITING

Have children create get-well cards. Suggest they decorate the front of the card and write a cheerful message inside using some words with suffixes.

ART

Have children create drawings to represent a word from the lesson. Pictures can be literal (*spoon, fruit, home*) or figurative (*sleepy, brightness, cheerful*). Display the pictures and have classmates guess the words.

 TECHNOLOGY **AstroWord** Suffixes

VISUAL LEARNERS GROUPS

Materials: tagboard squares or index cards

Write the suffixes *-ly, -ful, -less, -ness,* and *-y* on tagboard squares. Write the words *neat, care, fear, quick,* and *need* on the board. Invite volunteers to choose a suffix card, hold it next to a word on the board, read the word, and write it. Continue until all words are written for each base word.

CHALLENGE

Challenge children to create five word webs, one for each of the suffixes *-ly, -ful, -less, -ness,* and *-y.* Each suffix should be written in the center of a circle. Children then surround the circle with as many words as possible that end with that suffix.

EXTRA SUPPORT/INTERVENTION

Materials: index cards

Write several words with the suffixes *-ly, -ful, -less, -ness,* and *-y* on cards. Have children sort the cards by suffix, read each word aloud, and use it in a sentence. See Daily Phonics Practice, page 219.

Integrating Phonics and Reading

Guided Reading

Ask a volunteer to read the title and talk about the cover. Then, invite children to name and/or sing songs they know. You may also use the English Language Learners activity below.

First Reading Ask children to identify which song Sara sang to each person.

Second Reading Ask children to identify words in the story that end with suffixes.

Comprehension

After reading, ask children these questions:

• How did Sara's songs affect the people around her? *Recall/Details*

• Which of Sara's songs did you like best? *Reflective Analysis/Personal Response*

ESL/ELL **English Language Learners**

Have English language learners work with partners who are more English-proficient to explain the lyrics to each of Sara's songs.

Suffixes

Skill Focus

Children will

★ read and write words with the suffixes *-ion, -ment, -en, -able,* and *-ible.*

★ match words with the suffixes *-ion, -ment, -en, -able,* and *-ible* to their meanings.

Teach

Introduce Suffixes *-ion, -ment, -en, -able,* and *-ible* Introduce the lesson suffixes by writing these words on the board: *protection, excitement, darken, washable,* and *collectible.* Ask volunteers to underline the base words and identify the suffixes (*-ion, -ment, -en, -able, -ible*).

Remind children that suffixes have meanings and that their meanings can change a base word's meaning. Provide the following definitions:

> *-ion* = "the act of or condition of being"
> *-ment* = "condition of being"
> *-en* = "to make or become"
> *-able* and *-ible* = "can be"

Discuss with children the meanings of the words on the board. *(the condition of being protected, the condition of being excited, to make dark, can be washed, can be collected)*

Practice and Apply

Writing Review the rule at the top of page 115 and explain how it applies to the words *protection* and *excitement.* For the second activity on page 115, suggest that children try both word choices in each sentence before choosing a word to complete the sentence.

Read aloud the rule at the top of page 116. Point out that in the first activity on page 116, children may have to restore the *e* to some of the base words. For the crossword puzzle, tell children that the base word for most answers can be found in the clues. You may wish to demonstrate by completing the first item with the class.

Reading Use *At Home on the Earth,* MCP Phonics and Reading Word Study Skills Library 1, Level C, to provide additional practice in identifying words with suffixes.

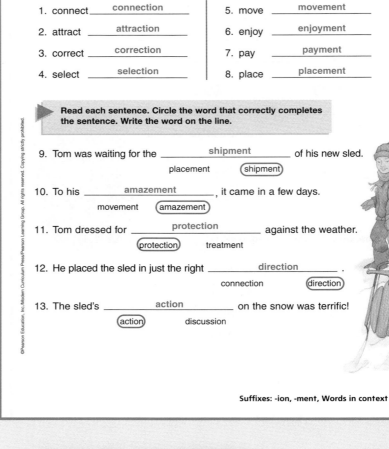

Name _____

RULE
The suffixes **ion** and **ment** form nouns. They usually mean "the condition of being." The suffix **ion** also means "the act of." Protect**ion** is the act of protecting. Excite**ment** is the condition of being excited.

Add the suffix to each word. Write the new words on the lines.

ion

1. connect ___connection___
2. attract ___attraction___
3. correct ___correction___
4. select ___selection___

ment

5. move ___movement___
6. enjoy ___enjoyment___
7. pay ___payment___
8. place ___placement___

Read each sentence. Circle the word that correctly completes the sentence. Write the word on the line.

9. Tom was waiting for the ___shipment___ of his new sled.
   placement   (shipment)

10. To his ___amazement___, it came in a few days.
    movement   (amazement)

11. Tom dressed for ___protection___ against the weather.
    (protection)   treatment

12. He placed the sled in just the right ___direction___.
    connection   (direction)

13. The sled's ___action___ on the snow was terrific!
    (action)   discussion

Suffixes: -ion, -ment, Words in context   **115**

FOCUS ON ALL LEARNERS

ESL/ELL ENGLISH LANGUAGE LEARNERS

Guide English language learners to complete the story at the bottom of page 115.

• Read aloud the directions. For the first item, help children respond with the word *shipment* by paraphrasing the sentence so the meaning of the suffix is clear. For example, say: *Tom was waiting for his new sled to be shipped. Which suffix can you add to ship to mean "the condition of being shipped"?*

• When all items have been completed, have children read the sentences aloud as a story. Confirm children's comprehension.

AUDITORY LEARNERS

As you say words with the target suffixes such as *breakable, sleepy, frighten, flexible, protection,* and *excitement,* ask volunteers to name the suffix and base word and explain what the word means.

VISUAL LEARNERS

Write the words *darken, likable, enjoyment, attraction,* and *flexible* on the board. Have children write a sentence for each word. Then, ask children to write five new sentences, using the base words without the suffixes.

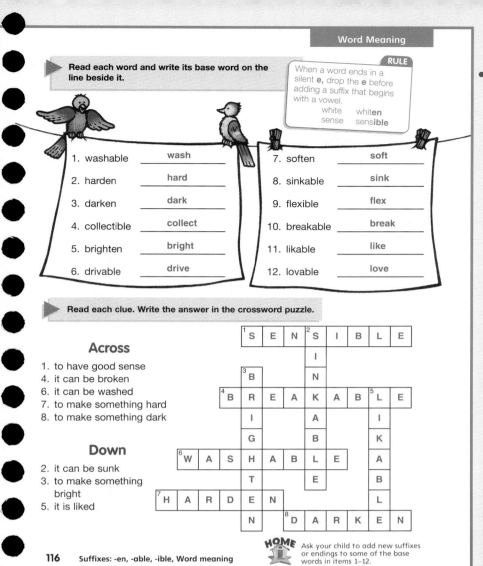

Word Meaning

Read each word and write its base word on the line beside it.

> **RULE**
> When a word ends in a silent **e**, drop the **e** before adding a suffix that begins with a vowel.
> white — whit**en**
> sense — sens**ible**

1. washable — wash
2. harden — hard
3. darken — dark
4. collectible — collect
5. brighten — bright
6. drivable — drive

7. soften — soft
8. sinkable — sink
9. flexible — flex
10. breakable — break
11. likable — like
12. lovable — love

Read each clue. Write the answer in the crossword puzzle.

Across
1. to have good sense
4. it can be broken
6. it can be washed
7. to make something hard
8. to make something dark

Down
2. it can be sunk
3. to make something bright
5. it is liked

Crossword answers:
- 1 Across: SENSIBLE
- 4 Across: BREAKABLE
- 6 Across: WASHABLE
- 7 Across: HARDEN
- 8 Across: DARKEN

Suffixes: -en, -able, -ible, Word meaning

 HOME Ask your child to add new suffixes or endings to some of the base words in items 1–12.

CURRICULUM CONNECTIONS

SPELLING

Have children write these words on the board in one column: *likable, brighten, soften, sinkable, breakable, tighten.* In another column write the words *loosen, darken, unbreakable, unlikable, harden, unsinkable.* Invite children to draw lines to connect words that are opposite in meaning.

WRITING

 PORTFOLIO

Have children write analogies using words with the suffixes *-ion, -ment, -en, -able,* and *-ible.* For example: *Dawn is to brighten as dusk is to darken.*

SCIENCE

Discuss with children what a meteorologist does. (*He or she studies, predicts, and reports the weather.*) Encourage children to name weather terms and record them on the board. Include words with suffixes, such as *rainy, frosty, precipitation, snowy, brighten, darken,* and *movement.* Some children might enjoy using weather terms as they role-play a meteorologist.

TECHNOLOGY 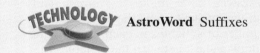 **AstroWord** Suffixes

---

KINESTHETIC LEARNERS   PARTNERS

Materials: tagboard, markers, scissors

Have partners work together to create jigsaw word puzzles by writing two words each for the suffixes *-ion, -ment, -en, -able,* and *-ible.* Then have children cut each word between the base word and suffix to make puzzle pieces.

CHALLENGE

Materials: dictionary

Challenge children to write a word with one of the suffixes they have learned so far for each letter of the alphabet from *adorable* to *zippy.* Suggest they refer to a dictionary if they need help thinking of a word.

EXTRA SUPPORT/INTERVENTION

Materials: index cards

Write several words with the suffixes *-ion, -ment, -en, -able,* and *-ible* on cards. Have children read and sort the words by suffix and give a meaning for each word. See Daily Phonics Practice, page 219.

Integrating Phonics and Reading

Guided Reading

Discuss the cover illustration. Then, have children turn to the back cover, read the summary aloud, and predict what the book will be about.

First Reading Ask children to explain the Native American attitude toward the earth.

Second Reading Read selected sentences and have children identify words with suffixes.

Comprehension

After reading, ask children these questions:

- Why did the Bruchac family found the Ndakinna Education Center and Nature Preserve? ***Inference/Main Idea***
- Would you like to spend some time at the Ndakinna Education Center? Why or why not? ***Reflective Analysis/Personal Response***

ESL/ELL **English Language Learners**

Explain that sometimes books include special features to give readers information. Then, have children locate several of the "Nature Notes" at the end of each chapter. Help children read these notes. Review by asking simple questions.

Review Suffixes and Syllables

Skill Focus

Children will

★ read and write words with the suffixes *-en, -able, -ible, -ion, -ment.*

★ write words with suffixes to complete sentences.

★ divide words with suffixes into syllables.

Teach

Introduce Suffixes and Syllables

Remind children that words are made of syllables. You hear one vowel sound in each syllable. Then, tell children you are going to say some words. They should hold up one hand if the word has one syllable. They should hold up two hands if the word has two syllables. Say *careful, helpless, darken, clap, slowly,* and *use.*

Write the following words on the board: *dark, play, trick, hard,* and *move.* Ask children to read the words and identify the number of syllables in each. *(one)* Then, add the suffixes *-ness, -ing, -y, -en,* and *-ment* to form *darkness, playing, tricky, harden,* and *movement.* Ask volunteers to read the words and identify the number of syllables in each. *(two)* Invite volunteers to draw a slash between the syllables in the words. Point out that when a suffix has a vowel sound it forms a syllable by itself.

Practice and Apply

Writing For the activity on the bottom of page 117, make sure children understand that they are to fill in only one circle. Suggest that children try each word choice in the sentence before choosing a word.

Review the rule at the top of page 118. For the activity on the page, suggest that children underline the suffix in each word before dividing it into syllables.

Reading Use *Josh and T.J.,* MCP Phonics and Reading Word Study Skills Library 1, Level C, to provide additional practice in identifying the number of syllables in words with suffixes.

Name _____

> Read each base word and add the suffix. Write the new word on the line.

1. move + ment ___movement___   2. dark + en ___darken___

3. invent + ion ___invention___   4. like + able ___likable___

5. pay + ment ___payment___   6. fright + en ___frighten___

7. break + able ___breakable___   8. sense +ible ___sensible___

> Fill in the circle beside the word that completes each sentence. Write the word on the line.

9. Jill needed to ___straighten___ out her room.
   ○ harden   ● straighten   ○ frighten

10. She began by sorting out her huge rock ___collection___.
    ● collection   ○ connection   ○ direction

11. Jill needed to get it down to a ___sensible___ size.
    ○ reversible   ○ flexible   ● sensible

12. She made her ___selection___ very carefully.
    ○ invention   ○ action   ● selection

13. Then she found a ___suitable___ place to put the rocks.
    ● suitable   ○ washable   ○ sinkable

14. Now, that was an ___improvement___!
    ○ payment   ● improvement   ○ pavement

Review suffixes: -en, -able, -ible, -ion, -ment   **117**

FOCUS ON ALL LEARNERS

ESL/ELL ENGLISH LANGUAGE LEARNERS

Use the activity on page 118 to assess English language learners' ability to recognize suffixes as syllables.

- Focus children's attention on the first item and the suffix *-ing.* Have children circle the *-ing.* Then, have them identify the base word *(play)* and the suffix *(-ing).* Finally, have them write the word on the line, separating the base word and the suffix with a hyphen. Help children apply the rule at the top of the page to the *-ing* suffix, identifying the vowel as the letter *i.*

- Continue in a similar manner with items 2–5. Then, have children work in pairs to complete the page.

KINESTHETIC LEARNERS GROUPS

Materials: index cards, watch or clock with a second hand

On index cards write the suffixes *-y, -ment, -ness, -less, -ly, -est, -ful,* and *-en* and the base words *dust, move, dark, care, slow, loud, help,* and *bright.* Have each child take a turn matching base words with suffixes while being timed.

► **Divide each word into syllables. Write the syllables on the lines.**

> **RULE**
> A suffix or ending that has one vowel sound forms a syllable by itself:
> hard-en   say-ing

1. playing _play-ing_
2. lighten _light-en_
3. spoonful _spoon-ful_
4. gladly _glad-ly_
5. needed _need-ed_
6. playful _play-ful_
7. cheerful _cheer-ful_
8. lovely _love-ly_
9. movement _move-ment_
10. loudest _loud-est_
11. useless _use-less_
12. darkness _dark-ness_
13. training _train-ing_
14. eating _eat-ing_
15. homeless _home-less_

16. shipment _ship-ment_
17. careful _care-ful_
18. laughing _laugh-ing_
19. patches _patch-es_
20. painting _paint-ing_
21. payment _pay-ment_
22. snowy _snow-y_
23. hopeful _hope-ful_
24. neatness _neat-ness_
25. slowly _slow-ly_
26. waiting _wait-ing_
27. careless _care-less_
28. rainy _rain-y_
29. brighten _bright-en_
30. useful _use-ful_

118 Syllables: Words with suffixes and endings

 HOME Help your child think of sentences using words from the page.

CURRICULUM CONNECTIONS

SPELLING

Ask volunteers to scramble the letters in each of the spelling words and write them on the board. Include the words *illness, likable, brighten, slowly, restful,* and *useless.* Children can then ask classmates to unscramble the letters and rewrite the words correctly.

WRITING

Have children try to write a paragraph using only words with one syllable. Then, ask them to write a paragraph using only words with two syllables. If children wish to compete, have them receive a point for each word with the correct number of syllables. The child with the most points wins.

SOCIAL STUDIES

Suggest that children create word webs entitled "Words That Tell About People." They can choose words from pages 117 and 118 and words of their own to write around the title. Invite children to discuss why they chose the words they did.

TECHNOLOGY **AstroWord** Suffixes

VISUAL LEARNERS

Materials: stapler, markers

Suggest that partners work together to make flip books featuring words with one suffix they have learned. A different base word is written on each of the pages. The suffix is written on a longer page at the back of the book, so it is shown with each base word as the pages are turned.

CHALLENGE

Materials: dictionary

Write *se-lec-tion* and *im-prove-ment* on the board, divided into syllables. Challenge children to write other multisyllabic words separating the syllables in a similar way. Encourage children to check their syllabication in a dictionary.

EXTRA SUPPORT/INTERVENTION

Say the words in the first column on page 118 slowly, separating the syllables. Ask children to repeat the words. Then, have them say the words in the second column, separating the syllables on their own. See *Daily Phonics Practice, pages 218–219.*

Integrating Phonics and Reading

Guided Reading

Have children look over the cover illustration. Then, have them turn to the back. Call on a volunteer to read the story summary. Invite children to predict what the story will be about.
First Reading Ask children how the Razzle Stones helped Josh make new friends.
Second Reading Read sentences from the story and ask children to identify words with suffixes.

Comprehension

After reading, ask children these questions:
- Why didn't Josh want to get to know his new neighbors? *Recall/Cause and Effect*
- How did Josh feel at the end of the story? *Reflective Analysis/Personal Response*

ESL/ELL **English Language Learners**
Review parts of the story by asking children simple questions. For example: *Who is Josh? Who is T.J.? Are they friends?* Provide picture clues to help children answer.

Syllables: Words with Suffixes and Endings

Skill Focus

Children will

★ match base words with suffixes to form new words.

★ identify the number of syllables in words with suffixes.

ESL/ELL Native speakers of Spanish will have little difficulty making the sound of *y*, since *y* in Spanish also functions as a vowel and a consonant. Other English language learners should consider the different sounds as they do long and short vowel differences—as two sounds for the same letter.

Teach

Introduce Syllables: Words with Suffixes
Tell children you are going to say some words. They should clap for each syllable they hear: Say: *pay, payment, wash, washable, kind, kindness, light, lightest, rest, restful, fly, flying, storm,* and *stormy.*

Write *run, use, neat, place, bright, act,* and *break* on the board. Ask a volunteer to read the words aloud. Then, ask children how many syllables are in each word. *(one)* Invite volunteers to turn the words into two- or three-syllable words by adding one of these suffixes: *-y, -ly, -ful, -ness, -less, -er, -est, -es, -able, -en, -ing, -ment, -ion,* and *-ed.* Ask children how they know that each new word has two or more syllables. *(Two or more vowel sounds are heard in each word.)*

Practice and Apply

Writing Read aloud the directions for the activity on page 119. Do the first item with children, making sure they understand that they are to draw a line from each base word to the suffix that matches it best.

For the activity on page 120, suggest that children identify the suffix in each word before deciding how many syllables the word has. Point out that the words may have one, two, or three syllables.

Reading Use *The Plant That Almost Ate the World,* MCP Phonics and Reading Word Study Skills Library 1, Level C, to provide additional practice in identifying the number of syllables in words with suffixes.

Name _____

> In each box draw a line from the base word in the first column with a suffix in the second column to make a new word. Write the word on the line.

1.
luck — able — lucky
cold — y — coldest
wash — ion — washable
protect — est — protection

2.
fly — less — flying
loud — ing — loudest
peach — est — peaches
meat — es — meatless

3.
safe — y — safely
pay — ing — payment
health — ly — healthy
say — ment — saying

4.
teach — less — teacher
home — ed — homeless
land — ful — landed
cup — er — cupful

5.
sink — y — sinkable
polite — ly — politely
cloud — en — cloudy
fright — able — frighten

6.
sleep — ful — sleepy
light — ment — lighten
spoon — y — spoonful
place — en — placement

7.
ax — ly — axes
sad — ible — sadly
use — ful — useful
collect — es — collectible

8.
fox — ed — foxes
hammer — ness — hammered
neat — able — neatness
break — es — breakable

Syllables: Words with suffixes and endings   **119**

FOCUS ON ALL LEARNERS

ESL/ELL ENGLISH LANGUAGE LEARNERS

Use the following strategies on page 119 to assess English language learners' ability to recognize suffixes and syllables.

- Have children identify the suffixes. Then, have them read aloud each base word with each suffix until they find a match. Write the new words on the board as they are identified.

- Help children count the syllables in each word by drawing a line between the base word and the suffix and saying the word. Children may not recognize that *-able* has two syllables. Sound out the word *washable* to help them hear the syllabication.

AUDITORY LEARNERS

Ask questions that include base words. The answer will be a new word made from the base word plus a suffix. Have children identify the word and tell how many syllables it has. For example: *What word describes a day with many clouds?* (*cloudy,* 2) Invite children to continue on their own with similar questions.

VISUAL LEARNERS INDIVIDUAL

Have children fold a sheet of paper into thirds and label the sections *1, 2, 3.* Have them look through the lesson for words with one, two, and three syllables to write in each section.

Write the number of syllables in each word.

1. knives	1	2. plays	1	3. shelves	1
4. boxes	2	5. payment	2	6. tagging	2
7. cleaned	1	8. parties	2	9. jumped	1
10. hopeful	2	11. thirsty	2	12. loving	2
13. loudly	2	14. action	2	15. sleepy	2
16. painful	2	17. darken	2	18. sickness	2
19. receiving	3	20. foxes	2	21. shipment	2
22. wives	1	23. days	1	24. harmless	2
25. purest	2	26. sensible	3	27. leaves	1
28. shining	2	29. running	2	30. gladly	2
31. cherries	2	32. cooking	2	33. patches	2
34. begging	2	35. flexible	3	36. wolves	1
37. skated	2	38. weakest	2	39. snowy	2
40. straighten	2	41. homeless	2	42. smoothest	2
43. pavement	2	44. axes	2	45. correction	3
46. turkeys	2	47. whitest	2	48. sinkable	3
49. breakable	3	50. raking	2	51. daisies	2

120 Syllables: Words with suffixes and endings

 Say a word on the page and ask your child to name the syllables.

CURRICULUM CONNECTIONS

SPELLING

Use these words and sentences as a posttest for writing words with suffixes.

1. **illness**   Ben's **illness** is not serious.
2. **likable**   Sally is a **likable** child.
3. **brighten**   A smile can **brighten** any face.
4. **slowly**   Snails move **slowly.**
5. **restful**   Blue is a **restful** color.
6. **useless**   This old glue is **useless.**

WRITING

Have children write a paragraph describing a career that interests them. Then, have them list some of the one-, two-, and three-syllable words they used.

SOCIAL STUDIES

Encourage children to find out about the work of a librarian by talking with their school librarian or by inviting a librarian to visit the class for an interview. Suggest that children set up a classroom library and take turns being in charge.

TECHNOLOGY   **AstroWord** Suffixes

Integrating Phonics and Reading

Guided Reading
Have children read the title and discuss the cover illustration. Then, invite children to talk about their favorite plants.
First Reading Ask children to describe the main character and explain her problem.
Second Reading Read story sentences and have children identify words with suffixes.

Comprehension
After reading, ask children these questions:
• Why did Janie decide to soak the seed pod? *Recall/Cause and Effect*
• What would have happened if Mr. Mercato hadn't figured out how to kill the monster plant? *Reflective Analysis/Speculation*
ESL/ELL **English Language Learners**
Review Chapter 5. Discuss what Janie's experiment was and how it resulted in the plant that almost ate the world. Use simple questions and picture clues to help children talk about the story.

KINESTHETIC LEARNERS

Materials: index cards

Have partners write base words from the lesson and these suffixes on cards: *-y, -ly, -ful, -ness, -less, -es, -er, -est, -able, -en, -ing, -ment,* and *-ed.* Place the base-word cards in one pile and the suffix cards in another. Have partners take turns drawing a card from each pile. A match earns one point.

CHALLENGE

Challenge children to make new words by adding as many different suffixes as they can to the words on page 119.

EXTRA SUPPORT/INTERVENTION

Work as a group to begin each page, having children take turns reading an item aloud. Before they begin working on their own, make sure each child has completed several items successfully. **See Daily Phonics Practice, pages 218–219.**

Review Contractions, Plurals, Suffixes, and Endings

Skill Focus

Children will

★ spell and write contractions, plurals, and words with suffixes and endings.

★ write questions for a news-story interview using contractions, plurals, and words with suffixes and endings.

Teach

Phonics and Spelling Review the fact that a contraction is formed by putting two words together and using an apostrophe to show where letters have been left out. List these word pairs on the board: *did not, you have, we will, that is*. Ask children to write each pair of words as a contraction. *(didn't, you've, we'll, that's)* Then, have them tell which letters have been left out. *(o, ha, wi, i)*

Point out that plurals name more than one thing. Then, write these words on the board: *coat, dish, cherry,* and *leaf*. Have children change each word to a plural. *(coats, dishes, cherries, leaves)*

Remind children that a suffix is a word part that is added to a base word. On the board, write *hopping, protection, teacher, washable, freezes, walked, excitement,* and *careless*. Have volunteers identify the suffix and the base word of each word.

Practice and Apply

Phonics and Spelling Make sure that children are able to read the words in the list on page 121 before they begin the activity. Then, review the rules for forming plurals, adding suffixes to base words with final *e*, and adding suffixes to short vowel base words ending with a single consonant.

Phonics and Writing Before children write their interview questions, invite them to brainstorm events that take place at school or in the community. Review with children the fact that their questions should lead to answers that tell *who, what, when, where,* and *why* of the event. Remind children to use some words from the box.

Reading Use *Let's Build a Playground*, MCP Phonics and Reading Word Study Skills Library 1, Level C, to provide additional practice in identifying the number of syllables in words with suffixes.

Name _____

Phonics & Spelling Say and spell each word. Write the words on the note pad where they belong.

bushes	chopped	foxes	gives	losses
lunches	nicer	padded	pencils	pillows
running	saved	tagging	takes	writing

Plurals
pillows
pencils
foxes
losses
lunches
bushes

Base Word with Final e
nicer
saved
writing
takes
gives

Final Consonant Doubled Before Adding Ending
running
tagging
chopped
padded

Pick a word from each column and write a complete sentence that uses the word.

1. _____

2. _____

3. _____

Review plurals, suffixes, and endings: Spelling   **121**

FOCUS ON ALL LEARNERS

ESL/ELL ENGLISH LANGUAGE LEARNERS

Do the activity on page 121 with English language learners to help them say and spell words with the target endings.

• Remind children that they have been learning about each type of word in this unit. Review word endings separately and give examples of each, including the appropriate spelling rules.

• Direct children's attention to the word *bushes* and the *-es* ending. Remind them that this word is plural. Have children each select a colored pencil, circle the word, and then circle the other words in the list that are plurals. Continue with each of the word groupings, choosing a different color for each one.

KINESTHETIC LEARNERS   GROUPS

Materials: index cards

Write contractions and matching word pairs on separate cards. Each child is dealt four cards and the others are placed face down in a pile. Players take turns asking for a specific card to make a match. If no one has it, the player can "go fish" in the pile. Play until all pairs are matched.

Phonics & Writing

A **news story** tells people facts about something interesting that has happened. It gives readers the *who, what, when, where,* and *why* of an event. The writer gathers information by reading, observing things, or asking people interview questions.

▶ Think of an interesting event in your school or community. Write the questions you would ask if you could interview someone who was involved in the event. Some of the words in the box may help you.

quickly	it's	helping	you've
action	useful	started	what's
happened	longer	where's	latest

Write the name of the person you will interview.

Begin questions with words like *who, what, when, where,* and *why.*

Try to **avoid** questions that can be answered with a simple yes or no.

122 Review contractions, suffixes, and endings: Writing

CURRICULUM CONNECTIONS

SPELLING

Use these words and sentences as a posttest for writing words with suffixes.

Note: If you wish to give a cumulative spelling test for Unit 4, including contractions and words with inflected endings, see the midunit cumulative test for Unit 4 in Lesson 50 on page 112.

1. **illness**   Measles is one **illness** I never had.
2. **likable**   My cousins are **likable** people.
3. **brighten**   Lamps would **brighten** the room.
4. **slowly**   The sun **slowly** set behind the hills.
5. **restful**   The sound of the waves is **restful.**
6. **useless**   The dirty mop was **useless.**

ART

Have children work in four groups to make posters presenting one of the rules for making plural words. Assign each group one of the four rules. Display all four posters on a bulletin board.

 **TECHNOLOGY**   **AstroWord** Suffixes

---

VISUAL LEARNERS  PARTNERS

One child secretly draws a picture of a group of objects or animals named by one of the plural words studied in this unit. Given a few clues, the partner guesses the subject of the picture by writing three plural words on paper. The first child checks the answers and the spelling of the words before revealing the picture. Then, children switch roles.

CHALLENGE

Challenge children to use as many words from pages 121 and 122 as they can in a single sentence. Here is an example: *Two **foxes** **started** **running** around the **bushes.***

EXTRA SUPPORT/INTERVENTION

Materials: index cards

Provide letter cards made from index cards and have children form a base word that ends with *x, ch, sh, ss,* or *y.* Then, have them change the word to its plural form. See Daily Phonics Practice, pages 217–219.

Integrating Phonics and Reading

Guided Reading

Have children read the title and discuss the cover illustration. Then, ask what kinds of things they think should be included in a playground.

First Reading Ask children to describe the steps involved in planning and building a playground.

Second Reading Have children identify story words with suffixes, contractions, and plurals.

Comprehension

After reading, ask children these questions:

• How can kids help with the planning and building of a community playground? *Recall/Details*

• What did you think of the playground that the community in the story built? *Reflective Analysis/Personal Response*

ESL/ELL **English Language Learners**

Point out that photographs can add information. Turn to the plan on page 13 as an example. Then, have children find other examples. Help children describe the pictures.

Take-Home Book

Review Contractions, Plurals, Suffixes and Endings

Skill Focus

Children will

★ read contractions, plurals, and words with suffixes and endings in the context of a story.

★ reread for fluency.

Teach

Build Background

- Remind children that the theme of this unit is "A Working World." Ask them to name jobs they have read about in this unit. Encourage children to add other kinds of work to the list of jobs, including work they do or would like to do.

- Write the word *zookeepers* on the board and read it aloud. Explain that zookeepers take care of animals in zoos. Ask children to speculate about the kinds of things a zookeeper does. Tell them that they will be reading a book about zookeeping.

Review Contractions, Plurals, and Suffixes   Write this sentence on the board: *Wouldn't working with animals in a zoo be interesting?* Ask a child to identify the contraction in the sentence. *(wouldn't)* Have other volunteers identify a plural *(animals)* and a word that has a suffix. *(working, interesting)*

Practice and Apply

Read the Book   Help children tear out and fold the pages to make their Take-Home Books. Encourage them to look through the book and talk about the pictures. Then, read the story together. After reading, discuss what children learned about being a zookeeper.

Sound to Symbol   Write the following headings on the board: *Contraction, Plurals, Words with Other Suffixes.* Have children look through the book and identify contractions *(you'd, they're)*, plurals *(animals, lions, elephants, tigers, monkeys, wolves, giraffes, zookeepers, kinds, jobs, places, homes, visitors, questions, volunteers)*, and words with suffixes besides -s and -es *(being, zookeeper, protection, brushing, bathing, making, healthy, treatment, quickly, working)*. Ask children to write the words on the board under the appropriate headings.

Reread for Fluency   Have children reread the book to increase their fluency and comprehension. Invite them to take their books home to read and share with family members.

FOCUS ON ALL LEARNERS

ESL/ELL ENGLISH LANGUAGE LEARNERS

After helping children make their Take-Home Books, use the following activities to teach English language learners.

- Ask children to identify the animal in each picture and describe what is happening.

- You may wish to help children make a main-idea chart to help them organize their ideas as they read.

- Read the story together.

- Have children identify familiar contractions, plurals, and words with suffixes in the story.

AUDITORY LEARNERS

Have one partner read the story aloud while the other listens for plurals and claps when one is read. Then, have the listener read aloud while the other claps when a word with a suffix is read.

VISUAL LEARNERS PARTNERS

Have partners each write a sentence that includes two words that could form a contraction. Then, have them exchange papers, circle the two words and rewrite the sentence with contractions. Have children repeat the activity with additional sentences.

2

Zookeepers provide clean water and food for the animals. They must know what kind of food is best for each animal and just how much the animal should eat. They also care for the animals by brushing them, bathing them, and making sure they get enough exercise.

3

Zookeepers make sure that the places where the animals live are clean and safe. The animals' homes must offer them protection from visitors and other animals. Zookeepers also watch the animals to be sure they're healthy. If an animal is sick, it must get treatment quickly.

124 Review contractions, plurals, suffixes, and endings: Take-home book

CURRICULUM CONNECTIONS

SCIENCE

Have children talk about why a zookeeper needs to study science in order to care for animals properly. List children's ideas on the board in categories such as *Behavior, Nutrition,* and *Environment.* Encourage children to do research to confirm their ideas or to find out more about the responsibilities and educational requirements of a zookeeper.

SOCIAL STUDIES

Play a guessing game about outdoor jobs. Have a volunteer draw a picture clue on the board and ask classmates to guess what job the picture shows. Write all correct responses on the board and underline suffixes in words. Possible jobs to be depicted include zookeeper, gardener, farmer, rancher, construction worker, house painter, and forest ranger.

WRITING

Invite pairs of children to write a script for an interview with a zookeeper. Suggest that one child play the role of the reporter and write the questions. The other child should play the role of the zookeeper and write the responses. Invite children to read their script aloud for the class.

TECHNOLOGY **AstroWord** Suffixes

KINESTHETIC LEARNERS GROUPS

Materials: paper bags, paper strips

Have children write plural forms and words with suffixes on paper strips and place them in a bag. Group members then take turns choosing a word from the bag to use in a sentence about zookeepers. Have groups trade bags and repeat the activity.

CHALLENGE

Materials: books, magazines

Explain to children that apostrophes may be used in informal written speech to indicate letters left out *(I'll wait here 'til you call.)* or in place of numbers left out *(class of '02).* Have children skim magazines and books for similar examples.

EXTRA SUPPORT/INTERVENTION

Some children may have difficulty reading the following story words: *giraffes, volunteers, exercise, studied, college.* Pronounce these words and explain their meanings as needed. See Daily Phonics Practice, pages 217–219.

Unit Checkup

Review Contractions, Plurals, Suffixes, and Endings

Skill Focus

Children will

★ read and write contractions, plurals, and words with suffixes and endings in context.

★ identify the two words that make up a contraction.

★ identify the correct spelling for plurals, words with inflected endings, and words with suffixes.

Teach

Review Contractions, Plurals, and Suffixes Write the headings *Contraction, Plural,* and *Word with a Suffix* on the board. Read the following words aloud and ask volunteers to write them under the correct headings: *raked, isn't, slowly, they'll, leaves, sixes, don't, you've, oldest, I'm, gifts, glasses, darkness, parties, putting, flexible, wearable,* and *treatment.*

Review the words in each of the columns. Help children identify the two words that make each contraction. Then, discuss the words with plural endings. Ask volunteers to explain the spelling rules for forming plurals. Finally, have children identify suffixes and base words. When appropriate, ask volunteers to explain the spelling rules for adding suffixes to specific words.

Practice and Apply

Assess Skills For the activity on page 125, suggest that children read each sentence with both word choices to make sure they choose the one that makes the most sense. Review the directions for both activities on page 126 to make sure children understand what to do.

UNIT **4** CHECKUP

Name _____

▶ Circle the word that will finish each sentence. Write the word on the line.

1. Our swim team ___collected___ newspapers to raise money. (collected) collecting

2. We worked with other school ___teams___ . team (teams)

3. People ___placed___ their papers at the curb. places (placed)

4. We ___picked___ up some yesterday. picker (picked)

5. Our swim ___coach___ drove the truck. (coach) coached

6. It was a ___windy___ day. wind (windy)

7. We ___chased___ a lot of loose papers! (chased) chasing

8. We did better than we had ___hoped___ . (hoped) hopped

9. Today my dad is ___driving___ the truck. drive (driving)

10. We already have fifty ___boxes___ of newspapers. box (boxes)

11. ___We're___ keeping them in a garage. Were (We're)

12. Some boxes are ___bigger___ than others. (bigger) biggest

13. We have to be ___careful___ lifting them. (careful) careless

14. Tomorrow ___we'll___ take them to be recycled. will (we'll)

Contractions, plurals, suffixes, endings: Assessment **125**

FOCUS ON ALL LEARNERS

ESL/ELL ENGLISH LANGUAGE LEARNERS

Help English language learners to identify the correct written forms of target words by doing the activities orally with them.

• For page 125, read aloud and confirm activity directions. Tell children that you will read aloud a sentence that uses one of the two answer choices. They are to circle the choice you say. Then, have them write the word on the line.

• Read aloud and confirm directions for both activities on page 126. Tell children that you will say each item along with the correct answer choice. They should fill in the circle beside the word you say.

KINESTHETIC LEARNERS

Write base words on the board and invite children to take turns choosing a word to rewrite as many times as they can, adding a different suffix or plural ending each time.

VISUAL LEARNERS

Materials: newspapers, markers

Provide each group with newspaper pages and ask them to read the headlines and circle words that are plurals or have suffixes. Have groups share the words they find with the class.

ASSESS UNDERSTANDING OF UNIT SKILLS

> ▶ Read the two words. Then fill in the circle beside the correct contraction.

1. you + will
   ○ you're   ● you'll

2. will + not
   ○ we'll   ● won't

3. here + is
   ○ he'll   ● here's

4. we + have
   ○ we'll   ● we've

5. does + not
   ● doesn't   ○ don't

6. it + is
   ○ its   ● it's

7. let + us
   ○ she's   ● let's

8. I + have
   ● I've   ○ I'll

9. we + will
   ● we'll   ○ we've

10. can + not
    ○ won't   ● can't

11. could + not
    ○ wouldn't   ● couldn't

12. are + not
    ● aren't   ○ can't

> ▶ Read the word and the ending. Fill in the circle next to the correct spelling.

13. lily + s
    ○ lilys   ● lilies

14. elf + s
    ○ elfs   ● elves

15. quick + ness
    ● quickness   ○ quickeness

16. rip + ed
    ● ripped   ○ riped

17. skate + ing
    ● skating   ○ skateing

18. rest + ed
    ○ restted   ● rested

19. toy + s
    ● toys   ○ toyes

20. glad + ly
    ● gladly   ○ gladdly

21. smart + est
    ● smartest   ○ smarttest

22. examine + ed
    ● examined   ○ examineed

23. break + able
    ○ breakle   ● breakable

24. protect + ion
    ● protection   ○ protecton

126   Contractions, plurals, suffixes, endings: Assessment

STUDENT PROGRESS ASSESSMENT

Review the observational notes you recorded as children completed the activities in this unit. You may find your notes useful in evaluating a child's progress with contractions, plurals, and words with suffixes.

PORTFOLIO ASSESSMENT

Review the materials children have collected in their portfolios to evaluate their progress. You may wish to have individual conferences with children to review their written work and evaluate how well they apply the phonics skills they are learning in their writing. Work with children to set future goals.

DAILY PHONICS PRACTICE

For children who need additional practice with contractions, plurals, and suffixes, quick reviews are provided on pages 217–219 in Daily Phonics Practice.

PHONICS POSTTEST

To assess children's mastery of contractions, plurals, and suffixes, use the posttest on pages 91g–91h.

AUDITORY LEARNERS

Have children sit in a circle. One member begins by saying two words that form a contraction to the person sitting to his or her left. That person says and spells the contraction and then says the next two words, and so on. Follow the same procedure for words with suffixes.

CHALLENGE

Challenge children to write exercises like those on page 126, exchange papers with classmates, and fill in the answers.

EXTRA SUPPORT/INTERVENTION

Materials: index cards

Write plurals and words with suffixes on separate cards. Ask partners to sort the words into two groups, placing plurals in one group and words with suffixes in the other. Then have children sort each group again into two groups: words that require spelling changes and those that do not. See Daily Phonics Practice, pages 217–219.

Teacher Notes

UNIT 5

Vowel Pairs, Digraphs, Diphthongs
THEME: BY THE SEA

CONTENTS

Student Performance Objectives

In Unit 5, children will learn about vowel pairs, vowel digraphs, and diphthongs within the context of the theme "By the Sea." As children begin to understand the ways vowels work together to affect the pronunciation of words, they will be able to

▶ Associate vowel pairs, vowel digraphs, and diphthongs with their sounds in words

▶ Distinguish among vowel pairs, vowel digraphs, and diphthongs

▶ Recognize syllables within words with vowel digraphs and diphthongs

Overview of Resources

| LESSON | MCP PHONICS AND READING LIBRARY, LEVEL C | | DAILY PHONICS PRACTICE |
	PROGRAM	TITLE	
Unit Opener			
58: Vowel pairs	RR, Stg Five, Bk 22	*Carla Gets a Pet*	219–220
59: Vowel pairs	RR, Stg Four, Bk 23	*Erik and the Three Goats*	219–220
60: Vowel digraphs *oo, ea, ei*	RR, Stg Five, Bk 23	*Heather's Book*	220
61: Vowel digraphs *oo, ea, ei, au, aw*	RR, Stg Five, Bk 27	*Dinosaur Days*	220
62: Vowel pairs and vowel digraphs	RR, Stg Five, Bk 24	*The House That Stood on Booker Hill*	219–220
63: Review vowel pairs and digraphs	RR, Stg Four, Bk 28	*Lobster Fishing at Dawn*	219–220
64: Diphthongs *oy, oi, ow, ou, ew*	RR, Stg Four, Bk 25	*Tiger's Tummy Ache*	220–221
65: Syllables with digraphs and diphthongs	RR, Stg Four, Bk 26	*Squirrels*	220–221
66: Review vowel pairs, vowel digraphs, and diphthongs	RR, Stg Four, Bk 29	*Molly's Broccoli*	219–221
67: Review vowel pairs, digraphs, diphthongs; Take-Home Book: "Octopuses"			219–221
68: Unit Checkup			219–221

RR–Ready Readers   Stg–Stage   Bk–Book

Assessment Options

In Unit 5, assess children's ability to read and write words with vowel pairs, vowel digraphs, and diphthongs. Use the Unit Pretest and Posttest for formal assessment. For ongoing informal assessment, you may wish to use children's work on the Review pages, Take-Home Books, and Unit Checkups. Encourage children to evaluate their own work and to participate in setting goals for their own learning.

ESL/ELL Vowel pairs, vowel digraphs, and diphthongs may be especially problematic for English language learners. Note pronunciation difficulties as they occur, but assess performance based upon children's ability to distinguish specific sounds when pronounced by a native speaker. For additional support for English language learners, see page 127j.

FORMAL ASSESSMENT

Use the Unit 5 Pretest, on pages 127e–127f, to help assess a child's knowledge at the beginning of a unit and to plan instruction.

ESL/ELL Before administering the Pretest, gather together items or pictures of items that match the visuals on page 127e. Select an item and have volunteers name it. Ask other children to write the word on the board and circle the vowel pair, vowel digraph, or diphthong. Some children may have difficulty understanding the directions. Read them aloud and model how to complete the test pages.

Use the Unit 5 Posttest, on pages 127g–127h, to help assess mastery of unit objectives and to plan for reteaching, if necessary.

INFORMAL ASSESSMENT

Use the Review pages, Unit Checkup, and Take-Home Books in the student book to provide an effective means of evaluating children's performance.

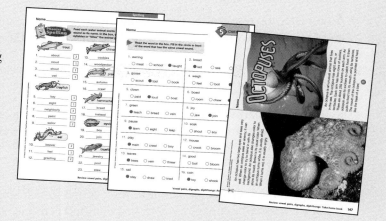

Unit 5 Skills	Review pages	Checkups	Take-Home Books
Vowel Pairs, Vowel Digraphs	138–140, 145–146	149–150	147–148
Diphthongs	142, 145–146	149–150	147–148
Syllables with Diphthongs	145–146	149–150	147–148

STUDENT PROGRESS CHECKLIST

Use the checklist on page 127i to record children's progress. You may want to cut the sections apart to place each child's checklist in his or her portfolio.

PORTFOLIO ASSESSMENT

This logo appears throughout the teaching plans. It signals opportunities for collecting children's work for individual portfolios. You may also want to include the Pretest and Posttest, the Review pages, the Unit Checkup, Phonics & Reading, and Phonics & Writing pages.

PHONEMIC AWARENESS AND PHONICS ASSESSMENT

Use PAPA to obtain an itemized analysis of children's decoding skills.

PAPA Skills	MCP Phonics Lessons in Unit 5
Deleting Sounds	Lesson 65
Vowel Pairs	Lessons 58, 59, 62, 63, 66
Vowel Digraphs	Lessons 60–63, 65, 66
Diphthongs	Lessons 64–66

Pretest and Posttest

DIRECTIONS

To help you assess children's progress in learning Unit 5 skills, tests are available on pages 127e–127h.

Administer the Pretest before children begin the unit. The results of the Pretest will help you identify each child's strengths and needs in advance, allowing you to structure lesson plans to meet individual needs. Administer the Posttest to assess children's overall mastery of skills taught in the unit and to identify specific areas that will require reteaching.

ESL/ELL Support English language learners by implementing any of the following suggestions before or during test taking, as appropriate.

- Model procedures for marking test answers. Complete several items together or in small groups to make sure children understand test-taking procedures.

- Conduct the test one-on-one with children who are unable to read independently in English or who need special pacing. Provide frequent support for their efforts.

- Administer the test orally. Try naming aloud the picture clues and saying the word choices so that children can hear the vowel sounds.

PERFORMANCE ASSESSMENT PROFILE

The following chart will help you identify specific skills as they appear on the tests and will enable you to identify and record specific information about an individual's or the class's performance on the tests.

Depending on the results of each test, refer to the Reteaching column for lesson-plan pages where you can find activities that will be useful for meeting individual needs or for daily phonics practice.

Answer Keys

Unit 5 Pretest, page 127e (BLM 29)

1. tail	4. leaf	7. soap
2. pie	5. jeans	8. hay
3. coat	6. train	9. wheel
10. stood	12. freight	14. draw
11. heavy	13. caught	15. moon

Unit 5 Pretest, page 127f (BLM 30)

16. mouth	18. enjoy	20. mouse
17. soil	19. screws	

21. 3	24. 2	27. 1	30. 1
22. 2	25. 1	28. 2	31. 2
23. 1	26. 3	29. 3	32. 3

Unit 5 Posttest, page 127g (BLM 31)

1. seal	4. boat	7. pail
2. feet	5. tie	8. mail
3. chain	6. tray	9. jeep
10. auto	12. ahead	14. crawl
11. took	13. weigh	15. soon

Unit 5 Posttest, page 127h (BLM 32)

16. joy	18. cloud	20. crew
17. loud	19. noise	

21. 2	24. 1	27. 2	30. 2
22. 1	25. 3	28. 1	31. 3
23. 2	26. 1	29. 2	32. 2

Performance Assessment Profile

Skill	Pretest Questions	Posttest Questions	Reteaching	
			Focus on All Learners	**Daily Phonics Practice**
Vowel Pairs	1–9	1–9	129–132, 137–139, 145–148	219–220
Vowel Digraphs	10–15	10–15	133–140, 145–148	220
Diphthongs	16–20	16–20	141–142, 145–148	220–221
Syllables with Vowel Digraphs and Diphthongs	21–32	21–32	143–144, 146	220–221

Name _____

> **Fill in the circle beside the word that names each picture.**

1. 
- ○ tree
- ○ pail
- ○ tail
- ○ toe

2. 
- ○ stay
- ○ play
- ○ pie
- ○ peel

3. 
- ○ coat
- ○ boat
- ○ cat
- ○ coal

4. 
- ○ load
- ○ lead
- ○ loaf
- ○ leaf

5. 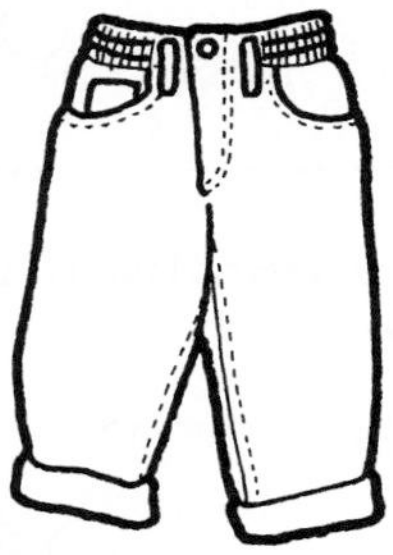
- ○ Jane
- ○ jeep
- ○ jet
- ○ jeans

6. 
- ○ trail
- ○ tie
- ○ tray
- ○ train

7. 
- ○ sail
- ○ seal
- ○ soap
- ○ seed

8. 
- ○ how
- ○ heat
- ○ heel
- ○ hay

9. 
- ○ wheel
- ○ wheat
- ○ well
- ○ wait

> **Fill in the circle beside the word that has the same vowel sound as the boldface word.**

10. **good**	○ food	○ stood	○ noon	○ loon
11. **head**	○ heavy	○ break	○ bead	○ team
12. **eight**	○ tie	○ freight	○ flies	○ fries
13. **taught**	○ caught	○ laugh	○ out	○ shout
14. **yawn**	○ draw	○ breath	○ sleigh	○ heat
15. **tooth**	○ took	○ door	○ moon	○ brook

Go to the next page.→

BLM 29 Unit 5 Pretest: Vowel pairs, vowel digraphs

Name_____

> ▶ **Fill in the circle beside the word that has the same vowel sound as the boldface word.**

16. **town**   ○ mouth   ○ north   ○ shown   ○ blown

17. **oil**   ○ girl   ○ loud   ○ soil   ○ four

18. **boy**   ○ crow   ○ enjoy   ○ bug   ○ brew

19. **news**   ○ nose   ○ noise   ○ now   ○ screws

20. **house**   ○ hose   ○ voice   ○ mouse   ○ joy

> ▶ **Say each word silently. Fill in the circle beside the number of syllables the word contains.**

21. **strawberry**   ○ 1   ○ 2   ○ 3

22. **fountain**   ○ 1   ○ 2   ○ 3

23. **bread**   ○ 1   ○ 2   ○ 3

24. **bookcase**   ○ 1   ○ 2   ○ 3

25. **seize**   ○ 1   ○ 2   ○ 3

26. **woodpecker**   ○ 1   ○ 2   ○ 3

27. **groom**   ○ 1   ○ 2   ○ 3

28. **August**   ○ 1   ○ 2   ○ 3

29. **allowing**   ○ 1   ○ 2   ○ 3

30. **bounce**   ○ 1   ○ 2   ○ 3

31. **feather**   ○ 1   ○ 2   ○ 3

32. **yesterday**   ○ 1   ○ 2   ○ 3

Possible score on Unit 5 Pretest is 32. Number correct _____

BLM 30 Unit 5 Pretest: Diphthongs, syllables with vowel digraphs and diphthongs

Name _____

> Fill in the circle beside the word that names each picture.

1. 
○ sow
○ song
○ seal
○ deal

2. 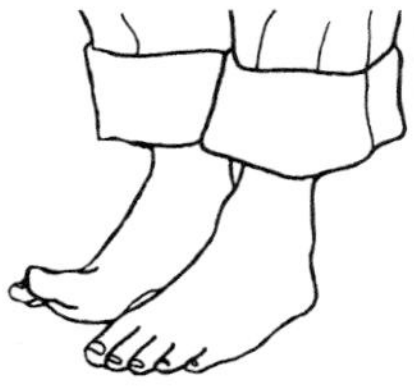
○ feet
○ teeth
○ foe
○ float

3. 
○ cheer
○ chair
○ chain
○ chart

4. 
○ oak
○ boat
○ bay
○ note

5. 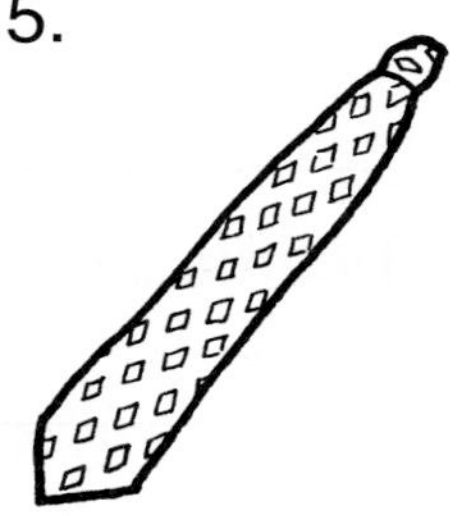
○ tie
○ tile
○ train
○ lie

6. 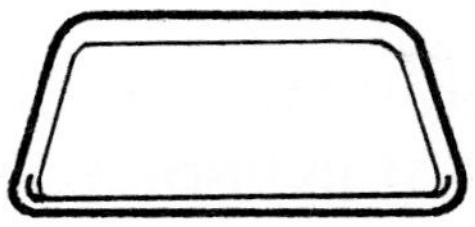
○ fray
○ tray
○ treat
○ tree

7. 
○ paint
○ peak
○ pail
○ plane

8. 
○ meet
○ make
○ meal
○ mail

9. 
○ jaw
○ jeep
○ joy
○ jail

> Fill in the circle beside the word that has the same vowel sound as the boldface word.

10. **naughty**   ○ auto   ○ laugh   ○ pout   ○ round

11. **look**   ○ loon   ○ took   ○ school   ○ too

12. **bread**   ○ each   ○ meat   ○ ahead   ○ easy

13. **vein**   ○ weigh   ○ ties   ○ lie   ○ wet

14. **lawn**   ○ eight   ○ crawl   ○ head   ○ spoon

15. **goose**   ○ soon   ○ good   ○ brook   ○ wool

Go to the next page.→

BLM 31 Unit 5 Posttest: Vowel pairs, vowel digraphs

Name _____

> **Fill in the circle beside the word that has the same vowel sound as the boldface word.**

16. **toy**   ○ town   ○ joy   ○ home   ○ show

17. **down**   ○ loud   ○ own   ○ blow   ○ day

18. **round**   ○ point   ○ soy   ○ rope   ○ cloud

19. **boil**   ○ noise   ○ out   ○ first   ○ count

20. **flew**   ○ found   ○ fled   ○ cow   ○ crew

> **Say each word silently. Fill in the circle beside the number of syllables the word contains.**

21. **somehow**   ○ 1   ○ 2   ○ 3

22. **draw**   ○ 1   ○ 2   ○ 3

23. **amount**   ○ 1   ○ 2   ○ 3

24. **neat**   ○ 1   ○ 2   ○ 3

25. **jewelry**   ○ 1   ○ 2   ○ 3

26. **sleigh**   ○ 1   ○ 2   ○ 3

27. **sooner**   ○ 1   ○ 2   ○ 3

28. **plowed**   ○ 1   ○ 2   ○ 3

29. **autumn**   ○ 1   ○ 2   ○ 3

30. **mountain**   ○ 1   ○ 2   ○ 3

31. **anyway**   ○ 1   ○ 2   ○ 3

32. **enjoy**   ○ 1   ○ 2   ○ 3

Possible score on Unit 5 Posttest is 32. Number correct _____

BLM 32 Unit 5 Posttest: Diphthongs, syllables with vowel digraphs and diphthongs

Student Progress Checklist

Make as many copies as needed to use for a class list. For individual portfolio use, cut apart each child's section. As indicated by the code, color in boxes next to skills satisfactorily assessed and insert an X by those requiring reteaching. Marked boxes can later be colored in to indicate mastery.

Student Progress Checklist

Code: ■ Satisfactory   ☒ Needs Reteaching

Student: _____ _____ Pretest Score: _____ Posttest Score: _____	**Skills** ☐ Vowel Pairs ☐ Vowel Digraphs ☐ Diphthongs ☐ Syllables with Vowel Digraphs/Diphthongs	**Comments / Learning Goals**
Student: _____ _____ Pretest Score: _____ Posttest Score: _____	**Skills** ☐ Vowel Pairs ☐ Vowel Digraphs ☐ Diphthongs ☐ Syllables with Vowel Digraphs/Diphthongs	**Comments / Learning Goals**
Student: _____ _____ Pretest Score: _____ Posttest Score: _____	**Skills** ☐ Vowel Pairs ☐ Vowel Digraphs ☐ Diphthongs ☐ Syllables with Vowel Digraphs/Diphthongs	**Comments / Learning Goals**
Student: _____ _____ Pretest Score: _____ Posttest Score: _____	**Skills** ☐ Vowel Pairs ☐ Vowel Digraphs ☐ Diphthongs ☐ Syllables with Vowel Digraphs/Diphthongs	**Comments / Learning Goals**

BLM 33 Unit 5 Checklist

Throughout Unit 5 there are opportunities to assess English language learners' ability to read and write words with vowel pairs, vowel digraphs, and diphthongs. Recognizing and pronouncing the vowel sounds represented by these letter teams may be especially problematic for English language learners. Children's home languages vary from having five pure vowel sounds in Spanish to 35 syllabic vowels in Cantonese. English language learners will need many opportunities to listen to and practice saying English vowel sounds before they can reasonably be expected to reproduce them without error. Take note of pronunciation difficulties as they occur, and assess progress based on their ability to distinguish vowel sounds when pronounced by a native speaker.

Lesson 58, pages 129–130 Native speakers of Spanish will likely sound *ai* and *ay* as the short, not long, *ai* sound; reinforce orally if you notice native-language interference.

Lesson 59, pages 131–132 Native speakers of Spanish may exhibit difficulty distinguishing the sounds of long *e* and short *i*, instead pronouncing both as long *e*. Practice with *check, chick; eat, it; neat, nit; seat, sit;* and *feet, fit.*

Lesson 60, pages 133–134 Children who have difficulty pronouncing *oo* vowel digraphs (*book/boot*) may need additional support and oral/listening practice with the long *oo* sound. Some children may also have difficulty pronouncing and distinguishing short vowels, including the sound of short *e*. In Tagalog, for example, short *e* sounds like *ay* in *say*. No similar vowel sound exists in Korean.

Lesson 61, pages 135–136 Children whose home language is Korean may introduce the sound /ya/ when they anticipate the sound of short *a* after *g* and have difficulty saying words like *August*. Listen for native-language interference with English pronunciation; offer additional practice as needed.

Lesson 64, pages 141–142 English language learners whose native languages identify one sound per letter may experience difficulty understanding that a vowel + a consonant can make a separate sound. Provide oral practice if you notice oral hesitation among these children.

Lesson 65, pages 143–144 Native speakers of Spanish are familiar with diphthongs formed by two vowels; but they are not familiar with diphthongs formed by a vowel and a consonant. Provide oral practice with words containing these sounds.

Spelling Connections

INTRODUCTION

The Unit Word List is a list of selected spelling words drawn from this unit. The words are grouped by vowel pairs and vowel digraphs, and diphthongs, vowel digraphs, and syllables. To incorporate spelling into your phonics program, use the activity in the Curriculum Connections section of each teaching plan.

ESL/ELL It is recommended that English language learners reach the intermediate fluency level of English proficiency before focusing on spelling.

For English language learners, introduce 6–8 words at a time. Help children understand the words' meanings by using visuals or realia.

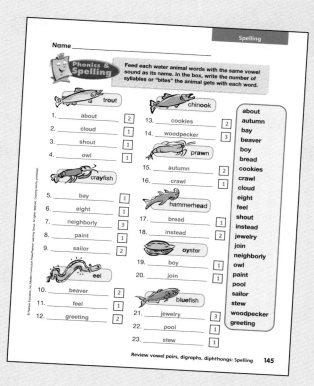

Review vowel pairs, digraphs, diphthongs: Spelling 145

The spelling lessons utilize the following approach for each word with a vowel digraph or diphthong.

1. Administer a pretest of the words, some of which have not yet been formally introduced. Dictation sentences are provided.

2. Provide practice.

3. Reassess. Dictation sentences are provided.

A midunit test focusing on words with vowel pairs and vowel digraphs is provided in Lesson 63. An end-of-unit review focusing on diphthongs and words with syllables containing vowel digraphs and diphthongs is provided in Lesson 66 with the option of a cumulative test for all spelling words in Unit 5.

DIRECTIONS

Make a copy of Blackline Master 34 for each child. After administering the pretest for vowel pairs and vowel digraphs or diphthongs, and syllables, give children a copy of the appropriate word list.

Children can work with a partner to practice spelling the words orally and identifying the vowel sound in each word. You may want to challenge children to make new words by substituting the consonants surrounding the vowel pairs, vowel digraphs, or diphthongs. Children can write words of their own on *My Own Word List* (see Blackline Master 34).

Have children store their list words in an envelope or plastic zipper bag in their books or notebooks. You may want to suggest that students keep a spelling notebook, listing words with similar patterns. Another idea is to build Word Walls with children and display them in the classroom. Each section of the wall can focus on words with a single phonics element. The walls will become a good resource for children to use when they are writing.

Unit Word List

Vowel Pairs; Vowel Digraphs
feel
paint
dried
cookies
bread
pool
eight
crawl

Diphthongs; Vowel Digraphs; Syllables
join
boy
about
owls
stew
autumn

Name _____

 **UNIT 5 WORD LIST**

Vowel Pairs; Vowel Digraphs

feel

paint

dried

cookies

bread

pool

eight

crawl

Diphthongs; Vowel Digraphs; Syllables

join

boy

about

owls

stew

autumn

My Own Word List

My Own Word List

Phonics Games, Activities, and Technology

The following collection of ideas offers a variety of opportunities to reinforce phonics skills while actively engaging children. The games, activities, and technology suggestions can easily be adapted to meet the needs of your group of learners. They vary in approach so as to consider children's different learning styles.

EGG-TRAY TOSS

For each small group of children, bend back or remove the top of an egg carton and write the numerals 1, 2, and 3 randomly inside the bottom sections. (Numeral stickers might also work well.) Make word cards, using one-, two-, or three-syllable words that have vowel pairs, vowel digraphs, or diphthongs, such as *chewy, flowerpots, autumn, breakfast, cloudy, clown, growl, spoiling, strawberry, bedspread, woodpecker, claw, mountain, reindeer, neighborly, measure, afternoon, wheelbarrow, today, dreamer,* and *treatment.*

To play, children spread the word cards face up nearby. They take turns to toss a marker such as a paper clip into the egg tray. They must find and read a word that has the number of syllables indicated by the marker. For each correct response, the word card is turned face down and the number of syllables recorded as points for the player. Encourage children to add to the game by making their own word cards.

SEA SERPENT VOWELS

> A sea serpent saw a big tanker,
> Bit a hole in her side, and
>   then sank her.
> It gulped down the crew
> In a minute or two—
> And then closed its teeth
>   on the anchor.

Write the poem at the left on the chalkboard. Invite children to find, underline, and read the words in the poem that have the vowel pairs, vowel digraphs, and diphthongs *ea, aw, ow, ew,* and *ee. (sea, saw, down, crew, teeth)* You also might use this poem to review vowel sounds in general.

CROSSWORDS IN NATURE

Provide copies of the crossword puzzle on Blackline Master 35 on page 127p. Have children read each clue, look in the word box for the answer, then write the word in the puzzle. (Answers: <u>Across</u> 1. bee 3. noises 4. outdoors 6. toad 7. owls 9. round 11. wheat <u>Down</u> 2. enjoy 4. oyster 5. soil 8. snout 10. dew)

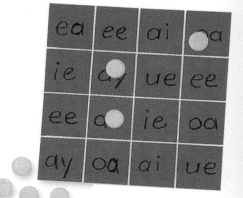

COVER UP THE VOWEL PAIRS

Have children fold a sheet of paper into 16 squares and randomly write the following vowel pairs as many times as necessary to fill the squares: *ea, ee, ai, oa, ie, ay, ue.* Hand out markers for children to play a version of bingo. As you say words with vowel pairs, children can cover the appropriate pairs on their game cards. When a player has covered vowel pairs in four squares across or down, the game ends and a new one begins.

WORD WEBBING

Invite children to create a word web about the sea. Begin by writing the title "Sea" in the center of a sheet of chart paper. Draw a circle around the title. Encourage children to suggest words and phrases associated with the sea that contain at least one vowel pair, vowel digraph, or diphthong. Draw a line from the title to each word or phrase as it is written. If children have difficulty, prompt them with clues for such words and phrases as those shown in the diagram.

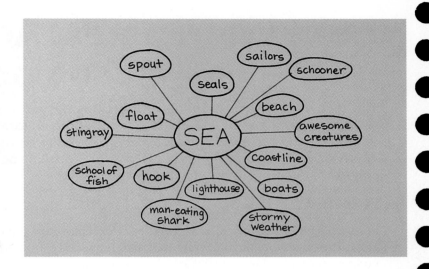

SEAWORTHY CLASS STORY

Invite children to use words and phrases from their word web to write a class story about a sea adventure. As children contribute ideas, form sentences to write on another sheet of chart paper. Encourage them to include as many words from the web as possible. When children have finished, read the story together and ask volunteers to underline the words with vowel pairs, vowel digraphs, and diphthongs.

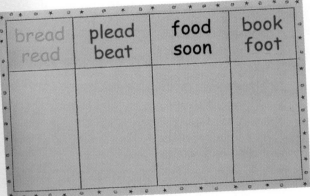

TEAM EFFORT

Make a chart on mural paper as shown at the left. Read the words together and establish that the vowels *ea* and *oo* each stand for two different sounds. Have children form four teams, one team to be responsible for each column on the chart. As you say words with *ea* and *oo*, the appropriate team should claim the word and one team member write the word on the chart. Then, invite members from each team to add their own words to each column. Display the chart and encourage children to continue adding words they encounter in their reading throughout the unit.

SORT AND RE-SORT

Provide sets of word cards featuring words with *aw, au, ow, ou, oo,* and *ew: fawn, draw, straw, awning, hawk; August, auto, taught, because, sausage; owl, flower, clown, growl, crowd; pouch, house, sound, cloud, mound; school, goose, tool, bloom, noodle; jewel, threw, stew, few, knew.*

Children can work independently, in pairs, or in small groups to sort the words into three groups by vowel sound and then re-sort each group according to spellings for the vowel sound.

FOLLOW THE TRAIL

Have children take the word cards from the previous activity and place them on a table or the floor to form a word trail. Using a game spinner or number cube, players can take turns moving a game marker along the trail, reading words as they go, and giving another word with the same vowel sound as the word landed on.

PASTE A MESSAGE

Provide newspapers and magazines and invite children to search large-print sections, such as ads and headlines, for words that have vowel pairs, vowel digraphs, or diphthongs, and cut out those words. When children have collected at least eight words, challenge them to piece the words together to make a message, filling in the message by writing other words. Provide glue and paper for children to paste down and write their messages. Encourage them to share their messages with the class.

WHAT'S THE WORD?

Invite children to write their own riddles with answers that contain vowel pairs, vowel digraphs, or diphthongs. To get them started, use some of the examples shown at right. When children are ready, have them read their riddles to ask one another.

What is a little animal with whiskers? (*mouse*)

What do you put on when it is cold outside? (*coat*)

What month comes after July? (*August*)

What do birds have all over their bodies? (*feathers*)

If you are not a girl, what are you? (*boy*)

What do horses eat? (*hay, oats, grain*)

RED ROVER

Have each child write a word with a vowel pair, vowel digraph, or diphthong on a sheet of tagboard or construction paper and thread a length of yarn through it so it can be worn around the neck. Make certain no words are duplicated.

Divide the class into two teams and have them line up about ten yards apart to play Red Rover. As teams choose a child to call over, they will chant "Red Rover, Red Rover, let _____ come over," inserting the word worn by the child in place of a name. The child wearing the word runs across to the other side and tries to break through the line of children with clasped hands. If the child breaks through, he or she chooses someone to take back to the other side. Play continues until all children are on one team.

 **TECHNOLOGY**

The following software products reinforce children's understanding of short vowels.

Reader Rabbit® 3

This product, the last in the *Reader Rabbit* series, is designed to teach six- to eight-year-olds writing skills through a series of games centered around Reader Rabbit's job as a newspaper reporter.

** Riverdeep The Learning Company
    500 Redwood Blvd.
    Novato, CA 94947
    (800) 825-4420
    www.learningcompanyschool.com

Reading Blaster™ Ages 6–8

Children ages 6–8 have fun playing games on different levels while learning critical reading skills in the latest edition of *Reading Blaster*.

** Sunburst Technology
    1900 South Batavia Avenue
    Geneva, IL 60134
    (800) 321-7511
    www.sunburst.com

Name _____

Read each clue. Find the answer to the clues in the word box.
Then, write the word in the crossword puzzle.

owls
toad
bee
enjoy
round
noises
oyster
outdoors
wheat
soil
dew
snout

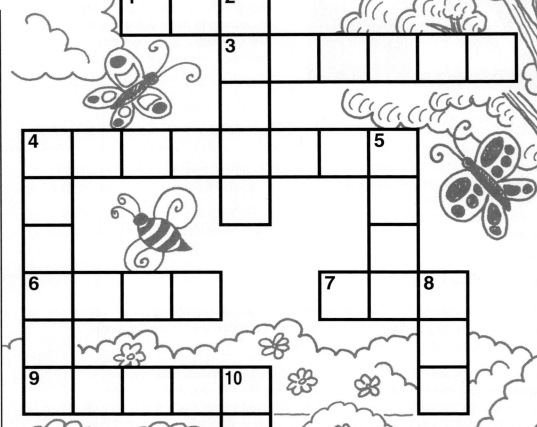

Across

1. an insect that buzzes
3. lots of sounds
4. the opposite of indoors
6. an animal like a frog
7. birds that hoot
9. the shape of the sun
11. grain made into bread

Down

2. have a good time
4. a creature in a shell
5. dirt to plant seeds in
8. a dog's nose
10. tiny drops of water

BLM 35 Unit 5 Activity

Home Connections

The Home Connections features of this program are intended to involve families in their children's learning and application of phonics skills. Three effective opportunities to make connections between home and school include the following.

- **HOME LETTER**
- **HOME NOTES**
- **TAKE-HOME BOOKS**

HOME LETTER

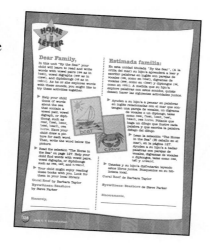

A letter is available to be sent home at the beginning of Unit 5. This letter informs family members that children will be learning to read and write words with vowel pairs, vowel digraphs, and diphthongs within the context of the unit theme, "By the Sea." The suggested home activity focuses on listing words about the sea that contain a vowel pair, vowel digraph, or diphthong and drawing a picture for each word. This activity promotes interaction between child and family members while supporting children's learning of the phonics elements taught in this unit. The letter, which is available in both English and Spanish, also suggests sea-theme books family members can read together.

HOME NOTES

Whenever the Home logo appears within the student book, a phonics activity is suggested to be done at home. The activities are simple to do, requiring little or no preparation or special materials, and are meant to reinforce the targeted phonics skill.

TAKE-HOME BOOKS

Within the student book are Take-Home Books that can be cut out and assembled. The story language in each book reinforces the targeted phonics skills. The books can be taken home and shared with family members. In Unit 5, one Take-Home Book is available, focusing on words with vowel pairs, vowel digraphs, and diphthongs as well as the unit theme, "By the Sea."

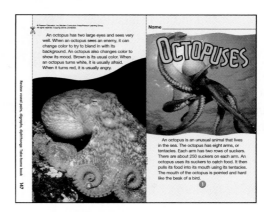

Home Notes in Spanish are also available for both teachers and parents to download and use from our website, www.PlaidPhonics.com.

Vowel Pairs, Digraphs, Diphthongs

Skill Focus

Assessing Prior Knowledge
To assess children's prior knowledge of vowel pairs, digraphs, and diphthongs, use the pretest on pages 127e–127f.

Unit Focus

Building Background

- Point out the unit theme "By the Sea!" on page 127. Have children discuss what they might expect to see in or near the sea.

- Ask children to identify the animal pictured on the page. Explain that it is a special kind of fish called a sea horse.

- Read the text aloud as children follow along. Tell children that there are many kinds of sea horses. Most are about five inches long. Sea horses move through the water in an upright position and are usually carried along by the sea's currents.

Introduce Vowel Pairs, Digraphs, Diphthongs

- On the board, write *sea, tail, seen, float*. Circle the letters that stand for the vowel sounds: *ea, ai, ee, oa*. Explain that these letters are vowel pairs. The first vowel has a long sound and the second is silent.

- Next, write the word *around*. Circle the letters *ou*. Point out that the two vowels blend to make a special sound called a diphthong.

- Then, write the words *pool* and *book*. Circle the letters *oo* in each word. Point out the special sound made by these letters together is called a digraph.

- Tell children they will learn more about vowel pairs, digraphs, and diphthongs as they do the lessons in the unit.

Critical Thinking Have children look at the picture on page 127 and consider the shape of a sea horse. Point out that its head is shaped somewhat like a horse's head, which makes the name *sea horse* a good one for this fish.

127

Read Aloud

The Horse in the Sea

A strange and beautiful horse lives among the many fish that swim in the sea. Of course, sea horses aren't really horses, but they are a kind of fish.

The body of a sea horse is covered with hard, spiny plates that protect it. A long tail that wraps around seaweed or coral keeps the sea horse from floating away.

Sea horses can change color. Changing color helps a sea horse blend in with the background so it can't be seen by enemies.

TALK About It Do you think a sea horse is a good name for a fish? Tell why or why not.

Unit 5 • Introduction
Critical Thinking 127

THEME FOCUS

BY THE SEA!

Have children share ideas they have related to the theme "By the Sea!" Encourage them to go beyond the information given in the selection. Invite children to talk about their experiences visiting or reading about the sea.

SEA-ANIMAL PUPPETS

Materials: construction paper, markers, glue, craft sticks

Have children make stick puppets of sea animals. Urge them to be imaginative. Some children may wish to look at books to get ideas as they work. Invite volunteers to put on puppet plays for the class.

FISHY TIC-TAC-TOE

Draw large tic-tac-toe grids on the board. Have volunteers write the names of fish and other sea animals in the grid spaces. Then, have pairs of children take turns playing tic-tac-toe, saying each word before making an *X* or an *O*.

Dear Family,

In this unit "By the Sea!" your child will learn to read and write words with vowel pairs (**oa** as in b**oa**t), vowel digraphs (**aw** as in cl**aw**), and diphthongs (**oi** as in c**oi**ns). As he or she explores words with these sounds, you might like to try these activities together.

▶ Help your child think of words about the sea that contain a vowel pair, vowel digraph, or diph-thong, such as s**ea**l, fl**oa**t, h**oo**k, b**oa**t, b**ea**ch, s**ea** horse. Have your child draw a pic-ture for each word. Then, write the word below the picture.

▶ Read the selection "The Horse in the Sea" on page 127. Help your child find words with vowel pairs, vowel digraphs, or diphthongs such as s**ea**, t**ai**l, and **a**r**ou**nd.

▶ Your child might enjoy reading these books with you. Look for them in your local library.

Coral Reef by Barbara Taylor
Eyewitness: Seashore by Steve Parker

Sincerely,

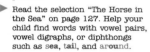

Estimada familia:

En esta unidad titulada "By the Sea!", (A la orilla del mar) su hijo/a aprenderá a leer y escribir palabras en inglés con parejas de vocales (**oa**, como en b**oa**t), digramas de vocales (**aw**, como en cl**aw**) y diptongos (**oi**, como en c**oi**n). A medida que su hijo/a explore palabras con estos sonidos, quizás deseen hacer las siguientes actividades juntos.

▶ Ayuden a su hijo/a a pensar en palabras en inglés relacionadas con el mar que con-tengan una pareja de vocales, un digrama de vocales o un diptongo, tales como s**ea**l, fl**oa**t, h**oo**k, b**oa**t, b**ea**ch, s**ea** horse. Pídanle que haga un dibujo que ilustre cada palabra y que escriba la palabra debajo del dibujo.

▶ Lean la selección "The Horse in the Sea" (El caballo en el mar), en la página 127. Ayuden a su hijo/a a hallar palabras con parejas de vocales, digramas de vocales o diptongos, tales como s**ea**, t**ai**l y **a**r**ou**nd.

▶ Ustedes y su hijo/a disfrutarán leyendo estos libros juntos. Búsquenlos en su bib-lioteca local.

Coral Reef de Barbara Taylor

Eyewitness: Seashore de Steve Parker

Sinceramente,

BULLETIN BOARD

Divide a seaside scene into the areas water, shore, and sky. Have children create paper cutouts of items to go in each area: stingray, eel, flounder, hammerhead shark (*water*); seashells, snails, seaweed, oysters (*shore*); seagull, eagle (*sky*). Have children label their pictures, underlining each vowel pair, digraph, or diphthong.

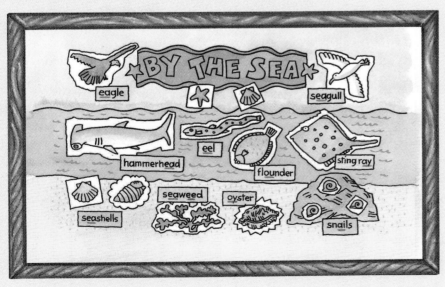

HOME CONNECTIONS

- The Home Letter on page 128 is intended to acquaint family members with the phonics skills children will be studying in this unit. Children can tear out page 128 and take it home.

- You might suggest that they complete the activities on the page with a family member. Encourage children to look in the library for the recommended books and read them with family members.

LEARNING CENTER ACTIVITIES

WRITING CENTER

Have children write a descriptive paragraph about a strange sea creature. Suggest that they begin by drawing a strange-looking sea animal, either realistic or imaginary. Then, children can refer to their drawing as they describe what the creature looks like, where it lives, and what makes it so strange.

SCIENCE CENTER

Provide children with an assortment of poster-making materials. Engage them in a discussion about the ways in which the seaside environment can be harmed and how it should be protected. Then, have partners work together to make posters reminding people to keep the sea and the shore clean and safe for the animals and plants that live there. Children can draw and/or cut out pictures to illustrate their posters.

MATH CENTER

Provide reference materials and ask children to do research to find out which animals are the largest and smallest sea creatures living today. Have children share and compare their findings. Some children may wish to make bar graphs comparing the sizes of the animals they have researched.

Vowel Pairs

Skill Focus

Children will

★ identify vowel pairs as two vowels together that make the long vowel sound of the first letter.

★ identify the sounds made by the vowel pairs *ai, ay, ea, ee, ie, oa, oe,* and *ue.*

ESL/ELL Native speakers of Spanish will likely sound *ai* and *ay* as the short, not long, *ai* sound; reinforce orally if you notice native-language interference.

Teach

Phonemic Awareness: Phoneme Identity
Model pronunciation of the following words: *tray, leaf, pie, goat,* and *blue.* Say each word and have children repeat chorally. Then, have children say the vowel sound in each word and offer another word with the same vowel sound. Ask whether the vowel sounds are long or short. (*The vowel sounds are long.*)

Sound to Symbol On the board, write the words from the Phonemic Awareness activity. Have volunteers circle the two vowels in each word. Explain that the *y* in *tray* acts as a vowel when it follows the *a.* Tell children that the two vowels in each word are called a vowel pair.

Say the words again, and ask whether children hear the long sound of the first or the second vowel. Point out that in a syllable with a vowel pair, the first vowel stands for the long sound and the second vowel is silent. Have volunteers identify the vowel whose long sound is heard in each pair.

Practice and Apply

Sound to Symbol As children complete the exercise on page 129, have them read the sentences softly to themselves, listening for words with long vowel sounds.

Critical Thinking For Talk About It, point out that item 5 contains clues to the autumn season in which the story takes place. This information will help them project what the scene would be like three months later.

Writing For page 130, suggest that children try each word choice before writing a word. Point out that each word is used once.

Reading Use *Carla Gets a Pet,* MCP Phonics and Reading Library, Super Skills Collection, Level C, to provide additional practice in reading words with vowel pairs.

Name _____

Read each sentence and underline the word with a vowel pair. Then, write the words on the lines at the bottom of the page.

RULE
In a vowel pair, two vowels come together to make one long vowel sound. When one syllable has a vowel pair, the first vowel stands for the long sound and the second vowel is silent.

true	boat	tree	pie
toe	leaf	train	tray

1. Ann and Ted went to the stable to <u>feed</u> the horses.
2. The horses like to <u>eat</u> <u>oats</u> from the large <u>pail</u>.
3. Ann and Ted <u>tried</u> to ride at <u>least</u> once a <u>week</u>.
4. The plan for <u>today</u> was to go riding on the <u>trail</u>.
5. It was chilly, and the <u>leaves</u> were changing colors.
6. There were many pretty <u>trees</u> and bushes.
7. Ann and Ted stopped for lunch by a <u>stream</u>.
8. A <u>toad</u> jumped along the grassy bank.
9. Ann wiggled her <u>toes</u> in the cool water.
10. Ted <u>lay</u> on the grass and gazed at the <u>blue</u> sky.
11. A tiny <u>boat</u> with a red <u>sail</u> drifted by them.

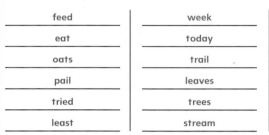

feed	week	toad
eat	today	toes
oats	trail	lay
pail	leaves	blue
tried	trees	boat
least	stream	sail

 If Ann and Ted rode on the same trail three months later, what would they see?

Vowel pairs: Words in context, critical thinking   **129**

FOCUS ON ALL LEARNERS

ESL/ELL ENGLISH LANGUAGE LEARNERS

As English language learners read the words in the box on page 130, have them cover up the second (silent) vowel in each vowel pair. This serves as a visual reminder that it is the long sound of the first vowel that is heard.

AUDITORY/VISUAL LEARNERS   INDIVIDUAL

Materials: index cards

Write the words *sleep, play, road, gain, toe, tail, feel, oats,* and *bead* on index cards. Have children work independently to say the words softly to themselves and sort them according to vowel sound. Then, have them resort the words according to vowel pairs.

KINESTHETIC LEARNERS   GROUPS

Have children pantomime words with vowel pairs for others to guess. Children may choose their own words, or select from word cards you have prepared. Try these words: *eat, paint, kneel, tie, play, toad, toes, glue.*

Copyright by Pearson Education, Inc., publishing as Modern Curriculum Press, an imprint of Pearson Learning Group.

▶ Find the word in the box that will complete the sentence. Write the word on the line.

breeze	blue	day	leaves
paint	boat	feels	green
playing	tries	sea	Joe

1. Kay wants to _____paint_____ a picture today.

2. She decides to paint a picture of the _____sea_____.

3. First, she shows the water with the color _____blue_____.

4. Then, she draws some _____green_____ sea plants.

5. The plants have long, green _____leaves_____.

6. Next, she draws a _____boat_____ sailing on the sea.

7. The boat has a red sail to catch the _____breeze_____.

8. Kay asks her friend _____Joe_____ what to draw next.

9. Then, she _____tries_____ to think of some sea animals.

10. She decides to show two seals _____playing_____ in the sea.

11. Finally, Kay is finished for the _____day_____.

12. She _____feels_____ proud of the picture she has made.

 TALK about it What would you draw in a picture of the sea?

 HOME Help your child make up a story about a day on the beach using the words in the box.

130 Vowel pairs ai, ay, ea, ee, ie, oa, oe, ue: Words in context

---

CHALLENGE

Challenge children to write pairs of words that begin and end with the same letters but have different vowel pairs. Examples include *soap, seep* and *mail, meal.*

EXTRA SUPPORT/INTERVENTION

Materials: a copy of the word search below

```
B O P M T F G X F R I E D
E V T A I L R S E E W A H
A Z R Y E C E T O A S T O
D H U O Y L E A N D A Y E
B E E Q Z X N Y C L U E W
```

Provide children with a copy of the word search puzzle. Encourage them to look for words that have vowel pairs and circle them. They should read words across or down. These words should be circled: UP-AND-DOWN—*bead, true, may, tie, green, stay, read, eat, hoe.* ACROSS—*fried, tail, see, toast, lean, day, bee, clue.* You may wish to list the words in the puzzle for children's reference. See Daily Phonics Practice, pages 219–220.

CURRICULUM CONNECTIONS

SPELLING

Use the following words and sentences as a pretest for writing words with vowel pairs and vowel digraphs.

1. **feel** How do you **feel** today?
2. **paint** Lucia likes to **paint** pictures.
3. **dried** The clothes **dried** in the sun.
4. **clue** This **clue** will help us do the puzzle.
5. **bread** Fresh **bread** smells good.
6. **pool** Carlos dove into the **pool**.
7. **eight** An octopus has **eight** arms.
8. **crawl** The baby learned to **crawl.**

WRITING

Have children write about a sailboat that can fly wherever its captain wishes to go. On the board, list words with vowel pairs that children can use in their stories. Invite volunteers to read their stories aloud.

PORTFOLIO

TECHNOLOGY **AstroWord** Long Vowels: *a, i;* Long Vowels: *i, o;* Long Vowels: *e, u*

Integrating Phonics and Reading

Guided Reading

Have children consider the cover and the book's title. Ask what they think will happen in the story. Then, have children talk about the duties that come with getting and caring for a pet.

First Reading Remind children that Carla's Mom decides that Carla is ready to get a dog. Ask: *Why does Carla change her mind?*

Second Reading Have children identify story words that have vowel pairs. Add these words to the classroom Word Wall.

Comprehension

After reading, ask these questions:
- What did Carla think when she found King's leash? *Inference/Character*
- How did you expect the story to end? *Reflective Analysis/Personal Response*

ESL/ELL English Language Learners

Draw an exclamation point on the board and make sure children understand that it is used to express strong feeling. Read the sentences *King! Come back! Stop!* expressively.

Vowel Pairs

Skill Focus

Children will

★ recognize words that contain any of the vowel pairs *ai, ay, ea, ee, ie, oa, oe,* or *ue.*

★ use words with vowel pairs in the context of complete sentences.

ESL/ELL Native speakers of Spanish may exhibit difficulty distinguishing the sounds of long *e* and short *i,* instead pronouncing both as long *e.* Practice with *check, chick; eat, it; neat, nit; seat, sit;* and *feet, fit.*

Teach

Phonological Awareness: Rhyme Explain to children that you will say a set of three words. Children are to identify the word in each set that does not rhyme with the other two.

- treat   feet   wet
- maid   had   played
- rod   toad   hoed

Sound to Symbol On the board, write the three groups of words from the Phonological Awareness activity. Ask volunteers to circle each vowel pair and identify its vowel sound. Then, ask children to identify two vowel pairs in each row that stand for the same sound. *(ea/ee, ai/ay, oa/oe)*

Then, call on volunteers to complete these sentences with words from the board.

- We _____ a game after lunch. *(played)*
- A ____ hopped out as we _____ the garden. *(toad, hoed)*

Practice and Apply

Sound to Symbol Before children begin the bottom of page 132, make sure they know the sound represented by each vowel pair. Ask volunteers to say the sound that each vowel pair stands for.

Writing For the cloze exercises on pages 131 and 132, suggest that children read each sentence after they have chosen a word to make sure the word makes sense in the sentence context.

Critical Thinking After children have completed the exercise on page 131, draw their attention to the Talk About It question. Discuss beach weather, food, games, activities.

Reading Use *Erik and the Three Goats,* MCP Phonics and Reading Library, Super Skills Collection, Level C, to provide additional practice with vowel pairs.

Erik and the Three Goats
Written by Gale Clifford Illustrated by Diane Fiedler

131

Name _____

> Read each sentence. Find the word or words from the box that best complete each sentence. Write each word on the line.

beach	day	tried	away
sailing	treat	cheese	Joe
boat	Sue	floated	sea gulls

1. It was a great _____ day _____ to go to the _____ beach _____.
2. Mom made us _____ cheese _____ sandwiches for lunch.
3. After lunch, Grandma and I _____ tried _____ to build a sand castle.
4. Later, the waves washed the sand castle _____ away _____.
5. Dean spotted some _____ sea gulls _____ flying.
6. My sister _____ Sue _____ spied some starfish on a rock.
7. Dad and _____ Joe _____ took the boat out _____ sailing _____.
8. They had to tow the _____ boat _____ to shore after the wind stopped.
9. Grandpa _____ floated _____ on a raft.
10. Going to the beach is a real _____ treat _____ for my family!

 What do you think you would like to do at the beach?

Vowel pairs ai, ay, ea, ee, ie, oa, oe, ue: Words in context, critical thinking   **131**

FOCUS ON ALL LEARNERS

ESL/ELL ENGLISH LANGUAGE LEARNERS

- For English language learners who have difficulty pronouncing long vowel sounds, point out that the long vowel sound is the same as the name of the letter in English.

- For the exercises on pages 131–132, discuss summer and winter activities. Use visuals to confirm meanings of unfamiliar words. Read aloud the completed sentences with children.

VISUAL LEARNERS

On the board, list the vowel pairs *ai, ay, ea, ee, ie, oa, oe, ue.* A player writes a word on the board, leaving a blank where the vowel pair should be. *(tr__n)* Classmates fill in the correct vowel pair to make a word. *(train)*

AUDITORY LEARNERS GROUPS

Read aloud words with short vowel sounds, such as *fed* and *sap.* For each word, have children replace the vowel with a vowel pair to make a new word. *(feed, soap)*

Fill in the circle next to the word that completes the sentence. Write the word on the line.

1. Jason and Jeff __played__ in the snow all day. ○ plain ● played
2. Making a snowman made them __feel__ very cold. ○ foam ● feel
3. They went inside to play with Jeff's __train__. ○ tree ● train
4. It felt good to remove their winter __coats__. ● coats ○ coal
5. Jeff's dog wagged its __tail__ to greet them. ○ tie ● tail
6. Jeff's mom made some hot apple cider for a __treat__. ● treat ○ tried
7. They sat on the __blue__ carpet to play. ● blue ○ blow
8. A __wheel__ on the train came off the track. ○ when ● wheel
9. Jason __tried__ to help Jeff fix it. ○ tray ● tried
10. Soon it was able to __coast__ along the rails. ● coast ○ crow
11. The train ran smoothly the rest of the __day__. ○ deal ● day

Read each clue. Then write the answer that contains the given vowel pair.

12. something to sail in — oa — __boat__
13. something we do to shoelaces — ie — __tie__
14. something that runs on tracks — ai — __train__
15. something on your foot — oe — __toe__
16. something we do at recess — ay — __play__
17. something that grows on a tree — ea — __leaf__

132 Vowel pairs ai, ay, ea, ee, ie, oa, oe, ue: Words in context

 HOME Help your child think of other words with vowel pairs *oa, ie, ai, oe, ay, ea* such as *float, dried,* or *wait.*

CURRICULUM CONNECTIONS

SPELLING

Write these spelling words on the board: *feel, paint, dried, clue.* Ask children to read the words. Then, call on volunteers to name the long vowel sound and circle the letters that spell the sound. Encourage children to write other words with these same vowel pairs.

WRITING

 **PORTFOLIO**

Have partners write a script for a dialogue between Jason and Jeff. When they have finished writing, children should underline words with vowel pairs. Invite volunteers to act out the script for the class.

SCIENCE/HEALTH

Have children list foods whose names contain vowel pairs. Some examples are *grains, cheese, pie, oatmeal, blueberries.* Invite children to plan meals including as many of these foods as possible.

TECHNOLOGY **AstroWord** Long Vowels: *a, i;* Long Vowels: *i, o;* Long Vowels: *e, u*

AUDITORY LEARNERS GROUPS

Materials: index cards

Ask each child to write a word with a vowel pair on a card. Make a card for yourself. Then, begin telling a story by saying a sentence that includes your word. Have each child continue the story, using his or her word in a sentence.

CHALLENGE

Encourage children to list pairs of words that sound the same but have a different spelling for the long vowel sound. One word in each pair should contain one of the vowel pairs studied in this lesson. Examples include *feet/feat, road/rowed, pain/pane, blue/blew.*

EXTRA SUPPORT/INTERVENTION

Make five columns on the board, labeled with the vowel pairs *ea, ai, oa, ie,* and *ue.* As you say words with these vowel pairs, have children spell the word aloud and say which column it belongs in. See Daily Phonics Practice, pages 219–220.

Integrating Phonics and Reading

Guided Reading

Read the title aloud as children look at the illustrations. Ask them what they think happens to Erik and the three goats.

First Reading Ask children to identify the main character and tell why he is crying.

Second Reading Ask children to identify story words that have vowel pairs.

Comprehension

After reading, ask children these questions:
• Why were Erik, the rabbit, and the fox all crying? ***Recall/Character***
• Why do you think the bees were able to get the goats to leave the grain? ***Inference/Cause and Effect***

ESL/ELL English Language Learners

Help children understand that the rabbit and the fox are crying in sympathy with Erik. Once they try to help him, they become involved in his problem and end up worrying along with him.

Vowel Digraphs

Skill Focus

Children will

★ identify vowel digraphs as two vowels together that make a long or a short sound or have a special sound.

★ identify the different sounds made by the digraphs *oo, ea,* and *ei.*

★ sort words by vowel digraph and sound.

ESL/ELL Children who have difficulty pronouncing *oo* vowel digraphs *(book/boot)* may need additional support and oral/listening practice with the long *oo* sound. Some children may also have difficulty pronouncing and distinguishing short vowels, including the sound of short *e.* In Tagalog, for example, short *e* sounds like *ay* in *say.* No similar vowel sound exists in Korean.

▶ Teach

Phonemic Awareness: Phoneme Categorization Explain to children that you will say groups of three words. Ask children to identify the word whose vowel sound is different.

- look   soon   tool
- head   meal   thread
- weigh   vein   knead

Sound to Symbol Write *look* and *soon* on the board and say the words with children. Ask if the vowel sounds are the same or different. *(different)* Explain that the sounds have their own special sound, which makes *oo* a vowel digraph.

Write the words *bread* and *vein* on the board. Ask children to read the words aloud and identify the vowels that make the vowel sound in each word. *(ea, ei)* Explain that these are also vowel digraphs.

▶ Practice and Apply

Sound to Symbol Review the rule on page 133. Then, have children read the rules on page 134. Review the sounds made by the digraphs *oo, ea,* and *ei.*

Critical Thinking Discuss the Talk About It question. Ask: *What would you do if you broke a window while playing ball?*

Writing On page 133, suggest that children say each word aloud if they are not sure in which column they should write a word. On page 134, tell children to read each sentence with their word choice.

Reading Use *Heather's Book,* MCP Phonics and Reading Library, Super Skills Collection, Level C, to provide practice in reading words with vowel digraphs.

133

Name _____

> Circle each word that has the vowel digraph **oo** or **ea.** Then write the words in the correct columns.

> **RULE**
> In a **vowel digraph,** two letters together stand for one vowel sound. It can be short or long, or have a special sound of its own. The vowel digraph **oo** stands for the vowel sound you hear in *book* and *pool.* The vowel digraph **ea** can stand for the short *e* sound you hear in *bread.*

1. Mike and Joe (looked) at the clock and saw that it was (noon.)
2. They (stood) up and left the (classroom.)
3. The (weather) was (cool,) so they grabbed their jackets.
4. They were (ready) to play a (good) game of (football.)
5. Mike threw the (heavy) ball, and it sailed over Joe's (head.)
6. The ball (took) a sudden turn toward the (school) wall.
7. Mike watched with (dread) as it went toward a window.
8. At the last minute, Joe (scooped) up the ball.

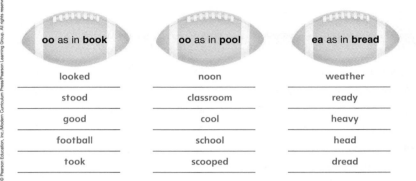

oo as in book	oo as in pool	ea as in bread
looked	noon	weather
stood	classroom	ready
good	cool	heavy
football	school	head
took	scooped	dread

TALK About It What would the boys have done if they had broken a window?

Vowel digraphs oo, ea: Sound to symbol, critical thinking   **133**

FOCUS ON ALL LEARNERS

ESL/ELL **ENGLISH LANGUAGE LEARNERS**

Focus children's attention on identifying the two different sounds of the vowel digraph *oo,* the short *e* sound made by the digraph *ea,* and the long *a* sound made by the digraph *ei.*

- Write the first sentence on page 133 on the board. Circle the target words *looked* and *noon.* Read these words aloud and have children repeat them. Then, ask children what two letters in each word make the vowel sound. Point out to the class the two different sounds produced by the vowel digraph *oo.*

- Read aloud the first rule on page 134 and the words in the colored box. Have children repeat chorally each word after you. Ask if the words all fit the rule. (yes) Have children circle the vowel digraph *ea* in each word. Do the same with the second rule on page 134.

VISUAL LEARNERS **PARTNERS**

Give partners the following list of words: *noon, good, book, soon, school, ready, bread, weighs, eight, freight.* Have each child choose four words to write in sentences, leaving out the vowel digraphs in the words. Partners trade papers and complete the words.

Find the word in the box that will complete the sentence. Write the word on the line.

> **RULE**
> Sometimes, **ea** has a short **e** sound, as in *head*.

bread	breakfast	headlines	heavy	ready	weather

1. Heather and Sid eat a large _____ **breakfast** _____ every day.
2. They have _____ **bread** _____ and jam with their milk and cereal.
3. Sid reads all the _____ **headlines** _____ in the newspaper first.
4. The _____ **weather** _____ report said that it would snow later.
5. Heather and Sid put on their _____ **heavy** _____ coats and boots.
6. Now they are _____ **ready** _____ for their long walk to school.

Find the word in the box that will complete the sentence. Write the word on the line.

> **RULE**
> In most words **ei** has a long **a** sound, as in *eight*.

eight	eighteen	neighbor	veins	weighs	weight

7. Lauren's health class grew from sixteen to _____ **eighteen** _____ students.
8. Her _____ **neighbor** _____, Mrs. Parkhurst, is the health teacher.
9. She teaches that _____ **veins** _____ carry blood to the heart.
10. Lauren learns how to read a scale to find her _____ **weight** _____.
11. It shows that Lauren _____ **weighs** _____ sixty pounds.
12. Lauren gained _____ **eight** _____ pounds since last year.

134 Vowel digraphs ea, ei: Words in context

HOME Have your child make up sentences using the words in the boxes such as, *Dan is ready for breakfast.*

CURRICULUM CONNECTIONS

SPELLING

Write *ea, oo,* and *ei* on the board. As you say the spelling words *bread, pool,* and *eight,* call on children to write the word on the board under the vowel digraph they hear in the word. Continue with the lesson words *noon, head, vein, look, lead, good, eight,* and *heavy.*

WRITING

Explain that *scoops* are news stories printed or told by one news organization before competitors report it. Have children write exciting headlines for news stories, using words with vowel digraphs.

SCIENCE/HEALTH

Help children make a class chart entitled "Here's to Your Good Health" by writing tips on how to stay healthy. Include words with vowel pairs and vowel digraphs, such as *eat breakfast every day, maintain a normal weight, wash hands with soap, brush teeth.*

TECHNOLOGY **AstroWord** Vowel Digraphs & Diphthongs

AUDITORY LEARNERS GROUPS

Write *school, book, bread,* and *vein* on the board as column heads. Say a word with the vowel digraph *oo, ea,* or *ei.* Have children repeat the word and write it on the board under the correct head.

CHALLENGE

Teach children the following tongue twister: *How much wood would a woodchuck chuck if a woodchuck could chuck wood?* Have them identify the vowel digraph that is used several times in the tongue twister. (*oo*) Then, suggest they write their own tongue twisters or alliterative sentences using words with the vowel digraph *oo, ea,* or *ei.*

EXTRA SUPPORT/INTERVENTION

As children complete the activities on pages 133 and 134, read the words and sentences with them to reinforce the sounds of vowel digraphs. See *Daily Phonics Practice,* page 220.

Integrating Phonics and Reading

Guided Reading
Direct children to look at the cover and read the title. Discuss diaries and what people write in them.
First Reading Help children identify the setting by talking about the year (1866) and the place (the American frontier).
Second Reading Ask children to identify story words with the vowel digraphs *oo, ea,* and *ie.*

Comprehension
After reading, ask:
• What did Heather and her family have to do to make a new home for themselves? ***Recall/Summarize***
• What do you think was the best part of Heather's new home? ***Reflective Analysis/ Personal Response***

ESL/ELL **English Language Learners**
Have children use pictures to name different tasks Heather and her family did, such as *carry water* and *bake bread.*

Vowel Digraphs

Skill Focus

Children will

★ recognize words that contain the vowel digraphs *aw, au, ea, ei,* or *oo.*

★ sort words with these vowel digraphs according to digraph and sound.

ESL/ELL Children whose home language is Korean may introduce the sound /ya/ when they anticipate the sound of short *a* after *g* and have difficulty saying words like *August.* Listen for native-language interference with English pronunciation; offer additional practice as needed.

▶ Teach

Phonemic Awareness: Phoneme Isolation
Read aloud each sentence below and have children say the vowel sound they hear repeated.

- **I saw a fawn on the lawn in August.**
- **Mrs. Day's baby weighed eight pounds.**
- **The cook took a look in the book.**
- **Is noon too soon for you, too?**
- **Fred spread jelly on the bread.**

Sound to Symbol Write the words *lawn* and *taught* on the board. Read the words aloud and ask what children notice about the vowel sounds in the words. (*They are the same.*) Then, circle the vowel digraph in each word. Ask what children notice about the vowel digraphs. (*They are spelled differently.*)

Write *good, pool, head,* and *weigh* on the board. Ask a child to read the words aloud. Then, have him or her circle the vowel digraph in each word and repeat the sound it stands for.

▶ Practice and Apply

Sound to Symbol For pages 135 and 136, suggest that children say the words softly to themselves and listen carefully for the vowel sound of each word. Have them note the vowel spelling as they say the word.

Critical Thinking After children complete the sentences on page 136, have them discuss the Talk About It question. Remind them to support their opinions with facts and details from the story.

Reading Use *Dinosaur Days,* MCP Phonics and Reading Library, Super Skills Collection, Level C, to provide additional practice in reading words with vowel digraphs.

▶ Circle each word that has the vowel digraph **aw, au,** or **ei.** Then write the words in the correct columns below.

> **RULE**
> The vowel digraphs **aw** and **au** have the sound you hear in *saw* and *caught.* The vowel digraph **ei** can have the long **a** sound you hear in *eight.*

1. (Shaun) sat on the (lawn) under a tree and (yawned.)
2. The (August) sun made him sleepy, and his book felt like a heavy (weight.)
3. He watched an ant (crawl) up a (vein) on a leaf.
4. He heard a (neighing) sound from his (neighbor's) horse.
5. He dreamed he was (drawing) an (awesome) (dinosaur.)
6. His art teacher had (taught) him how to sketch them.
7. The whistle of a (freight) train (caught) his attention, and he woke up.

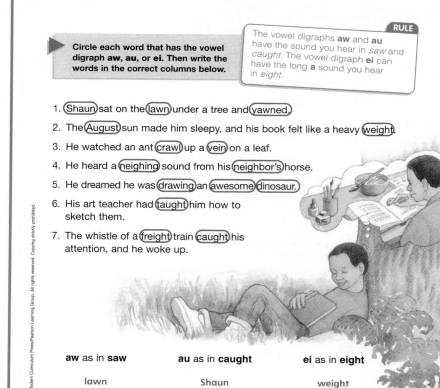

aw as in **saw**	**au** as in **caught**	**ei** as in **eight**
lawn	Shaun	weight
yawned	August	vein
crawl	dinosaur	neighing
drawing	taught	neighbor's
awesome	caught	freight

Vowel digraphs aw, au, ei: Sound to symbol   **135**

FOCUS ON ALL LEARNERS

ESL/ELL ENGLISH LANGUAGE LEARNERS

- Write the digraphs *oo, ea, ei,* and *aw/au* on chart paper in a four-column chart.
- Have children scan pages 135 and 136 and name words with each sound. Have volunteers write the words the group finds on the chart.
- Model pronunciation of unfamiliar words on the page and have children repeat.
- Have children complete pages 135 and 136 aloud as a group.

VISUAL LEARNERS INDIVIDUAL

Write these incomplete words on the board: *dr__, sp__l, w__ght, t__ght, c__k, thr__d.* Ask children to complete each word by supplying the digraph. Have them say each word and identify the sound its vowel digraph makes.

AUDITORY LEARNERS GROUPS

Form six teams and assign each team a vowel digraph: *oo* (book), *oo* (tool), *ea, aw, au, ei.* Give teams five minutes to write as many words as they can using their vowel digraph. Have groups read their lists aloud.

Circle each word that has a vowel digraph. Then, write the words in the correct column.

1. In (August) (Paul) mowed the (lawn) at his uncle's big farm.
2. He liked to start in the morning when it was (cool).
3. Sometimes he (hauled) bales of (straw) to the barn.
4. His uncle often helped him lift the (heavy) load.
5. During the hot (afternoon), his (head) began to (sweat).
6. He met his (neighbors) at the swimming (pool).
7. Before diving, he (looked) for the deepest water.
8. By (eight) o'clock he was so tired that he began to (yawn).
9. He went home to read a (good) (book) about lifting (weights).

oo as in **book**	oo as in **moon**	ei as in **sleigh**
looked	cool	neighbors
good	afternoon	eight
book	pool	weight

ea as in **thread**	aw as in **saw**	au as in **auto**
heavy	lawn	August
head	straw	Paul
sweat	yawn	hauled

TALK About It Do you think Paul likes to work on the farm? Why or why not?

HOME With your child, look in a newspaper for words that contain the vowel digraphs oo, ei, ea, aw, and au.

136 Vowel digraphs oo, ei, ea, aw, au: Sound to symbol, critical thinking

SPELLING

Write these words on slips of paper: *crawl, yawn, book, foot, noon, tool, head, bread, vein, reins*. Place the slips in a box. Have children select a word and act it out using gestures and pantomime for classmates to guess. Whoever guesses the word must spell it correctly in order to be the next player.

WRITING

Ask children to write a paragraph describing activities they like to do in August. Have them underline words with vowel digraphs.

SCIENCE

Have children research facts that tell about the sizes and weights of different marine animals. Children can work in small groups, recording their findings in a chart or table.

 **TECHNOLOGY** **AstroWord** Vowel Digraphs & Diphthongs

KINESTHETIC LEARNERS GROUPS

Distribute these sets of letters among five players: *pdrawtle, sweightna, cthreadwo, trclawxi, pspoolrt*. Each player must find and circle two hidden words with the same digraph and act out one of the words for his or her classmates to guess. Answers: *(draw/raw), (weight/weigh/eight), (thread/read), (claw/law), (spool/pool)*.

CHALLENGE

Have children add words to each list on page 136. Then, have them choose two words from a list, use the words to write a riddle or a rhyme, and share their work with the class.

EXTRA SUPPORT/INTERVENTION

Provide children with a list of words that contain the vowel digraphs used on page 136. Have children read and sort the words according to sound and spelling. See Daily Phonics Practice, page 220.

Integrating Phonics and Reading

Guided Reading
Have children talk about the cover illustration and the title. Ask what they think the book will be about.
First Reading Have children identify the main characters. Ask: *What do these characters have to do with dinosaurs?*
Second Reading Have children find words with the vowel digraphs *aw* and *au*.

Comprehension
After reading, ask children these questions:
• How did Paul and Dawn change during the course of the story? How did they stay the same? ***Recall/Comparisons***
• What ideas did this story give you about how to learn more about dinosaurs? ***Creative/Personal Response***

ESL/ELL English Language Learners
Help children understand that at the end of the story Paul and Dawn have become scientists who study dinosaurs.

Vowel Digraphs

Skill Focus

Children will

★ review vowel pairs and vowel digraphs.

★ identify and distinguish between vowel pairs and vowel digraphs.

Teach

Phonological Awareness: Rhyme Explain to children that you will say sets of three words, one set at a time. Children are to identify the word in each set that does not rhyme with the other two. Use these words.

- weigh   stay   tree
- pain   ran   main
- please   toes   freeze
- rein   vein   green
- peas   cries   lies
- bread   bead   instead
- glued   food   good
- boat   foot   goat

Sound to Symbol On the board, write the words from the previous activity. Have volunteers circle the words with vowel pairs. *(stay, tree, pain, main, please, toes, freeze, green, peas, cries, lies, bead, glued, boat, goat)* Ask how children know these words have vowel pairs. *(Each word has the long sound of the first vowel in the pair.)*

Have children name the words with vowel digraphs. *(weigh, rein, vein, bread, instead, food, good, foot)* Ask volunteers to underline the vowel digraphs and say their sounds.

Practice and Apply

Sound to Symbol Be sure children understand how to do the crossword puzzle on page 137. Suggest that children draw a line through each word in the box as they use it.

Writing For page 138, suggest that children say each underlined word softly to themselves in order to identify its vowel sound.

Reading Use *The House That Stood on Booker Hill*, MCP Phonics and Reading Library, Super Skills Collection, Level C, to provide additional practice in reading words with vowel pairs and vowel digraphs.

Name _____

▶ Read the clues. Find the word that matches each clue. Write the word in the puzzle.

| brook | eel | eight | snail | seaweed |
| coast | sailfish | prawn | sea horse | sawfish |

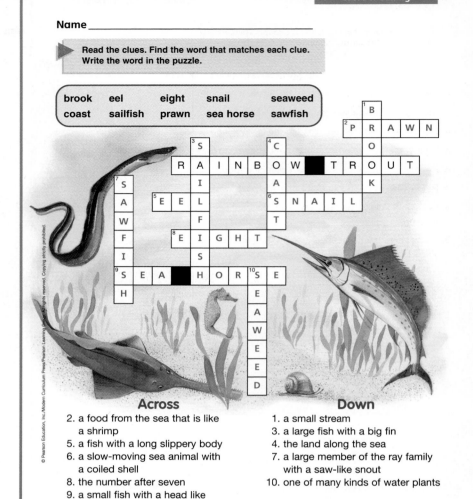

Across

2. a food from the sea that is like a shrimp
5. a fish with a long slippery body
6. a slow-moving sea animal with a coiled shell
8. the number after seven
9. a small fish with a head like a horse

Down

1. a small stream
3. a large fish with a big fin
4. the land along the sea
7. a large member of the ray family with a saw-like snout
10. one of many kinds of water plants

Vowel pairs and digraphs: Word meaning   137

FOCUS ON ALL LEARNERS

ESL/ELL ENGLISH LANGUAGE LEARNERS

English language learners may still have difficulty distinguishing between the two *oo* sounds. Give them extra help by writing these words on the board: *book, food, pool, good, wood, stoop, stood, fool, mood, took.* Exaggerate the *oo* sound and point out your lip position as you say each word. Have children repeat and sort the words by sound.

VISUAL LEARNERS

Have children create and illustrate hink-pinks—two-word rhymes—using words with vowel pairs or vowel digraphs. Here are examples: *weak beak, cool tool, bread head.* Challenge children to think of questions that can be answered by these rhymes, such as: *What does a duck have if it can't open its mouth?*

In the sentences below, underline each word that contains a vowel pair or a vowel digraph. Write the words in the correct columns.

1. The freezing rain and sleet beat on our gray home.
2. The streets looked awfully icy for a March day.
3. The news said a blue bus was caught in a ditch.
4. The news headline said, "No school today because of heavy snow."
5. The weather wasn't good for a sleigh ride.
6. My mother said that I could play with my neighbor, Kay.
7. I helped Mom bake raisin bread instead.
8. We feel that it is easy to have fun.

Vowel Pair	Vowel Digraph
freezing	looked
rain	awfully
sleet	caught
beat	headline
gray	school
streets	because
day	heavy
blue	weather
today	good
play	sleigh
Kay	neighbor
raisin	bread
feel	instead
easy	

138 Review vowel pairs and digraphs

 Have your child write a short story using as many words with vowel pairs or digraphs as he or she is able to.

CURRICULUM CONNECTIONS

SPELLING

Have children scramble the letters in each of the spelling words and write them on paper. Include the words *feel, paint, dried, clue, bread, pool, eight,* and *crawl.* Have partners exchange papers and unscramble the words.

WRITING

Suggest that children choose one of the animals from the crossword puzzle and imagine what it would be like to be that animal for a day. Have children write a paragraph describing one day in the life of the animal they chose.

SOCIAL STUDIES

Have children work in teams to find out where people find and how they make use of any of these animals: sailfish, eel, prawn, snail, sawfish, or starfish. Suggest that each team write their facts on fish-shaped paper for display in the Social Studies Center.

 AstroWord Vowel Digraphs & Diphthongs

KINESTHETIC LEARNERS GROUPS

On the board, draw a tree with branches labeled *ai, ee, ay, ea, oo, ei,* and *au.* Say words from this lesson and have volunteers write them on the branches labeled with the correct vowel pair or vowel digraph.

CHALLENGE

Have children work in groups to make posters that explain how to tell the difference between a vowel pair and a vowel digraph.

EXTRA SUPPORT/INTERVENTION

Children may need additional practice with vowel digraphs that have more than one pronunciation such as *height, vein; bread, bead; pool, good.* Work with children to find examples of words with digraphs that have more than one pronunciation. Then, sort the words according to digraph and sound. See Daily Phonics Practice, pages 219–220.

Integrating Phonics and Reading

Guided Reading

The House That Stood on Booker Hill

Have children preview the illustrations and predict what the book will be about.

First Reading Have children tell how many families lived in the house on Booker Hill and describe some of the things they did.

Second Reading Have children find story words with vowel digraphs and vowel pairs.

Comprehension

After reading, ask children these questions:
• What happened to the house on Booker Hill during the course of the story? ***Recall/Summarize***
• What might you do if you lived in the house on Booker Hill? ***Creative/Personal Response***

ESL/ELL English Language Learners

Point out the dates at the top of certain pages. Ask: *Why are the dates there? (The date tells when the story events shown and described on that page take place.)*

Phonics & Reading / Phonics & Writing

Review Vowel Pairs and Digraphs

Skill Focus

Children will

★ select words with vowel pairs and vowel digraphs to complete sentences.

★ write a friendly letter using words with vowel pairs and vowel digraphs.

▶ Teach

Phonics and Reading Review the definitions of vowel pair and vowel digraph. *(A vowel pair is two vowels that together make one long vowel sound as in* boat. *A vowel digraph is two vowels together that make a short vowel sound or have a special sound as in* look.*)* On the board, draw a two-column chart with the headings: **Vowel Pair, Vowel Digraph.**

Have children sort words by writing them in the appropriate column. Use words such as *boat, float, deep, see, blue, lagoon, foot, gray, weigh, soon, seemed, playful, look, rain, breathe.*

▶ Practice and Apply

Phonics and Reading Make sure children understand that they should complete the sentences on page 139 with words that have vowel pairs or vowel digraphs. Children can find the words to fill the blanks in the journal entry.

Critical Thinking For the Talk About It question, list children's ideas on the board. Have them use details from the journal entry to support their ideas.

Phonics and Writing Before children begin writing, use the callouts on page 140 to review the parts of a friendly letter. Remind children to include in their letter some of the words in the box.

Reading Use *Lobster Fishing at Dawn,* MCP Phonics and Reading Library, Super Skills Collection, Level C, to provide additional practice in reading words with vowel pairs and vowel digraphs.

139

Name _____

 **Phonics & Reading** Read the journal entry. Then, write words with vowel pairs and vowel digraphs to complete each sentence.

Gentle Giants   February 14

Our sightseeing boat floated deep in the blue waters of the lagoon. Within a short time, we spotted our first gray whale. This 40-foot giant was bigger than I could imagine! We were told they can weigh as much as 35 tons. We soon began to see one whale after another. The whales seemed very playful and curious. A friendly mother whale and her calf swam up to our boat to get a closer look at us. Suddenly, they dove into the water. When they burst up again, they spouted water. It felt like rain, and we got awfully wet. I learned that gray whales have two blowholes that help them to breathe. After seeing these beautiful animals up close, I understand why it is so important to take care of our oceans and respect all animals.

1. Our boat ____floated____ deep in the waters of the blue ____lagoon____.

2. We soon spotted our first 40-foot ____gray____ whale.

3. These gentle animals seemed very ____playful____ and curious.

4. A gray whale can ____weigh____ as much as 35 tons.

5. A friendly mother whale and her calf swam close to our ____boat____ to get a closer ____look____ at us.

6. We got ____awfully____ wet when the whales spouted water.

7. Gray whales have two blowholes to help them ____breathe____.

 Why do you think it is so important to keep our oceans clean?

Review vowel pairs and digraphs: Reading, critical thinking   **139**

FOCUS ON ALL LEARNERS

ESL/ELL ENGLISH LANGUAGE LEARNERS

Pair English language learners with native speakers to discuss the meanings of the words *sightseeing, lagoon, spouted, blowhole, respect,* and the phrase *burst up again.* Have children use visual aids and pantomime to demonstrate word meaning.

KINESTHETIC LEARNERS GROUPS

Materials: mural paper, markers, beanbag

Draw 12 fish on mural paper and label them with the words *teach, feel, rain, boat, tie, day, book, pool, head, eight, lawn, haul.* Place the paper on the floor. Have children toss a beanbag onto the paper and say and spell a word with the same vowel sound as the word on which the beanbag lands.

AUDITORY LEARNERS GROUPS

Materials: index cards

Have children write two words on separate cards for each of the vowel digraphs and vowel pairs. Then, have them use the cards to play a game of concentration, reading and matching words with the vowel sounds.

Phonics & Writing

Writing

A **friendly letter** helps us stay in touch with people we care about. We can share news, tell our feelings, or cheer a friend. We use words that are fun and friendly to tell about what we are doing.

▶ Imagine you are spending a day by the sea. Write a friendly letter to tell someone about the sights you saw and the things you did. Some of the words in the box may help you.

blue	coast	eight	floated	green
looked	play	ready	saw	tried

The **greeting** usually begins with Dear and the person's name.

The **heading** tells the date.

The **body**, or main part, tells about things you did.

End with a **closing**, such as Your friend, and your name.

140 Review vowel pairs and digraphs: Writing

 Invite your child to read his or her friendly letter aloud.

CURRICULUM CONNECTIONS

SPELLING

Use these words and sentences as a posttest for writing words with vowel pairs and vowel digraphs.

1. **paint**   Let's **paint** the door yellow.
2. **dried**   The paint **dried** quickly.
3. **bread**   Please buy a loaf of **bread.**
4. **pool**   There are goldfish in the **pool.**
5. **eight**   I set the alarm for **eight** o'clock.
6. **crawl**   I saw a snake **crawl** into a hole.
7. **feel**   **Feel** the smooth rock.
8. **clue**   The book gives a **clue** to the mystery.

MUSIC

Play a recording that blends music with sounds of the sea. Have children draw or write a description of what they picture in their mind as they listen.

SOCIAL STUDIES

Have children use the resources in the school library to find and share an interesting fact about the whaling history in the United States.

TECHNOLOGY   **AstroWord** Vowel Digraphs & Diphthongs

VISUAL LEARNERS *PARTNERS*

Have partners devise a code for vowel pairs and vowel digraphs and then use the code to write words. Partners can trade papers with another pair of children and try to crack each other's codes. Examples include b)!t *(boat)*, p))l *(pool)*, l!@n *(lawn)*.

CHALLENGE

Materials: dictionary

Suggest that children look in a dictionary to find new words with different vowel pairs and vowel digraphs. Have them write a sentence for each new word.

EXTRA SUPPORT/INTERVENTION

Have children read aloud the journal entry on page 139 individually or as a group. Then, help them identify the words with vowel pairs and vowel digraphs. Remind them that these words will help them complete the sentences. See Daily Phonics Practice, pages 219–220.

Integrating Phonics and Reading

Guided Reading

As children look at the book cover, ask them what they think is happening in the photograph.
First Reading Have children identify a fact about lobster fishing on each story page.
Second Reading Ask children to find story words with vowel pairs and vowel digraphs.

Comprehension

After reading, ask children these questions:
• Do you think the girl in the story enjoyed her day fishing for lobsters? How can you tell? *Inference/Character*
• Which part of the story did you think was the most interesting? *Reflective Analysis/ Personal Response*

ESL/ELL English Language Learners

Ask children who is telling the story. Have them identify the storyteller in one of the photographs. *(the man talking to the little girl)*

Diphthongs

Skill Focus

Children will

★ identify a diphthong as two vowels blended together to make one sound.

★ recognize the sound and spelling of the diphthongs *oy, oi, ow, ou, ew.*

ESL/ELL English language learners whose native languages identify one sound per letter may experience difficulty understanding that a vowel and consonant can make a separate sound. Provide oral practice if you notice oral hesitation among these children.

Teach

Phonemic Awareness: Phoneme Categorization Tell children that they will hear several sets of three words. Have them identify the word in each set that has a different vowel sound from the other two. Use these words.

- **sound   owl   grow**
- **town   blow   around**
- **noise   boys   loose**
- **blew   crowd   flew**

Sound to Symbol Write *spoil* and *joy* on the board. Say the words and ask a child to circle the letters that stand for the vowel sound in each word. Explain that the *oy* in *joy* and the *oi* in *spoil* blend together to make one vowel sound called a diphthong. You may wish to add that the *y* acts as a vowel in *joy.*

Say the words *cow, mouse,* and *flew* as you write them on the board. Ask children to repeat the vowel sound they hear in each word and tell what letters stand for these sounds. Lead children to identify *ow, ou,* and *ew* as diphthongs. Point out that, like *oy* and *oi, ow* and *ou* have the same sound.

Practice and Apply

Sound to Symbol Have volunteers read aloud the directions on pages 141 and 142. Ask children to reread the sentences on page 141 after completing the exercise to make sure that the words chosen make sense in this context.

Critical Thinking Have children discuss what qualities a good scientist would need to have. Ask children to support their opinions with details from the sentences.

Reading Use *Tiger's Tummy Ache,* MCP Phonics and Reading Library, Super Skills Collection, Level C, to provide additional practice in identifying words with diphthongs.

141

Name _____

RULE
A **diphthong** consists of two letters blended together to make one vowel sound.

oy=oi   ow=ou
boy boil   owl scout
        ew
        stew

▶ Circle the word that completes each sentence. Write the word on the line.

1. A team of scientists traveled to the ____South____ Pole.   (South)   Soil
2. They wanted to explore ____new____ places.   now   (new)
3. They asked a photographer to ____join____ them.   jewel   (join)
4. Everyone rejoiced when their goal ____drew____ near.   (drew)   blow
5. They ____knew____ they had succeeded.   know   (knew)
6. At first, the only ____sound____ they heard was the wind.   screw   (sound)
7. They wore face masks when the wind ____blew____.   blow   (blew)
8. They fell ____down____ on the ice and snow.   dew   (down)
9. Sometimes they had to ____shout____ to each other.   (shout)   show
10. They had to ____boil____ snow to cook their food.   (boil)   boy
11. Often they ate canned ____stew____.   (stew)   slow
12. Everyone ____grew____ tired and cold.   ground   (grew)
13. A chance to rest was cause for ____joy____.   (joy)   join
14. One day they heard a group of ____noisy____ seals.   (noisy)   choice
15. They saw a whale leap ____out____ of the water.   (out)   mouth
16. It blew air and water out of its ____spout____.   spoil   (spout)
17. The water looked like a ____fountain____.   (fountain)   found

TALK about it Why do you think the scientists traveled so far?

Diphthongs oy, oi, ow, ou, ew: Words in context, critical thinking   **141**

FOCUS ON ALL LEARNERS

ESL/ELL ENGLISH LANGUAGE LEARNERS

Provide pictures or samples of items named by the words *mouse, cloud, flower, crown, coins, toys, boys, stew, newspaper.* Write the words on the board. Point to a word, say it, and have an English language learner identify the picture or sample of the item named by the word. Ask the child to write the word on a label, say the word, and attach the label to the appropriate picture or sample.

AUDITORY LEARNERS

Have one partner write a word for each of these diphthongs: *oi, oy, ou, ow, ew.* Then, have the other partner read the words and write another word that rhymes with each.

KINESTHETIC LEARNERS

Play a version of Simon Says in which children do the action only if the command contains a word with a diphthong. You may wish to include commands such as *make **noise**, **shout** your name, **chew** your food, look **annoyed,*** and *take a **bow.***

▶ Read each clue. Choose the word from the box that matches the clue, and write it on the line. Circle the diphthong in each word you write.

1. a form of money ___coins___

2. drops of water on the grass at night ___dew___

3. things that children like to play with ___toys___

4. a place where people can live ___house___

5. the shape of a circle ___round___

6. a large number of people ___crowd___

7. what a ball can do ___bounce___

8. a headpiece for a king or queen ___crown___

9. an animal from which we get milk ___cow___

bounce	flowers
boy	house
cloud	mouse
coins	mouth
cow	owl
crowd	round
crown	stew
dew	toys

▶ Say the name of each picture. Choose the word from the box at the top of the page that names the picture, and write it on the line. Circle the diphthong.

10.
boy

11.
owl

12.
stew

13.
mouse

14.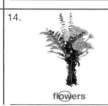
flowers

15.
cloud

142 Review diphthongs

 HOME Ask your child to name words with the same diphthong as the picture words.

CURRICULUM CONNECTIONS

SPELLING

Say the words and sentences below. Have volunteers write the words on the board. Others can check the spelling in a dictionary.

1. **join**   Please **join** our group.
2. **boy**   That **boy** is my neighbor.
3. **about**   What is the movie **about**?
4. **owls**   Many **owls** hunt at night.
5. **stew**   Mom made chicken **stew**.
6. **autumn**   The leaves fall in **autumn**.

WRITING

Have children choose two animal names, one with a diphthong (*mouse, cow*) and one with a vowel digraph (*woodpecker, raccoon*). Invite children to create a comic strip featuring the two animals.

PORTFOLIO

SOCIAL STUDIES

Ask children what they know about the South Pole. Invite volunteers to research the topic and report their findings to the class.

TECHNOLOGY   **AstroWord** Vowel Digraphs & Diphthongs

Integrating Phonics and Reading

Guided Reading
Discuss the book's title and cover. Ask children to share what they know about tigers.
First Reading Have children describe the characters Tiger and Rabbit.
Second Reading Have children identify story words that have diphthongs. You may wish to add the words to the Word Wall.

Tiger's Tummy Ache

Comprehension
After reading, ask children these questions:
• How did Rabbit trick Tiger into not eating him? *Recall/Plot*
• Which character did you like better? Why? *Reflective Analysis/Personal Response*

ESL/ELL English Language Learners
Remind children that quotation marks go around words that a story character says. Invite children to locate examples in the story and identify who the speaker is.

VISUAL/AUDITORY LEARNERS **GROUPS**

Materials: index cards

On index cards write letters and these phonograms: _ound, _oy, _oil, _ow, _ew. Provide each group with a set of phonogram cards and letter cards. Have children make as many words as they can with the cards. Add new words to the classroom Word Wall.

CHALLENGE

Challenge children to write sentences using words that repeat the sound of a diphthong, such as *Roy and Lloyd were noisy boys.*

EXTRA SUPPORT/INTERVENTION

Have children draw five ladders on paper and write one of these words on the bottom rung of each: *crown, stew, oil, mouse, boy.* Have them fill the other rungs with words that rhyme. See Daily Phonics Practice, pages 220–221.

Syllables

Skill Focus

Children will

★ identify the number of syllables in words that contain vowel digraphs or diphthongs.

★ recognize that the number of vowel sounds and the number of syllables in a word are the same.

ESL/ELL Native speakers of Spanish are familiar with diphthongs formed by two vowels; but they are not familiar with diphthongs formed by a vowel and a consonant. Provide oral practice with words containing these sounds.

Teach

Phonological Awareness: Phoneme Isolation Remind children that words are made up of syllables and that one vowel sound is heard in each syllable. Say the word *wooden*. Ask: *How many vowel sounds do you hear? (2) How many syllables does* wooden *have? (2)* Then, say the following words and have children identify the number of vowel sounds and syllables they hear: *newspaper, coolest, strawberries, shower, teacher, royal, choice,* and *neighborhood.*

Sound to Symbol Ask children to write the words from the previous activity on the board as you say them. Have children circle the letters that stand for each vowel sound and draw a vertical line between the syllables. Ask volunteers to identify the vowel digraph or diphthong in each word.

Point out the difference between the number of vowels in a word and the number of vowel sounds and syllables it has. Explain that *neighborhood* has five vowels but only three vowel sounds and three syllables.

Practice and Apply

Sound to Symbol Make sure children understand the directions on pages 143 and 144. When children have completed page 143, ask them why each word in the table has more vowels than vowel sounds. *(Each word has a vowel digraph.)* When children have completed page 144, ask them why some of the words have two vowels and only one vowel sound. *(They have a diphthong.)*

Reading Use *Squirrels,* MCP Phonics and Reading Library, Super Skills Collection, Level C, to provide additional practice in identifying syllables.

Name_____

▶ Read each word. On the first line, write the number of vowels you see. Say each word. On the second line, write the number of vowel sounds you hear. On the third line, write the number of syllables in the word.

a e i o u	Vowels You See	Vowel Sounds You Hear	Number of Syllables	a e i o u	Vowels You See	Vowel Sounds You Hear	Number of Syllables
1. autumn	3	2	2	17. measure	4	2	2
2. shook	2	1	1	18. instead	3	2	2
3. bread	2	1	1	19. neighborly	4	3	3
4. weigh	2	1	1	20. naughty	3	2	2
5. broom	2	1	1	21. headline	4	2	2
6. sweater	3	2	2	22. brook	2	1	1
7. bookcase	4	2	2	23. pause	3	1	1
8. school	2	1	1	24. eighteen	4	2	2
9. reindeer	4	2	2	25. leather	3	2	2
10. spool	2	1	1	26. haunted	3	2	2
11. sleigh	2	1	1	27. freight	2	1	1
12. feather	3	2	2	28. coins	2	1	1
13. bedspread	3	2	2	29. because	4	2	2
14. weighted	3	2	2	30. woodpile	4	2	2
15. woodpecker	4	3	3	31. raccoon	3	2	2
16. laundry	3	2	2	32. heavy	3	2	2

Vowel digraphs: Syllables   **143**

FOCUS ON ALL LEARNERS

ESL/ELL **ENGLISH LANGUAGE LEARNERS**

English language learners whose native language is monosyllabic may need help with multisyllabic words. Have them identify items whose names have vowel digraphs or diphthongs as well as more than one syllable, such as *bookshelf*. Say a word and point to the item named. Have children repeat. Write the word and draw a line between syllables. Have children say the word again with you as you point to each syllable.

KINESTHETIC LEARNERS

Write these and similar word pairs on cards: *goose/rooster, coil/boiling.* One partner says "1" or "2." The other partner says the word on the card with that number of syllables.

AUDITORY LEARNERS

List words from the lesson on the board. Have a child divide a word into syllables, either correctly or incorrectly. Classmates decide whether the word is divided correctly and verify it in a dictionary.

Say the name of the picture at the beginning of each row, and look at the letters circled in the picture name. Circle the same pair of letters in each word in the row. Then write the number of syllables in the word on the line.

1.

st(ew) __1__   ch(ew)y __2__
f(ew) __1__   cr(ew) __1__
j(ew)elry __3__   thr(ew) __1__
st(ew)

2.

p(oi)nter __2__   v(oi)ce __1__
br(oi)l __1__   j(oi)n __1__
(oi)lcan __2__   sp(oi)ling __2__
c(oi)ns

3.

b(oy) __1__   enj(oy) __2__
ann(oy) __2__   Tr(oy) __1__
r(oy)al __2__   t(oy) __1__
t(oy)s

4.

m(ou)se __1__   sh(ou)ted __2__
b(ou)nce __1__   cl(ou)dy __2__
(ou)tside __2__   h(ou)se __1__
sc(ou)t

5.

cr(ow)n __1__   n(ow) __1__
upt(ow)n __2__   br(ow)n __1__
fr(ow)ns __1__   fl(ow)erpot __3__
(ow)l

144   Words with diphthongs: Syllables

SPELLING

Make a chart on the board with six columns labeled *oi, oy, ow, ou, ew,* and *au.* Say the words *howl, join, autumn, enjoy, about,* and *chewing.* Call on children to write each word, spelled correctly, in the appropriate column. Volunteers may add their own words.

WRITING

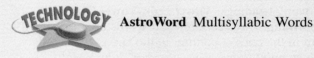

Suggest that children choose words with vowel digraphs and diphthongs to use in a haiku. Haiku is a Japanese verse form that has three lines of 5, 7, and 5 syllables—17 syllables in all. Here is an example:

> *Noisy woodpecker*
> *Tap, tap, tapping on the tree,*
> *Pausing to eat bugs.*

ART

Suggest that children copy their haiku on art paper and illustrate it however they wish.

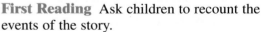 **AstroWord** Multisyllabic Words

---

VISUAL LEARNERS

Have each partner find in his or her book five two-syllable words that contain a vowel digraph or diphthong. Ask each child to write all the first syllables down the left side of a sheet of paper and all the second syllables in random order down the right side. Have partners exchange papers and match syllables.

CHALLENGE

Challenge children to list five words that have a vowel digraph or diphthong as well as four syllables. Suggest that they use a dictionary for reference. Then, have children identify the number of vowels, vowel sounds, and syllables in each word.

EXTRA SUPPORT/INTERVENTION

Suggest that children say each word on pages 143 and 144 to themselves and tap out the syllables on their desks. Have children check to see that each syllable contains letters that stand for a vowel sound. See Daily Phonics Practice, pages 220–221.

Integrating Phonics and Reading

Guided Reading
Have children look at the cover illustration and consider the book's title. Invite them to discuss what they already know about squirrels.
First Reading Ask children to recount the events of the story.
Second Reading Have children count the syllables in each multisyllabic word.
Comprehension
After reading, ask children these questions:
• What was the squirrel hiding and why? *Reflective Analysis/Cause and Effect*
• What facts in the story suggest that the boy liked squirrels? *Inference/Details*
ESL/ELL English Language Learners
Point out that this story is told in verse. Help English language learners see that line pairs 2 and 4, 6 and 8, 10 and 12, 14 and 16, 18 and 20 end in words that rhyme. Have children list the rhyming words.

Phonics & Spelling / Phonics & Writing

Review Vowel Pairs, Digraphs, and Diphthongs

Skill Focus

Children will

★ spell and write words with vowel pairs, vowel digraphs, and diphthongs.

★ write an informative paragraph using words with vowel pairs, digraphs, and diphthongs.

Teach

Phonics and Spelling Review the definitions of vowel pair, vowel digraph, and diphthong. *(A vowel pair is two vowels that together make a long vowel sound as in* coat. *A vowel digraph is two vowels together that make a short sound or have a special sound as in* took. *A diphthong is two vowels blended together to make one sound as in* blew, cloud, *and* toy.)

On the board, create a three-column chart with the following headings: **Vowel Pair, Vowel Digraph, Diphthong.** Have children sort words by arranging them in the correct column in the chart. Use words such as *paint, howl, raw, stay, boy, join, weight, book, boat.*

Practice and Apply

Phonics and Spelling Make sure that children are able to read the clue words on page 145 before they begin the activity. Suggest that they say each word in the list softly to themselves in order to hear the vowel sound before they write the word on the page. You also may wish to review the fact that each syllable in a word has one vowel sound.

Phonics and Writing Before children begin writing, have them brainstorm names of sea creatures and list them on the board. Remind children that once they have selected a topic, they should begin their paragraph with a topic sentence that states the main idea. The body of their paragraph should include facts and details that support the main idea.

Reading Use *Molly's Broccoli*, MCP Phonics and Reading Library, Super Skills Collection, Level C, to provide additional practice in identifying syllables.

145

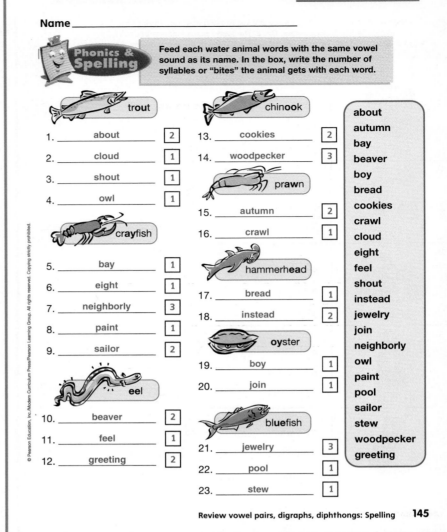

Name _____

Spelling

Phonics & Spelling Feed each water animal words with the same vowel sound as its name. In the box, write the number of syllables or "bites" the animal gets with each word.

trout
1. about — 2
2. cloud — 1
3. shout — 1
4. owl — 1

crayfish
5. bay — 1
6. eight — 1
7. neighborly — 3
8. paint — 1
9. sailor — 2

eel
10. beaver — 2
11. feel — 1
12. greeting — 2

chinook
13. cookies — 2
14. woodpecker — 3

prawn
15. autumn — 2
16. crawl — 1

hammerhead
17. bread — 1
18. instead — 2

oyster
19. boy — 1
20. join — 1

bluefish
21. jewelry — 3
22. pool — 1
23. stew — 1

| about |
| autumn |
| bay |
| beaver |
| boy |
| bread |
| cookies |
| crawl |
| cloud |
| eight |
| feel |
| shout |
| instead |
| jewelry |
| join |
| neighborly |
| owl |
| paint |
| pool |
| sailor |
| stew |
| woodpecker |
| greeting |

Review vowel pairs, digraphs, diphthongs: Spelling **145**

FOCUS ON ALL LEARNERS

ESL/ELL ENGLISH LANGUAGE LEARNERS

Materials: two index cards per child

Have English language learners color one card red and one green. Explain that you will say two words. If the vowel sounds are alike, children should hold up the green card. If the sounds are different, they should hold up the red card. Use word pairs such as *cow/cloud* (green), *boy/day* (red), *eight/hair* (red).

VISUAL/KINESTHETIC LEARNERS GROUPS

Write words from the lesson on slips of paper and place them in a box. Seat children in a circle. One child selects a word and reads it aloud. The word is passed to the next child who says and spells another word with the same vowel sound. That child selects a new word and the game continues.

VISUAL LEARNERS GROUPS

Before children begin writing their paragraphs, have them list details about their chosen animal. Encourage them to draw pictures to illustrate their paragraphs.

Phonics & Writing

An **informative paragraph** gives facts about a topic. One sentence tells the main idea. Other sentences tell details about the main idea.

Think about a real or make-believe sea creature, and write an informative paragraph about it. Some of the words in the box may help you.

about	autumn	boy	bread	bay
crawl	dried	eight	feel	float
join	owl	paint	pool	stew

Include the **main idea** in your first sentence.

Include **details** about the main idea in the other sentences.

146 Review vowel pairs, digraphs, diphthongs: Writing

HOME Ask your child to read the story he or she wrote.

CURRICULUM CONNECTIONS

SPELLING

Use these words and sentences to review vowel pairs, vowel digraphs, and diphthongs.

1. **join**   Let's **join** hands in a circle.
2. **boy**   That **boy** won the race.
3. **about**   The TV show is **about** the sea.
4. **owls**   Most **owls** have big eyes.
5. **stew**   Paula made **stew** for dinner.
6. **autumn**   **Autumn** comes after summer.

SCIENCE

Suggest that children expand their informative paragraphs into brief reports, using the resources in your classroom. Remind them to include a topic sentence and supporting details in every paragraph.

MUSIC

Have children write new lyrics for the song "There's a Hole in the Bottom of the Sea," using words with vowel pairs, vowel digraphs, and diphthongs.

 **TECHNOLOGY**   **AstroWord** Vowel Digraphs & Diphthongs

---

AUDITORY/KINESTHETIC LEARNERS   GROUPS

Materials: eight paper cups, beanbag

Write the name of an animal from page 145 on each cup. Place the cups on a table. Have children take turns tossing the beanbag at the cups. Players earn points by knocking over a cup and saying and spelling a word with the same vowel sound as the animal on the cup.

CHALLENGE

Ask children to think of additional words to go with each animal on page 145. Have children use a sheet of paper to list the words under the animals' names and write the number of syllables next to each word.

EXTRA SUPPORT/INTERVENTION

Materials: letter tiles

Have children use letter tiles or cards to build words with vowel pairs, vowel digraphs, or diphthongs. Children can then replace the beginning consonant to form new words. For example, *feel* can be changed to *heel* and then to *wheel*. See Daily Phonics Practice, pages 219–221.

Integrating Phonics and Reading

Guided Reading

Have children look at the cover and title. Ask them to explain what broccoli is, then tell how they feel about broccoli.

First Reading Have children identify things Molly would rather do than eat broccoli.

Second Reading Have children list story words with vowel pairs, vowel digraphs, and diphthongs.

Comprehension

After reading, ask children these questions:
- Why do you think everyone wanted Molly to eat broccoli? *Inference/Main Idea*
- Did this story make you feel any different about broccoli? Why? *Reflective Analysis/ Personal Response*

ESL/ELL English Language Learners

To help English language learners pronounce *oo* words, direct their attention to lip position and exaggerate vowel sounds as you say story words with *oo*. Have children repeat.

Take-Home Book

Review Vowel Pairs, Digraphs, and Diphthongs

Skill Focus

Children will

★ read and identify words with vowel pairs, vowel digraphs, and diphthongs in the context of a story.

★ reread for fluency.

Teach

Building Background Remind children that the theme of this unit is "By the Sea!" Ask children to name some of the animals they read about in the unit.

Tell children they will be reading a book about octopuses. Ask them to share what they know about octopuses. Point out that an octopus has eight arms and lives in the sea.

Phonemic Awareness: Phoneme Substitution Say the word *neat* and have children identify the vowel sound they hear. (*long* e) Have them change the initial consonant sound to make new words. (*beat, seat, feat, heat, meat*) Repeat with the word *pool.* (*cool, tool, stool, spool, fool*) Repeat again with the word *new.* (*stew, chew, threw, knew, few*)

Practice and Apply

Read the Book Help children tear out and fold the pages of their Take-Home Books. Have them look through the book and talk about the pictures. Then, read the story together.

Sound to Symbol Have volunteers read the book aloud. Ask children to identify words with vowel pairs, vowel digraphs, and diphthongs. Have children say the words and identify the vowel pair, vowel digraph, or diphthong and the sound it makes. List the words on the board in the three columns.

Reread for Fluency Have children reread the book to increase their fluency and comprehension. Urge children to take their books home to share with family members.

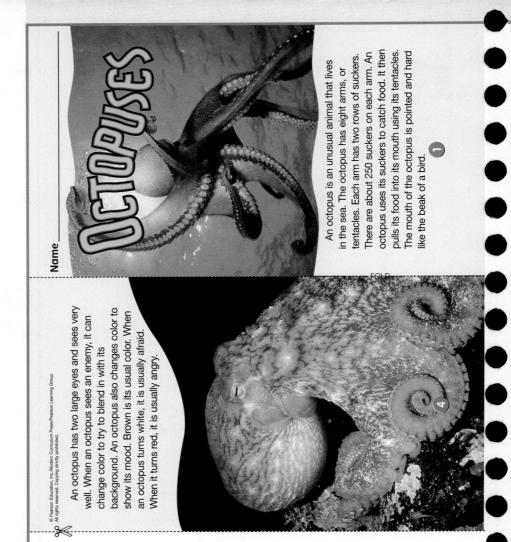

An octopus has two large eyes and sees very well. When an octopus sees an enemy, it can change color to try to blend in with its background. An octopus also changes color to show its mood. Brown is its usual color. When an octopus turns white, it is usually afraid. When it turns red, it is usually angry.

An octopus is an unusual animal that lives in the sea. The octopus has eight arms, or tentacles. Each arm has two rows of suckers. There are about 250 suckers on each arm. An octopus uses its suckers to catch food. It then pulls its food into its mouth using its tentacles. The mouth of the octopus is pointed and hard like the beak of a bird.

Review vowel pairs, digraphs, diphthongs: Take-home book   **147**

FOCUS ON ALL LEARNERS

ESL/ELL **ENGLISH LANGUAGE LEARNERS**

English language learners may have difficulty with these words in the Take-Home Book: *tentacles, suckers, well-developed, gills, squirts, sac, enemy, background, mood.* Pronounce the words and explain their meanings using the pictures in the book or other visual aids.

AUDITORY/KINESTHETIC LEARNERS

Write *oi, oy, ou, ow,* and *ew* on the board. As you say the words below, have children raise a hand when they hear a word with a diphthong. Have a volunteer identify the diphthong and continue. Use the words *speed, pointed, snout, coast, flew, brown, tail, join, boy, cool, deep, house, down, new.*

VISUAL LEARNERS

Draw and cut out three octopus shapes and label them *vowel pairs, vowel digraphs,* and *diphthongs.* Have children suggest words with any of these vowel terms and write the words on the appropriate octopus's arms.

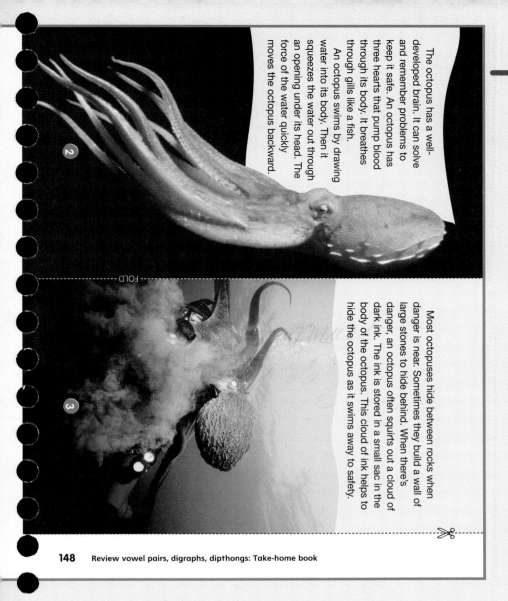

The octopus has a well-developed brain. It can solve and remember problems to keep it safe. An octopus has three hearts that pump blood through its body. It breathes through gills like a fish. An octopus swims by drawing water into its body. Then it squeezes the water out through an opening under its head. The force of the water quickly moves the octopus backward.

Most octopuses hide between rocks when danger is near. Sometimes they build a wall of large stones to hide behind. When there's danger, an octopus often squirts out a cloud of dark ink. The ink is stored in a small sac in the body of the octopus. This cloud of ink helps to hide the octopus as it swims away to safety.

148 Review vowel pairs, digraphs, dipthongs: Take-home book

CURRICULUM CONNECTIONS

SCIENCE

Materials: chart paper, felt-tip markers

Have children research octopuses and squids and create a chart showing how they are alike and how they are different. Suggest that children include pictures of both animals. Display the charts in the Science Center.

ART

Materials: art paper, watercolors or tempera paints, book about octopuses

Show children additional photographs of octopuses swimming, squirting ink, eating, hiding, or changing color. Have them paint a picture of an octopus doing any of these activities or doing something fantastic.

WRITING

Ask children to write a story about a fictional octopus. Encourage them to be creative.

 AstroWord Vowel Digraphs & Diphthongs

AUDITORY LEARNERS

Have children quiz each other orally about what they have learned about octopuses. Tell them to write questions and answers that they can ask one another. Suggest that children identify words with vowel pairs, vowel digraphs, and diphthongs in the questions and answers they write.

CHALLENGE

Provide children with the words below to use in sentences telling about something related to octopuses. Suggest that they include as many words as they can in each sentence. Use the words *sea, beak, sees, breathes, brain, squeezes, between, eight, mood, food, blood, mouth, pointed, brown, cloud.*

EXTRA SUPPORT/INTERVENTION

Write words with vowel pairs, vowel digraphs, and diphthongs on strips of paper. Then, cut the words apart, leaving the vowel teams together. Mix the pieces and have children use them to form words. **See Daily Phonics Practice, pages 219–221.**

Unit Checkup

Review Vowel Pairs, Digraphs, and Diphthongs

Skill Focus

Children will

★ review vowel pairs, vowel digraphs, and diphthongs.

★ use words with vowel pairs, vowel digraphs, or diphthongs in context.

Teach

Phonemic Awareness: Phoneme Isolation
Review the definition of a vowel pair with children. Then, have them identify the vowel sounds they hear in each of these words: *tail, tray, treat, trees, tied, toad, toes, true.*

Review the definition of a vowel digraph. Ask children to identify the vowel sounds heard in these words: *laundry, law, weather, weigh, boot, book.*

Review the definition of a diphthong. Have children identify the vowel sounds they hear in the words *broil, boy, bound, brown, brew.*

Sound to Symbol Write these groups of vowel teams on the board: (1) *ai, ay, ea, ee, ie, oa, oe, ue;* (2) *au, aw, ea, ei, oo;* (3) *oi, oy, ou, ow, ew.* Ask volunteers to name words with each of the vowel teams listed on the board.

Practice and Apply

Assess Skills Tell children that only one circle should be filled in for each item on page 149. For page 150, remind children to circle and write the words.

Name _____   5 CHECKUP

> Read the word in the box. Fill in the circle in front of the word that has the same vowel sound.

1. awning
   - ○ meat   ○ school   ● taught

2. bread
   - ● led   ○ sea   ○ say

3. goose
   - ○ scout   ● tool   ○ book

4. weigh
   - ○ feel   ○ boil   ● late

5. clown
   - ○ paid   ● loud   ○ boat

6. boast
   - ○ room   ○ chew   ● goat

7. green
   - ● teach   ○ bread   ○ vein

8. joy
   - ○ jaw   ● join   ○ wood

9. pause
   - ● lawn   ○ eight   ○ leap

10. soak
    - ○ shout   ○ soy   ● toe

11. play
    - ● main   ○ crawl   ○ boy

12. mouse
    - ○ crook   ○ broom   ● brown

13. leaves
    - ● trees   ○ vein   ○ threw

14. good
    - ○ boil   ○ bloom   ● look

15. sail
    - ● stay   ○ draw   ○ tried

16. coin
    - ● toy   ○ shook   ○ soon

Vowel pairs, digraphs, diphthongs: Assessment   **149**

FOCUS ON ALL LEARNERS

ESL/ELL ENGLISH LANGUAGE LEARNERS

Build background for the exercise on page 150 by discussing how animal sounds are represented in English. You may wish to pair fluent speakers with English language learners to work on the exercise together.

VISUAL LEARNERS PARTNERS

Materials: oak tag, scissors, markers

Assign each pair of children one vowel pair, vowel digraph, or diphthong. Then, have them create word slides with as many words as possible. Have pairs of children trade slides and read each other's words.

AUDITORY LEARNERS GROUPS

Have children take turns reading the riddles on page 150 for others to answer. Encourage children to add riddles of their own, featuring words with vowel pairs, vowel digraphs, and diphthongs.

Circle the word that best completes each sentence. Write the word on the line.

1. My brother and I _____played_____ a riddle game.   (played)   plowed

2. We _____took_____ turns making up animal riddles.   (took)   tied

3. What has a curly tail and says _____oink_____?   oats   (oink)

4. What is big and gray and _____weighs_____ up to 35 tons?   wait   (weighs)

5. What can fly and says _____cheep_____?   chime   (cheep)

6. What is a large black bird that makes a sound like _____caw_____?   (caw)   coo

7. What is small, yellow and says _____peep_____?   paw   (peep)

8. What gives milk and makes a _____moo_____ sound?   may   (moo)

9. What can you sit on that runs fast and makes a _____neigh_____ sound?   (neigh)   need

10. What sees well at night and can _____hoot_____?   cool   (hoot)

11. What is soft and quiet and says _____mew_____?   (mew)   mow

12. What is cute and furry and eats fish for _____meals_____?   mean   (meals)

13. "I _____feel_____ it's a cat," I said.   (feel)   feet

14. "No," he laughed. "It's a _____seal_____!"   south   (seal)

150   Vowel pairs, digraphs, diphthongs: Assessment

ASSESS UNDERSTANDING OF UNIT SKILLS

STUDENT PROGRESS ASSESSMENT

To assess the progress children have made with vowel pairs, vowel digraphs, and diphthongs, refer to the observational notes you made as children worked through this unit.

PORTFOLIO ASSESSMENT

To help you evaluate children's proficiency in applying phonics skills to written work, review the materials they have collected in their portfolios. You may wish to schedule interviews with children to discuss their progress and set immediate goals.

DAILY PHONICS PRACTICE

Quick reviews can be found on pages 219–221 in Daily Phonics Practice for children who need additional practice with vowel pairs, vowel digraphs, and diphthongs.

PHONICS POSTTEST

The posttest on pages 127g–127h will help you assess children's mastery of vowel pairs, vowel digraphs, and diphthongs.

KINESTHETIC LEARNERS GROUPS

Materials: bingo game boards, markers

Give children blank bingo game cards and have them fill in the spaces with these vowel teams: *ai, ay, ea, ee, ie, oa, oe, ue, au, aw, ea, ei, oo, oi, oy, ou, ow, ew.* Repeat vowel teams to fill the card. As you say a word, have children cover the letters that represent the vowel sound. The player who covers a row or column first is the winner.

CHALLENGE

Invite children to write riddle books to share with their classmates. Explain that the answer to each riddle should include a word that has a vowel pair, a vowel digraph, or a diphthong.

EXTRA SUPPORT/INTERVENTION

Preview the word choices on page 149 before children begin the Checkup exercise. Have children listen for and identify the vowel sound in each word. Explain that thinking of the answer to each riddle on page 150 may help them decide which word to choose. See Daily Phonics Practice, pages 219–221.

Teacher Notes

UNIT 6

Prefixes, Base Words, Suffixes, Syllables

THEME: TAKING CARE OF OUR EARTH

CONTENTS

UNIT 6 RESOURCES

TEACHING PLANS

Student Performance Objectives

In Unit 6, children will be introduced to the prefixes *re-, pre-, dis-, un-, mis-, ex-, de-, im-,* and *in-* and will review suffixes and syllabication rules within the context of the environmental theme "Taking Care of Our Earth." As children begin to understand and learn to apply the concept that prefixes and suffixes can be added to and change the meaning of words, they will be able to

▶ Recognize and identify the meanings of prefixes *re-, pre-, dis-, un-, mis-, ex-, de-, im-,* and *in-*

▶ Identify prefixes, base words, and suffixes

▶ Identify syllables in base words with prefixes and suffixes

▶ Learn and apply syllabication rules

Overview of Resources

LESSON	MCP PHONICS AND READING LIBRARY, LEVEL C PROGRAM	TITLE	DAILY PHONICS PRACTICE
69: Prefixes *im-, in-, un-, dis-, mis-*	NC, Set 1	*For a Better Life*	221
70: Prefixes *ex-, de-, re-, pre*	FC, Set 2	*Starfishers to the Rescue*	221
71: Prefixes, base words, suffixes, endings	RR, Stg Five, Bk 6	*Moon Stories*	222
72: Syllables: words with prefixes, suffixes, endings/Syllables in compound words	RR, Stg Five, Bk 10	*Sara's Lovely Songs*	222
73: Review compound words	RR, Stg Five, Bk 30	*The Junkpile Robot*	222
74: Syllables: words with suffixes	RR, Stg Five, Bk 7	*Bedtime at Aunt Carmen's*	222
75: Syllables: words with prefixes	FC, Set 4	*The Lost and Found Game*	222
76: Syllables: words with two or more consonants between vowels	NC, Set 3	*The Plant That Almost Ate the World*	222
77: Syllables in v-c-v words	RR, Stg Five, Bk 26	*Where Jeans Come From*	222
78: Syllables in v-c-v words	VFC, Set 4	*At the Top of the World*	222
79: Syllables: words with a vowel sounded alone	NC, Set 4	*The Living Desert*	222
80: Syllables: words with two vowels together	FC, Set 1	*Digging Dinosaurs*	222
81: Syllables: words with final *le*	RR, Stg Five, Bk 14	*Something Everyone Needs*	222
82: Review prefixes, base words, suffixes, endings, syllables	FC, Set 2	*Let's Build a Playground*	221–222
83: Take-Home Book: "David's Wonderful Idea"			221–222
84: Unit Checkup			221–222

RR—Reader Readers   Stg—Stage   Bk—Book   FC—First Chapters   NC—Next Chapters

Assessment Options

In Unit 6, assess children's ability to read and write words with prefixes and suffixes and their ability to identify syllables. Use the Unit Pretest and Posttest for formal assessment. For ongoing informal assessment, you may want to use children's work on the Review pages, Take-Home Books, and Unit Checkups. You may also want to encourage children to evaluate their own work and participate in setting goals for their learning.

ESL/ELL Provide frequent oral opportunities for English language learners to distinguish the prefix and its meaning from the base words. For English language learners who come from monosyllabic language backgrounds, the concepts of suffixes and multisyllable words may be perceived as being separate words. For additional support for English language learners, see page 151j.

FORMAL ASSESSMENT

Use the Unit 6 Pretest, on pages 151e–151f, to help assess a child's knowledge at the beginning of the unit and to plan instruction.

ESL/ELL Before administering the Pretest, English language learners may be unfamiliar with the testing format of filling in the circle next to the answer. Demonstrate how this is done. Inability to recognize words may require teacher support to preview them and read them aloud to the group. It may be more beneficial to conduct the pretest one-on-one with children who need special pacing.

Use the Unit 6 Posttest, on pages 152g–152h, to help assess mastery of unit objectives and to plan for reteaching, if necessary.

ESL/ELL Some children may continue to have difficulty with directions. Read the directions aloud and model how to mark the responses to complete the tests.

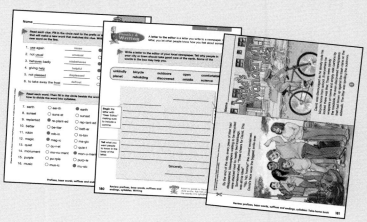

INFORMAL ASSESSMENT

Use the Review Pages, Unit Checkup, and Take-Home Book in the student book to provide an effective means of evaluating children's performance.

Unit 6 Skills	Review pages	Checkups	Take-Home Books
Prefixes	156	183–184	181–182
Prefixes, base words, suffixes, endings	179–180	183–184	181–182
Syllables	179–180	183–184	181–182

STUDENT PROGRESS CHECKLIST

Use the checklist on page 151i to record children's progress. You may want to cut the sections apart to place each child's checklist in his or her portfolio.

PORTFOLIO ASSESSMENT

This logo appears throughout the teaching plans. It signals opportunities for collecting student work for individual portfolios. You may also want to include the Pretest and Posttest, the Review pages, the Unit Checkup, Phonics & Reading, and Phonics & Writing pages.

Pretest and Posttest

DIRECTIONS

To help you assess children's progress in learning Unit 6 skills, tests are available on pages 151e–151h.

Administer the Pretest before children begin the unit. The results of the Pretest will help you identify each child's strengths and needs in advance, allowing you to structure lesson plans to meet individual needs. Administer the Posttest to assess children's overall mastery of skills taught in the unit to identify specific areas that will require reteaching.

ESL/ELL Since the objective of both the Unit 6 Pretest and Posttest is to choose the correct prefix or suffix to make a word that will match a given meaning or complete a sentence, it may be necessary to read aloud the definitions and sentences and to orally help children build the words.

To test the division of syllables, read the words aloud and have English language learners repeat the words before marking their test sheets.

PERFORMANCE ASSESSMENT PROFILE

The following chart will help you identify specific skills as they appear on the tests and will enable you to identify and record specific information about an individual's or the class's performance on the tests.

Depending on the results of each test, refer to the Reteaching column for lesson-plan pages where you can find activities that will be useful for meeting individual needs or for daily phonics practice.

Answer Keys

Unit 6 Pretest, page 151e (BLM 36)

1. re-	6. mis-	11. dis-
2. dis-	7. un-	12. un-
3. -ness	8. mis-	13. in-
4. un-	9. im-	
5. -ly	10. un-	

Unit 6 Pretest, page 151f (BLM 37)

14. spoiled	22. rush
15. exchanged	23. book-mark
16. playful	24. mak-ing
17. comfortable	25. re-fresh
18. biggest	26. but-ter
19. disliked	27. riv-er
20. deplane	28. la-zy
21. happiness	29. ra-di-a-tor

Unit 6 Posttest, page 151g (BLM 38)

1. dis-	6. re-	11. dis-
2. un-	7. un-	12. un-
3. -able	8. mis-	13. dis-
4. -ly	9. in-	
5. pre-	10. im-	

Unit 6 Posttest, page 151h (BLM 39)

14. harmless	22. vis-it
15. fastest	23. fix-ing
16. helpful	24. trick-y
17. derailed	25. mail-box
18. agreeable	26. pi-o-neer
19. exports	27. desk
20. slowly	28. bit-ter
21. discolored	29. re-do

Performance Assessment Profile

Skill	Pretest Questions	Posttest Questions	Reteaching	
			Focus on All Learners	**Daily Phonics Practice**
Prefixes	1, 2, 4, 6, 7–13, 15, 19, 20	1, 2, 5, 6, 7–13, 17, 19, 21	153–159, 165–166, 179–184	221–222
Suffixes	3, 5, 14, 16, 17, 18, 21	3, 4, 14, 15, 16, 18, 20	157–159, 163–164, 179–184	222
Syllables	22–29	22–29	160–184	222

Name _____

> ▶ **Read each clue. Then, fill in the circle under the correct prefix or suffix that should be added to the underlined word to make a new word that matches the clue.**

1. <u>ordered</u> again

    re ○   dis ○   un ○

2. opposite of <u>pleased</u>

    dis ○   ed ○   re ○

3. being <u>helpful</u>

    ing ○   ness ○   re ○

4. not <u>published</u>

    dis ○   ly ○   un ○

5. in a <u>wise</u> way

    ed ○   dis ○   ly ○

6. <u>use</u> incorrectly

    dis ○   ly ○   mis ○

> ▶ **Fill in the circle beside each prefix that should be added to the underlined word to give an opposite meaning to the sentence.**

7. He is a <u>kind</u> person.   ○ un   ○ in   ○ re

8. Mom <u>placed</u> her book in the room.   ○ un   ○ mis   ○ dis

9. The water was <u>pure</u>.   ○ im   ○ re   ○ un

10. Tammy <u>locked</u> the safe.   ○ re   ○ dis   ○ un

11. I <u>like</u> football games.   ○ dis   ○ un   ○ im

12. My homework is <u>finished</u>.   ○ un   ○ re   ○ dis

13. The answer was <u>correct</u>.   ○ re   ○ dis   ○ in

Go to the next page. →

Name _____

> Read each sentence. Fill in the circle beside the prefix or suffix that should be added to the base word so that the sentence makes sense.

14. Molly threw away the _____ milk.
    (spoil)

    ed ○   ful ○   er ○

15. Mom _____ the hat at the store.
    (changed)

    ex ○   dis ○   de ○

16. The cat is always _____.
    (play)

    ful ○   able ○   ness ○

17. I am not _____ sitting here.
    (comfort)

    er ○   ful ○   able ○

18. This is the _____ crowd ever!
    (big)

    ness ○   ful ○   est ○

19. We _____ the boring movie.
    (liked)

    dis ○   ex ○   un ○

20. The flight attendant helped us _____.
    (plane)

    ex ○   de ○   dis ○

21. Your _____ means a lot to me.
    (happy)

    ed ○   er ○   ness ○

> Read each word. Fill in the circle beside the correct way to divide the word into syllables.

22. **rush**   ○ rush   ○ r-ush   ○ ru-sh

23. **bookmark**   ○ boo-kmark   ○ book-mark   ○ bo-okmark

24. **making**   ○ mak-ing   ○ ma-king   ○ maki-ng

25. **refresh**   ○ re-fresh   ○ ref-resh   ○ r-efresh

26. **butter**   ○ butt-er   ○ bu-tter   ○ but-ter

27. **river**   ○ riv-er   ○ ri-ver   ○ river

28. **lazy**   ○ laz-y   ○ lazy   ○ la-zy

29. **radiator**   ○ radi-ator   ○ rad-ia-tor   ○ ra-di-a-tor

Possible score on Unit 6 Pretest is 29. Number correct _____

BLM 37 Unit 6 Pretest: Prefixes, suffixes, syllabication

Name _____

> Read each clue. Then, fill in the circle under the correct prefix or suffix that should be added to the underlined word to make a new word that matches the clue.

1. opposite of <u>obey</u>

dis	ed	re
○	○	○

2. not <u>happy</u>

mis	un	ly
○	○	○

3. can be <u>washed</u>

dis	able	un
○	○	○

4. in a <u>pleasant</u> way

ed	un	ly
○	○	○

5. to <u>pay</u> before

pre	dis	ful
○	○	○

6. to <u>fill</u> again

mis	re	es
○	○	○

> Fill in the circle beside each prefix that should be added to the underlined word to give an opposite meaning to the sentence.

7. The rows are <u>even</u>.   ○ un   ○ im   ○ re

8. Sue <u>spells</u> words with silent letters.   ○ un   ○ mis   ○ dis

9. The letter was <u>complete.</u>   ○ dis   ○ re   ○ in

10. The statue is <u>perfect</u>.   ○ re   ○ im   ○ un

11. The man <u>obeyed</u> the law.   ○ in   ○ dis   ○ re

12. Kevin <u>zipped</u> his jacket.   ○ dis   ○ un   ○ mis

13. Carol <u>likes</u> peas.   ○ re   ○ dis   ○ mis

Go to the next page. →

Name _____

> **Read each sentence. Fill in the circle beside the prefix or suffix that should be added to the base word so that the sentence will make sense.**

14. The tiny spider was _____.
    (harm)

    ly ◯   less ◯   est ◯

15. The _____ runner won the race.
    (fast)

    est ◯   ful ◯   able ◯

16. The kind salesclerk was _____.
    (help)

    ness ◯   er ◯   ful ◯

17. The train _____.
    (railed)

    de ◯   ex ◯   dis ◯

18. The warm weather is very _____.
    (agree)

    ness ◯   ful ◯   able ◯

19. China _____ many teas.
    (ports)

    dis ◯   ex ◯   un ◯

20. A snail moves _____.
    (slow)

    ly ◯   ness ◯   ing ◯

21. The rotten food was _____.
    (colored)

    re ◯   dis ◯   de ◯

> **Read each word. Then, fill in the circle beside the correct way to divide it into syllables.**

22. **visit**   ◯ vis-it   ◯ vi-sit   ◯ v-isit

23. **fixing**   ◯ fix-ing   ◯ fi-xing   ◯ fixi-ng

24. **tricky**   ◯ tric-ky   ◯ trick-y   ◯ tri-cky

25. **mailbox**   ◯ mail-box   ◯ mailb-ox   ◯ mai-lbox

26. **pioneer**   ◯ pio-neer   ◯ pio-ne-er   ◯ pi-o-neer

27. **desk**   ◯ d-esk   ◯ desk   ◯ de-sk

28. **bitter**   ◯ bitt-er   ◯ bit-ter   ◯ bi-tter

29. **redo**   ◯ r-edo   ◯ redo   ◯ re-do

Possible score on Unit 6 Posttest is 29. Number correct _____

BLM 39 Posttest: Prefixes, suffixes, syllabication

151h

Student Progress Checklist

Make as many copies as needed to use for a class list. For individual portfolio use, cut apart each child's section. As indicated by the code, color in boxes next to skills satisfactorily assessed and insert an *X* by those requiring reteaching. Marked boxes can later be colored in to indicate mastery.

Student Progress Checklist

Code: ■ Satisfactory   ☒ Needs Reteaching

Student: _____ _____ Pretest Score: _____ Posttest Score: _____	**Skills** ☐ Prefixes ☐ Suffixes ☐ Syllabication Rules	**Comments / Learning Goals**
Student: _____ _____ Pretest Score: _____ Posttest Score: _____	**Skills** ☐ Prefixes ☐ Suffixes ☐ Syllabication Rules	**Comments / Learning Goals**
Student: _____ _____ Pretest Score: _____ Posttest Score: _____	**Skills** ☐ Prefixes ☐ Suffixes ☐ Syllabication Rules	**Comments / Learning Goals**
Student: _____ _____ Pretest Score: _____ Posttest Score: _____	**Skills** ☐ Prefixes ☐ Suffixes ☐ Syllabication Rules	**Comments / Learning Goals**

BLM 40 Unit 6 Checklist

English Language Learners

Throughout Unit 6 there are opportunities to assess English language learners' ability to read and write words with prefixes and suffixes and their ability to identify syllables. Children whose home language is Cantonese, Hmong, Vietnamese, Korean, or Khmer come from monosyllabic language backgrounds. Overstressing the prefixes, suffixes, and syllables in words, especially compound words, may mislead English language learners into thinking two-syllable words are two separate words. Provide frequent oral opportunities for English language learners to distinguish the prefix and suffix in words and its meaning from the base words. Lead children to understand that syllabication will aid in word pronunciation and spelling.

Lesson 69, pages 153–154 Native speakers of Spanish are likely to be familiar with prefixes since they appear in their own language. Provide frequent oral opportunities for speakers of other languages to distinguish the prefix and its meaning from the base words.

Lesson 70, pages 155–156 Prefix is a concept English language learners will pick up quickly. Reinforce meanings and provide opportunities for children to hear and say *re-, de-, ex-,* and *pre-*, making the correct long or short vowel sounds.

Lesson 73, pages 161–172 Hmong, Vietnamese, and Cantonese are monosyllabic languages. Native speakers may need additional practice with compound words. Spanish speakers may also require additional practice, since few words in their native language are formed in this manner.

Lesson 75, pages 165–166 Point out to native speakers of Spanish that the prefix *des-* in Spanish often is *dis-* or *un-* in English. Provide frequent oral opportunities for speakers of other languages to identify and use these prefixes interchangeably in English.

Spelling Connections

INTRODUCTION

The Unit Word List is a list of selected spelling words drawn from this unit. The words are grouped by prefixes, suffixes, and syllables. To incorporate spelling into your phonics program, use the activity in the Curriculum Connections section of each teaching plan.

ESL/ELL It is recommended that English language learners reach the intermediate level of English proficiency before focusing on spelling. For English language learners, introduce one group of words at a time and their meanings through visuals, realia, or demonstrations.

The spelling lessons utilize the following approach for each set of words.

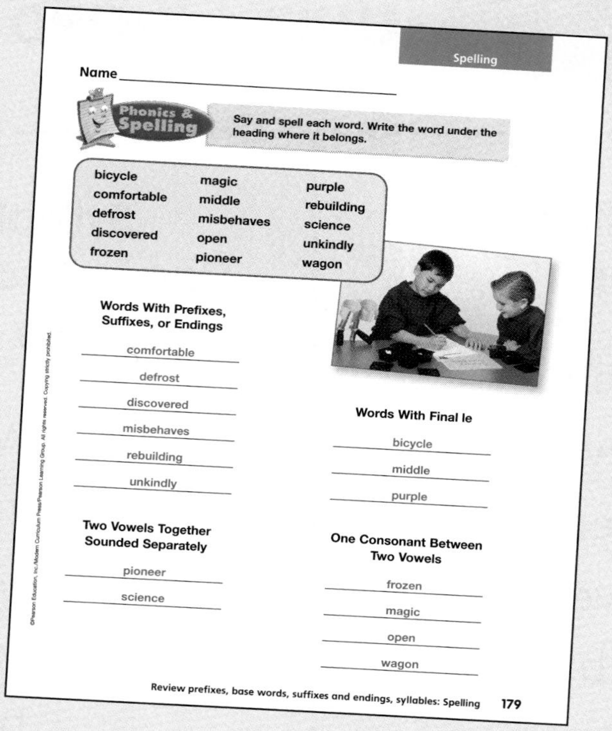

1. Administer a pretest of the words that have not yet been introduced. Dictation sentences are provided.

2. Provide practice.

3. Reassess. Dictation sentences are provided.

A final review of words with prefixes, suffixes, and syllables is provided at the end of the unit, on page 180.

DIRECTIONS

Make a copy of Blackline Master 41 for each child. After administering the pretest for prefixes, suffixes, and syllables, give children a copy of the appropriate word list.

Children can work with a partner to practice spelling the words orally and identifying the phonics element in each word. You may want to challenge children to make new words by adding prefixes and suffixes to different base words. Children can write words of their own on *My Own Word List* (see Blackline Master 41).

Have children store their list words in an envelope or plastic zipper bag in the back of their books. You may want to suggest that children keep a spelling notebook, listing words with similar patterns. Another idea is to build Word Walls with children and display them in the classroom. Each section of the wall could focus on words with a single phonics element. The walls will become a good resource for children to use when they are engaged in writing.

Unit Word List

Prefixes, Suffixes, Syllables
rebuilding
unkindly
discovered
misbehaves
comfortable
defrost

Syllables in v-c-v; 1–2 Vowel Sounds; Words Ending in *le*
wagon
magic
pioneer
open
bicycle
purple

Name _____

Phonics & Spelling

Say and spell each word. Write the word under the heading where it belongs.

bicycle	magic	purple
comfortable	middle	rebuilding
defrost	misbehaves	science
discovered	open	unkindly
frozen	pioneer	wagon

Words With Prefixes, Suffixes, or Endings
comfortable
defrost
discovered
misbehaves
rebuilding
unkindly

Words With Final le
bicycle
middle
purple

Two Vowels Together Sounded Separately
pioneer
science

One Consonant Between Two Vowels
frozen
magic
open
wagon

Review prefixes, base words, suffixes and endings, syllables: Spelling **179**

Name _____

 **UNIT 6 WORD LIST**

Prefixes, Suffixes, Syllables

rebuilding

unkindly

discovered

misbehaves

comfortable

defrost

Syllables in v-c-v, One to Two Vowel Sounds, Words Ending in le

wagon

magic

pioneer

open

bicycle

purple

My Own Word List

My Own Word List

Phonics Games, Activities, and Technology

The following collection of ideas offers a variety of opportunities to reinforce phonics skills while actively engaging children. The games, activities, and technology suggestions can easily be adapted to meet the needs of your group of learners. They vary in approach so as to consider children's different learning styles.

WORD WHEELS

Have children cut out two paper circles of different sizes to make a word wheel featuring words with prefixes *un-*, *dis-*, and *mis-*. Attach the two circles with a paper fastener placed in the center. Have them write the prefixes *un-*, *dis-*, and *mis-* in three places on the right side of the smaller circle, as shown. Around the bottom wheel children can add any base words that will form a word with one or more of the prefixes. Children can work in pairs to use one another's wheels to form and read words.

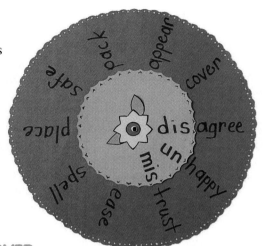

FLIPPING OVER SUFFIXES

Provide sheets of paper for children to staple together along one edge to make a flip book. The last sheet should be longer than the other pages of the book. Have children write a suffix such as *-ness*, *-less*, *-ful*, *-able*, *-y*, *-ment*, *-en*, or *-ly* on the last page and write base words to which the suffix can be added on the shorter pages. A new word is then formed with the suffix each time the page is flipped. Partners can work together to read and define one another's words.

KNOW AND DO-NOT-KNOW SORTS

Provide sets of word cards with words having prefixes *in-*, *im-*, *re-*, *dis-*, *un-*, *mis-*, *ex-*, *pre-*, and *de-* or suffixes *-ness*, *-less*, *-ful*, *-able*, *-y*, *-ment*, *-en*, and *-ly*. Children can work independently or with a partner to sort the words according to prefix or suffix. Then, have children sort the word cards again into those they know and can define and those they do not know. You may wish to provide children with an answer key for checking.

SYLLABLE RACE AGAINST TIME

Divide the class into five teams and assign one syllabication rule to each group. Challenge the teams to write as many words as possible to which the rule applies. They can use books as a reference. Set a time limit and check their words when time is up. Repeat the procedure using additional syllabication.

RECYCLING WORDS

Provide partners with large sheets of drawing paper to create game boards. Have them draw a wide path around the four sides of the paper as shown. Then, they can divide the path into sections large enough to write a word inside. Provide base words or have children select base words from lessons in Unit 6 and write one word in each square; for example, *please, certain, happy, able, appear, spell, look, like, claw, frost, change, fill, open, write, load, code, tie.* Partners take turns flipping a coin to move one space for heads and two spaces for tails. For each word landed on, they must "recycle" the word by adding a prefix or suffix to form a new word. Challenge children to not repeat words a partner has already used.

CALLING ALL V-C-V WORDS

Choose several two-syllable words with the vowel-consonant-vowel pattern to write on the board. As you write, insert a blank in place of one of the syllables in each word; for example, ___lac (lilac), spi ___ (spider), fro___ (frozen), ___on (wagon), shad ___ (shadow), fa___ (famous), drag___ (dragon). As you say a word, call on a volunteer to find and write the missing syllable to complete the word.

BEST FOOT FORWARD

Write several words with the prefixes and suffixes *ex-, de-, re-, pre-, un-, in-, im-, mis-, dis-, -able, -less, -ness, -ly, -y, -ment, -en,* and *-ful* on the chalkboard. Have children form a line across one side of the room. Invite children to take turns choosing a word from the board. A child may take one giant step forward for reading the word, a second step for identifying the base word, a third step for defining the word, and a fourth step for using the word correctly in a sentence. Circle words as they are used. Play until everyone has reached the opposite side of the room.

PREFIX WORD WALL

Invite children to create a Word Wall featuring words with prefixes. Form a chart with three columns as shown. Have children list prefixes in the left column and the meaning of the prefix in the next column. Invite volunteers to write word examples in the third column. Challenge children to choose words from the Word Wall to use in oral or written sentences.

PREFIX	MEANING	WORDS
re-	do again	revise, revisit, rewrite
dis-	not	dislike, disagree
un-	not	untie, undo
mis-	not	mistook, misunderstood
ex-	out of, from	exchange, exclaim
de-	from	depart

DISAPPEAR AND REAPPEAR

Invite children to write invisible words. Provide white crayons, white paper, and watercolors. Encourage children to experiment first by writing their name using the white crayon. Then, have them paint over their writing with watercolor paints. Their writing should show up clearly. If not, encourage children to press harder with the crayon. Once they have figured out how to write words that will show up, invite them to write words with prefixes *in-, im, ex-, de-, re-, pre-, un-, mis-,* and *dis-.* Partners can then exchange papers, paint over the page with watercolors, and read the words to one another. Students may also enjoy writing invisible messages that contain words with prefixes.

GREEN EARTH PICTURE SEARCH

Provide children with copies of Blackline Master 42 on page 151p. Have them read the list of animals and other items, find them in the picture, and circle them. They can check off each word as they find it. Then, ask children to write each word on the back of the sheet and divide it into syllables.

THE VOWEL STANDS ALONE

Display a set of large letter cards. Call on a number of children to hold up the letters and arrange themselves to form a word you say. Say words that apply to the syllabication rule: When a vowel is sounded alone, it forms a syllable by itself, such as *ocean, alive, unite, gasoline, ahead,* and *uniform.* Once children have arranged themselves, holding the letters to form the word for the group to see, ask the child who is holding the vowel that represents a syllable of its own to step forward.

The following software products reinforce children's understanding of a variety of phonics skills.

Word Munchers® Deluxe
Word recognition, rhyming, and phonics are the skill areas that children (ages 8–12) practice as they zoom through mazes with a "munching" character. The mazes contain words and objects to be munched according to rules displayed at the top of the screen.

** Riverdeep The Learning Company
   500 Redwood Blvd.
   Novato, CA 94947
   (800) 825-4420
   www.learningcompanyschool.com

Reading Explorer Deluxe
In this program, children learn basic reading skills of phonics and sentence construction. The 12 activities include games like What Am I?, Spell It Out, and Build-a-Sentence that teach letter recognition, word recognition, and sentence structure.

** DK Publishing, Inc.
   95 Madison Avenue
   New York, NY 10016
   (877) 342-5357
   www.DK.com

Name _____

▶ Read the words. Find the animals and other items in the picture and circle them. Then, write the words on the back of this sheet. Divide each word into syllables.

rabbit

robin

cabin

river

chimney

spider

dandelion

bicycle

canoe

paddle

turtle

balloon

railroad tracks

eagle

people

BLM 42 Unit 6 Activity

Home Connections

The Home Connections features of this program are intended to involve families in their children's learning and application of phonics skills. Three effective opportunities to make connections between home and school include the following.

- **HOME LETTER**
- **HOME NOTES**
- **TAKE-HOME BOOKS**

HOME LETTER

A letter is available to be sent home at the beginning of Unit 6. This letter informs family members that children will be learning to read and write words with prefixes, suffixes, and multiple syllables within the context of the unit theme, "Taking Care of Our Earth." The suggested home activity focuses on drawing a picture or creating something new to show what can be made using recycled materials. This activity promotes interaction between child and family members while supporting children's learning of reading and writing words with prefixes, suffixes, and syllabication. A letter, which is available in both English and Spanish, also suggests theme-related books family members can look for in a local library and enjoy reading together.

HOME NOTES

Whenever the Home logo appears within the student book, a phonics activity is suggested to be done at home. The activities are simple to do, requiring little or no preparation or special materials, and are meant to reinforce the targeted phonics skill.

Home Notes in Spanish are also available for both teachers and parents to download and use from our website, www.PlaidPhonics.com.

TAKE-HOME BOOKS

Within the student book are Take-Home Books that can be cut out and assembled. The story language in each book reinforces the targeted phonics skills. The books can be taken home and shared with family members. In Unit 6, one Take-Home Book is available, focusing on prefixes, suffixes, and words with multiple syllables as well as the unit theme, "Taking Care of Our Earth."

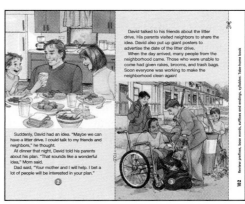

Prefixes, Base Words, Suffixes, Syllables

Skill Focus

Assess Prior Knowledge
To assess children's prior knowledge of prefixes, base words, suffixes, and syllables, use the pretest on pages 151e–151f.

Unit Focus

▶ Build Background

- Write the theme title "Taking Care of Our Earth" on the board and read it aloud. Talk about ways people can help keep the earth clean and safe.

- Draw children's attention to the photo on page 151. Explain that the house in the picture is made of used glass bottles that a man collected.

- Read the article aloud. Point out that Arsenault thought of an unusual and creative way to reuse bottles. Have children suggest ways in which they might use discarded items. Talk about why reusing and recycling things is important.

▶ Introduce Prefixes, Base Words, Suffixes, Syllables

- Write the word *beautiful* on the board. Underline *ful* and remind children that this word part is a suffix.

- Write *recycle* on the board. Circle *re* and explain that this word part is called a prefix. It comes at the beginning of a word. Ask a child to underline the base word. (*cycle*)

- To review syllables, ask children to name three-syllable words from the article, such as *everyone, recycling, important, wastefully, containers.*

Critical Thinking Talk about creative ways in which people might reuse recycled objects. Then, discuss the Talk About It question.

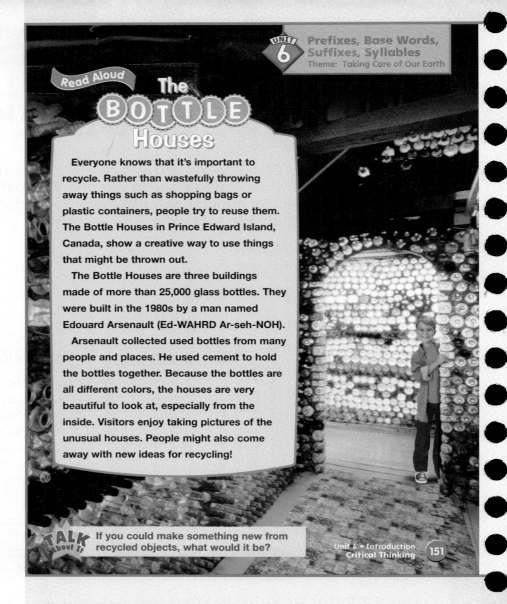

Read Aloud

The BOTTLE Houses

Everyone knows that it's important to recycle. Rather than wastefully throwing away things such as shopping bags or plastic containers, people try to reuse them. The Bottle Houses in Prince Edward Island, Canada, show a creative way to use things that might be thrown out.

The Bottle Houses are three buildings made of more than 25,000 glass bottles. They were built in the 1980s by a man named Edouard Arsenault (Ed-WAHRD Ar-seh-NOH).

Arsenault collected used bottles from many people and places. He used cement to hold the bottles together. Because the bottles are all different colors, the houses are very beautiful to look at, especially from the inside. Visitors enjoy taking pictures of the unusual houses. People might also come away with new ideas for recycling!

TALK about It If you could make something new from recycled objects, what would it be?

Unit 6 • Introduction
Critical Thinking **151**

THEME FOCUS

- -

TAKING CARE OF OUR EARTH

Point out to children that Edouard Arsenault collected thousands of used bottles in order to build his houses. Have children discuss things that are collected and recycled in their community. List their ideas on the board. Then, have children suggest ways in which the recycled materials might be used.

WHAT'S IN A WORD?

Write the following word pairs on the board: *disappear, reappear; careless, caring; helpful, helpless; displease, pleasing; displace, replace.* Read the words aloud with children and help them identify the base words, prefixes, and suffixes. Point out how the prefixes and suffixes change the meaning of the base words. Then, invite children to use the words in sentences about things people can do to take care of the earth.

REPORTS ON THE EARTH

Have children form groups, one for each of these topics: land, air, water, animals, and plants. Have each group research and write a list of several suggestions on what people can do to help take care of their group's topic. Have the groups present their ideas to the class.

Dear Family,

In this unit about "Taking Care of Our Earth," your child will learn to identify prefixes, such as **un-** in **un**like, and suffixes, such as **-ness** in kind**ness**. Your child will also learn the rules for dividing words into syllables. As your child becomes familiar with these skills, you might like to try these activities together.

▶ With your child, look through favorite stories and magazines for words that begin with a prefix or end with a suffix.

▶ Read the article on page 151 with your child. Ask him or her to identify the words with prefixes and suffixes. Then help your child to think up something new that could be made from recycled objects. Ask him or her to draw a picture to illustrate the idea or, if practical, to create it.

▶ Your child might enjoy reading these books with you. Look for them in your local library.

Miss Rumphius
by Barbara Cooney

And Still the Turtle Watched
by Sheila MacGill-Callahan

Sincerely,

_____

Estimada familia:

En esta unidad, que trata sobre "Taking Care of Our Earth" ("Cuidemos nuestra Tierra"), su hijo/a aprenderá a identificar prefijos, como **un-** en **un**like, y sufijos, como **-ness** en kind**ness**. También aprenderá las reglas para dividir las palabras en sílabas. A medida que su hijo/a se vaya familiarizando con estas destrezas, pueden hacer las siguientes actividades juntos.

▶ Con su hijo/a, busquen en revistas y cuentos favoritos palabras que comienzan con un prefijo o terminan en un sufijo.

▶ Lean juntos el artículo en la página 151. Pidan a su hijo/a que identifique las palabras con prefijos y con sufijos. Después, ayúdenlo/a a crear algo nuevo que pueda construirse a partir de objetos reciclados. Pídanle que haga un dibujo para ilustrar su idea o, si resulta posible, que lo construya.

▶ Ustedes y su hijo/a disfrutarán leyendo estos libros juntos. Búsquenlos en su biblioteca local.

Miss Rumphius
de Barbara Cooney

And Still the Turtle Watched
de Sheila MacGill-Callahan

Sinceramente,

_____

BULLETIN BOARD

Use colored paper to divide a "Take Care of Earth" bulletin board into fourths: Land (green); Air (white); Water (blue); Animals (brown). Post an environmental song or poem in the center. Suggest that children place appropriate photographs or drawings in each part.

HOME CONNECTIONS

- The Home Letter on page 152 will acquaint family members with the phonics skills children will be studying in this unit. Children can tear out the page and take it home.

- You may want to suggest that children complete the activities on the page with a family member. Encourage children to look in the school library or a local library for the books suggested and read them with family members.

LEARNING CENTER ACTIVITIES

WRITING CENTER

Invite children to write about an idea they have for recycling some particular kind of material in an interesting and useful way. Suggest they include drawings to help make their ideas clear. Then, gather children's work together for display in the Writing Center or the classroom.

SCIENCE CENTER

Provide children with chart paper, rulers, and markers. Ask them to make a chart, diagram, or poster that shows the importance of plants on the earth. Suggest that children list categories to which they might add words or pictures. Possible categories include: *Food for Us, Food for Animals, Homes for Animals, Shade, Lumber, Medicine.*

SOCIAL STUDIES CENTER

Have children look through newspapers and magazines for articles about the environment and taking care of our planet. Suggest that children photocopy or cut out the articles they find. Have them work together to arrange the articles by topic and display them for all to read and enjoy.

Prefixes

Skill Focus

Children will

★ identify the meanings of words with the prefixes *im-, in-, un-, dis-,* and *mis-.*

★ form new words by adding the prefixes *im-, in-, un-, dis-,* and *mis-* to base words.

ESL/ELL Native speakers of Spanish are likely to be familiar with prefixes since they appear in their own language. Provide frequent oral opportunities for speakers of other languages to distinguish the prefix and its meaning from the base words.

Teach

Introduce Prefixes *im-, in-, un-, dis-,* and *mis-* Write these word pairs on the board: *like, dislike; fair, unfair; trust, mistrust; proper, improper;* and *correct, incorrect.* Ask volunteers to circle the letters that have been added to the base word in each pair. Explain that these word parts are called prefixes. A prefix is added to the beginning of a base word to change its meaning or the way it is used in a sentence.

Point out that the prefixes *dis-, un-, mis-, im-,* and *in-* all mean "not." Have volunteers use the word *not* to tell what *dislike, unfair, mistrust, improper,* and *incorrect* mean. (*not like, not fair, not trust, not proper, not correct*)

Practice and Apply

Writing Have children read the *prefix* definition at the top of page 153 and explain how it applies to the words *dishonest, unbuckled, misplaced, improper,* and *inactive.* For the activity on page 153 and the first one on page 154, suggest to children that circling the prefix can help them identify the base word.

For the activity at the bottom of page 154, remind children to choose their answers from the words in items 1–10.

Reading Use *For a Better Life,* MCP Phonics and Reading Word Study Skills Library 1, Level C, to provide additional practice in identifying prefixes.

Name _____

> Read each word and write its base word on the line.

DEFINITION

A **prefix** is a word part that is added at the beginning of a base word to change the base word's meaning or the way it is used.
Dishonest means **not honest**.
Unbuckled means **not buckled**.
Misplaced means **not in the right place**.
Improper means **not proper**.
Inactive means **not active**.

1. displease _____please_____
2. incorrect _____correct_____
3. impure _____pure_____
4. misbehave _____behave_____
5. unfair _____fair_____
6. unhappy _____happy_____
7. dissatisfy _____satisfy_____
8. unfold _____fold_____
9. disagree _____agree_____
10. misfortune _____fortune_____
11. mislay _____lay_____
12. unpleasant _____pleasant_____
13. disobey _____obey_____
14. imperfect _____perfect_____

15. discharge _____charge_____
16. uncover _____cover_____
17. misspell _____spell_____
18. imprecise _____precise_____
19. disappear _____appear_____
20. unseen _____seen_____
21. misuse _____use_____
22. inaction _____action_____
23. untrue _____true_____
24. disable _____able_____
25. mistake _____take_____
26. uneven _____even_____
27. dislike _____like_____
28. incomplete _____complete_____

Prefixes: *im-, in-, un-, dis-,* and *mis-*   **153**

FOCUS ON ALL LEARNERS

ESL/ELL ENGLISH LANGUAGE LEARNERS

Reinforce oral pronunciation and auditory recognition of words with the prefixes *dis-, un-, mis-, im-,* and *in-.*

• Using a "same or different" activity, confirm children's ability to hear a prefix in lesson vocabulary.

• Have children write *dis-* on an index card.

• Say lesson vocabulary words aloud, such as *displease, agree, obey, disable, dislike.* Direct children to hold up their index cards if they hear *dis-* in the words you say. Confirm a response before proceeding to the next item.

• Write the words, using the prefix *dis-* on chart paper; have volunteers say the words, underline the prefix in each, and circle the base word. Post as a visual reference during the unit.

• Repeat the activity with the prefixes *un-, mis-, im-,* and *in-.*

KINESTHETIC LEARNERS

Have children draw a tic-tac-toe grid on paper. To play, children take turns saying a word with the prefix *dis-, un-, mis-, im-,* or *in-* and using the word in a sentence. If correct, the player writes *X* or *O* on the game board.

Read each word and write its base word on the line.

1. unable   _able_
2. unpleasant   _pleasant_
3. unhappy   _happy_
4. unmade   _made_
5. incorrect   _correct_

6. misprint   _print_
7. dislike   _like_
8. improper   _proper_
9. displease   _please_
10. impossible   _possible_

Read each sentence. Write a word from the examples above that means the same as the underlined words in the sentence.

11. Susan's mother thinks messy bedrooms are <u>not proper</u>.   _improper_
12. Susan's bed was <u>not made</u> yesterday morning.   _unmade_
13. Susan was <u>not able</u> to clean her room before school.   _unable_
14. Her mom was <u>not happy</u> and asked Susan to clean it.   _unhappy_
15. Susan would <u>not like</u> making her mother angry.   _dislike_
16. She cleaned the <u>not pleasant</u> mess.   _unpleasant_
17. Susan knows it's <u>not correct</u> to leave her room messy.   _incorrect_

154   Prefixes: im-, in-, un-, dis-, and mis-

 HOME With your child, look up words in the dictionary with the prefixes *im-, in-, un-, dis-,* and *mis-*.

CURRICULUM CONNECTIONS

SPELLING

Use the following words and sentences as a pretest for writing words with prefixes and suffixes.

1. **rebuilding**   Tim is **rebuilding** the house.
2. **unkindly**   Did she speak **unkindly**?
3. **discovered**   Iris **discovered** a way out.
4. **misbehaves**   That child **misbehaves**.
5. **comfortable**   Are you **comfortable**?
6. **defrost**   Please **defrost** the freezer.

WRITING

Ask children to write a story about Susan and a pet that misbehaves. Have them brainstorm a list of words with prefixes that they might use, such as *misbehaves, disobeys,* and *unhappy*.

PORTFOLIO

SCIENCE

Involve children in a discussion of why the future of Earth is uncertain unless we actively do things to take care of it. Suggest that children express their ideas in bumper sticker slogans.

 **TECHNOLOGY**   **AstroWord** Prefixes

AUDITORY LEARNERS GROUPS

Have children take turns giving an oral clue for a word with the prefix *dis-, un-, mis-, im-,* or *in-* for the others to guess. For example: *I'm thinking of a word that means "not pleasant." (unpleasant)*

CHALLENGE

Have partners take turns adding a prefix to base words. The base words must begin with each letter of the alphabet, in succession. For example, the first partner says *disable,* the second *misbehave,* and so on. If children get stuck, suggest that they look in a dictionary for ideas.

EXTRA SUPPORT/INTERVENTION

Write base words from page 153 on separate cards. Have children sort the cards according to the prefix that can be added, then add *dis-, un-, mis-, im-,* or *in-* and read each word aloud. See Daily Phonics Practice, page 221.

Integrating Phonics and Reading

Guided Reading
Ask a volunteer to read the title. Discuss the photograph on the cover. Then, ask children what they think the story will be about.
First Reading Invite children to describe what entering the country through Ellis Island was like.
Second Reading Have children identify story words with the target prefixes.

Comprehension
After reading, ask children these questions:
• What were some of the reasons why people wanted to come to the United States? *Recall/ Cause and Effect*
• In what ways was the Ellis Island experience more difficult for steerage passengers? *Reflective Analysis/Inference*

ESL/ELL **English Language Learners**
Have children turn to the Contents page, the Glossary, and the Index. Invite them to tell what the purpose of each part is.

Prefixes

Skill Focus

★ identify the prefixes *re-*, *de-*, *ex-*, and *pre-* and the base words to which they are attached.

★ write words with the prefixes *re-*, *de-*, *ex-*, and *pre-* to complete sentences.

ESL/ELL Prefix is a concept English language learners will pick up quickly. Reinforce meanings and provide opportunities for children to hear and say *re-*, *de-*, *ex-*, and *pre-*, making the correct long or short vowel sounds.

Teach

Introduce Prefixes *re-*, *de-*, *ex-*, and *pre-*
Remind children that a prefix is a word part added at the beginning of a base word to change its meaning or use. Have children identify prefixes by their recognition of base words as you read the following words aloud.

- **rebuild   export   deplane   preview**
- **express   derail   prepay   depart**
- **retell   reload   exclaim   prewash**

Write *rebuild*, *deplane*, *exclaim*, and *prepay* on the board. Have children draw a vertical line between the prefix and base word of each word. Explain the meaning of each prefix: *re-* means "do again," *de-* means "from," *ex-* means "out of" or "from," and *pre-* means "before." Have children tell the meanings of the words on the board. (*build again, go from the plane, call or cry out, pay before*)

Practice and Apply

Writing Have a volunteer read aloud the rule at the top of page 155 and explain the meanings of the words *repaint*, *depart*, *export*, and *premade*. For the activity on page 155 and the first one on page 156, suggest that children identify the prefix of each word before writing the base word.

For the second activity on page 156, have children try all three word choices in each sentence orally before writing the word that best completes it.

Reading Use *Starfishers to the Rescue*, MCP Phonics and Reading Word Study Skills Library 1, Level C, to provide additional practice in identifying prefixes.

155

Name _____

> Read each word and write its base word on the line.

RULE
The prefix **re** usually means **do again**. The prefix **de** usually means **from**. The prefix **ex** usually means **out of** or **from**. The prefix **pre** usually means **before**.
Repaint means **paint again**.
Depart means **go away from**.
Export means **send out of**.
Premade means **made before**.

1. prepay   pay
2. reread   read
3. defrost   frost
4. exchange   change
5. express   press
6. rebuild   build
7. refill   fill
8. derail   rail
9. reopen   open
10. rewrite   write
11. preview   view
12. redo   do
13. preshrunk   shrunk
14. depart   part

15. rewash   wash
16. preschool   school
17. exclaim   claim
18. detour   tour
19. decode   code
20. export   port
21. preset   set
22. deplane   plane
23. reteach   teach
24. demerit   merit
25. rewrap   wrap
26. reclaim   claim
27. retie   tie
28. decrease   crease

Prefixes: ex-, de-, re-, and pre-   **155**

FOCUS ON ALL LEARNERS

ESL/ELL ENGLISH LANGUAGE LEARNERS

Engage English language learners in reading and using prefixes.

- Complete items 1 through 8 on page 156 orally as a group. Review and correct any misconceptions.

- For items 9–15, have English language learners take turns reading the sentences aloud. Review word choices and guide children to agree on the word that best completes the sentence. Have children fill in the bubble and write the word.

- Children can take turns reading their completed sentences to each other in pairs or in small groups.

KINESTHETIC LEARNERS

Form small teams. Ask each team to draw on a sheet of paper six columns labeled with the prefixes *un-*, *mis-*, *re-*, *de-*, *ex-*, and *pre-*. At your signal, have team members write words in each column until you call time. The team with the most correctly spelled words wins the game.

AUDITORY LEARNERS

Invite partners to make up riddles with answers that are words with the prefixes *re-*, *de-*, *ex-*, and *pre-*. Here is an example: *You do this when you open something again.* (*reopen*)

155

▶ Read each word and write its base word on the line.

1. prepaid ___paid___
2. retell ___tell___
3. unable ___able___
4. dishonest ___honest___

5. mistake ___take___
6. exclaim ___claim___
7. inactive ___active___
8. depart ___part___

▶ Fill in the circle beside the word that completes each sentence. Write the word on the line.

9. Al ___reread___ Marie's invitation.
   ○ reloaded   ● reread   ○ refilled

10. He was ___unsure___ if he could go to the party.
    ● unsure   ○ unsaid   ○ unsafe

11. He ___disliked___ ice cream and cake.
    ○ disagreed   ○ disowned   ● disliked

12. He would go to the party, but he would ___depart___ early.
    ○ defend   ● depart   ○ defrost

13. At the party Marie ___unwrapped___ her gifts.
    ○ unchained   ○ unloaded   ● unwrapped

14. She could hardly wait to ___untie___ the bows.
    ● untie   ○ unpaid   ○ untrue

15. Al decided it would be ___improper___ to leave early.
    ○ impure   ○ imperfect   ● improper

 HOME Say a prefix (*im-, in-, un-, dis-, mis-, ex-, de-, re-, pre-*) to your child. Ask him or her to name a word with that prefix.

156 Review prefixes

CURRICULUM CONNECTIONS

SPELLING

Make a four-column chart on the board and label the columns *re-*, *de-*, *ex-*, and *pre-*. Ask a volunteer to write the words *exchange*, *rebuilding*, *preview*, and *defrost* in the appropriate columns. Have children add words from the lesson to the chart.

WRITING

Have children think about why Al decides to stay at Marie's party. Ask them to write a script for a conversation between Al and Marie. Have children use words with prefixes in their writing.

PORTFOLIO

MATH

Have children list on chart paper the names of things associated with birthday parties, such as *ice cream*, *cake*, *gifts*, *games*, *birthday cards*, *piñatas*, *balloons*, *party hats*, and *noisemakers*. Form two columns next to the items and label them *Like* and *Dislike*. Take a poll to determine how many children like and dislike each item on the list.

TECHNOLOGY **AstroWord** Prefixes

VISUAL LEARNERS **GROUPS**

Materials: index cards

Have children write on cards the prefixes *re-*, *de-*, *ex-*, and *pre-* as well as the base words *change*, *press*, *port*, *tour*, *part*, *frost*, *write*, *tie*, *read*, *pay*, *wash*, and *soak*. Ask children to take turns matching a prefix with a base word, reading the new word aloud, and making up a sentence.

CHALLENGE

Materials: index cards

Have children create two sets of cards. For each card in Set 1, children write a word with one of the prefixes *un-*, *mis-*, *dis-*, *im-*, *in-*, *re-*, *de-*, *ex-*, or *pre-*. For each card in Set 2, they write the meaning of one of the words in Set 1. Have children shuffle the two sets together, place the cards face down in a grid, and match words with meanings.

EXTRA SUPPORT/INTERVENTION

Materials: construction paper

Write the following words on separate strips of construction paper: *rewrite*, *refill*, *decode*, *defrost*, *export*, *exclaim*, *prepay*, and *preview*. Have children fold back the prefix portion of each strip and practice reading the word with and without its prefix by folding the flap back and forth. See Daily Phonics Practice, page 221.

Integrating Phonics and Reading

Guided Reading

Have a volunteer read the title and invite children to discuss the cover illustration. Then, ask children what they think the story will be about.

First Reading Ask children to describe how the Starfishers saved the people on the island.

Second Reading Have children identify story words with selected prefixes.

Comprehension

After reading, ask children these questions:
- How did Ana's idea help save the people on the island? *Recall/Summarizing*
- Do you think Ana deserves to be a Starfisher? Why or why not? *Reflective Analysis/ Personal Response*

ESL/ELL English Language Learners

Have children use word and picture clues to identify the story setting as being in the future.

Prefixes, Base Words, Suffixes, and Endings

Skill Focus

Children will

★ identify prefixes, base words, endings, and suffixes of words.

★ read and write words with both prefixes and suffixes or endings.

Teach

Introduce Words with Prefixes, Suffixes, and Endings Write the words *agreeable, properly, friendly,* and *painting* on the board. Ask volunteers to underline each base word and circle each suffix or ending. Talk about the meaning of each word.

Demonstrate how words can have both a prefix and a suffix or ending by adding a prefix to each of the words on the board to form the following words: *disagreeable, improperly, unfriendly,* and *repainting.* Discuss how the meaning of the words has been changed by the addition of the prefix.

Say the words below. After each, have a child repeat the word, pausing briefly after the prefix and after the base word.

- repainting
- disagreeable
- unwashable
- displeasing
- retelling
- unfairly
- distrustful
- unhealthy
- unhappiness
- unkindly

Practice and Apply

Writing Read aloud the definition at the top of page 157 and explain how it applies to the words *return* and *quickly.* You may wish to complete the first item in the activity on the page with children to make sure they understand what to do.

For the activity on page 158, invite a volunteer to restate the directions in his or her own words. Remind children to try both word choices in the sentence before deciding on one of them.

Reading Use *Moon Stories*, MCP Phonics and Reading Word Study Skills Library 1, Level C, to provide additional practice in identifying base words and suffixes.

Name _____

Read the definitions carefully. Then read each word below, and write its prefix, its base word, and its suffix or ending, in the correct columns.

> **DEFINITION**
> A **base word** is a word to which a prefix, suffix, or ending may be added to form a new word. A **prefix** is added at the beginning of a base word. A **suffix** or **ending** is added at the end of a base word.
> **re** + turn = return
> quick + **ly** = quickly

	prefix	base word	suffix or ending
1. rebuilding	re	build	ing
2. prepaying	pre	pay	ing
3. unkindly	un	kind	ly
4. uncomfortable	un	comfort	able
5. unhappiness	un	happy	ness
6. incorrectly	in	correct	ly
7. misbehaving	mis	behave	ing
8. displeasing	dis	please	ing
9. unpacking	un	pack	ing
10. exclaiming	ex	claim	ing
11. derailed	de	rail	ed
12. repainting	re	paint	ing
13. recycling	re	cycle	ing
14. immovable	im	move	able
15. defrosting	de	frost	ing

Prefixes, base words, suffixes, endings   **157**

FOCUS ON ALL LEARNERS

ESL/ELL ENGLISH LANGUAGE LEARNERS

Assess English language learners' ability to recognize prefixes, base words, endings, and suffixes by doing page 157 together.

- Ask a volunteer to read the first item aloud; assist with pronunciation if needed.
- Ask a child to identify the prefix in the word *rebuilding* and have the group write the prefix on the appropriate line. Follow a similar procedure for identification of the ending.
- Have children identify the base word *build* and write it on the appropriate line. Repeat with the remaining items.

KINESTHETIC LEARNERS

Have children form groups. One member in each group writes a base word and passes it around for other group members to add or remove a prefix, a suffix, or both each time writing a new word.

VISUAL LEARNERS

Write the following on the board and have children complete sentences by adding prefixes, endings, or suffixes to the words in parentheses: *This pie is (taste). This dog seems (friend). The silk blouse is (wash). The glass is (break). I am (frost) the freezer.*

Read each sentence. Use the code to make the two words under the sentence. Then circle the word that completes the sentence. Underline the prefix, the suffix, or the ending in each of the coded words. Some words have a prefix and a suffix or an ending.

1 = a	4 = e	7 = i	10 = m	13 = r	16 = u
2 = c	5 = f	8 = k	11 = n	14 = s	17 = w
3 = d	6 = h	9 = l	12 = p	15 = t	18 = y

1. Let's all try to be _____ caretakers of our planet!

c	a	r	e	l	e	s	s
2	1	13	4	9	4	14	14

h	e	l	p	f	u	l
6	4	9	12	5	16	9

2. Try to _____ shopping bags and plastic containers.

d	i	s	l	i	k	e
3	7	14	9	7	8	4

r	e	u	s	e
13	4	16	14	4

3. Pick up _____ newspapers, bottles, and boxes and recycle them.

k	i	n	d	l	y
8	7	11	3	9	18

u	n	c	l	a	i	m	e	d
16	11	2	9	1	7	10	4	3

4. Try not to be _____ when using water or electricity.

w	a	s	t	e	f	u	l
17	1	14	15	4	5	16	9

r	e	f	i	l	l	e	d
13	4	5	7	9	9	4	3

5. If people _____ say they cannot help, share these tips.

n	e	a	t	l	y
11	4	1	15	9	18

u	n	w	i	s	e	l	y
16	11	17	7	14	4	9	18

158 Prefixes, base words, suffixes, endings

HOME Using the code on the page, ask your child to make up words for you to decode.

CURRICULUM CONNECTIONS

SPELLING

Materials: tagboard strips, envelopes

Write the spelling words *rebuilding, unkindly, discovered, misbehaves, defrost,* and *comfortable* on tagboard strips. Then, cut the words into prefixes, base words, endings, and suffixes and store the pieces in an envelope. Invite children to work in pairs to match the pieces.

WRITING

Have pairs of children write poems about taking care of Earth. Ask them to use words with prefixes, endings, and suffixes such as *reusable, return, protecting, recycle, unlittered, beautiful, healthy,* and *helping*.

ART

Extend the theme "Taking Care of Our Earth" by inviting children to use magazines, greeting cards, calendars, and other paper products to create something new and useful.

TECHNOLOGY **AstroWord** Prefixes; Suffixes; Base Words and Endings

---

AUDITORY LEARNERS GROUPS

Say words that have prefixes and suffixes with the suffix and prefix reversed. Ask volunteers to correct the order and say each word aloud. Begin with these mixed-up words.

ing–paint–re	ful–thank–un	ness–happy–un
ly–fair–un	ing–tour–de	y–honest–dis
able–port–ex	able–agree–dis	ing–lock–un

CHALLENGE

Have children use the code from page 158 to write messages for their classmates to decode. Each message must contain at least two words with both a prefix and a suffix.

EXTRA SUPPORT/INTERVENTION

Materials: index cards, scissors, tape

Write words from page 157 on cards. As you cut apart a word between prefix, base word, and ending or suffix, have children say the prefix, base word, and ending or suffix. Then, mix the cards and have children match and tape the parts back together to re-form the words. See Daily Phonics Practice, page 222.

Integrating Phonics and Reading

Guided Reading

Have children read the title, look at the cover illustration, and leaf through the book. Invite them to predict what the story will be about.

First Reading Ask children to describe why the moon became sad and how Father Sky helped.

Second Reading Ask children to identify base words and suffixes used in the story. Invite them to add prefixes to story words such as *true, told, wise, pinned*.

Comprehension

After reading, ask children these questions:

• What was different about the moon at the beginning and end of the story? *Recall/ Comparisons*

• What natural behavior of the moon does this story try to explain? *Reflective Analysis/ Inference*

ESL/ELL English Language Learners

Invite children to use picture and word clues to retell the story in their own words.

Syllables

Skill Focus

Children will

★ read and write words with prefixes, endings, and suffixes and divide them into syllables.

★ read and write compound words and divide them into syllables.

Teach

Introduce Syllables Remind children that words can be divided into syllables. Each syllable has one vowel sound. Tell children you are going to say groups of words. Instruct children to clap for each syllable they hear. Use these words: *taste, tasteful, distasteful; paint, repaint, repainted; kind, unkind, unkindness; trust, mistrust, mistrusting.*

Ask a volunteer to write the word *mistrusting* on the board and circle the prefix (*mis-*) and the suffix (*-ing*). Explain that prefixes are always syllables. A suffix or an ending is a syllable if it contains a vowel sound. Rewrite the word, using hyphens to divide it into syllables. (*mis-trust-ing*)

Write *kind, tell, rest, safe, fly,* and *paint* on the board. Ask a volunteer to read the words aloud. Have children tell how many syllables are in each word. (*one*) Invite volunteers to turn the words into two- or three-syllable words by adding a prefix, an ending or suffix, or both. Ask children how they know that each new word has two or more syllables. (*Two or more vowel sounds are heard in each word.*)

Practice and Apply

Writing Read aloud the rule at the top of page 159. Point out that hyphens are often used to divide words into syllables. For the activity on the page, point out that some of the words have prefixes, some have suffixes, and some have both.

Ask a volunteer to read the rules at the top of page 160. If necessary, remind children that compound words are made up of two or more smaller words. Suggest that children say each word to themselves to hear the two words in each compound word.

Reading Use *Sara's Lovely Songs,* MCP Phonics and Reading Word Study Skills Library 1, Level C, to provide additional practice in dividing compound words and words with suffixes into syllables.

Name _____

RULE

Divide a word with a prefix, a suffix, or an ending between the prefix, suffix, or ending, and the base word. Use a hyphen (-) to divide the word.

unpacking	un-pack-ing
unfriendly	un-friend-ly
replanted	re-plant-ed

▶ **Divide each word into syllables. Remember to use hyphens.**

1. rewrite — re-write
2. movement — move-ment
3. untie — un-tie
4. dislike — dis-like
5. unpaid — un-paid
6. playing — play-ing
7. spoonful — spoon-ful
8. colder — cold-er
9. softest — soft-est
10. inside — in-side
11. unsafely — un-safe-ly
12. repainted — re-paint-ed
13. distasteful — dis-taste-ful
14. unhandy — un-hand-y
15. mistrust — mis-trust
16. renew — re-new

17. displease — dis-please
18. premix — pre-mix
19. amazement — a-maze-ment
20. sleepless — sleep-less
21. boxes — box-es
22. dampness — damp-ness
23. rested — rest-ed
24. flying — fly-ing
25. unwisely — un-wise-ly
26. returning — re-turn-ing
27. improve — im-prove
28. retelling — re-tell-ing
29. replanted — re-plant-ed
30. unkindly — un-kind-ly
31. excitement — ex-cite-ment
32. departing — de-part-ing

Syllables: Words with prefixes, suffixes, and endings   **159**

FOCUS ON ALL LEARNERS

ESL/ELL ENGLISH LANGUAGE LEARNERS

Use the activity on page 159 to assess English language learners' ability to recognize prefixes and endings or suffixes as syllables.

• Focus children's attention on the first item and the prefix *re-*. Have children use a pencil to circle *re-*. Then, have them identify the base word. (*write*) Ask children how many vowel sounds, or syllables, they hear in *rewrite*. Finally, have children write the word on the line, separating the base word syllable and the prefix syllable with a hyphen.

• Continue in a similar way with items 8 and 11 to review words with suffixes or endings and words with prefixes and suffixes. Then, have children work in pairs to complete the page.

KINESTHETIC LEARNERS GROUPS

Materials: paper strips, scissors

Have children write on a paper strip a silly headline using compound words, such as *Bloodhounds Find Popcorn.* Have children cut apart and mix the words in the headline for the class to unscramble and read.

> Study each rule about dividing words into syllables.

RULES

A one-syllable word is never divided.
house
Divide a compound word between the words that make up the compound word.
dog-house

> Divide each compound word into syllables. Remember to use hyphens.

1. into	in-to	2. doorman	door-man
3. birthday	birth-day	4. cowboy	cow-boy
5. rainbow	rain-bow	6. inside	in-side
7. tiptoe	tip-toe	8. someone	some-one
9. sidewalk	side-walk	10. sunshine	sun-shine
11. tonight	to-night	12. today	to-day
13. dishpan	dish-pan	14. highway	high-way
15. moonlight	moon-light	16. bedtime	bed-time
17. weekend	week-end	18. headline	head-line
19. dustpan	dust-pan	20. hillside	hill-side
21. sailboat	sail-boat	22. driveway	drive-way

160 Syllables: Compound words

HOME Challenge your child to think of more compound words and divide them into syllables.

CURRICULUM CONNECTIONS

SPELLING

Write the word *comfortable* on the board and have children identify the suffix, base word, and number of syllables. Ask children to add different prefixes and suffixes to *comfort*, writing as many words as possible and naming the number of syllables. (*uncomfortable, uncomfortably, comfortless, comforted, comforter, comforting, discomfort*)

SCIENCE

Ask children to use words such as *protection, restoring, renewal, misunderstanding, harmful, unknowingly, preserving, careless,* and *dishonesty* in a discussion about possible reasons for an animal to become threatened by pollution or a shrinking natural habitat.

TECHNOLOGY **AstroWord** Multisyllabic Words

VISUAL LEARNERS **GROUPS**

Materials: tagboard strips

Have each child write three words with a prefix, ending or suffix, or both on separate strips of tagboard. Then, have them cut their words apart between syllables to form puzzles. Ask children to swap puzzles, put them together, and use the words in sentences.

CHALLENGE

Challenge children to write sentences with fill-in blanks for partners to complete. The words that belong in the blanks must have a prefix, an ending or a suffix, or both.

EXTRA SUPPORT/INTERVENTION

Before children begin page 159, read the words aloud. Ask children to repeat each word, using a pencil to tap out the syllables. See Daily Phonics Practice, page 222.

Integrating Phonics and Reading

Guided Reading

Call on volunteers to read the title and describe the cover illustration. Then, invite children to name and/or sing songs they know. **First Reading** Have children describe how Sara's songs affected the people around her. **Second Reading** Guide children in dividing selected story words into syllables.

Sara's Lovely Songs

Comprehension

After reading, ask children these questions:
• How were Sara's songs related to what was happening? *Recall/Drawing Conclusions*
• Which of Sara's songs is your favorite? *Reflective Analysis/Personal Response*

ESL/ELL **English Language Learners**

Teach children the music and lyrics to one of Sara's songs. Then, have them read the lyrics aloud and tell in their own words what they mean.

Phonics and Reading / Phonics and Writing

Review Compound Words

Skill Focus

Children will

★ identify and read compound words in context.

★ write compound words to complete sentences about a story.

★ write a postcard, using compound words.

ESL/ELL Hmong, Vietnamese, and Cantonese are monosyllabic languages. Native speakers of these languages may need extra practice with compound words. Spanish speakers may also require extra practice, since few words in their native language are formed in this manner.

▶ Teach

Review Compound Words Remind children that a compound word is two or more words joined together to make a new word. Then, say the following word pairs. Ask children to put the words together to form a compound word.

day and *time*	*some* and *thing*
fire and *place*	*play* and *ground*
bath and *tub*	*side* and *walk*

Write the following on the board: *can____, side____, sun____, ____town, ____paper, ____one.* Ask children to add a word to each to form a compound word. (examples: *cannot, sidewalk, sunshine, uptown, newspaper, anyone*)

▶ Practice and Apply

Phonics and Reading For the activity on page 161, suggest that children look in the story for words to complete the sentences.

Critical Thinking For the Talk About It question at the bottom of page 161, talk about ways children can make people in their town aware of the problems litter can cause.

Phonics and Writing Before children begin writing their postcards on page 162, review the information in the callout boxes. Suggest that children reread the article on page 161 for ideas.

Reading Use *The Junkpile Robot*, MCP Phonics and Reading Word Study Skills Library 1, Level C, to provide additional practice in reading compound words.

161

Name _____

 Phonics & Reading Read the following article. Circle the compound words. Then write compound words to complete each sentence below.

Downtown or Trash Town?

When is a city (sidewalk) like a trash can? When it has litter on it! Old (newspapers) candy wrappers, soda cans, and other garbage make it look as if (nobody) cares about the place. That is what has happened to this city's (downtown) The ugly mess (cannot) be (overlooked)

Why don't people take better care of our (outside) areas? Litter not only is ugly, but also can turn (into) (something) unhealthy. Decaying litter and trash attract animals that can carry disease.

You can help your (hometown) with this problem. Organize a litter drive. Get (everyone) together to make a difference in a park or (playground) (uptown) or (downtown) or along the (highway.)

1. A city _____sidewalk_____ can look like a trash can.

2. Litter makes it look as if _____nobody_____ cares.

3. The ugly mess _____cannot_____ be _____overlooked_____.

4. Litter can turn into _____something_____ that is very unhealthy.

5. You can help your _____hometown_____ solve its litter problem.

6. Get _____everyone_____ involved by having a litter drive.

 TALK About It What can you do to help prevent litter?

Review compound words: Reading, critical thinking **161**

FOCUS ON ALL LEARNERS

ESL/ELL ENGLISH LANGUAGE LEARNERS

Use the story on page 161 to review compound words.

• Ask English language learners to scan the story and highlight words they recognize as compound words. Have children who need additional support work together.

• As children respond, verify that they are pronouncing the two shorter words together, without pausing between them.

• Have children print target story words on the board. Ask them to identify the words that make up each compound word.

KINESTHETIC LEARNERS GROUPS

Materials: index cards, marker

Give each child a card on which is written one of the following words: *pop, corn, cup, cake, high, way, down, town, out, doors, side,* and *walk.* Have children find partners with whom they can form compound words. List the words on the board.

VISUAL LEARNERS GROUPS

Ask children to list as many compound words as they can that contain the words *up, down, some,* or *any.* Afterward, have children compare their lists and identify the two words that make up each compound word.

Phonics & Writing

Writing

A **postcard** is a quick and easy way to send a message. The message should be short and to the point. One sentence should tell the main idea. The other sentences should tell details about the main idea.

▶ Write a postcard to the mayor of your town and give three reasons why it is important to organize a litter drive. Some of the words in the box may help you.

| downtown | anytime | backyard | cannot | citywide |
| weekend | somewhere | springtime | daylong | everyone |

Write today's date at the top of your postcard.

Dear _____ ,

Put the reason for writing in your first sentence.

_____
_____
_____

Write your ideas in the other sentences.

_____
_____

Sincerely,

_____

Don't forget to sign your name.

162 Review compound words: Writing

HOME Ask your child to make a sentence using some of the compound words from the box.

CURRICULUM CONNECTIONS

SPELLING

Write the words below on the board. Have a volunteer match words to form compound words.

sun	where
over	way
every	boy
high	shine
cow	walk
side	looked

WRITING

Review the parts of a business letter: date, address, greeting, body, and closing. Then, have children trade postcards with a partner, pretend to be mayor, and write a response to the classmate's postcard.

SOCIAL STUDIES

Invite children to choose any place in the world they would like to visit and make a list of things they might see there, focusing attention on things named by compound words.

PORTFOLIO

TECHNOLOGY **AstroWord** Compound Words

AUDITORY LEARNERS **PARTNERS**

Materials: spinner attached to a circle labeled *2* and *3*

Have partners take turns spinning the spinner and saying a compound word with either two or three syllables, as indicated by the number on which the arrow lands.

CHALLENGE

Ask children to write compound words beginning with as many different letters of the alphabet as possible. If children get stuck, suggest that they use a dictionary.

EXTRA SUPPORT/INTERVENTION

Materials: index cards

Write words that form compound words on separate cards. Then, invite children to match cards to form compound words, read the words they form, and use them in sentences. See Daily Phonics Practice, page 222.

Integrating Phonics and Reading

Guided Reading
Have children look over the cover illustration and read the title. Then, have them preview the illustrations in the book. Ask them what they think the book will be about.

First Reading Ask children to describe how Eddie and Bethann built J.R.

Second Reading Reread selected sentences and have children identify the compound word in each.

Comprehension
After reading, ask children these questions:
• Why did everyone end up liking the things J.R. did? *Recall/Cause and Effect*
• What might have happened if J.R. hadn't turned into a fountain? *Reflective Analysis/Inference*

ESL/ELL **English Language Learners**
Have children locate and say compound words they find in the story. Ask them to identify each of the shorter words that form the compound word.

Syllables: Words with Suffixes

Skill Focus

Children will

★ read and write words with suffixes or endings and divide them into syllables.

★ write words with suffixes or endings to complete sentences.

▶ Teach

Introduce Syllables: Words with Suffixes
Remind children that words are made of syllables. One vowel sound is heard in each syllable. Then, tell children you are going to say some words. They should hold up one hand if the word has one syllable. They should hold up two hands if the word has two syllables. Say: *care, careful, help, helpless, dark, darken, walk, walking, need, needy, sharp,* and *sharply.*

Write these words on the board: *say, help, kind, fast,* and *loud.* Have children read the words and identify the number of syllables in each. (*one*) Add the suffix or ending *-ing, -ful, -ness, -er,* and *-est* to form *saying, helpful, kindness, faster,* and *loudest.* Ask volunteers to read the words and identify the number of syllables. (*two*) Ask children to rewrite the words, using hyphens to separate the syllables. Point out that the first syllable in each word is a base word and the second syllable is a suffix or ending.

▶ Practice and Apply

Writing Ask a volunteer to read aloud the rule at the top of page 163 and explain how it applies to the word *kindness.* For the activity on page 163 and the first activity on page 164, suggest that children underline the base word in each word before dividing it into syllables.

For the second activity on page 164, remind children to choose from the words in the first activity to complete the sentences.

Reading Use *Bedtime at Aunt Carmen's,* MCP Phonics and Reading Word Study Skills Library 1, Level C, to provide additional practice in identifying the syllables in words with suffixes.

Name _____

▶ Study the rule. Then divide each word into syllables. Remember to use hyphens.

RULE
When a word has one suffix with a vowel sound in it, divide the word between the base word and the suffix.
kind-ness

1. saying   say-ing
2. sharpen   sharp-en
3. boxful   box-ful
4. cheated   cheat-ed
5. making   mak-ing
6. planted   plant-ed
7. pavement   pave-ment
8. homeless   home-less
9. needed   need-ed
10. walking   walk-ing
11. newest   new-est
12. flying   fly-ing
13. cupful   cup-ful
14. kindly   kind-ly
15. playing   play-ing
16. quicker   quick-er

17. foxes   fox-es
18. sleeping   sleep-ing
19. safely   safe-ly
20. treatment   treat-ment
21. fearless   fear-less
22. smallest   small-est
23. reading   read-ing
24. gladly   glad-ly
25. helpless   help-less
26. healthful   health-ful
27. rested   rest-ed
28. careless   care-less
29. colder   cold-er
30. loudest   loud-est
31. neatly   neat-ly
32. faster   fast-er

Syllables: Words with suffixes   **163**

FOCUS ON ALL LEARNERS

ESL/ELL ENGLISH LANGUAGE LEARNERS

Use the activity on page 163 to assess English language learners' ability to recognize suffixes or endings as syllables.

• Focus children's attention on the first item and the ending *-ing.* Have children circle *-ing.* Then, have them identify the base word. (*say*) Ask how many vowel sounds, or syllables, children hear in *saying.* Finally, have them write the word on the line, separating the base word and the ending with a hyphen.

• Continue in a similar manner with items 2–5. Then, have children work in pairs to complete the page.

VISUAL LEARNERS

Materials: index cards

Prepare two sets of cards that include the suffixes or endings *-er, -est, -ly, -ed, -ful, -ing, -es, -less* and the base words *late, hand, wish, fear, strong, clean, play, brush.* Have partners spread the cards face down, take turns choosing two cards, and try to match them to form a two-syllable word.

Divide the words into syllables, using hyphens.

1. painful   pain-ful
2. tallest   tall-est
3. playful   play-ful
4. scary   scar-y
5. watching   watch-ing
6. sickness   sick-ness

7. smarter   smart-er
8. darted   dart-ed
9. loudly   loud-ly
10. classes   class-es
11. learning   learn-ing
12. singing   sing-ing

Read each sentence. Choose one of the words above to complete the sentence. Write it on the line.

13. Two ___classes___ from our school visited the zoo.

14. We had fun ___watching___ the animals.

15. One ___playful___ monkey chased another.

16. The birds were ___singing___ joyfully.

17. A lion roared ___loudly___ .

18. Otters ___darted___ down a waterfall.

19. The alligator showed his ___scary___ sharp teeth.

20. We enjoyed ___learning___ new facts.

21. The ___tallest___ animal is the giraffe.

22. The elephant is ___smarter___ than most animals.

HOME Help your child use the words from numbers 1–12 in sentences.

164 Syllables: Words with suffixes

CURRICULUM CONNECTIONS

SPELLING

Have partners copy the spelling words on slips of paper: *rebuilding, unkindly, discovered, misbehaves, comfortable, defrost.* Suggest that children take turns saying the words for their partner to spell.

WRITING

Invite children to write a poem about an animal, following this format, using words with suffixes or endings:

animal name:	*Alligator*
two describing words:	*Scary, fearless*
three-word action:	*Darting after prey*
synonym for animal:	*Reptile*

SCIENCE

Challenge partners to choose words with suffixes that describe animals and write the word pairs on paper, such as *darting otters, scary iguanas, colorful chameleons, striped zebras.*

 AstroWord Multisyllabic Words

AUDITORY LEARNERS   GROUPS

Write one-syllable words, compound words, and words with suffixes or endings on the board. Have children form teams. Team members take turns reading a word and stating in their own words the rule for dividing it into syllables.

CHALLENGE

Challenge children to write ten pairs of words with opposite meanings. Each word should end with a suffix or ending. For example: *tallest, shortest; sickly, healthful; loudly, softly.*

EXTRA SUPPORT/INTERVENTION

Label five columns on the board with the suffixes or endings *-ing, -ful, -ed, -less,* and *-ly.* As you say words with the suffixes, have volunteers write the words with the syllables divided in the appropriate columns. See Daily Phonics Practice, page 222.

Integrating Phonics and Reading

Guided Reading

Ask volunteers to read the title and describe the cover illustration. Then, invite children to predict what the story will be about.

First Reading Have children tell why Edgar went to sleep on the couch and what happened.

Second Reading Ask children to identify words with suffixes or endings used in the story.

Comprehension

After reading, ask children these questions:

• Why did the girl in the story keep blaming her brother for things? *Recall/Drawing Conclusions*

• Did the story's ending surprise you? Why or why not? *Reflective Analysis/Personal Response*

ESL/ELL English Language Learners

Make sure children understand that the words *I* and *me* refer to the narrator of the story. Invite children to read the text as if they were the main character telling a story about themselves.

Syllables: Words with Prefixes

Skill Focus

Children will

★ read and write words with prefixes and divide them into syllables.

★ write words with prefixes to complete sentences.

ESL/ELL Point out to native speakers of Spanish that the prefix *des-* in Spanish often is *dis-* or *un-* in English. Provide frequent oral opportunities for speakers of other languages to identify and use these prefixes interchangeably in English.

Teach

Introduce Syllables: Words with Prefixes
Say the words below one at a time. Have children repeat each word and identify its base word and prefix. Use the words *depart, rewrite, displease, untie, exchange, input, impure,* and *preheat*.

Write the same words on the board. Ask children to choose a word and draw one line under the prefix and two lines under the base word. Explain that a word with a prefix is divided into syllables between the prefix and the base word. Ask children how many syllables are in each of the words on the board. (*two*) Then, have volunteers rewrite the words, using hyphens to divide them into syllables.

Practice and Apply

Writing Have a volunteer read aloud the rule at the top of page 165. For the activities on page 165 and at the top of page 166, suggest that children circle, underline, or highlight each prefix before dividing the word into syllables.

For the second activity on page 166, make sure children understand that they are to use words from the first activity to complete the sentences. Point out that each word is used once.

Reading Use *The Lost and Found Game*, MCP Phonics and Reading Word Study Skills Library 1, Level C, to provide additional practice in identifying syllables in words with prefixes.

Name _____

▶ Study the rule. Then write each word, dividing it into syllables.

> **RULE**
> When a word has a prefix, divide the word between the prefix and the base word.
> re-new

1. unable	un-a-ble	17. inform	in-form
2. reread	re-read	18. misfit	mis-fit
3. distrust	dis-trust	19. exchange	ex-change
4. impure	im-pure	20. unfair	un-fair
5. depart	de-part	21. preheat	pre-heat
6. express	ex-press	22. displease	dis-please
7. misprint	mis-print	23. import	im-port
8. return	re-turn	24. unscrew	un-screw
9. disown	dis-own	25. derail	de-rail
10. untie	un-tie	26. renew	re-new
11. replace	re-place	27. export	ex-port
12. exclaim	ex-claim	28. repaint	re-paint
13. undress	un-dress	29. discharge	dis-charge
14. premade	pre-made	30. unfold	un-fold
15. unkind	un-kind	31. input	in-put
16. display	dis-play	32. defrost	de-frost

Syllables: Words with prefixes   **165**

FOCUS ON ALL LEARNERS

ESL/ELL ENGLISH LANGUAGE LEARNERS

Use the activity on page 165 to assess English language learners' ability to recognize prefixes as syllables.

• Focus children's attention on the second item. (The first item is atypical in that its base word *able* has two syllables.) Have children circle the prefix *re-* and identify the base word. (*read*) Ask how many vowel sounds, or syllables, children hear in *reread*. (two) Finally, have them write the word on the line, separating the base word and the prefix with hyphens.

• Continue in a similar manner with items 3–6.

AUDITORY LEARNERS

Say the words *fold, cover, open, write, button, read, tie,* and *move*. Have children add the prefix *re-* or *un-* to each word to form a new word. Ask children to demonstrate the meaning of each new word, using pantomime and items in the classroom.

VISUAL LEARNERS

Write the prefixes *un-, re-, dis-, de-, ex-, mis-, pre-, im-,* and *in-* on the board. Ask children to write a word for each prefix on a sheet of paper. Collect the papers and randomly distribute them. Have children rewrite the words, dividing them into syllables.

▶ Divide the words into syllables using hyphens.

1. unable   un-a-ble
2. discomfort   dis-com-fort
3. repair   re-pair
4. pregame   pre-game
5. remove   re-move

6. delay   de-lay
7. depart   de-part
8. request   re-quest
9. displease   dis-please
10. unlock   un-lock

▶ Read each sentence. Choose one of the words above to complete the sentence. Write it on the line.

11. Beth used a key to _____ unlock _____ her trunk.

12. She had to _____ remove _____ her suitcases.

13. She felt some _____ discomfort _____ because of her heavy bag.

14. Beth had to _____ request _____ some help.

15. She was late because her car had needed a _____ repair _____.

16. Beth hadn't expected this _____ delay _____ in her plans.

17. She hoped she would make the _____ pregame _____ show.

18. It would _____ displease _____ Beth to miss the show.

19. Beth planned to _____ depart _____ tomorrow.

20. She was _____ unable _____ to stay longer.

HOME Ask your child to name other words with prefixes to divide into syllables.

166   Syllables: Words with prefixes

CURRICULUM CONNECTIONS

SPELLING

Ask a volunteer to write the spelling word *misbehaves* on the board. As you say the words *rebuilding*, *unkindly*, *discovered*, and *defrost*, have volunteers add the words to the board, forming a crossword puzzle. Then, have children add other words with prefixes, suffixes, or both.

WRITING

Ask children to write questions that begin with the words *What would you do if . . . .* The answer to each question must include a word with a prefix from page 165 or 166. Use these questions as models:

- **What would you do if your bike was rusted?** (*repaint it*)

- **What would you do if your clock was broken?** (*repair it*)

 AstroWord Multisyllabic Words

KINESTHETIC LEARNERS   PARTNERS

Materials: index cards, scissors

Write these mixed-up words on index cards: *disfold, exturn, replease, despell, unpress, misport.* Invite partners to cut the words apart into prefixes and base words. Then, have them match base words to the correct prefixes.

CHALLENGE

Materials: drawing paper, game markers

Invite children to fold a sheet of paper into 16 squares and write a base word in each space. Suggest that partners play a game by choosing a word, adding a prefix, and saying and spelling the new word. Game markers can be used to cover words as they are chosen.

EXTRA SUPPORT/INTERVENTION

Write the prefixes *un-, re-, dis-, de-, ex-, mis-, pre-, im-,* and *in-* on the board at the top of columns. As you say base words, have children add a prefix and write the word in the corresponding column, dividing the word into syllables as they write. See Daily Phonics Practice, page 222.

Integrating Phonics and Reading

Guided Reading

Have children read the title, discuss the cover illustration, and look over the Contents page. Then, invite them to predict what the story will be about.

First Reading Have children describe the idea the children in the story had for earning money.

Second Reading Have children identify story words with prefixes and divide them into syllables.

Comprehension

After reading, ask children these questions:
- What gave Ben an idea for raising money? *Recall/Cause and Effect*
- How do you think the Quincy Kids felt as they worked together to make Wari games? *Reflective Analysis/Character*

ESL/ELL English Language Learners

Review Chapter 7. Discuss how the children worked together to make and put together the Wari games.

Syllables

Skill Focus

Children will

★ recognize consonants and vowels in words.

★ divide words that have two or more consonants between vowels into syllables.

★ write words that have two or more consonants between vowels.

Name _____

> Study the rule. Then write each word, dividing it into syllables.

RULE
When two or more consonants come between two vowels in a word, the word is usually divided between the first two consonants.

hun-gry

1. picture	pic-ture		17. number	num-ber
2. pencil	pen-cil		18. silver	sil-ver
3. confess	con-fess		19. Kansas	Kan-sas
4. goblin	gob-lin		20. master	mas-ter
5. forgave	for-gave		21. finger	fin-ger
6. basket	bas-ket		22. invite	in-vite
7. admire	ad-mire		23. kidnap	kid-nap
8. princess	prin-cess		24. doctor	doc-tor
9. complete	com-plete		25. riddle	rid-dle
10. mistake	mis-take		26. almost	al-most
11. candy	can-dy		27. chapter	chap-ter
12. harbor	har-bor		28. surprise	sur-prise
13. plenty	plen-ty		29. dictate	dic-tate
14. children	chil-dren		30. butter	but-ter
15. pilgrim	pil-grim		31. window	win-dow
16. sudden	sud-den		32. problem	prob-lem

Syllables: Words with two or more consonants between two vowels   **167**

Teach

Introduce Syllables: Words with Consonants Between Vowels Say the words below, stressing each syllable. Ask volunteers to identify the number of syllables they hear in each word.

pencil   silver   supper   picnic   harbor

Write the word *pencil* on the board. Ask a child to circle the two consonants in the middle of the word. Point out that the two consonants come between two vowels. Explain that when two or more consonants come between two vowels in a word, the word is usually divided between the first two consonants. Demonstrate by rewriting the word *pencil*, divided into syllables: *pen-cil*.

Write the words *pilgrim*, *surprise*, *mistake*, and *sudden* on the board. Have volunteers rewrite and divide each word into syllables. (*pil-grim, sur-prise, mis-take, sud-den*)

Practice and Apply

Writing Read aloud the rule at the top of page 167 and explain how it applies to the word *hungry*. Suggest that children circle or highlight the two or more consonants that come between vowels in each word before deciding how to divide the word into syllables.

For the second activity on page 168, remind children to use words from the first activity to complete the sentences. Suggest that children say each sentence with their word choice in place to make sure it makes sense.

Reading Use *The Plant That Almost Ate the World*, MCP Phonics and Reading Word Study Skills Library 2, Level C, to provide additional practice in identifying the number of syllables in words with two or more consonants between two vowels.

FOCUS ON ALL LEARNERS

ESL/ELL ENGLISH LANGUAGE LEARNERS

Use the activity on page 167 to assess English language learners' ability to divide words into syllables.

- Reread the rule on page 167 aloud. Have children look at the first item. Ask a volunteer to name the consonants that come between vowels in *picture*. (ct)

- Ask children where *picture* should be divided. (*between* c *and* t) Then, rewrite the word, divided into syllables: *pic-ture*.

- Continue in a similar manner with items 2–5. Then, have children work in pairs to complete the page.

AUDITORY LEARNERS

Read these words aloud, stressing the syllables: *sun-set*, *for-got*, *fin-ger*, *rid-dle*, *chim-ney*, *whis-per*, *tip-toe*, *pup-py*, *con-test*, *tim-ber*. Ask children to name the two consonants between which each word is divided.

VISUAL LEARNERS GROUPS

Ask children to make a list of classroom items whose names have two syllables, such as *markers*, *pictures*, *windows*, *pencils*, *stapler*, and *scissors*. Have children identify the words that can be divided into syllables by applying the rule on page 167.

Write each word, dividing it into syllables.

1. magnet _____mag-net_____
2. sudden _____sud-den_____
3. blanket _____blan-ket_____
4. plenty _____plen-ty_____
5. invite _____in-vite_____
6. hungry _____hun-gry_____

7. circus _____cir-cus_____
8. confess _____con-fess_____
9. picnic _____pic-nic_____
10. almost _____al-most_____
11. puppy _____pup-py_____
12. bottom _____bot-tom_____

Read each sentence. Choose one of the words from above to complete the sentence. Write it on the line.

13. Dad and Meg took a delicious _____picnic_____ to the park.

14. They laid the food on a _____blanket_____.

15. They had _____plenty_____ of food to eat.

16. There was a _____sudden_____ tug on Meg's pants.

17. A _____puppy_____ was pulling on them.

18. Meg _____almost_____ fell over.

19. The puppy was very _____hungry_____, too.

20. Meg and Dad decided to _____invite_____ it to lunch.

168

Syllables: Words with two or more consonants between two vowels

HOME Help your child think of sentences using words from the page to continue the story.

CURRICULUM CONNECTIONS

SPELLING

Suggest that partners quiz one another on the spelling words *rebuilding*, *unkindly*, *discovered*, *misbehaves*, *comfortable*, and *defrost* as well as these words from pages 167 and 168: *almost*, *children*, *picnic*, *number*, *princess*, and *complete*.

MATH

Have children make a list of items they have thrown away during the past week that could have been recycled. For the next two weeks, suggest that children place a tally mark next to each item saved for recycling. At the end of the two weeks, have children compare the totals for the different recycled items.

TECHNOLOGY **AstroWord** Multisyllabic Words

KINESTHETIC LEARNERS **PARTNERS**

Materials: paper strips

Ask children to print these words in large letters on paper strips: *blanket*, *pencil*, *ginger*, *circus*, *garden*, *hornet*, *chapter*, *hungry*, *perfect*, and *surprise*. Have children take turns choosing a word and dividing it into syllables by folding the paper strip between the appropriate letters.

CHALLENGE

Challenge children by asking them to write as many animal names as they can that have two or more consonants between vowels. As children write the words, they should divide each into syllables.

EXTRA SUPPORT/INTERVENTION

Before children begin working on page 167, help them identify the two or more consonants that come together in each word. See Daily Phonics Practice, page 222.

Integrating Phonics and Reading

Guided Reading
Have children read the title and discuss the cover. Then, ask children to talk about their favorite plants and how to grow them.
First Reading Ask children to describe the events that take place once the plant begins to grow.
Second Reading Ask children to find story words that have one or more consonants between vowels.

Comprehension
After reading, ask children these questions:
• Why was Janie's teacher worried about the project she would come up with? *Inference/Character*
• Why do you think the strange plant grew the way it did? *Reflective Analysis/Inference*

ESL/ELL English Language Learners
Invite children to use picture clues to retell the story in their own words.

Syllables

Skill Focus

Children will

★ recognize consonants and short vowels in words.

★ divide words that follow the v-c-v pattern into syllables.

★ write words that follow the v-c-v pattern to complete sentences.

Teach

Introduce Syllables: V-C-V Words Write *v-c-v* on the board and explain that it stands for "vowel-consonant-vowel." Then, write the words *habit*, *finish*, *melon*, *magic*, and *wagon*. Have children identify the vowel-consonant-vowel pattern in each word and underline the letters in question. Then, ask children how many vowel sounds and syllables they hear in each word. (*two*). Ask if the vowel sounds are long or short. (*short*)

Point to the word *habit*. Explain that when a word follows the v-c-v pattern and the first vowel is short, the word is usually divided after the consonant. Demonstrate by rewriting *habit*: *hab-it*. Then, ask volunteers to divide the remaining words into syllables. (*fin-ish*, *mel-on*, *mag-ic*, *wag-on*)

Practice and Apply

Writing Ask a volunteer to read the rule at the top of page 169 and explain how it applies to the word *lemon*. For the first activity on pages 169 and 170, suggest that children circle or highlight the letters that follow the v-c-v pattern in each word before dividing the word into syllables.

For the second activity on page 169, suggest that children use the words *wagon*, *travel*, *palace*, *river*, *clever*, and *visit* in their paragraph.

Before children begin the second activity on page 170, remind them to use words from the first activity to complete the sentences.

Reading Use *Where Jeans Come From*, MCP Phonics and Reading Word Study Skills Library 1, Level C, to provide additional practice in identifying the syllables in v-c-v words.

Name _____

▶ **Read the rule. Then write each word, dividing it into syllables.**

> **RULE**
> When a single consonant comes between two vowels in a word, the word is usually divided after the consonant if the first vowel is short.
> **lem-on**

1. robin ____ rob-in ____
2. cabin ____ cab-in ____
3. figure ____ fig-ure ____
4. wagon ____ wag-on ____
5. travel ____ trav-el ____
6. palace ____ pal-ace ____
7. statue ____ stat-ue ____
8. finish ____ fin-ish ____

9. river ____ riv-er ____
10. clever ____ clev-er ____
11. cover ____ cov-er ____
12. visit ____ vis-it ____
13. shadow ____ shad-ow ____
14. model ____ mod-el ____
15. dozen ____ doz-en ____

▶ **Write a paragraph that tells about the picture. Try to use some of the words in numbers 1–15.**

_____

_____

_____

_____

_____

_____

Syllables: v-c-v words   **169**

FOCUS ON ALL LEARNERS

ESL/ELL ENGLISH LANGUAGE LEARNERS

Review examples of two-syllable words orally before engaging English language learners in written practice.

• Do items 1–5 at the top of page 169 orally as a group. Then, have children work in pairs to complete the activity.

• Read aloud the story on page 170, including the missing words, as English language learners listen. Read it again, one sentence at a time. Have children complete the sentences.

• Pair children to complete the story in writing. Check their work by having them read sentences aloud.

• Have children circle the v-c-v pattern in each word and identify the sound of the first vowel as either short or long.

KINESTHETIC LEARNERS GROUPS

Write v-c-v words and non-v-c-v words on the board, such as *metal*, *timid*, *slowly*, *circus*, *visit*, *shadow*, *wagon*, *monkey*, *unwrap*, *dragon*, and *magic*. Ask children to pick out the v-c-v words and rewrite them, dividing them into syllables.

▶ **Write each word, dividing it into syllables.**

1. cabin _____cab-in_____
2. travel _____trav-el_____
3. magic _____mag-ic_____
4. visit _____vis-it_____
5. figure _____fig-ure_____

6. palace _____pal-ace_____
7. ever _____ev-er_____
8. river _____riv-er_____
9. wagon _____wag-on_____
10. clever _____clev-er_____

▶ **Read each sentence. Choose one of the words in numbers 1–10 to complete the sentence. Write it on the line.**

11. There once lived a very _____clever_____ cat.
12. He lived in a tiny log _____cabin_____.
13. He liked to _____travel_____ to many places.
14. One day he set off with his red _____wagon_____.
15. When he got to a _____river_____, he swam across.
16. He came to the royal _____palace_____.
17. "I think I shall _____visit_____ the king," he said.
18. "I'll do some _____magic_____ tricks for him."
19. The king could not _____figure_____ out how the tricks were done.
20. He wondered if the cat would _____ever_____ visit him again.

HOME Say *CA-bin, CAB-in,* pausing between syllables. Ask your child to identify the correct way to divide the syllables (*cab-in*). Repeat with *figure* (*fig-ure*), *palace* (*pal-ace*), and *ever* (*ev-er*).

170 Syllables: v-c-v words

CURRICULUM CONNECTIONS

SPELLING

Use these words and sentences as a pretest for writing words with a v-c-v pattern—words with two vowels together that are sounded separately, and words that end in *le*.

1. **wagon** The **wagon** is full of pumpkins.
2. **magic** Did you go to the **magic** show?
3. **pioneer** **Pioneer** days were hard.
4. **open** Please **open** your books.
5. **bicycle** The **bicycle** has a flat tire.
6. **purple** We planted **purple** tulips.

WRITING

Ask children to continue the story on page 170 by writing about another visit with the king. Have children identify v-c-v words in their stories. Invite volunteers to read their stories aloud.

PORTFOLIO

TECHNOLOGY **AstroWord** Multisyllabic Words

AUDITORY LEARNERS

Materials: index cards

Use index cards to make letter cards. Invite children to take turns saying a word from the lesson for another group member to spell, using letter cards. A third group member can then manipulate the letter cards to divide the word into syllables.

CHALLENGE

Have partners draw a tic-tac-toe grid on paper and write v-c-v words in the squares. To play, children must divide the word into syllables correctly before writing an *X* or *O* in the square.

EXTRA SUPPORT/INTERVENTION

Help children divide the words on page 169 into syllables by asking them to find the letters that follow the v-c-v pattern and underline them. See Daily Phonics Practice, page 222.

Integrating Phonics and Reading

Guided Reading
Direct children to look at the cover and read the title. Then, invite them to tell what they think they will learn in the book.
First Reading Ask children to describe the steps in making jeans.
Second Reading Have children identify story words with the v-c-v pattern such as *color, denim, another.*

Comprehension
After reading, ask children these questions:
• What are jeans made of? *Recall/Main Ideas and Details*
• What did you learn about how jeans are made that you didn't know before? *Reflective Analysis/Personal Response*

ESL/ELL **English Language Learners**
Point to a picture in the book and ask children questions such as: *What kind of plant is this? What is the person doing?* Help children review the book, using picture clues.

Syllables

Skill Focus

Children will

★ recognize consonants and short and long vowels in words.

★ divide words that follow the v-c-v pattern into syllables.

★ write words that follow the v-c-v pattern to complete sentences.

Teach

Introduce Syllables: V-C-V Words Say the following words, emphasizing the syllables. Then, ask children how many vowel sounds and syllables they heard in each one. (*two*)

spider   label   music   frozen   polite

Write the words *spider*, *label*, *music*, *frozen*, and *polite* on the board. Call on volunteers to identify the vowel-consonant-vowel pattern in each word and underline the corresponding letters. Ask children if the first vowel sound is long or short. (*long*)

Point to the word *spider*. Tell children that when a word follows the v-c-v pattern and the first vowel is long, the word is usually divided before the consonant. Divide *spider* into syllables: *spi-der*. Ask volunteers to divide the remaining words into syllables. (*la-bel, mu-sic, fro-zen, po-lite*)

Practice and Apply

Writing Call on a volunteer to read the rule at the top of page 171 and explain how it applies to the word *tiny*. For the first activity on both pages 171 and 172, suggest that children say each word and listen for the sound of the first vowel before deciding how to divide the word into syllables.

For the second activity on page 172, remind children to use the words from the first activity to complete the sentences. Suggest that children say each sentence with their word choice in place to make sure it makes sense.

Reading Use *At the Top of the World*, MCP Phonics and Reading Word Study Skills Library 2, Level C, to provide additional practice in identifying syllables in words with the v-c-v pattern.

Name _____

> Study the rule. Then write each word, dividing it into syllables.

RULE
When a single consonant comes between two vowels in a word, the word is usually divided before the consonant if the first vowel is long.

ti-ny

1. lilac	li-lac	10. pilot	pi-lot
2. polar	po-lar	11. cozy	co-zy
3. spider	spi-der	12. motel	mo-tel
4. frozen	fro-zen	13. David	Da-vid
5. moment	mo-ment	14. music	mu-sic
6. lazy	la-zy	15. tiger	ti-ger
7. pupil	pu-pil	16. broken	bro-ken
8. lady	la-dy	17. famous	fa-mous
9. pirate	pi-rate	18. paper	pa-per

> Write a sentence using some of the words in numbers 1–18.

_____

_____

_____

Syllables: v-c-v words   **171**

FOCUS ON ALL LEARNERS

- -

ESL/ELL ENGLISH LANGUAGE LEARNERS

Review examples of two-syllable words orally.

• Do items 1–5 at the top of page 171 orally as a group. Then, have children work in pairs to complete the activity.

• Read aloud the story on page 172, including the missing words, as English language learners listen. Read it again, one sentence at a time. Have children complete each sentence.

• Pair children to complete the story in writing. Check their work by having them read sentences aloud.

• Have children circle the v-c-v pattern in each word and identify the sound of the first vowel as either short or long.

KINESTHETIC LEARNERS

Have partners each choose ten v-c-v words whose first vowel is long. Have them write their words on paper, leaving blanks for all the letters except for the v-c-v letters. Then, have partners trade papers and figure out each other's words.

VISUAL LEARNERS

Ask children to write stories, using words from the lesson such as *frozen*, *polar*, *famous*, and *pilot*. Have them circle the v-c-v words they used. Ask volunteers to read their stories aloud.

> Write each word, dividing it into syllables.

1. paper ___pa-per___
2. frozen ___fro-zen___
3. lilac ___li-lac___
4. cozy ___co-zy___
5. music ___mu-sic___
6. policeman ___po-lice-man___
7. spider ___spi-der___
8. pony ___po-ny___
9. sofa ___so-fa___
10. lazy ___la-zy___
11. grocer ___gro-cer___
12. basic ___ba-sic___

> Read each sentence. Choose a word from above to complete the sentence. Write it on the line.

13. A ___policeman___ gave us directions to the park.

14. A band was playing ___music___ .

15. First we took a ___pony___ ride.

16. Then we bought ___frozen___ ice cream.

17. We sat by a ___lilac___ bush to rest.

18. There we saw a ___spider___ spinning a web.

19. When I got home, I lay down on the ___sofa___ .

20. It was so warm and ___cozy___ that I fell asleep.

 HOME Help your child write new sentences using the words in numbers 1–12.

172 Syllables: v-c-v words

CURRICULUM CONNECTIONS

SPELLING

On the board, write the word *bicycle* without the letters that make up the v-c-v pattern: *b _ _ _ cle*. Identify the missing letters as a v-c-v combination and provide a clue, such as "something you pedal." Have the child who guesses the word finish writing it on the board. Continue with the words *bison, recent, lazy, tulip, frozen,* and *hotel*.

MUSIC

Focus on the lesson words *famous* and *music* by playing musical selections for children to enjoy while they attend to their work, such as "Tales of the Vienna Woods" by Johann Strauss, "Toy Symphony" by Joseph Haydn, and "The Carnival of Animals" by Camille Saint-Saëns.

 **TECHNOLOGY** **AstroWord** Multisyllabic Words

---

AUDITORY LEARNERS GROUPS

Have children take turns choosing a word from pages 171–172, saying aloud just the first syllable, and calling on a group member to finish the word. Responses may include words not in the lesson; for example, *la-* may become *lady, lazy, label, ladle,* or *laser*.

CHALLENGE

Have children make up crossword puzzles using words with the v-c-v pattern in the clues and/or in the answers. Suggest that children solve one another's puzzles.

EXTRA SUPPORT/INTERVENTION

Materials: index cards

Make letter cards and distribute them. Have children use the cards to build words and divide them into syllables before writing their responses to lesson items. See Daily Phonics Practice, page 222.

Integrating Phonics and Reading

Guided Reading
Have children look at the cover and read the title. Invite them to tell where they think the children are, based on their clothing and the snow.
First Reading Ask children to describe their favorite Arctic animal from the book.
Second Reading Have children identify story words with the v-c-v pattern such as *frozen, remember, polar*.

Comprehension
After reading, ask children these questions:
• What are some ways living things survive in the Arctic? *Recall/Main Ideas and Details*
• What did you learn about the Arctic that you didn't know before? *Reflective Analysis/ Personal Response*

ESL/ELL English Language Learners
Point to a picture in the book and ask children questions such as *What kind of animal is this? What is the person doing?* Help children review the book, using picture clues.

Syllables

Skill Focus

Children will

★ recognize vowels in words.

★ divide words with a vowel sounded alone into syllables.

★ write words that contain a vowel sounded alone to complete sentences.

Teach

Introduce Syllables: Words with a Vowel Sounded Alone Say the words below, stressing the syllables. Have children identify the vowel they hear sounded alone in each word. Use the words *alarm*, *unit*, *over*, *magazine*, *disobey*, *item*, and *telephone*. As children identify the vowel sounded alone in each word, write the word on the board and circle the vowel.

Explain that when a vowel is sounded alone in a word, it forms a syllable by itself. Demonstrate by dividing the word *alarm* into syllables: *a-larm*. Have children divide the other words on the board into syllables. (*u-nit*, *o-ver*, *mag-a-zine*, *dis-o-bey*, *i-tem*, *tel-e-phone*)

Practice and Apply

Writing Read aloud the rule at the top of page 173 and explain how it applies to the word *pyramid*. For the activity at the top of page 173, have children read the words aloud in order to hear the vowel that is sounded alone.

Before children begin page 174, point out that they should use the words in the box to complete sentences 1–10 and items 11–20.

Reading Use *The Living Desert*, MCP Phonics and Reading Word Study Skills Library 2, Level C, to provide additional practice in identifying syllables in words with vowels that stand alone.

Name _____

▶ Study the rule. Read each word and circle the vowel that is sounded by itself. Then write each word, dividing it into syllables.

> **RULE**
> When a vowel is sounded alone in a word, it forms a syllable by itself.
> pyr-a-mid

1. mag(a)zine — mag-a-zine
2. (o)pen — o-pen
3. un(i)form — un-i-form
4. dis(a)gree — dis-a-gree
5. (a)head — a-head
6. Can(a)da — Can-a-da
7. (u)nit — u-nit
8. tel(e)phone — tel-e-phone
9. dis(o)bey — dis-o-bey
10. (a)live — a-live
11. (o)cean — o-cean
12. (e)lectric — e-lec-tric
13. (a)gainst — a-gainst
14. doc(u)ment — doc-u-ment
15. gas(o)line — gas-o-line
16. Mex(i)co — Mex-i-co
17. (e)ternal — e-ter-nal
18. mon(u)ment — mon-u-ment
19. (o)dor — o-dor
20. (a)go — a-go

▶ Write a paragraph about a place you would like to visit, using as many of the words in numbers 1–20 as you can.

_____
_____
_____
_____
_____
_____
_____
_____

Syllables: Words with a vowel sounded alone   **173**

FOCUS ON ALL LEARNERS

ESL/ELL ENGLISH LANGUAGE LEARNERS

Assess English language learners' ability to recognize syllables.

• Do items 1–5 at the top of page 173 orally as a group. Then, have children work in pairs to complete the activity.

• Have English language learners listen as you read the story on page 174 aloud, with the missing words in place. Read it again, one sentence at a time, and have children complete each sentence with a word from the box.

• Say the target words again, slowly, and have children identify the vowel that is sounded alone in each one.

AUDITORY LEARNERS GROUPS

Have each child write the vowels *a*, *e*, *i*, *o*, and *u* on separate squares of paper. As you say words, invite children to hold up the vowel that forms a syllable by itself. Say the following words: *Mexico* (i), *eternal* (e), *Canada* (a), *unit* (u), *odor* (o), *items* (i), *ago* (a).

VISUAL LEARNERS GROUPS

Challenge children to choose words from the lesson to write in sentences. For example: *Long **ago** the people of **Mexico** built great **pyramids**. **Gasoline** does not have a pleasant **odor**.*

▶ **Read each sentence. Choose a word from the box to complete the sentence. Write it on the line.**

1. Tory's family went to ___Mexico___ .

2. Every day they swam in the ___ocean___ .

3. The marketplace was ___open___ .

4. Many ___items___ were for sale.

5. Tory brought a ___magazine___ to read.

6. The family climbed a huge ___pyramid___ .

7. It had been built a long time ___ago___ .

8. A man in a ___uniform___ explained its history.

9. Tory ran down the steps ___ahead___ of her parents.

10. Then she wanted to run up the steps ___again___ !

pyramid
magazine
uniform
items
ahead
ocean
again
ago
open
Mexico

▶ **Write the words from the box above, dividing them into syllables.**

11. ___pyr-a-mid___

12. ___mag-a-zine___

13. ___un-i-form___

14. ___i-tems___

15. ___a-head___

16. ___o-cean___

17. ___a-gain___

18. ___a-go___

19. ___o-pen___

20. ___Mex-i-co___

 HOME Using the words in the box, help your child to make up a new story.

174 Syllables: Words with a vowel sounded alone

CURRICULUM CONNECTIONS

SPELLING

Write the spelling word *open* on chart paper. Then, ask children to add prefixes and suffixes to spell as many new words as they can. (*opens, opened, opening, opener, openly, openness, reopen, reopened, unopened*)

WRITING

Ask children to write about a family trip in the form of a news story. Have them plan their stories by writing *who*, *what*, *when*, *where*, and *why* on a sheet of paper and jotting down ideas under each word. Ask children to circle story words with a vowel that is sounded alone.

SOCIAL STUDIES

Have children do research to learn interesting facts about Mexico, including tourist attractions, foods, customs, and celebrations. Suggest that children create travel brochures that include some of the information they learned.

TECHNOLOGY **AstroWord** Multisyllabic Words

KINESTHETIC LEARNERS GROUPS

Materials: index cards

Present scrambled words, using letter cards made with index cards. Have children rearrange the letters to spell each word correctly and then divide the words into syllables. Examples include *lcicrtee* (*e-lec-tric*), *uirmonf* (*u-ni-form*), *nmlaia* (*an-i-mal*), *cnaeo* (*o-cean*), and *livae* (*a-live*).

CHALLENGE

Challenge children to find two words for each vowel sound that forms a syllable by itself, one at the beginning of the word and one in the middle, for example, *ago* and *magazine*.

EXTRA SUPPORT/INTERVENTION

Materials: index cards

As children work on the activity on page 173, read each word aloud, exaggerating the syllables. See Daily Phonics Practice, page 222.

Integrating Phonics and Reading

Guided Reading
Direct children to look at the cover and read the title. Ask volunteers to share what they know about deserts and desert animals. You may also use the activity in the English Language Learners section below.
First Reading Have children tell how plants and animals survive in the hot desert.
Second Reading Invite children to identify story words that contain a vowel that is sounded alone, such as *evaporation, temperatures, anything, across, along,* and *unusual.*

Comprehension
After reading, ask children these questions:
• How do desert plants get the water they need? *Recall/Main Ideas and Details*
• What new facts did you learn about the desert? *Reflective Analysis/Personal Response*

ESL/ELL English Language Learners
Guide children in using word and picture clues to summarize their favorite chapter.

Syllables

Skill Focus

Children will

★ recognize vowel sounds in words.

★ identify syllables in words in which two vowels come together and are sounded separately.

Teach

Introduce Syllables: Words with Two Vowels Together that Are Sounded Separately
Write the word *idea* on the board. Pronounce it, emphasizing each syllable. Ask children how many syllables the word *idea* has and have them explain how they know. (*3, because there are three vowel sounds*)

Explain to children that when two vowels come together in a word and are sounded separately, the word is divided between the two vowels. Ask a volunteer to identify and circle the two vowels that come together in the word *idea* on the board. (*ea*) Then, demonstrate the rule by dividing *idea* into syllables: *i-de-a*.

Write the words *dial, giant, poet,* and *create* on the board. Ask children to identify the two vowels that come together and are sounded separately in each word. (*ia, ia, oe, ea*) Then, have them divide each word into syllables. (*di-al, gi-ant, po-et, cre-ate*)

Practice and Apply

Writing Ask a volunteer to read the rule at the top of page 175 and explain how it applies to the word *fluid*. For the first activity on page 175 and the activity on page 176, suggest that children circle or highlight the two vowels that come together in each word before they divide the words into syllables.

Reading Use *Digging Dinosaurs*, MCP Phonics and Reading Word Study Skills Library 2, Level C, to provide additional practice in identifying syllables in words with two vowels together that are sounded separately.

Name _____

▶ Study the rule. Then write each word, dividing it into syllables.

> **RULE**
> When two vowels come together in a word and are sounded separately, divide the word between the two vowels.
> **flu-id**

1. giant — gi-ant
2. quiet — qui-et
3. rodeo — ro-de-o
4. radiator — ra-di-a-tor
5. graduate — grad-u-ate
6. dial — di-al
7. usual — u-su-al
8. science — sci-ence
9. poem — po-em
10. radio — ra-di-o
11. lion — li-on
12. diet — di-et
13. ruin — ru-in
14. cruel — cru-el
15. pioneer — pi-o-neer
16. poet — po-et
17. create — cre-ate
18. idea — i-de-a
19. gradual — grad-u-al
20. oriole — o-ri-ole

▶ Write two sentences using some of the words in numbers 1–20.

_____

_____

_____

_____

_____

Syllables: Words with two vowels together that are sounded separately   **175**

FOCUS ON ALL LEARNERS

ESL/ELL ENGLISH LANGUAGE LEARNERS

Use page 175 to assess children's ability to recognize syllables in words with two vowels together that are sounded separately.

• Guide children in saying the first word—*giant*—with you.

• Have children name the two vowels that come together. (*ia*) Repeat the word so that they can hear the two vowel sounds.

• Tell children to draw a vertical line between the *i* and the *a* in the word *giant*. Then, have them rewrite the word, dividing it into syllables between the *i* and the *a*.

• Repeat the above procedure for items 2 through 5. Then, have children work with partners to complete the page.

KINESTHETIC LEARNERS

Form three teams and ask one member from each team to go to the board. Explain that you will say a word for them to write, divided into syllables. The first one to do so correctly wins three points. The next wins two points, and the third wins one point. Continue with three new players and a new word.

▶ **Write each word, dividing it into syllables.**

1. radio   ra-di-o
2. piano   pi-a-no
3. diet   di-et
4. mutual   mu-tu-al
5. quiet   qui-et
6. cruel   cru-el
7. graduate   grad-u-ate
8. poem   po-em
9. lion   li-on
10. violin   vi-o-lin
11. violet   vi-o-let
12. giant   gi-ant
13. guardian   guard-i-an
14. create   cre-ate
15. rodeo   ro-de-o
16. dandelion   dan-de-li-on

17. Ohio   O-hi-o
18. science   sci-ence
19. idea   i-de-a
20. denial   de-ni-al
21. radiator   ra-di-a-tor
22. fluid   flu-id
23. ruin   ru-in
24. trial   tri-al
25. defiant   de-fi-ant
26. pioneer   pi-o-neer
27. hyena   hy-e-na
28. celebrate   cel-e-brate
29. realize   re-al-ize
30. annual   an-nu-al
31. dial   di-al
32. violent   vi-o-lent

 HOME Ask your child questions that can be answered with words on the page, such as *What does a baby wear?* (diaper)

176 Syllables: Words with two vowels together that are sounded separately

---

CURRICULUM CONNECTIONS

SPELLING

Have partners challenge one another to spell three-syllable words from the lesson, beginning with the spelling word *pioneer.*

WRITING

Write the following on the board:

> **I am a ro-bot. Cre-at-ing me was dif-fi-cult.**
>
> **Do you re-a-lize that I am a sci-en-tif-ic won-der?**

Read what you have written in a monotone as if using a mechanical voice. Then, have children write several sentences as spoken by a robot, correctly dividing the words into syllables. Have them use words with two vowels together that are sounded separately. Invite children to read their sentences aloud as if they were robots.

 **TECHNOLOGY**   **AstroWord** Multisyllabic Words

---

VISUAL LEARNERS PARTNERS

Have each child write a word from the lesson on a sheet of paper. Tell children to insert blanks for the pair of vowels that come together: *g_ _ _ nt, tr _ _ l, r _ _ n* (*giant, trial, ruin*) Have partners trade papers and supply the missing vowels to write the word. Then, have them divide the word into syllables.

CHALLENGE

Challenge children to work together to list three- and four-syllable words that contain two vowels that come together and are sounded separately. Suggest that they begin with words from the lesson. Then, have them brainstorm other words or search for words in a dictionary.

EXTRA SUPPORT/INTERVENTION

Materials: paper strips, scissors

Write two-syllable words from page 175 on strips of paper. Have children name the two vowels that together are sounded separately. Then, have them cut the word apart between the vowels to divide it into syllables. See Daily Phonics Practice, page 222.

Integrating Phonics and Reading

Guided Reading
Direct children to look at the cover and read the title. Then, ask volunteers to name and describe dinosaurs.

First Reading Ask children to describe the type of dinosaur that they find the most interesting.

Second Reading Have children identify story words that contain two vowels together that are sounded separately, such as *ideas, period, giant, scientist, heaviest.*

Comprehension
After reading, ask children these questions:
• What are some ways in which scientists group dinosaurs? *Recall/Details*
• What dinosaur would you want to see alive? Why? *Reflective Analysis/Personal Reaction*

ESL/ELL English Language Learners
Tell children that dinosaur names are often hard to say. That is why the author of this book included a pronunciation guide for each name. Help children say examples correctly.

Syllables

Skill Focus

Children will

★ divide words ending in *le* into syllables.

★ read and identify words ending in *le* in the context of a story.

▶ Teach

Introduce Syllables: Words Ending in *le*
Write the word *gentle* on the board. Say it, emphasizing each syllable. Ask children how many syllables they hear in *gentle*. (*two*) Explain that when a word ends in a consonant plus *le*, you divide the word before the consonant. Ask a volunteer to circle the *le* at the end of the word. Then, demonstrate the rule by dividing *gentle* into syllables: *gen-tle*.

Write *sample*, *apple*, *purple*, *middle*, and *muscle* on the board. Ask volunteers to divide each word into syllables. (*sam-ple*, *ap-ple*, *pur-ple*, *mid-dle*, *mus-cle*) Provide assistance as needed.

▶ Practice and Apply

Writing Have a volunteer read the rule at the top of page 177 and explain how it applies to the word *nimble*. For each item at the top of page 177 and at the bottom of page 178, suggest that children identify the consonant preceding the *le* ending before dividing the word into syllables.

For the activity at the top of page 178, tell children that there are 15 words in the story that end in *le*.

Critical Thinking For the Talk About It question at the bottom of page 178, suggest that children reread the story to find clues about how Mary felt about canoeing with her dad.

Reading Use *Something Everyone Needs*, MCP Phonics and Reading Word Study Skills Library 2, Level C, to provide additional practice in identifying syllables in words that end in *le*.

Something Everyone Needs

Written by Marilyn Wakoff
Illustrated by Jane McCreary

Name _____

RULE

When a word ends in **le** preceded by a consonant, divide the word before that consonant.

nim-ble

▶ Study the rule. Then write each word, dividing it into syllables.

1. turtle	tur-tle	13. needle	nee-dle
2. puzzle	puz-zle	14. riddle	rid-dle
3. gentle	gen-tle	15. people	peo-ple
4. whistle	whis-tle	16. rattle	rat-tle
5. eagle	ea-gle	17. scramble	scram-ble
6. maple	ma-ple	18. cradle	cra-dle
7. pebble	peb-ble	19. dimple	dim-ple
8. simple	sim-ple	20. sample	sam-ple
9. thistle	this-tle	21. thimble	thim-ble
10. circle	cir-cle	22. temple	tem-ple
11. purple	pur-ple	23. tattle	tat-tle
12. bicycle	bi-cy-cle	24. middle	mid-dle

▶ Write a short paragraph using some of the words in numbers 1–24.

_____

_____

_____

_____

_____

Syllables: Words with le   **177**

FOCUS ON ALL LEARNERS

ESL/ELL ENGLISH LANGUAGE LEARNERS

Assess English language learners' ability to recognize syllables orally before engaging in written practice.

- Do items 1–5 at the top of page 177 orally as a group. Then, have children work in pairs to complete the activity.
- Have English language learners listen as you read the story on page 178 aloud. Read it again, one sentence at a time, and have children identify and say the words that end in *le*.
- Pair children to complete page 178. Check comprehension by having them tell how they divided the words into syllables.

KINESTHETIC LEARNERS 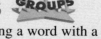 GROUPS

Have children take turns choosing a word with a consonant-plus-*le* ending and writing on the board only the first syllable, as in *wrin*. Whoever correctly guesses the word finishes writing it. (*wrinkle*) If no one guesses the word, clues can be given.

AUDITORY LEARNERS INDIVIDUAL

Ask children to write rhyming couplets with rhyming words ending in a consonant plus *le*. Suggest that children brainstorm rhyming *le* words before they begin writing. Invite volunteers to read their poems aloud as listeners identify the *le* words.

> Read the story. Circle each word that contains **le** preceded by a consonant. Then write each circled word below, dividing it into syllables.

A Day at the Lake

One day, Mary and her dad rode their (bicycles) to a small lake. They parked the bikes under a (maple) tree and headed for the boat dock. A (gentle) breeze made the water ripple.

"I'll show you how to (handle) a canoe," said Dad. "It's (simple). You'll be (able) to do it in no time."

The man at the dock untied a dark (purple) canoe and held it against the dock. Mary and her dad stepped squarely into the (middle) of the canoe so it wouldn't (topple).

Mary's dad showed her how to use the (paddle) as a rudder at the end of each stroke to keep the canoe from going in a (circle). Then Mary tried it.

"You're very (nimble)," said Dad. "You must have strong (muscles). You are really doing well."

Mary was proud. She had learned to manage a canoe without any (trouble).

1. bi-cy-cles
2. sim-ple
3. pad-dle
4. ma-ple
5. a-ble
6. cir-cle
7. gen-tle
8. pur-ple
9. nim-ble
10. rip-ple
11. mid-dle
12. mus-cles
13. han-dle
14. top-ple
15. trou-ble

 Will Mary and her dad go canoeing again? Why or why not?

HOME Help your child to continue the story using words from the page.

178 Syllables: Words with le, critical thinking

CURRICULUM CONNECTIONS

SPELLING

Use these words and sentences as a posttest for writing words with a v-c-v pattern, words with two vowels together that are sounded separately, and words that end in a consonant plus *le*.

1. **wagon**   This **wagon** is missing a wheel.
2. **magic**   Can Johnny do **magic** tricks?
3. **pioneer**   A **pioneer** must have courage.
4. **open**   Please **open** the window.
5. **bicycle**   Riding a **bicycle** is fun.
6. **purple**   Tami is wearing **purple** socks.

SOCIAL STUDIES

Invite children to work in groups to research the history of the canoe. Provide reference materials children can use to learn about and compare canoes built by different peoples such as Native Americans, Inuit, Polynesians, and Africans.

 **TECHNOLOGY**   **AstroWord** Multisyllabic Words

---

VISUAL LEARNERS   PARTNERS

Materials: drawing paper, crayons

Have each child fold a sheet of paper into fourths. In each section he or she should draw a picture of an item whose name ends with a consonant plus *le*. Examples include *apple*, *turtle*, *eagle*, *cradle*, *circle*, *people*, and *bicycle*. Suggest that children trade papers and write words to label one another's drawings.

CHALLENGE

Challenge children to write an original story using as many words as they can that end in a consonant plus *le*. When children have finished writing, ask them to underline the *le* words in their stories. Have volunteers read their stories aloud.

EXTRA SUPPORT/INTERVENTION

Materials: index cards

Write several words from the lesson on separate cards. Have children read and sort the words that have the same consonant-plus-*le* ending. Help children cut the cards to divide the words into syllables. See *Daily Phonics Practice*, page 222.

Integrating Phonics and Reading

Guided Reading
Direct children to look at the cover and read the title. Then, invite them to tell what they think the girl will do with all the things in front of her.
First Reading Have children describe what Nell made that her mother needed.
Second Reading Have children identify words in the story that end in a consonant plus *le*, such as *little*, *apple*, *table*.

Comprehension
After reading, ask children these questions:
- Why was the fair a big surprise for Nell? *Recall/Cause and Effect*
- Do you think Nell's seeder was a useful invention? Why or why not? *Reflective Analysis/Personal Response*

ESL/ELL English Language Learners
Have children turn to the title page. Explain that it includes the book's title, the author's name, and the illustrator's name. Help children identify each.

Phonics and Spelling / Phonics and Writing

Review Prefixes, Base Words, Suffixes, Endings, and Syllables

Skill Focus

Children will

★ spell words with prefixes and suffixes.

★ write and group words according to whether they have a v-c-v pattern, two vowels together that are sounded separately, or an *le* ending.

★ write a letter to the editor, using words with prefixes and suffixes.

Teach

Review Prefixes, Suffixes, Endings, Base Words, Syllables Review with children the fact that a suffix or ending is a word part that is added to the end of a base word, and a prefix is a word part that is added to the beginning of a base word. Then, write these words on the board: *rebuilding, unkindly, discover, misbehaves,* and *comfortable.* Ask volunteers to read a word and identify its prefix, suffix or ending, and its base word.

Remind children that words can be divided into syllables. Each syllable has a vowel sound. Add the following words to those on the board: *wagon, pioneer, purple, open,* and *bicycle.* Ask children to divide the words on the board into syllables. Have them identify the spelling rule they used to divide each word.

Practice and Apply

Phonics and Spelling For the activity on page 179, give children the following examples.

Words with Prefixes or Suffixes	*rereading*
Words with Two Vowels Together Sounded Separately	*trial*
Words with Final *le*	*simple*
V-C-V Words	*melon*

Phonics and Writing Before children begin writing, have them brainstorm reasons why people should take care of the earth. Review with them the tips in the callout boxes. Remind children to include in their letter some of the words in the box.

Reading Use *Let's Build a Playground,* MCP Phonics and Reading Word Study Skills Library 1, Level C, to provide additional practice in identifying prefixes, suffixes, base words, and syllables.

179

Name _____

Say and spell each word. Write the word under the heading where it belongs.

bicycle	magic	purple
comfortable	middle	rebuilding
defrost	misbehaves	science
discovered	open	unkindly
frozen	pioneer	wagon

Words With Prefixes, Suffixes, or Endings

comfortable

defrost

discovered

misbehaves

rebuilding

unkindly

Words With Final le

bicycle

middle

purple

Two Vowels Together Sounded Separately

pioneer

science

One Consonant Between Two Vowels

frozen

magic

open

wagon

Review prefixes, base words, suffixes and endings, syllables: Spelling   **179**

FOCUS ON ALL LEARNERS

ESL/ELL ENGLISH LANGUAGE LEARNERS

Review with English language learners key terms used to categorize the words they have been learning in this unit.

- List the words from page 179 on chart paper. Create four column heads alongside: *Prefixes & Suffixes, Two Vowels Sounded Separately, Final* le, and *V-C-V.*

- Tell children that this lesson reviews the different kinds of words they have been learning. Read aloud the column heads and give children an example of each type of word.

- Ask an English language learner to read aloud one word from the list. Model pronunciation and have children repeat.

- Ask a volunteer to say which column the word goes in.

- Confirm the reason for placing the word in that column, such as: *The word* bicycle *ends in* le.

- Continue in the same manner with all the words in the list.

KINESTHETIC LEARNERS GROUPS

Materials: large letter cards

Write letters on sheets of paper to make large letter cards. As you say words from the lesson, have volunteers hold letter cards and arrange themselves to form the word. Then, have them rearrange themselves to divide the word into syllables.

Phonics & Writing

A **letter to the editor** is a letter you write to a newspaper. In the letter, you let other people know how you feel about something.

Write a letter to the editor of your local newspaper. Tell why people in your city or town should take good care of the earth. Some of the words in the box may help you.

unkindly	bicycle	outdoors	open	comfortable
planet	rebuilding	discovered	middle	science

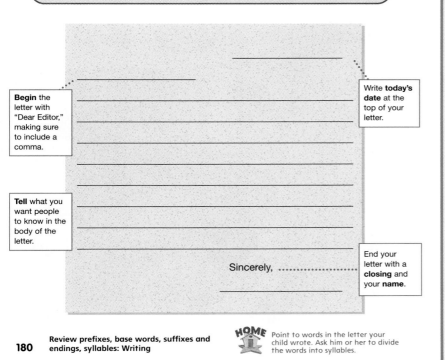

Write today's date at the top of your letter.

Begin the letter with "Dear Editor," making sure to include a comma.

Tell what you want people to know in the body of the letter.

Sincerely,

End your letter with a closing and your name.

180 Review prefixes, base words, suffixes and endings, syllables: Writing

 Point to words in the letter your child wrote. Ask him or her to divide the words into syllables.

CURRICULUM CONNECTIONS

SPELLING

Use these sentences to review Unit 6 words.

1. **rebuilding** — Joe is **rebuilding** the fence.
2. **unkindly** — Never treat a pet **unkindly**.
3. **discovered** — The cat **discovered** a mouse.
4. **misbehaves** — Betsy seldom **misbehaves**.
5. **comfortable** — Are your shoes **comfortable**?
6. **defrost** — Who will **defrost** the freezer?
7. **wagon** — Sam has a new red **wagon**.
8. **magic** — The fairy waved a **magic** wand.
9. **pioneer** — The **pioneer** trail leads west.
10. **open** — When does the store **open**?
11. **bicycle** — Our school has a **bicycle** rack.
12. **purple** — The seashell was **purple**.

WRITING

Have children compose a group thank-you note to Earth, each child describing one gift they are grateful to Earth for supplying. Begin each line with *Thank you, Earth, for . . ..*. Write the list on chart paper and display it in the classroom.

TECHNOLOGY **AstroWord** Multisyllabic Words

Integrating Phonics and Reading

Guided Reading
Have children read the title and discuss the cover illustration. Then, ask children what kinds of things they think should be included in a playground.

First Reading Ask children to describe how the children in the story helped build the playground.

Second Reading Have children identify words with prefixes, base words, and suffixes. Then, have them divide the words into syllables.

Comprehension
After reading, ask children these questions:

• What are the steps involved in planning and building a playground? *Recall/Sequence*
• What part of planning or building the playground did you find the most interesting? Why? *Reflective Analysis/Personal Response*

ESL/ELL **English Language Learners**
Have children turn to the Contents page and identify the chapter they liked best. Invite them to give a brief summary of the chapter.

AUDITORY LEARNERS GROUPS

Have children write riddles describing one or more spelling words (*rebuilding, unkindly, discovered, misbehaves, comfortable, defrost, wagon, magic, pioneer, open, bicycle, purple*). Call on volunteers to read their riddles for classmates to answer. Here is an example: *This word begins with a prefix and means "to thaw."* (*defrost*)

CHALLENGE

Challenge children to think of two or more additional words for each category on page 179. Encourage them to explain how each of their suggested words fits the category's description.

EXTRA SUPPORT/INTERVENTION

You may wish to have children work with partners as they write their letters on page 180. See Daily Phonics Practice, pages 221–222.

Take-Home Book

Review Prefixes, Base Words, Suffixes, Endings, and Syllables

Skill Focus

Children will

★ read words with prefixes, endings, or suffixes in the context of a story.

★ read multisyllabic words in the context of a story.

★ reread for fluency.

Teach

Build Background

• Remind children that the theme of this unit is "Taking Care of Our Earth." Ask children to name some ways in which people can help take care of our planet. List their ideas on the board.

• Write the Take-Home Book title *David's Wonderful Idea* on the board and ask a volunteer to read it aloud. Have children predict what David's idea might be.

Review Prefixes, Base Words, Suffixes, Endings, and Syllables Write these words on the board: *discourage, litter, wrappers, spoiling, recycle, wonderful, idea.* Have volunteers divide each word into syllables and then tell the rule for dividing each word. (*dis-cour-age; lit-ter; wrappers; spoil-ing; re-cy-cle; won-der-ful; i-de-a*)

Practice and Apply

Read the Book Help children tear out and fold the pages to make their Take-Home Books. Encourage them to look through the book and talk about the pictures. Then, read the story together. After reading, discuss what children learned about how they can help take care of Earth.

Prefixes, Base Words, Suffixes Write the following headings on the board: *Prefix, Base Word, Suffix.*

Have children look through the book and identify words with prefixes (*discouraged, discovered, unable, recycled, exclaimed*) and words with suffixes (*discouraged, slowly, discovered, spoiling, wonderful, working, waiting, neatly, biggest*). Encourage children to break the words into parts and write each part on the board under the correct heading.

Reread for Fluency Have children reread the book to increase their fluency and comprehension. Urge them to take their books home to read and share with family members.

181

By the end of the day, every piece of litter had disappeared. Newspapers waiting to be recycled were stacked next to neatly tied trashbags. Someone called, "Three cheers for David. This was all his idea!"

"Hip, hip, hooray!" the crowd exclaimed. David's face wore the biggest smile ever.

4

Name _____

David's Wonderful Idea

David was discouraged as he slowly rode his bicycle home from school. Everywhere he looked there was litter. There were candy wrappers on lawns and empty milk cartons by the roadside. He even discovered newspapers that had blown up against the trash cans on the sidewalk. The litter was spoiling the outdoors.

1

Review prefixes, base words, suffixes and endings, syllables: Take-home book   **181**

FOCUS ON ALL LEARNERS

ESL/ELL ENGLISH LANGUAGE LEARNERS

After assisting children with making the Take-Home Book, use the following activities to teach English language learners.

• Ask children to describe what is happening in each picture.

• You may wish to help children make a main-idea chart to organize their ideas.

• Read the story together.

• Have children find story words with prefixes, endings, or suffixes.

• Point to selected words and ask children to divide them into syllables.

VISUAL LEARNERS GROUPS

Materials: three plastic bins or cardboard boxes

Label each bin or cardboard box with one of the following: *Prefix, Suffix,* or *Prefix and Suffix.* Ask children to "recycle" words from the story by writing them on slips of paper and placing them into the appropriate bin or box.

Suddenly, David had an idea. "Maybe we can have a litter drive. I could talk to my friends and neighbors," he thought.

At dinner that night, David told his parents about his plan. "That sounds like a wonderful idea," Mom said.

Dad said, "Your mother and I will help. I bet a lot of people will be interested in your plan."

②

FOLD

③

David talked to his friends about the litter drive. His parents visited neighbors to share the idea. David also put up giant posters to advertise the date of the litter drive.

When the day arrived, many people from the neighborhood came. Those who were unable to come had given rakes, brooms, and trash bags. Soon everyone was working to make the neighborhood clean again!

182   Review prefixes, base words, suffixes and endings, syllables: Take-home book

---

CURRICULUM CONNECTIONS

MATH

Provide or help children obtain information from a local recycling center about the amount of trash they handle each day. Suggest that children figure out how much trash the center recycles in a week, in a month, and in a year.

SOCIAL STUDIES

Encourage children to brainstorm ideas about what they and others could do to improve their community. Provide art supplies and invite children to make posters expressing their ideas through slogans and art.

SCIENCE

Have children discuss the problems of waste disposal. Explain that organic waste (from plants and animals) decays and returns to the ground, enriching the soil and helping plants grow. Other trash piles up and never leaves the earth. Some is even poisonous and causes contamination. Ask children to create two word webs, one for *Biodegradable Trash* and one for *Harmful Trash*.

TECHNOLOGY   **AstroWord** Multisyllabic Words; Prefixes; Suffixes

---

KINESTHETIC LEARNERS   GROUPS

Materials: labels from cans and boxes, newspapers, magazines, greeting cards, scissors, glue, mural paper

Have children create a Word Wall, featuring words with prefixes, suffixes, v-c-v patterns, two vowels together that are sounded separately, and final *le*. Words can be cut from recycled materials, sorted, and glued on mural paper.

CHALLENGE

Invite children to continue the story about David's wonderful idea by writing about how David plans to keep the litter from spoiling the neighborhood in the future.

EXTRA SUPPORT/INTERVENTION

Some children may have difficulty reading or understanding the following story words and phrases: *litter, wrappers, milk cartons, spoiling the outdoors, litter drive, I bet, share the idea*. Read these words and phrases and explain their meanings as needed. **See Daily Phonics Practice, pages 221–222.**

Unit Checkup

Review Prefixes, Base Words, Suffixes, Endings, and Syllables

Skill Focus

Children will

★ recognize the meanings of prefixes, endings, and suffixes.

★ match prefixes and suffixes to base words.

★ identify words with prefixes and suffixes in sentences.

★ divide words into syllables.

Teach

Review Prefixes, Base Words, Suffixes, Endings, and Syllables Write these words on the board: *mislead, careful, airplane, picture, lemon, locate, radio, table,* and *animal.* Ask volunteers to choose a word and divide it into syllables. Continue until all the words have been rewritten and divided.

Have children briefly tell the rule used for dividing the words the way they did.

mis-lead	*between prefix and base word*
care-ful	*between base word and suffix*
air-plane	*between words in a compound*
pic-ture	*between two consonants*
lem-on	*v-c-v pattern, short vowel*
lo-cate	*v-c-v pattern, long vowel*
ra-di-o	*two vowels sounded separately*
ta-ble	*ending in consonant plus* -le
an-i-mal	*vowel sounded alone*

Practice and Apply

Assess Skills For the first activity on page 183, make sure children understand that the base word is the underlined word in each item. For the second activity on the page, have children read each word aloud to help them determine how it should be divided into syllables.

For page 184, point out that children must circle the words with prefixes, endings, or suffixes in the sentences in the first activity before writing the base words in the second activity.

Name _____

UNIT 6 CHECKUP

Read each clue. Fill in the circle next to the prefix or suffix that will make a new word that matches the clue. Write the new word on the line.

1. use again   _____reuse_____   ● re-   ○ -ful   ○ mis-
2. not usual   _____unusual_____   ○ -ly   ● un-   ○ re-
3. behaves badly   _____misbehaves_____   ● mis-   ○ un-   ○ de-
4. giving help   _____helpful_____   ● -ful   ○ -ly   ○ ex-
5. not pleased   _____displeased_____   ○ re-   ○ ex-   ● dis-
6. to take away the frost   _____defrost_____   ○ un-   ● de-   ○ -ly

Read each word. Then fill in the circle beside the word that shows how to divide the word into syllables.

7. earth   ○ ear-th   ● earth   ○ e-arth
8. sunset   ○ suns-et   ○ sunset   ● sun-set
9. replanted   ● re-plant-ed   ○ rep-lant-ed   ○ replant-ed
10. better   ○ be-tter   ○ bett-er   ● bet-ter
11. robin   ● rob-in   ○ ro-bin   ○ ro-bi-n
12. magic   ● mag-ic   ○ ma-gic   ○ magi-c
13. quiet   ○ qu-i-et   ○ quie-t   ● qui-et
14. monument   ○ mo-nu-ment   ● mon-u-ment   ○ monu-ment
15. purple   ○ pu-rple   ○ purp-le   ● pur-ple
16. music   ○ mus-ic   ● mu-sic   ○ m-u-sic

Prefixes, base words, suffixes and endings, syllables: Assessment   **183**

FOCUS ON ALL LEARNERS

ESL/ELL ENGLISH LANGUAGE LEARNERS

Ensure that children can recognize the correct written forms of target words by completing the activities orally with them.

• Read aloud and confirm that children understand the directions for both activities on page 183. Tell them that you will say each item along with the correct answer choice. They should fill in the circle beside the choice you say.

• For page 184, read aloud and confirm activity directions. Tell children that you will read aloud each sentence, one at a time. They should listen for words with prefixes or suffixes and circle the words you say. Then, help children identify the base word for each circled word and write it on the line.

KINESTHETIC LEARNERS GROUPS

Materials: paper bags, paper strips

Have groups write three syllabication rules each on a label and attach each label to a paper bag. Then, have children write words from the lessons on paper strips. Ask groups to trade bags and words and sort one another's words into the correct bags.

UNIT 6 CHECKUP

▶ **Read each sentence. Circle the word or words with a prefix, suffix, or ending.**

1. News about Earth may (discourage) you.
2. We cannot always (rebuild) what we harm.
3. We cannot turn (dirty) water into clean water overnight.
4. We know that the future of many kinds of animals is (uncertain.)
5. Many people treat Earth and animals (improperly.)
6. However, many more people are (thoughtful.)
7. Many people work hard for a (comfortable,) safe planet.
8. Earth can (renew) itself.
9. We must be (hopeful) about the future.
10. You can make a difference by (pitching) in to do your part!

▶ **Write the base word of each word you circled.**

11. _____courage_____
12. _____build_____
13. _____dirt_____
14. _____certain_____
15. _____proper_____
16. _____thought_____
17. _____comfort_____
18. _____new_____
19. _____hope_____
20. _____pitch_____

184   Prefixes, base words, suffixes and endings, syllables: Assessment

ASSESS UNDERSTANDING OF UNIT SKILLS

STUDENT PROGRESS ASSESSMENT

Review the observational notes you made as children worked on the activities in this unit. Your notes will help you evaluate children's understanding of prefixes, suffixes, base words, and syllabication.

PORTFOLIO ASSESSMENT

Review the papers collected in children's portfolios to assess the progress they have made with this unit's phonics skills. You may wish to schedule interviews with children to discuss their progress.

DAILY PHONICS PRACTICE

For children who need further practice with prefixes, suffixes, endings, base words, and syllables, quick reviews are provided on pages 221–222 in Daily Phonics Practice.

PHONICS POSTTEST

To assess children's mastery of prefixes, base words, suffixes, and syllables, use the posttest on pages 151g–151h.

VISUAL LEARNERS

Write these words on the board: *headline, moonlight, healthy, safely, watching, unlock, mistake, silver, admire, surprise, magic, shadow, moment, tiger, unit, document, create, whistle,* and *scramble.* Ask one group to divide the words into syllables and another group to explain the rules that were used to do so.

CHALLENGE

Suggest that pairs of children make up clues like those on page 183 for words with prefixes or suffixes and use the clues to quiz each other.

EXTRA SUPPORT/INTERVENTION

If children have difficulty dividing words into syllables for part two on page 183, have them read the three responses aloud and listen for the correct pronunciation of the word. See Daily Phonics Practice, pages 221–222.

Teacher Notes

UNIT 7

Synonyms, Antonyms, Homonyms, Dictionary Skills

THEME: EXPRESS YOURSELF!

CONTENTS

Student Performance Objectives

In Unit 7, children will be introduced to synonyms, antonyms, homonyms, multiple meanings of words, and dictionary skills within the context of the theme "Express Yourself!" As children begin to understand and learn synonyms, antonyms, homonyms, multiple meanings, and dictionary skills, they will be able to

▶ Recognize synonyms

▶ Recognize antonyms

▶ Recognize homonyms

▶ Recognize words with multiple meanings

▶ Use dictionary skills

Overview of Resources

LESSON	MCP PHONICS AND READING LIBRARY, LEVEL C PROGRAM	TITLE	DAILY PHONICS PRACTICE
85: Synonyms	NC, Set 2	*The Griffeys: Father and Son Baseball*	222–223
86: Antonyms	NC, Set 1	*The Mystery of the Spy's Diary*	222–223
87: Homonyms	FC, Set 3	*How Bullfrog Found His Sound*	222–223
88: Review homonyms	NC, Set 3	*Josh and T.J.*	222–223
89: Dictionary: alphabetical order/guide words	VFC, Set 1	*The Pet Show*	223
90: Dictionary: guide words	VFC, Set 2	*Hootie Joins In*	223
91: Dictionary: locating words	FC, Set 1	*Quackers, the Troublesome Duck*	223
92: Homographs: words with multiple meanings	FC, Set 4	*Secrets of the Rain Forest*	223
93: Review synonyms, antonyms, homonyms	FC, Set 1	*Digging Dinosaurs*	222–223
94: Take-Home Book "A Little Imagination"			222–223
95: Unit Checkup			222–223

VFC—Very First Chapters   FC—First Chapters   NC—Next Chapters

Assessment Options

In Unit 7, assess children's ability to recognize and use words that are synonyms, antonyms, and homonyms; use dictionary skills; and recognize multiple meanings of words. Use the Unit Pretest and Posttest for formal assessment. For ongoing informal assessment you may want to use children's work on the Review pages, Take-Home Books, and Unit Checkups. You may also want to encourage children to evaluate their own work and participate in setting goals for their own learning.

ESL/ELL Provide frequent oral opportunities for English language learners to hear and use words that are synonyms, antonyms, and homonyms, in personally meaningful contexts. Although children may experience these concepts in their home language, the sounds and spellings of English are new. For additional support for English language learners, see page 185j.

FORMAL ASSESSMENT

Use the Unit 7 Pretest, on pages 185e–185f, to help assess a child's knowledge at the beginning of the unit and to plan instruction.

ESL/ELL Before administering the Pretest, reinforce English language learners' use of the testing format of filling in the circle next to the answer. Read aloud each set of test directions and confirm understanding of the tasks by having volunteers restate in their own words what they are to do. Inability to recognize words may require teacher support to preview them and read them aloud to the group. It may be more beneficial to conduct the Pretest one-on-one with children who need special pacing.

Use the Unit 7 Posttest, on pages 185g–185h, to help assess mastery of unit objectives and to plan for reteaching, if necessary.

ESL/ELL Some children may continue to have difficulty with directions. Read the directions aloud and model how to mark the responses to complete the tests. If some are distracted by "text heaviness" of items 1–13, provide strips of paper to place under each test item to serve as a reading guide. In this way children can focus on one test item at a time.

INFORMAL ASSESSMENT

Use the Review pages, Unit Checkup, and Take-Home Book in the student book to provide an effective means of evaluating children's performance.

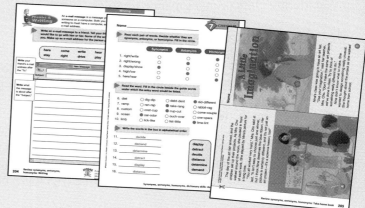

Unit 7 Skills	Review pages	Checkups	Take-Home Books
Synonyms	203–204	207–208	205–206
Antonyms	203–204	207–208	205–206
Homonyms	193–194	207–208	205–206
	203–204		
Dictionary skills	203–204	207–208	205–206
Multiple meanings	203–204	207–208	205–206

STUDENT PROGRESS CHECKLIST

Use the checklist on page 185i to record children's progress. You may want to cut the sections apart to place each child's checklist in his or her portfolio.

PORTFOLIO ASSESSMENT

This logo appears throughout the teaching plans. It signals opportunities for collecting student work for individual portfolios. You may also want to include the Pretest and Posttest, the Review pages, the Unit Checkup, Phonics & Reading, and Phonics & Writing pages.

Pretest and Posttest

DIRECTIONS

To help you assess children's progress in learning Unit 7 skills, tests are available on pages 185e–185h.

Administer the Pretest before children begin the unit. The results of the Pretest will help you identify each child's strengths and needs in advance, allowing you to structure lesson plans to meet individual needs. Administer the Posttest to assess children's overall mastery of skills taught in the unit to identify specific areas that will require reteaching.

ESL/ELL Since the objectives of both the Unit 7 Pretest and Posttest are to identify words that are synonyms, antonyms, or homonyms as well as test knowledge of multiple meanings of words and dictionary skills, it will be necessary to read each set of directions before children perform each part of the test.

- It may be necessary to read aloud word pairs and word meanings as children complete items 1–15 on the Pretest.

- For the second portion of the test, reassure students who are unsure of dictionary skills by explaining the task, perhaps give a board example, and make an alphabet chart available for use.

- You may want to have children who are unable to read independently in English complete the activity directly with you, during class or at a separate time.

PERFORMANCE ASSESSMENT PROFILE

The following chart will help you identify specific skills as they appear on the tests and will enable you to identify and record specific information about an individual's or the class's performance on the tests.

Depending on the results of each test, refer to the Reteaching column for lesson-plan pages where you can find activities that will be useful for meeting individual needs or for daily phonics practice.

Answer Keys

Unit 7 Pretest, page 185e (BLM 43)

1. H	5. H	8. S	11. H
2. S	6. A	9. H	12. A
3. S	7. A	10. A	13. H
4. S			

14. bank^1 15. bark^2

Unit 7 Pretest, page 185f (BLM 44)

16. cell   18. wigwam   20. sat
17. people   19. field

21. dense / detour
22. safe / salt
23. mope / most
24. candy / castle
25. join / juggle
26. remove / report
27. wizard / wrinkle
28. echo / exchange

Unit 7 Posttest, page 185g (BLM 45)

1. S	5. S	8. A	11. A
2. A	6. A	9. H	12. A
3. S	7. H	10. H	13. S
4. H			

14. light^1 15. bat^1

Unit 7 Post test, page 185h (BLM 46)

16. reach   18. sing   20. laugh
17. germ   19. come

21. recap / rescue
22. paint / panda
23. rift / river
24. ware / waste
25. blast / blow
26. hard / heat
27. foot / fork
28. look / lull

Performance Assessment Profile

Skill	Pretest Questions	Posttest Questions	Reteaching — Focus on All Learners	Reteaching — Daily Phonics Practice
Synonyms	2, 3, 4, 8	1, 3, 5, 13	187–188, 203–206	222–223
Antonyms	6, 7, 10, 12	2, 6, 8, 11, 12	189–190, 203–206	222–223
Homonyms	1, 5, 9, 11, 13	4, 7, 9, 10, 12	191–194, 203–206	222–223
Dictionary skills	14, 15, 16–28	14, 15, 16–28	195–200, 203–206	223
Multiple meanings	14, 15	14, 15	201–206	223

Name _____

	Synonyms	Antonyms	Homonyms
1. write, right	○	○	○
2. ill, sick	○	○	○
3. shut, close	○	○	○
4. plan, idea	○	○	○
5. nose, knows	○	○	○
6. climb, descend	○	○	○
7. heavy, light	○	○	○
8. repair, fix	○	○	○
9. here, hear	○	○	○
10. buy, sell	○	○	○
11. fair, fare	○	○	○
12. sharp, dull	○	○	○
13. dear, deer	○	○	○

▶ Read each sentence. Fill in the circle beside the dictionary entry whose definition fits the meaning of the underlined word in the sentence.

14. Mary walked along the river <u>bank</u>.

○ **bank**[1] land that borders a river

○ **bank**[2] a place to put money

15. Sap dripped from the hole in the <u>bark</u>.

○ **bark**[1] noise a dog makes

○ **bark**[2] outer covering of a tree trunk

Go to the next page. →

BLM 43 Unit 7 Pretest: Synonyms, homonyms, antonyms; multiple meanings

Name _____

> ▶ **Look at each pair of words. Fill in the circle under the word that comes between them in alphabetical order.**

16. celebrate, certain	certainly ○	cell ○	ceiling ○
17. peas, picture	peanut ○	pile ○	people ○
18. white, winner	winter ○	wigwam ○	while ○
19. feather, filled	fear ○	film ○	field ○
20. sailboat, saucer	sat ○	sack ○	save ○

> ▶ **Read each entry word. Fill in the circle beside the guide words under which the entry word would be listed.**

21. deposit	○ dessert / dew ○ dense / detour ○ depart / depend	25. journey	○ jiggle / journal ○ job / joke ○ join / juggle
22. sale	○ sad / sail ○ sage / salary ○ safe / salt	26. repair	○ remove / report ○ replace / reserve ○ regard / remain
23. mopping	○ mope / most ○ mostly / motel ○ modern / mop	27. wring	○ wiring / wish ○ wizard / wrinkle ○ wind / wrap
24. capital	○ cactus / candle ○ candy / castle ○ catch / cavity	28. elephant	○ eggplant / electric ○ escalator / exam ○ echo / exchange

Possible score on Unit 7 Pretest is 28. Number correct _____

BLM 44 Unit 7 Pretest: Dictionary skills

185f

Name _____

> Read each pair of words. Fill in the circle below Synonyms if the words are synonyms, Antonyms if they are antonyms, or Homonyms if they are homonyms.

	Synonyms	Antonyms	Homonyms
1. tale, story	○	○	○
2. finish, start	○	○	○
3. big, large	○	○	○
4. ads, adds	○	○	○
5. store, shop	○	○	○
6. back, front	○	○	○
7. one, won	○	○	○
8. far, near	○	○	○
9. four, for	○	○	○
10. whole, hole	○	○	○
11. pull, push	○	○	○
12. start, stop	○	○	○
13. unhappy, sad	○	○	○

> Read each sentence. Fill in the circle beside the dictionary entry whose definition fits the meaning of the underlined word in the sentence.

14. The small travel bag was very <u>light</u>.

○ **light¹** not weighing very much

○ **light²** to set on fire

15. Sam grabbed a <u>bat</u>, ready to play ball.

○ **bat¹** a wooden club used to hit a baseball

○ **bat²** a flying mammal

Go to the next page. →

Name _____

> Look at each pair of words. Fill in the circle under the word that comes between them in alphabetical order.

16. rattle, real   reach ○   rare ○   red ○

17. gentle, glass   glob ○   germ ○   gel ○

18. side, skunk   sky ○   sick ○   sing ○

19. color, cool   collect ○   come ○   copy ○

20. lap, law   laugh ○   lazy ○   lake ○

> Read each entry word. Fill in the circle beside the guide words under which the entry word would be listed.

21. reindeer
- ○ rear / regret
- ○ recap / rescue
- ○ relax / review

25. blister
- ○ blast / blow
- ○ blank / blind
- ○ blond / blue

22. pale
- ○ pack / palace
- ○ paint / panda
- ○ palm / pants

26. heart
- ○ hat / head
- ○ hard / heat
- ○ health / heart

23. ring
- ○ rib / rind
- ○ rip / rival
- ○ rift / river

27. forest
- ○ foot / fork
- ○ forgive / freckle
- ○ form / found

24. wash
- ○ ware / waste
- ○ wake / warn
- ○ wasp / wax

28. luck
- ○ lost / loyal
- ○ look / lull
- ○ lumber / lung

Possible score on Unit 7 Posttest is 28. Number correct _____

BLM 46 Unit 7 Posttest: Dictionary skills

Student Progress Checklist

Make as many copies as needed to use for a class list. For individual portfolio use, cut apart each child's section. As indicated by the code, color in boxes next to skills satisfactorily assessed and insert an *X* by those requiring reteaching. Marked boxes can later be colored in to indicate mastery.

Student Progress Checklist

Code: ■ Satisfactory ☒ Needs Reteaching

Student: _____ _____ Pretest Score: _____ Posttest Score: _____	**Skills** ☐ Synonyms ☐ Antonyms ☐ Homonyms ☐ Dictionary Skills ☐ Multiple Meanings	**Comments / Learning Goals**
Student: _____ _____ Pretest Score: _____ Posttest Score: _____	**Skills** ☐ Synonyms ☐ Antonyms ☐ Homonyms ☐ Dictionary Skills ☐ Multiple Meanings	**Comments / Learning Goals**
Student: _____ _____ Pretest Score: _____ Posttest Score: _____	**Skills** ☐ Synonyms ☐ Antonyms ☐ Homonyms ☐ Dictionary Skills ☐ Multiple Meanings	**Comments / Learning Goals**
Student: _____ _____ Pretest Score: _____ Posttest Score: _____	**Skills** ☐ Synonyms ☐ Antonyms ☐ Homonyms ☐ Dictionary Skills ☐ Multiple Meanings	**Comments / Learning Goals**

BLM 47 Unit 7 Checklist

Throughout Unit 7 there are opportunities to assess English language learners' ability to use and understand words that are synonyms, antonyms, and homonyms. English language learners may be familiar with these concepts in their home languages; however, keep in mind that the words, sounds, and spellings in English are not familiar to these children. Children will benefit from additional practice of synonyms, antonyms, and homonyms in meaningful contexts.

Lesson 85, pages 187–188 Although English language learners may experience these concepts in their home languages, the sounds and spellings of English are new. Reference pronunciation notes of issues with specific letters and blends in their respective lessons. Provide frequent opportunities for children to hear and use the words in personally meaningful contexts.

Lesson 86, pages 189–190 A strong emphasis on spelling may be inappropriate for English language learners who have not reached the intermediate level of proficiency. Allow children to use invented spelling and the phonics skills they are building upon as a foundation for future spelling success.

Lesson 87, pages 191–192 Native speakers of Spanish may be familiar with homonyms in their native language, due to similar pronunciation of *b* and *v*; soft *c, s,* and *z*; soft *g* and *j*; *ll* and *y*; and the silent *h*. Emphasize specific homonyms in context and have children memorize the different spellings of the word pairs.

Spelling Connections

INTRODUCTION

The Unit Word List is a list of selected spelling words drawn from this unit. To incorporate spelling into your phonics program, use the activity in the Curriculum Connections section of each teaching plan.

ESL/ELL It is recommended that English language learners reach the intermediate level of English proficiency before focusing on spelling. For English language learners introduce one group of words at a time and their meanings through visuals, realia, or demonstrations.

The spelling lessons utilize the following approach for each set of words.

1. Administer a pretest of the words that have not yet been introduced. Dictation sentences are provided.

2. Provide practice.

3. Reassess. Dictation sentences are provided.

A final review that covers synonyms, antonyms, and homonyms is provided on page 204.

DIRECTIONS

Make a copy of Blackline Master 48 for each child. After administering the pretest, give children a copy of the appropriate word list. Children can work with a partner to practice spelling the words orally. You may want to challenge children to think of new synonyms, antonyms, and homonyms. Children can write words of their own on *My Own Word List* (see Blackline Master 48).

Have children store their list words in an envelope in the back of their books. You may want to suggest that children keep a spelling notebook, listing words with similar patterns. Another idea is to build Word Walls with children and display them in the classroom. Each section of the wall can focus on words with a single phonics element. The walls will become a good resource for children to use when they are engaged in writing.

Unit Word List

Synonyms, Antonyms, Homonyms, ABC Order, Multiple Meanings

display
show
high
low
right
write

Name _____

Spelling

Phonics & Spelling — Find the synonym in the box for each word. Write it on the line.

| display | find | quick | raise |

1. show   display
2. locate   find
3. swift   quick
4. lift   raise

Find the antonym in the box for each word. Write it on the line.

| come | high | light | something |

5. nothing   something
6. low   high
7. heavy   light
8. go   come

Write a homonym for each word.

9. right   write
10. buy   by
11. dear   deer
12. stare   stair

Review synonyms, antonyms, homonyms: Spelling   **203**

185k

Name _____

UNIT 7 WORD LIST

Synonyms; Antonyms; Homonyms; ABC Order; Multiple Meanings	**My Own Word List Synonyms**	**My Own Word List Antonyms**
display show high low right write		
My Own Word List Homonyms	**My Own Word List ABC Order**	**My Own Word List Multiple Meanings**

BLM 48 Unit 7 Spelling Words

Phonics Games, Activities, and Technology

The following collection of ideas offers a variety of opportunities to reinforce skills while actively engaging children. The games, activities, and technology suggestions can easily be adapted to meet the needs of your group of learners. They vary in approach so as to consider children's different learning styles.

STAND UP FOR SYNONYMS

In advance, make word cards by writing pairs of words that are synonyms on separate cards. Seat children in a circle and randomly pass out the words. Begin by having one child stand and read the word on his or her card. The child holding a word that is a synonym responds by standing and reading the word. The group must agree that the words are synonyms before play continues. Use words such as the following for the word cards: *sparkle, glisten; reap, gather; look, search; quiet, silent; simple, easy; display, show; rush, hurry; woods, forest; pretty, beautiful; powerful, strong.* Follow a similar procedure using word pairs that are antonyms.

ANTONYM ANTICS

In advance, write word pairs that are antonyms on cards or sheets of paper, writing one word on each side of the card. You might use *big, little; young, old; over, under; in, out; come, go; full, empty; descend, climb; sharp, dull; joy, sorrow; nobody, anybody; join, separate;* and so on.

Play a game by placing the cards along a chalk ledge or in a pocket chart so that only one word is visible. Begin by pointing to the first word. Invite children to silently read the word and think of an antonym. See which child can be the first to name the antonym that is written on the back side of the card. Follow a similar procedure using synonym pairs such as *jump, leap; yell, shriek; squirm, wiggle; squeeze, hug; giggle, laugh; boast, brag.*

MEMORY MATCH GAME

Write the following words on separate slips of paper: *quiet, noisy; cut, chop; cent, scent; bare, bear; climb, scale; preferred, favorite; our, hour; wonderful, marvelous; light, heavy; awake, asleep; through, threw; hide, display.* You may want to make a master copy of the word cards so they can be reproduced and made available to several pairs of children. Have partners turn the cards face down. The first player turns over two words at a time to try to make a match of words that are synonyms, antonyms, or homonyms. If a match is made, the player explains the match, keeps the cards, and plays again. If no match is made, the cards are turned face down and the partner continues. Play until all pairs have been matched.

HOMONYM CHALLENGE

Write the following sets of homonyms on the board: *right-write, buy-by, weak-week, Bea-be-bee, sail-sale, wood-would, scent-cent-sent, nose-knows,* and *rain-reign-rein.* Challenge children to use homonyms in a single sentence that is a tongue twister to say. Start off with *How much wood would a woodchuck chuck if a woodchuck could chuck wood?* and *Sue saw several for sale signs for sailboats at a boat sale.*

FUNNY NEWSPAPER HEADLINES

Invite children to brainstorm homonyms and homographs. Then, encourage them to think of funny newspaper headlines that use words from their list, such as "A Weak Week for the Stock Market" or "Fish Scales Tip the Scales." Invite children to write the story that goes with their headlines and/or draw a picture that has a caption. You might compile children's work to make a class homonym/homograph newspaper.

ANIMAL OPPOSITES

Have partners choose a pair of words that are antonyms and think of an animal that can be described by each word. Then, invite partners to introduce their animal names to the group, pantomime an action to describe the animal, and have the others guess the antonym word pair. Some examples are: *mouse, giraffe (tall, short); hare, tortoise (swift, slow); bird, elephant (light, heavy); lion, kitten (fierce, gentle); wolf, dog (wild, tame).*

ABC MEMORY

Seat children in a circle. Explain that you will start a cumulative story with the words *I'm going to the market to buy apples.* The first child will repeat the story opener and the first object named (*apples*) and will add another item whose name begins with the letter *b.* The next child will repeat the story opener, repeat objects for *a* and *b,* add another object whose name begins with *c,* and so on. Challenge children to get all the way to *z!*

DICTIONARY DASH

Have children form groups of four. Group members will need paper, pencils, and a dictionary. Invite one child in each group to be the dictionary keeper. That child randomly opens the dictionary to any page, reads the guide words on the page, and writes them on a piece of paper for the other group members to see. Group members then each write a word that would appear on the same page as the guide words. They pass their words to the dictionary keeper, who must look for the words on the page. If a word does not appear on the page, the group should decide if it is a word that is not in that particular dictionary, or if it is a word that falls on a different page. Continue play with a different dictionary keeper.

CAN A KUMQUAT SKULK?

Invite children to use a dictionary to look up unusual and fun-sounding words. You might assign the following words to children: *kumquat, rutabaga, petunia, sassafras, hooligan, doily, skulk, beluga, dodo, cygnet*. Or choose words you think your class might enjoy knowing. (Make sure your dictionary includes all of the words!) After reading and pronouncing the words as a group, have children guess the word meanings. Then, invite partners to choose a word to find. Encourage them to write a brief definition and a sentence for each word.

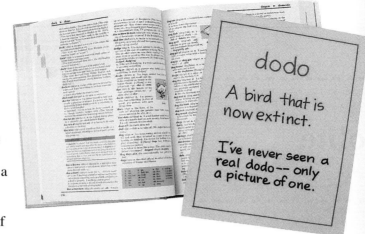

dodo
A bird that is now extinct.

I've never seen a real dodo -- only a picture of one.

ANTONYM DOMINOES

Make copies of Blackline Master 49 and give a copy to each pair of children. They can cut along the dashed lines to make a set of domino cards. Tell children to place one domino card in the center of their playing area and place all other cards face down. Each player takes three dominoes to begin. Partners take turns matching one antonym to build a domino chain. If a player is unable to make a match, that player draws another domino card and the partner takes a turn. The first player without any domino cards is the winner.

Variation: Have children write synonym pairs on the reverse side of the dominoes to make a domino chain with words that have the same meaning.

WHAT KIND OF WORDS?

Invite children to fold a sheet of paper in half and label one half with the word Synonyms and the other half with Antonyms. Provide counters for each child to use or have children design their own. Then, read word pairs and invite children to decide in which category the words fall and place a counter in the appropriate column. Have individuals check each other's work after each word pair and help each other as necessary.

synonyms	antonyms

TECHNOLOGY

The following software products reinforce children's understanding of a variety of phonics skills.

ClueFinders® 3rd Grade Adventure
An adventure awaits children (ages 7 to 9) as they travel to the rain forest to find Dr. Pythagoras. The program features 30 interactive games that teach more than 75 key third grade skills including vocabulary, spelling, grammar, synonyms, and antonyms.

** Riverdeep The Learning Company
   500 Redwood Blvd.
   Novato, CA 94947
   (800) 825-4420
   www.learningcompanyschool.com

Reading Blaster™ Ages 6–8
Children ages 6–8 have fun playing games on different levels while learning critical reading skills in the latest edition of *Reading Blaster*.

** Sunburst Technology
   1900 South Batavia Avenue
   Geneva, IL 60134
   (800) 321-7511
   www.sunburst.com

Antonym Dominoes

polite ◆ sharp	dull ◆ moist
thin ◆ messy	lost ◆ morning
first ◆ wealthy	far ◆ below
soft ◆ noisy	poor ◆ fast
slow ◆ hard	quiet ◆ rude
above ◆ thick	neat ◆ found
dry ◆ near	evening ◆ last

Home Connections

The Home Connections features of this program are intended to involve families in their children's learning and application of phonics skills. Three effective opportunities to make connections between home and school include the following.

- **HOME LETTER**
- **HOME NOTES**
- **TAKE-HOME BOOKS**

HOME LETTER

A letter is available to be sent home at the beginning of Unit 7. This letter informs family members that children will be learning about synonyms, antonyms, homonyms, and dictionary skills within the context of the unit theme, "Express Yourself!" The suggested home activity focuses on writing words that describe the child and then writing a second list of words that are synonyms. This activity promotes interaction between child and family members while supporting children's learning of word meanings. The letter, which is available in both English and Spanish, also suggests theme-related books family members can look for in a local library and enjoy reading together.

HOME NOTES

Whenever the Home logo appears within the student book, a phonics activity is suggested to be done at home. The activities are simple to do, requiring little or no preparation or special materials, and are meant to reinforce the targeted phonics skill.

Home Notes in Spanish are also available for both teachers and parents to download and use from our website, www.PlaidPhonics.com.

TAKE-HOME BOOKS

Within the student book are Take-Home Books that can be cut out and assembled. The story language in each book reinforces the targeted phonics skills. The books can be taken home and shared with family members. In Unit 7, one Take-Home Book is available, focusing on synonyms, antonyms, and homonyms, as well as the unit theme, "Express Yourself!"

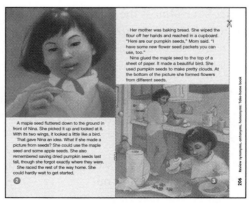

Synonyms, Antonyms, Homonyms, Homographs, Dictionary Skills

Skill Focus

Assess Prior Knowledge

To assess children's prior knowledge of synonyms, antonyms, homonyms, homographs, and dictionary skills, use the pretest on pages 185e–185f.

Unit Focus

Build Background

- Write the theme title "Express Yourself!" on the board. Say that in the poem "Changing," one person expresses a wish to be another person for a week in order to find out what that person is like.

- Read the poem aloud. Then, invite children to talk about how they feel about the poem.

Introduce Synonyms, Antonyms, Homonyms, Homographs

- Write the word *change* on the board. Have children suggest words that have almost the same meaning. List their ideas. (*replace*, *swap*, *trade*, *switch*) Tell children that words that mean almost the same thing are called synonyms.

- Ask children to suggest words that mean the opposite of *change*. List their ideas. (*stay*, *set*, *remain*, *stick*) Point out that words that have opposite meanings are called antonyms.

- Have children suggest two different meanings for *change*. (*money back*, *to exchange for*) Point out that words that are spelled alike but have different meanings are called homographs.

- Write *know*, *to*, and *week* on the board. Explain that words that sound the same but are spelled differently are called homonyms.

Critical Thinking Discuss ways people are special. Then, discuss the Talk About It question.

Read Aloud

Changing

by Mary Ann Hoberman

I know what I feel like;
I'd like to be *you*
And feel what *you* feel like
And do what *you* do.

I'd like to change places
For maybe a week
And look like your look-alike
And speak as you speak
And think what you're thinking
And go where you go
And feel what you're feeling
And know what you know.

I wish we could do it;
What fun it would be
If I could try you out
And you could try me.

UNIT 7 Synonyms, Antonyms, Homonyms, Homographs, Dictionary Skills
Theme: Express Yourself!

TALK About It What things about you make you special?

Unit 7 • Introduction
Critical Thinking **185**

THEME FOCUS

ME, MYSELF, AND YOU

Read the poem aloud one more time. Then, direct children to the illustration on page 185 and ask them how the children in the picture are alike yet different. Talk about ways in which a person can be like his or her friends but remain special at the same time.

SAME BUT DIFFERENT

Invite children to think about a friend or a family member. Have them write about ways in which they are like the other person and ways in which they are different. Model using synonyms and antonyms, as in this example: *My friend and I are both **nice**, **friendly** people. I can be **funny**, but I'm a little bit **shy**. My friend is **hilarious**. She is **outgoing** and can make anybody laugh, even people she doesn't know.*

EXPRESS YOURSELF

Make a large blank book. Include one page with each child's name. Invite children to write on their page at least one way in which they like to express their thoughts and feelings. For example, *I like to write poems. I like to sing songs. I like to make things.* Afterward, share children's ideas with the class.

HOME LETTER

Dear Family,

In this unit, called "Express Yourself," your child will learn about **synonyms** such as **big** and **large**; **antonyms** such as **lost** and **found**; **homonyms** such as **blue/blew**, and **homographs** such as **play**, which has several meanings. Your child will also be learning dictionary skills. As your child explores these skills, you might like to try these activities together.

▶ Have your child write a list of words that describe himself or herself. Then help your child write a second list of words that are synonyms and draw a picture to go with the words.

▶ With your child, read the poem on page 185. Ask your child to identify words with synonyms, antonyms, homonyms, and homographs.

▶ Your child might enjoy reading these books with you. Look for them in your local library.

How to Be Cool in the Third Grade by Betsy Duffey

Louise Goes Wild by Stephen Krensky

Sincerely,

Estimada familia:

En esta unidad, que trata sobre "Express Yourself" ("Expresándote"), su hijo/a estudiará **sinónimos** como **big** (grande) y **large** (amplio); **antónimos** como **lost** (perdido) y **found** (encontrado); **homónimos** como **blue** (azul)/**blew** (sopló) y **homógrafos** como **play** (jugar), que tienen varios significados. También aprenderá a usar un diccionario. A medida que su hijo/a se vaya familiarizando con estas destrezas, pueden hacer las siguientes actividades juntos.

▶ Pidan a su hijo/a que escriba una lista de palabras que lo/a describen. Ayuden a su hijo/a a escribir una segunda lista de palabras que son sinónimos. Pídanle que haga un dibujo de sí mismo/a para acompañar las palabras.

▶ Lean juntos el poema en la página 185. Pidan a su hijo/a que identifique las palabras con sinónimos, antónimos, homónimos, y homógrafos.

▶ Ustedes y su hijo/a disfrutarán leyendo estos libros juntos. Búsquenlos en su biblioteca local.

How to Be Cool in the Third Grade de Betsy Duffey

Louise Goes Wild de Stephen Krensky

Sinceramente,

HOME CONNECTIONS

- The Home Letter on page 186 will acquaint family members with the word study skills children will be studying in this unit. Children can tear out the page and take it home.

- You may want to suggest that children complete the activities on the page with a family member. Urge children to look in the library for the books suggested and read them with family members.

LEARNING CENTER ACTIVITIES

WRITING CENTER

Invite children to write character sketches, poems, or descriptive paragraphs about someone they know and like. Point out that they could write about a friend or relative. When children finish writing, suggest that they arrange their material in a display entitled "Our Friends."

MATH CENTER

Have each child make a list of ten things they like and ten things they dislike, such as particular sports, school subjects, colors, foods, games, and types of weather. Suggest that children share their lists with classmates to see what likes and dislikes they have in common. Then, ask volunteers to present the information in a bar graph showing the top five things children like and the top five things children dislike.

SOCIAL STUDIES CENTER

Teach children how to say the word *friends* in other languages, such as *amigos* (Spanish), *amis* (French), *rafiki* (Swahili), and *tomodachi* (Japanese). Talk about ways in which children all over the world are alike. Invite children of various cultural backgrounds to share some of their customs with the class.

BULLETIN BOARD

Provide children with pieces of butcher paper. Ask them to draw a picture of themselves with a large speech balloon. Then, have them write inside the balloon something to introduce themselves. Display children's drawings on a bulletin board with the title "Express Yourself."

Synonyms

Children will

★ define synonyms as words that have the same or almost the same meaning.

★ identify synonyms for given words.

★ write synonyms to complete sentences.

ESL/ELL Although English language learners may experience these concepts in their home languages, the sounds and spelling of English are new. Reference pronunciation notes of issues with specific letters and blends in their respective lessons. Provide frequent opportunities for children to hear and use the words in personally meaningful contexts.

Teach

Introduce Synonyms Say this sentence: *The whale is large.* Ask children if they can think of another word that has the same meaning as *large.* (*big*) Tell children that words that have the same or almost the same meaning—such as *large* and *big*—are called synonyms.

Say these word pairs and ask children what they notice about each pair: *fast, quick; small, little; afraid, scared.* Point out that the words in each pair have almost the same meaning. They are synonyms.

Write these words on the board: *near, pretty, silent.* Ask children to suggest a synonym for each word. (possible answers: *close, beautiful, quiet*)

Practice and Apply

Writing Have a volunteer read aloud the definition on page 187. For the activity on page 187 and the first activity on page 188, make sure children understand that they must find a word in the box that is a synonym for the underlined word in each sentence.

Critical Thinking After children have completed page 187, have them discuss the clues in the sentences that suggest a popular fairy tale.

Reading Use *The Griffeys: Father and Son Baseball*, MCP Phonics and Reading Word Study Skills Library 2, Level C, to provide practice in identifying and using synonyms.

187

Name _____

> Read each sentence. Then rewrite it, replacing the underlined word with a synonym from the box.

DEFINITION
Synonyms are words that have the same or almost the same meaning.
big—large   fall—drop

closes	discovers	field	forgets	glad
happens	loud	pretty	radio	silent
tale	teaches	unhappy	upset	woods

1. My dad enjoys reading me a <u>story</u> before bedtime. _____
   _____ My dad enjoys reading me a tale before bedtime. _____

2. I am <u>happy</u> when we spend time together. _____
   _____ I am glad when we spend time together. _____

3. He begins to read when I am <u>quiet</u>. _____
   _____ He begins to read when I am silent. _____

4. He always <u>finds</u> a new story to read. _____
   _____ He always discovers a new story to read. _____

5. This story is about a girl who lives in the <u>forest</u>. _____
   _____ This story is about a girl who lives in the woods. _____

6. She wears a <u>beautiful</u> red cape. _____
   _____ She wears a pretty red cape. _____

7. I can't wait to find out what <u>occurs</u>. _____
   _____ I can't wait to find out what happens. _____

 TALK About It What story do you think the girl's dad read to her? How can you tell?

Synonyms: Words in context, critical thinking   **187**

FOCUS ON ALL LEARNERS

ESL/ELL **ENGLISH LANGUAGE LEARNERS**

Assess English language learners' ability to identify synonyms by doing the activity on page 187 with them.

• Read the story aloud; have children take turns reading.

• Write the words *story, happy, quiet, finds, forest, beautiful,* and *occurs* in a column on the board. In another column, write *glad, tale, pretty, silent, happens, woods, discovers.*

• Have volunteers tell you what each word in the first column means. If they use a word in the second column to describe the first, draw a line between the two words.

• Tell children that words that have the same meaning, or almost the same meanings, are called synonyms.

VISUAL LEARNERS **PARTNERS**

Have each child write five phrases using a word that has a synonym, circling that word in each phrase. Have partners trade papers and rewrite the phrases, replacing words with synonyms.

Read each riddle. Write a word from the box to answer the riddle.

| big | beautiful | boat | close | funny | hear | woods |

1. I have four letters. I mean the same as <u>listen</u>. I am __hear__.
2. I have five letters. I mean the same as <u>comical</u>. I am __funny__.
3. I have four letters. I mean the same as <u>ship</u>. I am __boat__.
4. I have five letters. I mean the same as <u>near</u>. I am __close__.
5. I have three letters. I mean the same as <u>large</u>. I am __big__.
6. I have five letters. I mean the same as <u>forest</u>. I am __woods__.
7. I have nine letters. I mean the same as <u>pretty</u>. I am __beautiful__.

For each group of words, draw a line from the word in the first column to its synonym in the second column.

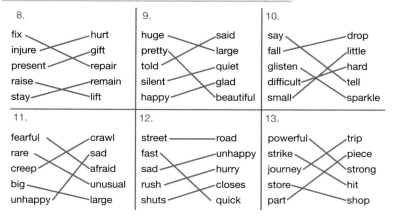

8.
fix — repair
injure — hurt
present — gift
raise — lift
stay — remain

9.
huge — large
pretty — beautiful
told — said
silent — quiet
happy — glad

10.
say — tell
fall — drop
glisten — sparkle
difficult — hard
small — little

11.
fearful — afraid
rare — unusual
creep — crawl
big — large
unhappy — sad

12.
street — road
fast — quick
sad — unhappy
rush — hurry
shuts — closes

13.
powerful — strong
strike — hit
journey — trip
store — shop
part — piece

Have your child use some of the words on the page to make up synonym riddles for you to answer, similar to those in numbers 1–7.

188 Synonyms: Word meaning

CURRICULUM CONNECTIONS

SPELLING

Use these words and sentences as a pretest for writing synonyms, antonyms, homonyms, and words with multiple meanings.

1. **display** Let's **display** our paintings.
2. **show** Please **show** me the way.
3. **high** How **high** is that mountain?
4. **low** The river runs through a **low** valley.
5. **right** Turn **right** at the corner.
6. **write** I will **write** the directions.

WRITING

Have children write titles of favorite books and then rewrite them using synonyms. Provide a thesaurus and model how it is used to find synonyms.

FINE ARTS

Invite partners to create "picture synonyms." Explain that one partner draws a picture and labels it. Then, the other partner draws a second version of the same picture and labels it with a synonym.

 **AstroWord** Vocabulary

Integrating Phonics and Reading

Guided Reading
Have children look at the cover illustration as you read the title aloud. Then, have them preview the illustrations. Ask what they think the book will be about.

First Reading Ask children to explain what is meant by "Father and Son Baseball" in the title.
Second Reading Reread sentences and have children suggest synonyms for selected words.

Comprehension
After reading, ask children these questions:
- How would you describe the relationship between Ken Griffey senior and his son? *Inference/Character*
- Do you think the Griffeys are good role models for young people? Why or why not? *Reflective Analysis/Personal Response*

ESL/ELL **English Language Learners**
Pair an English-proficient student with an English language learner to read a chapter in the book. Have children work together to orally summarize the chapter.

AUDITORY LEARNERS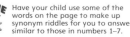

Have the class form two teams. List these words on the board: *harm, jump, strong, creep, fearful, drop, sad, bold, thin, trail, close.* Have teams take turns choosing a word from the board and naming as many synonyms for it as they can. Each synonym is worth one point. When all the words have been chosen, the team with the most points wins.

CHALLENGE

Have pairs of children play a game of verbal tennis. One child serves by saying a word, the other returns with a synonym. They keep exchanging synonyms until one misses. Then, the partner serves the next word.

EXTRA SUPPORT/INTERVENTION

Work with children to complete page 187. Suggest that they cross out each word in the box as they use it. See Daily Phonics Practice, pages 222–223.

Antonyms

Skill Focus

Children will

★ define antonyms as words that are opposite or almost opposite in meaning.

★ identify antonyms for given words.

★ complete sentences by choosing the correct antonym.

ESL/ELL A strong emphasis on spelling may be inappropriate for English language learners who have not reached the intermediate level of proficiency. Allow children to use invented spelling and the phonics skills they are building upon as a foundation for future spelling success.

Teach

Introduce Antonyms Ask children the following questions: *What is the opposite of* hot? (*cold*) *What is the opposite of* fast? (*slow*) Tell children that words that are opposite or almost opposite in meaning are called antonyms.

Say these word pairs and ask children what they notice about each pair: *big, little; young, old; soft, hard.* Point out that the words in each pair have opposite or nearly opposite meanings. They are antonyms.

Write these words on the board: *happy, near, quiet.* Ask children to suggest an antonym for each word. (possible answers: *sad, far, noisy*)

Practice and Apply

Writing Have a volunteer read aloud the definition on page 189 and apply it to the words *lost* and *found.* For the second activity on page 189, point out that each picture is a clue to the word children should choose to complete the sentence.

For page 190, suggest that children check off each word in the box as they use it. When children finish the puzzle, ask a volunteer to share the answer to the question at the bottom of the page.

Reading Use *The Mystery of the Spy's Diary,* MCP Phonics and Reading Word Study Skills Library 2, Level C, to provide practice in identifying and using antonyms.

189

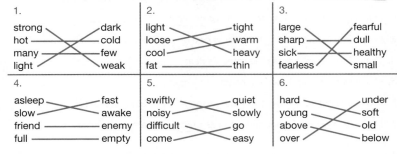

Name_____

For each group of words, draw a line from the word in the first column to its antonym in the second column.

1. strong — dark / hot — cold / many — few / light — weak

2. light — tight / loose — warm / cool — heavy / fat — thin

3. large — fearful / sharp — dull / sick — healthy / fearless — small

4. asleep — fast / slow — awake / friend — enemy / full — empty

5. swiftly — quiet / noisy — slowly / difficult — go / come — easy

6. hard — under / young — soft / above — old / over — below

Read each sentence. Circle the word that makes each sentence tell about the picture. Write the new sentence on the line.

7. Danny and Fran ((climbed) descended) a hill.
Danny and Fran climbed a hill.

8. It was (easy, (difficult)) to go up the steep hill.
It was difficult to go up the steep hill.

9. Along the path, they saw many (dull, (sharp)) rocks.
Along the path, they saw many sharp rocks.

10. When they reached the top, they were ((happy) sad).
When they reached the top, they were happy.

Antonyms: Words in context   **189**

FOCUS ON ALL LEARNERS

ESL/ELL ENGLISH LANGUAGE LEARNERS

Determine English language learners' ability to pair antonyms orally, using words from the lesson.

- Choose antonym pairs from pages 189 and 190. Write words from each pair on red sentence strips; write their antonyms on green strips.
- Post the red strips in one column on a bulletin board and the green strips in another column.
- Set a timer for a reasonable amount of time, and encourage English language learners to work together to "beat the clock," pairing antonyms.
- Review children's efforts; correct pairings if needed.

KINESTHETIC LEARNERS PARTNERS

Materials: index cards

Write words from antonym pairs on separate cards. Shuffle the cards and place them face down in a grid. Invite pairs of children to play "Concentration," in which partners take turns trying to match antonym pairs.

Read each word. Write its antonym in the blanks.
Write the letters from the boxes to answer the question.

above	clear	enemy	healthy	loose	outside
over	separate	sharp	simple	tall	wide

1. tight   l o **o** s e

2. friend   e n e m y

3. join   s e **p** a r a t e

4. difficult   s i m **p** l e

5. under   **o** v e r

6. inside   o u t **s** i d e

7. smoky   c l e a r

8. narrow   w **i** d e

9. short   **t** a l l

10. sick   h **e** a l t h y

11. below   a b o v e

12. dull   **s** h a r p

 What are antonyms?   opposites

 Help your child to name other antonym pairs and explain their meanings.

190   Antonyms: Word meaning

CURRICULUM CONNECTIONS

SPELLING

Practice spelling antonym pairs by having children take turns asking the group to name an antonym for a given word. Have children spell the words, using this format: *What is the opposite of* h-i-g-h? The response should follow a similar format: *The opposite of high is* l-o-w.

WRITING

Have partners work together to write synonym and antonym poems featuring adjectives. One child chooses a word with several synonyms and uses the format below to begin a poem.

> **Happy is . . . joyful, merry, cheerful, laughing, satisfied.**

The partner responds with antonyms.

> **Happy is not . . . sorrowful, sad, gloomy, weeping, complaining.**

TECHNOLOGY   **AstroWord** Vocabulary

VISUAL LEARNERS **GROUPS**

Write antonym pairs on the board. Scramble the letters in the second word of each pair and have children rewrite it. Use the words *large/yitn* (tiny), *sunny/kadr* (dark), *strong/ewak* (weak), *noisy/iquet* (quiet), *lost/nfuod* (found), *enemy/rnfdie* (friend), and *smile/onfrw* (frown).

CHALLENGE

Materials: a thesaurus listing both synonyms and antonyms

Explain that a thesaurus often lists antonyms as well as synonyms for words. Have children use the thesaurus to find additional antonyms for several of the words on pages 189 and 190. You may wish to add the words to the class Word Wall.

EXTRA SUPPORT/INTERVENTION

Draw a mountain shape on the board and write words from the lesson up one side and down the other. Have children travel up and down the mountain by reading the words and giving an antonym for each. See Daily Phonics Practice, pages 222–223.

Integrating Phonics and Reading

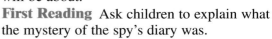

Guided Reading
Have children look at the cover illustration as you read the title aloud. Ask them what they think the children in the illustration are doing. Then, have them predict what they think the story will be about.

First Reading Ask children to explain what the mystery of the spy's diary was.

Second Reading Reread sentences and have children suggest antonyms for selected words.

Comprehension
After reading, ask children these questions:
- Why do you think Aunt Emma sent the diary to Karen? *Inference/Drawing Conclusions*
- What do you think might have happened if Mr. Connor hadn't shown up? *Inference/Plot*

ESL/ELL **English Language Learners**
Review a chapter with children. Ask simple questions to help them tell what happened in their own words. For example, in Chapter 1, point to the picture on page 7 and ask: *Who is the girl? What does she find in the box?*

Homonyms

Skill Focus

Children will

★ define homonyms as words that sound alike but have different spellings and meanings.

★ identify the correct homonym to complete sentences.

ESL/ELL Native speakers of Spanish may be familiar with homonyms in their native language, due to similar pronunciation of *b* and *v*; soft *c*, *s*, and *z*; soft *g* and *j*; *ll* and *y*; and the silent *h*. Emphasize specific homonyms in context and have children memorize the different spellings of the words in each pair.

Teach

Introduce Homonyms Say the sentences below. Have volunteers identify the two words in each sentence that sound the same.

- **Can you *see* the ship sailing on the *sea*?**
- **The wind *blew* the *blue* flag.**
- **I *ate eight* plums.**
- **She *won one* race.**

Tell children that words that sound alike but are spelled differently and have different meanings are called homonyms.

Write the word pairs below on the board. Say each pair aloud and ask children what they notice: *right*, *write*; *hour*, *our*; *knot*, *not*; *rode*, *road*. Point out that the words in each pair sound the same but are spelled differently. They are homonyms.

Practice and Apply

Writing Have a volunteer read aloud the definition on page 191 and apply it to the words *right* and *write*. For the activity on page 191 and the first activity on page 192, have children consider the meanings of the words before choosing one to complete the sentences.

Critical Thinking Involve children in a discussion about how the children feel about playing together as a team. Then, have volunteers respond to the Talk About It question.

Reading Use *How Bullfrog Found His Sound*, MCP Phonics and Reading Word Study Skills Library 2, Level C, to provide practice in identifying and using homonyms.

191

Name _____

DEFINITION
Homonyms are words that sound alike but have different spellings and meanings.
right—write

▶ **Read each sentence. Circle the word that completes the sentence and write it on the line.**

1. My soccer team (**beat**, beet) every team this year. _____ beat
2. We (maid, **made**) it to the city finals. _____ made
3. We (road, **rode**) to the big game in a bus. _____ rode
4. We wore our new (blew, **blue**) uniforms. _____ blue
5. "Play (**fair**, fare)," said our coach. _____ fair
6. Then he (**sent**, cent) us out onto the field. _____ sent
7. The time went (buy, **by**) fast. _____ by
8. We (eight, **ate**) oranges at half time. _____ ate
9. We couldn't (**wait**, weight) to continue the game. _____ wait
10. The game lasted one (our, **hour**). _____ hour
11. Katie's goal (**won**, one) the game for us. _____ won
12. The team's picture will (bee, **be**) in the newspaper. _____ be
13. Our trophy will arrive next (weak, **week**). _____ week

TALK About It How do you think the team will feel about playing together next year?

Homonyms: Words in context, critical thinking   **191**

FOCUS ON ALL LEARNERS

ESL/ELL ENGLISH LANGUAGE LEARNERS

Adapt the activities on pages 191 and 192 to provide homonym practice for English language learners.

- Copy each of the homonyms on page 191 onto individual index cards. Use a different color marker for each word pair.
- Shuffle cards. In small groups, have children pair homonyms. If children have difficulty, remind them to match words written in the same color, as well as words that sound the same.
- As children become more proficient, play again, adding more homonyms from page 192.

KINESTHETIC LEARNERS

Materials: index cards

Invite children to write words from six homonym pairs on 12 separate cards. Then, have them shuffle the cards, spread them face down in a grid, and play "Homonym Concentration."

VISUAL LEARNERS **GROUPS**

Write these words on the board: *ate*, *our*, *maid*, *eight*, *hour*, *write*, *would*, *right*, *wood*, and *maid*. Have volunteers identify two words in the list that are homonyms and use both words in a single sentence, such as *Mel ate breakfast at eight o'clock.*

> Read each sentence. Circle the word that completes the sentence. Write it on the line.

1. ___I___ have a favorite hobby.　Eye　(I)
2. I like to ___sail___ with my brother.　(sail)　sale
3. He ___knows___ many things about boats.　nose　(knows)
4. He is teaching me to tie a square ___knot___.　(knot)　not
5. Last week he ___made___ me practice.　maid　(made)
6. I still can't tie it the ___right___ way.　(right)　write
7. We sail ___our___ boat every weekend.　hour　(our)
8. We will sail today ___or___ tomorrow.　oar　(or)
9. We must ___wait___ for the wind to blow.　(wait)　weight

> For each group of words, draw a line from the word in the first column to its homonym in the second column.

10.
break — knot
not — stake
weight — wait
steak — brake

11.
ate — wrap
ring — wring
rap — eight
bare — bear

12.
right — dye
see — sea
die — road
rode — write

13.
I — pane
led — sale
sail — eye
pain — lead

HOME Help your child to name other homonym pairs and explain the meaning of each word.

192　Homonyms: Words in context

CURRICULUM CONNECTIONS

SPELLING

On the board, write a list of words from the lesson, scrambling the letters. Begin with the spelling word *write*: (*i w t e r*). Have children unscramble the letters to write the word and then write its homonym. Try the following word pairs: *write/right, rode/road, week/weak, sent/cent, knows/nose,* and *wait/weight.*

WRITING

PORTFOLIO

Invite children to work together to write tall tales for one of these homonym-inspired titles: *The Tale of a Tail; The Bear Who Was Barely There; "I'm Hoarse," Said the Horse; The Knight Who Was Afraid of the Night.* Then, have small groups gather to read their tales to one another.

SOCIAL STUDIES

Focus on the unit theme, "Express Yourself," by having children talk about their favorite hobbies. Suggest they give visual presentations, such as showing a collection or demonstrating a hobby.

TECHNOLOGY　**AstroWord**
Vocabulary

AUDITORY LEARNERS　PARTNERS

Materials: index cards

Write homonyms on individual cards. Give each child a card and have children walk around the room, saying their words aloud until partners find each other. Ask partners to use their words in sentences to tell about a sport such as softball, soccer, or sailing.

CHALLENGE

Challenge children to use homonyms to write coded messages in which the wrong homonym is used whenever a homonym appears. Here is an example: *Wood yew bee aloud two meat hymn inn won our?*

EXTRA SUPPORT/INTERVENTION

As children choose words to complete the sentences on pages 191 and 192, ask them to give the meanings of the word choices before writing them on the lines. See Daily Phonics Practice, pages 222–223.

Integrating Phonics and Reading

Guided Reading
Have children look at the cover illustration and read the title. Ask volunteers to tell what they know about bullfrogs. Then, have children predict what they think the story will be about.
First Reading Ask children to tell what Bullfrog's problem was and describe how he solved it.
Second Reading Have children identify homonyms in the story and give their meanings.
Comprehension
After reading, ask children these questions:
• Why did Bullfrog need to prove that he was special? *Recall/Drawing Conclusions*
• What lesson did Bullfrog learn? *Inference/Plot*
ESL/ELL English Language Learners
Invite children to turn to the glossary at the back of the book. Explain that the glossary lists words from the story that might be unfamiliar. Then, review each of the words. Ask volunteers to use the glossary words in sentences of their own.

Phonics and Reading / Phonics and Writing

Review Homonyms

Skill Focus

Children will

★ identify and read homonyms.

★ write words that have homonyms to complete sentences about a story.

★ write a narrative paragraph using homonyms.

Teach

Review Homonyms Remind children that homonyms are words that sound alike but have different spellings and meanings. Then, list these words on the board: *bare, hear, bee, wood, dear, sail,* and *weak*. Ask volunteers to read each word and write its homonym. Then, invite children to explain the difference in meaning for each pair of homonyms and use the words in sentences.

Practice and Apply

Phonics and Reading After children have read the passage on page 193, encourage them to reread it, looking for and underlining words that have homonyms. (*to, two, by, eight, for, buy, so, sea, hours, right, where, see*) Suggest that children choose from among the underlined words to complete each sentence.

Phonics and Writing Before children begin writing their narrative paragraphs on page 194, review the information in the callout boxes. Remind children to use some of the words in the box in their writing.

Critical Thinking For the Talk About It question at the bottom of page 193, invite children to talk about and share their artwork with the class.

Reading Use *Josh and T.J.*, MCP Phonics and Reading Word Study Skills Library 2, Level C, to provide additional practice in identifying and using words with homonyms.

193

Name _____

 **Phonics & Reading**

Read the passage. Then write a homonym from the passage to complete each sentence.

Art From the Paper World

George Pocheptsov, or "Georgie" as he is called, started to paint before he was two years old. He sold his first painting by the age of three. By the time he was eight, Georgie's art was selling for thousands of dollars apiece! Many people want to buy his paintings because they are so bright and colorful.

Georgie's favorite things to paint include animals, sea creatures, and people with musical instruments. He draws every day, sometimes for hours at a time. First he uses a pencil to make just the right sketch. Then he fills in the sketch with paints.

Before Georgie begins to paint, he visits his "paper world." This world is in his head. That's where all his ideas come from. Georgie says, "I want people to look at my paintings and see that the world is beautiful."

1. Georgie started to paint before he was _____two_____ .

2. By the time he was _____eight_____, his art was selling for thousands of dollars.

3. Many people want to _____buy_____ Georgie's paintings.

4. Georgie sometimes draws for _____hours_____ at a time.

5. Georgie uses a pencil to make just the _____right_____ sketch.

6. Georgie wants people to _____see_____ that the world is beautiful.

 What are your favorite things to draw or paint? Why are they your favorites?

Review homonyms: Reading, critical thinking   **193**

FOCUS ON ALL LEARNERS

ESL/ELL ENGLISH LANGUAGE LEARNERS

Use the story on page 193 to review homonyms with English language learners.

• Photocopy the story, one copy per child. You may wish to enlarge the print.

• Tell English language learners to scan the story and highlight words they recognize as homonyms. Have children who need additional support work together.

• Ask children to print target story words on the board. Invite volunteers to write a homonym for each word. To assess whether children understand the differences in meaning, have them use each homonym in a sentence.

KINESTHETIC LEARNERS

Dictate sentences with homonym pairs for volunteers to write on the board: *I ate eight rolls. The knight rode at night. Arrange these pears in pairs. The maid made the bed. How much is the fare to the fair? Our dad was an hour late.* Have children check the homonyms for correct spelling.

Phonics & Writing

A **narrative paragraph** tells a story about something that really happened. The events, characters, and setting are real. Often the writer is the main character.

Write a narrative paragraph to tell people about something interesting that you did or that happened to you. Some of the words in the box may help you.

I	right	eight	eye	wear
where	hour	ate	write	our

Begin with a **topic sentence** that tells who, when, and where.

Use words like *first*, *then*, and *later* to make the **order** of the story clear.

Use words that tell how things **looked**, **sounded**, **smelled**, **tasted**, and **felt**.

HOME Help your child to think of sentences that use homonyms, such as *The wind blew the blue boat.*

194 Review Homonyms: Writing

See Daily Phonics Practice, pages 222–223.

CURRICULUM CONNECTIONS

SPELLING

Use the following words and sentences as a midunit review of the spelling words.

1. **display** I like the window **display**.
2. **show** The **show** is an hour long.
3. **high** The bird flew **high** over the tree.
4. **low** The singer had a very **low** voice.
5. **right** Always try to do the **right** thing.
6. **write** I like to **write** poems.

WRITING

Invite children to write silly sentences using incorrect homonyms; for example, *Won knight, sum people road two town inn the rein.* Have children read their sentences aloud to a partner and then trade sentences. Have partners read the sentences again silently, identify each incorrect homonym, and rewrite the sentences correctly.

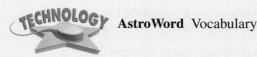 **AstroWord** Vocabulary

---

AUDITORY LEARNERS GROUPS

Have the class form two teams. Say a word from the lesson. Players from both teams write a homonym for the word on the board. The player who finishes first, with the word correctly spelled, earns a point for his or her team. Continue playing until everyone has had a turn. The team with more points wins.

CHALLENGE

Materials: index cards

Suggest that children write homonym word pairs on separate cards to share with learners who need extra support.

EXTRA SUPPORT/INTERVENTION

Materials: word cards (See Challenge activity above)

Invite children to use the homonym word cards to read and match words that are homonyms. Pair children with learners who are more proficient to talk about the meanings of the words. See Daily Phonics Practice, pages 222–223.

Integrating Phonics and Reading

Guided Reading
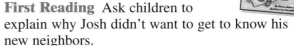
Have children read the title and look over the cover illustration. Then, have them read the story summary on the back cover silently as you read it aloud.
First Reading Ask children to explain why Josh didn't want to get to know his new neighbors.
Second Reading Read selected sentences from the story and ask children to identify homonyms.

Comprehension
After reading, ask children these questions:
- How did the Razzle Stones help Josh make new friends? *Recall/Cause and Effect*
- How did Josh feel at the end of the story? *Reflective Analysis/Personal Response*

ESL/ELL English Language Learners
Help children review the plot of the story by asking simple questions, such as *What are the names of the two boys who are friends? Which boy moves away?* Use picture clues to help children answer.

Alphabetical Order

Skill Focus

Children will

★ alphabetize words to the second and third letter.

★ use guide words to locate words in a dictionary.

Teach

Introduce Alphabetical Order Write the following two sets of words on the board:

- **bird   bat   begin   boat**
- **storm   still   stack   street**

Have children name the first letter of each word in the first set. (*b*) Ask children how they would put the words in alphabetical order when the first letters are the same. (*Look at the second letter.*) Ask a volunteer to write the first set of words in alphabetical order. (*bat, begin, bird, boat*)

Have children look at the second set of words. Explain that because each word begins with *st*, they must look at the third letter to determine the alphabetical order. Ask a volunteer to write the words in order. (*stack, still, storm, street*)

Introduce Dictionary Usage Display a dictionary page and direct children's attention to the guide words. Explain that these are the first and last words on the page. All the other words on the page are listed in alphabetical order between them. Then, write the words *lap* and *leap* on the board. Ask children to think of words that would appear on a dictionary page with these guide words.

Practice and Apply

Writing Have children read the hint on page 195. For the activity on page 195, suggest that children look at the first letter(s) in each word before deciding whether or not they need to alphabetize by the second or third letter.

Have children read the definition of "Guide Words" at the top of page 196. For the activity on that page, explain that each item has a set of guide words and other words that may or may not appear on a dictionary page with those guide words.

Reading Use *The Pet Show*, MCP Phonics and Reading Word Study Skills Library 2, Level C, to provide practice in alphabetizing and using guide words.

Name _____

▶ Read the hint. Then write each list of words in alphabetical order.

HINT Words in a dictionary are listed in alphabetical order. If the first letter of the words are the same, look at the second letter. If the first two letters are the same, look at the third letter.

1.		2.	
foxes	antelope	Danny	Ann
goat	beaver	Ann	Betty
beaver	camel	Frank	Carl
camel	deer	Carl	Danny
deer	elephant	Betty	Ellen
antelope	foxes	Ellen	Frank
elephant	goat	Gerry	Gerry

3.		4.	
bicycle	bat	cheese	chair
bat	bicycle	chop	cheese
bubbles	blocks	chrome	children
blocks	boat	chair	chop
boat	break	children	chrome
break	bubbles	chuckle	chuckle

Dictionary: Alphabetical order   **195**

FOCUS ON ALL LEARNERS

– – – – – – – – – – – – – – – – – – – –

ESL/ELL ENGLISH LANGUAGE LEARNERS

Adapt the activities on page 195 to provide English language learners practice with alphabetization.

- Review the letters of the alphabet. Provide a visual aid, such as an alphabet chart, to remind children of the letter order.
- Write each word from item 1 on page 195 on index cards. Mix the cards. Then, have children arrange them in alphabetical order, circling the first letter of each word. Continue in a similar way with items 3 and 4.

KINESTHETIC LEARNERS PARTNERS

Materials: index cards

Have children write words that begin with the same letter each on an index card. Then, have them mix the cards and work together to arrange them in alphabetical order.

VISUAL LEARNERS PARTNERS

Materials: dictionaries

Have children copy the guide words from a dictionary page. Then, have them close the dictionary and list other words that might appear on that page. Have them open the dictionary to the same page and check to see whether the words on their list are there.

> Look at each pair of guide words and the words below them. Circle the words in each list that you would find on a page with those guide words.

DEFINITION
Guide words appear at the top of each dictionary page. They tell you what the first and last words on the page are. All the words on the page are in alphabetical order between the guide words.

1. **mice • mop**	2. **fish • gate**	3. **dance • day**
(mile)	(five)	(dark)
men	(frogs)	deer
(mitt)	girl	doll
(moon)	gave	(date)
mask	(fun)	(dawn)

4. **rabbit • rake**	5. **wagon • wax**	6. **present • print**
(radio)	(wallet)	(pretzel)
(raccoon)	wooden	(princess)
rocket	(watching)	propeller
(radish)	(watermelon)	(principal)
(rain)	whale	(press)

196   Dictionary: Guide words

 HOME Help your child to think of other words that could be found between the guide words on this page.

CURRICULUM CONNECTIONS

SPELLING

On the board, have children write the words *display*, *show*, *high*, *low*, *write*, and *right* in alphabetical order. Then, have them brainstorm words that might appear in a dictionary just before and just after each word. Have children use a dictionary to check their work.

WRITING

Ask children to write a story with words that appear on one dictionary page, underlining each entry word they use. Have partners share stories and find the dictionary page each was based on.

PORTFOLIO

MATH

Have children list classmates' first names. Then, have them group the names by their first letter. Have children use this information to make a picture or bar graph to show how many names begin with different letters of the alphabet.

AUDITORY LEARNERS **GROUPS**

Write the guide words *mice* and *mop* on the board. Read these words: *mean*, *middle*, *mind*, *now*, *map*, *money*, *mood*, *mow*. Have children write only the words that would appear on the page with the guide words. Check children's choices by having them write the words on the board under the guide words. (*middle*, *mind*, *money*, *mood*)

CHALLENGE

Challenge children to alphabetize words by the third and fourth letter, such as *magazine*, *market*, *magic*, *magnet*, *marble*, *maple*, *maiden*.

EXTRA SUPPORT/INTERVENTION

To make alphabetizing easier for children, reduce the number of words in each activity on pages 195 and 196. Consider having them work with only two or three words at a time. See Daily Phonics Practice, page 223.

Integrating Phonics and Reading

Guided Reading

Have children look at the cover and read the title. Then, ask them to share their experiences with pets. You may also wish to use the activity in the English Language Learners section below.

First Reading Ask children to describe how Andy found a pet to take to the pet show.
Second Reading Have children list all the names of story characters in alphabetical order.

Comprehension

After reading, ask children these questions:
- Why was everyone surprised to find out that Andy had a pet snake? *Inference/Plot*
- Do you think it was a good idea for Andy to return Sammy to the wild? Why or why not? *Reflective Analysis/Personal Response*

ESL/ELL English Language Learners
After children have looked through the book, have them use picture and word clues to name different kinds of animals that appeared at the pet show.

Guide Words

Skill Focus

Children will

★ list words in alphabetical order.

★ use guide words to locate words in a dictionary.

Teach

Introduce Guide Words Write each of the following words on a large index card: *radio*, *rattle*, *raw*, *rayon*, *really*, *reason*, *reasonable*, and *record*. Pass out the cards to volunteers and ask them to go to the front of the room and hold up the cards, standing in random order. Invite the class to tell where the children should stand so that the words appear in alphabetical order from left to right.

Write the guide words *rabbit* and *reap* on the board. Ask children which words written on the cards would appear on a dictionary page with these guide words. (*radio*, *rattle*, *raw*, *rayon*, *really*) Have children explain their responses. Encourage children to name other words that might appear on a page with the guide words *rabbit* and *reap*. Invite them to write the words on the board.

Practice and Apply

Writing Read the directions for the first activity on page 197 aloud. Suggest that children look at the first three letters of each pair of guide words to help them decide which word would come between them alphabetically. The same suggestion applies to the second activity on the page, but you may wish to point out that the answer will be in the form of a page number.

For the activity on page 198, have a volunteer read the directions aloud and explain in his or her own words what children are expected to do.

Reading Use *Hootie Joins In*, MCP Phonics and Reading Word Study Skills Library 2, Level C, to provide practice in alphabetizing and using guide words.

Name _____

Look at each pair of guide words. Write the word from the box that belongs between the guide words.

| candle | drapes | jar | race | sandwiches | window |
| deal | flowers | lantern | rectangle | thirteen | zero |

1. sailboat ___ sandwiches ___ saw
2. dragon ___ drapes ___ dressing
3. flat ___ flowers ___ flute
4. jacket ___ jar ___ jay
5. ladder ___ lantern ___ lazy
6. record ___ rectangle ___ red
7. think ___ thirteen ___ thorn
8. camel ___ candle ___ candy
9. whiskers ___ window ___ wishbone
10. dazzle ___ deal ___ dear
11. zebra ___ zero ___ zigzag
12. rabbit ___ race ___ raffle

Look at each pair of guide words and the dictionary page number. Write the page number on which you would find each word listed below.

each • elevator 210

13. elephant ___ 210
16. easel ___ 210
19. family ___ 243

elf • escape 215

14. favorite ___ 243
17. English ___ 215
20. educate ___ 210

fake • frown 243

15. erase ___ 215
18. farmer ___ 243
21. eggplant ___ 210

Dictionary: Guide words   **197**

FOCUS ON ALL LEARNERS

ESL/ELL ENGLISH LANGUAGE LEARNERS

Adapt the activity on page 197 to provide English language learners practice using guide words.

- Display a dictionary page. Point to the first and last entry words on the page. Show children that these two entry words match the guide words at the top of the page.
- Do the first item on page 197 with children. Read the guide words aloud and then name the word from the box that comes between them. Have children write the word on the line.
- Do items 2–4 in a similar manner. Then, have children work in pairs to complete the activity on their own.

KINESTHETIC LEARNERS

Materials: strips of paper

Write guide-word pairs on the board. Then, write entry words that would be found between each set of guide words on paper strips and give one to each child. Have children stand under the pair of guide words that their word would come between.

Read each pair of guide words. Circle the five words in the box that would appear between those guide words. Then write the words you circled in alphabetical order on the lines.

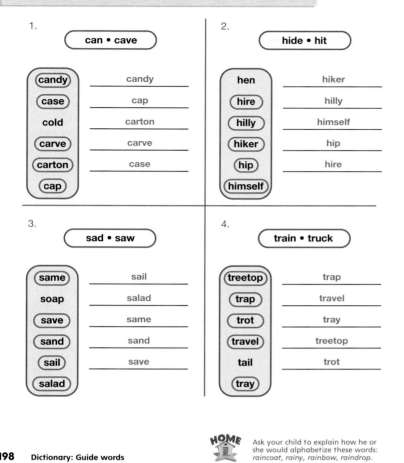

1. **can • cave**

candy	candy
case	cap
cold	carton
carve	carve
carton	case
cap	

2. **hide • hit**

hen	hiker
hire	hilly
hilly	himself
hiker	hip
hip	hire
himself	

3. **sad • saw**

same	sail
soap	salad
save	same
sand	sand
sail	save
salad	

4. **train • truck**

treetop	trap
trap	travel
trot	tray
travel	treetop
tail	trot
tray	

198 Dictionary: Guide words

HOME

Ask your child to explain how he or she would alphabetize these words: *raincoat, rainy, rainbow, raindrop.*

CURRICULUM CONNECTIONS

SPELLING

Write the spelling words *display*, *show*, *high*, *low*, *right*, and *write* on the board and read them aloud with children. Have children copy each word, find it in the dictionary, and record the guide words at the top of the page on which the word is found.

WRITING

Invite children to write sentences with words in alphabetical order. For example: *A big camel dances each fall*. The next sentence should begin where the previous sentence left off.

PORTFOLIO

SCIENCE

Have small groups of children use the index in a science book to choose a science topic. Then, have group members brainstorm words that relate to the topic and list them in alphabetical order. Suggest that two groups share their topics by talking about how the words in their lists relate.

VISUAL LEARNERS PARTNERS

Have partners select a favorite topic and a letter of the alphabet to write a free-verse poem, using words written in alphabetical order. For example: T *is for* tasty *foods*, tea, toast, tofu, tomatoes, tortillas, tuna, turnips, *and* TV *dinners*!

CHALLENGE

Challenge children to list at least four other words that would fall between each pair of guide words provided on page 198.

EXTRA SUPPORT/INTERVENTION

As children begin the activities on pages 197 and 198, provide them with an alphabet chart for easy reference. See Daily Phonics Practice, page 223.

Integrating Phonics and Reading

Guided Reading
Have children read the title and discuss what is happening in the cover illustration. Then, invite children to predict what the story will be about.
First Reading Ask children to describe how the songbirds and Hootie worked out their differences.
Second Reading Have children look up selected story words in a dictionary.

HOOTIE JOINS IN

Comprehension
After reading, ask children these questions:
• What problem did Hootie and the songbirds have? *Recall/Sequence*
• What do you think might have happened if Hootie and the Oak Tree Songbirds hadn't solved their problem? *Inference/Character*

ESL/ELL English Language Learners
Have children turn to Chapter 6. Point out that the songs the birds sing in this chapter rhyme. Then, have children identify the rhyming words.

Locating Words in a Dictionary

Skill Focus

Children will

★ list words in alphabetical order.

★ use guide words to locate words in a dictionary.

Teach

Introduce Locating Words in a Dictionary
Write *A–I*, *J–Q*, and *R–Z* each on a sheet of oak tag. Display the cards in the front of the room. Next, give each child a word to write on paper. Then, have children arrange themselves in three groups, standing in front of the card showing the range of first letters of the words they have written. Ask children in each group to arrange their words in alphabetical order, for a volunteer to read aloud.

Explain that it helps to think of a dictionary as having three parts: a "beginning" section for words beginning with the letters *A–I*; a "middle" section for words beginning with the letters *J–Q*; and an "end" section for words beginning with the letters *R–Z*. Then, say the words *bubble*, *flannel*, *mail*, *sudden*, *rooster*, and *wrestle*. Ask children to tell where the words would be found in the dictionary. (*beginning, beginning, middle, end, end, end*)

Practice and Apply

Writing Have children read the hint at the top of page 199. Read the directions aloud for both activities and make sure children understand what to do. For the first activity on the page, have children draw a line through each word as they use it. For the second activity, make sure children understand that they are to write *Beginning*, *Middle*, or *End* on the line and not the word itself.

For the activity on page 200, make sure children understand that for each item they are to write either *Beginning*, *Middle*, or *End* on the first line and *before*, *on*, or *after* on the second line.

Reading Use *Quackers, the Troublesome Duck,* MCP Phonics and Reading Word Study Skills Library 2, Level C, to provide practice in using a dictionary.

Dictionary

Name _____

▶ Where in the dictionary would you find the words in the box? Write each word where it belongs.

> **HINT**
> Dictionary words are listed in alphabetical order. You can find a word quickly if you think of the dictionary as having three parts: **Beginning Letters** (A–I), **Middle Letters** (J–Q), and **Ending Letters** (R–Z).

aunt	sister	doctor	myself	father
joy	love	teacher	family	write
read	brother	mother	uncle	neighbor

Beginning (A–I)	Middle (J–Q)	End (R–Z)
1. aunt	2. joy	3. read
4. brother	5. love	6. sister
7. doctor	8. mother	9. teacher
10. family	11. myself	12. uncle
13. father	14. neighbor	15. write

▶ Write Beginning, Middle, or End to tell where in the dictionary each word in bold print can be found.

16. People **express** themselves in different ways. ___Beginning___

17. Some people **write** books or poetry. ___End___

18. Athletes **play** many different sports. ___Middle___

19. Dancers such as Rosa express themselves with their **bodies**. ___Beginning___

20. How do you express **yourself**? ___End___

Dictionary: Locating words **199**

FOCUS ON ALL LEARNERS

ESL/ELL ENGLISH LANGUAGE LEARNERS

Adapt the activity on page 199 to provide English language learners practice using a dictionary.

• Look through a dictionary with children and talk about each of the three sections: *A–I*, *J–Q*, and *R–Z*. Call attention to tabs that indicate letters of the alphabet.

• Use bookmarks to divide the dictionary into the three sections. Write the letters covered in each section on the ends of the bookmarks.

• Suggest that children refer to the dictionary as they complete the activities on page 199.

KINESTHETIC LEARNERS

Materials: dictionaries

Have children sit in a circle. Provide them with one pencil and a sheet of paper. On the board, write two guide words from a dictionary page. Have each child take a turn writing a word that would fall between the guide words. Have children use the dictionary to check the words.

► Read the information in each exercise. Then answer the questions. Use page 199 to help you.

1.

You are writing a science report on dinosaurs. Look up the word *Tyrannosaurus.* In which section of the dictionary would you find this word? _____ **End**

You open the dictionary and see the guide words **unbroken • undergo**. Would *Tyrannosaurus* come **before, on,** or **after** a page with those guide words? _____ **before**

2.

While reading a recipe, you see the word *barbecue.* Where in the dictionary will you find this word? _____ **Beginning**

You open the dictionary and see the guide words **by • category**. Would *barbecue* come **before, on,** or **after** a page with those guide words? _____ **before**

3.

In a book of old Roman myths, you see the word *Hercules.* In which section of the dictionary should you look to find this word? _____ **Beginning**

You open the dictionary and see the guide words **hen • hero**. Would *Hercules* come **before, on,** or **after** a page with those guide words? _____ **on**

4.

You want to know more about North America. Look up *North America.* In which section of the dictionary would you find these words? _____ **Middle**

You open the dictionary and see the guide words **music • nap**. Would *North America* come **before, on,** or **after** a page with those guide words? _____ **after**

 Ask your child to name favorite activities such as *basketball* or *reading*, then tell you in which section of the dictionary those words would be found.

200 Dictionary: Locating words

CURRICULUM CONNECTIONS

SPELLING

Have children spell the words *show, display, high, low, right,* and *write* and then rewrite them in alphabetical order. Ask children to indicate in which section of a dictionary they would find each word—the beginning, middle, or end.

WRITING

Have children use the names of professionals, such as those found on page 199, to write riddles. Explain that the clues should include a job description along with alphabetical clues, such as *When I am on stage, I play the role of a character. My name comes between the words* activity *and* actual *in the dictionary. Who am I?* (an *actor*)

SOCIAL STUDIES

Invite children to apply dictionary skills to the telephone book. Suggest that they divide the phone book into three sections and see how quickly they can locate last names of family or friends by looking in the appropriate sections.

AUDITORY LEARNERS *PARTNERS*

Materials: dictionaries

One partner chooses a word from the dictionary and says it aloud. The other partner tells in which section of the dictionary it appears and locates the word. Partners then switch roles and begin with a new word.

CHALLENGE

Materials: watch with a second hand, dictionaries

Suggest that children have a contest to see who can locate a word in a dictionary in the shortest amount of time. Each player should have a dictionary, and children can take turns being the timekeeper.

EXTRA SUPPORT/INTERVENTION

Materials: dictionaries

Before children begin the activities on pages 199 and 200, provide them with an alphabet chart marked off into three sections: *beginning, middle,* and *end.* See Daily Phonics Practice, page 223.

Integrating Phonics and Reading

Guided Reading

Have children read the title and discuss what is shown on the cover. Invite children to share what they know about how ducks behave. Then, encourage them to predict what the story will be about.

First Reading Have children explain why Quackers kept returning to the school.

Second Reading Direct children to look up selected story words in a dictionary.

Comprehension

After reading, ask children these questions:
• Do you think the children should have been allowed to keep Quackers at school? Why or why not? *Inference/Drawing Conclusions*
• Why do you think Quackers flew away? *Recall/Drawing Conclusions*

ESL/ELL English Language Learners

Invite children to use chapter titles and picture clues to give a brief summary of the story in their own words.

Homographs

Skill Focus

Children will

★ define homographs as words that are spelled the same but have two or more meanings.

★ use picture clues to choose the correct meaning for a homograph.

★ choose the correct meaning for a homograph from how it is used in a sentence.

Teach

Introduce Homographs Write the following sentences on the board.

- I like to *bowl*.
- Ken ate a *bowl* of cereal.

Ask a volunteer to identify and circle the word that is common to both sentences. (*bowl*) Then, ask children what the word *bowl* means in the first sentence. (*a game*) What does it mean in the second sentence? (*a dish to eat from*) Explain that words that are spelled the same but have different meanings are called homographs. Then, direct children's attention to these sentence pairs:

- **They sell ribbon by the *yard*.**
  Daisies are growing in our *yard*.
- **There is no bread *left*.**
  Turn *left* at the corner.

Have children find the words *bowl*, *yard*, and *left* in the dictionary. Point out that the words are listed more than once with small numbers after them to show that they are homographs.

Practice and Apply

Writing Have children read the definition at the top of page 201. For the activity on the page, point out that children should write the number of the appropriate entry in the box.

For the activity on page 202, suggest that children read each sentence carefully, paying particular attention to how the underlined word is used.

Reading Use *Secrets of the Rain Forest*, MCP Phonics and Reading Word Study Skills Library 2, Level C, to provide practice in identifying homographs and their meanings.

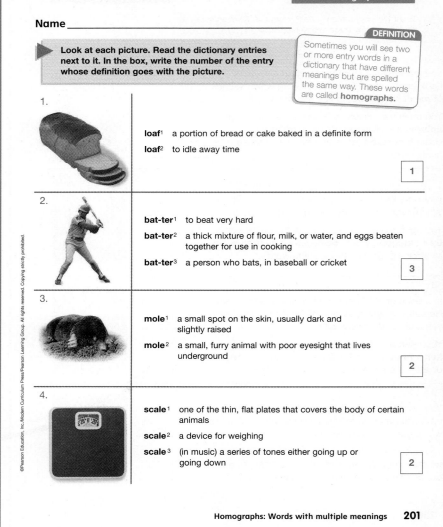

Name _____

> Look at each picture. Read the dictionary entries next to it. In the box, write the number of the entry whose definition goes with the picture.

DEFINITION
Sometimes you will see two or more entry words in a dictionary that have different meanings but are spelled the same way. These words are called **homographs**.

1.
loaf[1] a portion of bread or cake baked in a definite form
loaf[2] to idle away time

[1]

2.
bat-ter[1] to beat very hard
bat-ter[2] a thick mixture of flour, milk, or water, and eggs beaten together for use in cooking
bat-ter[3] a person who bats, in baseball or cricket

[3]

3.
mole[1] a small spot on the skin, usually dark and slightly raised
mole[2] a small, furry animal with poor eyesight that lives underground

[2]

4.
scale[1] one of the thin, flat plates that covers the body of certain animals
scale[2] a device for weighing
scale[3] (in music) a series of tones either going up or going down

[2]

Homographs: Words with multiple meanings   **201**

FOCUS ON ALL LEARNERS

ESL/ELL ENGLISH LANGUAGE LEARNERS

Assess English language learners' ability to identify the correct meanings for homographs.

- Ask volunteers to name each item pictured on page 201.
- Tell children that you are going to read each definition. They should decide which definition goes with the picture.
- Have children write the number of the correct definition in the box before moving on to the next item.
- When children finish page 201, pair them with English-proficient children to complete page 202.

KINESTHETIC LEARNERS   GROUPS

Write a list of homographs on the board, such as *tire*, *game*, *bark*, *fly*, *bowl*, *bat*, *rest*, *last*, *left*, and *page*. Have a volunteer choose a word and draw a sketch on the board or act out one meaning. Have others guess the word and the meaning.

VISUAL LEARNERS   PARTNERS

Materials: dictionaries

Have pairs of children find a homograph in the dictionary whose entries are numbered 1 and 2. One child uses the word in a sentence, and the other child identifies the correct meaning.

> Read each pair of dictionary entries and the sentence below them.
> Choose the entry whose definition fits the meaning of the underlined
> word. Write the entry number, 1 or 2, in the box.

1.
prune¹ a variety of plum that dries without spoiling

prune² to cut off or trim twigs or branches

Grandpa will <u>prune</u> the bushes in his garden. | **2**

2.
fine¹ very good

fine² money paid as a penalty for breaking a law

Meg did a <u>fine</u> job of painting the bookshelves. | **1**

3.
spoke¹ the past tense of **speak**

spoke² a bar coming out of the hub of a wheel

Danny had to repair two of the <u>spokes</u> on his bike. | **2**

4.
bat¹ a wooden club used to hit a ball, as in baseball or cricket

bat² a flying mammal, active at night

As they entered the cave, a <u>bat</u> flew out. | **2**

5.
ring¹ a circular band worn on the finger as an ornament

ring² to give forth a clear sound, as a doorbell or telephone bell

The bride and groom wore matching gold <u>rings</u>. | **1**

6.
case¹ a situation or condition, as in a *sad case*

case² a container

Janet put her new pin in her jewelry <u>case</u>. | **2**

7.
post¹ an upright piece of timber or metal

post² a position to which a person is assigned

Claude hammered the fence <u>post</u> into the ground. | **1**

8.
mail¹ letters or packages that are delivered by the post office

mail² armor made of metal rings linked together

Fran got <u>mail</u> from her pen pal in Australia. | **1**

202 Homographs: Words with multiple meanings

 Help your child think of a sentence using the other meaning in each set.

CURRICULUM CONNECTIONS

SPELLING

Invite children to write the spelling words *right* and *show* in sentences to demonstrate two different meanings for each word. (opposite of *left*, correct; to point out; a public display or program)

WRITING

Have children demonstrate their understanding of homographs by using the words to write silly questions for classmates to answer. For example: *Would someone who **loafs** bake a **loaf** every day? Would a **batter** use a bat to mix **batter**? Would a **mole** have a **mole** on its nose?*

MATH

Have children try their hand at using words that are homographs to write math word problems for others to solve. For example: *If one **loaf** takes 50 minutes to bake and three loaves will fit in the oven at one time, how much time will a person have to **loaf** for twelve loaves to finish baking?* (200 minutes, or 3 hours and 20 minutes)

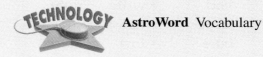 **AstroWord** Vocabulary

---

AUDITORY LEARNERS

Invite a child to say a sentence that demonstrates one meaning of a homograph, saying "blank" in place of the word. For example: *The bride wore a (blank) on her finger.* The listener who names the word to finish the sentence (*ring*) then provides a sentence to illustrate another meaning for the word.

CHALLENGE

Challenge children to use a homograph twice in a sentence to show two different meanings. For example: *When we left the highway, we turned left off the exit.*

EXTRA SUPPORT/INTERVENTION

Materials: dictionaries

Help children locate sample sentences that appear in dictionary entries for homographs. Explain that these sentences show how the homograph is used and can help them understand one of the word's meanings. Read the sentences and discuss how the homographs are used. See Daily Phonics Practice, page 223.

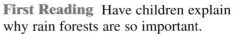

Guided Reading

Have children read the title. Invite children to share what they know about the rain forest and what they would like to know.

First Reading Have children explain why rain forests are so important.

Second Reading Have children identify homographs in selected story sentences.

Comprehension

After reading, ask children these questions:

- Why are the rain forests in danger? *Recall/Main Ideas and Details*
- What new facts did you learn about the rain forest? *Reflective Analysis/Personal Response*

ESL/ELL English Language Learners

Point out that this book used visual aids to help convey ideas. Then, invite children to leaf through the book, pointing out such features as maps and diagrams. Guide children in identifying what they show using the text.

Phonics and Spelling / Phonics and Writing

Review Synonyms, Antonyms, and Homonyms

Skill Focus

Children will

★ spell and write synonyms, antonyms, and homonyms.

★ write and group words according to whether they are synonyms, antonyms, or homonyms.

★ write an e-mail message using synonyms, antonyms, and homonyms in context.

Teach

Review Synonyms, Antonyms, Homonyms On the board, write the words *synonym*, *antonym*, and *homonym*. Have children give a definition for each term. You may wish to use prompts such as: *What do you call words that have the same or almost the same meaning?*

Write the following word pairs on the board.

• **good**	**bad**	• **write**	**right**
• **big**	**large**	• **tall**	**short**
• **bear**	**bare**	• **fast**	**quick**
• **happy**	**sad**	• **week**	**weak**

Ask volunteers to tell whether each pair is an example of synonyms, antonyms, or homonyms.

Practice and Apply

Phonics and Spelling Ask volunteers to state in their own words each set of directions on page 203. Then, read the list words aloud before children begin working. Point out that children must come up with their own words for the homonym activity at the bottom of the page.

Phonics and Writing Before children begin writing, invite them to brainstorm ideas of places friends can go together. Then, help children locate the "To," "Subject," and "Message" sections of the e-mail message. Ask volunteers to tell what kind of information goes in each section.

Reading Use *Digging Dinosaurs,* MCP Phonics and Reading Word Study Skills Library 2, Level C, to provide additional practice in identifying synonyms, antonyms, and homonyms.

203

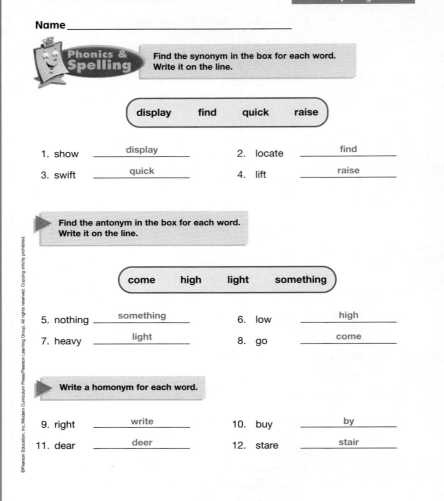

Name _____

Phonics & Spelling   Find the synonym in the box for each word. Write it on the line.

display	find	quick	raise

1. show _____ display _____   2. locate _____ find _____
3. swift _____ quick _____   4. lift _____ raise _____

Find the antonym in the box for each word. Write it on the line.

come	high	light	something

5. nothing _____ something _____   6. low _____ high _____
7. heavy _____ light _____   8. go _____ come _____

Write a homonym for each word.

9. right _____ write _____   10. buy _____ by _____
11. dear _____ deer _____   12. stare _____ stair _____

Review synonyms, antonyms, homonyms: Spelling   **203**

FOCUS ON ALL LEARNERS

ESL/ELL ENGLISH LANGUAGE LEARNERS

Preview with English language learners words used in this review lesson.

• In three columns, copy the activity words from page 203 onto chart paper.

• Tell children that this lesson reviews the skills they have been learning. Ask a child to read aloud one word from the list.

• Model correct pronunciation and have the group repeat.

• Ask a volunteer to tell what the word means.

• Confirm, in words, the skill, such as: *a synonym for* show *is* display.

• Continue to preview all the words in each of the activities.

KINESTHETIC LEARNERS   GROUPS

Materials: index cards

Write synonyms, antonyms, and homonyms, with each word on an index card. Give one card to each child. Have children walk around the room to find a matching word. Invite partners to identify their word relationships and use their words in sentences.

Phonics & Writing

An **e-mail message** is a message you write and send to someone on a computer. Both you and the person you're writing to must have a computer, access to the Internet, and an e-mail address.

▶ Write an e-mail message to a friend. Tell your friend about someplace you would like to go with him or her. Some of the words in the box may help you. Make up an e-mail address for the person you are writing to.

here	come	write	hear	park
stay	right	drive	play	there

Write your friend's e-mail address after the "To."

Write what the message is about after the "Subject."

Write your message in the box below the Subject line.

New Message

To...

Subject:

Send

204 Review synonyms, antonyms, homonyms: Writing

Point to words in the e-mail your child wrote. Ask him or her to identify any synonyms, antonyms, or homonyms for the words.

CURRICULUM CONNECTIONS

SPELLING

Use the following words and sentences as a posttest for writing words that are synonyms, antonyms, and homonyms.

1. **display**   I will **display** my painting.
2. **show**   Please **show** me your new book.
3. **high**   How **high** can you reach?
4. **low**   Golfers try for a **low** score.
5. **right**   Everything went **right** for me.
6. **write**   Can you **write** a song?

SCIENCE

Have children work in small groups to find out about different forms of communication and how they work, such as e-mail, television, telephone, radio, telegraph, and sign language. Invite each group to share what they learned with the class.

VISUAL LEARNERS GROUPS

Materials: poster board, game spinners and markers

Have small groups design a board game, writing homonyms in each space that makes up a path. Players use a spinner to move along the path, read aloud the word they land on, and use it in an original sentence.

CHALLENGE

Challenge children to write sentences that include two or more of these types of words: synonyms, antonyms, and homonyms.

EXTRA SUPPORT/INTERVENTION

Materials: index cards

Use index cards to make letter cards. Use the letter cards to spell out a word. Then, name a category, such as antonym. Invite children to use letter cards to spell out a word that is an antonym for the word you spelled. See Daily Phonics Practice, pages 222–223.

Integrating Phonics and Reading

Guided Reading

Direct children to look at the cover and read the title. Then, call on volunteers to share what they know about dinosaurs.

Digging Dinosaurs

First Reading Ask children to describe some ways in which dinosaurs can be grouped.

Second Reading Have children find story words that are synonyms, antonyms, or homonyms.

Comprehension

After reading, ask children these questions:

• What new fact did you learn about dinosaurs? *Recall/Details*

• Which type of dinosaur did you find the most interesting? Why? *Reflective Analysis/Personal Response*

ESL/ELL English Language Learners

Point out that this book has a glossary, a list of selected words with their meanings. Turn to the glossary and invite children to read aloud definitions of words they are unfamiliar with. Help children find the words in the text.

Take-Home Book

Review Synonyms, Antonyms, Homonyms, and Homographs

Skill Focus

Children will

★ read synonyms, antonyms, homonyms, and homographs in the context of a story.

★ reread for fluency.

Teach

Build Background

• Remind children that the theme of this unit is "Express Yourself!" Ask them to name some ways people express their thoughts, ideas, and feelings.

• Write the Take-Home Book title, *A Little Imagination,* on the board and read it aloud. Tell children they will learn how one person used her imagination to do a special art project as they read the story.

Review Synonyms, Antonyms, Homonyms, and Homographs Write these word pairs on the board and have children classify them: *happy/glad (synonyms), stare/stair (homonyms), fast/slow (antonyms).*

Remind children that a homograph is a word that can mean more than one thing. Then, write these homographs on the board: *bat, scale,* and *ring.* Ask volunteers to give two meanings for each word.

Practice and Apply

Read the Book Help children tear out and fold the pages to make their Take-Home Book. After children look through the book, read the story together. Talk about how Nina used her imagination to create something special.

Synonyms, Antonyms, Homonyms, Homographs Invite children to offer synonyms and antonyms for selected story words. For example: *different/unusual, same; pretty/beautiful, ugly; started/began, stopped.* Have children look through the story and identify words that have homonyms. Ask them to name the homonyms for each word they find. (*fair/fare, know/no, two/too/to, wait/weight, flour/flower, blue/blew*) Then, direct children to find homographs in the story, such as *ground, fall, rest,* and *top.* Have them give two or more meanings for each word.

Reread for Fluency Have children reread the book to increase their fluency and comprehension. Urge children to take their book home to share with their family.

205

A Little Imagination

Name

Nina's class was going to have an art fair. "Use your imagination," said her teacher, Mrs. Cho. "Don't make the same art projects we've done in class. Try to think of something really different to do."

Nina didn't know what to make. She wanted to design something really unusual. She thought about the project as she walked home from school.

1

The day of the art fair arrived, and the children set up their projects. As Mrs. Cho walked around the room, she paused in front of each work. She stayed by Nina's picture for a long time.

"You all worked very hard," Mrs. Cho said at last. "It isn't easy to choose just one winner, but I think Nina deserves the blue ribbon. Her picture is certainly different, and it's not just an art project—it's a science lesson, too!"

4

Review synonyms, antonyms, homonyms: Take-home book　**205**

FOCUS ON ALL LEARNERS

ESL/ELL ENGLISH LANGUAGE LEARNERS

After assisting children with making the Take-Home Book, use the following activities to teach English language learners.

• Ask children to describe what is happening in each picture.

• You may wish to help children make a main idea chart to help organize their ideas.

• Read the story together.

• Have children identify synonyms and antonyms for selected words in the story.

• Point out words that have homonyms or are homographs. Help children identify the homonyms and tell what the homograph means as it is used in the sentence.

KINESTHETIC LEARNERS GROUPS

Materials: construction paper, markers, tape

Write several words from Unit 7 on paper squares and display them around the classroom. Invite children to stand by a word of their choosing and talk about the word in terms of its being a synonym, antonym, homonym, or homograph.

A maple seed fluttered down to the ground in front of Nina. She picked it up and looked at it. With its two wings, it looked a little like a bird. That gave Nina an idea. What if she made a picture from seeds? She could use the maple seed and some apple seeds. She also remembered saving dried pumpkin seeds last fall, though she forgot exactly where they were. She raced the rest of the way home. She could hardly wait to get started.

2

FOLD

Her mother was baking bread. She wiped the flour off her hands and reached in a cupboard. "Here are our pumpkin seeds," Mom said. "I have some new flower seed packets you can use, too."

Nina glued the maple seed to the top of a sheet of paper. It made a beautiful bird. She used pumpkin seeds to make pretty clouds. At the bottom of the picture she formed flowers from different seeds.

3

206   Review synonyms, antonyms, homonyms: Take-home book

VISUAL LEARNERS

Materials: drawing paper, markers, tape

Have children write the headings *Synonyms, Antonyms, Homonyms,* and *Homographs* on separate sheets of paper. Then, have them find words from the Take-Home Book to list on each sheet, along with words of their own. Have them tape the sheets together, then fold them accordion style.

CHALLENGE

Invite children to work together to think of other ways Nina could have used her imagination to come up with an unusual and interesting art project. Have children write descriptions of their ideas to share with the class.

EXTRA SUPPORT/INTERVENTION

Encourage children to name a word that is a synonym, antonym, or homonym for a word selected from the story. See Daily Phonics Practice, pages 222–223.

CURRICULUM CONNECTIONS

LANGUAGE ARTS

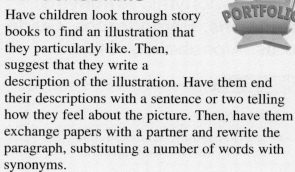

Have children look through story books to find an illustration that they particularly like. Then, suggest that they write a description of the illustration. Have them end their descriptions with a sentence or two telling how they feel about the picture. Then, have them exchange papers with a partner and rewrite the paragraph, substituting a number of words with synonyms.

FINE ARTS

Provide children with different kinds of seeds. Have them use the seeds to make pictures, as Nina did in the story. Warn children not to eat the seeds. Explain that they are only to be used for the art project. When the pictures are completed, display them in an art show for the class.

SCIENCE

Invite children to see how many different kinds of seeds they can find. Suggest that they look for seeds at home, outside, and in supermarkets, as well as in some of the foods they eat. Have children list the names of the seeds they find. Then, direct them to combine their lists to see how many different seeds they found in all.

 **AstroWord** Vocabulary

Unit Checkup

Review Synonyms, Antonyms, Homonyms, Homographs, Guide Words, Alphabetical Order

Skill Focus

Children will

★ identify synonyms, antonyms, homonyms, and homographs.

★ identify the correct guide words between which a particular dictionary entry will be found.

★ alphabetize words to the second and third letter.

★ identify the correct meaning for a homograph used in a sentence.

★ use homonyms to complete sentences.

Teach

Review Synonyms, Antonyms, Homonyms, Homographs Write word pairs on the board.

- **shut**   close   - **healthy**   sick
- **beet**   beat   - **mole**   mole

Ask children to identify each pair as either synonyms, antonyms, homonyms, or homographs. Discuss what children can use to discover the correct meaning or spelling of a word. (*dictionary*)

Review Guide Words, Alphabetical Order Ask a volunteer to locate the word *shut* in a dictionary. Ask if the word will be in the beginning, middle, or end of the dictionary. (*end*) Have the volunteer identify the guide words and read the definition. Ask if the dictionary verifies that the words *shut* and *close* are synonyms. Then, have children check the other word pairs on the board.

Practice and Apply

Assess Skills For the first activity on page 207, children fill in the circle under the term that describes each pair of words. For the second activity, children should fill in one circle next to each word. For the third activity, children may have to alphabetize to the second or third letter.

For the first activity on page 208, tell children that the listed words are homographs with their different meanings numbered. Children should read the sentence to determine which meaning is being used. Point out that answers will be a number. For the last activity, tell children to think about the meaning of each homonym before choosing one.

Name _____

▸ Read each pair of words. Decide whether they are synonyms, antonyms, or homonyms. Fill in the circle.

	Synonyms	Antonyms	Homonyms
1. right/write	○	○	●
2. right/wrong	○	●	○
3. display/show	●	○	○
4. high/low	○	●	○
5. here/hear	○	○	●

▸ Read the word. Fill in the circle beside the guide words under which the entry word would be listed.

6. diet	○ dig-dip	○ debt-dent	● did-different
7. ramp	○ ran-rap	● rake-rang	○ rabbit-rag
8. custom	○ cost-cup	● cup-cut	○ come-couple
9. ocean	● oar-odor	○ ouch-over	○ one-opera
10. limb	○ lick-like	○ list-little	● lima-lint

▸ Write the words in the box in alphabetical order.

11. _____ decide _____

12. _____ demand _____

13. _____ determine _____

14. _____ detract _____

15. _____ display _____

16. _____ distance _____

> display
> detract
> decide
> distance
> determine
> demand

Synonyms, antonyms, homonyms, dictionary skills: Assessment   **207**

FOCUS ON ALL LEARNERS

ESL/ELL ENGLISH LANGUAGE LEARNERS

Complete the activities orally with English language learners.

- Read aloud the directions for the first two activities on page 207. Tell children that you will say each item along with the correct answer choice. They should fill in the circle beside the choice you say.

- For the last activity on page 207, tell children that you will say the words in alphabetical order. They should write the words in the order in which you say them.

- Confirm activity directions for page 208. Tell children that you will read aloud each sentence one at a time. Then, they should write the number you say.

- For the activity on the bottom of page 208, tell children that you will read aloud each sentence. They should circle the word you spell.

KINESTHETIC LEARNERS GROUPS

Materials: three shoe boxes, index cards, marker

Write synonym, antonym, or homonym pairs on cards and stack the cards face down. Label the three boxes *Sound the Same, Mean the Same,* and *Opposites.* Children choose cards, read them aloud, and place them in the appropriate boxes.

> **Read the sentence. Choose the meaning of the word that is used in the sentence. Write the number of the meaning beside the sentence.**

scale¹   one of the thin, flat plates that cover the body of certain animals

scale²   a device for weighing

scale³   (in music) a series of tones either going up or going down

spoke¹   the past tense of speak

spoke²   a bar coming out of the hub of a wheel

batter¹   a thick mixture of flour, milk, or water, and eggs beaten together for use in cooking

batter²   a person who bats, in baseball or cricket

fine¹   very good

fine²   money paid as a penalty for breaking a law

___1___ 1. Amy mixed the **batter** for a surprise birthday cake.

___1___ 2. Jason **spoke** to his class about his favorite hobby.

___2___ 3. Mrs. Hadley paid a **fine** when her parking meter ran out.

___2___ 4. The school nurse weighed pupils on a new **scale**.

> **Circle the word that finishes each sentence.**

5. There is (no, know) person exactly like you.
6. You may like (to, too) play ball or swim.
7. Do you like the color (blew, blue)?
8. What day of the (weak, week) is your favorite?
9. Do you have a favorite poem or (tail, tale)?
10. What kind of music do you like to (here, hear)?
11. Do you like to learn (new, knew) sports?
12. (Wear, Where) is your favorite place to visit?

208   Synonyms, antonyms, homonyms, dictionary skills: Assessment

ASSESS UNDERSTANDING OF UNIT SKILLS

STUDENT PROGRESS ASSESSMENT

You may wish to review the observational notes you made as children worked on the activities in the unit. The notes will help you evaluate the progress children have made with these phonics skills.

PORTFOLIO ASSESSMENT

Review the materials children have collected in their portfolios to help you evaluate how well each child uses the phonics skills covered in this unit. Arrange an interview with each child to discuss the work and the progress made since the beginning of the unit.

DAILY PHONICS PRACTICE

For children who need further practice with the phonics skills covered in this unit, quick reviews are provided on pages 222–223 in Daily Phonics Practice.

PHONICS POSTTEST

To assess children's mastery of unit phonics skills, use the posttest on pages 185g–185h.

AUDITORY LEARNERS

Challenge children to say and spell words you describe, for example: *Say and spell three words in alphabetical order that begin with the letter* d. *Spell the homonym for* meet (meat) *and use both words in sentences. Use the word* mole *in two sentences to show different meanings.*

CHALLENGE

Challenge children to add two items to each section of the Unit Checkup.

EXTRA SUPPORT/INTERVENTION

Materials: index cards

Write several words from the unit on cards and have children read and match words that are synonyms, antonyms, or homonyms. Then, have all the cards arranged in alphabetical order. See Daily Phonics Practice, pages 222–223.

Teacher Notes

Daily Phonics Practice

Contents

Initial Consonants

◆ Ask children to sort objects or pictures into groups of things whose names have the same beginning sounds (for example, *button, ball, box, bag*). Children then place an alphabet card for that letter with the group.

◆ Play "beat the clock." Draw a clock face on the board, using these consonants instead of numbers: *l, d, p, h, m, b, n, t, r, k, s, f.* Children beat the clock by starting at twelve o'clock and saying words that begin with the sound each letter represents.

◆ Have children play a game of "I spy." Invite them to take turns giving clues to objects in the room whose names begin with consonants. For example, *I spy something you sit at and write on whose name begins with the sound of* d. (*desk*)

◆ Have children play "I'm going on a trip." Say, for example, *I'm going on a trip, and I'm bringing a ball and a bat. What will you bring?* Children respond with a word that has the same beginning sound as the words you say. (*bed, box, bike*)

Medial Consonants

◆ Say a letter and four words, asking children to raise their hands each time they hear the sound of that letter in the middle of a word. Use words such as these: *z—puzzle, zipper, buzz, dazzle; g—wagon, tiger, gift, argue.*

◆ Ask children to listen for a repeated middle sound as you say phrases, such as *warmest summer swimmers.* Invite volunteers to name the letter that stands for that sound.

◆ Distribute consonant letter cards. Tell children to listen to the words you say and to hold up their cards if they have the consonant that stands for the middle sound in the word. Say, for example, *tiger, happen, river, follow, pedal.*

◆ Distribute consonant letter cards. Say a word and ask the child who holds the appropriate card to identify the part or parts of the word in which the consonant sound is heard. For example, to a child who holds *l*, say the words *lemon, lily,* and *sell.* The child should reply with *beginning, beginning* and *middle,* and *end.*

Final Consonants

◆ Have children take turns making word ladders by changing the initial and final consonants of words. Demonstrate by changing *map* into *man* and *man* into *ran.*

◆ Say pairs of words and ask the class to say *Yes!* if the ending sounds match and *No!* if they don't—for example: *six, fox; glass, hill; moon, pan.*

◆ Invite children to help you create lists of words that begin with different consonants, such as *d, r, h,* and *p.* Then, name a final consonant. Have children find words in the list that end with that consonant and read the words aloud.

◆ Divide the group into "Beginnings," "Middles," and "Ends." Say a consonant and several words. Groups stand if they hear the consonant sound in the word in their position.

Hard and Soft c and g

◆ Shuffle word cards for words with hard and soft *c* and *g* sounds. Invite pairs of children to sort the words according to the sounds for *c* and *g*.

◆ Write the following on index cards: *soft* c, *hard* c, *soft* g, *hard* g. Place the cards in a pile. Invite volunteers to select a card and say two words in the category written on the card. Ask the class to guess the category.

◆ Divide the class into two groups, "Hard Sounds" and "Soft Sounds." Ask children to raise their hands when they hear their sound in these words: *stage, cork, dance, girl, giant, city, tiger, camel.*

◆ Make up riddles for words with hard and soft *c* and *g* sounds. Give clues that include the sound; for example, *This fruit, whose color is also its name, has a soft* g *sound in its name.* (*orange*)

Daily Phonics Practice

Short Vowels a, i, u, o, e

◆ Distribute index cards and have children write *a* on their cards. Ask children to hold up their cards when they hear a word that has the short *a* sound. Say words such as these: *beg, bag, big, bug.* Follow a similar procedure for other vowels and short vowel sounds.

◆ Write the following words in five columns on the board: *bag, sick, luck, hot, bed.* Have volunteers take turns making new words by changing the vowel in each word.

◆ Draw five bricks on the board. Call on volunteers to write words with the short *a* sound in each brick. Then, ask children to continue building the wall by drawing a second row of bricks containing words with the short *i* sound, and so on.

◆ Have children play a game of "I spy." Invite them to take turns giving clues to objects in the room. For example, *I spy something that tells time and has the short* o *sound.* (*clock*)

◆ Ask children to draw five equal columns on a sheet of paper and to write a different vowel letter at the top of each column. Have children write two or three short vowel words in each column. Encourage children to illustrate one of the words.

◆ Pass out word cards for short vowel words. Ask children with short *a* word cards to come to the front of the room. Have the entire class read the short *a* words aloud. Repeat for other short vowel sounds.

◆ Let two volunteers play "ping-pong rhymes." Player 1 names a short vowel word, and Player 2 gives a rhyming word. Children then reverse roles.

◆ Have children take turns making up riddles about words containing short vowel sounds. For example, *I am something a fish has. My name has the short* i *sound.* (*fin*)

◆ Play a word scramble game. Write a three-letter short vowel word on the board in random order. Ask children to write the word in the correct order. For example, *tle* becomes *let.*

Long Vowels a, i, u, o, e

◆ Ask children to wave their hands when they hear a word with long *a*. Then, say several words, one of which has the long *a* sound, such as *like, lake, leak* or *pale, pile, pole, peel*. Repeat for other long vowel sounds.

◆ Print the vowels *a, i, u, o,* and *e* on the board. Ask a volunteer to select a vowel, and then say and write a word that has the long sound for that vowel. Ask other children to name rhyming words for that word.

◆ Let children play musical chairs. Four children walk around three chairs while you say three short vowel words and one long vowel word, such as *sit, hat, dog, rake*. When children hear the long vowel word, they should sit down.

◆ Shuffle picture cards for words with long vowel sounds and show them one at a time. Ask volunteers to name the vowel sound in each picture's name. Have children categorize the picture cards according to their vowel sounds.

◆ Have children play a game of "change it." Write these words on the board: *cap, kit, cut, hop, bet*. Ask children to add *e* to each word and read the new word they make. (*cape, kite, cute, hope, beet*)

◆ On the board, draw five ladders with six rungs each. Have the class form five teams and assign each team a long vowel sound. Team members take turns writing words with their vowel sound on the rungs of their ladders.

◆ Divide the class into five groups and assign each group a long vowel sound. Draw five mountain outlines on the board. Team members climb the mountain by taking turns writing four words with their long vowel sound up one side of the mountain and four words down the other side.

Daily Phonics Practice

UNIT
3

Compound Words

◆ Print compound word equations on the board, such as *sun + shine = ___*. Invite volunteers to add the two words together to make a compound word.

◆ Print compound words on tagboard squares and arrange them on the floor in a hopscotch pattern. Let children take turns tossing a beanbag onto the squares. Have them read the word the beanbag lands on and tell what two words make up the compound word.

◆ Print the two parts of compound words on separate cards and place the cards face up. Have groups of children combine two cards to make a compound word and write the word on the board.

◆ Distribute the cards from the above activity randomly. Let children match their cards with others to form compound words. Together, pairs read aloud the compound word they have formed.

UNIT 3 LESSONS 24, 33, 37, 40

Syllables

◆ Read aloud a list of words—such as *ate, mailbox, hillside, beans, pancake, jeep*—and ask children to clap their hands for each syllable they hear.

◆ Label two bags 1 and 2. Spread out word cards for one- and two-syllable words. Invite two volunteers to "bag" as many words as they can in ten seconds by reading a word, telling how many syllables it has, and putting it in the correct bag.

◆ Have children play a game of "I spy." Invite them to take turns giving clues to objects in the classroom whose names have two syllables. For example, *I spy something you write on.* (*chalkboard*)

UNIT 3 LESSONS 25–28, 34, 39–40

Blends with r, l, s; Final Blends

◆ Place picture cards for words with *r, l,* and *s* blends face down and write several blends on the board. Call on volunteers to select a picture card, say the picture name, and place it on the chalkboard ledge below the correct blend.

◆ Prepare flashcards for words with a target blend and place them in a grab bag. Have children take turns drawing a card, reading the word, and using it in a sentence.

◆ Have children work in small groups to make up tongue twisters for words with blends. For example, *Trains travel on train tracks; Fred's flags fly free.*

◆ Invite pairs of children to play "ping-pong blends." Give the players a word with a beginning (or final) blend. They then alternate naming words with that blend until one can't think of a word.

◆ Print words with blends on index cards. Invite children to play "give me a clue." One child takes a card and gives a clue to the word. If no one can guess, the child gives another clue, and so on, until someone guesses correctly.

◆ Play "beat the clock." Draw a clock face on the board, using consonant blends instead of numbers. Children beat the clock by starting at twelve o'clock and saying a word for each consonant blend. Time the activity to see who can go around the clock before you say, *Time's up.*

◆ Ask children to create shopping lists using words with blends. A sample list might include *stamps, blankets, glasses, plates.*

UNIT 3 LESSONS 29–30, 39–40

y as a Vowel and as a Consonant

◆ Display a piece of yarn, a large number 20, and a question mark standing for *why.* Help children identify the items. Ask what the words have in common. (*the letter* y) Have children identify *y* as a consonant, the long *e* sound, and the long *i* sound.

◆ Use different colored chalk to print each of these words on the board: *you, tiny, why.* Then, say these words and ask volunteers to print them in the correct color under the word with the same *y* sound: *yes, fly, by, sunny, yard, city, dry, year, happy.*

◆ Shuffle word cards for words with *y* as a consonant and *y* with the long *e* and long *i* sounds. Invite pairs of children to sort the words according to the sound for *y*.

◆ Write *long e* and *long i* on two strips. Let volunteers hold up each strip. Distribute cards for words with *y* as a vowel. Call on children to read their words aloud and stand behind the child holding the name for the sound of *y* in their words.

◆ Place cards on which you have written *y* = long *e* and *y* = long *i* on the chalkboard ledge. Have the class form two teams. Then, read words such as *cry, baby, my, silly, funny,* and *fry*. The first player to pick up the correct card for the *y* sound scores a point.

◆ Have children form three groups. Assign one the consonant *y* sound, one the long *e* sound for *y*, and the third the long *i* sound for *y*. Have groups stand when they hear their sound in these words: *why, merry, yolk, yes, shy, tricky, lady, pry, windy, yell, try*.

UNIT 3 LESSONS 31–32, 34, 39–40

Consonant Digraphs

◆ Let children make up tongue twisters for consonant digraphs, such as *She sells seashells by the seashore*.

◆ Let pairs of children take turns writing a consonant digraph. The partner must finish writing a word that begins or ends with that digraph.

◆ Write consonant digraphs on cards and place the cards face down. Have children take turns picking up a digraph card; choose whether the digraph goes at the beginning, middle, or end; and write a word with the digraph in the position selected. For example, a word with *th* in the middle might be *mother*.

◆ Let children play "twenty questions" for words with consonant digraphs. Lead the first game yourself and then let the child who guesses correctly lead the next game.

◆ Ask children to write shopping lists using words with consonant digraphs. Assign categories, such as food (*cheese, peaches, wheat*) or clothes (*shirt, socks, shoes*).

◆ Play "beat the clock." Draw a clock face on the board, using consonant digraphs instead of numbers. Children beat the clock by starting at twelve o'clock and saying a word for each digraph. Challenge children to go around the clock before you say, *Time's up*.

◆ Make up riddles for consonant digraphs. Give clues that include the digraph, for example, *This place where you cook food has the digraph* ch *in the middle of its name*. (*kitchen*)

UNIT 3 LESSONS 35–40

r-Controlled Vowels ar, or, ir, ur, er

◆ Have children form five groups and assign each group one of the *r*-controlled vowels *ar, or, ir, ur, er*. Say several words with *r*-controlled vowels and have groups identify which words are theirs. Encourage children to write their words.

◆ Have children take turns making up riddles for words with *r*-controlled vowels. For example, *I'm a place where cows live*. (*farm*)

- Place word cards for words with *r*-controlled vowels in a grab bag. Have children take turns drawing a card from the bag, reading the word, and using it in a sentence.

- Print the letters *b, c, f, h, m, p, s,* and *t* on separate cards. On the board, print *ar, er, ir, or, ur.* Show one consonant card at a time, and invite children to name as many vowel + *r* words as they can that begin with that consonant. Print their suggestions on the board.

- Let children play "twenty questions" for words with *r*-controlled vowels. Lead the first game yourself and then let the child who guesses correctly lead the next game.

- Have children form five teams and assign each team an *r*-controlled vowel. Give teams five minutes in which to record as many words as they can think of with their *r*-controlled vowel.

- Let children play a game of "mystery cards," using picture cards for words with *r*-controlled vowels. One child chooses a card and describes the picture without naming it. The class is to guess the picture name and identify the *r*-controlled vowel.

Daily Phonics Practice

UNIT 4

UNIT 4 LESSONS 41–42, 55–57

Contractions

- Pronounce several words, such as *went, hasn't, fill, I'll, won't,* and *she's.* Ask children to raise their hands when they hear a contraction. As each contraction is identified, ask what two words were put together to form it.

- On the board, print contraction equations, such as *could + not = __.* Call on volunteers to write the contractions that solve the equations.

- Write ten contractions on the board and ask volunteers to write the two words that make up each one.

- On slips of paper write word pairs that can be contracted, spacing out the letters and words to allow for cutting. Invite volunteers to select and read a word pair; then cut the words apart, tape them together, and insert an apostrophe to make a contraction.

- Have pairs of children take turns showing the side of flashcards with two words and naming the contraction. Then, have children show the side with the contraction and name the words from which it was formed.

- Let children play "Concentration," using cards for pairs of words and their matching contractions. The object is to match words with their contractions.

- On the board, write in one column words that can be contracted and in a second column—randomly—their contractions. Have children take turns drawing lines to match words and contractions.

UNIT 4   LESSONS 43–45, 50, 55–57

Plural Endings -s, -es

◆ Print several sentences on the board, some of which contain plural nouns and some of which do not. For example: *The babies are playing. That lily is beautiful.* Call on volunteers to read each sentence, circle plural words, and underline singular words.

◆ Have children form two teams for base words and plural endings. Write these words on the board: *bushes, glass, boxes, jackets, rose, sandwich, benches, race.* Have members of the base word team write *B* next to base words, while members of the other team write *P* next to plural words.

◆ On the board, print words such as *box, dish, raincoat, glass, watch,* and *pet.* Give each child two index cards, one with *-s* on it and the other with *-es.* Point to each word and ask children to hold up the card that shows which ending they would add to make the word plural.

◆ Tell children that you will show them pictures and hold up one finger for a singular name and two fingers for a plural name. Have children name the pictures, using the singular or the plural form depending on the number of fingers, and then write the words on the board.

◆ Invite volunteers to write these words on the board as you say them aloud: *cherry, puppy, monkey, turkey, daisy, lily, pony, tray, donkey, toy, lady, boy, bunny, chimney.* Call on other children to write the plural form of each word and use it in a sentence.

◆ Ask volunteers to write these words on the board as you say them aloud: *loaf, shelf, knife, scarf, hoof, wife, wolf, calf.* Call on other children to write the plural form of each word and use it in a sentence.

UNIT 4   LESSONS 46–50, 53–57

Inflectional Endings -s, -ed, -ing;
Suffixes -er, -est; Syllables with Suffixes

◆ Write the suffixes *-s, -ed,* and *-ing* on tagboard squares. Then, write the words *jump, start, join, play, think,* and *paint* on the board. Ask volunteers to choose a suffix square, hold it next to a word, and write the new word.

◆ Have children add *-s* to these verbs and use them in sentences: *shake, drive, ripe, skate, rule.* Repeat for *-ing* and *-ed.* Discuss spelling changes with children.

◆ Write the suffixes *-s, -ed, -ing, -er,* and *-est* on the board. Challenge children to write math problems that show the suffixes added to base words. For example: *quick + er = quicker, sing + ing = singing.*

◆ On the board, write *Rabbit Running, Lion Leaping,* and the suffixes *-ing* and *-ed.* Say several base words. Have volunteers add one of the suffixes listed to the words and write them on the board under *Rabbit* if the final consonant is doubled and under *Lion* if it is not.

◆ Ask children to draw pictures of three things that vary in one quality. Let them exchange pictures and label each other's pictures with words that compare.

◆ Have children form groups of three and assign a word to each group, such as *cold, slow, neat, dark,* and *fast.* Have each group make up three sentences, using the base word and the *-er* and *-est* forms.

◆ Write these words on the chalkboard: *light, clean, slow.* Have children identify the number of syllables in each word. (*one*) Then, call on volunteers to turn the words into two-syllable words by adding one of these suffixes: *-ing, -er, -est.*

UNIT 4 LESSONS 51–57

Suffixes -ful, -ly, -less, -ness, -y, -en, -able, -ible, -ion, -ment; Syllables with Suffixes

◆ Shuffle flashcards for words with suffixes. Have children select a card, read the word aloud, tell its meaning, and use it in a sentence.

◆ On the board, print suffix equations, such as *care + less = __.* Call on volunteers to write the words that complete the equations.

◆ Invite children to create their own suffix equations showing suffixes added to base words. For example, *quick + ly = quickly.* Suggest that children create subtraction problems as well, such as *darken − en = dark.*

◆ Let pairs of children play a suffix guessing game. One partner writes a word with a suffix, such as *kindly,* and then gives the other a clue to the word. For example, *I'm thinking of a word that means "in a kind way."*

◆ Invite children to form mountain-climbing groups. Draw mountain shapes on the board, and print a base word at the bottom of each, such as *complete, pay, wood, wash, collect, care, rain, slow,* and *rest.* Climbers choose a word and climb by writing the base word plus a suffix going up the mountain.

◆ Write suffixes on the board. Name one suffix randomly and invite children to write words with that suffix. Have volunteers share their responses. Repeat with other suffixes.

◆ Encourage children to write on their paper some two-syllable words with the suffixes *-ful, -ly, -less,* or *-ness.* Have partners switch papers and count the syllables.

Daily Phonics Practice

UNIT 5 LESSONS 58–59, 62–63, 66–68

Vowel Pairs ai, ay, ea, ee, ie, oa

◆ On index cards, print words with vowel pairs. Put the cards in a paper bag. Invite children to take turns drawing three cards from the bag and making up a sentence using all three words.

◆ Have children work in pairs or small groups to write rhymes using words with vowel pairs that stand for the long *a, e, i,* and *o* vowel sounds.

◆ Print the vowel pairs *_ai_, _ay_, _ea_, _ee_ , _ie_,* and *_oa_* on the board, with blanks as shown. Challenge volunteers to make as many words as they can from each pair by filling in different consonants.

- Play "beat the clock." Draw a clock face on the board, using vowel pairs instead of numbers. Ask children to start at twelve o'clock and say a word for each vowel pair. Time the activity to see who can go around the clock before you say, *Time's up.*

- Write *bet* on the board and ask children to add a letter to make a new word with a long vowel sound. (*beat* or *beet*) Repeat for *ran* (*rain*), *got* (*goat*), and *pal* (*pail*).

- Have children form four teams. On the board, draw four ladders, labeled *long a*, *long e*, *long i*, and *long o*. Invite team members to take turns writing words with vowel pairs with their vowel sound on the rungs of their ladders.

- Challenge children to make up hink-pink riddles using words with vowel pairs. Offer this example, *What do you get when you think too hard?* (*brain strain*)

UNIT 5 LESSONS 60–63, 65–68

Vowel Digraphs oo, ea, ei, au, aw; Syllables

- Invite children to play a rhyming game. Give clues such as these *I am thinking of a word that rhymes with* saw *and begins with* cl. (*claw*) *I am thinking of a word that rhymes with* head *and begins with* br. (*bread*)

- Let children play "mystery cards," using picture cards for words with vowel digraphs. One child chooses a card and describes the picture without naming it. The class then guesses the picture name and identifies the vowel digraph.

- Write words on the board and ask children to use the words to form new words by changing the vowels into vowel digraphs, for example, *mean* (*moon*), *had* (*head, hood*), *case* (*cause*).

- Provide children with a foot or boot cut from paper. Challenge them to print on each as many *oo* words in five minutes as they can that have the corresponding sound of *oo*.

- Print these words on the board: *had, hop, hunt, red, fan, led, hot.* Challenge children to make new words by changing the vowels into vowel digraphs. Have them write their new words on the board and circle the digraphs.

- Print sets of four words on the board, three of which contain vowel digraphs—for example, *steal, stood, took, foot; crawl, dawn, rail, saw.* Ask pairs of children to say the words to each other and decide which word in each set does not belong.

- Assign one vowel digraph each to five teams. Give teams five minutes to record as many words as they can think of with their digraph. Award a point for each correct word.

- Have a volunteer explain the difference between the number of vowels and vowel sounds and the number of syllables. For example, *neighbor* has three vowels, two vowel sounds, and two syllables.

UNIT 5 LESSONS 64–68

Diphthongs oi, oy, ou, ow, ew; Syllables

- Invite children to play a rhyming game. Give clues such as these: *I am thinking of a word that rhymes with* new *and begins with* st. (*stew*) *I am thinking of a word that rhymes with* down *and begins with* cl. (*clown*)

◆ Play "beat the clock." Draw a clock face on the board, using diphthongs instead of numbers. Ask children to start at twelve o'clock and say a word for each diphthong. Time the activity to see who can go around the clock before you say, *Time's up.*

◆ Let children play "mystery cards," using picture cards for words with diphthongs. One child chooses a card and describes the picture without naming it. The class guesses the picture name and identifies the diphthong.

◆ Print these words on the board: *clod, spill, ton, fee, boo.* Challenge children to make new words by changing the vowels into the diphthong *oi, oy, ou, ow,* or *ew.* Have volunteers write their new words on the board and circle the diphthongs.

◆ Have children form five teams. Assign each team a diphthong. Give teams five minutes to record as many words as they can think of with their diphthong. Award one point for each correct word.

◆ Have children take turns making up riddles about words with diphthongs. For example, *I am a small, gray animal that runs around the house at night. What am I?* (*mouse*)

◆ Have partners write lists of words containing diphthongs. Partners then switch papers and divide each word into syllables.

Daily Phonics Practice

UNIT 6

UNIT 6 LESSONS 69–70, 83–84

Prefixes im-, in-, un-, dis-, mis-, ex-, de-, re-, pre-

◆ Have children form three prefix teams: *un-, dis-, mis-.* Read aloud base words and ask children to raise their hands if their team's prefix can be added to the base word. Have them say the new word. Say, for example, *happy, please, spell, obey, wrap, take.*

◆ In one column on the board, print words with prefixes, such as *dishonest, unfair,* and *misspell.* In a second column, print their meanings randomly: *not fair, spell incorrectly, not honest.* Invite volunteers to draw lines to match words with their meanings.

◆ Have children form six groups and assign each group a prefix. Ask groups to list words that begin with their prefix. Then, invite them to use the words in sentences.

◆ Challenge groups of children to look through a dictionary to find words with the prefixes *un-, dis-, mis-, ex-, de-, re-, im-, in-,* and *pre-.* Invite children to share their words and the words' meanings with the class.

◆ On the board, write words to which more than one prefix can be added, such as *wrap* (*unwrap, rewrap*). Ask volunteers to name the new words that can be made and tell what they mean.

◆ Have children form small groups. For each group, prepare sets of cards with base words and prefixes. Invite children to make as many words as they can in a given time by combining base words and prefixes.

◆ Let pairs of children play a guessing game. One partner writes a word with a prefix, such as *disagree,* and then gives the other a clue to the word. For example, *I'm thinking of a word that means "not agree."*

Prefixes, Base Words, Endings, and Suffixes

◆ On the board, print word equations, such as *dis + taste + ful = __*. Call on volunteers to write the words that solve the equations.

◆ Invite children to create their own word equations showing prefixes and suffixes added to base words. For example, *re + paint + ed = repainted*.

◆ Have children make a nine-square bingo card, writing three each of prefixes, base words, and suffixes in the squares. Call out words such as *un + happy + ly* and have children circle the word parts on their cards. The first to circle three in a row wins.

Syllables

◆ Label three bags 1, 2, and 3. Spread word cards for one-, two-, and three-syllable words next to the bags. Invite two volunteers to "bag" as many words as they can in ten seconds by telling how many syllables a word has and putting it in the correct bag.

◆ Let teams of children have a "syllable race." A member of each team comes to the board. Read aloud a one-, two-, or three-syllable word. The first to write the correct number of syllables in the word scores that many points for his or her team.

◆ Have children make a nine-square bingo card and write the numbers 1, 2, and 3 in any order in each row to fill the squares. Randomly call out one-, two-, and three-syllable words, telling children to cross out a number on their card for the number of syllables in the word. The first to mark three squares in a row wins.

◆ Appoint some children "writers" and others "dividers." Say the following words: *radio, flashlight, silent, sparkle, journey, travel, mislead, softness, monument*. Invite writers to write the words on the board and dividers to divide the words into syllables.

◆ Say these words and ask children how many syllables they hear: *careful, wrapper, idea, fireplace, flavor, lemon, sparkle, replanted*. Ask volunteers to write the words on the board, divide them into syllables, and give reasons for dividing the words as they did.

Daily Phonics Practice

UNIT 7

Synonyms, Antonyms, and Homonyms

◆ Say a word, such as *sparkle*, and call on a volunteer to name a synonym. (*glisten*) Invite that child to say another word and ask for a synonym. Repeat for antonyms.

◆ Write these words on index cards and distribute them to ten children: *present, gift, wonderful, marvelous, powerful, strong, glisten, sparkle, silent, quiet*. Have children read their words and pair up with those whose words are synonyms.

◆ Follow the same procedure as above for antonyms: *weak, strong, light, heavy, friend, enemy, full, empty, sharp, dull.*

◆ Give a group of children a list of words, such as *big, swift, glad,* and *tiny.* The leader says the first word, and the others race to name a synonym. The first to answer takes the list and serves as leader.

◆ Repeat the above activity for antonyms, with children providing words with opposite meanings from the ones on the list.

◆ Write the headings *Synonyms, Antonyms,* and *Homonyms* on the board and have children form three teams. Hold up a word card. Team members then write a synonym, antonym, or homonym for the word under the correct heading. Each correct answer scores a point.

◆ Write scrambled words on the board. Call on volunteers to unscramble and write each word and then write its homonym, for example, *wtia—wait, weight; bule—blue, blew.*

UNIT 7 LESSONS 85–95

Dictionary Skills

◆ Write these words on separate cards: *ratio, rattle, raw, rayon, really, reason, reasonable, record.* Distribute the words randomly to children and have them hold up their words. Encourage the class to tell how the children should stand so that the words are in alphabetical order.

◆ Write these words on the board: *soap, hill, carton, orchard, peep, class, backyard, absent, accept, sand.* Ask pairs of children to copy each word, find it in a dictionary, and write the guide words that appear on that page.

◆ Write guide words across the board, for example, *oil, olive; rainbow, rapid; be, beast.* Then, write entry words that would fall between those guide words on slips of paper and distribute them. Have children stand in alphabetical order under the appropriate guide words.

◆ Have groups of children sit in circles. On the board, write guide words chosen randomly from a dictionary. Challenge group members to take turns writing words that would fall between the two guide words. After a set period, check to see which group wrote the most words.

◆ Read guide word clues and encourage children to tell the answers. For example, *I am something in your kitchen found between* story *and* straight. (*stove*)

◆ Write these dictionary headings: *First A–C, Second D–L, Third M–R, Fourth S–Z.* Then, write these words: *nineteen, bounce, figure, jeep, railroad, bother, muffin, field, rapid, muddy.* Have children alphabetize the words and tell where each entry word would be found.

◆ Invite children to use a dictionary to write in random order ten entry words from one page. Have children exchange papers, alphabetize the words they receive, and identify the guide words.

◆ Provide pairs of children with a list of homographs, such as *like, line, top, can, down,* and *might.* Have children find each word in the dictionary and write two different meanings. Encourage children to write a sentence for each word.

Teacher Notes

Teacher Notes

Teacher Notes

Teacher Notes

Teacher Notes

Teacher Notes

Enhance *MCP Phonics* With These Additional Programs

**MCP Phonics
& Reading Libraries, K–3**

**Phonemic Awareness &
Phonics Assessment
(PAPA), K–4**

Spelling Workout, 1–8

Astroword, K–3

MCP Phonics
& Reading Libraries, K–3

Motivate success with on-level storybooks matched to specific decoding and reading skills with the *MCP Phonics & Reading Libraries*. A model for integrating phonics with each title is found at point-of-use throughout the *MCP Phonics Teacher Resource Guides*.

Phonemic Awareness
& Phonics Assessment
(PAPA), K–4

Phonemic Awareness & Phonics Assessment (PAPA) helps identify decoding strengths and needs, and guides instruction for students needing additional support. A correlated list of *PAPA* skills matched to specific lessons in *MCP Phonics* is presented within each Unit of the *MCP Phonics Teacher Resource Guide*.

Continued on reverse side

Return this card today for:
✔ Production Registration
✔ Free Gift

Title of the Product/Program You Purchased: _____

Grade Level: _____ Date of Purchase: _____

Your Name: _____ Date: _____

School Name: _____ County: _____

Your School/Home Address (circle one): _____

_____

Your E mail Address: _____

Your School/Home Phone Number (circle one): (_____) _____

---

1. I am a: (check all that apply)
- ☐ Teacher (T)
- ☐ Curriculum Supervisor (V)
- ☐ Principal/Administrator (N)
- ☐ Department Chair (C)
- ☐ Home School Teacher (H)
- ☐ Federal Funds Supervisor (F)

2. I teach level(s):
- ☐ K–2
- ☐ 3–6
- ☐ 7–12
- ☐ College /Adult Education
- ☐ Other _____

3. Areas of Instruction:
- ☐ Early Literacy/Phonics
- ☐ Reading/Language Arts
- ☐ Social Studies
- ☐ Staff Development
- ☐ Special Education
- ☐ ESL/ELL
- ☐ Math
- ☐ Science
- ☐ Gifted
- ☐ Assessment
- ☐ Family Literacy
- ☐ Other _____

4. How will you use *MCP Phonics* overall?
- ☐ As a primary phonics program
- ☐ As a supplement to a primary/core reading program

Please list your primary/core reading program_____Copyright_____
- ☐ As a supplement for use in a summer school/after school program

More specifically, **how will you use this product in your classroom?**
- ☐ Student material for classroom instruction
- ☐ Student material for homework assignments
- ☐ Student supplement for review or practice
- ☐ Remediation/Intervention
- ☐ Teacher Resource

5. How did you first hear about *MCP Phonics*?
- ☐ Sales Rep
- ☐ Online Store
- ☐ Catalog/Brochure
- ☐ Other _____

6. Please rank in order of importance the features that prompted you to purchase *MCP Phonics*:
- ☐ Systematic skills instruction & practice
- ☐ Alignment to current research
- ☐ Flexibility to support any reading program/methodology
- ☐ History of program success
- ☐ Other: _____

7. What time of year does your school place orders for consumable classroom materials?
- ☐ January–March
- ☐ April–June
- ☐ July–September
- ☐ October–December

8. How much money does your school spend a year on supplemental materials?
- ☐ Less than $500
- ☐ Between $500–$1,000
- ☐ Between $1,000–$2,000
- ☐ Over $2,000

9. Did you purchase *MCP Phonics* through a Grant?
- ☐ Yes   Please list Grant: _____
- ☐ No

10. ☐ Yes, I would like more information about the following programs:
- ☐ *MCP Phonics & Reading Libraries*
- ☐ *Phonemic Awareness & Phonics Assessment (PAPA)*
- ☐ *Spelling Workout*
- ☐ *Astroword*

11. ☐ Yes, I am interested in participating in studies to determine program effectiveness.

To complete mailer, fold twice and seal with adhesive tape. Do not staple. *Thank you*.

Thank you for purchasing *MCP "Plaid" Phonics.*

Please see the side panels for information regarding these related phonics programs!

Modern Curriculum Press
Globe Fearon
Celebration Press
Dale Seymour Publications
Good Year Books

Return This Card Today For:

✓Product Registration
Be the first to know of product updates and improvements as soon as we develop them.

✓Free Gift
To thank you for registering, we'll send you a special gift, while supplies last!

Visit Our Web site to register online: www.pearsonlearning.com.

Additional Programs, Continued

Spelling Workout, 1–8

Using the same scope and sequence found in *MCP Phonics*, *Spelling Workout* provides research-based spelling instruction that just makes sense. By using both programs, students hear and read the sounds, then write words as they progress from simple, letter-sound relationships to more complex spelling patterns.

Astroword, K–3

Astroword helps students practice and apply essential phonemic awareness, phonics, structural analysis, vocabulary, and spelling skills. A built-in management system also provides individual or class-summary performance measures. Correlated activities are referenced at point-of-use in the *MCP Phonics Teacher Resource Guides.*

Return the attached Product Registration Card or call today for more information about any of these programs.

Modern Curriculum Press
Globe Fearon
Celebration Press
Dale Seymour Publications
Good Year Books

www.pearsonlearning.com
Customer Service
1-800-321-3106